OXFORD WORLD'S CLASSICS

CAN YOU FORGIVE HER?

ANTHONY TROLLOPE (1815–82), the son of a failing London barrister, was brought up an awkward and unhappy youth amidst debt and privation. His mother maintained the family by writing, but Anthony's own first novel did not appear until 1847, when he had at length established a successful Civil Service career in the Post Office, from which he retired in 1867. After a slow start, he achieved fame with 47 novels and some 16 other books, and sales sometimes topping 100,000. He was acclaimed an unsurpassed portraitist of the lives of the professional and landed classes, especially in his perennially popular *Chronicles of Barsetshire* (1855–67), and his six brilliant Palliser novels (1864–80). His fascinating *Autobiography* (1883) recounts his successes with an enthusiasm which stems from memories of a miserable youth. Throughout the 1870s he developed new styles of fiction, but was losing critical favour by the time of his death.

LORD ST. JOHN OF FAWSLEY was Conservative MP for Chelmsford from 1964 to 1987 and has held cabinet posts in government and opposition. His publications include *Walter Bagehot* (1959) and *Law and Morals* (1964) and he has edited the collected works of Walter Bagehot.

KATE FLINT is Reader in English Language and Literature, and Fellow of Linacre College, Oxford. She is the author of *The Woman Reader, 1837–1914* (1993) and of numerous articles on nineteenth- and twentieth-century literature and cultural history. She has edited Virginia Woolf's *Flush* for Oxford World's Classics.

ANDREW SWARBRICK teaches English at Radley College. He has edited *The Art of Oliver Goldsmith* (1984) and assisted in the preparation of Sheridan Le Fanu's *Uncle Silas* for Oxford World's Classics. Among his other publications are essays and reviews in scholarly and literary magazines, and he has written studies of Philip Larkin and T. S. Eliot.

OXFORD WORLD'S CLASSICS

*For over 100 years Oxford World's Classics have brought
readers closer to the world's great literature. Now with over 700
titles—from the 4,000-year-old myths of Mesopotamia to the
twentieth century's greatest novels—the series makes available
lesser-known as well as celebrated writing.*

*The pocket-sized hardbacks of the early years contained
introductions by Virginia Woolf, T. S. Eliot, Graham Greene,
and other literary figures which enriched the experience of reading.
Today the series is recognized for its fine scholarship and
reliability in texts that span world literature, drama and poetry,
religion, philosophy and politics. Each edition includes perceptive
commentary and essential background information to meet the
changing needs of readers.*

OXFORD WORLD'S CLASSICS

——

ANTHONY TROLLOPE

Can You Forgive Her?

——

Introduced by
KATE FLINT

Edited by
ANDREW SWARBRICK

With a Preface by
LORD ST. JOHN OF FAWSLEY

With Illustrations by
LYNTON LAMB

OXFORD
UNIVERSITY PRESS

OXFORD
UNIVERSITY PRESS

Great Clarendon Street, Oxford OX2 6DP

Oxford University Press is a department of the University of Oxford.
It furthers the University's objective of excellence in research, scholarship,
and education by publishing worldwide in

Oxford New York

Athens Auckland Bangkok Bogotá Buenos Aires Calcutta
Cape Town Chennai Dar es Salaam Delhi Florence Hong Kong Istanbul
Karachi Kuala Lumpur Madrid Melbourne Mexico City Mumbai
Nairobi Paris São Paulo Singapore Taipei Tokyo Toronto Warsaw

with associated companies in Berlin Ibadan

Oxford is a registered trade mark of Oxford University Press
in the UK and in certain other countries

Published in the United States
by Oxford University Press Inc., New York

Preface © Lord St. John of Fawsley 1982
Introduction © Kate Flint 1982
Bibliography © W. J. McCormack 1982
Chronology © N. J. Hall 1991

First published as a World's Classics paperback 1982
Reissued as an Oxford World's Classics paperback 1999
Reissued 2008

British Library Cataloguing in Publication Data

Data available

Library of Congress Cataloging in Publication Data

Trollope, Anthony, 1815–1882.
Can you forgive her?
(The Centenary edition of Anthony Trollope's
Palliser novels) (Oxford world's classics)
Bibliography: p.
I. Swarbrick, Andrew. II. Title. III. Series.
Trollope, Anthony, 1815–1882. Palliser Novels.
PR5684.C27 1982 823'.8 82–6318

ISBN 978–0–19–953766–2

1

Printed in Great Britain by
Clays Ltd, St Ives plc

CONTENTS

PREFACE

ENGLISH fiction from about 1830 corresponded very closely in theme and treatment with the political and social changes of the nineteenth century. The death in that year of George IV marked a subtle change in the fabric of society, similar to the social upheavals of the Tudor period. At the same time, industrial progress, particularly in the form of travel and newspapers, put the ruling classes much more in the limelight, giving the nation more opportunities of observing its own mechanism. Institutions, up till then only open to the few, now practised more freedom in their admissions—especially the universities—and the great professions such as the Church became increasingly popular.

Against this background, one of Trollope's most enduring themes in the Palliser novels is that of property and rank asserting themselves against children (as in *The Duke's Children*) or against love (as in the case of Lady Glencora). In the end, however, such issues are usually resolved by a compromise dictated by reason. Plantagenet Palliser is a very representative Trollopian protagonist in that he has to make a compromise between his political hankerings and his domestic life, as does Lady Glencora, although in her case the compromise is forced on her rather than her making an independent decision. Thus, the traditional virtues of their class are maintained, albeit shakily, being permanently buffeted from without by forces that oppose, compromise, or destroy them (Burgo Fitzgerald poses a more insidious danger because he is, as it were, an insider challenging the status quo); and from within by their limitations and vices. The forces of decency, cultivation, and goodness have to struggle, and hard, to maintain themselves. Happiness is never achieved without some pain and uncertainty.

The interconnection between politics and private and

social lives permeates *Can You Forgive Her?* Vavasor uses Alice's money, and Palliser uses Lady Glencora's. Palliser's blindness to domesticity affects his career, just as his career affects his domestic life. He has to compromise and sacrifice, having found his private duty must overcome his political ambition. The reward in this case is prompt and longed-for—he finds his wife is pregnant during their sojourn abroad, and discovers that he would rather have this 'than to make a half dozen consecutive annual speeches in Parliament'.

It is interesting that two of Trollope's most repulsive villains, George Vavasor (in *Can You Forgive Her?*) and Ferdinand Lopez (in *The Prime Minister*), are unsuccessful politicians. Trollope is less interested by party politics than by moral distinctions. *Can You Forgive Her?* concerns itself with different kinds of political behaviour, and the extent to which such behaviour is conditioned by the nature of the political process and by the interconnections between political action and social influences. Vavasor was exactly the sort of would-be politician that Trollope hated, and he makes Palliser remark that the metropolitan seats (among which was the one George Vavasor sat for) 'should be left to rich commercial men who can afford to spend money on them'. For any one, politics is inseparable from money, and the novel is concerned to show how a man's spending his wife's money in furtherance of his ends can be done both honourably and dishonourably. Alice's money, which is used by Vavasor, is the nearest she can get to the political process. Her 'hankering after some second-hand political manoeuvring' is disastrous for her. Burgo Fitzgerald also pursues money, but he has not the public duty of a politician, so his downfall isn't so bad. Also, although selfish, he is in a way selfless. 'He seemed to think so little of himself' is the general opinion, and that is his major attraction and redeeming feature.

Better than anyone else Trollope shows what a chimera politics can be for those who enter it cynically, while retaining enough sensitivity to realize what they have missed. Part of this theme is the notion of politics as a game, and

George's election is typical. The disillusioning finale to all this is when Vavasor takes his seat in the chamber and is overwhelmed by a tremendous sense of anti-climax. And yet, for Vavasor, the game doesn't end with the election, but continues as he takes his seat and realizes that he doesn't possess the alchemy in himself—the integrity—to turn the process into gold.

LORD ST. JOHN OF FAWSLEY

INTRODUCTION

TROLLOPE AND SEXUAL POLITICS

I

Can You Forgive Her?, the first of the Palliser series, is conventionally counted among Trollope's political novels. It is our introduction to the sweep of Plantagenet Palliser's ministerial career which forms the basis for this classification, rather than any domination of the narrative by elections or Parliamentary intrigue. Yet the novel is centrally concerned with power structures in a far less restricted sense: if *Can You Forgive Her?* is legitimately to be termed a political novel, then it is the theme of sexual politics which is clearly predominant. 'What should a woman do with her life?', Alice Vavasor asked herself, and this theme is re-echoed by the presence of every other woman in the novel, from the uncomfortably married Lady Glencora to the nocturnal prostitutes; from the calculated coquetry of Mrs. Greenow to an early fictional prototype of the Odd Woman, Alice's cousin Kate. To pose this question in the mid-nineteenth century meant, in fiction at least, the consideration of a woman's position in relation to marriage. Hence the depiction of actual and potential partners, the evaluation of 'gentlemen', becomes as essential to a reading of the novel as does the consideration of Trollope's portrayal of women.

But it is on the predicament of women that Trollope overtly focuses. This aspect of sexual politics—the question of a woman's right to independence, to power over her own life—has been noted in criticism of the novel ever since its volume publication in 1864–5: the *Westminster Review* remarked that Alice 'has, half-consciously, become deeply infected with the nineteenth-century idea that there was something important to do with her life'.[1] This contagion

[1] *Westminster Review*, 75 (July 1865), p. 284.

manifested itself specifically in the now well-documented contemporary formation of feminist organizations concerned with suffrage and employment, and, more widely, was reflected in the many discussions on the position of women published throughout the 1850s and '60s. Trollope himself contributed to this debate with his lecture 'The Higher Education of Women' (1868).[2] Clearly, he believed in the maintenance of sexual difference: however much we may encourage a girl to adopt an intellectual regime to supplement Mudie's abundant supply of novels, the last thing we want, whether in the sphere of education or elsewhere, 'is to assimilate men and women'.[3] Despite admitting to a certain admiration for a woman who kicks against the pricks—as he puts it—he will always oppose her, since he sees the existing positioning of the sexes as the result of divine ordination, emanating

direct from nature,—or, in other words, from the wisdom of an all-wise and all-good Creator. It is to be seen everywhere,— in all the attributes, organs, capabilities, and gifts of the two sexes.[4]

Hence Trollope can allow himself to sympathize with Lady Glencora's outbursts at being married off, an heiress, to a coldly unromantic husband; appreciate her dash of devilry, her aptitude almost for wickedness, which alternates with her petulant sulkiness. Yet he expresses shock, in his *Autobiography*, that a distinguished Church dignitary could really believe he would allow Glencora to commit adultery.[5] The forbidden apple of Burgo Fitzgerald is expressly dangled, so that the reader may appreciate the moral strength involved in its rejection; the social attributes which recognize proprieties to be maintained while waltzing at Lady Monks's party; and the correct use of those reproductive organs which

[2] 'The Higher Education of Women' (1868), reprinted in Trollope, *Four Lectures*, ed. Morris L. Parrish (London, 1938).
[3] 'Higher Education', p. 73.   [4] ibid. p. 74.
[5] Trollope, *An Autobiography*, Oxford World's Classics (Oxford, 1980), p. 182.

produce the desirable fruit: a reconciliatory male heir to the Omnium title.

Trollope's attitude to committed feminists is made quite plain in the pages of *Can You Forgive Her?* There is some hope for Alice Vavasor, since her political ambitions are only at a secondary level—to play the role of supportive wife—and are absurdly naïve, as Trollope points out when he characterizes her daydreams in the image of her carrying seditious messages from the Tower in her stays. This is the stock material of romantic fiction, and hence to be dismissed lightly, belittlingly. Thankfully, Alice 'was not so far advanced as to think that women should be lawyers and doctors, or to wish that she might have the privilege of franchise for herself'. Clearly, she is unlikely to join the ranks of Iphigenia and Euphemia Palliser, devoting their lives to literature, fine arts, social economy, and the abstract sciences, and their energies to copious correspondence: representatives of the current movement which, as Trollope phrased it sourly in his lecture, he believed arose chiefly 'from a certain noble jealousy and high-minded ambition on the part of a certain class of ladies who grudge the other sex the superior privileges of manhood'.[6] Nowhere in his writing does Trollope exhibit sympathy for women who attempt voluntarily to act independently of men; indeed, he more than hints that such behaviour is far from voluntary, that it results from their bitterness at failing to secure a husband. 'Female Disabilities' is the none-too-subtle abbreviated title of the 'Rights of Women Institute, Established for the Relief of the Disabilities of Females', satirized in *Is He Popenjoy?*, an organization claimed by one character to have its origin in 'old maids who have gone crazy . . . because nobody has married them'.[7] Certainly the grunting, perspiring, moustached Baroness Banmann who typifies 'Female Disabilities' is presented as an unquestionable stereotype to illustrate

[6] 'Higher Education', p. 73.
[7] Trollope, *Is He Popenjoy?*, Oxford World's Classics (Oxford, 1986), i, p. 169.

this hypothesis, as is Wallachia Petrie, the boring women's rights enthusiast in *He Knew He Was Right*. Just as John Grey refuses to admit the seriousness of Alice's protests against the constraints imposed by an early marriage, removing them to the sphere of the abnormal by calling them 'the hallucination of a sickened imagination . . . a melancholy malady . . . your illness', so Trollope, commenting in his own paternalistic voice, here relegates women's demands to the status of a medical condition:

The hope in regard to all such women,—the hope entertained not by themselves, but by those who are solicitous for them,—is that they will be cured at last by a husband and half-a-dozen children.[8]

J. A. Banks, praising Trollope as one of the finest of sociological novelists, makes a valid point when he suggests that the writer may be read not for information about the feminist movement in any empirical sense, 'but for deep insights into the nature of the opposition which that movement had to face'.[9]

II

'Fall in love, marry the man, have two children, and live happy ever afterwards.' The glib phrasing of Trollope's solution to Alice's declared doubts concerning her future should alert us to the potential fragility of such a hypothetical proposal. Falling in love is not the only pre-nuptial requisite, as the case of Glencora all too clearly shows. Moreover, one's choice of marriage partner can prove a serious mistake, as demonstrated by the sombre example of Lady Midlothian, cited, rather aggressively, by Alice herself in the early pages of the novel. Nevertheless, provided the male protagonist is a 'gentleman', 'a man of honour, and with good means', and with the desirable amount of superior knowledge and reading—in other words, the qualities embodied in John

[8] Trollope, *He Knew He Was Right*, The World's Classics (Oxford, 1948), p. 720.

[9] J. A. Banks, 'The Way they Lived Then: Anthony Trollope and the 1870s', *Victorian Studies*, 12 (December 1968), p. 194.

Grey, as the text repetitively emphasizes—Trollope queries whether an answer with more wisdom in it could be given.

Husbands, however, were not necessarily to be had in mid-Victorian England, especially if the woman in question lacked the advantages of a respectable dowry. In Paris, Lady Glencora is transparently irritated by the avid interest which Alice shows in the figures quoted by the statistically-minded Mr. Palliser. Alice was 'glad to find that a hundred and fifty thousand female operatives were employed in Paris', but Glencora dismisses the fact of this work-force by declaring that they should eat conjugal cake: she 'said it was a great shame, and that they all ought to have husbands'. But 'Mr. Palliser explained that that was impossible, because of the redundancy of the female population'. The situation was no more favourable to female matrimony in England. Trollope is here surely quoting from the title of W. R. Greg's much discussed, and subsequently much reprinted essay of 1862, 'Why are Women Redundant?'[10] A similar question had been raised by F. P. Cobbe's piece of the same year, entitled, with equal provocation, 'What Shall We Do With Our Old Maids?'[11] The facts were clear. The 1861 census showed that the ratio of women to men in Great Britain was 1,053 to 1,000: a marked rise from the still unbalanced ratio of 1,042 to 1,000 in 1851. The greatest 'surplus', of 209,663 women, occurred in the age range 20–29: that is, in the bracket which included both Alice and Kate Vavasor.[12]

Modern criticism has certainly not ignored the themes

[10] W. R. Greg, 'Why are Women Redundant?', *National Review*, 1862, reprinted in his *Literary and Social Judgements* (London, 1868) and as a separate pamphlet in 1869.

[11] F. P. Cobbe, 'What Shall We Do With Our Old Maids?', *Fraser's Magazine*, 1862, reprinted in her *Essays on the Pursuits of Women* (London, 1863).

[12] B. R. Mitchell, *Abstract of British Historical Statistics* (Cambridge, 1962), p. 6, Table 2; General Report, Census, England and Wales (1861), *Parliamentary Papers* (1863), LIII Pt. 1 (3221), Appendix p. 115, Table 70.

of independence, choice, and subordination with regard to women in *Can You Forgive Her?*[13] But the discussion of Alice, Glencora, and Mrs. Greenow has primarily been pressed to the service of contradicting those who believed the novel to have a weak plot, a loose and straggling construction, who accused Trollope of having found his 1850 drama, *The Noble Jilt*, too slender to expand into a full-grown three-decker, of needing to introduce the more capricious Glencora to liven up a story dominated by the 'uninteresting and unintelligible' Alice.[14] Hence the triumvirate of unmarried woman, wife, and widow, each forced to discriminate between 'the worthy man and the wild man' in their lives, has been lauded as a triumph of planned equilibrium. But stressing these three tidy, parallel structures has led to the other women who appear in the novel being ignored. The structures of mid-Victorian society have been duplicated in subsequent analysis: those women who are marginal to the marriage structures of the plot have become marginal figures in critical discourse. Yet their very presence is used by Trollope to reinforce the promise of social and familial stability held out by the prize of marriage, a prize which it is foolish to disdain.

The strongest immediate threat to the stability of the circles portrayed by Trollope came not from the women's organizations, but from the prostitute—'a not unimportant type of the odd woman', as Gissing called her.[15] Victorian interest in this 'social evil' was at its greatest during the 1850s and 1860s—in 1860 the *Saturday Review* noted its popularity as a subject for discussion[16]—and opinion divided

[13] See especially John Halperin, *Trollope and Politics: A Study of the Pallisers and Others* (London, 1977).

[14] *Spectator*, 2 September 1865, XXXVIII, p. 978.

[15] George Gissing, *The Odd Women* (1893; reissued London, 1980), p. 299.

[16] Quoted in Paul McHugh, *Prostitution and Victorian Social Reform* (London, 1980), p. 17. See also E. M. Sigsworth and T. J. Wyke, 'A Study of Victorian Prostitution and Venereal Disease', in *Suffer and be Still*, ed. Martha Vicinus (Indiana, 1972).

on the necessity of the prostitute if the pre-marital virtue of upper-class females was to be preserved. As W. E. H. Lecky was to put it: 'Herself the supreme type of vice, she is ultimately the most efficient guardian of virtue.'[17] But the fact that Alice breaks off her engagement with George Vavasor when he dared weigh 'the value of his own low lusts against that of her holy love' is enough to place Trollope with regard to this argument. Moreover, in 1864, the year in which *Can You Forgive Her?* began appearing in monthly parts, the precise danger which prostitutes posed was being openly discussed, in the press and Parliament at least, due to the introduction of the Contagious Diseases Act, ostensibly designed to protect the armed forces from venereal infection.

In employing different dramatic presentations of 'fallen women', the novel highlights the dualism inherent in mid-Victorian reactions to the phenomenon. The thin, ragged, freezing girl who approaches Burgo Fitzgerald in Oxford Street for money to buy gin emphasizes, of course, the golden generosity of the likeable rake; a point reinforced when (by a coincidence for which De Quincey would have sold his soul) she later re-impinges on Burgo's melancholy. But her extreme youth—'sixteen, perhaps, at the most'— and remnants of extreme prettiness, of 'perfect innocence and pure faith', which bring out the pathos of her situation, seem designed to excite the reader's compassion for this social problem as it reflected specifically on the plight of young women. To some extent, the girl is allowed to retain her aura of innocence since sexual contact with her is, on both occasions, the last thing on Burgo's mind. Yet an unwholesome air surrounds the novel's other lost daughter of Eve, George's former mistress. Her bonnet flowers are parodic of past freshness; more seriously, disease, whether tubercular or worse, is hinted at in the hollowness of her jaws and peculiar brightness of her eyes. Since her pleas are no longer supported by the emotional power of youth,

[17] W. E. H. Lecky, *History of European Morals from Augustus to Charlemagne* (1869), 10th edn., 1892, II, p. 283.

Trollope, although not, perhaps, without some glancing sympathy for her typicality, presents her as a creature of whining weakness. As if George's heartless financial extortion and the murderous mind of the man were not already enough to damn him, the overt proof of their association is yet further evidence of his moral unsuitability for Alice, particularly since further sexual darkness and deception is hinted at on his part. Despite having discarded Jane, taken her evidently comfortable boudoir away from her, we learn early in the novel of George's nameless, carefully hidden third establishment, presumably occupied by some unrevealed successor. Trollope, already sailing close to Mudie's censorious wind by the introduction of these two prostitutes, could hardly have elaborated on this theme: unsuitable sexual behaviour is greeted with the silence of non-explanation. But since for Trollope 'mystery is a vice', necessary authorial taciturnity emphasizes yet again George's ungentlemanly social transgressions.

The case of Kate Vavasor presents a less blatant example of marginalization than does the prostitute. An underdeveloped character in the novel, and an ignored subject in criticism, she is—nearing thirty, unmarried, unoccupied except as a companion—a representative female type of the mid-century, yet one rarely portrayed in the fiction of the period, and one but awkwardly assimilated by Trollope. What occupation, indeed, could she have adopted? Her moneyed family connections preclude, no doubt, her stooping to the option of governess; in any case, since the opening of the new secondary schools for women, to be a graduate of one of these had, by the 1860s, become the generally accepted standard for governesses. The Society for Promoting the Employment of Women, founded in 1859, concentrated on work in telegraph offices, printing, lithography, and hairdressing, and, according to Bessie Parkes in 1860, it was usually the 'less refined' who took up such employment.[18]

[18] Quoted by A. James Hammerton, 'Feminism and Female Emancipation, 1861–1886', in *A Widening Sphere*, ed. Martha Vicinus (Indiana, 1977; London, 1980), p. 54.

Emigration was customarily seen, by Greg and others, to be the only feasible solution for women of a 'superior class' who proved unemployable, or unmarriable, in Britain. Yet it is George, her brother, who emigrates, if such a name can be given to unprincipled flight, and Kate, herself, keeps quiet on the subject of his mysterious disappearance. This is, perhaps, surprising, for, after all, it was her cousin Alice who was preoccupied by the question of 'What should a woman do with her life?'; Kate, earlier in the novel, had no doubts that she had found her occupation in unquestioning devotion to George. Unlike Alice, with her fanciful notions of what is entailed in giving political help to a man, Kate has a sound grasp both of means—willing to sacrifice her own inheritance to help her brother and with little compunction about dipping her hand by proxy into her cousin's pocket for the same ends—and of methods: she is, as Trollope points out, a capable intriguer.

Alice is more than a little envious of Kate's position. Clearly, the proximity of company and career allowed to a sister far exceeds those bounds of propriety which restricted an unmarried woman in relations with a man whom she could not marry: such a fraternal bond permitted political excitement without social danger. However, Trollope's attitude towards Kate's character, and hence his attitude towards Alice's assessment of her, is somewhat ambiguous. When first introduced, speaking with her 'little sarcastic smile', she is hardly a model of female delicacy, yet he uses her as a touchstone by which we are not initially allowed to see her brother as a complete villain, his scar as the mark of Cain—'There must have been something great about George Vavasor, or he would not have been so idolised by such a girl as his sister Kate.' Moreover, the thrust of some of her remarks is uncertain. When she epigrammatizes about women's characteristics: 'It's envy that makes us want to get married,—not love,' it is unclear whether she is referring to envying the independence of a bachelor's existence or the competitive nature of securing a husband. Several things do, however, emerge from Trollope's patchy portrayal of Kate. First, the intense nature of her passionate faith in her brother can only be explained by language which Trollope elsewhere reserves for more orthodox partnerships. 'The truth is, I'm married to George', Kate cries; she emits a howl of loneliness at the thought that if he were ever married elsewhere, even to Alice, she 'should have nothing to do in the world;—literally nothing—nothing—nothing—nothing!' Such incestuous sentiments are used to explain her lack of interest in other men. They also, obliquely, reflect on the ambience of sexual perversion which continually surrounds and blackens the exploitative George.

Secondly, Kate's discriminating avoidance of the pursuit of partner-hunting gives her an integrity in her independence which is ultimately lacking in the other young women. Aunt Greenow cannot understand why, with a very small fortune, Kate should not be 'desirous of being married with as little delay as possible'. Certainly, Trollope presents her discrimination, at times, as a type of haughtiness. Additionally, he hints, as she dresses for Alice's wedding, that she is lacking in the traditional instincts of her gender, not having much 'feminine taste for finery'. Yet by indicating that her devotion to George provides the major answer to such inexplicable behaviour, Trollope shows himself unable to think of female motivation existing outside the sphere of male–female pairings. As George's removal from the novel becomes inevitable, he grants Alice a respectable inheritance, releases her from the comic role of foil to her aunt's courtship, a potential Cheesacre-pairing, and so places her tidily in the marriage market: a conventional fictional dispatch for a character who otherwise, an odd woman in this carefully geometric design of choices, threatens to demonstrate a dangerous degree of clear-headed independence.

III

So far, this discussion of Trollope's sexual politics has restricted itself to the question of content, and the author's position, explicit or masked, with relation to his created characters and the attitudes they embody. From the politics of writing, however, let us turn to the politics of reading.

Can You Forgive Her? is a title which, in its interrogative form, involves the reader, and provokes a response. So regularly is the question reiterated by Trollope that no wonder certain critics reply, like Henry James, with bad-tempered impatience: 'Of course we can, and forget her, too, for that matter.'[19] But the inquiry deserves a far more sustained investigation, and not merely from the point of view of whether or not Alice was justified in holding back so long from marrying a man towards whom she felt increasingly unworthy. The pronoun on which the short query ends suggests, even before we open the novel, that we are to engage our moral judgement with the dubious behaviour, the peccadilloes of a specific, female, individual. Assessment of her conduct is necessarily related to her gender: a fact which immediately raises problems. To what extent is a late twentieth-century reader of this novel, particularly one alert to the specific conditions governing a woman's life in the mid-nineteenth century, going to respond in a way different to that programmed by Trollope in his more didactic textual comments? Moreover, to what degree can one postulate a difference in reaction between a male and a female reader of the story, whether at the time of its original publication, or today? We know that Trollope believed in the morally educative potential of fiction. In 'The Higher Education of Women', he advised his female listeners that, if they

will take some little trouble in the choice of your novels, the lessons which you will find taught in them are good lessons. Honour and honesty, modesty and self-denial, are as strongly

[19] Henry James, *Nation*, 28 September 1865, i, p. 409.

insisted on in our English novels as they are in our English sermons.[20]

But did he conceive of the reader of *Can You Forgive Her?* as being, in all probability, a woman, and was he primarily drawing his lessons for the benefit of this sex?

Today's readers are likely to start violently at various political assumptions in the novel—not least, at the possibility of describing George, without irony, as 'a stockbroker, a thoroughgoing Radical'. But it is in the terrain of relations between the sexes that our expectations have changed the most. It is thus far easier to sustain sympathy with the elements of frustration and rebellion in Alice's character, to notice the subordinate position which John Grey always demands of her, and the justice behind George's comment that Grey will 'make an upper servant of her; very respectable, no doubt, but still only an upper servant'. Not that George, with Kate's contrivance in the inn at Basle, is incapable of arranging the furniture so that Alice is a conversational 'prisoner'. However, it is her eventual husband who makes the most commanding use of his physical presence, and in relation to whom we ultimately judge the subjugation of Alice's self-possession. Before her marriage, Alice defiantly declares that, although Grey may offer his advice, he has no right to claim her obedience on any subject. In an age when obedience can safely be omitted from the marriage vows, the text has a far harder task in convincing the reader that Alice's capitulation is worthwhile, despite Grey's handsomeness and tediously indefatigable sense of honour. At least he satisfies one of her marital ambitions by taking up a Parliamentary seat: earlier he has failed to show any 'apparent solicitude' for that mid-nineteenth-century test of concern about social issues, 'Manchester and its cares'. Presumably, they will now be able to converse of an evening—as Alice shows herself well able to do in Mr. Palliser's company—whereas, during their uneasy courtship, John

[20] 'Higher Education', p. 85.

Grey employs his god-like mouth in drawing-room kisses rather than in eloquence. Nevertheless, we may choose to read Alice's reluctance to accept him not just, as Trollope ostensibly presents it, as a stubborn case of moral rectitude, but as a real unwillingness to give in to values, indeed, to demands, which she has not herself chosen. She has little option. In the Lucerne churchyard, Grey, rather coldly, claims her hand; speaks of his right to demand compliance, emotionally batters her with phrases about reconciling her conscience before God. Trollope employs a vocabulary of power, of omnipotence: Alice is pressed into compliance, 'pressed as in some countries the prisoner is pressed by the judge'. When she tells him he wins everything, always, there is little or no happiness in her surrender. As Grey leaves her alone for an hour's meditation, Trollope describes how, taking her fling at having her own will, 'She had assumed the command of the ship, and had thrown it upon the rocks, and she felt that she never ought to take the captain's place again.' No more masculine role-playing for Alice: the metaphor only serves to increase our latter-day apprehension over her projected future. We find ourselves contemplating whether or not we can forgive a quite different form of transgression from that envisaged by Trollope.

From the middle of the novel onwards, Trollope is keen to tell us that we should be ready to pardon Alice, that we must acknowledge her regret that she allowed herself to glory in her independence, that she had not allowed the sentiment of love to determine her marriage choice; that she had 'sinned against her sex'; that she had 'sinned with that sin which specially disgraces a woman'; that 'she had thrown off from her that wondrous aroma of precious delicacy, which is the greatest treasure of womanhood'. Betraying a slight apprehension that he is posing—and indeed answering—the question too early in the story, Trollope asks directly, for the first time, 'But can you forgive her, delicate reader?' For Trollope, the word 'delicate' was one heavily loaded with propriety; it is clearly a point

against Kate's womanhood that she should complain vehemently that this adjective, above all other words in the
language, reminds her of a whited sepulchre. His specific
designation of the reader as 'delicate', following on from the
application of the substantive in his preceding paragraph,
surely clarifies the reader's projected gender at this point.

When directly addressing his audience, Trollope does not
generally employ pronouns which make their sex explicit:
'you' is, on one level, neuter, enabling the addressee to
substitute his or her own position, although, in the sense
that it implies the application of a widely accepted moral
standard, it becomes invested with the dominant values of
the society within which it has been inscribed—values which,
in mid-nineteenth-century England, were unmistakably male-
determined. When Alice is deliberating on whether or not
to show George's letter to Kate, Trollope comments that the
reader will surmise that she was already half inclined to give
way, and to join her lot to that of George—'Alas, yes!
The reader will be right in his surmise.' But the author's
use of 'his' here seems to be the unconscious assumption of
the male gender as the neutral norm—an assumption as
likely to be questioned by today's reader, of course, as
Trollope's heart-felt lamentations at Alice's behaviour. For
Trollope makes it quite clear when he *is* addressing his own
sex alone. As George enters the House of Commons for the
first time, the author asks 'my male friend and reader'
whether he has never stood envying, in front of the members'
door, sorrowing to think—along with Trollope—that his
steps might never pass through it. Since, presenting the
character of Laura Standish in *Phineas Finn*, Trollope shows
us the slippery social slope which leads from a belief that a
woman's life is only half a life, since she cannot have a seat
in Parliament, he is understandably careful to exclude women
from this fervent aside.

On occasion, Trollope indicated that he envisaged novel
reading to be a predominantly female occupation. In 'Higher
Education', for example, it is the leisured woman whom he

singles out as the most likely sufferer from novel addiction. While not risking her valuable femininity in public life, she is rendered the more vulnerable when it comes to converting what should be a form of relaxation into a mode of life. But in a lecture of two years later, 'On English Prose Fiction as a Rational Amusement', when he speaks of the prevalence of novel reading in England, Trollope illustrates the uniformity of the habit through an image which includes all classes, both genders: 'Novels are in the hands of us all; from the Prime Minister down to the last-appointed scullery-maid.'[21] The rapid increase in novel consumption augments the case for their function as moral educators, particularly since almost all fictions deal with heterosexual love stories. Neither sex, for Trollope, has a monopoly on the need for such education, so

If novels, or any classes of novels, be bad for young women, then they are also bad for young men. I do not understand why it should be allowed, as by implication it is, that a man's thoughts may be impure. Of this I am sure, that he who condemns the reading of novels for his daughter, should condemn it for his son.[22]

But the lessons that a novel may teach remain specific to each sex. Thus Trollope asks whether the 'man-pupil' is to be taught that it is well to be false to the woman, to triumph over her, and to lie to her—in other words, to behave like George, nonchalantly throwing a dice to decide whether or not to send Alice his letter of proposal. Or is the male reader to be 'taught to be true and honest, and to be desirous of that which he seeks to win for noble and manly purposes?'[23]—to emulate John Grey. When it comes to the woman, is she to learn to be bold-faced, mean in spirit, fond of pleasure, and exacting, or is she to be taught the lesson which Alice herself finally assimilates—'to be modest, devoted, and unselfish?'[24]

[21] 'On English Prose Fiction as a Rational Amusement' (1870), reprinted in *Four Lectures*, p. 108.   [22] ibid. p. 107.
[23] ibid. pp. 109–10.   [24] ibid. p. 110.

We may query the values with which Trollope invests his version of sexual politics; may query, indeed, whether novels have the power to affect anyone in moral terms. In particular, we may now feel violent antagonism towards his stated position over the role of women. Hence, we can read with sympathy the desires of the female characters for a measure of independence, and question the fictional neatness when they are brought to marital heel. Among the protagonists, only Kate remains as an interesting reminder of the fact that in mid-Victorian England, not all women could be so neatly disposed of. But what we do have to credit Trollope with is the recognition that men and women do not read novels in the same way: that they approach them with separately constructed gender identities. Today, as in the nineteenth century, Trollope helps make us conscious of the way in which, when sexual difference is an important factor within society, such difference leads to difference in expectation, and difference in reading.

NOTE ON THE TEXT

Can You Forgive Her? was first published in monthly parts between January 1864 and August 1865 and in book form in two volumes, the first in October 1864 and the second in June 1865. A single volume edition was published in 1866.

The present edition follows that first published in The Oxford Trollope, under the general editorship of Michael Sadleir and Frederick Page, by Oxford University Press in 1948 (with illustrations by Lynton Lamb) and subsequently reissued in 1973. A number of printer's errors have been corrected but Trollope's variant spellings are retained. In the present edition each group of four chapters corresponds to a monthly instalment.

SELECT BIBLIOGRAPHY

The corpus of books on Trollope is large and still growing. As biography, N. John Hall's *Trollope: A Biography* (London, 1991), Victoria Glendinning's *Anthony Trollope* (London, 1992), Richard Mullen's *Anthony Trollope: A Victorian and his World* (London, 1990), and R. H. Super's *The Chronicler of Barsetshire* (Ann Arbor, Mich., 1988) supersede Michael Sadleir's pioneering *Trollope: A Commentary* (London, 1927). Sadleir also put together *Trollope: A Bibliography* (London, 1928). A splendidly pictorial account of Trollope's life and Civil Service career is given in C. P. Snow's *Trollope: His Life and Art* (London, 1975). N. John Hall has edited *The Letters of Anthony Trollope*, 2 vols. (Stanford, Calif., 1983). R. C. Terry compiles an eye- and earwitness portrait of the novelist in *Trollope: Interviews and Recollections* (London, 1987). Terry has also compiled the useful *A Trollope Chronology* (London, 1989). Trollope's own *An Autobiography* (London, 1883; repr. in Oxford World's Classics) remains the essential introduction to any reading of the fiction.

As a general introduction I would recommend James R. Kincaid, *The Novels of Anthony Trollope* (Oxford, 1977) and Ruth apRoberts, *Trollope, Artist and Moralist* (London, 1971). Some other very informative and useful critical books are: Bradford A. Booth, *Anthony Trollope: Aspects of his Life and Art* (London, 1958); Geoffrey Harvey, *The Art of Anthony Trollope* (London, 1980); W. J. Overton, *The Unofficial Trollope* (London, 1982); R. Polhemus, *The Changing World of Anthony Trollope* (Berkeley, Calif., 1968); A. Pollard, *Anthony Trollope* (London, 1978); R. C. Terry, *Anthony Trollope: The Artist in Hiding* (London, 1977); Andrew Wright, *Anthony Trollope: Dream and Art* (London, 1983). A particularly stimulating essay on *Barchester Towers* is included in D. A. Miller's *The Novel and the Police* (Berkeley, Calif., 1988).

For the critical reception of this and other Trollope fiction see: Donald Smalley (ed.), *Trollope: The Critical Heritage* (London, 1969), a selection of contemporary reviews; David Skilton, *Trollope and his Contemporaries* (London, 1972); J. C. Olmsted and J. E. Welch, *The Reputation of Trollope: An Annotated Bibliography 1925–75* (New York, 1978); Annette K. Lyons, *Anthony Trollope: An Annotated Bibliography* (Greenwood, Fla., 1985).

A CHRONOLOGY OF
ANTHONY TROLLOPE

Virtually all Trollope's fiction after *Framley Parsonage* (1860–1) appeared first in serial form, with book publication usually coming just prior to the final instalment of the serial.

1815   (24 Apr.) Born at 16 Keppel Street, Bloomsbury, the fourth son of Thomas and Frances Trollope.
(Summer ?) Family moves to Harrow-on-the-Hill.

1823   To Harrow School as a day-boy.

1825   To a private school at Sunbury.

1827   To school at Winchester College.

1830   Removed from Winchester and returned to Harrow.

1834   (Apr.) The family flees to Bruges to escape creditors.
(Nov.) Accepts a junior clerkship in the General Post Office, London.

1841   (Sept.) Made Postal Surveyor's Clerk at Banagher, King's County, Ireland.

1843   (mid-Sept.) Begins work on his first novel, *The Macdermots of Ballycloran*.

1844   (11 June) Marries Rose Heseltine.
(Aug.) Transferred to Clonmel, County Tipperary.

1846   (13 Mar.) Son, Henry Merivale Trollope, born.

1847   *The Macdermots of Ballycloran*, published in 3 vols. (Newby).
(27 Sept.) Son, Frederic James Anthony Trollope, born.

1848   *The Kellys and the O'Kellys; or Landlords and Tenants* 3 vols. (Colburn).
(Autumn) Moves to Mallow, County Cork.

1850   *La Vendée; An Historical Romance* 3 vols. (Colburn).
Writes *The Noble Jilt* (A play, published 1923).

1851   (1 Aug.) Sent to south-west of England on special postal mission.

1853   (29 July) Begins *The Warden* (the first of the Barsetshire novels).
(29 Aug.) Moves to Belfast as Acting Surveyor.

1854   (9 Oct.) Appointed Surveyor of Northern District of Ireland.

1855   *The Warden* 1 vol. (Longman).
Writes *The New Zealander*.
(June) Moves to Donnybrook, Dublin.

1857   *Barchester Towers* 3 vols. (Longman).

1858   *The Three Clerks* 3 vols. (Bentley).
Doctor Thorne 3 vols. (Chapman & Hall).

(Jan.) Departs for Egypt on Post Office business.
(Mar.) Visits Holy Land.
(Apr.–May) Returns via Malta, Gibraltar and Spain.
(May–Sept.) Visits Scotland and north of England on postal business.
(16 Nov.) Leaves for the West Indies on postal mission.

1859   *The Bertrams* 3 vols. (Chapman & Hall).
The West Indies and the Spanish Main 1 vol. (Chapman & Hall).
(3 July) Arrives home.
(Nov.) Leaves Ireland; settles at Waltham Cross, Hertfordshire, after being appointed Surveyor of the Eastern District of England.

1860   *Castle Richmond* 3 vols. (Chapman & Hall).
First serialized fiction, *Framley Parsonage*, published in the *Cornhill Magazine*.
(Oct.) Visits, with his wife, his mother and brother in Florence; makes the acquaintance of Kate Field, a 22-year-old American for whom he forms a romantic attachment.

1861   *Framley Parsonage* 3 vols. (Smith, Elder).
Tales of All Countries 1 vol. (Chapman & Hall).
(24 Aug.) Leaves for America to write a travel book.

1862   *Orley Farm* 2 vols. (Chapman & Hall).
North America 2 vols. (Chapman & Hall).
The Struggles of Brown, Jones and Robinson: By One of the Firm 1 vol. (New York, Harper—an American piracy; first English edition 1870, Smith, Elder).
(25 Mar.) Arrives home from America.
(5 Apr.) Elected to the Garrick Club.

1863   *Tales of All Countries*, Second Series, 1 vol. (Chapman & Hall).
Rachel Ray 2 vols. (Chapman & Hall).
(6 Oct.) Death of his mother, Mrs Frances Trollope.

1864   *The Small House at Allington* 2 vols. (Smith, Elder).
(12 Apr.) Elected a member of the Athenaeum Club.

1865   *Can You Forgive Her?* 2 vols. (Chapman & Hall).
Miss Mackenzie 1 vol. (Chapman & Hall).
Hunting Sketches 1 vol. (Chapman & Hall).

1866   *The Belton Estate* 3 vols. (Chapman & Hall).
Travelling Sketches 1 vol. (Chapman & Hall).
Clergymen of the Church of England 1 vol. (Chapman & Hall).

1867   *Nina Balatka* 2 vols. (Blackwood).
The Claverings 2 vols. (Smith, Elder).
The Last Chronicle of Barset 2 vols. (Smith, Elder).
Lotta Schmidt and Other Stories 1 vol. (Strahan).
(1 Sept.) Resigns from the Post Office.
Assumes editorship of *Saint Pauls Magazine*.

1868 *Linda Tressel* 2 vols. (Blackwood).
    (11 Apr.) Leaves London for the United States on postal mission.
    (26 July) Returns from America.
    (Nov.) Stands unsuccessfully as Liberal candidate for Beverley, Yorkshire.

1869 *Phineas Finn; the Irish Member* 2 vols. (Virtue & Co).
    He Knew He Was Right 2 vols. (Strahan).
    Did He Steal It? A Comedy in Three Acts (a version of *The Last Chronicle of Barset*, privately printed by Virtue & Co).

1870 *The Vicar of Bullhampton* 1 vol. (Bradbury, Evans).
    An Editor's Tales 1 vol. (Strahan).
    The Commentaries of Caesar 1 vol. (Blackwood).
    (Jan.–July) Eased out of *Saint Pauls Magazine*.

1871 *Sir Harry Hotspur of Humblethwaite* 1 vol. (Hurst & Blackett).
    Ralph the Heir 3 vols. (Hurst & Blackett).
    (Apr.) Gives up house at Waltham Cross.
    (24 May) Sails to Australia to visit his son.
    (27 July) Arrives at Melbourne.

1872 *The Golden Lion of Granpere* 1 vol. (Tinsley).
    (Jan.–Oct.) Travelling in Australia and New Zealand.
    (Dec.) Returns via the United states.

1873 *The Eustace Diamonds* 3 vols. (Chapman & Hall).
    Australia and New Zealand 2 vols. (Chapman & Hall).
    (Apr.) Settles in Montagu Square, London.

1874 *Phineas Redux* 2 vols. (Chapman & Hall).
    Lady Anna 2 vols. (Chapman & Hall).
    Harry Heathcote of Gangoil. A Tale of Australian Bush Life 1 vol. (Sampson Low).

1875 *The Way We Live Now* 2 vols. (Chapman & Hall).
    (1 Mar.) Leaves for Australia via Brindisi, the Suez Canal, and Ceylon.
    (4 May) Arrives in Australia.
    (Aug.–Oct.) Sailing homewards.
    (Oct.) Begins *An Autobiography*.

1876 *The Prime Minister* 4 vols. (Chapman & Hall).

1877 *The American Senator* 3 vols. (Chapman & Hall).
    (29 June) Leaves for South Africa.
    (11 Dec.) Sails for home.

1878 *South Africa* 2 vols. (Chapman & Hall).
    Is He Popenjoy? 3 vols. (Chapman & Hall).
    (June–July) Travels to Iceland in the yacht 'Mastiff'.
    How the 'Mastiffs' Went to Ireland 1 vol. (privately printed, Virtue & Co).

1879 *An Eye for an Eye* 2 vols. (Chapman & Hall).

Thackeray 1 vol. (Macmillan).
John Candigate 3 vols. (Chapman & Hall).
Cousin Henry 2 vols. (Chapman & Hall).

1880   *The Duke's Children* 3 vols. (Chapman & Hall).
The Life of Cicero 2 vols. (Chapman & Hall).
(July) Settles at South Harting, Sussex, near Petersfield.

1881   *Dr Wortle's School* 2 vols. (Chapman & Hall).
Ayala's Angel 3 vols. (Chapman & Hall).

1882   *Why Frau Frohmann Raised Her Prices; and Other Stories* 1 vol. (Isbister).
The Fixed Period 2 vols. (Blackwood).
Marion Fay 3 vols. (Chapman & Hall).
Lord Palmerston 1 vol. (Isbister).
Kept in the Dark 2 vols. (Chatto & Windus).
(May) Visits Ireland to collect material for a new Irish novel.
(Aug.) Returns to Ireland a second time.
(2 Oct.) Takes rooms for the winter at Garlant's Hotel, Suffolk St., London.
(3 Nov.) Suffers paralytic stroke.
(6 Dec.) Dies in nursing home, 34 Welbeck St., London.

1883   *Mr. Scarborough's Family* 3 vols. (Chatto & Windus).
The Landleaguers (unfinished) 3 vols. (Chatto & Windus).
An Autobiography 2 vols. (Blackwood).

1884   *An Old Man's Love* 2 vols. (Blackwood).

1923   *The Noble Jilt* 1 vol. (Constable).

1927   *London Tradesmen* 1 vol. (Elkin Mathews and Marrat).

1972   *The New Zealander* 1 vol. (Oxford University Press).

CONTENTS

Volume I

CONTENTS

CONTENTS
Volume II

CONTENTS

CONTENTS

CAN YOU FORGIVE HER?

VOLUME I

CHAPTER I

Mr. Vavasor and His Daughter

WHETHER or no, she, whom you are to forgive, if you can, did or did not belong to the Upper Ten Thousand* of this our English world, I am not prepared to say with any strength of affirmation. By blood she was connected with big people,—distantly connected with some very big people indeed, people who belonged to the Upper Ten Hundred if there be any such division; but of these very big relations she had known and seen little, and they had cared as little for her. Her grandfather, Squire Vavasor of Vavasor Hall, in Westmoreland, was a country gentleman, possessing some thousand a year at the outside, and he therefore never came up to London, and had no ambition to have himself numbered as one in any exclusive set. A hot-headed, ignorant, honest old gentleman, he lived ever at Vavasor Hall, declaring, to any who would listen to him, that the country was going to the mischief, and congratulating himself that at any rate, in his county, parliamentary reform had been powerless to alter the old political arrangements. Alice Vavasor, whose offence against the world I am to tell you, and if possible to excuse, was the daughter of his younger son; and as her father, John Vavasor, had done nothing to raise the family name to eminence, Alice could not lay claim to any high position from her birth as a Vavasor. John Vavasor had come up to London early in life as a barrister, and had failed.* He had failed at least in attaining either much wealth or much repute, though he had succeeded in earning, or perhaps I might better say, in obtaining, a livelihood. He had married a lady somewhat older than himself, who was in possession of four hundred a year, and who was related to those big people to whom I have alluded. Who these were, and the special nature of the relationship, I shall be called upon to explain hereafter, but at present it will suffice to say that Alice Macleod gave great offence to all her friends by her marriage.

1

She did not, however, give them much time for the indulgence of their anger. Having given birth to a daughter within twelve months of her marriage, she died, leaving in abeyance that question as to whether the fault of her marriage should or should not be pardoned by her family.

When a man marries an heiress for her money, if that money be within her own control, as was the case with Miss Macleod's fortune, it is generally well for the speculating lover that the lady's friends should quarrel with him and with her. She is thereby driven to throw herself entirely into the gentleman's arms, and he thus becomes possessed of the wife and the money without the abominable nuisance of stringent settlements. But the Macleods, though they quarrelled with Alice, did not quarrel with her à l'outrance.* They snubbed herself and her chosen husband; but they did not so far separate themselves from her and her affairs as to give up the charge of her possessions. Her four hundred a year was settled very closely on herself and on her children, without even a life interest having been given to Mr. Vavasor, and therefore when she died the mother's fortune became the property of the little baby. But, under these circumstances, the big people did not refuse to interest themselves to some extent on behalf of the father. I do not suppose that any actual agreement or compact was made between Mr. Vavasor and the Macleods; but it came to be understood between them that if he made no demand upon them for his daughter's money, and allowed them to have charge of her education, they would do something for him. He was a practising barrister, though his practice had never amounted to much; and a practising barrister is always supposed to be capable of filling any situation which may come in his way. Two years after his wife's death Mr. Vavasor was appointed assistant commissioner in some office which had to do with insolvents, and which was abolished three years after his appointment. It was at first thought that he would keep his eight hundred a year for life and be required to do nothing for it; but a wretched cheeseparing Whig government, as John Vavasor called it when describing the circumstances of the arrangement to his father, down in Westmoreland, would not permit this; it gave him the option of taking four hundred a year for doing nothing, or of keeping his whole income and attending three days a week for three hours a day during term time, at a miserable dingy little office near Chancery*Lane, where his duty would consist in signing his name to accounts which he never read, and at which he was never supposed even to look. He had sulkily elected to keep the money, and this signing had now been for nearly twenty years the business of his life. Of course he considered himself to be a very hardly-used man. One Lord Chancellor*after another he petitioned, begging that he might be relieved from the cruelty of his position, and allowed to take his salary without doing any-thing in return for it. The amount of work which he did perform was certainly a minimum of labour. Term time, as terms were counted in Mr. Vavasor's office, hardly comprised half the year, and the hours of weekly attendance did not do more than make one day's work a week for a working man; but Mr. Vavasor had been appointed an assistant commissioner, and with every Lord Chancellor he argued that all Westminster Hall, and Lincoln's Inn*to boot, had no right to call upon him to degrade himself by signing his name to accounts. In answer to every memorial he was offered the alternative of freedom with half his income; and so the thing went on.

There can, however, be no doubt that Mr. Vavasor was better off and happier with his almost nominal employment than he would have been without it. He always argued that it kept him in London; but he would undoubtedly have lived in London with or without his official occupation. He had become so habituated to London life in a small way, before the choice of leaving London was open to him, that nothing would have kept him long away from it. After his wife's death he dined at his club every day on which a dinner was not given to him by some friend elsewhere, and was rarely happy except when so dining. They who have seen him scanning the steward's list of dishes, and giving the necessary orders for his own and his friend's dinner, at about half-past four in the afternoon, have seen John Vavasor at the only moment of the day at which he is ever much in earnest. All other things are light and easy to him,—to be taken easily and to be dismissed easily. Even the eating of the dinner calls forth from him no special sign of energy. Sometimes a frown will gather on his brow as he tastes the first half glass from his bottle of claret; but as a rule that which he has prepared for himself with so much elaborate care, is consumed with only pleasant enjoyment. Now and again it will happen that the cook is treacherous even to him, and then he can hit hard; but in hitting he is quiet, and strikes with a smile on his face.

Such had been Mr. Vavasor's pursuits and pleasures in life up to the time at which my story commences. But I must not allow the reader to suppose that he was a man without good qualities. Had he when young possessed the gift of industry I think that he might have shone in his profession, and have been well spoken of and esteemed in the world. As it was he was a discontented man, but nevertheless he was popular, and to some extent esteemed. He was liberal as far as his means would permit; he was a man of his word; and he understood well that code of by-laws which was presumed to constitute the character of a gentleman in his circle. He knew how to carry himself well among men, and understood thoroughly what might be said, and what might not; what might be done among those with whom he lived, and what should be left undone. By nature, too, he was kindly disposed, loving many persons a little if he loved few or none passionately. More-over, at the age of fifty, he was a handsome man, with a fine forehead, round which the hair and beard was only beginning to show itself to be grey. He stood well, with a large person, only now beginning to become corpulent. His eyes were bright and grey, and his mouth and chin were sharply cut, and told of gentle birth. Most men who knew John Vavasor well, declared it to be a pity that he should spend his time in signing accounts in Chancery Lane.

I have said that Alice Vavasor's big relatives cared but little for her in her early years; but I have also said that they were

4

careful to undertake the charge of her education, and I must
explain away this little discrepancy. The biggest of these big
people had hardly heard of her; but there was a certain Lady

Macleod, not very big herself, but, as it were, hanging on to
the skirts of those who were so, who cared very much for
Alice. She was the widow of a Sir Archibald Macleod, K.C.B.,*
who had been a soldier, she herself having also been a Macleod
by birth; and for very many years past—from a time previous
to the birth of Alice Vavasor—she had lived at Cheltenham,
making short sojourns in London during the spring, when the
contents of her limited purse would admit of her doing so.

5

Of old Lady Macleod I think I may say that she was a good woman;—that she was a good woman, though subject to two of the most serious drawbacks to goodness which can afflict a lady. She was a Calvinistic Sabbatarian* in religion, and in worldly matters she was a devout believer in the high rank of her noble relatives. She could almost worship a youthful marquis, though he lived a life that would disgrace a heathen among heathens; and she could and did, in her own mind, condemn crowds of commonplace men and women to all eternal torments which her imagination could conceive, because they listened to profane music in a park on Sunday. Yet she was a good woman. Out of her small means she gave much away. She owed no man anything. She strove to love her neighbours. She bore much pain with calm unspeaking endurance, and she lived in trust of a better world. Alice Vavasor, who was after all only her cousin, she loved with an exceeding love, and yet Alice had done very much to extinguish such love. Alice, in the years of her childhood, had been brought up by Lady Macleod; at the age of twelve she had been sent to a school at Aix-la-Chapelle,—a comitatus*of her relatives having agreed that such was to be her fate, much in opposition to Lady Macleod's judgment; at nineteen she had returned to Cheltenham, and after remaining there for little more than a year, had expressed her unwillingness to remain longer with her cousin. She could sympathise neither with her relative's faults or virtues. She made an arrangement, therefore, with her father, that they two would keep house together in London, and so they had lived for the last five years;—for Alice Vavasor when she will be introduced to the reader had already passed her twenty-fourth birthday.

Their mode of life had been singular and certainly not in all respects satisfactory. Alice when she was twenty-one had the full command of her own fortune; and when she induced her father, who for the last fifteen years had lived in lodgings, to take a small house in Queen Anne Street,* of course she offered to incur a portion of the expense. He had warned her that his habits were not those of a domestic man, but he had been content simply so to warn her. He had not felt it to be his duty to decline the arrangement because he knew himself to be unable to give to his child all that attention which a widowed father under such circumstances should pay to an only daughter. The house had been taken, and Alice and he had lived together, but their lives had been quite apart. For a short time, for a month or two, he had striven to dine at home and even to remain at home through the evening; but the work had been too hard for him and he had utterly broken down. He had said to her and to himself that his health would fail him under the effects of so great a change made so late in life, and I am not sure that he had not spoken truly. At any rate the effort had been abandoned, and Mr. Vavasor now never dined at home. Nor did he and his daughter ever dine out together. Their joint means did not admit of their giving dinners, and therefore they could not make their joint way in the same circle. It thus came to pass that they lived apart,—quite apart. They saw each other, probably, daily; but they did little more than see each other. They did not even breakfast together, and after three o'clock in the day Mr. Vavasor was never to be found in his own house.

Miss Vavasor had made for herself a certain footing in society, though I am disposed to doubt her right to be considered as holding a place among the Upper Ten Thousand. Two classes of people she had chosen to avoid, having been driven to such avoidings by her aunt's preferences; marquises and such-like, whether wicked or otherwise, she had eschewed, and had eschewed likewise all Low Church tendencies. The eschewing of marquises is not generally very difficult. Young ladies living with their fathers on very moderate incomes in or about Queen Anne Street are not usually much troubled on that matter. Nor can I say that Miss Vavasor was so troubled. But with her there was a certain definite thing to be done towards such eschewal. Lady Macleod by no means avoided her noble relatives, nor did she at all avoid Alice Vavasor. When in London she was persevering in her visits to Queen Anne Street, though she considered herself, nobody knew why, not to be on speaking terms with Mr. Vavasor. And she strove hard to produce an intimacy between Alice and her noble relatives—such an intimacy as that which she herself enjoyed;—an intimacy which gave her a footing in their houses but no footing in their hearts, or even in their habits. But all this Alice declined with as much consistency as she did those other struggles which her old cousin made on her behalf,—strong, never-flagging, but ever-failing efforts to induce the girl to go to such places of worship as Lady Macleod herself frequented.

A few words must be said as to Alice Vavasor's person; one fact also must be told, and then, I believe, I may start upon my story. As regards her character, I will leave it to be read in the story itself. The reader already knows that she appears upon the scene at no very early age, and the mode of her life had perhaps given to her an appearance of more years than those which she really possessed. It was not that her face was old, but that there was nothing that was girlish in her manners. Her demeanour was as staid, and her voice as self-possessed, as though she had already been ten years married. In person she was tall and well made, rather large in her neck and shoulders, as were all the Vavasors, but by no means fat. Her hair was brown, but very dark, and she wore it rather lower upon her forehead than is customary at the present day. Her eyes, too, were dark, though they were not black, and her complexion, though not quite that of a brunette, was far away from being fair. Her nose was somewhat broad, and retroussé too, but to my thinking it was a charming nose, full of character, and giving to her face at times a look of pleasant humour, which it would otherwise have lacked. Her mouth was large, and full of character, and her chin oval, dimpled, and finely chiselled, like her father's. I beg you, in taking her for all in all, to admit that she was a fine, handsome, high-spirited young woman.

And now for my fact. At the time of which I am writing she was already engaged to be married.

CHAPTER II

Lady Macleod

I CANNOT say that the house in Queen Anne Street was a pleasant house. I am now speaking of the material house, made up of the walls and furniture, and not of any pleasantness or unpleasantness supplied by the inmates. It was a small house on the south side of the street, squeezed in between two large mansions which seemed to crush it, and by which its fair proportion of doorstep and area was in truth curtailed. The stairs were narrow; the dining-room was dark, and possessed none of those appearances of plenteous hospitality which a dining-room should have. But all this would have been as nothing if the drawing-room had been pretty as it is the bounden duty of all drawing-rooms to be. But Alice Vavasor's drawing-room was not pretty. Her father had had the care of furnishing the house, and he had intrusted the duty to a tradesman who had chosen green paper, a green carpet, green curtains, and green damask chairs. There was a green damask sofa, and two green armchairs opposite to each other at the two sides of the fireplace. The room was altogether green, and was not enticing. In shape it was nearly square, the very small back room on the same floor not having been, as is usual, added to it. This had been fitted up as a 'study' for Mr. Vavasor, and was very rarely used for any purpose.

Most of us know when we enter a drawing-room whether it is a pretty room or no; but how few of us know how to make a drawing-room pretty! There has come up in London in these latter days a form of room so monstrously ugly that I will venture to say that no other people on earth but Londoners would put up with it. Londoners, as a rule, take their houses as they can get them, looking only to situation, size, and price. What Grecian, what Roman, what Turk, what Italian would endure, or would ever have endured, to use a room with a monstrous cantle* in the form of a parallelogram cut sheerly out of one corner of it? This is the shape of room we have now adopted,—or rather which the builders have adopted for us,—

9

in order to throw the whole first floor into one apartment which may be presumed to have noble dimensions,—with such drawback from it as the necessities of the staircase may require. A sharp unadorned corner projects itself into these would-be noble dimensions, and as ugly a form of chamber is produced as any upon which the eye can look. I would say more on the subject if I dared to do so here, but I am bound now to confine myself to Miss Vavasor's room. The monstrous deformity of which I have spoken was not known when that house in Queen Anne Street was built. There is to be found no such abomination of shape in the buildings of our ancestors,— not even in the days of George the Second. But yet the draw-ing-room of which I speak was ugly, and Alice knew that it was so. She knew that it was ugly, and she would greatly have liked to banish the green sofa, to have re-papered the wall, and to have hung up curtains with a dash of pink through them. With the green carpet she would have been contented. But her father was an extravagant man; and from the day on which she had come of age she had determined that it was her special duty to avoid extravagance.

'It's the ugliest room I ever saw in my life,' her father once said to her.

'It is not very pretty,' Alice replied.

'I'll go halves with you in the expense of redoing it,' said Mr. Vavasor.

'Wouldn't that be extravagant, papa? The things have not been here quite four years yet.'

Then Mr. Vavasor had shrugged his shoulders and said nothing more about it. It was little to him whether the draw-ing-room in Queen Anne Street was ugly or pretty. He was on the committee of his club, and he took care that the furniture there should be in all respects comfortable.

It was now June; and that month Lady Macleod was in the habit of spending among her noble relatives in London when she had succeeded in making both ends so far overlap each other at Cheltenham as to give her the fifty pounds necessary for this purpose. For though she spent her month in London among her noble friends, it must not be supposed that her noble friends gave her bed and board. They sometimes gave her tea, such as it was, and once or twice in the month they gave the old lady a second-rate dinner. On these occasions she hired a little parlour and bedroom behind it in King Street, Saint James's,* and lived a hot, uncomfortable life, going about at nights to gatherings of fashionable people of which she in her heart disapproved, seeking for smiles which seldom came to her, and which she excused herself for desiring because they were the smiles of her kith and her kin, telling herself always that she made this vain journey to the modern Babylon*for the good of Alice Vavasor, and telling herself as often that she now made it for the last time. On the occasion of her preceding visit she had reminded herself that she was then seventy-five years old, and had sworn to herself that she would come to London no more; but here she was again in London, having justified the journey to herself on the plea that there were circumstances in Alice's engagement which made it desirable that she should for a while be near her niece. Her niece, as she thought, was hardly managing her own affairs discreetly.

'Well, aunt,' said Alice, as the old lady walked into the drawing-room one morning at eleven o'clock. Alice always called Lady Macleod her aunt, though, as has been before explained, there was no such close connexion between them. During Lady Macleod's sojourn in London these morning visits were made almost every day. Alice never denied herself, and even made a point of remaining at home to receive them unless she had previously explained that she would be out; but I am not prepared to say that they were, of their own nature, agreeable to her.

'Would you mind shutting the window, my dear?' said Lady Macleod, seating herself stiffly on one of the small ugly green chairs. She had been educated at a time when easy-chairs were considered vicious, and among people who regarded all easy postures as being so; and she could still boast, at seventy-six, that she never leaned back. 'Would you mind shutting the window? I'm so warm that I'm afraid of the draught.'

'You don't mean to say that you've walked from King Street,' said Alice, doing as she was desired.

'Indeed I do,—every step of the way. Cabs are so ruinous. It's a most unfortunate thing; they always say it's just over the two miles here. I don't believe a word of it, because I'm only a little more than the half-hour walking it; and those men will say anything. But how can I prove it, you know?'

'I really think it's too far for you to walk when it's so warm.'

'But what can I do, my dear? I must come, when I've specially come up to London to see you. I shall have a cab back again, because it'll be hotter then, and dear Lady Midlothian has promised to send her carriage at three to take me to the concert. I do so wish you'd go, Alice.'

'It's out of the question, aunt. The idea of my going in that way at the last moment, without any invitation!'

'It wouldn't be without an invitation, Alice. The marchioness has said to me over and over again how glad she would be to see you, if I would bring you.'

'Why doesn't she come and call if she is so anxious to know me?'

'My dear, you've no right to expect it; you haven't indeed. She never calls even on me.'

'I know I've no right, and I don't expect it, and I don't want it. But neither has she a right to suppose that, under such circumstances, I shall go to her house. You might as well give it up, aunt. Cart-ropes wouldn't drag me there.'

'I think you are very wrong,—particularly under your present circumstances. A young woman that is going to be married, as you are——'

'As I am,——perhaps.'

'That's nonsense, Alice. Of course you are; and for his sake you are bound to cultivate any advantages that naturally belong to you. As to Lady Midlothian or the marchioness coming to call on you here in your father's house, after all that has passed, you really have no right to look for it.'

'And I don't look for it.'

'That sort of people are not expected to call. If you'll think of it, how could they do it with all the demands they have on their time?'

'My dear aunt, I wouldn't interfere with their time for worlds.'

'Nobody can say of me, I'm sure, that I run after great people or rich people. It does happen that some of the nearest relations I have,—indeed I may say the nearest relations,— are people of high rank; and I do not see that I'm bound to turn away from my own flesh and blood because of that, particularly when they are always so anxious to keep up the connexion.'

'I was only speaking of myself, aunt. It is very different with you. You have known them all your life.'

'And how are you to know them if you won't begin? Lady Midlothian said to me only yesterday that she was glad to hear that you were going to be married so respectably, and then——'

'Upon my word I'm very much obliged to her ladyship. I wonder whether she considered that she married respectably when she took Lord Midlothian?'

Now Lady Midlothian had been unfortunate in her marriage, having united herself to a man of bad character, who had used her ill, and from whom she had now been for some years separated. Alice might have spared her allusion to this mis-fortune when speaking of the countess to the cousin who was so fond of her, but she was angered by the application of that odious word respectable to her own prospects; and perhaps the more angered as she was somewhat inclined to feel that the epithet did suit her own position. Her engagement, she had sometimes told herself, was very respectable, and had as often told herself that it lacked other attractions which it should have possessed. She was not quite pleased with herself in having accepted John Grey,—or rather perhaps was not satis-fied with herself in having loved him. In her many thoughts on the subject, she always admitted to herself that she had accepted him simply because she loved him;—that she had given her quick assent to his quick proposal simply because he had won her heart. But she was sometimes almost angry with herself that she had permitted her heart to be thus easily taken from her, and had rebuked herself for her girlish facility. But the marriage would be at any rate respectable. Mr. Grey was a man of high character, of good though moderate means; he was, too, well educated, of good birth, a gentleman, and a man of talent. No one could deny that the marriage would be highly respectable, and her father had been more than satisfied. Why Miss Vavasor herself was not quite satisfied will, I hope, in time make itself appear. In the meanwhile it can be understood that Lady Midlothian's praise would gall her.

'Alice, don't be uncharitable,' said Lady Macleod severely. 'Whatever may have been Lady Midlothian's misfortunes no one can say that they have resulted from her own fault.'

'Yes, they can, aunt, if she married a man whom she knew to be a scapegrace because he was very rich and an earl.'

'She was the daughter of a nobleman herself, and only married in her own degree. But I don't want to discuss that. She meant to be good-natured when she mentioned your marriage, and you should take it as it was meant. After all she was only your mother's second cousin——'

'Dear aunt, I make no claim on her cousinship.'

'But she admits the claim, and is quite anxious that you should know her. She has been at the trouble to find out everything about Mr. Grey, and told me that nothing could be more satisfactory.'

'Upon my word I am very much obliged to her.'

Lady Macleod was a woman of much patience, and possessed also of considerable perseverance. For another half-hour she went on expatiating on the advantages which would accrue to Alice as a married woman from an acquaintance with her noble relatives, and endeavouring to persuade her that no better opportunity than the present would present itself. There would be a place in Lady Midlothian's carriage, as none other of the daughters were going but Lady Jane. Lady Midlothian would take it quite as a compliment, and a concert was not like a ball or any customary party. An unmarried girl might very properly

14

go to a concert under such circumstances as now existed without any special invitation. Lady Macleod ought to have known her adopted niece better. Alice was immoveable. As a matter of course she was immoveable. Lady Macleod had seldom been able to persuade her to anything, and ought to have been well sure that, of all things, she could not have persuaded her to this.

Then, at last, they came to another subject, as to which Lady Macleod declared that she had specially come on this special morning, forgetting, probably, that she had already made the same assertion with reference to the concert. But in truth the last assertion was the correct one, and on that other subject she had been hurried on to say more than she meant by the eagerness of the moment. All the morning she had been full of the matter on which she was now about to speak. She had discussed it quite at length with Lady Midlothian;—though she was by no means prepared to tell Alice Vavasor that any such discussion had taken place. From the concert, and the effect which Lady Midlothian's countenance might have upon Mr. Grey's future welfare, she got herself by degrees round to a projected Swiss tour which Alice was about to make. Of this Swiss tour she had heard before, but had not heard who were to be Miss Vavasor's companions until Lady Midlothian had told her. How it had come to pass that Lady Midlothian had interested herself so much in the concerns of a person whom she did not know, and on whom she in her greatness could not be expected to call, I cannot say; but from some quarter she had learned who were the proposed companions of Alice Vavasor's tour, and she had told Lady Macleod that she did not at all approve of the arrangement.

'And when do you go, Alice?' said Lady Macleod.

'Early in July, I believe. It will be very hot, but Kate must be back by the middle of August.' Kate Vavasor was Alice's first cousin.

'Oh! Kate is to go with you?'

'Of course she is. I could not go alone, or with no one but George. Indeed it was Kate who made up the party.'

'Of course you could not go alone with George,' said Lady

Macleod, very grimly. Now George Vavasor was Kate's brother, and was therefore also first cousin to Alice. He was heir to the old squire down in Westmoreland, with whom Kate lived, their father being dead. Nothing, it would seem, could be more rational than that Alice should go to Switzerland with her cousins; but Lady Macleod was clearly not of this opinion; she looked very grim as she made this allusion to cousin George, and seemed to be preparing herself for a fight.

'That is exactly what I say,' answered Alice. 'But, indeed, he is simply going as an escort to me and Kate, as we don't like the rôle of unprotected females. It is very good-natured of him, seeing how much his time is taken up.'

'I thought he never did anything.'

'That's because you don't know him, aunt.'

'No; certainly I don't know him.' She did not add that she had no wish to know Mr. George Vavasor, but she looked it. 'And has your father been told that he is going?'

'Of course he has.'

'And does——' Lady Macleod hesitated a little before she went on, and then finished her question with a little spasmodic assumption of courage. 'And does Mr. Grey know that he is going?'

Alice remained silent for a full minute before she answered this question, during which Lady Macleod sat watching her grimly, with her eyes very intent upon her niece's face. If she supposed such silence to have been in any degree produced by shame in answering the question, she was much mistaken. But it may be doubted whether she understood the character of the girl whom she thought she knew so well, and it is probable that she did make such mistake.

'I might tell you simply that he does,' said Alice at last, 'seeing that I wrote to him yesterday, letting him know that such were our arrangements; but I feel that I should not thus answer the question you mean to ask. You want to know whether Mr. Grey will approve of it. As I only wrote yesterday of course I have not heard, and therefore cannot say. But

I can say this, aunt, that much as I might regret his dis-approval, it would make no change in my plans.'

'Would it not? Then I must tell you, you are very wrong. It ought to make a change. What! the disapproval of the man you are going to marry make no change in your plans?'

'Not in that matter. Come, aunt, if we must discuss this matter let us do it at any rate fairly. In an ordinary way, if Mr. Grey had asked me to give up for any reason my trip altogether, I should have given it up certainly, as I would give up any other indifferent project at the request of so dear a friend,— a friend with whom I am so—so—so—closely connected. But if he asked me not to travel with my cousin George, I should refuse him absolutely, without a word of parley on the subject, simply because of the nature and closeness of my connection with him. I suppose you understand what I mean, aunt?'

'I suppose I do. You mean that you would refuse to obey him on the very subject on which he has a right to claim your obedience.'

'He has no right to claim my obedience on any subject,' said Alice; and as she spoke Aunt Macleod jumped up with a little start at the vehemence of the words, and of the tone in which they were expressed. She had heard that tone before, and might have been used to it; but, nevertheless, the little jump was involuntary. 'At present he has no right to my obedience on any subject, but least of all on that,' said Alice. 'His advice he may give me, but I am quite sure he will not ask for obedience.'

'And if he advises you you will slight his advice.'

'If he tells me that I had better not travel with my cousin George I shall certainly not take his advice. Moreover, I should be careful to let him know how much I was offended by any such counsel from him. It would show a littleness on his part, and a suspicion of which I cannot suppose him to be capable.' Alice, as she said this, got up from her seat and walked about the room. When she had finished she stood at one of the windows with her back to her visitor. There was silence between them for a minute or two, during which Lady

Macleod was deeply considering how best she might speak the terrible words, which, as Alice's nearest female relative, she felt herself bound to utter. At last she collected her thoughts and her courage, and spoke out.

'My dear Alice, I need hardly say that if you had a mother living, or any person with you filling the place of a mother, I should not interfere in this matter.'

'Of course, Aunt Macleod, if you think I am wrong you have quite a right to say so.'

'I do think you are wrong,—very wrong, indeed; and if you persist in this I am afraid I must say that I shall think you wicked. Of course Mr. Grey cannot like you to travel with George Vavasor.'

'And why not, aunt?' Alice, as she asked this question, turned round and confronted Lady Macleod boldly. She spoke with a steady voice, and fixed her eyes upon the old lady's face, as though determined to show that she had no fear of what might be said to her.

'Why not, Alice? Surely you do not wish me to say why not.'

'But I do wish you to say why not. How can I defend myself till the accusation is made?'

'You are now engaged to marry Mr. Grey, with the consent and approbation of all your friends. Two years ago you had—had——'

'Had what, aunt? If you mean to say that two years ago I was engaged to my cousin George you are mistaken. Three years ago I told him that under certain conditions I would become engaged to him. But my conditions did not suit him, nor his me, and no engagement was ever made. Mr. Grey knows the history of the whole thing. As far as it was possible I have told him everything that took place.'

'The fact was, Alice, that George Vavasor's mode of life was such that an engagement with him would have been absolute madness.'

'Dear aunt, you must excuse me if I say that I cannot discuss George Vavasor's mode of life. If I were thinking of becoming his wife you would have a perfect right to discuss it, because of your constant kindness to me. But as matters are he is simply a cousin; and as I like him and you do not, we had better say nothing about him.'

'I must say this,—that after what has passed, and at the present crisis of your life——'

'Dear aunt, I'm not in any crisis.'

'Yes, you are, Alice; in the most special crisis of a girl's life. You are still a girl, but you are the promised wife of a very worthy man, who will look to you for all his domestic happiness. George Vavasor has the name, at least, of being very wild.'

'The worthy man and the wild man must fight it out between them. If I were going away with George by himself, there might be something in what you say.'

'That would be monstrous.'

'Monstrous or not, it isn't what I'm about to do. Kate and I have put our purses together, and are going to have an outing for our special fun and gratification. As we should be poor travellers alone, George has promised to go with his sister. Papa knows all about it, and never thought of making any objection.'

Lady Macleod shook her head. She did not like to say anything against Mr. Vavasor before his daughter; but the shaking of her head was intended to signify that Mr. Vavasor's assent in such a matter was worth nothing.

'I can only say again,' said Lady Macleod, 'that I think Mr. Grey will be displeased,—and that he will have very great cause for displeasure. And I think, moreover, that his approbation ought to be your chief study. I believe, my dear, I'll ask you to let Jane get me a cab. I shan't have a bit too much time to dress for the concert.'

Alice simply rang the bell, and said no further word on the subject which they had been discussing. When Lady Macleod got up to go away, Alice kissed her, as was customary with them, and the old lady as she went uttered her customary valediction. 'God bless you, my dear. Good-bye! I'll come to-morrow if I can.' There was therefore no quarrel between them. But both of them felt that words had been spoken which must probably lead to some diminution of their past intimacy.

When Lady Macleod had gone Alice sat alone for an hour thinking of what had passed between them,—thinking rather of those two men, the worthy man and the wild man, whose names had been mentioned in close connection with herself. John Grey was a worthy man, a man worthy at all points, as far as she knew him. She told herself that it was so. And she told herself, also, that her cousin George was wild,—very wild. And yet her thoughts were, I fear, on the whole more kindly towards her cousin than towards her lover. She had declared to her aunt that John Grey would be incapable of such suspicion as would be shown by any objection on his part to the arrangements made for the tour. She had said so, and had so believed; and yet she continued to brood over the position which her affairs would take, if he did make the objection which Lady Macleod anticipated. She told herself over and over again, that under such circumstances she would not give way an inch. 'He is free to go,' she said to herself. 'If he does not trust me he is quite free to go.' It may almost be said that she came at last to anticipate from her lover that very answer to her own letter which she had declared him to be incapable of making.

CHAPTER III

John Grey, the Worthy Man

M R. GREY's answer to Alice Vavasor's letter, which was duly sent by return of post and duly received on the morning after Lady Macleod's visit, may perhaps be taken as giving a sample of his worthiness. It was dated from Nethercoats, a small country-house in Cambridgeshire which belonged to him, at which he already spent much of his time, and at which he intended to live altogether after his marriage.

'Nethercoats, June, 186—.

'DEAREST ALICE,

'I am glad you have settled your affairs,—foreign affairs, I mean,—so much to your mind. As to your home affairs they are not, to my thinking, quite so satisfactorily arranged. But as I am a party interested in the latter my opinion may perhaps have an undue bias. Touching the tour, I quite agree with you that you and Kate would have been uncomfortable alone. It's a very fine theory, that of women being able to get along without men as well as with them; but, like other fine theories, it will be found very troublesome by those who first put it in practice. Gloved hands, petticoats, feminine softness, and the general homage paid to beauty, all stand in the way of success. These things may perhaps some day be got rid of, and possibly with advantage; but while young ladies are still encumbered with them a male companion will always be found to be a comfort. I don't quite know whether your cousin George is the best possible knight you might have chosen. I should consider myself to be infinitely preferable, had my going been upon the cards. Were you in danger of meeting Paynim*foes, he, no doubt, would kill them off much quicker than I could do, and would be much more serviceable in liberating you from the dungeons of oppressors, or even from stray tigers in the Swiss forests. But I doubt his being punctual with the luggage. He will want you or Kate to keep the accounts, if any are kept. He will be slow in getting you glasses of water at the railway stations, and will always keep you waiting at breakfast. I hold that a man with two ladies on a tour should be an absolute slave to them, or they will not fully enjoy themselves. He should simply be an upper servant, with the privilege of sitting at the same table with his mistresses. I have my doubts as to whether your cousin is fit for the place; but, as to myself, it is just the thing that I was made for. Luckily, however, neither you nor Kate are without wills of your own, and perhaps you may be able to reduce Mr. Vavasor to obedience.

'As to the home affairs I have very little to say here,—in this letter. I shall of course run up and see you before you start, and shall probably stay a week in town. I know I ought not to do so, as it will be a week of idleness, and yet not a week of happiness. I'd sooner have an hour with you in the country than a whole day in London. And I always feel in town that

I've too much to do to allow of my doing anything. If it were sheer idleness I could enjoy it, but it is a feverish idleness, in which one is driven here and there, expecting some gratification which not only never comes, but which never even begins to come. I will, however, undergo a week of it,—say the last seven days of this month, and shall trust to you to recompense me by as much of yourself as your town doings will permit.

'And now again as to those home affairs. If I say nothing now I believe you will understand why I refrain. You have cunningly just left me to imply, from what you say, that all my arguments have been of no avail; but you do not answer them, or even tell me that you have decided. I shall therefore imply nothing, and still trust to my personal eloquence for success. Or rather not trust,—not trust, but hope.

'The garden is going on very well. We are rather short of water, and therefore not quite as bright as I had hoped; but we are preparing with untiring industry for future brightness. Your commands have been obeyed in all things, and Morrison always says "The mistress didn't mean this," or "The mistress did intend that." God bless the mistress is what I now say, and send her home, to her own home, to her flowers, and her fruit, and her house, and her husband, as soon as may be, with no more of those delays which are to me so grievous, and which seem to me to be so unnecessary. That is my prayer.

'Yours ever and always,

'J. G.'

'I didn't give commands,' Alice said to herself, as she sat with the letter at her solitary breakfast-table. 'He asked me how I liked the things, and of course I was obliged to say. I was obliged to seem to care, even if I didn't care.' Such were her first thoughts as she put the letter back into its envelope, after reading it the second time. When she opened it, which she did quickly, not pausing a moment lest she should suspect herself of fearing to see what might be its contents, her mind was full of that rebuke which her aunt had anticipated, and which she had almost taught herself to expect. She had torn

the letter open rapidly, and had dashed at its contents with
quick eyes. In half a moment she had seen what was the nature
of the reply respecting the proposed companion of her tour,
and then she had completed her reading slowly enough. 'No;

I gave no commands,' she repeated to herself, as though she
might thereby absolve herself from blame in reference to some
possible future accusations, which might perhaps be brought
against her under certain circumstances which she was contemplating.

Then she considered the letter bit by bit, taking it backwards, and sipping her tea every now and then amidst her
thoughts. No; she had no home, no house, there. She had no
husband;—not as yet. He spoke of their engagement as though
it were a betrothal, as betrothals used to be of yore; as though
they were already in some sort married. Such betrothals were

not made now-a-days. There still remained, both to him and to her, a certain liberty of extricating themselves from this engagement. Should he come to her and say that he found that their contemplated marriage would not make him happy, would not she release him without a word of reproach? Would not she regard him as much more honourable in doing so than in adhering to a marriage which was distasteful to him? And if she would so judge him,—judge him and certainly acquit him, was it not reasonable that she under similar circumstances should expect a similar acquittal? Then she declared to herself that she carried on this argument within her own breast simply as an argument, induced to do so by that assertion on his part that he was already her husband,—that his house was even now her home. She had no intention of using that power which was still hers. She had no wish to go back from her pledged word. She thought that she had no such wish. She loved him much, and admired him even more than she loved him. He was noble, generous, clever, good,—so good as to be almost perfect; nay, for aught she knew he was perfect. Would that he had some faults! Would that he had! Would that he had! How could she, full of faults as she knew herself to be,—how could she hope to make happy a man perfect as he was! But then there would be no doubt as to her present duty. She loved him, and that was everything. Having told him that she loved him, and having on that score accepted his love, nothing but a change in her heart towards him could justify her in seeking to break the bond which bound them together. She did love him, and she loved him only.

But she had once loved her cousin. Yes, truly it was so. In her thoughts she did not now deny it. She had loved him, and was tormented by a feeling that she had had a more full delight in that love than in this other that had sprung up subsequently. She had told herself that this had come of her youth;—that love at twenty was sweeter than it could be afterwards. There had been a something of rapture in that earlier dream which could never be repeated,—which could never live, indeed, except in a dream. Now, now that she was older and perhaps wiser, love meant a partnership, in which each partner would be honest to the other, in which each would wish and strive for the other's welfare, so that thus their joint welfare might be insured. Then, in those early girlish days, it had meant a total abnegation of self. The one was of earth, and therefore possible. The other had been a ray from heaven,—and impossible, except in a dream.

And she had been mistaken in her first love. She admitted that frankly. He whom she had worshipped had been an idol of clay,* and she knew that it was well for her to have abandoned that idolatry. He had not only been untrue to her, but, worse than that, had been false in excusing his untruth. He had not only promised falsely, but had made such promises with a deliberate, premeditated falsehood. And he had been selfish, coldly selfish, weighing the value of his own low lusts against that of her holy love. She had known this, and had parted from him with an oath to herself that no promised contrition on his part should ever bring them again together. But she had pardoned him as a man, though never as a lover, and had bade him welcome again as a cousin and as her friend's brother. She had again become very anxious as to his career, not hiding her regard, but professing that anxiety aloud. She knew him to be clever, ambitious, bold,—and she believed even yet, in spite of her own experience, that he might not be bad at heart. Now, as she told herself that in truth she loved the man to whom her troth was plighted, I fear that she almost thought more of that other man from whom she had torn herself asunder.

'Why should he find himself unhappy in London?' she said, as she went back to the letter. 'Why should he pretend to condemn the very place which most men find the fittest for all their energies? Were I a man, no earthly consideration should induce me to live elsewhere. It is odd how we differ in all things. However brilliant might be his own light, he would be contented to hide it under a bushel.'

And at last she recurred to that matter as to which she had been so anxious when she first opened her lover's letter. It will be remembered how assured she had expressed herself that Mr. Grey would not condescend to object to her travelling with her cousin. He had not so condescended. He had written on the matter with a pleasant joke, like a gentleman as he was, disdaining to allude to the past passages in the life of her whom he loved, abstaining even from expressing anything that might be taken as a permission on his part. There had been in Alice's words, as she told him of their proposed plan, a something that had betrayed a tremor in her thoughts. She had studiously striven so to frame her phrases that her tale might be told as any other simple statement,—as though there had been no trembling in her mind as she wrote. But she had failed, and she knew that she had failed. She had failed; and he had read all her effort and all her failure. She was quite conscious of this; she felt it thoroughly; and she knew that he was noble and a gentleman to the last drop of his blood. And yet—yet—yet there was almost a feeling of disappointment in that he had not written such a letter as Lady Macleod had anticipated.

During the next week Lady Macleod still came almost daily to Queen Anne Street, but nothing further was said between her and Miss Vavasor as to the Swiss tour; nor were any questions asked about Mr. Grey's opinion on the subject. The old lady of course discovered that there was no quarrel, or, as she believed, any probability of a quarrel; and with that she was obliged to be contented. Nor did she again on this occasion attempt to take Alice to Lady Midlothian's. Indeed, their usual subjects of conversation were almost abandoned, and Lady Macleod's visits, though they were as constant as heretofore, were not so long. She did not dare to talk about Mr. Grey, and because she did not so dare, was determined to regard herself as in a degree ill-used. So she was silent, reserved, and fretful. At length came the last day of her London season, and her last visit to her niece. 'I would come because it's my last day,' said Lady Macleod; 'but really I'm so hurried, and have so many things to do, that I hardly know how to manage it.'

'It's very kind,' said Alice, giving her aunt an affectionate squeeze of the hand.

'I'm keeping the cab, so I can stay just twenty-five minutes. I've marked the time accurately, but I know the man will swear it's over the half-hour.'

'You'll have no more trouble about cabs, aunt, when you are back in Cheltenham.'

'The flys*are worse, my dear. I really think they're worse. I pay the bill every month, but they've always one down that I didn't have. It's the regular practice, for I've had them from all the men in the place.'

'It's hard enough to find honest men anywhere, I suppose.'

'Or honest women either. What do you think of Mrs. Green wanting to charge me for an extra week, because she says I didn't give her notice till Tuesday morning? I won't pay her, and she may stop my things if she dares. However, it's the last time. I shall never come up to London again, my dear.'

'Oh, aunt, don't say that!'

'But I do say it, my dear. What should an old woman like me do, trailing up to town every year, merely because it's what people choose to call the season?'

'To see your friends, of course. Age doesn't matter when a person's health is so good as yours.'

'If you knew what I suffer from lumbago,—though I must say coming to London always does cure that for the time. But as for friends——! Well, I suppose one has no right to complain when one gets to be as old as I am; but I declare I believe that those I love best would sooner be without me than with me.'

'Do you mean me, aunt?'

'No, my dear, I don't mean you. Of course my life would have been very different if you could have consented to remain with me till you were married. But I didn't mean you. I don't know that I meant any one. You shouldn't mind what an old woman like me says.'

'You're a little melancholy because you're going away.'

'No, indeed. I don't know why I stayed the last week. I did say to Lady Midlothian that I thought I should go on the 20th; and, though I know that she knew that I really didn't go, she has not once sent to me since. To be sure they've been out every night; but I thought she might have asked me to come and lunch. It's so very lonely dining by myself in lodgings in London.'

'And yet you never will come and dine with me.'

'No, my dear; no. But we won't talk about that. I've just one word more to say. Let me see. I've just six minutes to stay. I've made up my mind that I'll never come up to town again,—except for one thing.'

'And what's that, aunt?' Alice, as she asked the question, well knew what that one thing was.

'I'll come for your marriage, my dear. I do hope you will not keep me waiting long.'

'Ah! I can't make any promise. There's no knowing when that may be.'

'And why should there be no knowing? I always think that when a girl is once engaged the sooner she's married the better. There may be reasons for delay on the gentleman's part.'

'There very often are, you know.'

'But, Alice, you don't mean to say that Mr. Grey is putting it off?'

Alice was silent for a moment, during which Lady Macleod's face assumed a look of almost tragic horror. Was there something wrong on Mr. Grey's side of which she was altogether unaware? Alice, though for a second or two she had been guilty of a slight playful deceit, was too honest to allow the impression to remain. 'No, aunt,' she said; 'Mr. Grey is not putting it off. It has been left to me to fix the time.'

'And why don't you fix it?'

'It is such a serious thing! After all it is not more than four months yet since I—I accepted him. I don't know that there has been any delay.'

'But you might fix the time now, if he wishes it.'

'Well, perhaps I shall,—some day, aunt. I'm going to think about it, and you mustn't drive me.'

'But you should have some one to advise you, Alice.'

'Ah! that's just it. People always do seem to think it so

28

terrible that a girl should have her own way in anything. She mustn't like any one at first; and then, when she does like some one, she must marry him directly she's bidden. I haven't much of my own way at present; but you see, when I'm married I shan't have it at all. You can't wonder that I shouldn't be in a hurry.'

'I am not advocating anything like hurry, my dear. But, goodness gracious me! I've been here twenty-eight minutes, and that horrid man will impose upon me. Good-bye; God bless you! Mind you write.' And Lady Macleod hurried out of the room more intent at the present moment upon saving her sixpence than she was on any other matter whatsoever.

And then John Grey came up to town, arriving a day or two after the time that he had fixed. It is not, perhaps, improbable that Alice had used some diplomatic skill in preventing a meeting between Lady Macleod and her lover. They both were very anxious to obtain the same object, and Alice was to some extent opposed to their views. Had Lady Macleod and John Grey put their forces together she might have found herself unable to resist their joint endeavours. She was resolved that she would not at any rate name any day for her marriage before her return from Switzerland; and she may therefore have thought it wise to keep Mr. Grey in the country till after Lady Macleod had gone, even though she thereby cut down the time of his sojourn in London to four days. On the occasion of that visit Mr. Vavasor did a very memorable thing. He dined at home with the view of welcoming his future son-in-law. He dined at home, and asked, or rather assented to Alice's asking, George and Kate Vavasor to join the dinner-party. 'What an auspicious omen for the future nuptials!' said Kate, with her little sarcastic smile. 'Uncle John dines at home, and Mr. Grey joins in the dissipation of a dinner-party. We shall all be changed soon, I suppose, and George and I will take to keeping a little cottage in the country.'

'Kate,' said Alice, angrily, 'I think you are about the most unjust person I ever met. I would forgive your raillery, however painful it might be, if it were only fair.'

'And to whom is it unfair on the present occasion;—to your father?'

'It was not intended for him.'

'To yourself?'

'I care nothing as to myself; you know that very well.'

'Then it must have been unfair to Mr. Grey.'

'Yes; it was Mr. Grey whom you meant to attack. If I can forgive him for not caring for society, surely you might do so.'

'Exactly; but that's just what you can't do, my dear. You don't forgive him. If you did you might be quite sure that I should say nothing. And if you choose to bid me hold my tongue I will say nothing. But when you tell me all your own thoughts about this thing you can hardly expect but what I should let you know mine in return. I'm not particular; and if you are ready for a little good, wholesome, useful hypocrisy, I won't balk you. I mayn't be quite so dishonest as you call me, but I'm not so wedded to truth but what I can look, and act, and speak a few falsehoods if you wish it. Only let us understand each other.'

'You know I wish for no falsehood, Kate.'

'I know it's very hard to understand what you do wish. I know that for the last year or two I have been trying to find out your wishes, and, upon my word, my success has been very indifferent. I suppose you wish to marry Mr. Grey, but I'm by no means certain. I suppose the last thing on earth you'd wish would be to marry George.'

'The very last. You're right there at any rate.'

'Alice——! sometimes you drive me too hard; you do, indeed. You make me doubt whether I hate or love you most. Knowing what my feelings are about George, I cannot understand how you can bring yourself to speak of him to me with such contempt!' Kate Vavasor, as she spoke these words, left the room with a quick step, and hurried up to her own chamber. There Alice found her in tears, and was driven by her friend's real grief into the expression of an apology, which she knew was not properly due from her. Kate was acquainted with all the circumstances of that old affair between her brother and

Alice. She had given in her adhesion*to the propriety of what Alice had done. She had allowed that her brother George's behaviour had been such as to make any engagement between them impossible. The fault, therefore, had been hers in making any reference to the question of such a marriage. Nor had it been by any means her first fault of the same kind. Till Alice had become engaged to Mr. Grey she had spoken of George only as her brother, or as her friend's cousin, but now she was constantly making allusion to those past occurrences, which all of them should have striven to forget. Under these circumstances was not Lady Macleod right in saying that George Vavasor should not have been accepted as a companion for the Swiss tour?

The little dinner-party went off very quietly; and if no other ground existed for charging Mr. Grey with London dissipation than what that afforded, he was accused most unjustly. The two young men had never before met each other; and Vavasor had gone to his uncle's house, prepared not only to dislike but to despise his successor in Alice's favour. But in this he was either disappointed or gratified, as the case may be. 'He has plenty to say for himself,' he said to Kate on his way home.

'Oh yes; he can talk.'

'And he doesn't talk like a prig either, which was what I expected. He's uncommonly handsome.'

'I thought men never saw that in each other. I never see it in any man.'

'I see it in every animal,—in men, women, horses, dogs, and even pigs. I like to look on handsome things. I think people always do who are ugly themselves.'

'And so you're going into raptures in favour of John Grey.'

'No, I'm not. I very seldom go into raptures about anything. But he talks in the way I like a man to talk. How he bowled my uncle over about those actors; and yet if my uncle knows anything about anything it is about the stage twenty years ago.' There was nothing more said then about John Grey; but Kate understood her brother well enough to be aware that this

31

praise meant very little. George Vavasor spoke sometimes from his heart, and did so more frequently to his sister than to any one else; but his words came generally from his head.

On the day after the little dinner in Queen Anne Street, John Grey came to say good-bye to his betrothed;—for his betrothed she certainly was, in spite of those very poor arguments which she had used in trying to convince herself that she was still free if she wished to claim her freedom. Though he had been constantly with Alice during the last three days, he had not hitherto said anything as to the day of their marriage. He had been constantly with her alone, sitting for hours in that ugly green drawing-room, but he had never touched the subject. He had told her much of Switzerland, which she had never yet seen but which he knew well. He had told her much of his garden and house, whither she had once gone with her father, whilst paying a visit nominally to the colleges at Cambridge. And he had talked of various matters, matters bearing in no immediate way upon his own or her affairs; for Mr. Grey was a man who knew well how to make words pleasant; but previous to this last moment he had said nothing on that subject on which he was so intent.

'Well, Alice,' he said, when the last hour had come, 'and about that question of home affairs?'

'Let us finish off the foreign affairs first.'

'We have finished them; haven't we?'

'Finished them! why, we haven't started yet.'

'No; you haven't started. But we've had the discussion. Is there any reason why you'd rather not have this thing settled?'

'No; no special reason.'

'Then why not let it be fixed? Do you fear coming to me as my wife?'

'No.'

'I cannot think that you repent your goodness to me.'

'No; I don't repent it;—what you call my goodness ! I love you too entirely for that.'

'My darling!' And now he passed his arm round her waist as they stood near the empty fireplace. 'And if you love me——'

'I do love you.'

'Then why should you not wish to come to me?'

'I do wish it. I think I wish it.'

'But, Alice, you must have wished it altogether when you consented to be my wife.'

'A person may wish for a thing altogether, and yet not wish for it instantly.'

'Instantly! Come; I have not been hard on you. This is still June. Will you say the middle of September, and we shall still be in time for warm pleasant days among the lakes? Is that asking for too much?'

'It is not asking for anything.'

33

'Nay, but it is, love. Grant it, and I will swear that you have granted me everything.'

She was silent, having things to say but not knowing in what words to put them. Now that he was with her she could not say the things which she had told herself that she would utter to him. She could not bring herself to hint to him that his views of life were so unlike her own, that there could be no chance of happiness between them, unless each could strive to lean somewhat towards the other. No man could be more gracious in word and manner than John Grey; no man more chivalrous in his carriage towards a woman; but he always spoke and acted as though there could be no question that his manner of life was to be adopted, without a word or thought of doubting, by his wife. When two came together, why should not each yield something, and each claim something? This she had meant to say to him on this day; but now that he was with her she could not say it.

'John,' she said at last, 'do not press me about this till I return.'

'But then you will say the time is short. It would be short then.'

'I cannot answer you now;—indeed, I cannot. That is, I cannot answer in the affirmative. It is such a solemn thing.'

'Will it ever be less solemn, dearest?'

'Never, I hope never.'

He did not press her further then, but kissed her and bade her farewell.

CHAPTER IV

George Vavasor, the Wild Man

IT will no doubt be understood that George Vavasor did not roam about in the woods unshorn, or wear leathern trappings and sandals, like Robinson Crusoe, instead of coats and trousers. His wildness was of another kind. Indeed, I don't know that he was in truth at all wild, though Lady Macleod had called him so, and Alice had assented to her use of the word.

George Vavasor had lived in London since he was twenty, and now, at the time of the beginning of my story, he was a year or two over thirty. He was and ever had been the heir to his grandfather's estate; but that estate was small, and when George first came to London his father was a strong man of forty, with as much promise of life in him as his son had. A profession had therefore been absolutely necessary to him; and he had, at his uncle John's instance, been placed in the office of a parliamentary land agent. With this parliamentary land agent he had quarrelled to the knife, but not before he had by his talents made himself so useful that he had before him the prospects of a lucrative partnership in the business. George Vavasor had many faults, but idleness—absolute idleness—was not one of them. He would occasionally postpone his work to pleasure. He would be at Newmarket when he should have been at Whitehall. But it was not usual with him to be in bed when he should be at his desk, and when he was at his desk he did not whittle his ruler, or pick his teeth, or clip his nails. Upon the whole his friends were pleased with the first five years of his life in London—in spite of his having been found to be in debt on more than one occasion. But his debts had been paid; and all was going on swimmingly, when one day he knocked down the parliamentary agent with a blow between the eyes, and then there was an end of that. He himself was wont to say that he had known very well what he was about, that it had behoved him to knock down the man who was to have been his partner, and that he regretted nothing in the matter. At any rate the deed was looked upon with approving eyes by many men of good standing,—or, at any rate, sufficient standing to help George to another position; and within six weeks of the time of his leaving the office at Whitehall, he had become a partner in an established firm of wine merchants. A great-aunt had just then left him a couple of thousand pounds, which no doubt assisted him in his views with the wine merchants.

In this employment he remained for another period of five years, and was supposed by all his friends to be doing very well. And indeed he did not do badly, only that he did not do well enough to satisfy himself. He was ambitious of making the house to which he belonged the first house in the trade in London, and scared his partners by the boldness and extent of his views. He himself declared that if they would only have gone along with him he would have made them princes in the wine market. But they were men either of more prudence or of less audacity than he, and they declined to walk in his courses. At the end of the five years Vavasor left the house, not having knocked any one down on this occasion, and taking with him a very nice sum of money.

The last two of these five years had certainly been the best period of his life, for he had really worked very hard, like a man, giving up all pleasure that took time from him,—and giving up also most pleasures which were dangerous on account of their costliness. He went to no races, played no billiards, and spoke of Cremorne*as a childish thing, which he had abandoned now that he was no longer a child. It was during these two years that he had had his love passages with his cousin; and it must be presumed that he had, at any rate, intended at one time to settle himself respectably as a married man. He had, however, behaved very badly to Alice, and the match had been broken off.

He had also during the last two years quarrelled with his grandfather. He had wished to raise a sum of money on the Vavasor estate, which, as it was unentailed,* he could only do with his grandfather's concurrence. The old gentleman would not hear of it,—would listen with no patience to the proposition. It was in vain that George attempted to make the squire understand that the wine business was going on very well, that he himself owed no man anything, that everything with him was flourishing;—but that his trade might be extended indefinitely by the use of a few thousand pounds at moderate interest. Old Mr. Vavasor was furious. No documents and no assurances could make him lay aside a belief that the wine merchants, and the business, and his grandson were all ruined and ruinous together. No one but a ruined man would attempt to raise money on the family estate! So they had quarrelled, and had never spoken or seen each other since. 'He shall have the estate for his life,' the squire said to his son John. 'I don't think I have a right to leave it away from him. It never has been left away from the heir. But I'll tie it up so that he shan't cut a tree on it.' John Vavasor perhaps thought that the old rule of primogeniture might under such circumstances have been judiciously abandoned—in this one instance, in his own favour. But he did not say so. Nor would he have said it had there been a chance of his doing so with success. He was a man from whom no very noble deed could be expected; but he was also one who would do no ignoble deed.

After that George Vavasor had become a stockbroker, and a stockbroker he was now. In the first twelve months after his leaving the wine business,—the same being the first year after his breach with Alice,—he had gone back greatly in the estimation of men. He had lived in open defiance of decency. He had spent much money and had apparently made none, and had been, as all his friends declared, on the high road to ruin. Aunt Macleod had taken her judgment from this period of his life when she had spoken of him as a man who never did anything. But he had come forth again suddenly as a working man; and now they who professed to know, declared that he was by no means poor. He was in the City every day; and during the last two years had earned the character of a shrewd fellow who knew what he was about, who might not perhaps be very mealy-mouthed in affairs of business, but who was fairly and decently honourable in his money transactions. In fact, he stood well on 'Change.

And during these two years he had stood a contest for a seat in Parliament, having striven to represent the metropolitan borough of Chelsea,* on the extremely Radical interest. It is true that he had failed, and that he had spent a considerable sum of money in the contest. 'Where on earth does your nephew get his money?' men said to John Vavasor at his club. 'Upon my word I don't know,' said Vavasor. 'He doesn't get it from me, and I'm sure he doesn't get it from my father.' But

George Vavasor, though he failed at Chelsea, did not spend his money altogether fruitlessly. He gained reputation by the struggle, and men came to speak of him as though he were one who would do something. He was a stockbroker, a thorough-going Radical, and yet he was the heir to a fine estate, which had come down from father to son for four hundred years! There was something captivating about his history and adventures, especially as just at the time of the election he became engaged to an heiress, who died a month before the marriage should have taken place. She died without a will, and her money all went to some third cousins.

George Vavasor bore this last disappointment like a man, and it was at this time that he again became fully reconciled to his cousin. Previous to this they had met; and Alice, at her cousin Kate's instigation, had induced her father to meet him. But at first there had been no renewal of real friendship. Alice had given her cordial assent to her cousin's marriage with the heiress, Miss Grant, telling Kate that such an engagement was the very thing to put him thoroughly on his feet. And then she had been much pleased by his spirit at that Chelsea election. 'It was grand of him, wasn't it?' said Kate, her eyes brimming full of tears. 'It was very spirited,' said Alice. 'If you knew all, you would say so. They could get no one else to stand but that Mr. Travers, and he wouldn't come forward, unless they would guarantee all his expenses.' 'I hope it didn't cost George much,' said Alice. 'It did, though; nearly all he had got. But what matters? Money's nothing to him, except for its uses. My own little mite*is my own now, and he shall have every farthing of it for the next election, even though I should go out as a housemaid the next day.' There must have been something great about George Vavasor, or he would not have been so idolized by such a girl as his sister Kate.

Early in the present spring, before the arrangements for the Swiss journey were made, George Vavasor had spoken to Alice about that intended marriage which had been broken off by the lady's death. He was sitting one evening with his cousin in the drawing-room in Queen Anne Street, waiting for Kate, who was to join him there before going to some party. I wonder whether Kate had had a hint from her brother to be late! At any rate, the two were together for an hour, and the talk had been all about himself. He had congratulated her on her engagement with Mr. Grey, which had just become known to him, and had then spoken of his own last intended marriage.

'I grieved for her,' he said, 'greatly.'

'I'm sure you did, George.'

'Yes, I did;—for her, herself. Of course the world has given me credit for lamenting the loss of her money. But the truth is, that as regards both herself and her money, it is much better for me that we were never married.'

'Do you mean even though she should have lived?'

'Yes;—even had she lived.'

'And why so? If you liked her, her money was surely no drawback.'

'No; not if I had liked her.'

'And did you not like her?'

'No.'

'Oh, George!'

'I did not love her as a man should love his wife, if you mean that. As for my liking her, I did like her. I liked her very much.'

'But you would have loved her?'

'I don't know. I don't find that task of loving so very easy. It might have been that I should have learned to hate her.'

'If so, it is better for you, and better for her, that she has gone.'

'It is better. I am sure of it. And yet I grieve for her, and in thinking of her I almost feel as though I were guilty of her death.'

'But she never suspected that you did not love her?'

'Oh no. But she was not given to think much of such things. She took all that for granted. Poor girl! she is at rest now, and her money has gone, where it should go, among her own relatives.'

'Yes; with such feelings as yours are about her, her money would have been a burden to you.'

'I would not have taken it. I hope, at least, that I would not have taken it. Money is a sore temptation, especially to a poor man like me. It is well for me that the trial did not come in my way.'

'But you are not such a very poor man now, are you, George? I thought your business was a good one.'

'It is, and I have no right to be a poor man. But a man will be poor who does such mad things as I do. I had three or four thousand pounds clear, and I spent every shilling of it on the Chelsea election. Goodness knows whether I shall have a shilling at all when another chance comes round; but if I have I shall certainly spend it, and if I have not, I shall go in debt wherever I can raise a hundred pounds.'

'I hope you will be successful at last.'

'I feel sure that I shall. But, in the mean time, I cannot but know that my career is perfectly reckless. No woman ought to join her lot to mine unless she has within her courage to be as reckless as I am. You know what men do when they toss up for shillings?'

'Yes, I suppose I do.'

'I am tossing up every day of my life for every shilling that I have.'

'Do you mean that you're—gambling?'

'No. I have given that up altogether. I used to gamble, but I never do that now, and never shall again. What I mean is this,—that I hold myself in readiness to risk everything at any moment, in order to gain any object that may serve my turn. I am always ready to lead a forlorn hope. That's what I mean by tossing up every day for every shilling that I have.'

Alice did not quite understand him, and perhaps he did not intend that she should. Perhaps his object was to mystify her imagination. She did not understand him, but I fear that she admired the kind of courage which he professed. And he had not only professed it: in that matter of the past election he had certainly practised it.

In talking of beauty to his sister he had spoken of himself as being ugly. He would not generally have been called ugly by women, had not one side of his face been dreadfully scarred by a cicatrice, which in healing, had left a dark indented line down from his left eye to his lower jaw. That black ravine running through his cheek was certainly ugly. On some occasions, when he was angry or disappointed, it was very hideous; for he would so contort his face that the scar would, as it were, stretch itself out, revealing all its horrors, and his countenance would become all scar. 'He looked at me like the devil himself—making the hole in his face gape at me,' the old squire had said to John Vavasor in describing the interview in which the grandson had tried to bully his grandfather into assenting to his own views about the mortgage. But in other respects George's face was not ugly, and might have been thought handsome by many women. His hair was black, and was parted in the front. His forehead, though low, was broad. His eyes were dark and bright, and his eyebrows were very full, and perfectly black. At those periods of his anger, all his face which was not scar, was eye and eyebrow. He wore a thick black moustache, which covered his mouth, but no whiskers. People said of him that he was so proud of his wound that he would not grow a hair to cover it. The fact, however, was that no whisker could be made to come sufficiently forward to be of service, and therefore he wore none.

The story of that wound should be told. When he was yet hardly more than a boy, before he had come up to London, he was living in a house in the country which his father then occupied. At the time his father was absent, and he and his sister only were in the house with the maid-servants. His sister had a few jewels in her room, and an exaggerated report of them having come to the ears of certain enterprising burglars, a little plan was arranged for obtaining them. A small boy was hidden in the house, a window was opened, and at the proper witching hour of night*a stout individual crept upstairs in his stocking-feet, and was already at Kate Vavasor's door,—when, in the dark, dressed only in his nightshirt, wholly unarmed,

41

George Vavasor flew at the fellow's throat. Two hours elapsed before the horror-stricken women of the house could bring men to the place. George's face had then been ripped open from the eye downwards, with some chisel, or housebreaking instrument. But the man was dead. George had wrenched from him his own tool, and having first jobbed*him all over with insufficient wounds, had at last driven the steel through his windpipe. The small boy escaped, carrying with him two shillings and threepence which Kate had left upon the drawing-room mantelpiece.

George Vavasor was rather low in stature, but well made, with small hands and feet, but broad in the chest and strong in the loins. He was a fine horseman and a hard rider; and men who had known him well said that he could fence and shoot with a pistol as few men care to do in these peaceable days. Since volunteering had come up, he had become a captain of Volunteers,* and had won prizes with his rifle at Wimbledon.

Such had been the life of George Vavasor, and such was his character, and such his appearance. He had always lived alone in London, and did so at present; but just now his sister was much with him, as she was staying up in town with an aunt, another Vavasor by birth, with whom the reader will, if he persevere, become acquainted in course of time. I hope he will persevere a little, for of all the Vavasors Mrs. Greenow was perhaps the best worth knowing. But Kate Vavasor's home was understood to be in her grandfather's house in Westmoreland.

On the evening before they started for Switzerland, George and Kate walked from Queen Anne Street, where they had been dining with Alice, to Mrs. Greenow's house. Everything had been settled about luggage, hours of starting, and routes as regarded their few first days; and the common purse had been made over to George. That portion of Mr. Grey's letter had been read which alluded to the Paynims and the glasses of water, and everything had passed in the best of good-humour. 'I'll endeavour to get the cold water for you,' George had said; 'but as to the breakfasts, I can only hope you won't put

me to severe trials by any very early hours. When people go
out for pleasure it should be pleasure.'

The brother and sister walked through two or three streets
in silence, and then Kate asked a question.

'George, I wonder what your wishes really are about Alice?'

'That she shouldn't want her breakfast too early while we
are away.'

'That means I'm to hold my tongue, of course.'

'No, it doesn't.'

'Then it means that you intend to hold yours.'

'No; not that either.'

'Then what does it mean?'

'That I have no fixed wishes on the subject. Of course she'll
marry this man John Grey, and then no one will hear another
word about her.'

'She will no doubt, if you don't interfere. Probably she will
whether you interfere or not. But if you wish to interfere——'

'She's got four hundred a year, and is not so good-looking
as she was.'

'Yes; she has got four hundred a year, and she is more handsome now than ever she was. I know that you think so;—and
that you love her and love no one else—unless you have a
sneaking fondness for me.'

'I'll leave you to judge of that last.'

'And as for me,—I only love two people in the world; her
and you. If ever you mean to try, you should try now.'

CHAPTER V

The Balcony at Basle

I AM not going to describe the Vavasors' Swiss tour. It would
not be fair on my readers. 'Six Weeks in the Bernese Ober-
land, by a party of three,' would have but very small chance of
success in the literary world at present, and I should consider
myself to be dishonest if I attempted to palm off such matter
on the public in the pages of a novel. It is true that I have just

returned from Switzerland, and should find such a course of writing very convenient. But I dismiss the temptation, strong as it is. Retro age, Satanas.* No living man or woman any longer wants to be told anything of the Grimsell or of the Gemmi. Ludgate Hill is now-a-days more interesting than the Jungfrau.*

The Vavasors were not very energetic on their tour. As George had said, they had gone out for pleasure and not for work. They went direct to Interlaken and then hung about between that place and Grindelwald and Lauterbrunnen. It delighted him to sit still on some outer bench, looking at the mountains, with a cigar in his mouth, and it seemed to delight them to be with him. Much that Mr. Grey prophesied had come true. The two girls were ministers to him, instead of having him as their slave.

'What fine fellows those Alpine club*men think themselves,' he said on one of these occasions, 'and how thoroughly they despise the sort of enjoyment I get from mountains. But they're mistaken.'

'I don't see why either need be mistaken,' said Alice.

'But they are mistaken,' he continued. 'They rob the mountains of their poetry, which is or should be their greatest charm. Mont Blanc can have no mystery for a man who has been up it half a dozen times. It's like getting behind the scenes at a ballet, or making a conjuror explain his tricks.'

'But is the exercise nothing?' said Kate.

'Yes; the exercise is very fine;—but that avoids the question.'

'And they all botanize,' said Alice.

'I don't believe it. I believe that the most of them simply walk up the mountain and down again. But if they did, that avoids the question also. The poetry and mystery of the mountains are lost to those who make themselves familiar with their details, not the less because such familiarity may have useful results. In this world things are beautiful only because they are not quite seen, or not perfectly understood. Poetry is precious chiefly because it suggests more than it declares. Look in there, through that valley, where you just see the distant little peak at the end. Are you not dreaming of the unknown beautiful world that exists up there;—beautiful, as heaven is beautiful, because you know nothing of the reality? If you make your way up there and back to-morrow, and find out all about it, do you mean to say that it will be as beautiful to you when you come back?'

'Yes;—I think it would,' said Alice.

'Then you've no poetry in you. Now I'm made up of poetry.' After that they began to laugh at him and were very happy.

I think that Mr. Grey was right in answering Alice's letter as he did; but I think that Lady Macleod was also right in saying that Alice should not have gone to Switzerland in company with George Vavasor. A peculiar familiarity sprang up, which, had all its circumstances been known to Mr. Grey, would not have entirely satisfied him, even though no word was said which might in itself have displeased him. During the first weeks of their travelling no word was said which would have displeased him; but at last, when the time for their return was drawing nigh, when their happiness was nearly over, and that feeling of melancholy was coming on them which always pervades the last hours of any period that has been pleasant,— then words became softer than they had been, and references were made to old days,—allusions which never should have been permitted between them.

Alice had been very happy,—more happy perhaps in that she had been a joint minister with Kate to her cousin George's idle fantasies, than she would have been hurrying about with him as her slave. They had tacitly agreed to spoil him with comforts; and girls are always happier in spoiling some man than in being spoiled by men. And he had taken it all well, doing his despotism pleasantly, exacting much, but exacting nothing that was disagreeable. And he had been amusing always, as Alice thought, without any effort. But men and women, when they show themselves at their best, seldom do so without an effort. If the object be near the heart the effort will be pleasant to him who makes it, and if it be made well, it will be hidden;

45

but, not the less, will the effort be there. George Vavasor had on the present occasion done his very best to please his cousin.

They were sitting at Basle one evening in the balcony of the big hotel*which overlooks the Rhine. This big hotel is always full of tourists who are either just beginning or just completing their Swiss doings. The balcony runs the length of the house, and is open to all the company; but it is spacious, and little parties can be formed there with perfect privacy. The swift broad Rhine runs underneath, rushing through from the bridge which here spans the river; and every now and then on summer evenings loud shouts come up from strong swimmers in the water, who are glorying in the swiftness of the current. The three were sitting there, by themselves, at the end of the balcony. Coffee was before them on a little table, and George's cigar, as usual, was in his mouth.

'It's nearly all over,' said he, after they had remained silent for some minutes.

'And I do think it has been a success,' said Kate. 'Always excepting about the money. I'm ruined for ever.'

'I'll make your money all straight,' said George.

'Indeed you'll do nothing of the kind,' said Kate. 'I'm ruined, but you are ruineder. But what signifies? It is such a great thing ever to have had six weeks' happiness, that the ruin is, in point of fact, a good speculation. What do you say, Alice? Won't you vote, too, that we've done it well?'

'I think we've done it very well. I have enjoyed myself thoroughly.'

'And now you've got to go home to John Grey and Cambridgeshire! It's no wonder you should be melancholy.' That was the thought in Kate's mind, but she did not speak it out on this occasion.

'That's good of you, Alice,' said Kate. 'Is it not, George? I like a person who will give a hearty meed*of approbation.'

'But I am giving the meed of approbation to myself.'

'I like a person even to do that heartily,' said Kate. 'Not that George and I are thankful for the compliment. We are

46

prepared to admit that we owe almost everything to you,—
are we not, George?'

'I'm not; by any means,' said George.

'Well, I am, and I expect to have something pretty said to
me in return. Have I been cross once, Alice?'

'No; I don't think you have. You are never cross, though
you are often ferocious.'

'But I haven't been once ferocious,—nor has George.'

'He would have been the most ungrateful man alive if he
had,' said Alice. 'We've done nothing since we've started but
realize for him that picture in "Punch" of the young gentleman at Jeddo who had a dozen ladies to wait upon him.'

'And now he has got to go home to his lodgings, and wait
upon himself again. Poor fellow! I do pity you, George.'

'No, you don't;—nor does Alice. I believe girls always
think that a bachelor in London has the happiest of all lives.
It's because they think so that they generally want to put an
end to the man's condition.'

'It's envy that makes us want to get married,—not love,'
said Kate.

'It's the devil in some shape, as often as not,' said he. 'With a
man, marriage always seems to him to be an evil at the instant.'

'Not always,' said Alice.

'Almost always;—but he does it, as he takes physic, because something worse will come if he don't. A man never likes having his tooth pulled out, but all men do have their teeth pulled out,—and they who delay it too long suffer the very mischief.'

'I do like George's philosophy,' said Kate, getting up from her chair as she spoke; 'it is so sharp, and has such a pleasant acid taste about it; and then we all know that it means nothing. Alice, I'm going up-stairs to begin the final packing.'

'I'll come with you, dear.'

'No, don't. To tell the truth I'm only going into that man's room because he won't put up a single thing of his own decently. We'll do ours, of course, when we go up to bed. Whatever you disarrange to-night, Master George, you must re-arrange for yourself to-morrow morning, for I promise I won't go into your room at five o'clock.'

'How I do hate that early work,' said George.

'I'll be down again very soon,' said Kate. 'Then we'll take one turn on the bridge and go to bed.'

Alice and George were left together sitting in the balcony. They had been alone together before many times since their travels had commenced; but they both of them felt that there was something to them in the present moment different from any other period of their journey. There was something that each felt to be sweet, undefinable, and dangerous. Alice had known that it would be better for her to go up-stairs with Kate; but Kate's answer had been of such a nature that had she gone she would have shown that she had some special reason for going. Why should she show such a need? Or why, indeed, should she entertain it?

Alice was seated quite at the end of the gallery, and Kate's chair was at her feet in the corner. When Alice and Kate had seated themselves, the waiter had brought a small table for the coffee-cups, and George had placed his chair on the other side of that. So that Alice was, as it were, a prisoner. She could not slip away without some special preparation for going, and

Kate had so placed her chair in leaving, that she must actually have asked George to move it before she could escape. But why should she wish to escape? Nothing could be more lovely and enticing than the scene before her. The night had come on, with quick but still unperceived approach, as it does in those parts; for the twilight there is not prolonged as it is with us more northern folk. The night had come on, but there was a rising moon, which just sufficed to give a sheen to the water beneath her. The air was deliciously soft;—of that softness which produces no sensation either of warmth or cold, but which just seems to touch one with loving tenderness, as though the unseen spirits of the air kissed one's forehead as they passed on their wings. The Rhine was running at her feet, so near, that in the soft half light it seemed as though she might step into its ripple. The Rhine was running by with that delicious sound of rapidly moving waters, that fresh refreshing gurgle of the river, which is so delicious to the ear at all times. If you be talking, it wraps up your speech, keeping it for yourselves, making it difficult neither to her who listens nor to him who speaks. If you would sleep, it is of all lullabies the sweetest. If you are alone and would think, it aids all your thoughts. If you are alone, and, alas! would not think,—if thinking be too painful,—it will dispel your sorrow, and give the comfort which music alone can give. Alice felt that the air kissed her, that the river sang for her its sweetest song, that the moon shone for her with its softest light,—that light which lends the poetry of half-developed beauty to everything that it touches. Why should she leave it?

Nothing was said for some minutes after Kate's departure, and Alice was beginning to shake from her that half feeling of danger which had come over her. Vavasor had sat back in his chair, leaning against the house, with his feet raised upon a stool; his arms were folded across his breast, and he seemed to have divided himself between his thoughts and his cigar. Alice was looking full upon the river, and her thoughts had strayed away to her future home among John Grey's flower-beds and shrubs; but the river, though it sang to her pleasantly.

seemed to sing a song of other things than such a home as that,—a song full of mystery, as are all river songs when one tries to understand their words.

'When are you to be married, Alice?' said George at last.

'Oh, George!' said she. 'You ask me a question as though you were putting a pistol to my ear.'

'I'm sorry the question was so unpleasant.'

'I didn't say that it was unpleasant; but you asked it so suddenly! The truth is, I didn't expect you to speak at all just then. I suppose I was thinking of something.'

'But if it be not unpleasant,—when are you to be married?'

'I do not know. It is not fixed.'

'But about when, I mean? This summer?'

'Certainly not this summer, for the summer will be over when we reach home.'

'This winter? Next spring? Next year?—or in ten years' time?'

'Before the expiration of the ten years, I suppose. Anything more exact than that I can't say.'

'I suppose you like it?' he then said.

'What; being married? You see I've never tried yet.'

'The idea of it,—the anticipation. You look forward with satisfaction to the kind of life you will lead at Nethercoats? Don't suppose I am saying anything against it, for I have no conception what sort of a place Nethercoats is. On the whole I don't know that there is any kind of life better than that of an English country gentleman in his own place;—that is, if he can keep it up, and not live as the old squire does, in a state of chronic poverty.'

'Mr. Grey's place doesn't entitle him to be called a country gentleman.'

'But you like the prospect of it?'

'Oh, George, how you do cross-question one! Of course I like it, or I shouldn't have accepted it.'

'That does not follow. But I quite acknowledge that I have no right to cross-question you. If I ever had such right on the score of cousinship, I have lost it on the score of——; but we

50

won't mind that, will we, Alice?' To this she at first made no answer, but he repeated the question. 'Will we, Alice?'

'Will we what?'

'Recur to the old days.'

'Why should we recur to them? They are passed, and as we are again friends and dear cousins the sting of them is gone.'

'Ah, yes! The sting of them is gone. It is for that reason, because it is so, that we may at last recur to them without danger. If we regret nothing,—if neither of us has anything to regret, why not recur to them, and talk of them freely?'

'No, George; that would not do.'

'By heavens, no! It would drive me mad; and if I know aught of you, it would hardly leave you as calm as you are at present.'

'As I would wish to be left calm——'

'Would you? Then I suppose I ought to hold my tongue. But, Alice, I shall never have the power of speaking to you again as I speak now. Since we have been out together, we have been dear friends; is it not so?'

'And shall we not always be dear friends?'

'No, certainly not. How will it be possible? Think of it. How can I really be your friend when you are the mistress of that man's house in Cambridgeshire?'

'George!'

'I mean nothing disrespectful. I truly beg your pardon if it has seemed so. Let me say that gentleman's house;—for he is a gentleman.'

'That he certainly is.'

'You could not have accepted him were he not so. But how can I be your friend when you are his wife? I may still call you cousin Alice, and pat your children on the head if I chance to see them; and shall stop in the street and shake hands with him if I meet him;—that is if my untoward fate does not induce him to cut my acquaintance;—but as for friendship, that will be over when you and I shall have parted next Thursday evening at London Bridge.'

'Oh, George, don't say so!'

'But I do.'

'And why on Thursday? Do you mean that you won't come to Queen Anne Street any more?'

'Yes, that is what I do mean. This trip of ours has been very successful, Kate says. Perhaps Kate knows nothing about it.'

'It has been very pleasant,—at least to me.'

'And the pleasure has had no drawback?'

'None to me.'

'It has been very pleasant to me, also;—but the pleasure has had its alloy. Alice, I have nothing to ask from you,—nothing.'

'Anything that you should ask, I would do for you.'

'I have nothing to ask;—nothing. But I have one word to say.'

'George, do not say it. Let me go up-stairs. Let me go to Kate.'

'Certainly; if you wish it you shall go.' He still held his foot against the chair which barred her passage, and did not attempt to rise as he must have done to make way for her passage out. 'Certainly you shall go to Kate, if you refuse to hear me. But after all that has passed between us, after these six weeks of intimate companionship, I think you ought to listen to me. I tell you that I have nothing to ask. I am not going to make love to you.'

Alice had commenced some attempt to rise, but she had again settled herself in her chair. And now, when he paused for a moment, she made no further sign that she wished to escape, nor did she say a word to intimate her further wish that he should be silent.

'I am not going to make love to you,' he said again. 'As for making love, as the word goes, that must be over between you and me. It has been made and marred, and cannot be remade. It may exist, or it may have been expelled; but where it does not exist, it will never be brought back again.'

'It should not be spoken of between you and me.'

'So, no doubt, any proper-going duenna*would say, and so, too, little children should be told; but between you and me there can be no necessity for falsehood. We have grown beyond our sugar-toothed ages, and are now men and women. I perfectly understood your breaking away from me. I understood you, and in spite of my sorrow knew that you were right. I am not going to accuse or to defend myself; but I knew that you were right.'

'Then let there be no more about it.'

'Yes; there must be more about it. I did not understand you when you accepted Mr. Grey. Against him I have not a whisper to make. He may be perfect for aught I know. But, knowing you as I thought I did, I could not understand your loving such a man as him. It was as though one who had lived on brandy should take himself suddenly to a milk diet,—and enjoy the change! A milk diet is no doubt the best. But men who have lived on brandy can't make those changes very suddenly. They perish in the attempt.'

'Not always, George.'

'It may be done with months of agony;—but there was no such agony with you.'

'Who can tell?'

'But you will tell me the cure was made. I thought so, and therefore thought that I should find you changed. I thought that you, who had been all fire, would now have turned yourself into soft-flowing milk and honey, and have become fit for the life in store for you. With such a one I might have travelled from Moscow to Malta without danger. The woman fit to be John Grey's wife would certainly do me no harm,—could not touch my happiness. I might have loved her once,—might still love the memory of what she had been; but her, in her new form, after her new birth,—such a one as that, Alice, could be nothing to me. Don't mistake me. I have enough of wisdom in me to know how much better, ay, and happier a woman she might be. It was not that I thought you had descended in the scale; but I gave you credit for virtues which you have not acquired. Alice, that wholesome diet of which I spoke is not your diet. You would starve on it, and perish.'

He had spoken with great energy, but still in a low voice, having turned full round upon the table, with both his arms

upon it, and his face stretched out far over towards her. She
was looking full at him; and, as I have said before, that scar
and his gloomy eyes and thick eyebrows seemed to make up
the whole of his face. But the scar had never been ugly to her.
She knew the story, and when he was her lover she had taken
pride in the mark of the wound. She looked at him, but though
he paused she did not speak. The music of the river was still
in her ears, and there came upon her a struggle as though she
were striving to understand its song. Were the waters also
telling her of the mistake she had made in accepting Mr. Grey
as her husband? What her cousin was now telling her,—was
it not a repetition of words which she had spoken to herself
hundreds of times during the last two months? Was she not
telling herself daily,—hourly,—always,—in every thought of
her life, that in accepting Mr. Grey she had assumed herself
to be mistress of virtues which she did not possess? Had she
not, in truth, rioted upon brandy, till the innocence of milk was
unfitted for her? This man now came and rudely told her all
this,—but did he not tell her the truth? She sat silent and con-
victed; only gazing into his face when his speech was done.

'I have learned this since we have been again together,
Alice; and finding you, not the angel I had supposed, finding
you to be the same woman I had once loved,—the safety that
I anticipated has not fallen to my lot. That's all. Here's Kate,
and now we'll go for our walk.'

CHAPTER VI

The Bridge over the Rhine

'GEORGE,' said Kate, speaking before she quite got up to
them, 'will you tell me whether you have been preparing
all your things for an open sale by auction?' Then she stole a
look at Alice, and having learned from that glance that something had occurred which prevented Alice from joining her in
her raillery, she went on with it herself rapidly, as though to
cover Alice's confusion and give her time to rally before they

should all move. 'Would you believe it? he had three razors
laid out on his table——'

'A man must shave,—even at Basle.'

'But not with three razors at once; and three hair-brushes,
and half a dozen tooth-brushes, and a small collection of combs,
and four or five little glass bottles, looking as though they
contained poison,—all with silver tops. I can only suppose
you desired to startle the weak mind of the chambermaid. I
have put them all up; but remember this, if they are taken out
again you are responsible. And I will not put up your boots,
George. What can you have wanted with three pairs of boots
at Basle?'

'When you have completed the list of my wardrobe we'll
go out upon the bridge. That is, if Alice likes it.'

'Oh, yes; I shall like it.'

'Come along then,' said Kate. And so they moved away.

When they got upon the bridge Alice and Kate were together, while George strolled behind them, close to them, but
not taking any part in their conversation,—as though he had
merely gone with them as an escort. Kate seemed to be perfectly content with this arrangement, chattering to Alice, so
that she might show that there was nothing serious on the
minds of any of them. It need hardly be said that Alice at this
time made no appeal to George to join them. He followed
them at their heels, with his hands behind his back, looking
down upon the pavement and simply waiting upon their
pleasure.

'Do you know,' said Kate, 'I have a very great mind to run
away.'

'Where do you want to run to?'

'Well;—that wouldn't much signify. Perhaps I'd go to the
little inn at Handek.* It's a lonely place, where nobody would
hear of me,—and I should have the waterfall. I'm afraid they'd
want to have their bill paid. That would be the worst of it.'

'But why run away just now?'

'I won't, because you wouldn't like going home with George
alone,—and I suppose he'd be bound to look after me, as he's

doing now. I wonder what he thinks of having to walk over the bridge after us girls. I suppose he'd be in that place down there drinking beer, if we weren't here.'

'If he wanted to go, I dare say he would, in spite of us.'

'That's ungrateful of you, for I'm sure we've never been kept in a moment by his failing us. But as I was saying, I do dread going home. You are going to John Grey, which may be pleasant enough; but I'm going—to Aunt Greenow.'

'It's your own choice.'

'No, it's not. I haven't any choice in the matter. Of course I might refuse to speak to Aunt Greenow, and nobody could make me;—but practically I haven't any choice in the matter. Fancy a month at Yarmouth with no companion but such a woman as that!'

'I shouldn't mind it. Aunt Greenow always seems to me to be a very good sort of woman.'

'She may be a good woman, but I must say I think she's of a bad sort. You've never heard her talk about her husband?'

'No, never; I think she did cry a little the first day she came to Queen Anne Street, but that wasn't unnatural.'

'He was thirty years older than herself.'

'But still he was her husband. And even if her tears are assumed, what of that? What's a woman to do? Of course she was wrong to marry him. She was thirty-five, and had nothing, while he was sixty-five, and was very rich. According to all accounts she made him a very good wife, and now that she's got all his money, you wouldn't have her go about laughing within three months of his death.'

'No; I wouldn't have her laugh; but neither would I have her cry. And she's quite right to wear weeds; but she needn't be so very outrageous in the depth of her hems, or so very careful that her caps are becoming. Her eyes will be worn out by their double service. They are always red with weeping, and yet she is ready every minute with a full battery of execution for any man that she sees.'

'Then why have you consented to go to Yarmouth with her?'

'Just because she's got forty thousand pounds. If Mr. Greenow had left her with a bare maintenance I don't suppose I should ever have held out my hand to her.'

'Then you're as bad as she is.'

'Quite as bad;—and that's what makes me want to run away. But it isn't my own fault altogether. It's the fault of the world at large. Does anybody ever drop their rich relatives? When she proposed to take me to Yarmouth, wasn't it natural that the squire should ask me to go? When I told George, wasn't it natural that he should say, "Oh, go by all means. She's got forty thousand pounds!" One can't pretend to be wiser or better than one's relatives. And after all what can I expect from her money?'

'Nothing, I should say.'

'Not a halfpenny. I'm nearly thirty and she's only forty, and of course she'll marry again. I will say of myself, too, that no person living cares less for money.'

'I should think no one.'

'Yet one sticks to one's rich relatives. It's the way of the world.' Then she paused a moment. 'But shall I tell you, Alice, why I do stick to her? Perhaps you'll think the object as mean as though I wanted her money myself.'

'Why is it?'

'Because it is on the cards that she may help George in his career. I do not want money, but he may. And for such purposes as his, I think it fair that all the family should contribute. I feel sure that he would make a name for himself in Parliament; and if I had my way I would spend every shilling of Vavasor money in putting him there. When I told the squire so I thought he would have eaten me. I really did think he would have turned me out of the house.'

'And serve you right too after what had happened.'

'I didn't care. Let him turn me out. I was determined he should know what I thought. He swore at me; and then he was so unhappy at what he had done that he came and kissed me that night in my bedroom, and gave me a ten-pound note. What do you think I did with it? I sent it as a contribution to

57

the next election, and George has it now locked up in a box. Don't you tell him that I told you.'

Then they stopped and leaned for a while over the parapet of the bridge. 'Come here, George,' said Kate; and she made room for him between herself and Alice. 'Wouldn't you like to be swimming down there as those boys were doing when we went out into the balcony? The water looks so enticing.'

'I can't say I should;—unless it might be a pleasant way of swimming into the next world.'

'I should so like to feel myself going with the stream,' said Kate; 'particularly by this light. I can't fancy in the least that I should be drowned.'

'I can't fancy anything else,' said Alice.

'It would be so pleasant to feel the water gliding along one's limbs, and to be carried away headlong,—knowing that you were on the direct road to Rotterdam.'

'And so arrive there without your clothes,' said George.

'They would be brought after in a boat. Didn't you see that those boys had a boat with them? But if I lived here, I'd never do it except by moonlight. The water looks so clear and bright now, and the rushing sound of it is so soft! The sea at Yarmouth won't be anything like that, I suppose.'

Neither of them any longer answered her, and yet she went on talking about the river, and their aunt, and her prospects at Yarmouth. Neither of them answered her, and yet it seemed that they had not a word to say to each other. But still they stood there looking down upon the river, and every now and then Kate's voice was to be heard, preventing the feeling which might otherwise have arisen that their hearts were too full for speech.

At last Alice seemed to shiver. There was a slight trembling in her arms, which George felt rather than saw. 'You are cold,' he said.

'No indeed.'

'If you are, let us go in. I thought you shivered with the night air.'

'It wasn't that. I was thinking of something. Don't you ever think of things that make you shiver?'

'Indeed I do, very often;—so often that I have to do my shivering inwardly. Otherwise people would think I had the palsy.'

'I don't mean things of moment,' said Alice. 'Little bits of things make me do it;—perhaps a word that I said and ought not to have said ten years ago;—the most ordinary little mistakes, even my own past thoughts to myself about the merest trifles. They are always making me shiver.'

'It's not because you have committed any murder then.'

'No; but it's my conscience all the same, I suppose.'

'Ah! I'm not so good as you. I doubt it's not my conscience at all. When I think of a chance I've let go by, as I have thousands, then it is that I shiver. But, as I tell you, I shiver inwardly. I've been in one long shiver ever since we came out because of one chance that I let go by. Come, we'll go in. We've to be up at five o'clock, and now it's eleven. I'll do the rest of my shivering in bed.'

'Are you tired of being out?' said Kate, when the other two began to move.

'Not tired of being out, but George reminds me that we have to be up at five.'

'I wish George would hold his tongue. We can't come to the bridge at Basle every night in our lives. If one found oneself at the top of Sinai I'm afraid the first feeling would be one of fear lest one wouldn't be down in time to dress for dinner. Are you aware, George, that the king of rivers is running beneath your feet, and that the moon is shining with a brilliance you never see at home?'

'I'll stay here all night if you'll put off going to-morrow,' said George.

'Our money wouldn't hold out,' said Kate.

'Don't talk about Sinai any more after that,' said he, 'but let's go in to bed.'

They walked across the bridge back to the hotel in the same manner as before, the two girls going together with the young man after them, and so they went up the front steps of the hotel, through the hall, and on to the stairs. Here George handed Alice her candle, and as he did so he whispered a few words to her. 'My shivering fit has to come yet,' said he, 'and will last me the whole night.' She would have given much to have been able to answer him lightly, as though what he had said had meant nothing;—but she couldn't do it; the light speech would not come to her. She was conscious of all this, and went away to her own room without answering him at all. Here she sat down at the window looking out upon the river till Kate should join her. Their rooms opened through from one to the other, and she would not begin her packing till her cousin should come.

But Kate had gone with her brother, promising, as she did so, that she would be back in half a minute. That half-minute was protracted beyond half an hour. 'If you'll take my advice,' said Kate, at last, standing up with her candle in her hand, 'you'll ask her in plain words to give you another chance. Do it to-morrow at Strasbourg; you'll never have a better opportunity.'

'And bid her throw John Grey over!'

'Don't say anything about John Grey; leave her to settle that matter with herself. Believe me that she has quite courage enough to dispose of John Grey, if she has courage enough to accept your offer.'

'Kate, you women never understand each other. If I were to do that, all her most powerful feelings would be arrayed in arms against me. I must leave her to find out first that she wishes to be rid of her engagement.'

'She has found that out long ago. Do you think I don't know what she wishes? But if you can't bring yourself to speak to her, she'll marry him in spite of her wishes.'

'Bring myself! I've never been very slow in bringing myself to speak to any one when there was need. It isn't very pleasant sometimes, but I do it, if I find occasion.'

'But surely it must be pleasant with her. You must be glad to find that she still loves you. You still love her, I suppose?'

'Upon my word I don't know.'

'Don't provoke me, George. I'm moving heaven and earth to bring you two together; but if I didn't think you loved her, I'd go to her at once and bid her never see you again.'

'Upon my word, Kate, I sometimes think it would be better if you'd leave heaven and earth alone.'

'Then I will. But of all human beings, surely you're the most ungrateful.'

'Why shouldn't she marry John Grey if she likes him?'

'But she doesn't like him. And I hate him. I hate the sound of his voice, and the turn of his eye, and that slow, steady movement of his,—as though he was always bethinking himself that he wouldn't wear out his clothes.'

'I don't see that your hating him ought to have anything to do with it.'

'If you're going to preach morals, I'll leave you. It's the darling wish of my heart that she should be your wife. If you ever loved anybody,—and I sometimes doubt whether you ever did,—but if you did, you loved her.'

'Did and do are different things.'

'Very well, George; then I have done. It has been the same in every twist and turn of my life. In everything that I have striven to do for you, you have thrown yourself over, in order that I might be thrown over too. But I believe you say this merely to vex me.'

'Upon my word, Kate, I think you'd better go to bed.'

'But not till I've told her everything. I won't leave her to be deceived and ill-used again.'

'Who is ill-using her now? Is it not the worst of ill-usage, trying to separate her from that man?'

'No;—if I thought so, I would have no hand in doing it. She would be miserable with him, and make him miserable as well. She does not really love him. He loves her, but I've nothing to do with that. It's nothing to me if he breaks his heart.'

'I shall break mine if you don't let me go to bed.'

With that she went away and hurried along the corridor,

till she came to her cousin's room. She found Alice still seated at the window, or rather kneeling on the chair, with her head out through the lattice. 'Why, you lazy creature,' said Kate; 'I declare you haven't touched a thing.'

'You said we'd do it together.'

'But he has kept me. Oh, what a man he is! If he ever does get married, what will his wife do with him?'

'I don't think he ever will,' said Alice.

'Don't you? I dare say you understand him better than I do. Sometimes I think that the only thing wanting to make him thoroughly good, is a wife. But it isn't every woman that would do for him. And the woman who marries him should have high courage. There are moments with him when he is very wild; but he never is cruel and hard. Is Mr. Grey ever hard?'

'Never;—nor yet wild.'

'Oh, certainly not that. I'm quite sure he's never wild.'

'When you say that, Kate, I know that you mean to abuse him.'

'No; upon my word. What's the good of abusing him to you? I like a man to be wild,—wild in my sense. You knew that before.'

'I wonder whether you'd like a wild man for yourself?'

'Ah! that's a question I've never asked myself. I've been often curious to consider what sort of husband would suit you, but I've had very few thoughts about a husband for myself. The truth is, I'm married to George. Ever since——'

'Ever since what?'

'Since you and he were parted, I've had nothing to do in life but to stick to him. And I shall do so to the end,—unless one thing should happen.'

'And what's that?'

'Unless you should become his wife after all. He will never marry anybody else.'

'Kate, you shouldn't allude to such a thing now. You know that it's impossible.'

'Well; perhaps so. As far as I'm concerned, it is all the

better for me. If George ever married, I should have nothing to do in the world;—literally nothing—nothing—nothing—nothing!'

'Kate, don't talk in that way,' and Alice came up to her and embraced her.

'Go away,' said she. 'Go, Alice; you and I must part. I cannot bear it any longer. You must know it all. When you are

married to John Grey, our friendship must be over. If you became George's wife I should become nobody. I've nothing else in the world. You and he would be so all-sufficient for each other, that I should drop away from you like an old garment. But I'd give up all, everything, every hope I have, to see you become George's wife. I know myself not to be good. I know myself to be very bad, and yet I care nothing for myself. Don't, Alice, don't; I don't want your caresses. Caress him, and I'll kneel at your feet, and cover them with kisses.' She had now thrown herself upon a sofa, and had turned her face away to the wall.

'Kate, you shouldn't speak in that way.'

'Of course I shouldn't,—but I do.'

'You, who know everything, must know that I cannot marry your brother,—even if he wished it.'

'He does wish it.'

'Not though I were under no other engagement.'

'And why not?' said Kate, again starting up. 'What is there

to separate you from George now, but that unfortunate affair, that will end in the misery of you all? Do you think I can't see? Don't I know which of the two men you like best?'

'You are making me sorry, Kate, that I have ventured to come here in your brother's company. It is not only unkind of you to talk to me in this way, but worse than that—it is indelicate.'

'Oh, indelicate! How I do hate that word. If any word in the language reminds me of a whited sepulchre it is that;— all clean and polished outside with filth and rottenness within. Are your thoughts delicate? that's the thing. You are engaged to marry John Grey. That may be delicate enough if you love him truly, and feel yourself fitted to be his wife; but it's about the most indelicate thing you can do, if you love any one better than him. Delicacy with many women is like their cleanliness. Nothing can be nicer than the whole outside get-up, but you wouldn't wish to answer for anything beneath.'

'If you think ill of me like that——'

'No; I don't think ill of you. How can I think ill of you when I know that all your difficulties have come from him? It hasn't been your fault; it has been his throughout. It is he who has driven you to sacrifice yourself on this altar. If we can, both of us, manage to lay aside all delicacy and pretence, and dare to speak the truth, we shall acknowledge that it is so. Had Mr. Grey come to you while things were smooth between you and George, would you have thought it possible that he could be George's rival in your estimation? It is Hyperion to a Satyr.'*

'And which is the Satyr?'

'I'll leave your heart to tell you. You know what is the darling wish of my heart. But, Alice, if I thought that Mr. Grey was to you Hyperion,—if I thought that you could marry him with that sort of worshipping, idolatrous love which makes a girl proud as well as happy in her marriage, I wouldn't raise a little finger to prevent it.'

To this Alice made no answer, and then Kate allowed the matter to drop. Alice made no answer, though she felt that she was allowing judgment to go against her by default in not doing so. She had intended to fight bravely, and to have maintained the excellence of her present position as the affianced bride of Mr. Grey, but she felt that she had failed. She felt that she had, in some sort, acknowledged that the match was one to be deplored;—that her words in her own defence would by no means have satisfied Mr. Grey, if Mr. Grey could have heard them;—that they would have induced him to offer her back her troth rather than have made him happy as a lover. But she had nothing further to say. She could do something. She would hurry home and bid him name the earliest day he pleased. After that her cousin would cease to disturb her in her career.

It was nearly one o'clock before the two girls began to prepare for their morning start, and Alice, when they had finished their packing, seemed to be worn out with fatigue. 'If you are tired, dear, we'll put it off,' said Kate. 'Not for worlds,' said Alice. 'For half a word we'll do it,' continued Kate. 'I'll slip out to George and tell him, and there's nothing he'd like so much.' But Alice would not consent.

About two they got into bed, and punctually at six they were at the railway station. 'Don't speak to me,' said George, when he met them at their door in the passage. 'I shall only yawn in your face.' However, they were in time,—which means abroad that they were at the station half an hour before their train started,—and they went on upon their journey to Strasbourg.

There is nothing further to be told of their tour. They were but two days and nights on the road from Basle to London; and during those two days and nights neither George nor Kate spoke a word to Alice of her marriage, nor was any allusion made to the balcony at the inn, or to the bridge over the river.

CHAPTER VII

Aunt Greenow

KATE VAVASOR remained only three days in London before she started for Yarmouth; and during those three days she was not much with her cousin. 'I'm my aunt's, body and soul, for the next six weeks,' she said to Alice, when she did come to Queen Anne Street on the morning after her arrival. 'And she is exigeant in a manner I can't at all explain to you. You mustn't be surprised if I don't even write a line. I've escaped by stealth now. She went up-stairs to try on some new weeds for the seaside, and then I bolted.' She did not say a word about George; nor during those three days, nor for some days afterwards, did George show himself. As it turned out afterwards, he had gone off to Scotland, and had remained a week among the grouse. Thus, at least, he had accounted for himself and his movements; but all George Vavasor's friends knew that his goings-out and comings-in were seldom accounted for openly like those of other men.

It will perhaps be as well to say a few words about Mrs. Greenow before we go with her to Yarmouth. Mrs. Greenow was the only daughter and the youngest child of the old squire at Vavasor Hall. She was just ten years younger than her brother John, and I am inclined to think that she was almost justified in her repeated assertion that the difference was much greater than ten years, by the freshness of her colour, and by the general juvenility of her appearance. She certainly did not look forty, and who can expect a woman to proclaim herself to be older than her looks? In early life she had been taken from her father's house, and had lived with relatives in one of the large towns in the north of England. It is certain she had not been quite successful as a girl. Though she had enjoyed the name of being a beauty, she had not the usual success which comes from such repute. At thirty-four she was still unmarried. She had, moreover, acquired the character of being a flirt; and I fear that the stories which were told of her, though doubtless more than half false, had in them sufficient of truth to justify the character. Now this was very sad, seeing that Arabella Vavasor had no fortune, and that she had offended her father and brothers by declining to comply with their advice at certain periods of her career. There was, indeed, considerable trouble in the minds of the various male Vavasors with reference to Arabella, when tidings suddenly reached the Hall that she was going to be married to an old man.

She was married to the old man; and the marriage fortunately turned out satisfactorily, at any rate for the old man and for her family. The Vavasors were relieved from all further trouble, and were as much surprised as gratified when they heard that she did her duty well in her new position. Arabella had long been a thorn in their side, never having really done anything which they could pronounce to be absolutely wrong, but always giving them cause for fear. Now they feared no longer. Her husband was a retired merchant, very rich, not very strong in health, and devoted to his bride. Rumours soon made their way to Vavasor Hall, and to Queen Anne Street, that Mrs. Greenow was quite a pattern wife, and that Mr. Greenow considered himself to be the happiest old man in Lancashire. And now in her prosperity she quite forgave the former slights which had been put upon her by her relatives. She wrote to her dear niece Alice, and to her dearest niece Kate, and sent little presents to her father. On one occasion she took her husband to Vavasor Hall, and there was a regular renewal of all the old family feelings. Arabella's husband was an old man, and was very old for his age; but the whole thing was quite respectable, and there was, at any rate, no doubt about the money. Then Mr. Greenow died; and the widow, having proved the will, came up to London and claimed the commiseration of her nieces.

'Why not go to Yarmouth with her for a month?' George had said to Kate. 'Of course it will be a bore. But an aunt with forty thousand pounds has a right to claim attention.' Kate acknowledged the truth of the argument, and agreed to go to Yarmouth for a month. 'Your aunt Arabella has shown herself to be a very sensible woman,' the old squire had written; 'much more sensible than anybody thought her before her marriage. Of course you should go with her if she asks you.' What aunt, uncle, or cousin, in the uncontrolled possession of forty thousand pounds was ever unpopular in the family?

Yarmouth is not a very prepossessing place to the eye. To my eye, at any rate, it is not so.* There is an old town with which summer visitors have little or nothing to do; and there are the new houses down by the seaside, to which, at any rate, belongs the full advantage of sea air. A kind of esplanade runs for nearly a mile along the sands, and there are built, or in the course of building, rows of houses appropriated to summer visitors all looking out upon the sea. There is no beauty unless the yellow sandy sea can be called beautiful. The coast is low and straight, and the east wind blows full upon it. But the place is healthy; and Mrs. Greenow was probably right in thinking that she might there revive some portion of the health which she had lost in watching beside the couch of her departing lord.

'Omnibus;—no, indeed. Jeannette, get me a fly.' These were the first words Mrs. Greenow spoke as she put her foot upon the platform at the Yarmouth station. Her maid's name was Jenny; but Kate had already found, somewhat to her dismay, that orders had been issued before they left London that the girl was henceforth to be called Jeannette. Kate had also already found that her aunt could be imperious; but this taste for masterdom had not shown itself so plainly in London as it did from the moment that the train had left the station at Shoreditch.* In London Mrs. Greenow had been among Londoners, and her career had hitherto been provincial. Her spirit, no doubt, had been somewhat cowed by the novelty of her position. But when she felt herself to be once beyond the stones,* as the saying used to be, she was herself again; and at Ipswich she had ordered Jeannette to get her a glass of sherry with an air that had created a good deal of attention among the guards and porters.

The fly was procured; and with considerable exertion all Mrs. Greenow's boxes, together with the more moderate belongings of her niece and maid, were stowed on the top of it, round upon the driver's body on the coach box, on the maid's lap, and I fear in Kate's also, and upon the vacant seat.

'The large house in Montpelier Parade,' said Mrs. Greenow.

'They is all large, ma'am,' said the driver.

'The largest,' said Mrs. Greenow.

'They're much of a muchness,' said the driver.

'Then Mrs. Jones's,' said Mrs. Greenow. 'But I was particularly told it was the largest in the row.'

'I know Mrs. Jones's well,' said the driver, and away they went.

Mrs. Jones's house was handsome and comfortable; but I fear Mrs. Greenow's satisfaction in this respect was impaired by her disappointment in finding that it was not perceptibly bigger than those to the right and left of her. Her ambition in this and in other similar matters would have amused Kate greatly had she been a bystander, and not one of her aunt's party. Mrs. Greenow was good-natured, liberal, and not by nature selfish; but she was determined not to waste the good things which fortune had given, and desired that all the world should see that she had forty thousand pounds of her own. And in doing this she was repressed by no feeling of false shame. She never hesitated in her demands through bashfulness. She called aloud for such comfort and grandeur as Yarmouth could afford her, and was well pleased that all around should hear her calling. Joined to all this was her uncontrolled grief for her husband's death.

'Dear Greenow! sweet lamb! Oh, Kate, if you'd only known that man!' When she said this she was sitting in the best of Mrs. Jones's sitting-rooms, waiting to have dinner announced. She had taken a drawing-room and dining-room, 'because,' as she had said, 'she didn't see why people should be stuffy when they went to the sea-side;—not if they had means to make themselves comfortable.'

'Oh, Kate, I do wish you'd known him!'

'I wish I had,' said Kate,—very untruly. 'I was unfortunately away when he went to Vavasor Hall.'

'Ah, yes; but it was at home, in the domestic circle, that

Greenow should have been seen to be appreciated. I was a happy woman, Kate, while that lasted.' And Kate was surprised to see that real tears—one or two on each side—were making their way down her aunt's cheeks. But they were soon checked with a handkerchief of the broadest hem and of the finest cambric.

'Dinner, ma'am,' said Jeannette, opening the door.

'Jeannette, I told you always to say that dinner was served.'

'Dinner's served then,' said Jeannette in a tone of anger.

'Come, Kate,' said her aunt. 'I've but little appetite myself, but there's no reason you shouldn't eat your dinner. I specially wrote to Mrs. Jones to have some sweetbread. I do hope she's got a decent cook. It's very little I eat myself, but I do like to see things nice.'

The next day was Sunday; and it was beautiful to see how Mrs. Greenow went to church in all the glory of widowhood. There had been a great unpacking after that banquet on the sweetbread, and all her funereal millinery had been displayed before Kate's wondering eyes. The charm of the woman was in this,—that she was not in the least ashamed of anything that she did. She turned over all her wardrobe of mourning, showing the richness of each article, the stiffness of the crape, the fineness of the cambric, the breadth of the frills,—telling the price of each to a shilling, while she explained how the whole had been amassed without any consideration of expense. This she did with all the pride of a young bride when she shows the glories of her trousseau to the friend of her bosom. Jeannette stood by the while, removing one thing and exhibiting another. Now and again through the performance, Mrs. Greenow would rest a while from her employment, and address the shade of the departed one in terms of most endearing affection. In the midst of this Mrs. Jones came in; but the widow was not a whit abashed by the presence of the stranger. 'Peace be to his manes!'*she said at last, as she carefully folded up a huge black crape mantilla. She made, however, but one syllable of the classical word, and Mrs. Jones thought that her lodger had addressed herself to the mortal 'remains' of her deceased lord.

'He is left her uncommon well off, I suppose,' said Mrs. Jones to Jeannette.

'You may say that, ma'am. It's more nor a hundred thousand of pounds!'

'No!'

'Pounds of sterling, ma'am! Indeed it is;—to my knowledge.'

'Why don't she have a carriage?'

'So she do;—but a lady can't bring her carriage down to the sea when she's only just buried her husband, as one may say. What'd folks say if they saw her in her own carriage? But it ain't because she can't afford it, Mrs. Jones. And now we're talking of it you must order a fly for church to-morrow, that'll look private, you know. She said I was to get a man that had a livery coat and gloves.'

The man with the coat and gloves was procured; and Mrs. Greenow's entry into church made quite a sensation. There was a thoughtfulness about her which alone showed that she was a woman of no ordinary power. She foresaw all necessities, and made provision for all emergencies. Another would not have secured an eligible sitting, and been at home in Yarmouth church, till half the period of her sojourn there was over. But Mrs. Greenow had done it all. She walked up the middle aisle with as much self-possession as though the chancel had belonged to her family for years; and the respectable pew-opener absolutely deserted two or three old ladies whom she was attending, to show Mrs. Greenow into her seat. When seated, she was the cynosure*of all eyes. Kate Vavasor became immediately aware that a great sensation had been occasioned by their entrance, and equally aware that none of it was due to her. I regret to say that this feeling continued to show itself throughout the whole service. How many ladies of forty go to church without attracting the least attention! But it is hardly too much to say that every person in that church had looked at Mrs. Greenow. I doubt if there was present there a single married lady who, on leaving the building, did not speak to her husband of the widow. There had

prevailed during the whole two hours a general though un-
expressed conviction that something worthy of remark had
happened that morning. It had an effect even upon the curate's
reading; and the incumbent, while preaching his sermon, could
not keep his eyes off that wonderful bonnet and veil.

On the next morning, before eleven, Mrs. Greenow's name
was put down at the Assembly Room. 'I need hardly say that
in my present condition I care nothing for these things. Of
course I would sooner be alone. But, my dear Kate, I know
what I owe to you.'

Kate, with less intelligence than might have been expected
from one so clever, began to assure her aunt that she required
no society; and that, coming thus with her to the seaside in
the early days of her widowhood, she had been well aware
that they would live retired. But Mrs. Greenow soon put her
down, and did so without the slightest feeling of shame or
annoyance on her own part. 'My dear,' she said, 'in this matter
you must let me do what I know to be right. I should consider
myself to be very selfish if I allowed my grief to interfere with
your amusements.'

'But, aunt, I don't care for such amusements.'

'That's nonsense, my dear. You ought to care for them.
How are you to settle yourself in life if you don't care for
them?'

'My dear aunt, I am settled.'

'Settled!' said Mrs. Greenow, astounded, as though there
must have been some hidden marriage of which she had not
heard. 'But that's nonsense. Of course you're not settled; and
how are you to be, if I allow you to shut yourself up in such a
place as this,—just where a girl has a chance?'

It was in vain that Kate tried to stop her. It was not easy
to stop Mrs. Greenow when she was supported by the full
assurance of being mistress of the place and of the occasion.
'No, my dear; I know very well what I owe to you, and I shall
do my duty. As I said before, society can have no charms now
for such a one as I am. All that social intercourse could ever
do for me lies buried in my darling's grave. My heart is

desolate, and must remain so. But I'm not going to immolate you on the altars of my grief. I shall force myself to go out for your sake, Kate.'

'But, dear aunt, the world will think it so odd, just at present.'

'I don't care twopence for the world. What can the world do to me? I'm not dependent on the world,—thanks to the care of that sainted lamb. I can hold my own; and as long as I can do that the world won't hurt me. No, Kate, if I think a thing's right I shall do it. I mean to make the place pleasant to you if I can, and the world may object if it likes.'

Mrs. Greenow was probably right in her appreciation of the value of her independence. Remarks may perhaps have been made by the world of Yarmouth as to her early return to society. People, no doubt, did remind each other that old Greenow was hardly yet four months buried. Mrs. Jones and Jeannette probably had their little jokes down stairs. But this did not hurt Mrs. Greenow. What was said, was not said in her hearing. Mrs. Jones's bills were paid every Saturday with admirable punctuality; and as long as this was done, everybody about the house treated the lady with that deference which was due to the respectability of her possessions. When a recently bereaved widow attempts to enjoy her freedom without money, then it behoves the world to speak aloud;— and the world does its duty.

Numerous people came to call at Montpelier Parade, and Kate was astonished to find that her aunt had so many friends. She was indeed so bewildered by these strangers that she could hardly ascertain whom her aunt had really known before, and whom she now saw for the first time. Somebody had known somebody who had known somebody else, and that was allowed to be a sufficient introduction,—always presuming that the existing somebody was backed by some known advantages of money or position. Mrs. Greenow could smile from beneath her widow's cap in a most bewitching way. 'Upon my word then she is really handsome,' Kate wrote one day to Alice. But she could also frown, and knew well how to put aside, or, if need be, to reprobate any attempt at familiarity from those whose worldly circumstances were supposed to be disadvantageous.

'My dear aunt,' said Kate one morning after their walk upon the pier, 'how you did snub that Captain Bellfield!'

'Captain Bellfield, indeed! I don't believe he's a captain at all. At any rate he has sold out,* and the tradesmen have had a scramble for the money. He was only a lieutenant when the 97th were in Manchester, and I'm sure he's never had a shilling to purchase since that.'

'But everybody here seems to know him.'

'Perhaps they do not know so much of him as I do. The idea of his having the impudence to tell me I was looking very well! Nothing can be so mean as men who go about in that way when they haven't money enough in their pockets to pay their washerwomen.'

'But how do you know, aunt, that Captain Bellfield hasn't paid his washerwoman?'

'I know more than you think, my dear. It's my business. How could I tell whose attentions you should receive and whose you shouldn't, if I didn't inquire into these things?'

It was in vain that Kate rebelled, or attempted to rebel against this more than maternal care. She told her aunt that she was now nearly thirty, and that she had managed her own affairs, at any rate with safety, for the last ten years;—but it was to no purpose. Kate would get angry; but Mrs. Greenow never became angry. Kate would be quite in earnest; but Mrs. Greenow would push aside all that her niece said as though it were worth nothing. Kate was an unmarried woman with a very small fortune, and therefore, of course, was desirous of being married with as little delay as possible. It was natural that she should deny that it was so, especially at this early date in their mutual acquaintance. When the niece came to know her aunt more intimately, there might be confidence between them, and then they would do better. But Mrs. Greenow would spare neither herself nor her purse on Kate's behalf, and she would be a dragon of watchfulness in protecting her from the evil desires of such useless men as Captain Bellfield.

'I declare, Kate, I don't understand you,' she said one morning to her niece as they sat together over a late breakfast. They had fallen into luxurious habits, and I am afraid it was past eleven o'clock, although the breakfast things were still on the table. Kate would usually bathe before breakfast, but Mrs. Greenow was never out of her room till half-past ten. 'I like the morning for contemplation,' she once said. 'When a woman has gone through all that I have suffered she has a great deal to think of.' 'And it is so much more comfortable to be a-thinking when one's in bed,' said Jeannette, who was present at the time. 'Child, hold your tongue,' said the widow. 'Yes, ma'am,' said Jeannette. But we'll return to the scene at the breakfast-table.

'What don't you understand, aunt?'

'You only danced twice last night, and once you stood up with Captain Bellfield.'

'On purpose to ask after that poor woman who washes his clothes without getting paid for it.'

'Nonsense, Kate; you didn't ask him anything of the kind, I'm sure. It's very provoking. It is indeed.'

'But what harm can Captain Bellfield do me?'

'What good can he do you? That's the question. You see, my dear, years will go by. I don't mean to say you ain't quite as young as ever you were, and nothing can be nicer and fresher than you are;—especially since you took to bathing.'

'Oh, aunt, don't!'

'My dear, the truth must be spoken. I declare I don't think I ever saw a young woman so improvident as you are. When are you to begin to think about getting married if you don't do it now?'

'I shall never begin to think about it, till I buy my wedding clothes.'

'That's nonsense,—sheer nonsense. How are you to get wedding clothes if you have never thought about getting a husband? Didn't I see Mr. Cheesacre ask you to dance last night?'

'Yes, he did; while you were talking to Captain Bellfield yourself, aunt.'

'Captain Bellfield can't hurt me, my dear. And why didn't you dance with Mr. Cheesacre?'

'He's a fat Norfolk farmer, with not an idea beyond the virtues of stall-feeding.'

'My dear, every acre of it is his own land,—every acre! And he bought another farm for thirteen thousand pounds only last autumn. They're better than the squires,—some of those gentlemen farmers; they are indeed. And of all men in the world they're the easiest managed.'

'That's a recommendation, no doubt.'

'Of course it is;—a great recommendation.'

Mrs. Greenow had no idea of joking when her mind was intent on serious things. 'He's to take us to the picnic to-morrow, and I do hope you'll manage to let him sit beside you. It'll be the place of honour, because he gives all the wine. He's picked up with that man Bellfield, and he's to be there; but if you allow your name to be once mixed up with his, it will be all over with you as far as Yarmouth is concerned.'

'I don't at all want to be mixed up with Captain Bellfield, as you call it,' said Kate. Then she subsided into her novel, while Mrs. Greenow busied herself about the good things for the picnic. In truth, the aunt did not understand the niece. Whatsoever might be the faults of Kate Vavasor, an un-maidenly desire of catching a husband for herself was certainly not one of them.

CHAPTER VIII

Mr. Cheesacre

Yarmouth is not a happy place for a picnic. A picnic should be held among green things. Green turf is absolutely an essential. There should be trees, broken ground, small paths, thickets, and hidden recesses. There should, if possible, be rocks, old timber, moss, and brambles. There should certainly be hills and dales,—on a small scale, and, above all, there should be running water. There should be no expanse. Jones should not be able to see all Greene's movements, nor should Augusta always have her eye upon her sister Jane. But the spot chosen for Mr. Cheesacre's picnic at Yarmouth had none of the virtues above described. It was on the sea-shore. Nothing was visible from the site but sand and sea. There were no trees there and nothing green;—neither was there any running water. But there was a long, dry, flat strand; there was an old boat half turned over, under which it was proposed to dine; and in addition to this, benches, boards, and some amount of canvas for shelter were provided by the liberality of Mr. Cheesacre. Therefore it was called Mr. Cheesacre's picnic.

But it was to be a marine picnic, and therefore the essential attributes of other picnics were not required. The idea had come from some boating expeditions, in which mackerel had been caught, and during which food had been eaten, not altogether comfortably, in the boats. Then a thought had suggested itself to Captain Bellfield that they might land and eat their food, and his friend Mr. Cheesacre had promised his substantial aid. A lady had surmised that Ormesby sands would be the very place for dancing in the cool of the evening. They might 'Dance on the sand,' she said, 'and yet no footing seen.'* And so the thing had progressed, and the picnic been inaugurated.

It was Mr. Cheesacre's picnic undoubtedly. Mr. Cheesacre was to supply the boats, the wine, the cigars, the music, and the carpenter's work necessary for the turning of the old boat into a banqueting saloon. But Mrs. Greenow had promised to provide the eatables, and enjoyed as much of the éclat*as the master of the festival. She had known Mr. Cheesacre now for ten days and was quite intimate with him. He was a stout, florid man, of about forty-five, a bachelor, apparently much attached to ladies' society, bearing no sign of age except that he was rather bald, and that grey hairs had mixed themselves with his whiskers, very fond of his farming, and yet somewhat ashamed of it when he found himself in what he considered to be polite circles. And he was, moreover, a little inclined to seek the honour which comes from a well-filled and liberally-opened purse. He liked to give a man a dinner and then to boast of the dinner he had given. He was very proud when he could talk of having mounted, for a day's hunting, any man who might be supposed to be of higher rank than himself. 'I had Grimsby with me the other day,—the son of old Grimsby of Hatherwick, you know. Blessed if he didn't stake my bay mare. But what matters? I mounted him again the next day just the same.' Some people thought he was soft, for it was very well known throughout Norfolk that young Grimsby would take a mount wherever he could get it. In these days Mrs. Greenow had become intimate with Mr. Cheesacre, and had already learned that he was the undoubted owner of his own acres.

'It wouldn't do for me,' she had said to him, 'to be putting myself forward, as if I were giving a party myself, or anything of that sort;—would it now?'

'Well, perhaps not. But you might come with us.'

'So I will, Mr. Cheesacre, for that dear girl's sake. I should never forgive myself if I debarred her from all the pleasures of youth, because of my sorrows. I need hardly say that at such a time as this nothing of that sort can give me any pleasure.'

'I suppose not,' said Mr. Cheesacre, with a solemn look.

'Quite out of the question.' And Mrs. Greenow wiped away her tears. 'For though as regards age I might dance on the sands as merrily as the best of them——'

'That I'm sure you could, Mrs. Greenow.'

'How's a woman to enjoy herself if her heart lies buried?'

'But it won't be so always, Mrs. Greenow.'

Mrs. Greenow shook her head to show that she hardly knew how to answer such a question. Probably it would be so always;—but she did not wish to put a damper on the present occasion by making so sad a declaration. 'But as I was saying,' continued she—'if you and I do it between us won't that be the surest way of having it come off nicely?'

Mr. Cheesacre thought that it would be the best way.

'Exactly so;—I'll do the meat and pastry and fruit, and you shall do the boats and the wine.'

'And the music,' said Cheesacre, 'and the expenses at the place.' He did not choose that any part of his outlay should go unnoticed.

'I'll go halves in all that if you like,' said Mrs. Greenow. But Mr. Cheesacre had declined this. He did not begrudge the expense, but only wished that it should be recognized.

'And, Mr. Cheesacre,' continued Mrs. Greenow, 'I did mean to send the music; I did, indeed.'

'I couldn't hear of it, Mrs. Greenow.'

'But I mention it now, because I was thinking of getting Blowehard to come. That other man, Flutey, wouldn't do at all out in the open air.'

'It shall be Blowehard,' said Mr. Cheesacre; and it was Blowehard. Mrs. Greenow liked to have her own way in these little things, though her heart did lie buried.

On the morning of the picnic Mr. Cheesacre came down to Montpelier Parade with Captain Bellfield, whose linen on that occasion certainly gave no outward sign of any quarrel between him and his washerwoman. He was got up wonderfully, and was prepared at all points for the day's work. He had on a pseudo-sailor's jacket, very liberally ornamented with brass buttons, which displayed with great judgment the exquisite shapes of his pseudo-sailor's duck trousers. Beneath them there was a pair of very shiny patent-leather shoes, well adapted for dancing on the sand, presuming him to be anxious of doing so, as Venus offered to do, without leaving any footmarks. His waistcoat was of a delicate white fabric, ornamented with very many gilt buttons. He had bejewelled studs in his shirt, and yellow kid gloves on his hands; having, of course, another pair in his pocket for the necessities of the evening. His array was quite perfect, and had stricken dismay into the heart of his friend Cheesacre, when he joined that gentleman. He was a well-made man, nearly six feet high, with dark hair, dark whiskers, and dark moustache, nearly black, but of that suspicious hue which to the observant beholder seems always to tell a tale of the hairdresser's shop. He was handsome, too, with well-arranged features,—but carrying, perhaps, in his

nose some first symptoms of the effects of midnight amusements. Upon the whole, however, he was a nice man to look
on,—for those who like to look on nice men of that kind.

Cheesacre, too, had adopted something of a sailor's garb.
He had on a jacket of a rougher sort, coming down much
lower than that of the Captain, being much looser, and perhaps somewhat more like a garment which a possible seaman
might possibly wear. But he was disgusted with himself the
moment that he saw Bellfield. His heart had been faint, and
he had not dared to ornament himself boldly as his friend had
done. 'I say, Guss, you are a swell,' he exclaimed. It may be
explained that Captain Bellfield had been christened Gustavus.

'I don't know much about that,' said the Captain; 'my fellow
sent me this toggery, and said that it was the sort of thing.
I'll change with you if you like it.' But Cheesacre could not
have worn that jacket, and he walked on, hating himself.

It will be remembered that Mrs. Greenow had spoken with
considerable severity of Captain Bellfield's pretensions when
discussing his character with her niece; but, nevertheless, on
the present occasion she received him with most gracious
smiles. It may be that her estimate of his character had been
altered, or that she was making sacrifice of her own feelings
in consideration of Mr. Cheesacre, who was known to be the
Captain's intimate friend. But she had smiles for both of them.
She had a wondrous power of smiling; and could, upon occasion, give signs of peculiar favour to half a dozen different
gentlemen in as many minutes. They found her in the midst of
hampers which were not yet wholly packed, while Mrs. Jones,
Jeannette, and the cook of the household moved around her,
on the outside of the circle, ministering to her wants. She had
in her hand an outspread clean napkin, and she wore fastened
round her dress a huge coarse apron, that she might thus be
protected from some possible ebullition of gravy, or escape
of salad mixture, or cream; but in other respects she was
clothed in the fullest honours of widowhood. She had not miti-
gated her weeds by half an inch. She had scorned to make any
compromise between the world of pleasure and the world of

woe. There she was, a widow, declared by herself to be of four months' standing, with a buried heart, making ready a dainty banquet with skill and liberality. She was ready on the instant to sit down upon the basket in which the grouse pie had been just carefully inhumed, and talk about her sainted lamb with a deluge of tears. If anybody didn't like it, that person—might do the other thing. Mr. Cheesacre and Captain Bellfield thought that they did like it.

'Oh, Mr. Cheesacre, if you haven't caught me before I've half done! Captain Bellfield, I hope you think my apron becoming.'

'Everything that you wear, Mrs. Greenow, is always becoming.'

'Don't talk in that way when you know——; but never mind—we will think of nothing sad to-day if we can help it. Will we, Mr. Cheesacre?'

'Oh dear no; I should think not;—unless it should come on to rain.'

'It won't rain—we won't think of such a thing. But, by the by, Captain Bellfield, I and my niece do mean to send out a few things, just in a bag you know, so that we may tidy ourselves up a little after the sea. I don't want it mentioned, because if it gets about among the other ladies, they'd think we wanted to make a dressing of it;—and there wouldn't be room for them all; would there?'

'No; there wouldn't,' said Mr. Cheesacre, who had been out on the previous evening, inspecting, and perhaps limiting, the carpenters in their work.

'That's just it,' said Mrs. Greenow. 'But there won't be any harm, will there, Mr. Cheesacre, in Jeannette going out with our things? She'll ride in the cart, you know, with the eatables. I know Jeannette's a friend of yours.'

'We shall be delighted to have Jeannette,' said Mr. Cheesacre.

'Thank ye, sir,' said Jeannette, with a curtsey.

'Jeannette, don't you let Mr. Cheesacre turn your head; and mind you behave yourself and be useful. Well; let me see;

—what else is there? Mrs. Jones, you might as well give me that ham now. Captain Bellfield, hand it over. Don't you put it into the basket, because you'd turn it the wrong side down. There now, if you haven't nearly made me upset the apricot pie.' Then, in the transfer of the dishes between the Captain and the widow, there occurred some little innocent by-play, which seemed to give offence to Mr. Cheesacre; so that that gentleman turned his back upon the hampers and took a step away towards the door.

Mrs. Greenow saw the thing at a glance, and immediately applied herself to cure the wound. 'What do you think, Mr. Cheesacre?' said she, 'Kate wouldn't come down because she didn't choose that you should see her with an apron on over her frock!'

'I'm sure I don't know why Miss Vavasor should care about my seeing her.'

'Nor I neither. That's just what I said. Do step up into the drawing-room; you'll find her there, and you can make her answer for herself.'

'She wouldn't come down for me,' said Mr. Cheesacre. But he didn't stir. Perhaps he wasn't willing to leave his friend with the widow.

At length the last of the dishes was packed, and Mrs. Greenow went up stairs with the two gentlemen. There they found Kate and two or three other ladies who had promised to embark under the protection of Mrs. Greenow's wings. There were the two Miss Fairstairs, whom Mrs. Greenow had especially patronized, and who repaid that lady for her kindness by an amount of outspoken eulogy which startled Kate by its audacity.

'Your dear aunt!' Fanny Fairstairs had said on coming into the room. 'I don't think I ever came across a woman with such genuine milk of human kindness!'

'Nor with so much true wit,' said her sister Charlotte,— who had been called Charlie on the sands of Yarmouth for the last twelve years.

When the widow came into the room, they flew at her and

devoured her with kisses, and swore that they had never seen her looking so well. But as the bright new gloves which both the girls wore had been presents from Mrs. Greenow, they certainly did owe her some affection. There are not many ladies who would venture to bestow such gifts upon their friends after so very short an acquaintance; but Mrs. Greenow had a power that was quite her own in such matters. She was already on a very confidential footing with the Miss Fairstairs, and had given them much useful advice as to their future prospects.

And then was there a Mrs. Green, whose husband was first-lieutenant on board a man-of-war on the West Indian Station.* Mrs. Green was a quiet, ladylike little woman, rather pretty, very silent, and, as one would have thought, hardly adapted for the special intimacy of Mrs. Greenow. But Mrs. Greenow had found out that she was alone, not very rich, and in want of the solace of society. Therefore she had, from sheer good-nature, forced herself upon Mrs. Green, and Mrs. Green, with much trepidation, had consented to be taken to the picnic. 'I know your husband would like it,' Mrs. Greenow had said, 'and I hope I may live to tell him that I made you go.'

There came in also a brother of the Fairstairs girls, Joe Fairstairs, a lanky, useless, idle young man, younger than them, who was supposed to earn his bread in an attorney's office at Norwich, or rather to be preparing to earn it at some future time, and who was a heavy burden upon all his friends. 'We told Joe to come to the house,' said Fanny to the widow, apologetically, 'because we thought he might be useful in carrying down the cloaks.' Mrs. Greenow smiled graciously upon Joe, and assured him that she was charmed to see him, without any reference to such services as those mentioned.

And then they started. When they got to the door both Cheesacre and the Captain made an attempt to get possession of the widow's arm. But she had it all arranged. Captain Bellfield found himself constrained to attend to Mrs. Green, while Mr. Cheesacre walked down to the beach beside Kate Vavasor. 'I'll take your arm, Mr. Joe,' said the widow, 'and the girls shall come with us.' But when they got to the boats, round which the other comers to the picnic were already assembled, Mr. Cheesacre,—although both the boats were for the day his own,—found himself separated from the widow. He got into that which contained Kate Vavasor, and was shoved off from the beach while he saw Captain Bellfield arranging Mrs. Greenow's drapery. He had declared to himself that it should be otherwise; and that as he had to pay the piper, the piper should play as he liked it. But Mrs. Greenow with a word or two had settled it all, and Mr. Cheesacre had found himself to be powerless. 'How absurd Bellfield looks in that jacket, doesn't he?' he said to Kate, as he took his seat in the boat.

'Do you think so? I thought it was so very pretty and becoming for the occasion.'

Mr. Cheesacre hated Captain Bellfield, and regretted more than ever that he had not done something for his own personal adornment. He could not endure to think that his friend, who paid for nothing, should carry away the honours of the morning and defraud him of the delights which should justly belong to him. 'It may be becoming,' said Cheesacre; 'but don't you think it's awfully extravagant?'

'As to that I can't tell. You see I don't at all know what is the price of a jacket covered all over with little brass buttons.'

'And the waistcoat, Miss Vavasor!' said Cheesacre, almost solemnly.

'The waistcoat I should think must have been expensive.'

'Oh, dreadful! and he's got nothing, Miss Vavasor; literally nothing. Do you know,'—and he reduced his voice to a whisper as he made this communication,—'I lent him twenty pounds the day before yesterday; I did indeed. You won't mention it again, of course. I tell you, because, as you are seeing a good deal of him just now, I think it right that you should know on what sort of a footing he stands.' It's all fair, they say, in love and war, and this small breach of confidence was, we must presume, a love stratagem on the part of Mr. Cheesacre. He was at this time smitten with the charms both of the widow and of the niece, and he constantly found that the captain was interfering with him on whichever side he turned himself. On the present occasion he had desired to take the widow for his share, and was, upon the whole, inclined to think that the widow was the more worthy of his attentions. He had made certain little inquiries within the last day or two, the answers to which had been satisfactory. These he had by no means communicated to his friend, to whom, indeed, he had expressed an opinion that Mrs. Greenow was after all only a flash in the pan. 'She does very well pour passer le temps,'*the captain had answered. Mr. Cheesacre had not quite understood the exact gist of the captain's meaning, but had felt certain that his friend was playing him false.

'I don't want it to be mentioned again, Miss Vavasor,' he continued.

'Such things should not be mentioned at all,' Kate replied, having been angered at the insinuation that the nature of Captain Bellfield's footing could be a matter of any moment to her.

'No, they shouldn't; and therefore I know that I'm quite safe with you, Miss Vavasor. He's a very pleasant fellow, very; and has seen the world,—uncommon; but he's better for eating and drinking with than he is for buying and selling with, as we say in Norfolk. Do you like Norfolk, Miss Vavasor?'

'I never was in it before, and now I've only seen Yarmouth.'

'A nice place, Yarmouth, very; but you should come up and see our lands. I suppose you don't know that we feed one-third of England during the winter months.'

'Dear me!'

'We do, though; nobody knows what a county Norfolk is. Taking it altogether, including the game you know, and Lord Nelson,* and its watering-places and the rest of it, I don't think there's a county in England to beat it. Fancy feeding one-third of all England and Wales!'

'With bread and cheese, do you mean, and those sort of things?'

'Beef!' said Mr. Cheesacre, and in his patriotic energy he repeated the word aloud. 'Beef! Yes indeed; but if you were to tell them that in London they wouldn't believe you. Ah! you should certainly come down and see our lands. The 7.45 A.M. train would take you through Norwich to my door, as one may say, and you would be back by the 6.22 P.M.' In this way he brought himself back again into good-humour, feeling, that in the absence of the widow, he could not do better than make progress with the niece.

In the mean time Mrs. Greenow and the Captain were getting on very comfortably in the other boat. 'Take an oar, Captain,' one of the men had said to him as soon as he had placed the ladies. 'Not to-day, Jack,' he had answered. 'I'll content myself with being bo'san this morning.' 'The best thing as the bo'san does is to pipe all hands to grog,' said the man. 'I won't be behind in that either,' said the Captain; and so they all went on swimmingly.

'What a fine generous fellow your friend, Mr. Cheesacre, is!' said the widow.

'Yes, he is; he's a capital fellow in his way. Some of these Norfolk farmers are no end of good fellows.'

'And I suppose he's something more than a common farmer. He's visited by the people about where he lives, isn't he?'

'Oh, yes, in a sort of a way. The county people, you know, keep themselves very much to themselves.'

'That's of course. But his house;—he has a good sort of place, hasn't he?'

'Yes, yes;—a very good house;—a little too near to the horse-pond for my taste. But when a man gets his money out of the till, he musn't be ashamed of the counter;—must he, Mrs. Greenow?'

'But he could live like a gentleman if he let his own land, couldn't he?'

'That depends upon how a gentleman wishes to live.' Here the privacy of their conversation was interrupted by an exclamation from a young lady to the effect that Charlie Fairstairs was becoming sick. This Charlie stoutly denied, and proved the truth of her assertion by her behaviour. Soon after this they completed their marine adventures, and prepared to land close to the spot at which the banquet was prepared.

CHAPTER IX

The Rivals

THERE had been a pretence of fishing, but no fish had been caught. It was soon found that such an amusement would interfere with the ladies' dresses, and the affairs had become too serious to allow of any trivial interruption. 'I really think, Mr. Cheesacre,' an anxious mother had said, 'that you'd better give it up. The water off the nasty cord has got all over Maria's dress, already.' Maria made a faint protest that it did not signify in the least; but the fishing was given up,—not without an inward feeling on the part of Mr. Cheesacre that if Maria chose to come out with him in his boat, having been invited especially to fish, she ought to have put up with the natural results. 'There are people who like to take everything and never like to give anything,' he said to Kate afterwards, as he was walking up with her to the picnic dinner. But he was unreasonable and unjust. The girls had graced his party with their best hats and freshest muslins, not that they might see him catch a mackerel, but that they might flirt and dance to the best advantage. 'You can't suppose that any girl will like to be drenched with sea-water when she has taken so much trouble with her starch,' said Kate. 'Then she shouldn't come fishing,' said Mr. Cheesacre. 'I hate such airs.'

But when they arrived at the old boat, Mrs. Greenow shone forth pre-eminently as the mistress of the occasion, altogether overshadowing Mr. Cheesacre by the extent of her authority. There was a little contest for supremacy between them, invisible to the eyes of the multitude; but Mr. Cheesacre in such a matter had not a chance against Mrs. Greenow. I am disposed to think that she would have reigned even though she had not contributed the eatables; but with that point in her favour, she was able to make herself supreme. Jeannette, too, was her servant, which was a great thing. Mr. Cheesacre soon gave way; and though he bustled about and was conspicuous, he bustled about in obedience to orders received, and became a head servant. Captain Bellfield also made himself useful, but he drove Mr. Cheesacre into paroxysms of suppressed anger by giving directions, and by having those directions obeyed. A man to whom he had lent twenty pounds the day before yesterday, and who had not contributed so much as a bottle of champagne!

'We're to dine at four, and now it's half-past three,' said Mrs. Greenow, addressing herself to the multitude.

'And to begin to dance at six,' said an eager young lady.

'Maria, hold your tongue,' said the young lady's mother.

'Yes, we'll dine at four,' said Mr. Cheesacre. 'And as for the music, I've ordered it to be here punctual at half-past five. We're to have three horns, cymbals, triangle, and a drum.'

'How very nice; isn't it, Mrs. Greenow?' said Charlie Fairstairs.

'And now suppose we begin to unpack,' said Captain Bellfield. 'Half the fun is in arranging the things.'

'Oh, dear, yes; more than half,' said Fanny Fairstairs.

'Bellfield, don't mind about the hampers,' said Cheesacre. 'Wine is a ticklish thing to handle, and there's my man there to manage it.'

'It's odd if I don't know more about wine than the boots from the hotel,' said Bellfield. This allusion to the boots almost cowed Mr. Cheesacre, and made him turn away, leaving Bellfield with the widow.

There was a great unpacking, during which Captain Bellfield and Mrs. Greenow constantly had their heads in the same hamper. I by no means intend to insinuate that there was anything wrong in this. People engaged together in unpacking pies and cold chickens must have their heads in the same hamper. But a great intimacy was thereby produced, and the widow seemed to have laid aside altogether that prejudice of hers with reference to the washerwoman. There was a long table placed on the sand, sheltered by the upturned boat from the land side, but open towards the sea, and over this, supported on poles, there was an awning. Upon the whole the arrangement was not an uncomfortable one for people who had selected so very uncomfortable a dining-room as the sand of the sea-shore. Much was certainly due to Mr. Cheesacre for the expenditure he had incurred,—and something perhaps to Captain Bellfield for his ingenuity in having suggested it.

Now came the placing of the guests for dinner, and Mr. Cheesacre made another great effort. 'I'll tell you what,' said he, aloud, 'Bellfield and I will take the two ends of the table, and Mrs. Greenow shall sit at my right hand.' This was not only boldly done, but there was a propriety in it which at first sight seemed to be irresistible. Much as he had hated and did hate the Captain, he had skilfully made the proposition in such a way as to flatter him, and it seemed for a few moments as though he were going to have it all his own way. But Captain Bellfield was not a man to submit to defeat in such a matter as this without an effort. 'I don't think that will do,' said he. 'Mrs. Greenow gives the dinner, and Cheesacre gives the wine. We must have them at the two ends of the table. I am sure Mrs. Greenow won't refuse to allow me to hand her to the place which belongs to her. I will sit at her right hand and be her minister.' Mrs. Greenow did not refuse,—and so the matter was adjusted.

Mr. Cheesacre took his seat in despair. It was nothing to him that he had Kate Vavasor at his left hand. He liked talking to Kate very well, but he could not enjoy that pleasure while Captain Bellfield was in the very act of making progress with the widow. 'One would think that he had given it himself; wouldn't you?' he said to Maria's mother, who sat at his right hand.

The lady did not in the least understand him. 'Given what?' said she.

'Why, the music and the wine and all the rest of it. There are some people full of that kind of impudence. How they manage to carry it on without ever paying a shilling, I never could tell. I know I have to pay my way, and something over and beyond generally.'

Maria's mother said, 'Yes, indeed.' She had other daughters there besides Maria, and was looking down the table to see whether they were judiciously placed. Her beauty, her youngest one, Ophelia, was sitting next to that ne'er-do-well Joe Fairstairs, and this made her unhappy. 'Ophelia, my dear, you are dreadfully in the draught; there's a seat up here, just opposite, where you'll be more comfortable.'

'There's no draught here, mamma,' said Ophelia, without the slightest sign of moving. Perhaps Ophelia liked the society of that lanky, idle, useless young man.

The mirth of the table certainly came from Mrs. Greenow's end. The widow had hardly taken her place before she got up again and changed with the Captain. It was found that the Captain could better carve the great grouse pie from the end than from the side. Cheesacre, when he saw this, absolutely threw down his knife and fork violently upon the table. 'Is anything the matter?' said Maria's mother.

'Matter!' said he. Then he shook his head in grief of heart and vexation of spirit, and resumed his knife and fork. Kate watched it all, and was greatly amused. 'I never saw a man so nearly broken-hearted,' she said, in her letter to Alice the next day. 'Eleven, thirteen, eighteen, twenty-one,' said Cheesacre to himself, reckoning up in his misery the number of pounds sterling which he would have to pay for being ill-treated in this way.

'Ladies and gentlemen,' said Captain Bellfield, as soon as the eating was over, 'if I may be permitted to get upon my legs for two minutes, I am going to propose a toast to you.' The real patron of the feast had actually not yet swallowed his last bit of cheese. The thing was indecent in the violence of its injustice.

'If you please, Captain Bellfield,' said the patron, indifferent to the cheese in his throat, 'I'll propose the toast.'

'Nothing on earth could be better, my dear fellow,' said the Captain, 'and I'm sure I should be the last man in the world to take the job out of the hands of one who would do it so much better than I can; but as it's your health that we're going to drink, I really don't see how you are to do it.'

Cheesacre grunted and sat down. He certainly could not

propose his own health, nor did he complain of the honour that was to be done him. It was very proper that his health should be drunk, and he had now to think of the words in which he would return thanks. But the extent of his horror may be imagined when Bellfield got up and made a most brilliant speech in praise of Mrs. Greenow. For full five minutes he went on without mentioning the name of Cheesacre. Yarmouth, he said, had never in his days been so blessed as it had been this year by the presence of the lady who was now with them. She had come among them, he declared, forgetful of herself and of her great sorrows, with the sole desire of adding something to the happiness of others. Then Mrs. Greenow had taken out her pocket-handkerchief, sweeping back the broad ribbons of her cap over her shoulders. Altogether the scene was very affecting, and Cheesacre was driven to madness. They were the very words that he had intended to speak himself.

'I hate all this kind of thing,' he said to Kate. 'It's so fulsome.'

'After-dinner speeches never mean anything,' said Kate.

At last, when Bellfield had come to an end of praising Mrs. Greenow, he told the guests that he wished to join his friend Cheesacre in the toast, the more so as it could hardly be hoped that Mrs. Greenow would herself rise to return thanks. There was no better fellow than his friend Cheesacre, whom he had known for he would not say how many years. He was quite sure they would all have the most sincere pleasure in joining the health of Mr. Cheesacre with that of Mrs. Greenow. Then there was a clattering of glasses and a murmuring of healths, and Mr. Cheesacre slowly got upon his legs.

'I'm very much obliged to this company,' said he, 'and to my friend Bellfield, who really is,—but perhaps that doesn't signify now. I've had the greatest pleasure in getting up this little thing, and I'd made up my mind to propose Mrs. Greenow's health; but, h'm, ha, no doubt it has been in better hands. Perhaps, considering all things, Bellfield might have waited.'

'With such a subject on my hands, I couldn't wait a moment.'

'I didn't interrupt you, Captain Bellfield, and perhaps you'll let me go on without interrupting me. We've all drunk Mrs. Greenow's health, and I'm sure she's very much obliged. So am I for the honour you've done me. I have taken some trouble in getting up this little thing, and I hope you like it. I think somebody said something about liberality. I beg to assure you that I don't think of that for a moment. Somebody must pay for these sort of things, and I'm always very glad to take my turn. I dare say Bellfield will give us the next picnic, and if he'll appoint a day before the end of the month, I shall be happy to be one of the party.' Then he sat down with some inward satisfaction, fully convinced that he had given his enemy a fatal blow.

'Nothing on earth would give me so much pleasure,' said Bellfield. After that he turned again to Mrs. Greenow and went on with his private conversation.

There was no more speaking, nor was there much time for other after-dinner ceremonies. The three horns, the cymbals, the triangle, and the drum were soon heard tuning-up behind the banqueting-hall, and the ladies went to the further end of the old boat to make their preparations for the dance. Then it was that the thoughtful care of Mrs. Greenow, in having sent Jeannette with brushes, combs, clean handkerchiefs, and other little knick-knackeries, became so apparent. It was said that the widow herself actually changed her cap,—which was considered by some to be very unfair, as there had been an understanding that there should be no dressing. On such occasions ladies are generally willing to forego the advantage of dressing on the condition that other ladies shall forego the same advantage; but when this compact is broken by any special lady, the treason is thought to be very treacherous. It is as though a fencer should remove the button from the end of his foil. But Mrs. Greenow was so good-natured in tendering the services of Jeannette to all the young ladies, and was so willing to share with others those good things of the toilet which her care had provided, that her cap was forgiven her by the most of those present.

When ladies have made up their minds to dance they will

dance let the circumstances of the moment be ever so antagonistic to that exercise. A ploughed field in February would not
be too wet, nor the side of a house too uneven. In honest truth
the sands of the seashore are not adapted for the exercise. It
was all very well for Venus to make the promise, but when
making it she knew that Adonis would not keep her to her
word. Let any lightest-limbed nymph try it, and she will find
that she leaves most palpable footing. The sands in question
were doubtless compact, firm, and sufficiently moist to make
walking on them comfortable; but they ruffled themselves most
uncomfortably under the unwonted pressure to which they
were subjected. Nevertheless our friends did dance on the
sands; finding, however, that quadrilles and Sir Roger de
Coverley*suited them better than polkas and waltzes.

'No, my friend, no,' Mrs. Greenow said to Mr. Cheesacre
when that gentleman endeavoured to persuade her to stand
up; 'Kate will be delighted I am sure to join you,—but as for
me, you must excuse me.'

But Mr. Cheesacre was not inclined at that moment to ask
Kate Vavasor to dance with him. He was possessed by an undefined idea that Kate had snubbed him, and as Kate's fortune
was, as he said, literally nothing, he was not at all disposed to
court her favour at the expense of such suffering to himself.

'I'm not quite sure that I'll dance myself,' said he, seating
himself in a corner of the tent by Mrs. Greenow's side. Captain Bellfield at that moment was seen leading Miss Vavasor
away to a new place on the sands, whither he was followed by
a score of dancers; and Mr. Cheesacre saw that now at last
he might reap the reward for which he had laboured. He was
alone with the widow, and having been made bold by wine,
had an opportunity of fighting his battle, than which none
better could ever be found. He was himself by no means a poor
man, and he despised poverty in others. It was well that there
should be poor gentry, in order that they might act as satellites
to those who, like himself, had money. As to Mrs. Greenow's
money, there was no doubt. He knew it all to a fraction. She
had spread for herself, or some one else had spread for her, a

report that her wealth was almost unlimited; but the forty thousand pounds was a fact, and any such innocent fault as that little fiction might well be forgiven to a woman endorsed with such substantial virtues. And she was handsome too. Mr. Cheesacre, as he regarded her matured charms, sometimes felt that he should have been smitten even without the forty thousand pounds. 'By George! there's flesh and blood,' he had once said to his friend Bellfield before he had begun to suspect the man's treachery. His admiration must then have been sincere, for at that time the forty thousand pounds was not an ascertained fact. Looking at the matter in all its bearings Mr. Cheesacre thought that he couldn't do better. His wooing should be fair, honest, and above-board. He was a thriving man, and what might not they two do in Norfolk if they put their wealth together?

'Oh, Mr. Cheesacre, you should join them,' said Mrs. Greenow; 'they'll not half enjoy themselves without you. Kate will think that you mean to neglect her.'

'I shan't dance, Mrs. Greenow, unless you like to stand up for a set.'

'No, my friend, no; I shall not do that. I fear you forget how recent has been my bereavement. Your asking me is the bitterest reproach to me for having ventured to join your festive board.'

'Upon my honour I didn't mean it, Mrs. Greenow. I didn't mean it, indeed.'

'I do not suspect you. It would have been unmanly.'

'And nobody can say that of me. There isn't a man or woman in Norfolk that wouldn't say I was manly.'

'I'm quite sure of that.'

'I have my faults, I'm aware.'

'And what are your faults, Mr. Cheesacre?'

'Well; perhaps I'm extravagant. But it's only in these kind of things you know, when I spend a little money for the sake of making my friends happy. When I'm about, on the lands at home, I ain't extravagant, I can tell you.'

'Extravagance is a great vice.'

'Oh, I ain't extravagant in that sense;—not a bit in the world. But when a man's enamoured, and perhaps looking out for a wife, he does like to be a little free, you know.'

'And are you looking out for a wife, Mr. Cheesacre?'

'If I told you I suppose you'd only laugh at me.'

'No; indeed I would not. I am not given to joking when any one that I regard speaks to me seriously.'

'Ain't you though? I'm so glad of that. When one has really got a serious thing to say, one doesn't like to have fun poked at one.'

'And, besides, how could I laugh at marriage, seeing how happy I have been in that condition?—so—very—happy,' and Mrs. Greenow put up her handkerchief to her eyes.

'So happy that you'll try it again some day; won't you?'

'Never, Mr. Cheesacre; never. Is that the way you talk of serious things without joking? Anything like love—love of that sort—is over for me. It lies buried under the sod with my poor dear departed saint.'

'But, Mrs. Greenow,'—and Cheesacre, as he prepared to argue the question with her, got nearer to her in the corner behind the table,—'But, Mrs. Greenow, care killed a cat, you know.'

'And sometimes I think that care will kill me.'

'No, by George; not if I can prevent it.'

'You're very kind, Mr. Cheesacre; but there's no preventing such care as mine.'

'Isn't there though? I'll tell you what, Mrs. Greenow; I'm in earnest, I am indeed. If you'll inquire, you'll find there isn't a fellow in Norfolk pays his way better than I do, or is better able to do it. I don't pay a sixpence of rent, and I sit upon seven hundred acres of as good land as there is in the county. There's not an acre that won't do me a bullock and a half. Just put that and that together, and see what it comes to. And, mind you, some of these fellows that farm their own land are worse off than if they'd rent to pay. They've borrowed so much to carry on with, that the interest is more than rent. I don't owe a sixpence to ere a man or ere a company in the world. I can walk into every bank in Norwich without seeing my master. There ain't any of my paper*flying about, Mrs. Greenow. I'm Samuel Cheesacre of Oileymead, and it's all my own.' Mr. Cheesacre, as he thus spoke of his good fortunes and firm standing in the world, became impetuous in the energy of the moment, and brought down his fist powerfully on the slight table before them. The whole fabric rattled, and the boat resounded, but the noise he had made seemed to assist him. 'It's all my own, Mrs. Greenow, and the half of it shall be yours if you'll please to take it;' then he stretched out his hand to her, not as though he intended to grasp hers in a grasp of love, but as if he expected some hand-pledge from her as a token that she accepted the bargain.

'If you'd known Greenow, Mr. Cheesacre——'

'I've no doubt he was a very good sort of man.'

'If you'd known him, you would not have addressed me in this way.'

'What difference would that make? My idea is that care killed a cat, as I said before. I never knew what was the good of being unhappy. If I find early mangels*don't do on a bit of land, then I sow late turnips; and never cry after spilt milk. Greenow was the early mangels; I'll be the late turnips. Come then, say the word. There ain't a bedroom in my house,—not one of the front ones,—that isn't mahogany furnished!'

'What's furniture to me?' said Mrs. Greenow, with her handkerchief to her eyes.

Just at this moment Maria's mother stepped in under the canvas. It was most inopportune. Mr. Cheesacre felt that he was progressing well, and was conscious that he had got safely over those fences in the race which his bashfulness would naturally make difficult to him. He knew that he had done this under the influence of the champagne, and was aware that it might not be easy to procure again a combination of circumstances that would be so beneficial to him. But now he was interrupted just as he was expecting success. He was interrupted, and felt himself to be looking like a guilty creature under the eye of the strange lady. He had not a word to say;

but drawing himself suddenly a foot and a half away from the widow's side, sat there confessing his guilt in his face.

Mrs. Greenow felt no guilt, and was afraid of no strange eyes. 'Mr. Cheesacre and I are talking about farming,' she said.

'Oh; farming!' answered Maria's mother.

'Mr. Cheesacre thinks that late turnips are better than early mangels,' said Mrs. Greenow.

'Yes, I do,' said Cheesacre.

'I prefer the early mangels,' said Mrs. Greenow. 'I don't think nature ever intended those late crops. What do you say, Mrs. Walker?'

'I daresay Mr. Cheesacre understands what he's about when he's at home,' said the lady.

'I know what a bit of land can do as well as any man in Norfolk,' said the gentleman.

'It may be very well in Norfolk,' said Mrs. Greenow, rising from her seat; 'but the practice isn't thought much of in the other counties with which I am better acquainted.'

'I'd just come in to say that I thought we might be getting to the boats,' said Mrs. Walker. 'My Ophelia is so delicate.' At this moment the delicate Ophelia was to be seen, under the influence of the music, taking a distant range upon the sands with Joe Fairstairs' arm round her waist. The attitude was justified by the tune that was in progress, and there is no reason why a galop on the sands should have any special termination in distance, as it must have in a room. But, under such circumstances, Mrs. Walker's solicitude was not unreasonable.

The erratic steps of the distant dancers were recalled and preparations were made for the return journey. Others had strayed besides the delicate Ophelia and the idle Joe, and some little time was taken up in collecting the party. The boats had to be drawn down, and the boatmen fetched from their cans and tobacco-pipes. 'I hope they're sober,' said Mrs. Walker, with a look of great dismay.

'Sober as judges,' said Bellfield, who had himself been looking after the remains of Mr. Cheesacre's hampers, while that gentleman had been so much better engaged in the tent.

'Because,' continued Mrs. Walker, 'I know that they play all manner of tricks when they're—in liquor. They'd think nothing of taking us out to sea, Mrs. Greenow.'

'Oh, I do wish they would,' said Ophelia.

'Ophelia, mind you come in the boat with me,' said her mother, and she looked very savage when she gave the order. It was Mrs. Walker's intention that that boat should not carry Joe Fairstairs. But Joe and her daughter together were too clever for her. When the boats went off she found herself to be in that one over which Mr. Cheesacre presided, while the sinning Ophelia with her good-for-nothing admirer were under the more mirthful protection of Captain Bellfield.

'Mamma will be so angry,' said Ophelia, 'and it was all your fault. I did mean to go into the other boat. Don't, Mr. Fairstairs.' Then they got settled down in their seats, to the satisfaction, let us hope, of them both.

Mr. Cheesacre had vainly endeavoured to arrange that Mrs. Greenow should return with him. But not only was Captain Bellfield opposed to such a change in their positions, but so also was Mrs. Greenow. 'I think we'd better go back as we came,' she said, giving her hand to the Captain.

'Oh, certainly,' said Captain Bellfield. 'Why should there be any change? Cheesacre, old fellow, mind you look after Mrs. Walker. Come along, my hearty.' It really almost appeared that Captain Bellfield was addressing Mrs. Greenow as 'his hearty,' but it must be presumed that the term of genial endearment was intended for the whole boat's load. Mrs. Greenow took her place on the comfortable broad bench in the stern, and Bellfield seated himself beside her, with the tiller in his hand.

'If you're going to steer, Captain Bellfield, I beg that you'll be careful.'

'Careful,—and with you on board!' said the Captain. 'Don't you know that I would sooner perish beneath the waves than that a drop of water should touch you roughly?'

'But you see, we might perish beneath the waves together.'

'Together! What a sweet word that is;—perish together!

If it were not that there might be something better even than that, I would wish to perish in such company.'

'But I should not wish anything of the kind, Captain Bellfield, and therefore pray be careful.'

There was no perishing by water on that occasion. Mr. Cheesacre's boat reached the pier at Yarmouth first, and gave up its load without accident. Very shortly afterwards Captain Bellfield's crew reached the same place in the same state of preservation. 'There,' said he, as he handed out Mrs. Greenow. 'I have brought you to no harm, at any rate as yet.'

'And, as I hope, will not do so hereafter.'

'May the heavens forbid it, Mrs. Greenow! Whatever may be our lots hereafter,—yours I mean and mine,—I trust that yours may be free from all disaster. Oh, that I might venture to hope that, at some future day, the privilege might be mine of protecting you from all danger!'

'I can protect myself very well, I can assure you. Good night, Captain Bellfield. We won't take you and Mr. Cheesacre out of your way;—will we, Kate? We have had a most pleasant day.'

They were now upon the esplanade, and Mrs. Greenow's house was to the right, whereas the lodgings of both the gentlemen were to the left. Each of them fought hard for the privilege of accompanying the widow to her door; but Mrs. Greenow was self-willed, and upon this occasion would have neither of them. 'Mr. Joe Fairstairs must pass the house,' said she, 'and he will see us home. Mr. Cheesacre, good night. Indeed you shall not;—not a step.' There was that in her voice which induced Mr. Cheesacre to obey her, and which made Captain Bellfield aware that he would only injure his cause if he endeavoured to make further progress in it on the present occasion.

'Well, Kate, what do you think of the day?' the aunt said when she was alone with her niece.

'I never think much about such days, aunt. It was all very well, but I fear I have not the temperament fitted for enjoying the fun. I envied Ophelia Walker because she made herself thoroughly happy.'

'I do like to see girls enjoy themselves,' said Mrs. Greenow, 'I do indeed;—and young men too. It seems so natural; why shouldn't young people flirt?'

'Or old people either, for the matter of that?'

'Or old people either,—if they don't do any harm to anybody. I'll tell you what it is, Kate; people have become so very virtuous, that they're driven into all manner of abominable resources for amusement and occupation. If I had sons and daughters I should think a little flirting the very best thing for them as a safety-valve. When people get to be old, there's a difficulty. They want to flirt with the young people and the young people don't want them. If the old people would be content to flirt together, I don't see why they should ever give it up;—till they're obliged to give up everything, and go away.'

That was Mrs. Greenow's doctrine on the subject of flirtation.

CHAPTER X
Nethercoats

WE will leave Mrs. Greenow with her niece and two suitors at Yarmouth, and returning by stages to London, will call upon Mr. Grey at his place in Cambridgeshire* as we pass by. I believe it is conceded by all the other counties, that Cambridgeshire possesses fewer rural beauties than any other county in England. It is very flat; it is not well timbered; the rivers are merely dikes; and in a very large portion of the county the farms and fields are divided simply by ditches—not by hedgerows. Such arrangements are, no doubt, well adapted for agricultural purposes, but are not conducive to rural beauty. Mr. Grey's residence was situated in a part of Cambridgeshire in which the above-named characteristics are very much marked. It was in the Isle of Ely, some few miles distant from the Cathedral town, on the side of a long straight road, which ran through the fields for miles without even a bush to cheer it. The name of his place was Nethercoats, and here he lived generally throughout the year, and here he intended to live throughout his life.

His father had held a prebendal stall*at Ely in times when prebendal stalls were worth more than they are at present, and having also been possessed of a living in the neighbourhood, had amassed a considerable sum of money. With this he had during his life purchased the property of Nethercoats, and had built on it the house in which his son now lived. He had married late in life, and had lost his wife soon after the birth of an only child. The house had been built in his own parish, and his wife had lived there for a few months and had died there. But after that event the old clergyman had gone back to his residence in the close at Ely, and there John Grey had had the home of his youth. He had been brought up under his father's eye, having been sent to no public school. But he had gone to Cambridge, had taken college honours, and had then, his father dying exactly at this time, declined to accept a fellowship. His father had left to him an income of some fifteen hundred a year, and with this he sat himself down, near to his college friends, near also to the old cathedral which he loved, in the house which his father had built.

But though Nethercoats possessed no beauty of scenery, though the country around it was in truth as uninteresting as any country could be, it had many delights of its own. The house itself was as excellent a residence for a country gentleman of small means as taste and skill together could construct. I doubt whether prettier rooms were ever seen than the drawing-room, the library, and the dining-room at Nethercoats. They were all on the ground-floor, and all opened out on to the garden and lawn. The library, which was the largest of the three, was a handsome chamber, and so filled as to make it well known in the University as one of the best private collections in that part of England. But perhaps the gardens of Nethercoats constituted its greatest glory. They were spacious and excellently kept up, and had been originally laid out with that knowledge of gardening without which no garden, merely as a garden, can be effective. And such, of necessity, was the garden of Nethercoats. Fine single forest trees there were none there, nor was it possible that there should have been any such.

Nor could there be a clear rippling stream with steep green banks, and broken rocks lying about its bed. Such beauties are beauties of landscape, and do not of their nature belong to a garden. But the shrubs of Nethercoats were of the rarest kind, and had been long enough in their present places to have reached the period of their beauty. Nothing had been spared that a garden could want. The fruit-trees were perfect in their kind, and the glass-houses were so good and so extensive that John Grey in his prudence was sometimes tempted to think that he had too much of them.

It must be understood that there were no grounds, according to the meaning usually given to that word, belonging to the house at Nethercoats. Between the garden and the public road there was a paddock belonging to the house, along the side of which, but divided from it by a hedge and shrubbery, ran the private carriage-way up to the house. This swept through the small front flower-garden, dividing it equally; but the lawns and indeed the whole of that which made the beauty of the place lay on the back of the house, on which side opened the windows from the three sitting-rooms. Down on the public road there stood a lodge at which lived one of the gardeners. There was another field of some six or seven acres, to which there was a gate from the corner of the front paddock, and which went round two sides of the garden. This was Nethercoats, and the whole estate covered about twelve acres.

It was not a place for much bachelor enjoyment of that sort generally popular with bachelors, nevertheless Mr. Grey had been constant in his residence there for the seven years which had now elapsed since he had left his college. His easy access to Cambridge had probably done much to mitigate what might otherwise have been the too great tedium of his life; and he had, prompted thereto by early associations, found most of his society in the close of Ely Cathedral. But, with all the delight he could derive from these two sources, there had still been many solitary hours in his life, and he had gradually learned to feel that he of all men wanted a companion in his home.

His visits to London had generally been short and far between, occasioned probably by some need in the library, or by the necessity of some slight literary transaction with the editor or publisher of a periodical. In one of these visits he had met Alice Vavasor, and had remained in Town,—I will not say till Alice had promised to share his home in Cambridgeshire, but so long that he had resolved before he went that he would ask her to do so. He had asked her, and we know that he had been successful. He had obtained her promise, and from that moment all his life had been changed for him. Hitherto at Nethercoats his little smoking-room, his books, and his plants had been everything to him. Now he began to surround himself with an infinity of feminine belongings, and to promise himself an infinity of feminine blessings, wondering much that he should have been content to pass so long a portion of his life in the dull seclusion which he had endured. He was not by nature an impatient man; but now he became impatient, longing for the fruition of his new idea of happiness,—longing to have that as his own which he certainly loved beyond all else in the world, and which, perhaps, was all he had ever loved with the perfect love of equality. But though impatient, and fully aware of his own impatience, he acknowledged to himself that Alice could not be expected to share it. He could plan nothing now,— could have no pleasure in life that she was not expected to share. But as yet it could not be so with her. She had her house in London, her town society, and her father. And, inasmuch as the change for her would be much greater than it would be for him, it was natural that she should require some small delay. He had not pressed her. At least he had not pressed her with that eager pressure which a girl must resist with something of the opposition of a contest, if she resist at all. But in truth his impatience was now waxing strong, and during the absence in Switzerland of which we have spoken, he resolved that a marriage very late in the autumn,—that a marriage even in winter, would be better than a marriage postponed till the following year. It was not yet late in August when the party returned from their tour. Would not a further delay of two months suffice for his bride?

Alice had written to him occasionally from Switzerland, and her first two letters had been very charming. They had referred almost exclusively to the tour, and had been made pleasant with some slightly coloured account of George Vavasor's idleness, and of Kate's obedience to her brother's behests. Alice had never written much of love in her love-letters, and Grey was well enough contented with her style, though it was not impassioned. As for doubting her love, it was not in the heart of the man to do so after it had been once assured to him by her word. He could not so slightly respect himself or her as to leave room for such a doubt in his bosom. He was a man who could never have suggested to himself that a woman loved him till the fact was there before him; but who having ascertained, as he might think, the fact, could never suggest to himself that her love would fail him. Her first two letters from Switzerland had been very pleasant; but after that there had seemed to have crept over her a melancholy which she unconsciously transferred to her words, and which he could not but taste in them,—at first unconsciously, also, but soon with so plain a flavour that he recognized it, and made it a matter of mental inquiry. During the three or four last days of the journey, while they were at Basle and on their way home, she had not written. But she did write on the day after her arrival, having then received from Mr. Grey a letter, in which he told her how very much she would add to his happiness if she would now agree that their marriage should not be postponed beyond the end of October. This letter she found in her room on her return, and this she answered at once. And she answered it in such words that Mr. Grey resolved that he would at once go to her in London. I will give her letter at length, as I shall then be best able to proceed with my story quickly.

'Queen Anne Street,—August, 186–.

'DEAREST JOHN,—

'We reached home yesterday tired enough, as we came through from Paris without stopping. I may indeed say that we came through from Strasbourg, as we only slept in Paris. I don't like Strasbourg. A steeple,* after all, is not everything, and putting the steeple aside, I don't think the style is good. But the hotel was uncomfortable, which goes for so much;—and then we were saturated with beauty of a better kind.

'I got your letter directly I came in last night, and I suppose I had better dash at it at once. I would so willingly delay doing so, saying nice little things the while, did I not know that this would be mere cowardice. Whatever happens I won't be a coward, and therefore I will tell you at once that I cannot let you hope that we should be married this year. Of course you will ask me why, as you have a right to do, and of course I am bound to answer. I do not know that I can give any answer with which you will not have a right to complain. If it be so, I can only ask your pardon for the injury I am doing you.

'Marriage is a great change in life,—much greater to me than to you, who will remain in your old house, will keep your old pursuits, will still be your own master, and will change in nothing,—except in this, that you will have a companion who probably may not be all that you expect. But I must change everything. It will be to me as though I were passing through a grave to a new world. I shall see nothing that I have been accustomed to see, and must abandon all the ways of life that I have hitherto adopted. Of course I should have thought of this before I accepted you; and I did think of it. I made up my mind that, as I truly loved you, I would risk the change;—that I would risk it for your sake and for mine, hoping that I might add something to your happiness, and that I might secure my own. Dear John, do not suppose that I despair that it may be so; but, indeed, you must not hurry me. I must tune myself to the change that I have to make. What if I should wake some morning after six months living with you, and tell you that the quiet of your home was making me mad?

'You must not ask me again till the winter shall have passed away. If in the meantime I shall find that I have been wrong, I will humbly confess that I have wronged you, and ask you to forgive me. And I will freely admit this. If the delay which I now purpose is so contrary to your own plans as to make your marriage, under such circumstances, not that which you had expected, I know that you are free to tell me so, and to say that our engagement shall be over. I am well aware that I can have no right to bind you to a marriage at one period which you had only contemplated as to take place at another period. I think I may promise that I will obey any wish you may express in anything,—except in that one thing which you urged in your last letter.

'Kate is going down to Yarmouth with Mrs. Greenow, and I shall see no more of her probably till next year, as she will be due in Westmoreland after that. George left me at the door when he brought me home, and declared that he intended to vanish out of London. Whether in town or out, he is never to be seen at this period of the year. Papa offers to go to Ramsgate for a fortnight, but he looks so wretched when he makes the offer, that I shall not have the heart to hold him to it. Lady Macleod very much wants me to go to Cheltenham. I very much want not to go, simply because I can never agree with her about anything; but it will probably end in my going there for a week or two. Over and beyond that, I have no prospects before Christmas which are not purely domestic. There is a project that we shall all eat our Christmas dinner at Vavasor Hall,—of course not including George,—but this project is quite in the clouds, and, as far as I am concerned, will remain there.

'Dear John, let me hear that this letter does not make you unhappy.

'Most affectionately yours,
'ALICE VAVASOR.'

At Nethercoats, the post was brought in at breakfast-time, and Mr. Grey was sitting with his tea and eggs before him, when he read Alice's letter. He read it twice before he began to think what he would do in regard to it, and then referred to one or two others which he had received from Switzerland,— reading them also very carefully. After that, he took up the slouch hat which he had been wearing in the garden before he was called to his breakfast, and, with the letters in his hand, sauntered down among the shrubs and lawns.

He knew, he thought he knew, that there was more in Alice's mind than a mere wish for delay. There was more in it than that hesitation to take at once a step which she really desired to take, if not now, then after some short interval. He felt that

she was unhappy, and unhappy because she distrusted the results of her marriage; but it never for a moment occurred to him that, therefore, the engagement between them should be broken. In the first place he loved her too well to allow of his admitting such an idea without terrible sorrow to himself. He was a constant, firm man, somewhat reserved, and unwilling to make new acquaintances, and, therefore, specially unwilling to break away from those which he had made. Undoubtedly, had he satisfied himself that Alice's happiness demanded such a sacrifice of himself, he would have made it, and made it without a word of complaint. The blow would not have prostrated him, but the bruise would have remained on his heart, indelible, not to be healed but by death. He would have submitted, and no man would have seen that he had been injured. But it did not once occur to him that such a proceeding on his part would be beneficial to Alice. Without being aware of it, he reckoned himself to be the nobler creature of the two, and now thought of her as of one wounded, and wanting a cure. Some weakness had fallen on her, and strength must be given to her from another. He did not in the least doubt her love, but he knew that she had been associated, for a few weeks past, with two persons whose daily conversation would be prone to weaken the tone of her mind. He no more thought of giving her up than a man thinks of having his leg cut off because he has sprained his sinews. He would go up to town and see her, and would not even yet abandon all hope that she might be found sitting at his board when Christmas should come. By that day's post he wrote a short note to her.

'Dearest Alice,' he said, 'I have resolved to go to London at once. I will be with you in the evening at eight, the day after to-morrow.

'Yours, J. G.'

There was no more in the letter than that.

'And now,' she said, when she received it, 'I must dare to tell him the whole truth.'

CHAPTER XI

John Grey goes to London

AND what was the whole truth? Alice Vavasor, when she declared to herself that she must tell her lover the whole truth, was expressing to herself her intention of putting an end to her engagement with Mr. Grey. She was acknowledging that that which had to be told was not compatible with the love and perfect faith which she owed to the man who was her affianced husband. And yet, why should it be so? She did not intend to tell him that she had been false in her love to him. It was not that her heart had again veered itself round and given itself to that wild cousin of hers. Though she might feel herself constrained to part from John Grey, George Vavasor could never be her husband. Of that she assured herself fifty times during the two days' grace which had been allowed her. Nay, she went farther than that with herself, and pronounced a verdict against any marriage as possible to her if she now decided against this marriage which had for some months past been regarded as fixed by herself and all her friends.

People often say that marriage is an important thing, and should be much thought of in advance, and marrying people are cautioned that there are many who marry in haste and repent at leisure. I am not sure, however, that marriage may not be pondered over too much; nor do I feel certain that the leisurely repentance does not as often follow the leisurely marriages as it does the rapid ones. That some repent no one can doubt; but I am inclined to believe that most men and women take their lots as they find them, marrying as the birds do by force of nature, and going on with their mates with a general, though not perhaps an undisturbed satisfaction, feeling inwardly assured that Providence, if it have not done the very best for them, has done for them as well as they could do for themselves with all the thought in the world. I do not know that a woman can assure to herself, by her own prudence and taste, a good husband any more than she can add two cubits to her stature; but husbands have been made to be decently good,—and wives too, for the most part, in our country,—so that the thing does not require quite so much thinking as some people say.

That Alice Vavasor had thought too much about it, I feel quite sure. She had gone on thinking of it till she had filled herself with a cloud of doubts which even the sunshine of love was unable to drive from her heavens. That a girl should really love the man she intends to marry,—that, at any rate, may be admitted. But love generally comes easily enough. With all her doubts Alice never doubted her love for Mr. Grey. Nor did she doubt his character, nor his temper, nor his means. But she had gone on thinking of the matter till her mind had become filled with some undefined idea of the importance to her of her own life. What should a woman do with her life? There had arisen round her a flock of learned ladies*asking that question, to whom it seems that the proper answer has never yet occurred. Fall in love, marry the man, have two children, and live happy ever afterwards. I maintain that answer has as much wisdom in it as any other that can be given;—or perhaps more. The advice contained in it cannot, perhaps, always be followed to the letter; but neither can the advice of the other kind, which is given by the flock of learned ladies who ask the question.

A woman's life is important to her,—as is that of a man to him,—not chiefly in regard to that which she shall do with it. The chief thing for her to look to is the manner in which that something shall be done. It is of moment to a young man when entering life to decide whether he shall make hats or shoes; but not of half the moment that will be that other decision, whether he shall make good shoes or bad. And so with a woman;—if she shall have recognized the necessity of truth and honesty for the purposes of her life, I do not know that she need ask herself many questions as to what she will do with it.

Alice Vavasor was ever asking herself that question, and had by degrees filled herself with a vague idea that there was a something to be done; a something over and beyond, or perhaps altogether beside that marrying and having two children; —if she only knew what it was. She had filled herself, or had been filled by her cousins, with an undefined ambition that made her restless without giving her any real food for her mind. When she told herself that she would have no scope for action in that life in Cambridgeshire which Mr. Grey was preparing for her, she did not herself know what she meant by action. Had any one accused her of being afraid to separate herself from London society, she would have declared that she went very little into society and disliked that little. Had it been whispered to her that she loved the neighbourhood of the shops, she would have scorned the whisperer. Had it been suggested that the continued rattle of the big city was necessary to her happiness, she would have declared that she and her father had picked out for their residence the quietest street in London because she could not bear noise;—and yet she told herself that she feared to be taken into the desolate calmness of Cambridgeshire.

When she did contrive to find any answer to that question as to what she should do with her life,—or rather what she would wish to do with it if she were a free agent, it was generally of a political nature. She was not so far advanced as to think that women should be lawyers and doctors, or to wish that she might have the privilege of the franchise for herself; but she had undoubtedly a hankering after some second-hand political manœuvring. She would have liked, I think, to have been the wife of the leader of a Radical opposition, in the time when such men were put into prison, and to have kept up for him his seditious correspondence while he lay in the Tower. She would have carried the answers to him inside her stays,— and have made long journeys down into northern parts without any money, if the cause required it. She would have liked to have around her ardent spirits, male or female, who would have talked of 'the cause,' and have kept alive in her some flame of political fire. As it was, she had no cause. Her father's political views were very mild. Lady Macleod's were deadly Conservative. Kate Vavasor was an aspiring Radical just now, because her brother was in the same line; but during the year of the love-passages between George and Alice, George Vavasor's politics had been as Conservative as you please. He did not become a Radical till he had quarrelled with his grandfather. Now, indeed, he was possessed of very advanced views, —views with which Alice felt that she could sympathize. But what would be the use of sympathizing down in Cambridgeshire? John Grey had, so to speak, no politics. He had decided views as to the treatment which the Roman Senate received from Augustus,* and had even discussed with Alice the conduct of the Girondists*at the time of Robespierre's triumph; but for Manchester and its cares*he had no apparent solicitude, and had declared to Alice ·that he would not accept a seat in the

British House of Commons if it were offered to him free of expense. What political enthusiasm could she indulge with such a companion down in Cambridgeshire?

She thought too much of all this,—and was, if I may say, over-prudent in calculating the chances of her happiness and of his. For, to give her credit for what was her due, she was quite as anxious on the latter head as on the former. 'I don't care for the Roman Senate,' she would say to herself. 'I don't care much for the Girondists. How am I to talk to him day after day, night after night, when we shall be alone together?'

No doubt her tour in Switzerland with her cousin had had some effect in making such thoughts stronger now than they had ever been. She had not again learned to love her cousin. She was as firmly sure as ever that she could never love him more. He had insulted her love; and though she had forgiven him and again enrolled him among her dearest friends, she could never again feel for him that passion which a woman means when she acknowledges that she is in love. That, as regarded her and George Vavasor, was over. But, nevertheless, there had been a something of romance during those days in Switzerland which she feared she would regret when she found herself settled at Nethercoats. She envied Kate. Kate could, as his sister, attach herself on to George's political career, and obtain from it all that excitement of life which Alice desired for herself. Alice could not love her cousin and marry him; but she felt that if she could do so without impropriety she would like to stick close to him like another sister, to spend her money in aiding his career in Parliament as Kate would do, and trust herself and her career into the boat which he was to command. She did not love her cousin; but she still believed in him,—with a faith which he certainly did not deserve.

As the two days passed over her, her mind grew more and more fixed as to its purpose. She would tell Mr. Grey that she was not fit to be his wife—and she would beg him to pardon her and to leave her. It never occurred to her that perhaps he might refuse to let her go. She felt quite sure that she would be free as soon as she had spoken the word which she intended to speak. If she could speak it with decision she would be free, and to attain that decision she would school herself with her utmost strength. At one moment she thought of telling all to her father and of begging him to break the matter to Mr. Grey; but she knew that her father would not understand her, and that he would be very hostile to her,—saying hard, uncomfortable words, which would probably be spared if the thing were done before he was informed. Nor would she write to Kate, whose letters to her at this time were full of wit at the expense of Mrs. Greenow. She would tell Kate as soon as the thing was done, but not before. That Kate would sympathize with her, she was quite certain.

So the two days passed by and the time came at which John Grey was to be there. As the minute hand on the drawing-room clock came round to the full hour, she felt that her heart was beating with a violence which she could not repress. The thing seemed to her to assume bigger dimensions than it had hitherto done. She began to be aware that she was about to be guilty of a great iniquity, when it was too late for her to change her mind. She could not bring herself to resolve that she would, on the moment, change her mind. She believed that she could never pardon herself such weakness. But yet she felt herself to be aware that her purpose was wicked. When the knock at the door was at last heard she trembled and feared that she would almost be unable to speak to him. Might it be possible that there should yet be a reprieve for her? No; it was his step on the stairs, and there he was in the room with her.

'My dearest,' he said, coming to her. His smile was sweet and loving as it ever was, and his voice had its usual manly, genial, loving tone. As he walked across the room Alice felt that he was a man of whom a wife might be very proud. He was tall and very handsome, with brown hair, with bright blue eyes, and a mouth like a god. It was the beauty of his mouth,— beauty which comprised firmness within itself, that made Alice afraid of him. He was still dressed in his morning clothes; but he was a man who always seemed to be well dressed. 'My dearest,' he said, advancing across the room, and before she knew how to stop herself or him, he had taken her in his arms and kissed her.

He did not immediately begin about the letter, but placed her upon the sofa, seating himself by her side, and looked into her face with loving eyes,—not as though to scrutinize what might be amiss there, but as though determined to enjoy to the full his privilege as a lover. There was no reproach at any rate in his countenance;—none as yet; nor did it seem that he thought that he had any cause for fear. They sat in this way for a moment or two in silence, and during those moments Alice was summoning up her courage to speak. The palpitation at her heart was already gone, and she was determined that she would speak.

'Though I am very glad to see you,' she said, at last, 'I am sorry that my letter should have given you the trouble of this journey.'

'Trouble!' he said. 'Nay, you ought to know that it is no trouble. I have not enough to do down at Nethercoats to make the running up to you at any time an unpleasant excitement. So your Swiss journey went off pleasantly?'

'Yes; it went off very pleasantly.' This she said in that tone of voice which clearly implies that the speaker is not thinking of the words spoken.

'And Kate has now left you?'

'Yes; she is with her aunt, at the seaside.'

'So I understand;—and your cousin George?'

'I never know much of George's movements. He may be in Town, but I have not seen him since I came back.'

'Ah! that is the way with friends living in London. Unless circumstances bring them together, they are in fact further apart than if they lived fifty miles asunder in the country. And he managed to get through all the trouble without losing your luggage for you very often?'

'If you were to say that we did not lose his, that would be nearer the mark. But, John, you have come up to London in this sudden way to speak to me about my letter to you. Is it not so?'

'Certainly it is so. Certainly I have.'

'I have thought much, since, of what I then wrote, very much,—very much, indeed; and I have learned to feel sure that we had better——'

'Stop, Alice; stop a moment, love. Do not speak hurriedly. Shall I tell you what I learned from your letter?'

'Yes; tell me, if you think it better that you should do so.'

'Perhaps it may be better. I learned, love, that something had been said or done during your journey,—or perhaps only something thought, that had made you melancholy, and filled your mind for a while with those unsubstantial and indefinable regrets for the past which we are all apt to feel at certain moments of our life. There are few of us who do not encounter, now and again, some of that irrational spirit of sadness which, when over-indulged, drives men to madness and self-destruction. I used to know well what it was before I knew you; but since I have had the hope of having you in my house, I have banished it utterly. In that I think I have been stronger than you. Do not speak under the influence of that spirit till you have thought whether you, too, cannot banish it.'

'I have tried, and it will not be banished.'

'Try again, Alice. It is a damned spirit, and belongs neither to heaven nor to earth. Do not say to me the words that you were about to say till you have wrestled with it manfully. I think I know what those words were to be. If you love me, those words should not be spoken. If you do not——'

'If I do not love you, I love no one upon earth.'

'I believe it. I believe it as I believe in my own love for you. I trust your love implicitly, Alice. I know that you love me. I think I can read your mind. Tell me that I may return to Cambridgeshire, and again plead my cause for an early marriage from thence. I will not take such speech from you to mean more than it says!'

She sat quiet, looking at him—looking full into his face. She had in nowise changed her mind, but after such words from him, she did not know how to declare to him her resolution. There was something in his manner that awed her,—and something also that softened her.

'Tell me,' said he, 'that I may see you again to-morrow morning in our usual quiet, loving way, and that I may return home to-morrow evening. Pronounce a yea to that speech from me, and I will ask for nothing further.'

'No; I cannot do so,' she said. And the tone of her voice, as she spoke, was different to any tone that he had heard before from her mouth.

'Is that melancholy fiend too strong for you?' He smiled as he said this, and as he smiled, he took her hand. She did not attempt to withdraw it, but sat by him in a strange calmness, looking straight before her into the middle of the room. 'You have not struggled with it. You know, as I do, that it is a bad fiend and a wicked one,—a fiend that is prompting you to the worst cruelty in the world. Alice! Alice! Alice! Try to think of all this as though some other person were concerned. If it were your friend, what advice would you give her?'

'I would bid her tell the man who had loved her,—that is, if he were noble, good, and great,—that she found herself to be unfit to be his wife; and then I would bid her ask his pardon humbly on her knees.' As she said this, she sank before him on the floor, and looked up into his face with an expression of sad contrition which almost drew him from his purposed firmness.

He had purposed to be firm,—to yield to her in nothing, resolving to treat all that she might say as the hallucination of a sickened imagination,—as the effect of absolute want of health, for which some change in her mode of life would be the best cure. She might bid him begone in what language she would. He knew well that such was her intention. But he would not allow a word coming from her in such a way to disturb arrangements made for the happiness of their joint lives. As a loving husband would treat a wife, who, in some exceptional moment of a melancholy malady, should declare herself unable to remain longer in her home, so would he treat her. As for accepting what she might say as his dismissal, he would as soon think of taking the fruit-trees from the southern wall because the sun sometimes shines from the north. He could not treat either his interests or hers so lightly as that.

116

'But what if he granted no such pardon, Alice? I will grant none such. You are my wife, my own, my dearest, my chosen one. You are all that I value in the world, my treasure and my comfort, my earthly happiness and my gleam of something better that is to come hereafter. Do you think that I shall let you go from me in that way? No, love. If you are ill I will wait till your illness is gone by; and, if you will let me, I will be your nurse.'

'I am not ill.'

'Not ill with any defined sickness. You do not shake with ague, nor does your head rack you with aching; but yet you may be ill. Think of what has passed between us. Must you not be ill when you seek to put an end to all that without any cause assigned?'

'You will not hear my reasons,'—she was still kneeling before him and looking up into his face.

'I will hear them if you will tell me that they refer to any supposed faults of my own.'

'No, no, no!'

'Then I will not hear them. It is for me to find out your faults, and when I have found out any that require complaint, I will come and make it. Dear Alice, I wish you knew how I long for you.' Then he put his hand upon her hair, as though he would caress her.

But this she would not suffer, so she rose slowly, and stood with her hand upon the table in the middle of the room. 'Mr. Grey——' she said.

'If you will call me so, I shall think it only a part of your malady.'

'Mr. Grey,' she continued, 'I can only hope that you will take me at my word.'

'Oh, but I will not; certainly I will not, if that would be adverse to my own interests.'

'I am thinking of your interests; I am, indeed;—at any rate as much as of my own. I feel quite sure that I should not make you happy as your wife,—quite sure; and feeling that, I think that I am right, even after all that has passed, to ask your forgiveness, and to beg that our engagement may be over.'

'No, Alice, no; never with my consent. I cannot tell you with what contentment I would marry you to-morrow,—to-morrow, or next month, or the month after. But if it cannot be so, then I will wait. Nothing but your marriage with some one else would convince me.'

'I cannot convince you in that way,' she said, smiling.

'You will convince me in no other. You have not spoken to your father of this as yet?'

'Not as yet.'

'Do not do so, at any rate for the present. You will own that it might be possible that you would have to unsay what you had said.'

'No; it is not possible.'

'Give yourself and me the chance. It can do no harm. And, Alice, I ask you now for no reasons. I will not ask your reasons, or even listen to them, because I do not believe that they will long have effect even on yourself. Do you still think of going to Cheltenham?'

'I have decided nothing as yet.'

'If I were you, I would go. I think a change of air would be good for you.'

'Yes; you treat me as though I were partly silly, and partly insane; but it is not so. The change you speak of should be in my nature, and in yours.'

He shook his head and still smiled. There was something in the imperturbed security of his manner which almost made her angry with him. It seemed as though he assumed so great a superiority that he felt himself able to treat any resolve of hers as the petulance of a child. And though he spoke in strong language of his love, and of his longing that she should come to him, yet he was so well able to command his feelings, that he showed no sign of grief at the communication she had made to him. She did not doubt his love, but she believed him to be so much the master of his love,—as he was the master of everything else, that her separation from him would cause him no uncontrollable grief. In that she utterly failed to understand his character. Had she known him better, she might have been sure that such a separation now would with him have carried its mark to the grave. Should he submit to her decision, he would go home and settle himself to his books the next day; but on no following day would he be again capable of walking forth among his flowers with an easy heart. He was a strong, constant man, perhaps over-conscious of his own strength; but then his strength was great. 'He is perfect!' Alice had said to herself often. 'Oh that he were less perfect!'

He did not stay with her long after the last word that has been recorded. 'Perhaps,' he said, as for a moment he held her hand at parting, 'I had better not come to-morrow.'

'No, no; it is better not.'

'I advise you not to tell your father of this, and doubtless you will think of it before you do so. But if you do tell him, let me know that you have done so.'

'Why that?'

'Because in such case I also must see him. God bless you, Alice! God bless you, dearest, dearest Alice!' Then he went, and she sat there on the sofa without moving, till she heard her father's feet as he came up the stairs.

'What, Alice, are you not in bed yet?'

'Not yet, papa.'

'And so John Grey has been here. He has left his stick in the hall. I should know it among a thousand.'

'Yes; he has been here.'

'Is anything the matter, Alice?'

'No, papa, nothing is the matter.'

'He has not made himself disagreeable, has he?'

'Not in the least. He never does anything wrong. He may defy man or woman to find fault with him.'

'So that is it, is it? He is just a shade too good. Well, I have always thought that myself. But it's a fault on the right side.'

'It's no fault, papa. If there be any fault, it is not with him. But I am yawning and tired, and I will go to bed.'

'Is he to be here to-morrow?'

'No; he returns to Nethercoats early. Good-night, papa.'

Mr. Vavasor, as he went up to his bedroom, felt sure that there had been something wrong between his daughter and her lover. 'I don't know how she'll ever put up with him,' he said to himself, 'he is so terribly conceited. I shall never forget how he went on about Charles Kemble,* and what a fool he made of himself.'

Alice, before she went to bed, sat down and wrote a letter to her cousin Kate.

CHAPTER XII

Mr. George Vavasor at Home

IT cannot perhaps fairly be said that George Vavasor was an inhospitable man, seeing that it was his custom to entertain his friends occasionally at Greenwich, Richmond, or such places; and he would now and again have a friend to dine with him at his club. But he never gave breakfasts, dinners, or suppers under his own roof. During a short period of his wine-selling career, at which time he had occupied handsome rooms over his place of business in New Burlington Street, he had presided at certain feasts given to customers or expectant customers by the firm; but he had not found this employment to be to his taste, and had soon relinquished it to one of the other partners. Since that he had lived in lodgings in Cecil Street,—down at the bottom of that retired nook, near to the river and away from the Strand. Here he had simply two rooms on the first floor, and hither his friends came to him very rarely. They came very rarely on any account. A stray man might now and then pass an hour with him here; but on such occasions the chances were that the visit had some reference, near or distant, to affairs of business. Eating or drinking there was never any to be found here by the most intimate of his allies. His lodgings were his private retreat, and they were so private that but few of his friends knew where he lived.

And had it been possible he would have wished that no one should have known his whereabouts. I am not aware that he had any special reason for this peculiarity, or that there was anything about his mode of life that required hiding; but he was a man who had always lived as though secrecy in certain matters might at any time become useful to him. He had a mode of dressing himself when he went out at night that made it almost impossible that any one should recognize him. The people at his lodgings did not even know that he had relatives, and his nearest relatives hardly knew that he had lodgings. Even Kate had never been at the rooms in Cecil Street, and addressed all her letters to his place of business or his club. He was a man who would bear no inquiry into himself. If he had been out of view for a month, and his friends asked him where he had been, he always answered the question falsely, or left it unanswered. There are many men of whom every-body knows all about all their belongings;—as to whom every-body knows where they live, whither they go, what is their means, and how they spend it. But there are others of whom no man knows anything, and George Vavasor was such a one. For myself I like the open babbler the best. Babbling may be a weakness, but to my thinking mystery is a vice.

Vavasor also maintained another little establishment, down in Oxfordshire; but the two establishments did not even know of each other's existence. There was a third, too, very closely hidden from the world's eye, which shall be nameless; but of the establishment in Oxfordshire he did sometimes speak, in very humble words, among his friends. When he found him-self among hunting men, he would speak of his two nags at Roebury, saying that he had never yet been able to mount a regular hunting stable, and that he supposed he never would; but that there were at Roebury two indifferent beasts of his if any one chose to buy them. And men very often did buy Vava-sor's horses. When he was on them they always went well and sold themselves readily. And though he thus spoke of two, and perhaps did not keep more during the summer, he always seemed to have horses enough when he was down in the coun-try. No one ever knew George Vavasor not to hunt because he was short of stuff. And here, at Roebury, he kept a trusty servant, an ancient groom with two little bushy grey eyes which looked as though they could see through a stable door. Many were the long whisperings which George and Bat Smithers carried on at the stable door, in the very back depth of the yard attached to the hunting inn at Roebury. Bat regarded his master as a man wholly devoted to horses, but often wondered why he was not more regular in his sojournings in Oxfordshire. Of any other portion of his master's life Bat knew nothing. Bat could give the address of his master's club in London, but he could give no other address.

But though Vavasor's private lodgings were so very private, he had, nevertheless, taken some trouble in adorning them. The furniture in the sitting-room was very neat, and the book-shelves were filled with volumes that shone with gilding on their backs. The inkstand, the paper-weight, the envelope case on his writing-table were all handsome. He had a single good portrait of a woman's head hanging on one of his walls. He had a special place adapted for his pistols, others for his foils, and again another for his whips. The room was as pretty a bachelor's room as you would wish to enter, but you might see, by the position of the single easy-chair that was brought forward, that it was seldom appropriated to the comfort of more than one person. Here he sat lounging over his break-fast, late on a Sunday morning in September, when all the world was out of town. He was reading a letter which had just been brought down to him from his club. Though the writer of it was his sister Kate, she had not been privileged to address it to his private lodgings. He read it very quickly, running rapidly over its contents, and then threw it aside from him as though it were of no moment, keeping, however, an enclosure in his hand. And yet the letter was of much moment, and made him think deeply. 'If I did it at all,' said he, 'it would be more with the object of cutting him out than with any other.'

The reader will hardly require to be told that the 'him' in question was John Grey, and that Kate's letter was one in-stigating her brother to renew his love affair with Alice. And Vavasor was in truth well inclined to renew it, and would have begun the renewing it at once, had he not doubted his power with his cousin. Indeed it has been seen that he had already attempted some commencement of such renewal at Basle. He had told Kate more than once that Alice's fortune was not much, and that her beauty was past its prime; and he would no doubt repeat the same objections to his sister with some pretence of disinclination. It was not his custom to show his hand to the players at any game that he played. But he was, in truth, very anxious to obtain from Alice a second promise of her hand. How soon after that he might marry her, would be another question.

Perhaps it was not Alice's beauty that he coveted, nor yet her money exclusively. Nevertheless he thought her very beautiful, and was fully aware that her money would be of great service to him. But I believe that he was true in that word that he spoke to himself, and that his chief attraction was the delight which he would have in robbing Mr. Grey of his wife. Alice had once been his love, had clung to his side, had whispered love to him, and he had enough of the weakness of humanity in him to feel the soreness arising from her affection for another. When she broke away from him he had acknowledged that he had been wrong, and when, since her engagement with Mr. Grey, he had congratulated her, he had told her in his quiet, half-whispered, impressive words how right she was; but not the less, therefore, did he feel himself hurt that John Grey should be her lover. And when he had met this man he had spoken well of him to his sister, saying that he was a gentleman, a scholar, and a man of parts; but not the less had he hated him from the first moment of his seeing him. Such hatred under such circumstances was almost pardonable. But George Vavasor, when he hated, was apt to follow up his hatred with injury. He could not violently dislike a man and yet not wish to do him any harm. At present, as he sat lounging in his chair, he thought that he would like to marry his cousin Alice; but he was quite sure that he would like to be the means of putting a stop to the proposed marriage between Alice and John Grey.

Kate had been very false to her friend, and had sent up to her brother the very letter which Alice had written to her after that meeting in Queen Anne Street which was described in the last chapter,—or rather a portion of it, for with the reserve common to women she had kept back the other half. Alice had declared to herself that she would be sure of her cousin's sympathy, and had written out all her heart on the matter, as was her wont when writing to Kate. 'But you must understand,' she wrote, 'that all that I said to him went with him for nothing. I had determined to make him know that everything between us must be over, but I failed. I found that I had no words at command, but that he was able to talk to me as though I were a child. He told me that I was sick and full of phantasies, and bade me change the air. As he spoke in this way, I could not help feeling how right he was to use me so; but I felt also that he, in his mighty superiority, could never be a fitting husband for a creature so inferior to him as I am. Though I altogether failed to make him understand that it was so, every moment that we were together made me more fixed in my resolution.'

This letter from Alice to Kate, Vavasor read over and over again, though Kate's letter to himself, which was the longer one, he had thrown aside after the first glance. There was nothing that he could learn from that. He was as good a judge of the manner in which he would play his own game as Kate could be; but in this matter he was to learn how he would play his game from a knowledge of the other girl's mind. 'She'll never marry him, at any rate,' he said to himself, 'and she is right. He'd make an upper servant of her; very respectable, no doubt, but still only an upper servant. Now with me;—well, I hardly know what I should make of her. I cannot think of myself as a man married.' Then he threw her letter after Kate's, and betook himself to his newspaper and his cigar.

It was two hours after this, and he still wore his dressing-gown, and he was still lounging in his easy-chair, when the waiting-maid at the lodgings brought him up word that a gentleman wished to see him. Vavasor kept no servant of his own except that confidential groom down at Bicester.* It was a

rule with him that people could be better served and cheaper
served by other people's servants than by their own. Even in
the stables at Bicester the innkeeper had to find what assistance
was wanted, and charge for it in the bill. And George Vavasor
was no Sybarite.* He did not deem it impracticable to put on

his own trousers without having a man standing at his foot to
hold up the leg of the garment. A valet about a man knows a
great deal of a man's ways, and therefore George had no valet.

'A gentleman!' said he to the girl. 'Does the gentleman look
like a public-house keeper?'

'Well, I think he do,' said the girl.

'Then show him up,' said George.

And the gentleman was a public-house keeper. Vavasor was
pretty sure of his visitor before he desired the servant to give
him entrance. It was Mr. Grimes from the Handsome Man
public-house and tavern, in the Brompton Road, and he had
come by appointment to have a little conversation with Mr.
Vavasor on matters political. Mr. Grimes was a man who

knew that business was business, and as such had some considerable weight in his own neighbourhood. With him politics was business, as well as beer, and omnibus-horses, and foreign wines;—in the fabrication of which latter article Mr. Grimes was supposed to have an extended experience. To such as him, when intent on business, Mr. Vavasor was not averse to make known the secrets of his lodging-house; and now, when the idle London world was either at morning church or still in bed, Mr. Grimes had come out by appointment to do a little political business with the lately-rejected member for the Chelsea Districts.

Vavasor had been, as I have said, lately rejected, and the new member who had beaten him at the hustings had sat now for one session in Parliament. Under his present reign he was destined to the honour of one other session, and then the period of his existing glory,—for which he was said to have paid nearly six thousand pounds,—would be over. But he might be elected again, perhaps for a full period of six sessions; and it might be hoped that this second election would be conducted on more economical principles. To this, the economical view of the matter, Mr. Grimes was very much opposed, and was now waiting upon George Vavasor in Cecil Street, chiefly with the object of opposing the new member's wishes on this head. No doubt Mr. Grimes was personally an advocate for the return of Mr. Vavasor, and would do all in his power to prevent the re-election of the young Lord Kilfenora, whose father, the Marquis of Bunratty, had scattered that six thousand pounds among the electors and non-electors of Chelsea; but his main object was that money should be spent. "Tain't altogether for myself,' he said to a confidential friend in the same way of business; 'I don't get so much on it. Perhaps sometimes not none. May be I've a bill agin some of those gents not paid this werry moment. But it's the game I looks to. If the game dies away, it'll never be got up again;—never. Who'll care about elections then? Anybody'd go and get hisself elected if we was to let the game go by!' And so, that the game might not go by, Mr. Grimes was now present in Mr. George Vavasor's rooms.

'Well, Mr. Grimes,' said George, 'how are you this morn-ing? Sit down, Mr. Grimes. If every man were as punctual as you are, the world would go like clock-work; wouldn't it?'

'Business is business, Mr. Vavasor,' said the publican, after having made his salute, and having taken his chair with some little show of mock modesty. 'That's my maxim. If I didn't stick to that, nothing wouldn't ever stick to me; and nothing doesn't much, as it is. Times is very bad, Mr. Vavasor.'

'Of course they are. They're always bad. What was the Devil made for, except that they should be bad? But I should have thought you publicans were the last men who ought to complain.'

'Lord love you, Mr. Vavasor; why, I suppose of all the men as is put upon, we're put upon the worst. What's the good of drawing of beer, if the more you draw the more you don't make? Yesterday as ever was was Saturday, and we drawed three pound ten and nine. What'll that come to, Mr. Vavasor, when you reckons it up with the brewer? Why, it's a next to nothing. You knows that well enough.'

'Upon my word I don't. But I know you don't sell a pint of beer without getting a profit out of it.'

'Lord love you, Mr. Vavasor. If I hadn't nothink to look to but beer I couldn't keep a house over my head; no, I couldn't. That house of mine belongs to Meux's people; and very good people they are too;—have made a sight of money; haven't they, Mr. Vavasor? I has to get my beer from them in course. Why not, when it's their house? But if I sells their stuff as I gets it, there ain't a halfpenny coming to me out of a gallon. Look at that, now.'

'But then you don't sell it as you get it. You stretch it.'

'That's in course. I'm not going to tell you a lie, Mr. Vava-sor. You know what's what as well as I do, and a sight better, I expect. There's a dozen different ways of handling beer, Mr. Vavasor. But what's the use of that, when they can take four or five pounds a day over the counter for their rot-gut stuff at the "Cadogan Arms," and I can't do no better nor yet per-haps so well, for a real honest glass of beer? Stretch it! It's my belief the more you poison their liquor, the more the people likes it!'

Mr. Grimes was a stout man, not very tall, with a mottled red face, and large protruding eyes. As regards his own person, Mr. Grimes might have been taken as a fair sample of the English innkeeper, as described for many years past. But in his outer garments he was very unlike that description. He wore a black, swallow-tailed coat, made, however, to set very loose upon his back, a black waistcoat, and black pantaloons. He carried, moreover, in his hands a black chimney-pot hat. Not only have the top-boots and breeches vanished from the costume of innkeepers, but also the long, particoloured waist-coat, and the birds'-eye fogle* round their necks. They get themselves up to look like Dissenting ministers or undertakers, except that there is still a something about their rosy gills which tells a tale of the spigot*and corkscrew.

Mr. Grimes had only just finished the tale of his own hard ways as a publican, when the door-bell was again rung. 'There's Scruby,' said George Vavasor, 'and now we can go to business.'

CHAPTER XIII

Mr. Grimes gets his Odd Money

THE handmaiden at George Vavasor's lodgings announced 'another gent,' and then Mr. Scruby entered the room in which were seated George, and Mr. Grimes the publican from the 'Handsome Man' on the Brompton Road. Mr. Scruby was an attorney from Great Marlborough Street, supposed to be very knowing in the ways of metropolitan elections; and he had now stepped round, as he called it, with the object of saying a few words to Mr. Grimes, partly on the subject of the forth-coming contest at Chelsea, and partly on that of the contest just past. These words were to be said in the presence of Mr. Vavasor, the person interested. That some other words had been spoken between Mr. Scruby and Mr. Grimes on the same subjects behind Mr. Vavasor's back I think very probable. But even though this might have been so I am not prepared to say that Mr. Vavasor had been deceived by their combinations.

The two men were very civil to each other in their salutations, the attorney assuming an air of patronizing condescension, always calling the other Grimes; whereas Mr. Scruby was treated with considerable deference by the publican, and was always called Mr. Scruby. 'Business is business,' said the publican as soon as these salutations were over; 'isn't it now, Mr. Scruby?'

'And I suppose Grimes thinks Sunday morning a particularly good time for business,' said the attorney, laughing.

'It's quiet, you know,' said Grimes. 'But it warn't me as named Sunday morning. It was Mr. Vavasor here. But it is quiet; ain't it, Mr. Scruby?'

Mr. Scruby acknowledged that it was quiet, especially looking out over the river, and then they proceeded to business. 'We must pull the governor through better next time than we did last,' said the attorney.

'Of course we must, Mr. Scruby; but, Lord love you, Mr. Vavasor, whose fault was it? What notice did I get,—just tell me that? Why, Travers's name was up on the Liberal interest ever so long before the governor had ever thought about it.'

'Nobody is blaming you, Mr. Grimes,' said George.

'And nobody can't, Mr. Vavasor. I done my work true as steel, and there ain't another man about the place as could have done half as much. You ask Mr. Scruby else. Mr. Scruby knows, if ere a man in London does. I tell you what it is, Mr. Vavasor, them Chelsea fellows, who lives mostly down by the river, ain't like your Maryboners or Finsburyites. It wants something of a man to manage them. Don't it, Mr. Scruby?'

'It wants something of a man to manage any of them as far as my experience goes,' said Mr. Scruby.

'Of course it do; and there ain't no one in London knows so much about it as you do, Mr. Scruby. I will say that for you. But the long and the short of it is this;—business is business, and money is money.'

'Money is money, certainly,' said Mr. Scruby. 'There's no

doubt in the world about that, Grimes;—and a deal of it you had out of the last election.'

'No, I hadn't; begging your pardon, Mr. Scruby, for making so free. What I had to my own cheek*wasn't nothing to speak of. I wasn't paid for my time; that's what I wasn't. You look how a publican's business gets cut up at them elections;—and then the state of the house afterwards! What would the governor say to me if I was to put down painting inside and out in my little bill?'

'It doesn't seem to make much difference how you put it down,' said Vavasor. 'The total is what I look at.'

'Just so, Mr. Vavasor; just so. The total is what I looks at too. And I has to look at it a deuced long time before I gets it. I ain't a got it yet; have I, Mr. Vavasor?'

'Well; if you ask me I should say you had,' said George. 'I know I paid Mr. Scruby three hundred pounds on your account.'

'And I got every shilling of it, Mr. Vavasor. I'm not a going to deny the money, Mr. Vavasor. You'll never find me doing that. I'm as round as your hat, and as square as your elbow,— I am. Mr. Scruby knows me; don't you, Mr. Scruby?'

'Perhaps I know you too well, Grimes.'

'No, you don't, Mr. Scruby; not a bit too well. Nor I don't know you too well, either. I respect you, Mr. Scruby, because you're a man as understands your business. But as I was saying, what's three hundred pounds when a man's bill is three hundred and ninety-two thirteen and fourpence?'

'I thought that was all settled, Mr. Scruby,' said Vavasor.

'Why, you see, Mr. Vavasor, it's very hard to settle these things. If you ask me whether Mr. Grimes here can sue you for the balance, I tell you very plainly that he can't. We were a little short of money when we came to a settlement, as is generally the case at such times, and so we took Mr. Grimes's receipt for three hundred pounds.'

'Of course you did, Mr. Scruby.'

'Not on account, but in full of all demands.'

'Now, Mr. Scruby!' and the publican as he made this appeal

looked at the attorney with an expression of countenance which was absolutely eloquent. 'Are you going to put me off with such an excuse as that?' so the look spoke plainly enough. 'Are you going to bring up my own signature against me, when you know very well that I shouldn't have got a shilling at all for the next twelvemonths if I hadn't given it? Oh, Mr. Scruby!' That's what Mr. Grimes' look said, and both Mr. Scruby and Mr. Vavasor understood it perfectly.

'In full of all demands,' said Mr. Scruby, with a slight tone of triumph in his voice, as though to show that Grimes' appeal had no effect at all upon his conscience. 'If you were to go into a court of law, Grimes, you wouldn't have a leg to stand upon.'

'A court of law? Who's a going to law with the governor, I should like to know? not I; not if he didn't pay me them ninety-two pounds thirteen and fourpence for the next five years.'

'Five years or fifteen would make no difference,' said Scruby. 'You couldn't do it.'

'And I ain't a going to try. That's not the ticket I've come here about, Mr. Vavasor, this blessed Sunday morning. Going to law, indeed! But, Mr. Scruby, I've got a family.'

'Not in the vale of Taunton,* I hope,' said George.

'They is at the Handsome Man in the Brompton Road, Mr. Vavasor; and I always feels that I owes my first duty to them. If a man don't work for his family, what do he work for?'

'Come, come, Grimes,' said Mr. Scruby. 'What is it you're at? Out with it, and don't keep us here all day.'

'What is it I'm at, Mr. Scruby? As if you didn't know very well what I'm at. There's my house;—in all them Chelsea Districts it's the most convenientest of any public as is open for all manner of election purposes. That's given up to it.'

'And what next?' said Scruby.

'The next is, I myself. There isn't one of the lot of 'em can work them Chelsea fellows down along the river unless it is me. Mr. Scruby knows that. Why, I've been a getting of them up with a view to this very job ever since;—why, ever since they was a talking of the Chelsea Districts. When Lord Robert was a coming in for the county on the religious dodge, he couldn't have worked them fellows anyhow, only for me. Mr. Scruby knows that.'

'Let's take it all for granted, Mr. Grimes,' said Vavasor. 'What comes next?'

'Well;—them Bunratty people; it is them as come next. They know which side their bread is like to be buttered; they do. They're a bidding for the Handsome Man already; they are.'

'And you'd let your house to the Tory party, Grimes!' said Mr. Scruby, in a tone in which disgust and anger were blended.

'Who said anything of my letting my house to the Tory party, Mr. Scruby? I'm as round as your hat, Mr. Scruby, and as square as your elbow; I am. But suppose as all the Liberal gents as employs you, Mr. Scruby, was to turn again you and not pay you your little bills, wouldn't you have your eyes open for customers of another kind? Come now, Mr. Scruby?'

'You won't make much of that game, Grimes.'

'Perhaps not; perhaps not. There's a risk in all these things; isn't there, Mr. Vavasor? I should like to see you a Parliament gent; I should indeed. You'd be a credit to the Districts; I really think you would.'

'I'm much obliged by your good opinion, Mr. Grimes,' said George.

'When I sees a gent coming forward I knows whether he's fit for Parliament, or whether he ain't. I says you are fit. But, lord love you, Mr. Vavasor; it's a thing a gentleman always has to pay for.'

'That's true enough; a deal more than it's worth, generally.'

'A thing's worth what it fetches. I'm worth what I'll fetch; that's the long and the short of it. I want to have my balance, that's the truth. It's the odd money in a man's bill as always carries the profit. You ask Mr. Scruby else;—only with a lawyer it's all profit, I believe.'

'That's what you know about it,' said Scruby.

'If you cut off a man's odd money,' continued the publican, 'you break his heart. He'd almost sooner have that and leave the other standing. He'd call the hundreds capital, and if he lost them at last, why, he'd put it down as being in the way of trade. But the odd money;—he looks at that, Mr. Vavasor, as in a manner the very sweat of his brow, the work of his own hand; that's what goes to his family, and keeps the pot a boiling downstairs. Never stop a man's odd money, Mr. Vavasor; that is, unless he comes it very strong indeed.'

'And what is it you want now?' said Scruby.

'I wants ninety-two pounds thirteen and fourpence, Mr. Scruby, and then we'll go to work for the new fight with contented hearts. If we're to begin at all, it's quite time; it is indeed, Mr. Vavasor.'

'And what you mean us to understand is, that you won't begin at all without your money,' said the lawyer.

'That's about it, Mr. Scruby.'

'Take a fifty-pound note, Grimes,' said the lawyer.

'Fifty-pound notes are not so ready,' said George.

'Oh, he'll be only too happy to have your acceptance; won't you, Grimes?'

'Not for fifty pounds, Mr. Scruby. It's the odd money that I wants. I don't mind the thirteen and four, because that's neither here nor there among friends, but if I didn't get all them ninety-two pounds I should be a broken-hearted man; I should indeed, Mr. Vavasor. I couldn't go about your work for next year so as to do you justice among the electors. I couldn't indeed.'

'You'd better give him a bill for ninety pounds at three months, Mr. Vavasor. I have no doubt he has got a stamp in his pocket.'

'That I have, Mr. Scruby; there ain't no mistake about that. A bill stamp is a thing that often turns up convenient with gents as mean business like Mr. Vavasor and you. But you must make it ninety-two; you must indeed, Mr. Vavasor. And do make it two months if you can, Mr. Vavasor; they do charge* so unconscionable on ninety days at them branch banks; they do indeed.'

George Vavasor and Mr. Scruby, between them, yielded at

last, so far as to allow the bill to be drawn for ninety-two pounds, but they were stanch*as to the time. 'If it must be, it must,' said the publican, with a deep sigh, as he folded up the paper and put it into the pocket of a huge case which he carried. 'And now, gents, I'll tell you what it is. We'll make safe work of this here next election. We know what's to be our little game in time, and if we don't go in and win, my name ain't Jacob Grimes, and I ain't the landlord of the Handsome Man. As you gents has perhaps got something to say among yourselves, I'll make so bold as to wish you good morning.' So, with that, Mr. Grimes lifted his hat from the floor, and bowed himself out of the room.

'You couldn't have done it cheaper; you couldn't, indeed,' said the lawyer, as soon as the sound of the closing front door had been heard.

'Perhaps not; but what a thief the man is! I remember your telling me that the bill was about the most preposterous you had ever seen.'

'So it was, and if we hadn't wanted him again of course we shouldn't have paid him. But we'll have it all off his next account, Mr. Vavasor,—every shilling of it. It's only lent; that's all;—it's only lent.'

'But one doesn't want to lend such a man money, if one could help it.'

'That's true. If you look at it in that light, it's quite true. But you see we cannot do without him. If he hadn't got your bill, he'd have gone over to the other fellows before the week was over; and the worst of it would have been that he knows our hand. Looking at it all round you've got him cheap, Mr. Vavasor;—you have, indeed.'

'Looking at it all round is just what I don't like, Mr. Scruby. But if a man will have a whistle, he must pay for it.'

'You can't do it cheap*for any of these metropolitan seats; you can't, indeed, Mr. Vavasor. That is, a new man can't. When you've been in four or five times, like old Duncombe, why then, of course, you may snap your fingers at such men as Grimes. But the Chelsea Districts ain't dear. I don't call them by any means dear. Now Marylebone is dear,—and so is Southwark. It's dear, and nasty; that's what the Borough is. Only that I never tell tales, I could tell you a tale, Mr. Vavasor, that'd make your hair stand on end; I could indeed.'

'Ah! the game is hardly worth the candle, I believe.'

'That depends on what way you choose to look at it. A seat in Parliament is a great thing to a man who wants to make his way;—a very great thing;—specially when a man's young, like you, Mr. Vavasor.'

'Young!' said George. 'Sometimes it seems to me as though I've been living for a hundred years. But I won't trouble you with that, Mr. Scruby, and I believe I needn't keep you any longer.' With that, he got up and bowed the attorney out of the room, with just a little more ceremony than he had shown to the publican.

'Young!' said Vavasor to himself, when he was left alone. 'There's my uncle, or the old squire,—they're both younger men than I am. One cares for his dinner, and the other for his bullocks and his trees. But what is there that I care for, unless it is not getting among the sheriff's officers*for debt?' Then he took out a little memorandum-book from his breast-pocket, and having made in it an entry as to the amount and date of that bill which he had just accepted on the publican's behalf, he conned over the particulars of its pages. 'Very blue; very blue, indeed,' he said to himself when he had completed the study. 'But nobody shall say I hadn't the courage to play the game out, and that old fellow must die some day, one supposes. If I were not a fool, I should make it up with him before he went; but I am a fool, and shall remain so to the last.' Soon after that he dressed himself slowly, reading a little every now and then as he did so. When his toilet was completed, and his Sunday newspapers sufficiently perused, he took up his hat and umbrella and sauntered out.

CHAPTER XIV

Alice Vavasor becomes Troubled

KATE VAVASOR had sent to her brother only the first half of her cousin's letter, that half in which Alice had attempted to describe what had taken place between her and Mr. Grey. In doing this, Kate had been a wicked traitor,—a traitor to that feminine faith against which treason on the part of one woman is always unpardonable in the eyes of other women. But her treason would have been of a deeper dye had she sent the latter portion, for in that Alice had spoken of George Vavasor himself. But even of this treason, Kate would, I think, have been guilty, had the words which Alice wrote been of a nature to serve her own purpose if read by her brother. But they had not been of this nature. They had spoken of George as a man with whom any closer connection than that which existed at present was impossible, and had been written with the view of begging Kate to desist from making futile attempts in that direction. 'I feel myself driven,' Alice had said, 'to write all this, as otherwise,—if I were simply to tell you that I have resolved to part from Mr. Grey,—you would think that the other thing might follow. The other thing cannot follow. I should think myself untrue in my friendship to you if I did not tell you about Mr. Grey; and you will be untrue in your friendship to me if you take advantage of my confidence by saying more about your brother.' This part of Alice's letter Kate had not sent to George Vavasor;—'But the other thing shall follow,' Kate had said, as she read the words for the second time, and then put the papers into her desk. 'It shall follow.'

To give Kate Vavasor her due, she was, at any rate, unselfish in her intrigues. She was obstinately persistent, and she was moreover unscrupulous, but she was not selfish. Many years ago she had made up her mind that George and Alice should be man and wife, feeling that such a marriage would be good at any rate for her brother. It had been almost brought

about, and had then been hindered altogether through a fault
on her brother's part. But she had forgiven him this sin as she
had forgiven many others, and she was now at work in his
behalf again, determined that they two should be married, even
though neither of them might be now anxious that it should
be so. The intrigue itself was dear to her, and success in it
was necessary to her self-respect.

She answered Alice's letter with a pleasant, gossiping epistle,
which shall be recorded, as it will tell us something of Mrs.
Greenow's proceedings at Yarmouth. Kate had promised to
stay at Yarmouth for a month, but she had already been there
six weeks, and was still under her aunt's wing.

'Yarmouth, October, 186–.

'DEAREST ALICE,

'Of course I am delighted. It is no good saying that I am
not. I know how difficult it is to deal with you, and therefore
I sit down to answer your letter with fear and trembling, lest
I should say a word too much, and thereby drive you back, or
not say quite enough and thereby fail to encourage you on. Of
course I am glad. I have long thought that Mr. Grey could not
make you happy, and as I have thought so, how can I not be
glad? It is no use saying that he is good and noble, and all that
sort of thing. I have never denied it. But he was not suited to
you, and his life would have made you wretched. Ergo, I rejoice. And as you are the dearest friend I have, of course I
rejoice mightily.

'I can understand accurately the sort of way in which the
interview went. Of course he had the best of it. I can see him so
plainly as he stood up in unruffled self-possession, ignoring all
that you said, suggesting that you were feverish or perhaps
bilious, waving his hand over you a little, as though that might
possibly do you some small good, and then taking his leave
with an assurance that it would be all right as soon as the wind
changed. I suppose it's very noble in him, not taking you at
your word, and giving you, as it were, another chance; but
there is a kind of nobility which is almost too great for this

137

world. I think very well of you, my dear, as women go, but I do not think well enough of you to believe that you are fit to be Mr. John Grey's wife.

'Of course I'm very glad. You have known my mind from the first to the last, and, therefore, what would be the good of my mincing matters? No woman wishes her dearest friend to marry a man to whom she herself is antipathetic. You would have been as much lost to me, had you become Mrs. Grey of Nethercoats, Cambridgeshire, as though you had gone to heaven. I don't say but what Nethercoats may be a kind of heaven,—but then one doesn't wish one's friend that distant sort of happiness. A flat Eden I can fancy it, hemmed in by broad dykes, in which cream and eggs are very plentiful, where an Adam and an Eve might drink the choicest tea out of the finest china, with toast buttered to perfection, from year's end to year's end; into which no money troubles would ever find their way, nor yet any naughty novels. But such an Eden is not tempting to me, nor, as I think, to you. I can fancy you stretching your poor neck over the dyke, longing to fly away that you might cease to be at rest, but knowing that the matrimonial dragon was too strong for any such flight. If ever bird banged his wings to pieces against gilded bars, you would have banged yours to pieces in that cage.

'You say that you have failed to make him understand that the matter is settled. I need not say that of course it is settled, and that he must be made to understand it. You owe it to him now to put him out of all doubt. He is, I suppose, accessible to the words of a mortal, god though he be. But I do not fear about this, for, after all, you have as much firmness about you as most people;—perhaps as much as he has at bottom, though you may not have so many occasions to show it.

'As to that other matter I can only say that you shall be obliged, as far as it is in my power to obey you. For what may come out from me by word of mouth when we are together, I will not answer with certainty. But my pen is under better control, and it shall not write the offending name.

'And now I must tell you a little about myself;—or rather,

I am inclined to spin a yarn, and tell you a great deal. I have got such a lover! But I did describe him before. Of course it's Mr. Cheesacre. If I were to say that he hasn't declared himself, I should hardly give you a fair idea of my success. And yet he has not declared himself,—and, which is worse, is very anxious to marry a rival. But it's a strong point in my favour that my rival wants him to take me, and that he will assuredly be driven to make me an offer sooner or later, in obedience to her orders. My aunt is my rival, and I do not feel the least doubt as to his having offered to her half a dozen times. But then she has another lover, Captain Bellfield, and I see that she prefers him. He is a penniless scamp and looks as though he drank. He paints his whiskers too, which I don't like; and, being forty, tries to look like twenty-five. Otherwise he is agreeable enough, and I rather approve of my aunt's taste in preferring him.

'But my lover has solid attractions, and allures me on by a description of the fat cattle which he sends to market. He is a man of substance, and should I ever become Mrs. Cheesacre, I have reason to think that I shall not be left in want. We went up to his place on a visit the other day. Oileymead is the name of my future home;—not so pretty as Nethercoats, is it? And we had such a time there! We reached the place at ten and left it at four, and he managed to give us three meals. I'm sure we had before our eyes at different times every bit of china, delf, glass, and plate in the establishment. He made us go into the cellar, and told us how much wine he had got there, and how much beer. "It's all paid for, Mrs. Greenow, every bottle of it," he said, turning round to my aunt, with a pathetic earnestness, for which I had hardly given him credit. "Everything in this house is my own; it's all paid for. I don't call anything a man's own till it's paid for. Now that jacket that Bellfield swells about with on the sands at Yarmouth,—that's not his own,—· and it's not like to be either." And then he winked his eye as though bidding my aunt to think of that before she encouraged such a lover as Bellfield. He took us into every bedroom, and disclosed to us all the glories of his upper chambers. It would have done you good to see him lifting the counterpanes, and bidding my aunt feel the texture of the blankets! And then to see her turn round to me and say:—"Kate, it's simply the best-furnished house I ever went over in my life!"—"It does seem very comfortable," said I. "Comfortable!" said he. "Yes, I don't think there's anybody can say that Oileymead isn't comfortable." I did so think of you and Nethercoats. The attractions are the same;—only in the one place you would have a god for your keeper, and in the other a brute. For myself, if ever I'm to have a keeper at all, I shall prefer a man. But when we got to the farmyard his eloquence reached the highest pitch. "Mrs. Greenow," said he, "look at that," and he pointed to heaps of manure raised like the streets of a little city. "Look at that!" "There's a great deal," said my aunt. "I believe you," said he. "I've more muck upon this place here than any farmer in Norfolk, gentle or simple; I don't care who the other is." Only fancy, Alice; it may all be mine; the blankets, the wine, the muck, and the rest of it. So my aunt assured me when we got home that evening. When I remarked that the wealth had been exhibited to her and not to me, she did not affect to deny it, but treated that as a matter of no moment. "He wants a wife, my dear," she said, "and you may pick him up to-morrow by putting out your hand." When I remarked that his mind seemed to be intent on low things, and specially named the muck, she only laughed at me. "Money's never dirty," she said, "nor yet what makes money." She talks of taking lodgings in Norwich for the winter, saying that in her widowed state she will be as well there as anywhere else, and she wants me to stay with her up to Christmas. Indeed she first proposed the Norwich plan on the ground that it might be useful to me,—with a view to Mr. Cheesacre, of course; but I fancy that she is unwilling to tear herself away from Captain Bellfield. At any rate to Norwich she will go, and I have promised not to leave her before the second week in November. With all her absurdities I like her. Her faults are terrible faults, but she has not the fault of hiding them by falsehood. She is never stupid, and she is very good-natured. She would have allowed me to equip myself from head to foot at her expense, if I would have accepted her liberality, and absolutely offered to give me my trousseau if I would marry Mr. Cheesacre.

'I live in the hope that you will come down to the old place at Christmas. I won't offend you more than I can help. At any rate he won't be there. And if I don't see you there, where am I to see you? If I were you I would certainly not go to Cheltenham. You are never happy there.

'Do you ever dream of the river at Basle? I do;—so often.

'Most affectionately yours,

'KATE VAVASOR.'

Alice had almost lost the sensation created by the former portion of Kate's letter by the fun of the latter, before she had quite made that sensation her own. The picture of the Cambridgeshire Eden would have displeased her had she dwelt upon it, and the allusion to the cream and toast would have had the very opposite effect to that which Kate had intended. Perhaps Kate had felt this, and had therefore merged it all in her stories about Mr. Cheesacre. 'I will go to Cheltenham,' she said to herself. 'He has recommended it. I shall never be his wife;—but, till we have parted altogether, I will show him that I think well of his advice.' That same afternoon she told her father that she would go to Lady Macleod's at Cheltenham before the end of the month. She was, in truth, prompted to this by a resolution, of which she was herself hardly conscious, that she would not at this period of her life be in any way guided by her cousin. Having made up her mind about Mr. Grey, it was right that she should let her cousin know her purpose; but she would never be driven to confess to herself that Kate had influenced her in the matter. She would go to Cheltenham. Lady Macleod would no doubt vex her by hourly solicitations that the match might be renewed; but, if she knew herself, she had strength to withstand Lady Macleod.

She received one letter from Mr. Grey before the time came for her departure, and she answered it, telling him of her

intention;—telling him also that she now felt herself bound to
explain to her father her present position. 'I tell you this,' she
said, 'in consequence of what you said to me on the matter.
My father will know it to-morrow, and on the following morning I shall start for Cheltenham. I have heard from Lady Macleod and she expects me.'

On the following morning she did tell her father, standing
by him as he sat at his breakfast. 'What!' said he, putting down
his tea-cup and looking up into her face; 'What! not marry
John Grey!'

'No, papa; I know how strange you must think it.'

'And you say that there has been no quarrel.'

'No;—there has been no quarrel. By degrees I have learned
to feel that I should not make him happy as his wife.'

'It's d—d nonsense,' said Mr. Vavasor. Now such an expression as this from him, addressed to his daughter, showed
that he was very deeply moved.

'Oh, papa! don't talk to me in that way.'

'But it is. I never heard such trash in my life. If he comes to
me I shall tell him so. Not make him happy! Why can't you
make him happy?'

'We are not suited to each other.'

'But what's the matter with him? He's a gentleman.'

'Yes; he's a gentleman.'

'And a man of honour, and with good means, and with all
that knowledge and reading which you profess to like. Look
here, Alice; I am not going to interfere, nor shall I attempt
to make you marry any one. You are your own mistress as
far as that is concerned. But I do hope, for your sake and for
mine,—I do hope that there is nothing again between you and
your cousin.'

'There is nothing, papa.'

'I did not like your going abroad with him, though I didn't
choose to interrupt your plan by saying so. But if there were
anything of that kind going on, I should be bound to tell you
that your cousin's position at present is not a good one. Men
do not speak well of him.'

'There is nothing between us, papa; but if there were, men speaking ill of him would not deter me.'

'And men speaking well of Mr. Grey will not do the other thing. I know very well that women can be obstinate.'

'I haven't come to this resolution without thinking much about it, papa.'

'I suppose not. Well;—I can't say anything more. You are your own mistress, and your fortune is in your own keeping. I can't make you marry John Grey. I think you very foolish, and if he comes to me I shall tell him so. You are going down to Cheltenham, are you?'

'Yes, papa; I have promised Lady Macleod.'

'Very well. I'd sooner it should be you than me; that's all I can say.' Then he took up his newspaper, thereby showing that he had nothing further to say on the matter, and Alice left him alone.

The whole thing was so vexatious that even Mr. Vavasor was disturbed by it. As it was not term time he had no signing to do in Chancery Lane, and could not, therefore, bury his unhappiness in his daily labour,—or rather in his labour that was by no means daily. So he sat at home till four o'clock, expressing to himself in various phrases his wonder that 'any man alive should ever rear a daughter.' And when he got to his club the waiters found him quite unmanageable about his dinner, which he ate alone, rejecting all propositions of companionship. But later in the evening he regained his composure over a glass of whiskey-toddy and a cigar. 'She's got her own money,' he said to himself, 'and what does it matter? I don't suppose she'll marry her cousin. I don't think she's fool enough for that. And after all she'll probably make it up again with John Grey.' And in this way he determined that he might let this annoyance run off him, and that he need not as a father take the trouble of any interference.

But while he was at his club there came a visitor to Queen Anne Street, and that visitor was the dangerous cousin of whom, according to his uncle's testimony, men at present did not speak well. Alice had not seen him since they had parted on the day of their arrival in London,—nor, indeed, had heard of his whereabouts. In the consternation of her mind at this step which she was taking,—a step which she had taught herself to regard as essentially her duty before it was taken, but which seemed to herself to be false and treacherous the moment she had taken it,—she had become aware that she had been wrong to travel with her cousin. She felt sure,—she thought that she was sure,—that her doing so had in nowise affected her dealings with Mr. Grey. She was very certain,—she thought that she was certain,—that she would have rejected him just the same had she never gone to Switzerland. But every one would say of her that her journey to Switzerland with such companions had produced that result. It had been unlucky and she was sorry for it, and she now wished to avoid all communication with her cousin till this affair should be altogether over. She was especially unwilling to see him; but she had not felt it necessary to give any special injunctions as to his admittance; and now, before she had time to think of it,—on the eve of her departure for Cheltenham,—he was in the room with her, just as the dusk of the October evening was coming on. She was sitting away from the fire, almost behind the window-curtains, thinking of John Grey and very unhappy in her thoughts, when George Vavasor was announced. It will of course be understood that Vavasor had at this time received his sister's letter. He had received it, and had had time to consider the matter since the Sunday morning on which we saw him in his own rooms in Cecil Street. 'She can turn it all into capital to-morrow, if she pleases,' he had said to himself when thinking of her income. But he had also reminded himself that her grandfather would probably enable him to settle an income out of the property upon Alice, in the event of their being married. And then he had also felt that he could have no greater triumph than 'walking atop of John Grey,' as he called it. His return for the Chelsea Districts would hardly be sweeter to him than that.

'You must have thought I had vanished out of the world,' said George, coming up to her with his extended hand.

Alice was confused, and hardly knew how to address him. 'Somebody told me that you were shooting,' she said after a pause.

'So I was, but my shooting is not like the shooting of your great Nimrods,*—men who are hunters upon the earth. Two days among the grouse and two more among the partridges are about the extent of it. Capel Court*is the preserve in which I am usually to be found.'

Alice knew nothing of Capel Court, and said, 'Oh, indeed.'

'Have you heard from Kate?' George asked.

'Yes, once or twice; she is still at Yarmouth with Aunt Greenow.'

'And is going to Norwich, as she says. Kate seems to have made a league with Aunt Greenow. I, who don't pretend to be very disinterested in money matters, think that she is quite right. No doubt Aunt Greenow may marry again, but friends with forty thousand pounds are always agreeable.'

'I don't believe that Kate thinks much of that,' said Alice.

'Not so much as she ought, I dare say. Poor Kate is not a rich woman, or, I fear, likely to become one. She doesn't seem to dream of getting married, and her own fortune is less than a hundred a year.'

'Girls who never dream of getting married are just those who make the best marriages at last,' said Alice.

'Perhaps so, but I wish I was easier about Kate. She is the best sister a man ever had.'

'Indeed she is.'

'And I have done nothing for her as yet. I did think, while I was in that wine business, that I could have done anything I pleased for her. But my grandfather's obstinacy put me out of that; and now I'm beginning the world again,—that is, comparatively. I wonder whether you think I'm wrong in trying to get into Parliament?'

'No; quite right. I admire you for it. It is just what I would do in your place. You are unmarried, and have a right to run the risk.'

'I am so glad to hear you speak like that,' said he. He had

145

now managed to take up that friendly, confidential, almost affectionate tone of talking which he had so often used when abroad with her, and which he had failed to assume when first entering the room.

'I have always thought so.'

'But you have never said it.'

'Haven't I? I thought I had.'

'Not heartily like that. I know that people abuse me;—my own people, my grandfather, and probably your father,—saying that I am reckless and the rest of it. I do risk everything for my object; but I do not know that any one can blame me,—unless it be Kate. To whom else do I owe anything?'

'Kate does not blame you.'

'No; she sympathizes with me; she, and she only, unless it be you.' Then he paused for an answer, but she made him none. 'She is brave enough to give me her hearty sympathy. But perhaps for that very reason I ought to be the more chary in endangering the only support that she is like to have. What is ninety pounds a year for the maintenance of a single lady?'

'I hope that Kate will always live with me,' said Alice; 'that is, as soon as she has lost her home at Vavasor Hall.'

He had been very crafty and had laid a trap for her. He had laid a trap for her, and she had fallen into it. She had determined not to be induced to talk of herself; but he had brought the thing round so cunningly that the words were out of her mouth before she remembered whither they would lead her. She did remember this as she was speaking them, but then it was too late.

'What;—at Nethercoats?' said he. 'Neither she nor I doubt your love, but few men would like such an intruder as that into their household, and of all men Mr. Grey, whose nature is retiring, would like it the least.'

'I was not thinking of Nethercoats,' said Alice.

'Ah, no; that is it, you see. Kate says so often to me that when you are married she will be alone in the world.'

'I don't think she will ever find that I shall separate myself from her.'

'No; not by any will of your own. Poor Kate! You cannot be surprised that she should think of your marriage with dread. How much of her life has been made up of her companionship with you;—and all the best of it too! You ought not to be angry with her for regarding your withdrawal into Cambridge-shire with dismay.'

Alice could not act the lie which now seemed to be incumbent on her. She could not let him talk of Nethercoats as though it were to be her future home. She made the struggle, and she found that she could not do it. She was unable to find the words which should tell no lie to the ear, and which should yet deceive him. 'Kate may still live with me,' she said slowly. 'Everything is over between me and Mr. Grey.'

'Alice!—is that true?'

'Yes, George; it is true. If you will allow me to say so, I would rather not talk about it;—not just at present.'

'And does Kate know it?'

'Yes, Kate knows it.'

'And my uncle?'

'Yes, papa knows it also.'

'Alice, how can I help speaking of it? How can I not tell you that I am rejoiced that you are saved from a thraldom which I have long felt sure would break your heart?'

'Pray do not talk of it further.'

'Well; if I am forbidden I shall of course obey. But I own it is hard to me. How can I not congratulate you?' To this she answered nothing, but beat with her foot upon the floor as though she were impatient of his words. 'Yes, Alice, I understand. You are angry with me,' he continued. 'And yet you have no right to be surprised that when you tell me this I should think of all that passed between us in Switzerland. Surely the cousin who was with you then has a right to say what he thinks of this change in your life; at any rate he may do so, if as in this case he approves altogether of what you are doing.'

'I am glad of your approval, George; but pray let that be an end to it.'

After that the two sat silent for a minute or two. She was waiting for him to go, but she could not bid him leave the house. She was angry with herself, in that she had allowed herself to tell him of her altered plans, and she was angry with him because he would not understand that she ought to be spared all conversation on the subject. So she sat looking through the window at the row of gaslights as they were being lit, and he remained in his chair with his elbow on the table and his head resting on his hand.

'Do you remember asking me whether I ever shivered,' he said at last; '—whether I ever thought of things that made me shiver? Don't you remember; on the bridge at Basle?'

'Yes; I remember.'

'Well, Alice;—one cause for my shivering is over. I won't say more than that now. Shall you remain long at Cheltenham?'

'Just a month.'

'And then you come back here?'

'I suppose so. Papa and I will probably go down to Vavasor Hall before Christmas. How much before I cannot say.'

'I shall see you at any rate after your return from Cheltenham? Of course Kate will know, and she will tell me.'

'Yes; Kate will know. I suppose she will stay here when she comes up from Norfolk. Good-bye.'

'Good-bye, Alice. I shall have fewer fits of that inward shivering that you spoke of,—many less, on account of what I have now heard. God bless you, Alice; good-bye.'

'Good-bye, George.'

As he went he took her hand and pressed it closely between his own. In those days when they were lovers,—engaged lovers, a close, long-continued pressure of her hand had been his most eloquent speech of love. He had not been given to many kisses,—not even to many words of love. But he would take her hand and hold it, even as he looked away from her, and she remembered well the touch of his palm. It was ever cool,—cool, and with a surface smooth as a woman's,—a small hand that had a firm grip. There had been days when she had loved to feel that her own was within it, when she trusted in

148

it, and intended that it should be her staff through life. Now she distrusted it; and as the thoughts of the old days came upon her, and the remembrance of that touch was recalled, she drew her hand away rapidly. Not for that had she driven from her as honest a man as had ever wished to mate with a woman. He, George Vavasor, had never so held her hand since the day when they had parted, and now on this first occasion of her freedom she felt it again. What did he think of her? Did he suppose that she could transfer her love in that way, as a flower may be taken from one buttonhole and placed in another? He read it all, and knew that he was hurrying on too quickly. 'I can understand well,' he said in a whisper, 'what your present feelings are; but I do not think you will be really angry with me because I have been unable to repress my joy at what I cannot but regard as your release from a great misfortune.' Then he went.

'My release!' she said, seating herself on the chair from which he had risen. 'My release from a misfortune! No;—but my fall from heaven! Oh, what a man he is! That he should have loved me, and that I should have driven him away from me!' Her thoughts travelled off to the sweetness of that home at Nethercoats, to the excellence of that master who might have been hers; and then in an agony of despair she told herself that she had been an idiot and a fool, as well as a traitor. What had she wanted in life that she should have thus quarrelled with as happy a lot as ever had been offered to a woman? Had she not been mad, when she sent from her side the only man that she loved,—the only man that she had ever truly respected? For hours she sat there, all alone, putting out the candles which the servant had lighted for her, and leaving untasted the tea that was brought to her.

Poor Alice! I hope that she may be forgiven. It was her special fault, that when at Rome* she longed for Tibur, and when at Tibur she regretted Rome. Not that her cousin George is to be taken as representing the joys of the great capital, though Mr. Grey may be presumed to form no inconsiderable part of the promised delights of the country. Now that she had sacrificed her Tibur, because it had seemed to her that the sunny quiet of its pastures lacked the excitement necessary for the happiness of life, she was again prepared to quarrel with the heartlessness of Rome, and already was again sighing for the tranquillity of the country.

Sitting there, full of these regrets, she declared to herself that she would wait for her father's return, and then, throwing herself upon his love and upon his mercy, would beg him to go to Mr. Grey and ask for pardon for her. 'I should be very humble to him,' she said; 'but he is so good, that I may dare to be humble before him.' So she waited for her father. She waited till twelve, till one, till two;—but still he did not come. Later than that she did not dare to wait for him. She feared to trust him on such business returning so late as that,—after so many cigars; after, perhaps, some superfluous beakers of club nectar. His temper at such a moment would not be fit for such work as hers. But if he was late in coming home, who had sent him away from his home in unhappiness? Between two and three she went to bed, and on the following morning she left Queen Anne Street for the Great Western Station before her father was up.

CHAPTER XV

Paramount Crescent

LADY MACLEOD lived at No. 3, Paramount Crescent, in Cheltenham, where she occupied a very handsome first-floor drawing-room, with a bedroom behind it, looking over a stable-yard, and a small room which would have been the dressing-room had the late Sir Archibald been alive, but which was at present called the dining-room: and in it Lady Macleod did dine whenever her larger room was to be used for any purposes of evening company. The vicinity of the stable-yard was not regarded by the tenant as among the attractions of the house; but it had the effect of lowering the rent, and Lady Macleod was a woman who regarded such matters. Her income, though small, would have sufficed to enable her to live removed from

such discomforts; but she was one of those women who regard
it as a duty to leave something behind them,—even though it
be left to those who do not at all want it; and Lady Macleod
was a woman who wilfully neglected no duty. So she pinched
herself, and inhaled the effluvia of the stables, and squabbled
with the cabmen, in order that she might bequeath a thousand
pounds or two to some Lady Midlothian, who cared, perhaps,
little for her, and would hardly thank her memory for the
money.

Had Alice consented to live with her, she would have merged
that duty of leaving money behind her in that other duty of
finding a home for her adopted niece. But Alice had gone away,
and therefore the money was due to Lady Midlothian rather
than to her. The saving, however, was postponed whenever
Alice would consent to visit Cheltenham; and a bedroom was
secured for her which did not look out over the stables. Accommodation was also found for her maid much better than that
provided for Lady Macleod's own maid. She was a hospitable,
good old woman, painfully struggling to do the best she could
in the world. It was a pity that she was such a bore, a pity that
she was so hard to cabmen and others, a pity that she suspected all tradesmen, servants, and people generally of a rank
of life inferior to her own, a pity that she was disposed to condemn for ever and ever so many of her own rank because they
played cards on week days, and did not go to church on Sun-
days,—and a pity, as I think above all, that while she was so
suspicious of the poor she was so lenient to the vices of earls,
earls' sons, and such like.

Alice, having fully considered the matter, had thought it
most prudent to tell Lady Macleod by letter what she had done
in regard to Mr. Grey. There had been many objections to the
writing of such a letter, but there appeared to be stronger
objection to that telling it face to face which would have been
forced upon her had she not written. There would in such case
have arisen on Lady Macleod's countenance a sternness of
rebuke which Alice did not choose to encounter. The same
sternness of rebuke would come upon the countenance on receipt

of the written information; but it would come in its most aggravated form on the immediate receipt of the letter, and some of its bitterness would have passed away before Alice's arrival. I think that Alice was right. It is better for both parties that any great offence should be confessed by letter.

But Alice trembled as the cab drew up at No. 3, Paramount Crescent. She met her aunt, as was usual, just inside the drawing-room door, and she saw at once that if any bitterness had passed away from that face, the original bitterness must indeed have been bitter. She had so timed her letter that Lady Macleod should have no opportunity of answering it. The answer was written there in the mingled anger and sorrow of those austere features.

'Alice!' she said, as she took her niece in her arms and kissed her; 'oh, Alice, what is this?'

'Yes, aunt; it is very bad, I know,' and poor Alice tried to make a jest of it. 'Young ladies are very wicked when they don't know their own minds. But if they haven't known them and have been wicked, what can they do but repent?'

'Repent!' said Lady Macleod. 'Yes; I hope you will repent. Poor Mr. Grey;—what must he think of it?'

'I can only hope, aunt, that he won't think of it at all for very long.'

'That's nonsense, my dear. Of course he'll think of it, and of course you'll marry him.'

'Shall I, aunt?'

'Of course you will. Why, Alice, hasn't it been all settled among the families? Lady Midlothian knew all the particulars of it just as well as I did. And is not your word pledged to him? I really don't understand what you mean. I don't see how it is possible you should go back. Gentlemen when they do that kind of thing are put out of society;—but I really think it is worse in a woman.'

'Then they may if they please put me out of society;—only that I don't know that I'm particularly in it.'

'And the wickedness of the thing, Alice! I'm obliged to say so.'

'When you talk to me about society, aunt, and about Lady Midlothian, I give up to you, willingly;—the more willingly, perhaps, because I don't care much for one or the other.' Here Lady Macleod tried to say a word; but she failed, and Alice went on, boldly looking up into her aunt's face, which became a shade more bitter than ever. 'But when you tell me about wickedness and my conscience, then I must be my own judge. It is my conscience, and the fear of committing wickedness, that has made me do this.'

'You should submit to be guided by your elders, Alice.'

'No; my elders in such a matter as this cannot teach me. It cannot be right that I should go to a man's house and be his wife, if I do not think that I can make him happy.'

'Then why did you accept him?'

'Because I was mistaken. I am not going to defend that. If you choose to scold me for that, you may do so, aunt, and I will not answer you. But as to marrying him or not marrying him now,—as to that, I must judge for myself.'

'It was a pity you did not know your own mind earlier.'

'It was a pity,—a great pity. I have done myself an injury that is quite irretrievable;—I know that, and am prepared to bear it. I have done him, too, an injustice which I regret with my whole heart. I can only excuse myself by saying that I might have done him a worse injustice.'

All this was said at the very moment of her arrival, and the greeting did not seem to promise much for the happiness of the next month; but perhaps it was better for them both that the attack and the defence should thus be made suddenly, at their first meeting. It is better to pull the string at once when you are in the shower-bath, and not to stand shivering, thinking of the inevitable shock which you can only postpone for a few minutes. Lady Macleod in this case had pulled the string, and thus reaped the advantage of her alacrity.

'Well, my dear,' said her ladyship, 'I suppose you will like to go up stairs and take off your bonnet. Mary shall bring you some tea when you come down.' So Alice escaped, and when she returned to the comfort of her cup of tea in the drawing-room, the fury of the storm had passed away. She sat talking of other things till dinner; and though Lady Macleod did during the evening make one allusion to 'poor Mr. Grey,' the subject was allowed to drop. Alice was very tender as to her aunt's ailments, was more than ordinarily attentive to the long list of Cheltenham iniquities which was displayed to her, and refrained from combating any of her aunt's religious views. After a while they got upon the subject of Aunt Greenow, for whose name Lady Macleod had a special aversion,—as indeed she had for all the Vavasor side of Alice's family; and then Alice offered to read, and did read to her aunt many pages out of one of those terrible books of wrath, which from time to time come forth and tell us that there is no hope for us. Lady Macleod liked to be so told; and as she now, poor woman, could not read at nights herself, she enjoyed her evening.

Lady Macleod no doubt did enjoy her niece's sojourn at Cheltenham, but I do not think it could have been pleasant to Alice. On the second day nothing was said about Mr. Grey, and Alice hoped that by her continual readings in the book of wrath her aunt's heart might be softened towards her. But it seemed that Lady Macleod measured the periods of respite, for on the third day and on the fifth she returned to the attack. 'Did John Grey still wish that the match should go on?' she asked, categorically. It was in vain that Alice tried to put aside the question, and begged that the matter might not be discussed. Lady Macleod insisted on her right to carry on the examination, and Alice was driven to acknowledge that she believed he did wish it. She could hardly say otherwise, seeing that she had at that moment a letter from him in her pocket, in which he still spoke of his engagement as being absolutely binding on him, and expressed a hope that this change from London to Cheltenham would bring her round and set everything to rights. He certainly did, in a fashion, wave his hand over her, as Kate had said of him. This letter Alice had resolved that she would not answer. He would probably write again, and she would beg him to desist. Instead of Cheltenham bringing her round, Cheltenham had made her firmer than ever in her resolution. I am inclined to think that the best mode of bringing her round at this moment would have been a course of visits from her cousin George, and a series of letters from her cousin Kate. Lady Macleod's injunctions would certainly not bring her round.

After ten days, ten terrible days, devoted to discussions on

matrimony in the morning, and to the book of wrath in the evening,—relieved by two tea-parties, in which the sins of Cheltenham were discussed at length,—Lady Macleod herself got a letter from Mr. Grey. Mr. Grey's kindest compliments to Lady Macleod. He believed that Lady Macleod was aware of the circumstances of his engagement with Miss Vavasor. Might he call on Miss Vavasor at Lady Macleod's house in Cheltenham? and might he also hope to have the pleasure of making Lady Macleod's acquaintance? Alice had been in the room when her aunt received this letter, but her aunt had said nothing, and Alice had not known from whom the letter had come. When her aunt crept away with it after breakfast she had suspected nothing, and had never imagined that Lady Macleod, in the privacy of her own room looking out upon the stables, had addressed a letter to Nethercoats. But such a letter had been addressed to Nethercoats, and Mr. Grey had been informed that he would be received in Paramount Crescent with great pleasure.

Mr. Grey had even indicated the day on which he would come, and on the morning of that day Lady Macleod had presided over the two teacups in a state of nervous excitement which was quite visible to Alice. More than once Alice asked little questions, not supposing that she was specially concerned in the matter which had caused her aunt's fidgety restlessness, but observing it so plainly that it was almost impossible not to allude to it. 'There's nothing the matter, my dear, at all,' at last Lady Macleod said; but as she said so she was making up her mind that the moment had not come in which she must apprise Alice of Mr. Grey's intended visit. As Alice had questioned her at the breakfast table she would say nothing about it then, but waited till the teacups were withdrawn, and till the maid had given her last officious poke to the fire. Then she began. She had Mr. Grey's letter in her pocket, and as she prepared herself to speak, she pulled it out and held it on the little table before her.

'Alice,' she said, 'I expect a visitor here to-day.'

Alice knew instantly who was the expected visitor. Probably any girl under such circumstances would have known equally well. 'A visitor, aunt !' she said, and managed to hide her knowledge admirably.

'Yes, Alice, a visitor. I should have told you before, only I thought,—I thought I had better not. It is Mr.—Mr. Grey.'

'Indeed, aunt! Is he coming to see you?'

'Well;—he is desirous no doubt of seeing you more especially; but he has expressed a wish to make my acquaintance, which I cannot, under the circumstances, think is unnatural. Of course, Alice, he must want to talk over this affair with your friends.'

'I wish I could have spared them,' said Alice,—'I wish I could.'

'I have brought his letter here, and you can see it if you please. It is very nicely written, and as far as I am concerned I should not think of refusing to see him. And now comes the question. What are we to do with him? Am I to ask him to dinner? I take it for granted that he will not expect me to offer him a bed, as he knows that I live in lodgings.'

'Oh no, aunt; he certainly will not expect that.'

'But ought I to ask him to dinner? I should be most happy to entertain him, though you know how very scanty my means of doing so are;—but I really do not know how it might be,—between you and him, I mean.'

'We should not fight, aunt.'

'No, I suppose not;—but if you cannot be affectionate in your manner to him——'

'I will not answer for my manners, aunt; but you may be sure of this,—that I should be affectionate in my heart. I shall always regard him as a dearly loved friend; though for many years, no doubt, I shall be unable to express my friendship.'

'That may be all very well, Alice, but it will not be what he will want. I think upon the whole that I had better not ask him to dinner.'

'Perhaps not, aunt.'

'It is a period of the day in which any special constraint among people is more disagreeable than at any other time, and then at dinner the servants must see it. I think there might be some awkwardness if he were to dine here.'

'I really think there would,' said Alice, anxious to have the subject dropped.

'I hope he won't think that I am inhospitable. I should be so happy to do the best I could for him, for I regard him, Alice, quite as though he were to be your husband. And when anybody at all connected with me has come to Cheltenham I always have asked them to dine, and then I have Gubbins's man to come and wait at table,—as you know.'

'Of all men in the world Mr. Grey is the last to think about it.'

'That should only make me the more careful. But I think it would perhaps be more comfortable if he were to come in the evening.'

'Much more comfortable, aunt.'

'I suppose he will be here in the afternoon, before dinner, and we had better wait at home for him. I dare say he'll want to see you alone, and therefore I'll retire to my own room,'—

looking over the stables! Dear old lady. 'But if you wish it, I will receive him first—and then Martha,'—Martha was Alice's maid—'can fetch you down.'

This discussion as to the propriety or impropriety of giving her lover a dinner had not been pleasant to Alice, but, nevertheless, when it was over she felt grateful to Lady Macleod. There was an attempt in the arrangement to make Mr. Grey's visit as little painful as possible; and though such a discussion at such a time might as well have been avoided, the decision to which her ladyship had at last come with reference both to the dinner and the management of the visit was, no doubt, the right one.

Lady Macleod had been quite correct in all her anticipations. At three o'clock Mr. Grey was announced, and Lady Macleod, alone, received him in her drawing-room. She had intended to give him a great deal of good advice, to bid him still keep up his heart and as it were hold up his head, to confess to him how very badly Alice was behaving, and to express her entire concurrence with that theory of bodily ailment as the cause and origin of her conduct. But she found that Mr. Grey was a man to whom she could not give much advice. It was he who did the speaking at this conference, and not she. She was overawed by him after the first three minutes. Indeed her first glance at him had awed her. He was so handsome,— and then, in his beauty, he had so quiet and almost saddened an air! Strange to say that after she had seen him, Lady Macleod entertained for him an infinitely higher admiration than before, and yet she was less surprised than she had been at Alice's refusal of him. The conference was very short; and Mr. Grey had not been a quarter of an hour in the house before Martha attended upon her mistress with her summons.

Alice was ready and came down instantly. She found Mr. Grey standing in the middle of the room waiting to receive her, and the look of majesty which had cowed Lady Macleod had gone from his countenance. He could not have received her with a kinder smile, had she come to him with a promise that she would at this meeting name the day for their marriage.

'At any rate it does not make him unhappy,' she said to herself.

'You are not angry,' he said, 'that I should have followed you all the way here, to see you.'

'No, certainly; not angry, Mr. Grey. All anger that there may be between us must be on your side. I feel that thoroughly.'

'Then there shall be none on either side. Whatever may be done, I will not be angry with you. Your father advised me to come down here to you.'

'You have seen him, then?'

'Yes, I have seen him. I was in London the day you left.'

'It is so terrible to think that I should have brought upon you all this trouble.'

'You will bring upon me much worse trouble than that, unless——. But I have not now come down here to tell you that. I believe that according to rule in such matters I should not have come to you at all, but I don't know that I care much about such rules.'

'It is I that have broken all rules.'

'When a lady tells a gentleman that she does not wish to see more of him——'

'Oh, Mr. Grey, I have not told you that.'

'Have you not? I am glad at any rate to hear you deny it. But you will understand what I mean. When a gentleman gets his dismissal from a lady he should accept it,—that is, his dismissal under such circumstances as I have received mine. But I cannot lay down my love in that way; nor, maintaining my love, can I give up the battle. It seems to me that I have a right at any rate to know something of your comings and goings as long as,—unless, Alice, you should take another name than mine.'

'My intention is to keep my own.' This she said in the lowest possible tone,—almost in a whisper,—with her eyes fixed upon the ground.

'And you will not deny me that right?'

'I cannot hinder you. Whatever you may do, I myself have sinned so against you that I can have no right to blame you.'

'There shall be no question between us of injury from one to the other. In any conversation that we may have, or in any correspondence——'

'Oh, Mr. Grey, do not ask me to write.'

'Listen to me. Should there be any on either side, there shall be no idea of any wrong done.'

'But I have done you wrong;—great wrong.'

'No, Alice; I will not have it so. When I asked you to accept my hand,—begging the greatest boon which it could ever come to my lot to ask from a fellow-mortal,—I knew well how great was your goodness to me when you told me that it should be mine. Now that you refuse it, I know also that you are good, thinking that in doing so you are acting for my welfare,—thinking more of my welfare than of your own.'

'Oh yes, yes; it is so, Mr. Grey; indeed it is so.'

'Believing that, how can I talk of wrong? That you are wrong in your thinking on this subject,—that your mind has become twisted by false impressions,—that I believe. But I cannot therefore love you less,—nor, so believing, can I consider myself to be injured. Nor am I even so little selfish as you are. I think if you were my wife that I could make you happy; but I feel sure that my happiness depends on your being my wife.'

She looked up into his face, but it was still serene in all its manly beauty. Her cousin George, if he were moved to strong feeling, showed it at once in his eyes,—in his mouth, in the whole visage of his countenance. He glared in his anger, and was impassioned in his love. But Mr. Grey when speaking of the happiness of his entire life, when confessing that it was now at stake with a decision against him that would be ruinous to it, spoke without a quiver in his voice, and had no more sign of passion in his face than if he were telling his gardener to move a rose tree.

'I hope—and believe that you will find your happiness elsewhere, Mr. Grey.'

'Well; we can but differ, Alice. In that we do differ. And now I will say one word to explain why I have come here. If

I were to write to you against your will, it would seem that I were persecuting you. I cannot bring myself to do that, even though I had the right. But if I were to let you go from me, taking what you have said to me and doing nothing, it would seem that I had accepted your decision as final. I do not do so. I will not do so. I come simply to tell you that I am still your suitor. If you will let me, I will see you again early in January, —as soon as you have returned to town. You will hardly refuse to see me.'

'No,' she said; 'I cannot refuse to see you.'

'Then it shall be so,' he said, 'and I will not trouble you with letters, nor will I trouble you longer now with words. Tell your aunt that I have said what I came to say, and that I give her my kindest thanks.' Then he took her hand and pressed it,—not as George Vavasor had pressed it,— and was gone. When Lady Macleod returned, she found that the question of the evening's tea arrangements had settled itself.

CHAPTER XVI

The Roebury Club

IT has been said that George Vavasor had a little establishment at Roebury, down in Oxfordshire, and thither he betook himself about the middle of November. He had been long known in this county, and whether or no men spoke well of him as a man of business in London, men spoke well of him down there, as one who knew how to ride to hounds. Not that Vavasor was popular among fellow-sportsmen. It was quite otherwise. He was not a man that made himself really popular in any social meetings of men. He did not himself care for the loose little talkings, half flat and half sharp, of men when they meet together in idleness. He was not open enough in his nature for such popularity. Some men were afraid of him, and some suspected him. There were others who made up to him, seeking his intimacy, but these he usually snubbed, and always

161

kept at a distance. Though he had indulged in all the ordinary pleasures of young men, he had never been a jovial man. In his conversations with men he always seemed to think that he should use his time towards serving some purpose of business. With women he was quite the reverse. With women he could be happy. With women he could really associate. A woman he could really love;—but I doubt whether for all that he could treat a woman well.

But he was known in the Oxfordshire country as a man who knew what he was about, and such men are always welcome. It is the man who does not know how to ride that is made uncomfortable in the hunting field by cold looks or expressed censure. And yet it is very rarely that such men do any real harm. Such a one may now and then get among the hounds or override the hunt, but it is not often so. Many such complaints are made; but in truth the too forward man, who presses the dogs, is generally one who can ride, but is too eager or too selfish to keep in his proper place. The bad rider, like the bad whist player, pays highly for what he does not enjoy, and should be thanked. But at both games he gets cruelly snubbed. At both games George Vavasor was great and he never got snubbed.

There were men who lived together at Roebury in a kind of club,—four or five of them, who came thither from London, running backwards and forwards as hunting arrangements enabled them to do so,—a brewer or two and a banker, with a would-be fast attorney, a sporting literary gentleman,* and a young unmarried Member of Parliament who had no particular home of his own in the country. These men formed the Roebury Club, and a jolly life they had of it. They had their own wine closet at the King's Head,—or Roebury Inn as the house had come to be popularly called,—and supplied their own game. The landlord found everything else; and as they were not very particular about their bills, they were allowed to do pretty much as they liked in the house. They were rather imperious, very late in their hours, sometimes, though not often, noisy, and once there had been a hasty quarrel which had made the landlord in his anger say that the club should be turned out of his house. But they paid well, chaffed*the servants much oftener than they bullied them, and on the whole were very popular.

To this club Vavasor did not belong, alleging that he could not afford to live at their pace, and alleging, also, that his stays at Roebury were not long enough to make him a desirable member. The invitation to him was not repeated and he lodged elsewhere in the little town. But he occasionally went in of an evening, and would make up with the members a table at whist.

He had come down to Roebury by mail train, ready for hunting the next morning, and walked into the club-room just at midnight. There he found Maxwell the banker, Grindley the would-be fast attorney, and Calder Jones the Member of Parliament, playing dummy. Neither of the brewers were there, nor was the sporting literary gentleman.

'Here's Vavasor,' said Maxwell, 'and now we won't play this blackguard game any longer. Somebody told me, Vavasor, that you were gone away.'

'Gone away;—what, like a fox?'

'I don't know what it was; that something had happened to you since last season; that you were married, or dead, or gone abroad. By George, I've lost the trick after all! I hate dummy like the devil. I never hold a card in dummy's hand. Yes, I know; that's seven points on each side. Vavasor, come and cut. Upon my word if any one had asked me, I should have said you were dead.'

'But you see, nobody ever does think of asking you anything.'

'What you probably mean,' said Grindley, 'is that Vavasor was not returned for Chelsea last February; but you've seen him since that. Are you going to try it again, Vavasor?'

'If you'll lend me the money I will.'

'I don't see what on earth a man gains by going into the house,' said Calder Jones. 'I couldn't help myself as it happened, but, upon my word it's a deuce of a bore. A fellow

163

thinks he can do as he likes about going,—but he can't. It wouldn't do for me to give it up, because——'

'Oh no, of course not; where should we all be?' said Vavasor.

'It's you and me, Grindems,' said Maxwell. 'D— parliament, and now let's have a rubber.'

They played till three and Mr. Calder Jones lost a good deal of money,—a good deal of money in a little way, for they never played above ten-shilling points, and no bet was made for more than a pound or two. But Vavasor was the winner, and when he left the room he became the subject of some ill-natured remarks.

'I wonder he likes coming in here,' said Grindley, who had himself been the man to invite him to belong to the club, and who had at one time indulged the ambition of an intimacy with George Vavasor.

'I can't understand it,' said Calder Jones, who was a little bitter about his money. 'Last year he seemed to walk in just when he liked, as though he were one of us.'

'He's a bad sort of fellow,' said Grindley; 'he's so uncommonly dark. I don't know where on earth he gets his money from. He was heir to some small property in the north, but he lost every shilling of that when he was in the wine trade.'

'You're wrong there, Grindems,' said Maxwell,—making use of a playful nickname which he had invented for his friend. 'He made a pot of money at the wine business, and had he stuck to it he would have been a rich man.'

'He's lost it all since then, and that place in the north into the bargain.'

'Wrong again, Grindems, my boy. If old Vavasor were to die to-morrow, Vavasor Hall would go just as he might choose to leave it. George may be a ruined man for aught I know——'

'There's no doubt about that, I believe,' said Grindley.

'Perhaps not, Grindems; but he can't have lost Vavasor Hall, because he has never as yet had an interest in it. He's the natural heir, and will probably get it some day.'

'All the same,' said Calder Jones, 'isn't it rather odd he should come in here?'

'We've asked him often enough,' said Maxwell; 'not because we like him, but because we want him so often to make up a rubber. I don't like George Vavasor, and I don't know who does; but I like him better than dummy. And I'd sooner play whist with men I don't like, Grindems, than I'd not play at all.' A bystander might have thought from the tone of Mr. Maxwell's voice that he was alluding to Mr. Grindley himself, but Mr. Grindley didn't seem to take it in that light.

'That's true, of course,' said he. 'We can't pick men just as we please. But I certainly didn't think that he'd make it out for another season.'

The club breakfasted the next morning at nine o'clock, in order that they might start at half-past for the meet at Edgehill. Edgehill*is twelve miles from Roebury, and the hacks would do it in an hour and a half,—or perhaps a little less. 'Does anybody know anything about that brown horse of Vavasor's?' said Maxwell. 'I saw him coming into the yard yesterday with that old groom of his.'

'He had a brown horse last season,' said Grindley;—'a little thing that went very fast, but wasn't quite sound on the road.'

'That was a mare,' said Maxwell, 'and he sold her to Cinquebars.'*

'For a hundred and fifty,' said Calder Jones, 'and she wasn't worth the odd fifty.'

'He won seventy with her at Leamington,' said Maxwell, 'and I doubt whether he'd take his money now.'

'Is Cinquebars coming down here this year?'

'I don't know,' said Maxwell. 'I hope not. He's the best fellow in the world, but he can't ride, and he don't care for hunting, and he makes more row than any fellow I ever met. I wish some fellow could tell me something about that fellow's brown horse.'

'I'd never buy a horse of Vavasor's if I were you,' said Grindley. 'He never has anything that's all right all round.'

---

* Ah, my friend [Thackeray], from whom I have borrowed this scion of the nobility! Had he been left with us he would have forgiven me my little theft, and now that he has gone I will not change the name.*

'And who has?' said Maxwell, as he took into his plate a second mutton chop, which had just been brought up hot into the room especially for him. 'That's the mistake men make about horses, and that's why there's so much cheating. I never ask for a warranty with a horse, and don't very often have a horse examined. Yet I do as well as others. You can't have perfect horses any more than you can perfect men, or perfect women. You put up with red hair, or bad teeth, or big feet,— or sometimes with the devil of a voice. But a man when he wants a horse won't put up with anything! Therefore those who've got horses to sell must lie. When I go into the market with three hundred pounds I expect a perfect animal. As I never do that now I never expect a perfect animal. I like 'em to see; I like 'em to have four legs; and I like 'em to have a little wind. I don't much mind anything else.'

'By jove, you're about right,' said Calder Jones. The reader will therefore readily see that Mr. Maxwell the banker reigned as king in that club.

Vavasor had sent two horses on in charge of Bat Smithers, and followed on a pony about fourteen hands high, which he had ridden as a cover hack*for the last four years. He did not start till near ten, but he was able to catch Bat with his two horses about a mile and a half on that side of Edgehill. 'Have you managed to come along pretty clean?' the master asked as he came up with his servant.

'They be the most beastly roads in all England,' said Bat, who always found fault with any county in which he happened to be located. 'But I'll warrant I'm cleaner than most on 'em. What for any county should make such roads as them I never could tell.'

'The roads about here are bad, certainly;—very bad. But I suppose they would have been better had Providence sent better materials. And what do you think of the brown horse, Bat?'

'Well, sir.' He said no more, and that he said with a drawl.

'He's as fine an animal to look at as ever I put my eye on,' said George.

'He's all that,' said Bat.

'He's got lots of pace too.'

'I'm sure he has, sir.'

'And they tell me you can't beat him at jumping.'

'They can mostly do that, sir, if they're well handled.'

'You see he's a deal over my weight.'

'Yes, he is, Mr. Vavasor. He is a fourteen stoner.'

'Or fifteen,' said Vavasor.

'Perhaps he may, sir. There's no knowing what a 'orse can carry till he's tried.'

George asked his groom no more questions, but felt sure that he had better sell his brown horse if he could. Now I here protest that there was nothing specially amiss with the brown horse. Towards the end of the preceding season he had overreached himself and had been lame, and had been sold by some owner with more money than brains who had not cared to wait for a cure. Then there had gone with him a bad character, and a vague suspicion had attached itself to him, as there does to hundreds of horses which are very good animals in their way. He had come thus to Tattersall's,* and Vavasor had bought him cheap, thinking that he might make money of him, from his form and action. He had found nothing amiss with him,—nor, indeed, had Bat Smithers. But his character went with him, and therefore Bat Smithers thought it well to be knowing. George Vavasor knew as much of horses as most men can,—as, perhaps, any man can who is not a dealer, or a veterinary surgeon; but he, like all men, doubted his own knowledge, though on that subject he would never admit that he doubted it. Therefore he took Bat's word and felt sure that the horse was wrong.

'We shall have a run from the big wood,' said George.

'If they make un break,* you will, sir,' said Bat.

'At any rate I'll ride the brown horse,' said George. Then, as soon as that was settled between them, the Roebury Club overtook them.

There was now a rush of horses on the road together, and they were within a quarter of a mile of Edgehill church, close to which was the meet. Bat with his two hunters fell a little behind, and the others trotted on together. The other grooms with their animals were on in advance, and were by this time employed in combing out forelocks, and rubbing stirrup leathers and horses' legs free from the dirt of the roads;—but Bat Smithers was like his master, and did not congregate much with other men, and Vavasor was sure to give orders to his servant different from the orders given by others.

'Are you well mounted this year?' Maxwell asked of George Vavasor.

'No, indeed; I never was what I call well mounted yet. I generally have one horse and three or four cripples. That brown horse behind there is pretty good, I believe.'

'I see your man has got the old chestnut mare with him.'

'She's one of the cripples,—not but what she's as sound as a bell, and as good a hunter as ever I wish to ride; but she makes a little noise when she's going.'

'So that you can hear her three fields off,' said Grindley.

'Five if the fields are small enough and your ears are sharp enough,' said Vavasor. 'All the same I wouldn't change her for the best horse I ever saw under you.'

'Had you there, Grindems,' said Maxwell.

'No he didn't,' said Grindley. 'He didn't have me at all.'

'Your horses, Grindley, are always up to all the work they have to do,' said George; 'and I don't know what any man wants more than that.'

'Had you again, Grindems,' said Maxwell.

'I can ride against him any day,' said Grindley.

'Yes; or against a brick wall either, if your horse didn't know any better,' said George.

'Had you again, Grindems,' said Maxwell. Whereupon Mr. Grindley trotted on, round the corner by the church, and into the field in which the hounds were assembled. The fire had become too hot for him, and he thought it best to escape. Had it been Vavasor alone he would have turned upon him and snarled, but he could not afford to exhibit any ill temper to the king of the club. Mr. Grindley was not popular, and were Maxwell to turn openly against him his sporting life down at Roebury would decidedly be a failure.

The lives of such men as Mr. Grindley—men who are tolerated in the daily society of others who are accounted their superiors—do not seem to have many attractions. And yet how many such men does one see in almost every set? Why Mr. Grindley should have been inferior to Mr. Maxwell the banker, or to Stone, or to Prettyman who were brewers, or even to Mr. Pollock the heavy-weight literary gentleman, I can hardly say. An attorney by his trade is at any rate as good as a brewer, and there are many attorneys who hold their heads high anywhere. Grindley was a rich man,—or at any rate rich enough for the life he led. I don't know much about his birth, but I believe it was as good as Maxwell's. He was not ignorant, or a fool;—whereas I rather think Maxwell was a fool. Grindley had made his own way in the world, but Maxwell would certainly not have made himself a banker if his father had not been a banker before him; nor could the bank have gone on and prospered had there not been partners there who were better men of business than our friend. Grindley knew that he had a better intellect than Maxwell; and yet he allowed Maxwell to snub him, and he toadied Maxwell in return. It was not on the score of riding that Maxwell claimed and held his superiority, for Grindley did not want pluck, and every one knew that Maxwell had lived freely and that his nerves were not what they had been. I think it had come from the outward look of the men, from the form of each, from the gait and visage which in one was good and in the other insignificant. The nature of such dominion of man over man is very singular, but this is certain, that when once obtained in manhood it may be easily held.

Among boys at school the same thing is even more conspicuous, because boys have less of conscience than men, are more addicted to tyranny, and when weak are less prone to feel the misery and disgrace of succumbing. Who has been through a large school and does not remember the Maxwells and Grindleys,—the tyrants and the slaves,—those who domineered and those who submitted? Nor was it, even then, personal strength, nor always superior courage, that gave the power of command.

169

Nor was it intellect, or thoughtfulness, nor by any means such qualities as make men and boys loveable. It is said by many who have had to deal with boys, that certain among them claim and obtain ascendancy by the spirit within them; but I doubt whether the ascendancy is not rather thrust on them than claimed by them. Here again I think the outward gait of the boy goes far towards obtaining for him the submission of his fellows.

But the tyrant boy does not become the tyrant man, or the slave boy the slave man, because the outward visage, that has been noble or mean in the one, changes and becomes so often mean or noble in the other.

'By George, there's Pollock!' said Maxwell, as he rode into the field by the church. 'I'll bet half a crown that he's come down from London this morning, that he was up all night last night, and that he tells us so three times before the hounds go out of the paddock.' Mr. Pollock was the heavy-weight sporting literary gentleman.

CHAPTER XVII

Edgehill

OF all sights in the world there is, I think, none more beautiful than that of a pack of fox-hounds seated, on a winter morning, round the huntsman, if the place of meeting has been chosen with anything of artistic skill. It should be in a grassy field, and the field should be small. It should not be absolutely away from all buildings, and the hedgerows should not have been clipped and pared, and made straight with reference to modern agricultural economy. There should be trees near, and the ground should be a little uneven, so as to mark some certain small space as the exact spot where the dogs and servants of the hunt should congregate.

There are well-known grand meets in England, in the parks of noblemen, before their houses, or even on what are called their lawns; but these magnificent affairs have but little of the beauty of which I speak. Such assemblies are too grand and too ornate, and, moreover, much too far removed from true sporting proprieties. At them, equipages are shining, and ladies' dresses are gorgeous, and crowds of tradesmen from the neighbouring town have come there to look at the grand folk. To my eye there is nothing beautiful in that. The meet I speak of is arranged with a view to sport, but the accident of the locality may make it the prettiest thing in the world.

Such, in a special degree, was the case at Edgehill. At Edgehill the whole village consisted of three or four cottages; but there was a small old church, with an old grey tower, and a narrow, green, almost dark, churchyard, surrounded by elmtrees. The road from Roebury to the meet passed by the church stile, and turning just beyond it came upon the gate which led into the little field in which the hounds felt themselves as much at home as in their kennels. There might be six or seven acres in the field, which was long and narrow, so that the huntsman had space to walk leisurely up and down with the pack clustering round him, when he considered that longer sitting might

171

chill them. The church tower was close at hand, visible through the trees, and the field itself was green and soft, though never splashing with mud or heavy with holes.

Edgehill was a favourite meet in that country, partly because foxes were very abundant in the great wood adjacent, partly because the whole country around is grass-land, and partly, no doubt, from the sporting propensities of the neighbouring population. As regards my own taste, I do not know that I do like beginning a day with a great wood,—and if not beginning it, certainly not ending it. It is hard to come upon the cream of hunting, as it is upon the cream of any other delight. Who can always drink Lafitte of the finest, can always talk to a woman who is both beautiful and witty, or can always find the right spirit in the poetry he reads? A man has usually to work through much mud before he gets his nugget. It is so certainly in hunting, and a big wood too frequently afflicts the sportsman, as the mud does the miner. The small gorse cover is the happy, much-envied bit of ground in which the gold is sure to show itself readily. But without the woods the gorse would not hold the foxes, and without the mud the gold would not have found its resting-place.

But, as I have said, Edgehill was a popular meet, and, as regarded the meet itself, was eminently picturesque. On the present occasion the little field was full of horsemen, moving about slowly, chatting together, smoking cigars, getting off from their hacks and mounting their hunters, giving orders to their servants, and preparing for the day. There were old country gentlemen there, greeting each other from far sides of the county; sporting farmers who love to find themselves alongside their landlords, and to feel that the pleasures of the country are common to both; men down from town, like our friends of the Roebury club, who made hunting their chosen pleasure, and who formed, in number, perhaps the largest portion of the field; officers from garrisons round about; a cloud of servants, and a few nondescript stragglers who had picked up horses, hither and thither, round the country. Outside the gate on the road were drawn up a variety of vehicles, open carriages, dog-carts, gigs, and waggonettes,* in some few of which were seated ladies who had come over to see the meet. But Edgehill was, essentially, not a ladies' meet. The distances to it were long, and the rides in Cranby Wood—the big wood —were not adapted for wheels. There were one or two ladies on horseback, as is always the case; but Edgehill was not a place popular, even with hunting ladies. One carriage, that of the old master of the hounds, had entered the sacred precincts of the field, and from this the old baronet was just descending, as Maxwell, Calder Jones, and Vavasor rode into the field.

'I hope I see you well, Sir William,' said Maxwell, greeting the master. Calder Jones also made his little speech, and so did Vavasor.

'Humph—well, yes, I'm pretty well, thank'ee. Just move on, will you? My mare can't stir here.' Then some one else spoke to him, and he only grunted in answer. Having slowly been assisted up on to his horse,—for he was over seventy years of age,—he trotted off to the hounds, while all the farmers round him touched their hats to him. But his mind was laden with affairs of import, and he noticed no one. In a whispered voice he gave his instructions to his huntsman, who said, 'Yes, Sir William,' 'No, Sir William,' 'No doubt, Sir William.' One long-eared, long-legged fellow, in a hunting-cap and scarlet coat, hung listening by, anxious to catch something of the orders for the morning. 'Who the devil's that fellow, that's all breeches and boots?' said Sir William aloud to some one near him, as the huntsman moved off with the hounds. Sir William knew the man well enough, but was minded to punish him for his discourtesy. 'Where shall we find first, Sir William?' said Calder Jones, in a voice that was really very humble. 'How the mischief am I to know where the foxes are?' said Sir William, with an oath; and Calder Jones retired unhappy, and for the moment altogether silenced.

And yet Sir William was the most popular man in the county, and no more courteous gentleman ever sat at the bottom of his own table. A mild man he was, too, when out of his saddle, and one by no means disposed to assume special supremacy.

But a master of hounds, if he have long held the country,—and
Sir William had held his for more than thirty years,—obtains
a power which that of no other potentate can equal. He may
say and do what he pleases, and his tyranny is always respected.
No conspiracy against him has a chance of success; no sedition
will meet with sympathy;—that is, if he be successful in showing sport. If a man be sworn at, abused, and put down without
cause, let him bear it and think that he has been a victim for
the public good. And let him never be angry with the master.
That rough tongue is the necessity of the master's position.
They used to say that no captain could manage a ship without
swearing at his men. But what are the captain's troubles in
comparison with those of the master of hounds? The captain's
men are under discipline, and can be locked up, flogged, or have
their grog stopped. The master of hounds cannot stop the grog
of any offender, and he can only stop the tongue, or horse, of
such an one by very sharp words.

'Well, Pollock, when did you come?' said Maxwell.

'By George,' said the literary gentleman, 'just down from
London by the 8.30 from Euston Square, and got over here
from Winslow in a trap,* with two fellows I never saw in my
life before. We came tandem in a fly, and did the nineteen
miles in an hour.'

'Come, Athenian, draw it mild,' said Maxwell.

'We did, indeed. I wonder whether they'll pay me their
share of the fly. I had to leave Onslow Crescent at a quarter
before eight, and I did three hours' work before I started.'

'Then you did it by candle-light,' said Grindley.

'Of course I did; and why shouldn't I? Do you suppose no
one can work by candle-light except a lawyer? I suppose you
fellows were playing whist, and drinking hard. I'm uncommon
glad I wasn't with you, for I shall be able to ride.'

'I bet you a pound,' said Jones, 'if there's a run, I see more
of it than you.'

'I'll take that bet with Jones,' said Grindley, 'and Vavasor
shall be the judge.'

'Gentlemen, the hounds can't get out, if you will stop up the gate,' said Sir William. Then the pack passed through, and they all trotted on for four miles, to Cranby Wood.

Vavasor, as he rode on to the wood, was alone, or speaking, from time to time, a few words to his servant. 'I'll ride the chestnut mare in the wood,' he said, 'and do you keep near me.'

'I bean't to be galloping up and down them rides, I suppose,' said Bat, almost contemptuously.

'I shan't gallop up and down the rides, myself; but do you mark me, to know where I am, so that I can change if a fox should go away.'

'You'll be here all day, sir. That's my belief.'

'If so, I won't ride the brown horse at all. But do you take care to let me have him if there's a chance. Do you understand?'

'Oh, yes, I understand, sir. There ain't no difficulty in my understanding;—only I don't think, sir, you'll ever get a fox out of that wood to-day. Why, it stands to reason. The wind's from the north-east.'

Cranby Wood is very large,—there being, in truth, two or three woods together. It was nearly twelve before they found; and then for an hour there was great excitement among the men, who rode up and down the rides as the hounds drove the fox from one end to another of the enclosure. Once or twice the poor animal did try to go away, and then there was great hallooing, galloping, and jumping over unnecessary fences; but he was headed back again, or changed his mind, not liking the north-east wind of which Bat Smithers had predicted such bad things. After one, the crowd of men became rather more indifferent, and clustered together in broad spots, eating their lunch, smoking cigars, and chaffing each other. It was singular to observe the amazing quantity of ham sandwiches and of sherry that had been carried into Cranby Wood on that day. Grooms appeared to have been laden with cases, and men were as well armed with flasks at their saddle-bows* as they used to be with pistols. Maxwell and Pollock formed the centre of one of these crowds, and chaffed each other with the utmost industry, till, tired of having inflicted no wounds, they turned upon Grindley and drove him out of the circle. 'You'll make that man cut his throat, if you go on at that,' said Pollock. 'Shall I? said Maxwell. 'Then I'll certainly stick to him for the sake of humanity in general.' During all this time Vavasor sat apart, quite alone, and Bat Smithers grimly kept his place, about three hundred yards from him.

'We shan't do any good to-day,' said Grindley, coming up to Vavasor.

'I'm sure I don't know,' said Vavasor.

'That old fellow has got to be so stupid, he doesn't know what he's about,' said Grindley, meaning Sir William.

'How can he make the fox break?' said Vavasor; and as his voice was by no means encouraging Grindley rode away.

Lunch and cigars lasted till two, during which hour the hounds, the huntsmen, the whips, and old Sir William were hard at work, as also were some few others who persistently followed every chance of the game. From that till three there were two or three flashes in the pan, and false reports as to foxes which had gone away, which first set men galloping, and then made them very angry. After three, men began to say naughty things, to abuse Cranby Wood, to wish violently that they had remained at home or gone elsewhere, and to speak irreverently of their ancient master. 'It's the cussidest place in all creation,' said Maxwell. 'I often said I'd not come here any more, and now I say it again.'

'And yet you'll be here the next meet,' said Grindley, who had sneaked back to his old companions in weariness of spirit.

'Grindems, you know a sight too much,' said Maxwell; 'you do indeed. An ordinary fellow has no chance with you.'

Grindley was again going to catch it, but was this time saved by the appearance of the huntsman, who came galloping up one of the rides, with a lot of the hounds at his heels.

'He isn't away, Tom, surely?' said Maxwell.

'He's out of the wood somewheres,' said Tom;—and off they all went. Vavasor changed his horse, getting on to the brown one, and giving up his chestnut mare to Bat Smithers, who suggested that he might as well go home to Roebury now. Vavasor gave him no answer, but, trotting on to the point where the rides met, stopped a moment and listened carefully. Then he took a path diverging away from that by which the huntsmen and the crowd of horsemen had gone, and made the best of his way through the wood. At the end of this he came upon Sir William, who, with no one near him but his servant, was standing in the pathway of a little hunting-gate.

'Hold hard,' said Sir William. 'The hounds are not out of the wood yet.'

'Is the fox away, sir?'

'What's the good of that if we can't get the hounds out?— Yes, he's away. He passed out where I'm standing.' And then he began to blow his horn lustily, and by degrees other men and a few hounds came down the ride. Then Tom, with his horse almost blown, made his appearance outside the wood, and soon there came a rush of men, nearly on the top of one another, pushing on, not knowing whither, but keenly alive to the fact that the fox had at last consented to move his quarters.

Tom touched his hat, and looked at his master, inquiringly. 'He's gone for Claydon's,' said the master. 'Try them up that hedgerow.' Tom did try them up the hedgerow, and in half a minute the hounds came upon the scent. Then you might see men settling their hats on their heads, and feeling their feet in their stirrups. The moment for which they had so long waited had come, and yet there were many who would now have preferred that the fox should be headed back into cover. Some had but little confidence in their half-blown horses;— with many the waiting, though so abused and anathematized, was in truth more to their taste than the run itself;—with others the excitement had gone by, and a gallop over a field or two was necessary before it would be restored. With most men at such a moment there is a little nervousness, some fear of making a bad start, a dread lest others should have more of the success of the hunt than falls to them. But there was a great rush and a mighty bustle as the hounds made out their game, and Sir William felt himself called upon to use the rough side of his tongue to more than one delinquent.

And then certain sly old stagers might be seen turning off to the left, instead of following the course of the game as indicated by the hounds. They were men who had felt the air as they came out, and knew that the fox must soon run down wind, whatever he might do for the first half mile or so,— men who knew also which was the shortest way to Claydon's by the road. Ah, the satisfaction that there is when these men are thrown out, and their dead knowledge proved to be of no avail! If a fox will only run straight, heading from the cover on his real line, these very sagacious gentlemen seldom come to much honour and glory.

In the present instance the beast seemed determined to go straight enough, for the hounds ran the scent along three or four hedgerows in a line. He had managed to get for himself full ten minutes' start, and had been able to leave the cover and all his enemies well behind him before he bethought himself as to his best way to his purposed destination. And here, from field to field, there were little hunting-gates at which men crowded lustily, poking and shoving each other's horses, and hating each other with a bitterness of hatred which is, I think, known nowhere else. No hunting man ever wants to jump if he can help it, and the hedges near the gate were not alluring. A few there were who made lines for themselves, taking the next field to the right, or scrambling through the corners of the fences while the rush was going on at the gates; and among these was George Vavasor. He never rode in a crowd, always keeping himself somewhat away from men as well as hounds. He would often be thrown out, and then men would hear no more of him for that day. On such occasions he did not show himself, as other men do, twenty minutes after the fox had been killed or run to ground,—but betook himself home by himself, going through the byeways and lanes, thus leaving no report of his failure to be spoken of by his compeers.

As long as the line of gates lasted, the crowd continued as

thick as ever, and the best man was he whose horse could shove the hardest. After passing some four or five fields in this way they came out upon a road, and, the scent holding strong, the dogs crossed it without any demurring. Then came doubt into the minds of men, many of whom, before they would venture away from their position on the lane, narrowly watched the leading hounds to see whether there was indication of a turn to the one side or the other. Sir William, whose seventy odd years excused him, turned sharp to the left, knowing that he could make Claydon's that way; and very many were the submissive horsemen who followed him; a few took the road to the right, having in their minds some little game of their own. The hardest riders there had already crossed from the road into the country, and were going well to the hounds, ignorant, some of them, of the brook before them, and others unheeding. Foremost among these was Burgo Fitzgerald,—Burgo Fitzgerald, whom no man had ever known to crane at a fence, or to hug a road, or to spare his own neck or his horse's. And yet poor Burgo seldom finished well,—coming to repeated grief in this matter of his hunting, as he did so constantly in other matters of his life.

But almost neck and neck with Burgo was Pollock, the sporting literary gentleman. Pollock had but two horses to his stud, and was never known to give much money for them;—and he weighed without his boots, fifteen stones! No one ever knew how Pollock did it;—more especially as all the world declared that he was as ignorant of hunting as any tailor. He could ride, or when he couldn't ride he could tumble,—men said that of him,—and he would ride as long as the beast under him could go. But few knew the sad misfortunes which poor Pollock sometimes encountered;—the muddy ditches in which he was left; the despair with which he would stand by his unfortunate horse when the poor brute could no longer move across some deep-ploughed field; the miles that he would walk at night beside a tired animal, as he made his way slowly back to Roebury!

Then came Tom the huntsman, with Calder Jones close to

him, and Grindley intent on winning his sovereign. Vavasor had also crossed the road somewhat to the left, carrying with him one or two who knew that he was a safe man to follow. Maxwell had been ignominiously turned by the hedge, which, together with its ditch, formed a fence such as all men do not love at the beginning of a run. He had turned from it, acknowledging the cause. 'By George!' said he, 'that's too big for me yet awhile; and there's no end of a river at the bottom.' So he had followed the master down the road.

All those whom we have named managed to get over the brook, Pollock's horse barely contriving to get up his hind legs from the broken edge of the bank. Some nags refused it, and their riders thus lost all their chance of sport for that day. Such is the lot of men who hunt. A man pays five or six pounds for his day's amusement, and it is ten to one that the occurrences of the day disgust rather than gratify him! One or two got in, and scrambled out on the other side, but Tufto Pearlings, the Manchester man from Friday Street, stuck in the mud at the bottom, and could not get his mare out till seven men had come with ropes to help him. 'Where the devil is my fellow?' Pearlings asked of the countrymen; but the countrymen could not tell him that 'his fellow' with his second horse was riding the hunt with great satisfaction to himself.

George Vavasor found that his horse went with him uncommonly well, taking his fences almost in the stride of his gallop, and giving unmistakeable signs of good condition. 'I wonder what it is that's amiss with him,' said George to himself, resolving, however, that he would sell him that day if he got an opportunity. Straight went the line of the fox, up from the brook, and Tom began to say that his master had been wrong about Claydon's.

'Where are we now?' said Burgo, as four or five of them dashed through the open gate of a farmyard.

'This is Bulby's farm,' said Tom, 'and we're going right away for Elmham Wood.'

'Elmham Wood be d——,' said a stout farmer, who had come as far as that with them. 'You won't see Elmham Wood to-day.'

'I suppose you know best,' said Tom; and then they were through the yard, across another road, and down a steep ravine by the side of a little copse. 'He's been through them firs, any way,' said Tom. 'To him, Gaylass!' Then up they went the other side of the ravine, and saw the body of the hounds almost a field before them at the top.

'I say,—that took some of the wind out of a fellow,' said Pollock.

'You mustn't mind about wind now,' said Burgo, dashing on.

'Wasn't the pace awful, coming up to that farm-house?' said Calder Jones, looking round to see if Grindley was shaken off. But Grindley, with some six or seven others, was still there. And there, also, always in the next field to the left, was George Vavasor. He had spoken no word to any one since the hunt commenced, nor had he wished to speak to any one. He desired to sell his horse,—and he desired also to succeed in the run for other reasons than that, though I think he would have found it difficult to define them.

Now they had open grass land for about a mile, but with very heavy fences,—so that the hounds gained upon them a little, and Pollock's weight began to tell. The huntsman and Burgo were leading with some fortunate country gentleman whose good stars had brought him in upon them at the farm-yard gate. It is the injustice of such accidents as this that breaks the heart of a man who has honestly gone through all the heat and work of the struggle! And the hounds had veered a little round to the left, making, after all, for Claydon's. 'Darned if the Squire warn't right,' said Tom. Sir William, though a baronet, was familiarly called the Squire throughout the hunt.

'We ain't going for Claydon's now?' asked Burgo.

'Them's Claydon beeches we sees over there,' said Tom. '''Tain't often the Squire's wrong.'

Here they came to a little double rail and a little quickset* hedge. A double rail is a nasty fence always if it has been made any way strong, and one which a man with a wife and a family is justified in avoiding. They mostly can be avoided, having gates; and this could have been avoided. But Burgo never avoided anything, and went over it beautifully. The difficulty is to be discreet when the man before one has been indiscreet. Tom went for the gate, as did Pollock, who knew that he could have no chance at the double rails. But Calder Jones came to infinite grief, striking the top bar of the second rail, and going head-foremost out of his saddle, as though thrown by a catapult. There we must leave him. Grindley, rejoicing greatly at this discomfiture, made for the gate; but the country gentleman with the fresh horse accomplished the rails, and was soon alongside of Burgo.

'I didn't see you at the start,' said Burgo.

'And I didn't see you,' said the country gentleman; 'so it's even.'

Burgo did not see the thing in the same light, but he said no more. Grindley and Tom were soon after them, Tom doing his utmost to shake off the attorney. Pollock was coming on also; but the pace had been too much for him, and though the ground rode light his poor beast laboured and grunted sorely. The hounds were still veering somewhat to the left, and Burgo, jumping over a small fence into the same field with them, saw that there was a horseman ahead of him. This was George Vavasor, who was going well, without any symptom of distress.

And now they were at Claydon's, having run over some seven miles of ground in about thirty-five minutes. To those who do not know what hunting is, this pace does not seem very extraordinary; but it had been quite quick enough, as was testified by the horses which had gone the distance. Our party entered Claydon's Park at back, through a gate in the park palings that was open on hunting days; but a much more numerous lot was there almost as soon as them, who had come in by the main entrance. This lot was headed by Sir William, and our friend Maxwell was with him.

'A jolly thing so far,' said Burgo to Maxwell; 'about the best we've had this year.'

'I didn't see a yard of it,' said Maxwell. 'I hadn't nerve to get off the first road, and I haven't been off it ever since.' Maxwell was a man who never lied about his hunting, or had the slightest shame in riding roads. 'Who's been with you?' said he.

'There've been Tom and I;—and Calder Jones was there for a while. I think he killed himself somewhere. And there was Pollock, and your friend Grindley, and a chap whose name I don't know who dropped out of heaven about half-way in the run; and there was another man whose back I saw just now; there he is,—by heavens, it's Vavasor! I didn't know he was here.'

They hung about the Claydon covers for ten minutes, and then their fox went off again,—their fox or another, as to which there was a great discussion afterwards; but he who would have suggested the idea of a new fox to Sir William would have been a bold man. A fox, however, went off, turning still to the left from Claydon's towards Roebury. Those ten minutes had brought up some fifty men; but it did not bring up Calder Jones nor Tufto Pearlings, nor some half-dozen others who had already come to serious misfortune; but Grindley was there, very triumphant in his own success, and already talking of Jones's sovereign. And Pollock was there also, thankful for that ten minutes' law,* and trusting that wind might be given to his horse to finish the run triumphantly.

But the pace on leaving Claydon's was better than ever. This may have come from the fact that the scent was keener, as they got out so close upon their game. But I think they must have changed their fox. Maxwell, who saw him go, swore that he was fresh and clean. Burgo said that he knew it to be the same fox, but gave no reason. 'Same fox! in course it was; why shouldn't it be the same?' said Tom. The country gentleman who had dropped from heaven was quite sure that they had changed, and so were most of those who had ridden the road. Pollock confined himself to hoping that he might soon be killed, and that thus his triumph for the day might be assured.

On they went, and the pace soon became too good for the poor author. His horse at last refused a little hedge, and there was not another trot to be got out of him. That night Pollock turned up at Roebury about nine o'clock, very hungry,—and it was known that his animal was alive;—but the poor horse ate not a grain of oats that night, nor on the next morning. Vavasor had again taken a line to himself, on this occasion a little to the right of the meet; but Maxwell followed him and rode close with him to the end. Burgo for a while still led the body of the field, incurring at first much condemnation from Sir William, —nominally for hurrying on among the hounds, but in truth because he got before Sir William himself. During this latter part of the run Sir William stuck to the hounds in spite of his seventy odd years. Going down into Marham Bottom, some four or five were left behind, for they feared the soft ground near the river, and did not know the pass through it. But Sir William knew it, and those who remained close to him got over that trouble. Burgo, who would still lead, nearly foundered in the bog;—but he was light, and his horse pulled him through,—leaving a fore-shoe in the mud. After that Burgo was contented to give Sir William the lead.

Then they came up by Marham Pits to Cleshey Small Wood, which they passed without hanging there a minute, and over the grass lands of Cleshey Farm. Here Vavasor and Maxwell joined the others, having gained some three hundred yards in distance by their course, but having been forced to jump the Marham Stream which Sir William had forded. The pace now was as good as the horses could make it,—and perhaps something better as regarded some of them. Sir William's servant had been with him, and he had got his second horse at Claydon's; Maxwell had been equally fortunate; Tom's second horse had not come up, and his beast was in great distress; Grindley had remained behind at Marham Bottom, being contented perhaps with having beaten Calder Jones,—from whom by-the-by I may here declare that he never got his sovereign. Burgo, Vavasor, and the country gentleman still held on; but it was devoutly desired by all of them that the fox might soon come to the end of his tether. Ah! that intense longing that the fox may fail, when the failing powers of the horse begin to make themselves known,—and the consciousness comes on that all that one has done will go for nothing unless the thing can be brought to a close in a field or two! So far you have triumphed, leaving scores of men behind; but of what good is all that, if you also are to be left behind at the last?

It was manifest now to all who knew the country that the fox was making for Thornden Deer Park, but Thornden Deer Park was still two miles ahead of them, and the hounds were so near to their game that the poor beast could hardly hope to live till he got there. He had tried a well-known drain near Cleshey Farm House; but it had been inhospitably, nay cruelly, closed against him. Soon after that he threw himself down in a ditch, and the eager hounds overran him, giving him a moment's law,—and giving also a moment's law to horses that wanted it as badly. 'I'm about done for,' said Burgo to Maxwell. 'Luckily for you,' said Maxwell, 'the fox is much in the same way.'

But the fox had still more power left in him than poor Burgo Fitzgerald's horse. He gained a minute's check and then he started again, being viewed away by Sir William himself. The country gentleman of whom mention has been made also viewed him, and holloa'd as he did so: 'Yoicks, tally; gone away!' The unfortunate man! 'What the d—— are you roaring at?' said Sir William. 'Do you suppose I don't know where the fox is?' Whereupon the country gentleman retreated, and became less conspicuous than he had been.

Away they went again, off Cleshey and into Thornden parish, on the land of Sorrell Farm,—a spot well to be remembered by one or two ever afterwards. Here Sir William made for a gate which took him a little out of the line; but Maxwell and Burgo Fitzgerald, followed by Vavasor, went straight ahead. There was a huge ditch and boundary bank there which Sir William had known and had avoided. Maxwell, whose pluck had returned to him at last, took it well. His horse was comparatively fresh and made nothing of it. Then came poor Burgo! Oh, Burgo, hadst thou not have been a very child, thou shouldst have known that now, at this time of the day,—after all that thy gallant horse had done for thee,—it was impossible to thee or him. But when did Burgo Fitzgerald know anything? He rode at the bank as though it had been the first fence of the day, striking his poor beast with his spurs, as though muscle, strength, and new power could be imparted by their rowels.* The animal rose at the bank, and in some way got upon it, scrambling as he struck it with his chest, and then fell headlong into the ditch at the other side, a confused mass of head, limbs, and body. His career was at an end, and he had broken his heart! Poor noble beast, noble in vain! To his very last gasp he had done his best, and had deserved that he should have been in better hands. His master's ignorance had killed him. There are men who never know how little a horse can do,—or how much!

There was to some extent a gap in the fence when Maxwell had first ridden it and Burgo had followed him; a gap, or break in the hedge at the top, indicating plainly the place at which a horse could best get over. To this spot Vavasor followed, and was on the bank at Burgo's heels before he knew what had happened. But the man had got away and only the horse lay there in the ditch. 'Are you hurt?' said Vavasor; 'can I do anything?' But he did not stop. 'If you can find a chap just send him to me,' said Burgo in a melancholy tone. Then he sat down, with his feet in the ditch, and looked at the carcase of his horse.

There was no more need of jumping that day. The way was open into the next field,—a turnip field,—and there amidst the crisp breaking turnip-tops, with the breath of his enemies hot upon him, with their sharp teeth at his entrails, biting at them impotently in the agonies of his death struggle, poor Reynard finished his career. Maxwell was certainly the first there,—but Sir William and George Vavasor were close upon him. That taking of brushes of which we used to hear is a little out of fashion; but if such honour were due to any one it was due to Vavasor, for he and he only had ridden the hunt throughout. But he claimed no honour, and none was specially given to him. He and Maxwell rode homewards together, having sent assistance to poor Burgo Fitzgerald; and as they went along the road, saying but little to each other, Maxwell, in a very indifferent voice, asked him a question.

'What do you want for that horse, Vavasor?'

'A hundred and fifty,' said Vavasor.

'He's mine,' said Maxwell. So the brown horse was sold for about half his value, because he had brought with him a bad character.

CHAPTER XVIII

Alice Vavasor's Great Relations

BURGO FITZGERALD, of whose hunting experiences something has been told in the last chapter, was a young man born in the purple of the English aristocracy. He was related to half the dukes in the kingdom, and had three countesses for his aunts. When he came of age he was master of a sufficient fortune to make it quite out of the question that he should be asked to earn his bread; and though that, and other windfalls that had come to him, had long since been spent, no one had ever made to him so ridiculous a proposition as that. He was now thirty, and for some years past had been known to be much worse than penniless; but still he lived on in the same circles, still slept softly and drank of the best, and went about with his valet and his groom and his horses, and fared sumptuously every day. Some people said the countesses did it for him, and some said that it was the dukes;—while others, again, declared that the Jews were his most generous friends. At any rate he still seemed to live as he had always lived, setting tradesmen at defiance, and laughing to scorn all the rules which regulate the lives of other men.

About eighteen months before the time of which I am now speaking, a great chance had come in this young man's way, and he had almost succeeded in making himself one of the richest men in England. There had been then a great heiress in the land, on whom the properties of half-a-dozen ancient families had concentrated; and Burgo, who in spite of his iniquities still kept his position in the drawing-rooms of the great, had almost succeeded in obtaining the hand and the wealth,—as people still said that he had obtained the heart,— of the Lady Glencora M'Cluskie. But sundry mighty magnates, driven almost to despair at the prospect of such a sacrifice, had sagaciously put their heads together, and the result had been that the Lady Glencora had heard reason. She had listened,— with many haughty tossings indeed of her proud little head, with many throbbings of her passionate young heart; but in the end she listened and heard reason. She saw Burgo, for the last time, and told him that she was the promised bride of Plantagenet Palliser, nephew and heir of the Duke of Omnium.

He had borne it like a man,—never having groaned openly, or quivered once before any comrade at the name of the Lady Glencora. She had married Mr. Palliser at St. George's Square,* and on the morning of the marriage he had hung about his club door in Pall Mall, listening to the bells, and saying a word or two about the wedding, with admirable courage. It had been for him a great chance,—and he had lost it. Who can say, too, that his only regret was for the money? He had spoken once of it to a married sister of his, in whose house he had first met Lady Glencora. 'I shall never marry now,—that is all,' he said—and then he went about, living his old reckless life, with the same recklessness as ever. He was one of those young men with dark hair and blue eyes,—who wear no beard, and are certainly among the handsomest of all God's creatures. No more handsome man than Burgo Fitzgerald lived in his days; and this merit at any rate was his,—that he thought nothing of his own beauty. But he lived ever without conscience, without purpose,—with no idea that it behoved him as a man to do anything but eat and drink,—or ride well to hounds till some poor brute, much nobler than himself, perished beneath him.

He chiefly concerns our story at this present time because the Lady Glencora who had loved him,—and would have married him had not those sagacious heads prevented it,—was a cousin of Alice Vavasor's. She was among those very great relations with whom Alice was connected by her mother's side,—being indeed so near to Lady Macleod, that she was first cousin to that lady, only once removed. Lady Midlothian was aunt to the Lady Glencora, and our Alice might have called cousins, and not been forbidden, with the old Lord of the Isles, Lady Glencora's father,—who was dead, however, some time previous to that affair with Burgo,—and with the Marquis of Auld Reekie, who was Lady Glencora's uncle, and had been her guardian. But Alice had kept herself aloof from her grand relations on her mother's side, choosing rather to hold herself as belonging to those who were her father's kindred. With Lady Glencora, however, she had for a short time,—for some week or ten days,—been on terms of almost affectionate intimacy. It had been then, when the wayward heiress with the bright waving locks had been most strongly minded to give herself and her wealth to Burgo Fitzgerald. Burgo had had money dealings with George Vavasor, and knew him,—knew him intimately, and had learned the fact of this cousinship between the heiress and his friend's cousin. Whereupon in the agony of those weeks in which the sagacious heads were resisting her love, Lady Glencora came to her cousin in Queen Anne Street, and told Alice all that tale. 'Was Alice,' she asked, 'afraid of the marquises and the countesses, or of all the rank and all the money which they boasted?' Alice answered that she was not at all afraid of them. 'Then would she permit Lady Glencora and Burgo to see each other in the drawing-room at Queen Anne Street, just once!' Just once,—so that they might arrange that little plan of an elopement. But Alice could not do that for her newly found cousin. She endeavoured to explain that it was not the dignity of the sagacious heads which stood in her way, but her woman's feeling of what was right and wrong in such a matter.

'Why should I not marry him?' said Lady Glencora, with her eyes flashing. 'He is my equal.'

Alice explained that she had no word to say against such a marriage. She counselled her cousin to be true to her love if her love was in itself true. But she, an unmarried woman, who had hitherto not known her cousin, might not give such help as that! 'If you will not help me, I am helpless!' said the Lady Glencora, and then she kneeled at Alice's knees and threw her wavy locks abroad on Alice's lap. 'How shall I bribe you?' said Lady Glencora. 'Next to him I will love you better than all the world.' But Alice, though she kissed the fair forehead and owned that such reward would be worth much to her, could not take any bribe for such a cause. Then Lady Glencora had been angry with her, calling her heartless, and threatening her that she too might have sorrow of her own and want assistance. Alice told nothing of her own tale,—how she had loved her cousin and had been forced to give him up, but said what kind words she could, and she of the waving hair and light blue eyes had been pacified. Then she had come again,—had come daily while the sagacious heads were at work,—and Alice in her trouble had been a comfort to her.

But the sagacious heads were victorious, as we know, and Lady Glencora M'Cluskie became Lady Glencora Palliser with all the propriety in the world, instead of becoming wife to poor Burgo, with all imaginable impropriety. And then she wrote a letter to Alice, very short and rather sad; but still with a certain sweetness in it. 'She had been counselled that it was not fitting for her to love as she had thought to love, and she had resolved to give up her dream. Her cousin Alice, she knew, would respect her secret. She was going to become the wife of the best man, she thought, in all the world; and it should be the one care of her life to make him happy.' She said not a word in all her letter of loving this newly found lord. 'She was to be married at once. Would Alice be one among the bevy of bridesmaids who were to grace the ceremony?'

Alice wished her joy heartily,—'heartily,' she said, but had declined that office of bridesmaid. She did not wish to undergo the cold looks of the Lady Julias and Lady Janes who all would know each other, but none of whom would know her. So she sent her cousin a little ring, and asked her to keep it amidst all that wealthy tribute of marriage gifts which would be poured forth at her feet.

From that time to this present Alice had heard no more of Lady Glencora. She had been married late in the preceding season and had gone away with Mr. Palliser, spending her honeymoon amidst the softnesses of some Italian lake. They had not returned to England till the time had come for them to encounter the magnificent Christmas festivities of Mr. Palliser's uncle, the Duke. On this occasion Gatherum Castle,* the vast palace which the Duke had built at a cost of nearly a quarter of a million, was opened, as it had never been opened before;— for the Duke's heir had married to the Duke's liking, and the Duke was a man who could do such things handsomely when he was well pleased. Then there had been a throng of bridal guests, and a succession of bridal gaieties which had continued themselves even past the time at which Mr. Palliser was due at Westminster;—and Mr. Palliser was a legislator who served his country with the utmost assiduity. So the London season commenced, progressed, and was consumed; and still Alice heard nothing more of her friend and cousin Lady Glencora.

But this had troubled her not at all. A chance circumstance, the story of which she had told to no one, had given her a short intimacy with this fair child of the gold mines, but she had felt that they two could not live together in habits of much intimacy. She had, when thinking of the young bride, only thought of that wild love episode in the girl's life. It had been strange to her that she should in one week have listened to the most passionate protestations from her friend of love for one man, and then have been told in the next that another man was to be her friend's husband! But she reflected that her own career was much the same,—only with the interval of some longer time.

But her own career was not the same. Glencora had married Mr. Palliser,—had married him without pausing to doubt;— but Alice had gone on doubting till at last she had resolved that she would not marry Mr. Grey. She thought of this much in those days at Cheltenham, and wondered often whether Glencora lived with her husband in the full happiness of conjugal love.

One morning, about three days after Mr. Grey's visit, there came to her two letters, as to neither of which did she know the writer by the handwriting. Lady Macleod had told her,—with some hesitation, indeed, for Lady Macleod was afraid of her,—but had told her, nevertheless, more than once, that those noble relatives had heard of the treatment to which Mr. Grey was being subjected, and had expressed their great sorrow,—if not dismay or almost anger. Lady Macleod, indeed, had gone as far as she dared, and might have gone further without any sacrifice of truth. Lady Midlothian had said that it would be disgraceful to the family, and Lady Glencora's aunt, the Marchioness of Auld Reekie, had demanded to be told what it was the girl wanted.

When the letters came Lady Macleod was not present, and I am disposed to think that one of them had been written by concerted arrangement with her. But if so she had not dared to watch the immediate effect of her own projectile. This one was from Lady Midlothian. Of the other Lady Macleod certainly knew nothing, though it also had sprung out of the discussions which had taken place as to Alice's sins in the Auld Reekie-Midlothian set. This other letter was from Lady Glencora. Alice opened the two, one without reading the other, very slowly. Lady Midlothian's was the first opened, and there came a spot of anger on Alice's cheeks as she saw the signature, and caught a word or two as she allowed her eye to glance down the page. Then she opened the other, which was shorter, and when she saw her cousin's signature, 'Glencora Palliser,' she read that letter first,—read it twice before she went back to the disagreeable task of perusing Lady Midlothian's lecture. The reader shall have both the letters, but that from the Countess shall have precedence.

'Castle Reekie, N. B.—Oct. 186–.
'MY DEAR MISS VAVASOR,

'I have not the pleasure of knowing you personally, though I have heard of you very often from our dear mutual friend and relative Lady Macleod, with whom I understand that you are at present on a visit. Your grandmother,—by the mother's side,—Lady Flora Macleod, and my mother the Countess of Leith, were half-sisters; and though circumstances since that have prevented our seeing so much of each other as is desirable, I have always remembered the connection, and have ever regarded you as one in whose welfare I am bound by ties of blood to take a warm interest.'

(' "Since that!"—what does she mean by "since that"?' said Alice to herself. 'She has never set eyes on me at all. Why does she talk of not having seen as much of me as is desirable?')

'I had learned with great gratification that you were going to be married to a most worthy gentleman, Mr. John Grey of Nethercoats, in Cambridgeshire. When I first heard this I made it my business to institute some inquiries, and I was heartily glad to find that your choice had done you so much credit.' (If the reader has read Alice's character as I have meant it should be read, it will thoroughly be understood that this was wormwood to her.) 'I was informed that Mr. Grey is in every respect a gentleman,—that he is a man of most excellent habits, and one to whom any young woman could commit her future happiness with security, that his means are very good for his position, and that there was no possible objection to such a marriage. All this gave great satisfaction to me, in which I was joined by the Marchioness of Auld Reekie, who is connected with you almost as nearly as I am, and who, I can assure you, feels a considerable interest in your welfare. I am staying with her now, and in all that I say, she agrees with me.

'You may feel then how dreadfully we were dismayed when we were told by dear Lady Macleod that you had told Mr. Grey that you intended to change your mind! My dear Miss Vavasor, can this be true? There are things in which a young lady has no right to change her mind after it has been once made up; and certainly when a young lady has accepted a gentleman, that is one of them. He cannot legally make you become his wife, but he has a right to claim you before God and man. Have you considered that he has probably furnished his house in consequence of his intended marriage,—and perhaps in compliance with your own especial wishes?' (I think that Lady Macleod must have told the Countess something that she had heard about the garden.) 'Have you reflected that he has of course told all his friends? Have you any reason to give? I am told, none! Nothing should ever be done without a reason; much less such a thing as this in which your own interests and, I may say, respectability are involved. I hope you will think of this before you persist in destroying your own happiness and perhaps that of a very worthy man.

'I had heard, some years ago, when you were much younger, that you had become imprudently attached in another direction —with a gentleman with none of those qualities to recommend him which speak so highly for Mr. Grey. It would grieve me very much, as it would also the Marchioness, who in this matter thinks exactly as I do, if I were led to suppose that your rejection of Mr. Grey had been caused by *any renewal of that project*. Nothing, my dear Miss Vavasor, could be more unfortunate,—and I might almost add a stronger word.

'I have been advised that a line from me as representing your poor mother's family, especially as I have at the present moment the opportunity of expressing Lady Auld Reekie's sentiments as well as my own, might be of service. I implore you, my dear Miss Vavasor, to remember what you owe to God and man, and to carry out an engagement made by yourself, that is in all respects comme il faut, and which will give entire satisfaction to your friends and relatives.

'If you do this you will always find me to be your sincere friend,

'MARGARET M. MIDLOTHIAN.'

I think that Lady Macleod had been wrong in supposing that this could do any good. She should have known Alice better; and should also have known the world better. But her own reverence for her own noble relatives was so great that she could not understand, even yet, that all such feeling was wanting to her niece. It was to her impossible that the expressed opinion of such an one as the Countess of Midlothian, owning her relationship and solicitude, and condescending at the same time to express friendship,—she could not, I say, understand that the voice of such an one, so speaking, should have no weight whatever. But I think that she had been quite right in keeping out of Alice's way at the moment of the arrival of the letter. Alice read it, slowly, and then replacing it in its envelope, leaned back quietly in her chair,—with her eyes fixed upon the teapot on the table. She had, however, the other letter on which to occupy her mind, and thus relieve her from the effects of too deep an animosity against the Countess.

The Lady Glencora's letter was as follows:

'Matching Priory, Thursday.

'DEAR COUSIN,

'I have just come home from Scotland, where they have been telling me something of your little troubles. I had little troubles once too, and you were so good to me! Will you come to us here for a few weeks? We shall be here till Christmas-time, when we go somewhere else. I have told my husband that you are a great friend of mine as well as a cousin, and that he must be good to you. He is very quiet, and works very hard at politics; but I think you will like him. Do come! There will be a good many people here, so that you will not find it dull. If you will name the day we will send the carriage for you to Matching Station, and I dare say I can manage to come myself.

'Yours affectionately,

'G. PALLISER.'

'P.S. I know what will be in your mind. You will say, why did not she come to me in London? She knew the way to Queen Anne Street well enough. Dear Alice, don't say that. Believe me, I had much to do and think of in London. And if I was wrong, yet you will forgive me. Mr. Palliser says I am to give you his love,—as being a cousin,—and say that you must come!'

This letter was certainly better than the other, but Alice, on reading it, came to a resolve that she would not accept the invitation. In the first place, even that allusion to her little troubles jarred upon her feelings; and then she thought that her rejection of Mr. Grey could be no special reason why she should go to Matching Priory. Was it not very possible that she had been invited that she might meet Lady Midlothian there, and encounter all the strength of a personal battery from the Countess? Lady Glencora's letter she would of course answer, but to Lady Midlothian she would not condescend to make any reply whatever.

About eleven o'clock Lady Macleod came down to her. For half-an-hour or so Alice said nothing; nor did Lady Macleod ask any question. She looked inquisitively at Alice, eyeing the letter which was lying by the side of her niece's workbasket, but she said no word about Mr. Grey or the Countess. At last Alice spoke.

'Aunt,' she said, 'I have had a letter this morning from your friend, Lady Midlothian.'

'She is my cousin, Alice; and yours as much as mine.'

'Your cousin then, aunt. But it is of more moment that she is your friend. She certainly is not mine, nor can her cousinship afford any justification for her interfering in my affairs.'

'Alice,—from her position——'

'Her position can be nothing to me, aunt. I will not submit to it. There is her letter, which you can read if you please. After that you may burn it. I need hardly say that I shall not answer it.'

'And what am I to say to her, Alice?'

'Nothing from me, aunt;—from yourself, whatever you please, of course.' Then there was silence between them for a few minutes. 'And I have had another letter, from Lady Glencora, who married Mr. Palliser, and whom I knew in London last spring.'

'And has that offended you, too?'

'No, there is no offence in that. She asks me to go and see her at Matching Priory, her husband's house; but I shall not go.'

But at last Alice agreed to pay this visit, and it may be as well to explain here how she was brought to do so. She wrote to Lady Glencora, declining, and explaining frankly that she did decline, because she thought it probable that she might there meet Lady Midlothian. Lady Midlothian, she said, had interfered very unwarrantably in her affairs, and she did not wish to make her acquaintance. To this Lady Glencora replied, post haste, that she had intended no such horrid treachery as that for Alice; that neither would Lady Midlothian be there, nor any of that set; by which Alice knew that Lady Glencora referred specially to her aunt the Marchioness; that no one would be at Matching who could torment Alice, either with right or without it, 'except so far as I myself may do so,' Lady Glencora said; and then she named an early day in November, at which she would herself undertake to meet Alice at the Matching Station. On receipt of this letter, Alice, after two days' doubt, accepted the invitation.

CHAPTER XIX

Tribute from Oileymead

KATE VAVASOR, in writing to her cousin Alice, felt some little difficulty in excusing herself for remaining in Norfolk with Mrs. Greenow. She had laughed at Mrs. Greenow before she went to Yarmouth, and had laughed at herself for going there. And in all her letters since, she had spoken of her aunt as a silly, vain, worldly woman, weeping crocodile tears for an old husband whose death had released her from the tedium of his company, and spreading lures to catch new lovers. But yet she agreed to stay with her aunt, and remain with her in lodgings at Norwich for a month.

But Mrs. Greenow had about her something more than Kate had acknowledged when she first attempted to read her aunt's character. She was clever, and in her own way persuasive. She was very generous, and possessed a certain power

197

of making herself pleasant to those around her. In asking Kate
to stay with her she had so asked as to make it appear that
Kate was to confer the favour. She had told her niece that she
was all alone in the world. 'I have money,' she had said, with
more appearance of true feeling than Kate had observed before. 'I have money, but I have nothing else in the world.
I have no home. Why should I not remain here in Norfolk,
where I know a few people? If you'll say that you'll go anywhere else with me, I'll go to any place you'll name.' Kate
had believed this to be hardly true. She had felt sure that her
aunt wished to remain in the neighbourhood of her seaside
admirers; but, nevertheless, she had yielded, and at the end
of October the two ladies, with Jeannette, settled themselves
in comfortable lodgings within the precincts of the Close at
Norwich.

Mr. Greenow at this time had been dead very nearly six
months, but his widow made some mistake in her dates and
appeared to think that the interval had been longer. On the
day of their arrival at Norwich it was evident that this error
had confirmed itself in her mind. 'Only think,' she said, as she
unpacked a little miniature of the departed one, and sat with
it for a moment in her hands, as she pressed her handkerchief
to her eyes, 'only think, that it is barely nine months since he
was with me?'

'Six, you mean, aunt,' said Kate, unadvisedly.

'Only nine months!' repeated Mrs. Greenow, as though she
had not heard her niece. 'Only nine months!' After that Kate
attempted to correct no more such errors. 'It happened in
May, Miss,' Jeannette said afterwards to Miss Vavasor, 'and
that, as we reckons, will be just a twelvemonth come Christmas.' But Kate paid no attention to this.

And Jeannette was very ungrateful, and certainly should
have indulged herself in no such sarcasms. When Mrs. Greenow
made a slight change in her mourning, which she did on her
arrival at Norwich, using a little lace among her crapes, Jeannette reaped a rich harvest in gifts of clothes. Mrs. Greenow
knew well enough that she expected more from a servant than

mere service;—that she wanted loyalty, discretion, and perhaps sometimes a little secrecy;—and as she paid for these things, she should have had them.

Kate undertook to stay a month with her aunt at Norwich, and Mrs. Greenow undertook that Mr. Cheesacre should declare himself as Kate's lover, before the expiration of the month. It was in vain that Kate protested that she wanted no such lover, and that she would certainly reject him if he came. 'That's all very well, my dear,' Aunt Greenow would say. 'A girl must settle herself some day, you know;—and you'd have it all your own way at Oileymead.'

But the offer certainly showed much generosity on the part of Aunt Greenow, inasmuch as Mr. Cheesacre's attentions were apparently paid to herself rather than to her niece. Mr. Cheesacre was very attentive. He had taken the lodgings in the Close, and had sent over fowls and cream from Oileymead, and had called on the morning after their arrival; but in all his attentions he distinguished the aunt more particularly than the niece. 'I am all for Mr. Cheesacre, Miss,' said Jeannette once. 'The Captain is perhaps the nicerer-looking gentleman, and he ain't so podgy like; but what's good looks if a gentleman hasn't got nothing? I can't abide anything that's poor; neither can't Missus.' From which it was evident that Jeannette gave Miss Vavasor no credit in having Mr. Cheesacre in her train.

Captain Bellfield was also at Norwich, having obtained some quasi-military employment there in the matter of drilling volunteers. Certain capacities in that line it may be supposed that he possessed, and, as his friend Cheesacre said of him, he was going to earn an honest penny once in his life. The Captain and Mr. Cheesacre had made up any little differences that had existed between them at Yarmouth, and were close allies again when they left that place. Some little compact on matters of business must have been arranged between them,—for the Captain was in funds again. He was in funds again through the liberality of his friend,—and no payment of former loans had been made, nor had there been any speech of such. Mr.

Cheesacre had drawn his purse-strings liberally, and had declared that if all went well the hospitality of Oileymead should not be wanting during the winter. Captain Bellfield had nodded his head and declared that all should go well.

'You won't see much of the Captain, I suppose,' said Mr. Cheesacre to Mrs. Greenow on the morning of the day after her arrival at Norwich. He had come across the whole way from Oileymead to ask her if she found herself comfortable,—and perhaps with an eye to the Norwich markets at the same time. He now wore a pair of black riding boots over his trousers, and a round topped hat, and looked much more at home than he had done by the seaside.

'Not much, I dare say,' said the widow. 'He tells me that he must be on duty ten or twelve hours a day. Poor fellow!'

'It's a deuced good thing for him, and he ought to be very much obliged to me for putting him in the way of getting it. But he told me to tell you that if he didn't call, you were not to be angry with him.'

'Oh, no;—I shall remember, of course.'

'You see, if he don't work now he must come to grief. He hasn't got a shilling that he can call his own.'

'Hasn't he really?'

'Not a shilling, Mrs. Greenow;—and then he's awfully in debt. He isn't a bad fellow, you know, only there's no trusting him for anything.' Then after a few further inquiries that were almost tender, and a promise of further supplies from the dairy, Mr. Cheesacre took his leave, almost forgetting to ask after Miss Vavasor.

But as he left the house he had a word to say to Jeannette. 'He hasn't been here, has he, Jenny?' 'We haven't seen a sight of him yet, sir,—and I have thought it a little odd.' Then Mr. Cheesacre gave the girl half-a-crown, and went his way. Jeannette, I think, must have forgotten that the Captain had looked in after leaving his military duties on the preceding evening.

The Captain's ten or twelve hours of daily work was performed, no doubt, at irregular intervals,—some days late and some days early,—for he might be seen about Norwich almost at all times, during the early part of that November;—and he might be very often seen going into the Close. In Norwich there are two weekly market-days, but on those days the Captain was no doubt kept more entirely to his military employment, for at such times he never was seen near the Close. Now Mr. Cheesacre's visits to the town were generally made on market-days, and so it happened that they did not meet. On such occasions Mr. Cheesacre always was driven to Mrs. Greenow's door in a cab,—for he would come into town by railway,—and he would deposit a basket bearing the rich produce of his dairy. It was in vain that Mrs. Greenow protested against these gifts,—for she did protest and declared that if they were continued, they would be sent back. They were, however, continued, and Mrs. Greenow was at her wits' end about them. Cheesacre would not come up with them; but leaving them, would go about his business, and would return to see the ladies. On such occasions he would be very particular in getting his basket from Jeannette. As he did so he would generally ask some question about the Captain, and Jeannette would give him answers confidentially,—so that there was a strong friendship between these two.

'What am I to do about it?' said Mrs. Greenow, as Kate came into the sitting-room one morning, and saw on the table a small hamper lined with a clean cloth. 'It's as much as Jeannette has been able to carry.'

'So it is, ma'am,—quite; and I'm strong in the arm, too, ma'am.'

'What am I to do, Kate? He is such a good creature.'

'And he do admire you both so much,' said Jeannette.

'Of course I don't want to offend him for many reasons,' said the aunt, looking knowingly at her niece.

'I don't know anything about your reasons, aunt, but if I were you, I should leave the basket just as it is till he comes in the afternoon.'

'Would you mind seeing him yourself, Kate, and explaining to him that it won't do to go on in this way. Perhaps you wouldn't mind telling him that if he'll promise not to bring any more, you won't object to take this one.'

'Indeed, aunt, I can't do that. They're not brought to me.'

'Oh, Kate!'

'Nonsense, aunt;—I won't have you say so;—before Jeannette, too.'

'I think it's for both, ma'am; I do indeed. And there certainly ain't any cream to be bought like it in Norwich;—nor yet eggs.'

'I wonder what there is in the basket.' And the widow lifted up the corner of the cloth. 'I declare if there isn't a turkey poult already.'

'My!' said Jeannette. 'A turkey poult!*Why, that's worth ten and sixpence in the market if it's worth a penny.'

'It's out of the question that I should take upon myself to say anything to him about it,' said Kate.

'Upon my word I don't see why you shouldn't, as well as I,' said Mrs. Greenow.

'I'll tell you what, ma'am,' said Jeannette: 'let me just ask him who they're for;—he'll tell me anything.'

'Don't do anything of the kind, Jeannette,' said Kate. 'Of course, aunt, they're brought for you. There's no doubt about that. A gentleman doesn't bring cream and turkeys to—— I never heard of such a thing!'

'I don't see why a gentleman shouldn't bring cream and turkeys to you just as well as to me. Indeed, he told me once as much himself.'

'Then, if they're for me, I'll leave them down outside the front door, and he may find his provisions there.' And Kate proceeded to lift the basket off the table.

'Leave it alone, Kate,' said Mrs. Greenow, with a voice that was rather solemn; and which had, too, something of sadness in its tone. 'Leave it alone. I'll see Mr. Cheesacre myself.'

'And I do hope you won't mention my name. It's the most absurd thing in the world. The man never spoke two dozen words to me in his life.'

'He speaks to me, though,' said Mrs. Greenow.

'I dare say he does,' said Kate.

'And about you, too, my dear.'

'He doesn't come here with those big flowers in his button-hole for nothing,' said Jeannette,—'not if I knows what a gentleman means.'

'Of course he doesn't,' said Mrs. Greenow.

'If you don't object, aunt,' said Kate, 'I will write to grand-papa and tell him that I will return home at once.'

'What!—because of Mr. Cheesacre?' said Mrs. Greenow. 'I don't think you'll be so silly as that, my dear.'

On the present occasion Mrs. Greenow undertook that she would see the generous gentleman, and endeavour to stop the supplies from his farmyard. It was well understood that he would call about four o'clock, when his business in the town would be over; and that he would bring with him a little boy, who would carry away the basket. At that hour Kate of course was absent, and the widow received Mr. Cheesacre alone. The basket and cloth were there, in the sitting-room, and on the table were laid out the rich things which it had contained;— the turkey poult first, on a dish provided in the lodging-house, then a dozen fresh eggs in a soup-plate, then the cream in a little tin can, which, for the last fortnight, had passed regularly between Oileymead and the house in the Close, and as to which Mr. Cheesacre was very pointed in his inquiries with Jean-nette. Then behind the cream there were two or three heads of brocoli, and a stick of celery as thick as a man's wrist. Altogether the tribute was a very comfortable assistance to the housekeeping of a lady living in a small way in lodgings.

Mr. Cheesacre, when he saw the array on the long sofa-table, knew that he was to prepare himself for some resistance; but that resistance would give him, he thought, an opportunity of saying a few words that he was desirous of speaking, and he did not altogether regret it. 'I just called in,' he said, 'to see how you were.'

'We are not likely to starve,' said Mrs. Greenow, pointing to the delicacies from Oileymead.

'Just a few trifles that my old woman asked me to bring in,' said Cheesacre. 'She insisted on putting them up.'

'But your old woman is by far too magnificent,' said Mrs. Greenow. 'She really frightens Kate and me out of our wits.'

Mr. Cheesacre had no wish that Miss Vavasor's name should be brought into play upon the occasion. 'Dear Mrs. Greenow,' said he, 'there is no cause for you to be alarmed, I can assure you. Mere trifles;—light as air, you know. I don't think anything of such things as these.'

'But I and Kate think a great deal of them,—a very great deal, I can assure you. Do you know, we had a long debate this morning whether or no we would return them to Oiley-mead?'

'Return them, Mrs. Greenow!'

'Yes, indeed: what are women, situated as we are, to do under such circumstances? When gentlemen will be too liberal, their liberality must be repressed.'

'And have I been too liberal, Mrs. Greenow? What is a young turkey and a stick of celery when a man is willing to give everything that he has in the world?'

'You've got a great deal more in the world, Mr. Chees-acre, than you'd like to part with. But we won't talk of that, now.'

'When shall we talk of it?'

'If you really have anything to say, you had by far better speak to Kate herself.'

'Mrs. Greenow, you mistake me. Indeed you mistake me.' Just at this moment, as he was drawing close to the widow, she heard, or fancied that she heard, Jeannette's step, and, going to the sitting-room door, called to her maid. Jeannette did not hear her, but the bell was rung, and then Jeannette came. 'You may take these things down, Jeannette,' she said. 'Mr. Cheesacre has promised that no more shall come.'

'But I haven't promised,' said Mr. Cheesacre.

'You will oblige me and Kate, I know;—and, Jeannette, tell Miss Vavasor that I am ready to walk with her.'

Then Mr. Cheesacre knew that he could not say those few words on that occasion; and as the hour of his train was near, he took his departure, and went out of the Close, followed by the little boy, carrying the basket, the cloth, and the tin can.

CHAPTER XX

Which shall it be?

THE next day was Sunday, and it was well known at the lodging-house in the Close that Mr. Cheesacre would not be seen there then. Mrs. Greenow had specially warned him that she was not fond of Sunday visitors, fearing that otherwise he might find it convenient to give them too much of his society on that idle day. In the morning the aunt and niece both went to the Cathedral, and then at three o'clock they dined. But on this occasion they did not dine alone. Charlie Fairstairs, who, with her family, had come home from Yarmouth, had been asked to join them; and in order that Charlie might not feel it dull, Mrs. Greenow had, with her usual good-nature, invited Captain Bellfield. A very nice little dinner they had. The Captain carved the turkey, giving due honour to Mr. Cheesacre as he did so; and when he nibbled his celery with his cheese, he was prettily jocose about the richness of the farmyard at Oileymead.

'He is the most generous man I ever met,' said Mrs. Greenow.

'So he is,' said Captain Bellfield, 'and we'll drink his health. Poor old Cheesy! It's a great pity he shouldn't get himself a wife.'

'I don't know any man more calculated to make a young woman happy,' said Mrs. Greenow.

'No, indeed,' said Miss Fairstairs. 'I'm told that his house and all about it is quite beautiful.'

'Especially the straw-yard and the horse-pond,' said the Captain. And then they drank the health of their absent friend.

It had been arranged that the ladies should go to church in the evening, and it was thought that Captain Bellfield would, perhaps, accompany them; but when the time for starting came, Kate and Charlie were ready, but the widow was not, and she remained,—in order, as she afterwards explained to Kate, that Captain Bellfield might not seem to be turned out of the house.

He had made no offer churchwards, and,—'Poor man,' as Mrs. Greenow said in her little explanation, 'if I hadn't let him stay there, he would have had no resting-place for the sole of his foot, but some horrid barrack-room!' Therefore the Captain was allowed to find a resting-place in Mrs. Greenow's drawing-room; but on the return of the young ladies from church, he was not there, and the widow was alone, 'looking back,' she said, 'to things that were gone;—that were gone. But come, dears, I am not going to make you melancholy.' So they had tea, and Mr. Cheesacre's cream was used with liberality.

Captain Bellfield had not allowed the opportunity to slip idly from his hands. In the first quarter of an hour after the younger ladies had gone, he said little or nothing, but sat with a wine-glass before him, which once or twice he filled from the decanter. 'I'm afraid the wine is not very good,' said Mrs. Greenow. 'But one can't get good wine in lodgings.'

'I'm not thinking very much about it, Mrs. Greenow; that's the truth,' said the Captain. 'I daresay the wine is very good of its kind.' Then there was another period of silence between them.

'I suppose you find it rather dull, living in lodgings; don't you?' asked the Captain.

'I don't know quite what you mean by dull, Captain Bellfield; but a woman circumstanced as I am, can't find her life very gay. It's not a full twelvemonth yet, since I lost all that made life desirable, and sometimes I wonder at myself for holding up as well as I do.'

'It's wicked to give way to grief too much, Mrs. Greenow.'

'That's what my dear Kate always says to me, and I'm sure I do my best to overcome it.' Upon this some soft tears trickled down her cheek, showing in their course that she at any rate used no paint in producing that freshness of colour which was one of her great charms. Then she pressed her handkerchief to her eyes, and removing it, smiled faintly on the Captain. 'I didn't intend to treat you to such a scene as this, Captain Bellfield.'

'There is nothing on earth, Mrs. Greenow, I desire so much, as permission to dry those tears.'

'Time alone can do that, Captain Bellfield;—time alone.'

'But cannot time be aided by love and friendship and affection?'

'By friendship, yes. What would life be worth without the solace of friendship?'

'And how much better is the warm glow of love?' Captain Bellfield, as he asked this question, deliberately got up, and moved his chair over to the widow's side. But the widow as deliberately changed her position to the corner of a sofa. The Captain did not at once follow her, nor did he in any way show that he was aware that she had fled from him.

'How much better is the warm glow of love?' he said again, contenting himself with looking into her face with all his eyes. He had hoped that he would have been able to press her hand by this time.

'The warm glow of love, Captain Bellfield, if you have ever felt it——'

'If I have ever felt it! Do I not feel it now, Mrs. Greenow? There can be no longer any mask kept upon my feelings. I never could restrain the yearnings of my heart when they have been strong.'

'Have they often been strong, Captain Bellfield?'

'Yes, often;—in various scenes of life; on the field of battle——'

'I did not know that you had seen active service.'

'What!—not on the plains of Zululand, when with fifty picked men I kept five hundred Caffres*at bay for seven weeks; —never knew the comfort of a bed, or a pillow to my head, for seven long weeks!'

'Not for seven weeks?' said Mrs. Greenow.

'No. Did I not see active service at Essequibo, on the burning coast of Guiana, when all the wild Africans from the woods rose up to destroy the colony; or again at the mouth of the Kitchyhomy River,*when I made good the capture of a slaver by my own hand and my own sword!'

'I really hadn't heard,' said Mrs. Greenow.

'Ah, I understand. I know. Cheesy is the best fellow in the

world in some respects, but he cannot bring himself to speak
well of a fellow behind his back. I know who has belittled me.
Who was the first to storm the heights of Inkerman?'*demanded the Captain, thinking in the heat of the moment that
he might as well be hung for a sheep as a lamb.

'But when you spoke of yearnings, I thought you meant
yearnings of a softer kind.'

'So I did. So I did. I don't know why I have been led away
to speak of deeds that are very seldom mentioned, at any rate
by myself. But I cannot bear that a slanderous backbiting tongue
should make you think that I have seen no service. I have
served her Majesty in the four quarters of the globe, Mrs.
Greenow; and now I am ready to serve you in any way in
which you will allow me to make my service acceptable.'
Whereupon he took one stride over to the sofa, and went down
upon his knees before her.

'But, Captain Bellfield, I don't want any services. Pray get
up, now; the girl will come in.'

'I care nothing for any girl. I am planted here till some
answer shall have been made to me; till some word shall have
been said that may give me a little hope.' Then he attempted
to get hold of her hand, but she put them behind her back and
shook her head. 'Arabella,' he said, 'will you not speak a word
to me?'

'Not a word, Captain Bellfield, till you get up; and I
won't have you call me Arabella. I am the widow of Samuel
Greenow, than whom no man was more respected where he
was known, and it is not fitting that I should be addressed in
that way.'

'But I want you to become my wife,—and then——'

'Ah, then indeed! But that then isn't likely to come. Get up,
Captain Bellfield, or I'll push you over and then ring the bell.
A man never looks so much like a fool as when he's kneeling
down,—unless he's saying his prayers, as you ought to be do-
ing now. Get up, I tell you. It's just half-past seven, and I told
Jeannette to come to me then.'

There was that in the widow's voice which made him get

up, and he rose slowly to his feet. 'You've pushed all the chairs about, you stupid man,' she said. Then in one minute she had restored the scattered furniture to their proper places, and had rung the bell. When Jeannette came she desired that tea might be ready by the time that the young ladies returned, and asked Captain Bellfield if a cup should be set for him. This he declined, and bade her farewell while Jeannette was still in the room. She shook hands with him without any sign of anger, and even expressed a hope that they might see him again before long.

'He's a very handsome man, is the Captain,' said Jeannette, as the hero of the Kitchyhomy River descended the stairs.

'You shouldn't think about handsome men, child,' said Mrs. Greenow.

'And I'm sure I don't,' said Jeannette. 'Not no more than anybody else; but if a man is handsome, ma'am, why, it stands to reason that he is handsome.'

'I suppose Captain Bellfield has given you a kiss and a pair of gloves.'

'As for gloves and such like, Mr. Cheesacre is much better for giving than the Captain; as we all know; don't we, ma'am? But in regard to kisses, they're presents as I never takes from anybody. Let everybody pay his debts. If the Captain ever gets a wife, let him kiss her.'

On the following Tuesday morning Mr. Cheesacre as usual called in the Close, but he brought with him no basket. He merely left a winter nosegay made of green leaves and laurestinus*flowers, and sent up a message to say that he should call at half-past three, and hoped that he might then be able to see Mrs. Greenow,—on particular business.

'That means you, Kate,' said Mrs. Greenow.

'No, it doesn't; it doesn't mean me at all. At any rate he won't see me.'

'I dare say it's me he wishes to see. It seems to be the fashionable plan now for gentlemen to make offers by deputy. If he says anything, I can only refer him to you, you know.'

'Yes, you can; you can tell him simply that I won't have him. But he is no more thinking of me than——'

'Than he is of me, you were going to say.'

'No, aunt; I wasn't going to say that at all.'

'Well, we shall see. If he does mean anything, of course you can please yourself; but I really think you might do worse.'

'But if I don't want to do at all?'

'Very well; you must have your own way. I can only tell you what I think.'

At half-past three o'clock punctually Mr. Cheesacre came to the door, and was shown up stairs. He was told by Jeannette that Captain Bellfield had looked in on the Sunday afternoon, but that Miss Fairstairs and Miss Vavasor had been there the whole time. He had not got on his black boots nor yet had his round topped hat. And as he did wear a new frock coat, and had his left hand thrust into a kid glove, Jeannette was quite sure that he intended business of some kind. With new boots, creaking loudly, he walked up into the drawing-room, and there he found the widow alone.

'Thanks for the flowers,' she said at once. 'It was so good of you to bring something that we could accept.'

'As for that,' said he, 'I don't see why you should scruple about a trifle of cream, but I hope that any such feeling as that will be over before long.' To this the widow made no answer, but she looked very sweetly on him as she bade him sit down.

He did sit down; but first he put his hat and stick carefully away in one corner, and then he pulled off his glove—somewhat laboriously, for his hand was warm. He was clearly prepared for great things. As he pushed up his hair with his hands there came from his locks an ambrosial perfume,—as of marrow-oil, and there was a fixed propriety of position of every hair of his whiskers, which indicated very plainly that he had been at a hairdresser's shop since he left the market. Nor do I believe that he had worn that coat when he came to the door earlier in the morning. If I were to say that he had called at his tailor's also, I do not think that I should be wrong.

'How goes everything at Oileymead?' said Mrs. Greenow,

seeing that her guest wanted some little assistance in leading off the conversation.

'Pretty well, Mrs. Greenow; pretty well. Everything will go very well if I am successful in the object which I have on hand to-day.'

'I'm sure I hope you'll be successful in all your undertakings.'

'In all my business undertakings I am, Mrs. Greenow. There isn't a shilling due on my land to e'er a bank in Norwich; and I haven't thrashed out a quarter of last year's corn yet, which is more than many of them can say. But there ain't many of them who don't have to pay rent, and so perhaps I oughtn't to boast.'

'I know that Providence has been very good to you, Mr. Cheesacre, as regards worldly matters.'

'And I haven't left it all to Providence, either. Those who do, generally go to the wall, as far as I can see. I'm always at work late and early, and I know when I get a profit out of a man's labour and when I don't, as well as though it was my only chance of bread and cheese.'

'I always thought you understood farming business, Mr. Cheesacre.'

'Yes, I do. I like a bit of fun well enough, when the time for it comes, as you saw at Yarmouth. And I keep my three or four hunters, as I think a country gentleman should; and I shoot over my own ground. But I always stick to my work. There are men, like Bellfield, who won't work. What do they come to? They're always borrowing.'

'But he has fought his country's battles, Mr. Cheesacre.'

'He fight! I suppose he's been telling you some of his old stories. He was ten years in the West Indies, and all his fighting was with the musquitoes.'

'But he was in the Crimea. At Inkerman, for instance——'

'He in the Crimea! Well, never mind. But do you inquire before you believe that story. But as I was saying, Mrs. Greenow, you have seen my little place at Oileymead.'

'A charming house. All you want is a mistress for it.'

'That's it; that's just it. All I want is a mistress for it. And there's only one woman on earth that I would wish to see in that position. Arabella Greenow, will you be that woman?' As he made the offer he got up and stood before her, placing his right hand upon his heart.

'I, Mr. Cheesacre!' she said.

'Yes, you. Who else? Since I saw you what other woman has been anything to me; or, indeed, I may say before? Since the first day I saw you I felt that there my happiness depended.'

'Oh, Mr. Cheesacre, I thought you were looking elsewhere.'

'No, no, no. There never was such a mistake as that. I have the highest regard and esteem for Miss Vavasor, but really——'

'Mr. Cheesacre, what am I to say to you?'

'What are you to say to me? Say that you'll be mine. Say that I shall be yours. Say that all I have at Oileymead shall be yours. Say that the open carriage for a pair of ponies to be driven by a lady which I have been looking at this morning shall be yours. Yes, indeed; the sweetest thing you ever saw in your life,—just like one that the lady of the Lord Lieutenant drives about in always. That's what you must say. Come, Mrs. Greenow!'

'Ah, Mr. Cheesacre, you don't know what it is to have buried the pride of your youth hardly yet twelve months.'

'But you have buried him, and there let there be an end of it. Your sitting here all alone, morning, noon, and night, won't bring him back. I'm sorry for him; I am indeed. Poor Greenow! But what more can I do?'

'I can do more, Mr. Cheesacre. I can mourn for him in solitude and in silence.'

'No, no, no. What's the use of it,—breaking your heart for nothing,—and my heart too? You never think of that.' And Mr. Cheesacre spoke in a tone that was full of reproach.

'It cannot be, Mr. Cheesacre.'

'Ah, but it can be. Come, Mrs. Greenow. We understand each other well enough now, surely. Come, dearest.' And he approached her as though to put his arm round her waist. But at that moment there came a knock at the door, and Jeannette, entering the room, told her mistress that Captain Bellfield was below, and wanted to know whether he could see her for a minute on particular business.

'Show Captain Bellfield up, certainly,' said Mrs. Greenow.

'D—— Captain Bellfield!' said Mr. Cheesacre.

CHAPTER XXI

Alice is taught to grow Upwards, towards the Light

BEFORE the day came on which Alice was to go to Matching Priory, she had often regretted that she had been induced to make the promise, and yet she had as often resolved that there was no possible reason why she should not go to Matching Priory. But she feared this commencement of a closer connexion with her great relations. She had told herself so often that she was quite separated from them, that the slight accident of blood in no way tied her to them or them to her,—this lesson had been so thoroughly taught to her by the injudicious attempts of Lady Macleod to teach an opposite lesson, that she did not like the idea of putting aside the effect of that teaching. And perhaps she was a little afraid of the great folk whom she might probably meet at her cousin's house. Lady Glencora herself she had liked,—and had loved too with that momentary love which certain circumstances of our life will sometimes produce, a love which is strong while it lasts, but which can be laid down when the need of it is passed. She had liked and loved Lady Glencora, and had in no degree been afraid of her during those strange visitings in Queen Anne Street;—but she was by no means sure that she should like Lady Glencora in the midst of her grandeur and surrounded by the pomp of her rank. She would have no other friend or acquaintance in that house, and feared that she might find herself desolate, cold, and wounded in her pride. She had been tricked into the visit, too, or rather had tricked herself into it. She had been sure that there had been a joint scheme between her cousin and Lady Midlothian, and could not resist the temptation of repudiating it in her letter to Lady Glencora. But there had been no such scheme; she had wronged Lady Glencora, and had therefore been unable to resist her second request. But she felt unhappy, fearing that she would be out of her element, and more than once half made up her mind to excuse herself.

Her aunt had, from the first, thought well of her going, believing that it might probably be the means of reconciling her to Mr. Grey. Moreover, it was a step altogether in the right direction. Lady Glencora would, if she lived, become a Duchess, and as she was decidedly Alice's cousin, of course Alice should go to her house when invited. It must be acknowledged that Lady Macleod was not selfish in her worship of rank. She had played out her game in life, and there was no probability that she would live to be called cousin by a Duchess of Omnium. She bade Alice go to Matching Priory, simply because she loved her niece, and therefore wished her to live in the best and most eligible way within her reach. 'I think you owe it as a duty to your family to go,' said Lady Macleod.

What further correspondence about her affairs had passed between Lady Macleod and Lady Midlothian Alice never knew. She steadily refused all entreaty made that she would answer the Countess's letter, and at last threatened her aunt that if the request were further urged she would answer it,—telling Lady Midlothian that she had been very impertinent.

'I am becoming a very old woman, Alice,' the poor lady said, piteously, 'and I suppose I had better not interfere any further. Whatever I have said I have always meant to be for your good.' Then Alice got up, and kissing her aunt, tried to explain to her that she resented no interference from her, and felt grateful for all that she both said and did; but that she could not endure meddling from people whom she did not know, and who thought themselves entitled to meddle by their rank.

'And because they are cousins as well,' said Lady Macleod, in a softly sad, apologetic voice.

Alice left Cheltenham about the middle of November on her road to Matching Priory. She was to sleep in London one night, and go down to Matching in Yorkshire with her maid on the following day. Her father undertook to meet her at the Great Western Station, and to take her on the following morning to the Great Northern.* He said nothing in his letter about dining with her, but when he met her, muttered something about an engagement, and taking her home graciously promised that he would breakfast with her on the following morning.

'I'm very glad you are going, Alice,' he said when they were in the cab together.

'Why, papa?'

'Why?—because I think it's the proper thing to do. You know I've never said much to you about these people. They're not connected with me, and I know that they hate the name of Vavasor;—not but what the name is a deal older than any of theirs, and the family too.'

'And therefore I don't understand why you think I'm specially right. If you were to say I was specially wrong, I should be less surprised, and of course I shouldn't go.'

'You should go by all means. Rank and wealth are advantages, let anybody say what they will to the contrary. Why else does everybody want to get them?'

'But I shan't get them by going to Matching Priory.'

'You'll get part of their value. Take them as a whole, the nobility of England are pleasant acquaintances to have. I haven't run after them very much myself, though I married, as I may say, among them. That very thing rather stood in my way than otherwise. But you may be sure of this, that men and women ought to grow, like plants, upwards. Everybody should endeavour to stand as well as he can in the world, and if I had a choice of acquaintance between a sugar-baker and a peer, I should prefer the peer,—unless, indeed, the sugar-baker had something very strong on his side to offer. I don't call that tuft-hunting,* and it does not necessitate toadying. It's simply growing up, towards the light, as the trees do.'

Alice listened to her father's worldly wisdom with a smile,

but she did not attempt to answer him. It was very seldom, indeed, that he took upon himself the labour of lecturing her, or that he gave her even as much counsel as he had given now. 'Well, papa, I hope I shall find myself growing towards the light,' she said as she got out of the cab. Then he had not entered the house, but had taken the cab on with him to his club.

On her table Alice found a note from her cousin George. 'I hear you are going down to the Pallisers at Matching Priory to-morrow, and as I shall be glad to say one word to you before you go, will you let me see you this evening,—say at nine?—G. V.' She felt immediately that she could not help seeing him, but she greatly regretted the necessity. She wished that she had gone directly from Cheltenham to the North,— regardless even of those changes of wardrobe which her purposed visit required. Then she set herself to considering. How had George heard of her visit to the Priory, and how had he learned the precise evening which she would pass in London? Why should he be so intent on watching all her movements as it seemed that he was? As to seeing him she had no alternative, so she completed her arrangements for her journey before nine, and then awaited him in the drawing-room.

'I'm so glad you're going to Matching Priory,' were the first words he said. He, too, might have taught her to grow towards the light, if she had asked him for his reasons;—but this she did not do just then.

'How did you learn that I was going?' she said.

'I heard it from a friend of mine. Well;—from Burgo Fitzgerald, if you must know.'

'From Mr. Fitzgerald?' said Alice, in profound astonish-' ment. 'How could Mr. Fitzgerald have heard of it?'

'That's more than I know, Alice. Not directly from Lady Glencora, I should say.'

'That would be impossible.'

'Yes; quite so, no doubt. I think she keeps up her intimacy with Burgo's sister, and perhaps it got round to him in that way.'

'And did he tell you also that I was going to-morrow? He must have known all about it very accurately.'

'No; then I asked Kate, and Kate told me when you were going. Yes; I know. Kate has been wrong, hasn't she? Kate was cautioned, no doubt, to say nothing about your comings and goings to so inconsiderable a person as myself. But you must not be down upon Kate. She never mentioned it till I showed by my question to her that I knew all about your journey to Matching. I own I do not understand why it should be necessary to keep me so much in the dark.'

Alice felt that she was blushing. The caution had been given to Kate because Kate still transgressed in her letters, by saying little words about her brother. And Alice did not even now believe Kate to have been false to her; but she saw that she herself had been imprudent.

'I cannot understand it,' continued George, speaking without looking at her. 'It was but the other day that we were such dear friends! Do you remember the balcony at Basle? and now it seems that we are quite estranged;—nay, worse than estranged; that I am, as it were, under some ban. Have I done anything to offend you, Alice? If so, speak out, like a woman of spirit as you are.'

'Nothing,' said Alice.

'Then why am I tabooed? Why was I told the other day that I might not congratulate you on your happy emancipation? I say boldly, that had you resolved on that while we were together in Switzerland, you would have permitted me, as a friend, almost as a brother, to discuss it with you.'

'I think not, George.'

'I am sure you would. And why has Kate been warned not to tell me of this visit to the Pallisers? I know she has been warned though she has not confessed it.'

Alice sat silent, not knowing what to say in answer to this charge brought against her,—thinking, perhaps, that the questioner would allow his question to pass without an answer. But Vavasor was not so complaisant. 'If there be any reason, Alice, I think that I have a right to ask it.'

For a few seconds she did not speak a word, but sat considering. He also remained silent with his eyes fixed upon her. She looked at him and saw nothing but his scar,—nothing but his scar and the brightness of his eyes, which was almost fierce. She knew that he was in earnest, and therefore resolved that she would be in earnest also. 'I think that you have such a right,' she said at last.

'Then let me exercise it.'

'I think that you have such a right, but I think also that you are ungenerous to exercise it.'

'I cannot understand that. By heavens, Alice, I cannot be left in this suspense! If I have done anything to offend you, perhaps I can remove the offence by apology.'

'You have done nothing to offend me.'

'Or if there be any cause why our friendship should be dropped,—why we should be on a different footing to each other in London than we were in Switzerland, I may acknowledge it, if it be explained to me. But I cannot put up with the doubt, when I am told that I have a right to demand its solution.'

'Then I will be frank with you, George, though my being so will, as you may guess, be very painful.' She paused again, looking at him to see if yet he would spare her; but he was all scar and eyes as before, and there was no mercy in his face.

'Your sister, George, has thought that my parting with Mr. Grey might lead to a renewal of a purpose of marriage between you and me. You know her eagerness, and will understand that it may have been necessary that I should require silence from her on that head. You ought now to understand it all.'

'I then am being punished for her sins,' he said; and suddenly the scar on his face was healed up again, and there was something of the old pleasantness in his eyes.

'I have said nothing about any sins, George, but I have found it necessary to be on my guard.'

'Well,' he said, after a short pause, 'you are an honest

woman, Alice,—the honestest I ever knew. I will bring Kate to order,—and, now, we may be friends again; may we not?' And he extended his hand to her across the table.

'Yes,' she said, 'certainly; if you wish it.' She spoke doubtingly, with indecision in her voice, as though remembering at the moment that he had given her no pledge. 'I certainly do wish it very much,' said he; and then she gave him her hand.

'And I may now talk about your new freedom?'

'No,' said she; 'no. Do not speak of that. A woman does not do what I have done in that affair without great suffering. I have to think of it daily; but do not make me speak of it.'

'But this other subject, this visit to Matching; surely I may speak of that?' There was something now in his voice so bright, that she felt the influence of it, and answered him cheerfully, 'I don't see what you can have to say about it.'

'But I have a great deal. I am so glad you are going. Mind you cement a close intimacy with Mr. Palliser.'

'With Mr. Palliser?'

'Yes; with Mr. Palliser. You must read all the blue books* about finance. I'll send them to you if you like it.'

'Oh, George!'

'I'm quite in earnest. That is, not in earnest about the blue books, as you would not have time; but about Mr. Palliser. He will be the new Chancellor of the Exchequer without a doubt.'

'Will he indeed? But why should I make a bosom friend of the Chancellor of the Exchequer? I don't want any public money.'

'But I do, my girl. Don't you see?'

'No; I don't.'

'I think I shall get returned at this next election.'

'I'm sure I hope you will.'

'And if I do, of course it will be my game to support the ministry;—or rather the new ministry; for of course there will be changes.'

'I hope they will be on the right side.'

'Not a doubt of that, Alice.'

'I wish they might be changed altogether.'

'Ah! that's impossible. It's very well as a dream; but there are no such men as you want to see,—men really from the people,—strong enough to take high office. A man can't drive four horses because he's a philanthropist,—or rather a phil-horseophist, and is desirous that the team should be driven without any hurt to them. A man can't govern well, simply because he is genuinely anxious that men should be well governed.'

'And will there never be any such men?'

'I won't say that. I don't mind confessing to you that it is my ambition to be such a one myself. But a child must crawl before he can walk. Such a one as I, hoping to do something in politics, must spare no chance. It would be something to me that Mr. Palliser should become the friend of any dear friend of mine,—especially of a dear friend bearing the same name.'

'I'm afraid, George, you'll find me a bad hand at making any such friendship.'

'They say he is led immensely by his wife, and that she is very clever. But I mean this chiefly, Alice, that I do hope I shall have all your sympathy in any political career that I may make, and all your assistance also.'

'My sympathy I think I can promise you. My assistance, I fear, would be worthless.'

'By no means worthless, Alice; not if I see you take that place in the world which I hope to see you fill. Do you think women now-a-days have no bearing upon the politics of the times? Almost as much as men have.' In answer to which Alice shook her head; but, nevertheless, she felt in some way pleased and flattered.

George left her without saying a word more about her marriage prospects past or future, and Alice as she went to bed felt glad that this explanation between them had been made.

CHAPTER XXII

Dandy and Flirt

ALICE reached the Matching Road Station about three o'clock in the afternoon without adventure, and immediately on the stopping of the train became aware that all trouble was off her own hands. A servant in livery came to the open window, and touching his hat to her, inquired if she were Miss Vavasor. Then her dressing-bag and shawls and cloaks were taken from her, and she was conveyed through the station by the station-master on one side of her, the footman on the other, and by the railway porter behind. She instantly perceived that she had become possessed of great privileges by belonging even for a time to Matching Priory, and that she was essentially growing upwards towards the light.

Outside, on the broad drive before the little station, she saw an omnibus that was going to the small town of Matching, intended for people who had not grown upwards as had been her lot; and she saw also a light stylish-looking cart which she would have called a Whitechapel*had she been properly instructed in such matters, and a little low open carriage with two beautiful small horses, in which was sitting a lady enveloped in furs. Of course this was Lady Glencora. Another

222

servant was standing on the ground, holding the horses of the
carriage and the cart.

'Dear Alice, I'm so glad you've come,' said a voice from the
furs. 'Look here, dear; your maid can go in the dog-cart with
your things,'—it wasn't a dog-cart, but Lady Glencora knew
no better;—'she'll be quite comfortable there; and do you get
in here. Are you very cold?'

'Oh, no; not cold at all.'

'But it is awfully cold. You've been in the stuffy carriage,
but you'll find it cold enough out here, I can tell you.'

'Oh! Lady Glencora, I am so sorry that I've brought you
out on such a morning,' said Alice, getting in and taking the
place assigned her next to the charioteer.

'What nonsense! Sorry! Why, I've looked forward to meeting you all alone, ever since I knew you were coming. If it
had snowed all the morning I should have come just the same.
I drive out almost every day when I'm down here,—that is,
when the house is not too crowded, or I can make an excuse.
Wrap these things over you; there are plenty of them. You
shall drive if you like.' Alice, however, declined the driving,
expressing her gratitude in what prettiest words she could find.

'I like driving better than anything, I think. Mr. Palliser
doesn't like ladies to hunt, and of course it wouldn't do as he
does not hunt himself. I do ride, but he never gets on horseback. I almost fancy I should like to drive four-in-hand,—only
I know I should be afraid.'

'It would look very terrible,' said Alice.

'Yes; wouldn't it? The look would be the worst of it; as it is
all the world over. Sometimes I wish there were no such things
as looks. I don't mean anything improper, you know; only one
does get so hampered, right and left, for fear of Mrs. Grundy.*
I endeavour to go straight, and get along pretty well on the
whole, I suppose. Baker, you must put Dandy in the bar; he
pulls so, going home, that I can't hold him in the check.' She
stopped the horses, and Baker, a very completely-got-up groom
of some forty years of age, who sat behind, got down and put
the impetuous Dandy 'in the bar,' thereby changing the rein,

so that the curb was brought to bear on him. 'They're called Dandy and Flirt,' continued Lady Glencora, speaking to Alice. 'Ain't they a beautiful match? The Duke gave them to me and named them himself. Did you ever see the Duke?'

'Never,' said Alice.

'He won't be here before Christmas, but you shall be introduced some day in London. He's an excellent creature and I'm a great pet of his; though, after all, I never speak half a dozen words to him when I see him. He's one of those people who never talk. I'm one of those who like talking, as you'll find out. I think it runs in families; and the Pallisers are non-talkers. That doesn't mean that they are not speakers, for Mr. Palliser has plenty to say in the House, and they declare that he's one of the few public men who've got lungs enough to make a financial statement without breaking down.'

Alice was aware that she had as yet hardly spoken herself, and began to bethink herself that she didn't know what to say. Had Lady Glencora paused on the subject of Dandy and Flirt, she might have managed to be enthusiastic about the horses, but she could not discuss freely the general silence of the Palliser family, nor the excellent lungs, as regarded public purposes, of the one who was the husband of her present friend. So she asked how far it was to Matching Priory.

'You're not tired of me already, I hope,' said Lady Glencora.

'I didn't mean that,' said Alice. 'I delight in the drive. But somehow one expects Matching Station to be near Matching.'

'Ah, yes; that's a great cheat. It's not Matching Station at all, but Matching Road Station, and it's eight miles. It is a great bore, for though the omnibus brings our parcels, we have to be constantly sending over, and it's very expensive, I can assure you. I want Mr. Palliser to have a branch,* but he says he would have to take all the shares himself, and that would cost more, I suppose.'

'Is there a town at Matching?'

'Oh, a little bit of a place. I'll go round by it if you like, and in at the further gate.'

'Oh, no!' said Alice.

'Ah, but I should like. It was a borough once, and belonged to the Duke; but they put it out at the Reform Bill.* They made some kind of bargain;—he was to keep either Silverbridge or Matching, but not both. Mr. Palliser sits for Silverbridge, you know. The Duke chose Silverbridge,—or rather his father did, as he was then going to build his great place in Barsetshire;—that's near Silverbridge. But the Matching people haven't forgiven him yet. He was sitting for Matching himself when the Reform Bill passed. Then his father died, and he hasn't lived here much since. It's a great deal nicer place than Gatherum Castle, only not half so grand. I hate grandeur; don't you?'

'I've never tried much of it, as you have.'

'Come now; that's not fair. There's no one in the world less grand than I am.'

'I mean that I've not had grand people about me.'

'Having cut all your cousins,—and Lady Midlothian in particular, like a naughty girl as you are. I was so angry with you when you accused me of selling you about that. You ought to have known that I was the last person in the world to have done such a thing.'

'I did not think you meant to sell me, but I thought——'

'Yes, you did, Alice. I know what you thought; you thought that Lady Midlothian was making a tool of me that I might bring you under her thumb, so that she might bully you into Mr. Grey's arms. That's what you thought. I don't know that I was at all entitled to your good opinion, but I was not entitled to that special bad opinion.'

'I had no bad opinion;—but it was so necessary that I should guard myself.'

'You shall be guarded. I'll take you under my shield. Mr. Grey shan't be named to you, except that I shall expect you to tell me all about it; and you must tell me all about that dangerous cousin, too, of whom they were saying such terrible things down in Scotland. I had heard of him before.' These last words Lady Glencora spoke in a lower voice and in an altered tone,—slowly, as though she were thinking of something that pained her. It was from Burgo Fitzgerald that she had heard of George Vavasor.

Alice did not know what to say. She found it impossible to discuss all the most secret and deepest of her feelings out in that open carriage, perhaps in the hearing of the servant behind, on this her first meeting with her cousin,—of whom, in fact, she knew very little. She had not intended to discuss these things at all, and certainly not in such a manner as this. So she remained silent. 'This is the beginning of the park,' said Lady Glencora, pointing to a grand old ruin of an oak tree, which stood on the wide margin of the road, outside the rounded corner of the park palings, propped up with a skeleton of supporting sticks all round it. 'And that is Matching oak, under which Cœur de Lion or Edward the Third, I forget which, was met by Sir Guy de Palisere as he came from the war, or from hunting, or something of that kind. It was the king, you know, who had been fighting or whatever it was, and Sir Guy entertained him when he was very tired. Jeffrey Palliser, who is my husband's cousin, says that old Sir Guy luckily pulled out his brandy-flask. But the king immediately gave him all the lands of Matching,—only there was a priory then and a lot of monks, and I don't quite understand how that was. But I know one of the younger brothers always used to be abbot and sit in the House of Lords. And the king gave him Littlebury at the same time, which is about seven miles away from here. As Jeffrey Palliser says, it was a great deal of money for a pull at his flask. Jeffrey Palliser is here now, and I hope you'll like him. If I have no child, and Mr. Palliser were not to marry again, Jeffrey would be the heir.' And here again her voice was low and slow, and altogether changed in its tone.

'I suppose that's the way most of the old families got their estates.'

'Either so, or by robbery. Many of them were terrible thieves, my dear, and I dare say Sir Guy was no better than he should be. But since that they have always called some of the Pallisers Plantagenet. My husband's name is Plantagenet. The Duke is called George Plantagenet and the king was his godfather. The queen is my godmother, I believe, but I don't know that I'm much the better for it. There's no use in god-fathers and godmothers;—do you think there is?'

'Not much as it's managed now.'

'If I had a child,—Oh, Alice, it's a dreadful thing not to have a child when so much depends on it!'

'But you're such a short time married yet.'

'Ah, well; I can see it in his eyes when he asks me questions; but I don't think he'd say an unkind word, not if his own posi-tion depended on it. Ah, well; this is Matching. That other gate we passed, where Dandy wanted to turn in,—that's where we usually go up, but I've brought you round to show you the town. That's the inn,—whoever can possibly come to stay there I don't know; I never saw anybody go in or out. That's the baker who bakes our bread,—we baked it at the house at first, but nobody could eat it; and I know that that man there mends Mr. Palliser's shoes. He's very particular about his shoes. We shall see the church as we go in at the other gate. It is in the park, and is very pretty,—but not half so pretty as the priory ruins close to the house. The ruins are our great lion. I do so love to wander about them at moonlight. I often think of you when I do; I don't know why.—But I do know why, and I'll tell you some day. Come, Miss Flirt!'

As they drove up through the park, Lady Glencora pointed out first the church and then the ruins, through the midst of which the road ran, and then they were at once before the front door. The corner of the modern house came within two hundred yards of the gateway of the old priory. It was a large building, very pretty, with two long fronts; but it was no more than a house. It was not a palace, nor a castle, nor was it hardly to be called a mansion. It was built with gabled roofs, four of which formed the side from which the windows of the drawing-rooms opened out upon a lawn which separated the house from the old ruins, and which indeed surrounded the ruins, and went inside them, forming the present flooring of the old chapel, and the old refectory, and the old cloisters. Much of the cloisters indeed was standing, and there the stone pavement remained;

but the square of the cloisters was all turfed, and in the middle
of it stood a large modern stone vase, out of the broad basin
of which hung flowering creepers and green tendrils.

As Lady Glencora drove up to the door, a gentleman, who
had heard the sound of the wheels, came forth to meet them.
'There's Mr. Palliser,' said she; 'that shows that you are an
honoured guest, for you may be sure that he is hard at work
and would not have come out for anybody else. Plantagenet,
here is Miss Vavasor, perished. Alice, my husband.' Then Mr.
Palliser put forth his hand and helped her out of the carriage.

'I hope you've not found it very cold,' said he. 'The winter
has come upon us quite suddenly.'

He said nothing more to her than this, till he met her again
before dinner. He was a tall thin man, apparently not more
than thirty years of age, looking in all respects like a gentleman, but with nothing in his appearance that was remarkable.
It was a face that you might see and forget, and see again and
forget again; and yet when you looked at it and pulled it to
pieces, you found that it was a fairly good face, showing intellect in the forehead, and much character in the mouth. The
eyes too, though not to be called bright, had always something
to say for themselves, looking as though they had a real meaning. But the outline of the face was almost insignificant, being
too thin; and he wore no beard to give it character. But, indeed, Mr. Palliser was a man who had never thought of assisting his position in the world by his outward appearance. Not
to be looked at, but to be read about in the newspapers, was
his ambition. Men said that he was to be Chancellor of the
Exchequer, and no one thought of suggesting that the insignifi-
cance of his face would stand in his way.

'Are the people all out?' his wife asked him.

'The men have not come in from shooting;—at least I think
not;—and some of the ladies are driving, I suppose. But I
haven't seen anybody since you went.'

'Of course you haven't. He never has time, Alice, to see any
one. But we'll go up stairs, dear. I told them to let us have tea
in my dressing-room, as I thought you'd like that better than

going into the drawing-room before you had taken off your
things. You must be famished, I know. Then you can come
down, or if you want to avoid two dressings you can sit over
the fire up stairs till dinner-time.' So saying she skipped up
stairs and Alice followed her. 'Here's my dressing-room, and

here's your room all but opposite. You look out into the park.
It's pretty, isn't it? But come into my dressing-room, and see
the ruins out of the window.'

Alice followed Lady Glencora across the passage into what
she called her dressing-room, and there found herself surrounded by an infinitude of feminine luxuries. The prettiest
of tables were there;—the easiest of chairs;—the most costly of
cabinets;—the quaintest of old china ornaments. It was bright
with the gayest colours,—made pleasant to the eye with the
binding of many books, having nymphs painted on the ceiling
and little Cupids on the doors. 'Isn't it pretty?' she said, turning quickly on Alice. 'I call it my dressing-room because in
that way I can keep people out of it, but I have my brushes and
soap in a little closet there, and my clothes,—my clothes are

everywhere I suppose, only there are none of them here. Isn't it pretty?'

'Very pretty.'

'The Duke did it all. He understands such things thoroughly. Now to Mr. Palliser a dressing-room is a dressing-room, and a bedroom a bedroom. He cares for nothing being pretty; not even his wife, or he wouldn't have married me.'

'You wouldn't say that if you meant it.'

'Well, I don't know. Sometimes when I look at myself, when I simply am myself, with no making up or grimacing, you know, I think I'm the ugliest young woman the sun ever shone on. And in ten years' time I shall be the ugliest old woman. Only think,—my hair is beginning to get gray, and I'm not twenty-one yet. Look at it;' and she lifted up the wavy locks just above her ear. 'But there's one comfort; he doesn't care about beauty. How old are you?'

'Over five-and-twenty,' said Alice.

'Nonsense;—then I oughtn't to have asked you. I am so sorry.'

'That's nonsense at any rate. Why should you think I should be ashamed of my age?'

'I don't know why, only, somehow, people are; and I didn't think you were so old. Five-and-twenty seems so old to me. It would be nothing if you were married; only, you see, you won't get married.'

'Perhaps I may yet; some day.'

'Of course you will. You'll have to give way. You'll find that they'll get the better of you. Your father will storm at you, and Lady Macleod will preach at you, and Lady Midlothian will jump upon you.'

'I'm not a bit afraid of Lady Midlothian.'

'I know what it is, my dear, to be jumped upon. We talk with such horror of the French people giving their daughters in marriage, just as they might sell a house or a field, but we do exactly the same thing ourselves. When they all come upon you in earnest how are you to stand against them? How can any girl do it?'

'I think I shall be able.'

'To be sure you're older,—and you are not so heavily weighted. But never mind; I didn't mean to talk about that;—not yet at any rate. Well, now, my dear, I must go down. The Duchess of St. Bungay is here, and Mr. Palliser will be angry if I don't do pretty to her. The Duke is to be the new President of the Council, or rather, I believe he is President now. I try to remember it all, but it is so hard when one doesn't really care two pence how it goes. Not but what I'm very anxious that Mr. Palliser should be Chancellor of the Exchequer. And now, will you remain here, or will you come down with me, or will you go to your own room, and I'll call for you when I go down to dinner? We dine at eight.'

Alice decided that she would stay in her own room till dinner time, and was taken there by Lady Glencora. She found her maid unpacking her clothes, and for a while employed herself in assisting at the work; but that was soon done, and then she was left alone. 'I shall feel so strange, ma'am, among all those people down stairs,' said the girl. 'They all seem to look at me as though they didn't know who I was.'

'You'll get over that soon, Jane.'

'I suppose I shall; but you see, they're all like knowing each other, miss.'

Alice, when she sat down alone, felt herself to be very much in the same condition as her maid. What would the Duchess of St. Bungay or Mr. Jeffrey Palliser,—who himself might live to be a duke if things went well for him,—care for her? As to Mr. Palliser, the master of the house, it was already evident to her that he would not put himself out of his way for her. Had she not done wrong to come there? If it were possible for her to fly away, back to the dulness of Queen Anne Street, or even to the preachings of Lady Macleod, would she not do so immediately? What business had she,—she asked herself,—to come to such a house as that? Lady Glencora was very kind to her, but frightened her even by her kindness. Moreover, she was aware that Lady Glencora could not devote herself especially to any such guest as she was. Lady Glencora must of course look after her duchesses, and do pretty, as she called it, to her husband's important political alliances.

And then she began to think about Lady Glencora herself. What a strange, weird creature she was,—with her round blue eyes and wavy hair, looking sometimes like a child and sometimes almost like an old woman! And how she talked! What things she said, and what terrible forebodings she uttered of stranger things that she meant to say! Why had she at their first meeting made that allusion to the mode of her own betrothal,—and then, checking herself for speaking of it so soon, almost declared that she meant to speak more of it hereafter? 'She should never mention it to any one,' said Alice to herself. 'If her lot in life has not satisfied her, there is so much the more reason why she should not mention it.' Then Alice protested to herself that no father, no aunt, no Lady Midlothian should persuade her into a marriage of which she feared the consequences. But Lady Glencora had made for herself excuses which were not altogether untrue. She had been very young, and had been terribly weighted with her wealth.

And it seemed to Alice that her cousin had told her everything in that hour and a half that they had been together. She had given a whole history of her husband and of herself. She had said how indifferent he was to her pleasures, and how vainly she strove to interest herself in his pursuits. And then, as yet, she was childless and without prospect of a child, when, as she herself had said,—'so much depended on it.' It was very strange to Alice that all this should have been already told to her. And why should Lady Glencora think of Alice when she walked out among the priory ruins by moonlight?

The two hours seemed to her very long,—as though she were passing her time in absolute seclusion at Matching. Of course she did not dare to go down stairs. But at last her maid came to dress her.

'How do you get on below, Jane?' her mistress asked her.

'Why, miss, they are uncommon civil, and I don't think after all it will be so bad. We had our teas very comfortable in the housekeeper's room. There are five or six of us altogether, all ladies'-maids, miss; and there's nothing on earth to do all the day long, only sit and do a little needlework over the fire.'

A few minutes before eight Lady Glencora knocked at Alice's door, and took her arm to lead her to the drawing-room. Alice saw that she was magnificently dressed, with an enormous expanse of robe, and that her locks had been so managed that no one could suspect the presence of a gray hair. Indeed, with all her magnificence, she looked almost a child. 'Let me see,' she said, as they went down stairs together. 'I'll tell Jeffrey to take you in to dinner. He's about the easiest young man we have here. He rather turns up his nose at everything, but that doesn't make him the less agreeable; does it, dear?—unless he turns up his nose at you, you know.'

'But perhaps he will.'

'No; he won't do that. That would be uncourteous,—and he's the most courteous man in the world. There's nobody here, you see,' she said as they entered the room, 'and I didn't suppose there would be. It's always proper to be first in one's own house. I do so try to be proper,—and it is such trouble. Talking of people earning their bread, Alice;—I'm sure I earn mine. Oh dear!—what fun it would be to be sitting somewhere in Asia, eating a chicken with one's fingers, and lighting a big fire outside one's tent to keep off the lions and tigers. Fancy your being on one side of the fire and the lions and tigers on the other, grinning at you through the flames!' Then Lady Glencora strove to look like a lion, and grinned at herself in the glass.

'That sort of grin wouldn't frighten me,' said Alice.

'I dare say not. I have been reading about it in that woman's travels. Oh, here they are, and I mustn't make any more faces. Duchess, do come to the fire. I hope you've got warm again. This is my cousin, Miss Vavasor.'

The Duchess made a stiff little bow of condescension, and then declared that she was charmingly warm. 'I don't know how you manage in your house, but the staircases are so comfortable. Now at Longroyston we've taken all the trouble in the world,—put down hot-water pipes all over the house, and everything else that could be thought of, and yet, you can't move about the place without meeting with draughts at every corner of the passages.' The Duchess spoke with an enormous emphasis on every other word, sometimes putting so great a stress on some special syllable, as almost to bring her voice to a whistle. This she had done with the word 'pipes' to a great degree,—so that Alice never afterwards forgot the hot-water pipes of Longroyston. 'I was telling Lady Glencora, Miss Palliser, that I never knew a house so warm as this,—or, I'm sorry to say,'—and here the emphasis was very strong on the word sorry,—'so cold as Longroyston.' And the tone in which Longroyston was uttered would almost have drawn tears from a critical audience in the pit of a playhouse. The Duchess was a woman of about forty, very handsome, but with no meaning in her beauty, carrying a good fixed colour in her face, which did not look like paint, but which probably had received some little assistance from art. She was a well-built, sizeable woman, with good proportions and fine health,—but a fool. She had addressed herself to one Miss Palliser; but two Miss Pallisers, cousins of Plantagenet Palliser, had entered the room at the same time, of whom I may say, whatever other traits of character they may have possessed, that at any rate they were not fools.

'It's always easy to warm a small house like this,' said Miss Palliser, whose Christian names, unfortunately for her, were Iphigenia Theodata, and who by her cousin and sister was called Iphy—'and I suppose equally difficult to warm a large one such as Longroyston.' The other Miss Palliser had been christened Euphemia.

'We've got no pipes, Duchess, at any rate,' said Lady Glencora; and Alice, as she sat listening, thought she discerned in Lady Glencora's pronunciation of the word pipes an almost hidden imitation of the Duchess's whistle. It must have been so, for at the moment Lady Glencora's eye met Alice's for an instant, and was then withdrawn, so that Alice was compelled to think that her friend and cousin was not always quite successful in those struggles she made to be proper.

Then the gentlemen came in one after another, and other ladies, till about thirty people were assembled. Mr. Palliser came up and spoke another word to Alice in a kind voice,— meant to express some sense of connection if not cousinship. 'My wife has been thinking so much of your coming. I hope we shall be able to amuse you.' Alice, who had already begun to feel desolate, was grateful, and made up her mind that she would try to like Mr. Palliser.

Jeffrey Palliser was almost the last in the room, but directly he entered Lady Glencora got up from her seat, and met him as he was coming into the crowd. 'You must take my cousin, Alice Vavasor, in to dinner,' she said, 'and;—will you oblige me to-day?'

'Yes;—as you ask me like that.'

'Then try to make her comfortable.' After that she introduced them, and Jeffrey Palliser stood opposite to Alice, talking to her, till dinner was announced.

CHAPTER XXIII

Dinner at Matching Priory

ALICE found herself seated near to Lady Glencora's end of the table, and, in spite of her resolution to like Mr. Palliser, she was not sorry that such an arrangement had been made. Mr. Palliser had taken the Duchess out to dinner, and Alice wished to be as far removed as possible from her Grace. She found herself seated between her bespoken friend Jeffrey Palliser and the Duke, and as soon as she was seated Lady Glencora introduced her to her second neighbour. 'My cousin, Duke,' Lady Glencora said, 'and a terrible Radical.'

'Oh, indeed; I'm glad of that. We're sadly in want of a few leading Radicals, and perhaps I may be able to gain one now.'

Alice thought of her cousin George, and wished that he, instead of herself, was sitting next to the Duke of St. Bungay. 'But I'm afraid I never shall be a leading Radical,' she said.

'You shall lead me at any rate, if you will,' said he.

'As the little dogs lead the blind men,' said Lady Glencora.

'No, Lady Glencora, not so. But as the pretty women lead the men who have eyes in their head. There is nothing I want so much, Miss Vavasor, as to become a Radical;—if I only knew how.'

'I think it's very easy to know how,' said Alice.

'Do you? I don't. I've voted for every Liberal measure that has come seriously before Parliament since I had a seat in either House, and I've not been able to get beyond Whiggery yet.'

'Have you voted for the ballot?' asked Alice, almost trembling at her own audacity as she put the question.

'Well; no, I've not. And I suppose that is the crux. But the ballot has never been seriously brought before any House in which I have sat. I hate it with so keen a private hatred, that I doubt whether I could vote for it.'

'But the Radicals love it,' said Alice.

'Palliser,' said the Duke, speaking loudly from his end of the table, 'I'm told you can never be entitled to call yourself a Radical till you've voted for the ballot.'

'I don't want to be called a Radical,' said Mr. Palliser,—'or to be called anything at all.'

'Except Chancellor of the Exchequer,' said Lady Glencora in a low voice.

'And that's about the finest ambition by which a man can be moved,' said the Duke. 'The man who can manage the purse-

strings of this country can manage anything.' Then that conversation dropped and the Duke ate his dinner.

'I was especially commissioned to amuse you,' said Mr.
Jeffrey Palliser to Alice. 'But when I undertook the task I had
no conception that you would be calling Cabinet Ministers
over the coals about their politics.'

'I did nothing of the kind, surely, Mr. Palliser. I suppose
all Radicals do vote for the ballot, and that's why I said it.'

'Your definition was perfectly just, I dare say, only——'

'Only what?'

'Lady Glencora need not have been so anxious to provide
specially for your amusement. Not but what I'm very much
obliged to her,—of course. But, Miss Vavasor, unfortunately
I'm not a politician. I haven't a chance of a seat in the House,
and so I despise politics.'

'Women are not allowed to be politicians in this country.'

'Thank God, they can't do much in that way;—not directly,
I mean. Only think where we should be if we had a feminine
House of Commons, with feminine debates, carried on, of
course, with feminine courtesy. My cousins Iphy and Phemy
there would of course be members. You don't know them yet?'

'No; not yet. Are they politicians?'

'Not especially. They have their tendencies, which are decidedly Liberal. There has never been a Tory Palliser known,
you know. But they are too clever to give themselves up to
anything in which they can do nothing. Being women they live
a depressed life, devoting themselves to literature, fine arts,
social economy, and the abstract sciences. They write wonderful letters; but I believe their correspondence lists are quite
full, so that you have no chance at present of getting on either
of them.'

'I haven't the slightest pretension to ask for such an honour.'

'Oh! if you mean because you don't know them, that has
nothing to do with it.'

'But I have no claim either private or public.'

'That has nothing to do with it either. They don't at all seek
people of note as their correspondents. Free communication

with all the world is their motto, and Rowland Hill*is the god they worship. Only they have been forced to guard themselves against too great an accession of paper and ink. Are you fond of writing letters, Miss Vavasor?'

'Yes, to my friends; but I like getting them better.'

'I shrewdly suspect they don't read half what they get. Is it possible any one should go through two sheets of paper filled by our friend the Duchess there? No; their delight is in writing. They sit each at her desk after breakfast, and go on till lunch. There is a little rivalry between them, not expressed to each other, but visible to their friends. Iphy certainly does get off the greater number, and I'm told crosses* quite as often as Phemy, but then she has the advantage of a bolder and a larger hand.'

'Do they write to you?'

'Oh, dear no. I don't think they ever write to any relative. They don't discuss family affairs and such topics as that. Architecture goes a long way with them, and whether women ought to be clerks in public offices. Iphy has certain American correspondents that take up much of her time, but she acknowledges she does not read their letters.'

'Then I certainly shall not write to her.'

'But you are not American, I hope. I do hate the Americans.* It's the only strong political feeling I have. I went there once, and found I couldn't live with them on any terms.'

'But they please themselves. I don't see they are to be hated because they don't live after our fashion.'

'Oh; it's jealousy of course. I know that. I didn't come across a cab-driver who wasn't a much better educated man than I am. And as for their women, they know everything. But I hated them, and I intend to hate them. You haven't been there?'

'Oh no.'

'Then I will make bold to say that any English lady who spent a month with them and didn't hate them would have very singular tastes. I begin to think they'll eat each other up, and then there'll come an entirely new set of people of a different sort. I always regarded the States as a Sodom and Gomorrah, prospering in wickedness, on which fire and brimstone were sure to fall sooner or later.'

'I think that's wicked.'

'I am wicked, as Topsy*used to say. Do you hunt?'

'No.'

'Do you shoot?'

'Shoot! What; with a gun?'

'Yes. I was staying in a house last week with a lady who shot a good deal.'

'No; I don't shoot.'

'Do you ride?'

'No; I wish I did. I have never ridden because I've no one to ride with me.'

'Do you drive?'

'No; I don't drive either.'

'Then what do you do?'

'I sit at home, and——'

'Mend your stockings?'

'No; I don't do that, because it's disagreeable; but I do work a good deal. Sometimes I have amused myself by reading.'

'Ah; they never do that here. I have heard that there is a library, but the clue to it has been lost, and nobody now knows the way. I don't believe in libraries. Nobody ever goes into a library to read, any more than you would into a larder to eat. But there is this difference;—the food you consume does come out of the larders, but the books you read never come out of the libraries.'

'Except Mudie's,*said Alice.

'Ah, yes; he is the great librarian. And you mean to read all the time you are here, Miss Vavasor?'

'I mean to walk about the priory ruins sometimes.'

'Then you must go by moonlight, and I'll go with you. Only isn't it rather late in the year for that?'

'I should think it is,—for you, Mr. Palliser.'

Then the Duke spoke to her again, and she found that she got on very well during dinner. But she could not but feel angry with herself in that she had any fear on the subject;—and yet she could not divest herself of that fear. She acknowledged to herself that she was conscious of a certain inferiority to Lady Glencora and to Mr. Jeffrey Palliser, which almost made her unhappy. As regarded the Duke on the other side of her, she had no such feeling. He was old enough to be her father, and was a Cabinet Minister; therefore he was entitled to her reverence. But how was it that she could not help accepting the other people round her as being indeed superior to herself? Was she really learning to believe that she could grow upwards by their sunlight?

'Jeffrey is a pleasant fellow, is he not?' said Lady Glencora to her as they passed back through the billiard-room to the drawing-room.

'Very pleasant;—a little sarcastic, perhaps.'

'I should think you would soon find yourself able to get the better of that if he tries it upon you,' said Lady Glencora; and then the ladies were all in the drawing-room together.

'It is quite deliciously warm, coming from one room to another,' said the Duchess, putting her emphasis on the 'one' and the 'other.'

'Then we had better keep continually moving,' said a certain Mrs. Conway Sparkes, a literary lady, who had been very handsome, who was still very clever, who was not perhaps very goodnatured, and of whom the Duchess of St. Bungay was rather afraid.

'I hope we may be warm here too,' said Lady Glencora.

'But not deliciously warm,' said Mrs. Conway Sparkes.

'It makes me tremble in every limb when Mrs. Sparkes attacks her,' Lady Glencora said to Alice in Alice's own room that night, 'for I know she'll tell the Duke; and he'll tell that tall man with red hair whom you see standing about, and the tall man with red hair will tell Mr. Palliser, and then I shall catch it.'

'And who is the tall man with red hair?'

'He's a political link between the Duke and Mr. Palliser. His name is Bott, and he's a Member of Parliament.'

'But why should he interfere?'

'I suppose it's his business. I don't quite understand all
the ins and outs of it. I believe he's to be one of Mr. Palliser's
private secretaries if he becomes Chancellor of the Exchequer.
Perhaps he doesn't tell;—only I think he does all the same.
He always calls me Lady Glen-cowrer. He comes out of Lancashire, and made calico as long as he could get any cotton.'*
But this happened in the bedroom, and we must go back for a
while to the drawing-room.

The Duchess had made no answer to Mrs. Sparkes, and so
nothing further was said about the warmth. Nor, indeed, was
there any conversation that was comfortably general. The number of ladies in the room was too great for that, and ladies do
not divide themselves nicely into small parties, as men and
women do when they are mixed. Lady Glencora behaved pretty
by telling the Duchess all about her pet pheasants; Mrs. Conway Sparkes told ill-natured tales of some one to Miss Euphemia
Palliser; one of the Duchess's daughters walked off to a distant piano with an admiring friend and touched a few notes;
while Iphigenia Palliser boldly took up a book, and placed herself at a table. Alice, who was sitting opposite to Lady Glencora, began to speculate whether she might do the same; but
her courage failed her, and she sat on, telling herself that she
was out of her element. 'Alice Vavasor,' said Lady Glencora
after a while, suddenly, and in a somewhat loud voice, 'can you
play billiards?'

'No,' said Alice, rather startled.

'Then you shall learn to-night, and if nobody else will teach
you, you shall be my pupil.' Whereupon Lady Glencora rang
the bell and ordered that the billiard-table might be got ready.
'You'll play, Duchess, of course,' said Lady Glencora.

'It is so nice and warm, that I think I will,' said the Duchess;
but as she spoke she looked suspiciously to that part of the
room where Mrs. Conway Sparkes was sitting.

'Let us all play,' said Mrs. Conway Sparkes, 'and then it
will be nicer,—and perhaps warmer, too.'

The gentlemen joined them just as they were settling themselves round the table, and as many of them stayed there, the

billiard-room became full. Alice had first a cue put into her hand, and making nothing of that was permitted to play with a mace.* The duty of instructing her devolved on Jeffrey Palliser, and the next hour passed pleasantly;—not so pleasantly, she thought afterwards, as did some of those hours in Switzerland when her cousins were with her. After all, she could get more out of her life with such associates as them, than she could with any of these people at Matching. She felt quite sure of that;—though Jeffrey Palliser did take great trouble to teach her the game, and once or twice made her laugh heartily by quizzing the Duchess's attitude as she stood up to make her stroke.

'I wish I could play billiards,' said Mrs. Sparkes, on one of these occasions; 'I do indeed.'

'I thought you said you were coming to play,' said the Duchess, almost majestically, and with a tone of triumph evidently produced by her own successes.

'Only to see your Grace,' said Mrs. Sparkes.

'I don't know that there is anything more to see in me than in anybody else,' said the Duchess. 'Mr. Palliser, that was a cannon.* Will you mark that for our side?'

'Oh no, Duchess, you hit the same ball twice.'

'Very well;—then I suppose Miss Vavasor plays now. That was a miss. Will you mark that, if you please?' This latter demand was made with great stress, as though she had been defrauded in the matter of the cannon, and was obeyed. Before long, the Duchess, with her partner, Lady Glencora, won the game,—which fact, however, was, I think, owing rather to Alice's ignorance than to her Grace's skill. The Duchess, however, was very triumphant, and made her way back into the drawing-room with a step which seemed to declare loudly that she had trumped Mrs. Sparkes at last.

Not long after this the ladies went up stairs on their way to bed. Many of them, perhaps, did not go to their pillows at once, as it was as yet not eleven o'clock, and it was past ten when they all came down to breakfast. At any rate, Alice, who had been up at seven, did not go to bed then, nor for the next

two hours. 'I'll come into your room just for one minute,' Lady
Glencora said as she passed on from the door to her own room;
and in about five minutes she was back with her cousin. 'Would
you mind going into my room—it's just there, and sitting with
Ellen for a minute?' This Lady Glencora said in the sweetest
possible tone to the girl who was waiting on Alice; and then,
when they were alone together, she got into a little chair by
the fireside and prepared herself for conversation.

'I must keep you up for a quarter of an hour while I tell you
something. But first of all, how do you like the people? Will
you be able to be comfortable with them?' Alice of course said
that she thought she would; and then there came that little
discussion in which the duties of Mr. Bott, the man with the
red hair, were described.

'But I've got something to tell you,' said Lady Glencora,
when they had already been there some twenty minutes. 'Sit
down opposite to me, and look at the fire while I look at
you.'

'Is it anything terrible?'

'It's nothing wrong.'

'Oh, Lady Glencora, if it's——'

'I won't have you call me Lady Glencora. Don't I call you
Alice? Why are you so unkind to me? I have not come to you
now asking you to do for me anything that you ought not
to do.'

'But you are going to tell me something.' Alice felt sure that
the thing to be told would have some reference to Mr. Fitzgerald, and she did not wish to hear Mr. Fitzgerald's name
from her cousin's lips.

'Tell you something;—of course I am. I'm going to tell you
that,—that in writing to you the other day I wrote a fib. But
it wasn't that I wished to deceive you;—only I couldn't say it
all in a letter.'

'Say all what?'

'You know I confessed that I had been very bad in not coming
to you in London last year.'

'I never thought of it for a moment.'

'You did not care whether I came or not; was that it? But never mind. Why should you have cared? But I cared. I told you in my letter that I didn't come because I had so many things on hand. Of course that was a fib.'

'Everybody makes excuses of that kind,' said Alice.

'But they don't make them to the very people of all others whom they want to know and love. I was longing to come to you every day. But I feared I could not come without speaking of him;—and I had determined never to speak of him again.' This she said in that peculiar low voice which she assumed at times.

'Then why do it now, Lady Glencora?'

'I won't be called Lady Glencora. Call me Cora. I had a sister once, older than I, and she used to call me Cora. If she had lived——. But never mind that now. She didn't live. I'll tell you why I do it now. Because I cannot help it. Besides, I've met him. I've been in the same room with him, and have spoken to him. What's the good of any such resolution now?'

'And you have met him?'

'Yes; he—Mr. Palliser—knew all about it. When he talked of taking me to the house, I whispered to him that I thought Burgo would be there.'

'Do not call him by his Christian name,' said Alice, almost with a shudder.

'Why not?—why not his Christian name? I did when I told my husband. Or perhaps I said Burgo Fitzgerald.'

'Well.'

'And he bade me go. He said it didn't signify, and that I had better learn to bear it. Bear it, indeed! If I am to meet him, and speak to him, and look at him, surely I may mention his name.' And then she paused for an answer. 'May I not?'

'What am I to say?' exclaimed Alice.

'Anything you please, that's not a falsehood. But I've got you here because I don't think you will tell a falsehood. Oh, Alice, I do so want to go right, and it is so hard!'

Hard, indeed, poor creature, for one so weighted as she had been, and sent out into the world with so small advantages of previous training or of present friendship! Alice began to feel now that she had been enticed to Matching Priory because her cousin wanted a friend, and of course she could not refuse to give the friendship that was asked from her. She got up from her chair, and kneeling down at the other's feet put up her face and kissed her.

'I knew you would be good to me,' said Lady Glencora. 'I knew you would. And you may say whatever you like. But I could not bear that you should not know the real reason why I neither came to you nor sent for you after we went to London. You'll come to me now; won't you, dear?'

'Yes;—and you'll come to me,' said Alice, making in her mind a sort of bargain that she was not to be received into Mr. Palliser's house after the fashion in which Lady Midlothian had proposed to receive her. But it struck her at once that this was unworthy of her, and ungenerous. 'But I'll come to you,' she added, 'whether you come to me or not.'

'I will go to you,' said Lady Glencora, 'of course,—why shouldn't I? But you know what I mean. We shall have dinners and parties and lots of people.'

'And we shall have none,' said Alice, smiling.

'And therefore there is so much more excuse for your coming to me;—or rather I mean so much more reason, for I don't want excuses. Well, dear, I'm so glad I've told you. I was afraid to see you in London. I should hardly have known how to look at you then. But I've got over that now.' Then she smiled and returned the kiss which Alice had given her. It was singular to see her standing on the bedroom rug with all her magnificence of dress, but with her hair pushed back behind her ears, and her eyes red with tears,—as though the burden of the magnificence remained to her after its purpose was over.

'I declare it's ever so much past twelve. Good night, now, dear. I wonder whether he's come up. But I should have heard his step if he had. He never treads lightly. He seldom gives over work till after one, and sometimes goes on till three. It's the only thing he likes, I believe. God bless you! good night.

I've such a deal more to say to you; and, Alice, you must tell me something about yourself, too; won't you, dear?' Then without waiting for an answer Lady Glencora went, leaving Alice in a maze of bewilderment. She could hardly believe that all she had heard, and all she had done, had happened since she left Queen Anne Street that morning.

CHAPTER XXIV
Three Politicians

MR. PALLISER was one of those politicians in possessing whom England has perhaps more reason to be proud than of any other of her resources, and who, as a body, give to her that exquisite combination of conservatism and progress which is her present strength and best security for the future. He could afford to learn to be a statesman, and had the industry wanted for such training. He was born in the purple, noble himself, and heir to the highest rank as well as one of the greatest fortunes of the country, already very rich, surrounded by all the temptations of luxury and pleasure; and yet he devoted himself to work with the grinding energy of a young penniless barrister labouring for a penniless wife, and did so without any motive more selfish than that of being counted in the roll of the public servants of England. He was not a brilliant man, and understood well that such was the case. He was now listened to in the House, as the phrase goes; but he was listened to as a laborious man, who was in earnest in what he did, who got up his facts with accuracy, and who, dull though he be, was worthy of confidence. And he was very dull. He rather prided himself on being dull, and on conquering in spite of his dulness. He never allowed himself a joke in his speeches, nor attempted even the smallest flourish of rhetoric. He was very careful in his language, labouring night and day to learn to express himself with accuracy, with no needless repetition of words, perspicuously with regard to the special object he might have in view. He had taught himself to believe that

oratory, as oratory, was a sin against that honesty in politics
by which he strove to guide himself. He desired to use words
for the purpose of teaching things which he knew and which
others did not know; and he desired also to be honoured for
his knowledge. But he had no desire to be honoured for the
language in which his knowledge was conveyed. He was an upright, thin, laborious man; who by his parts alone could have
served no political party materially, but whose parts were
sufficient to make his education, integrity, and industry useful
in the highest degree. It is the trust which such men inspire
which makes them so serviceable;—trust not only in their
labour,—for any man rising from the mass of the people may be
equally laborious; nor yet simply in their honesty and patriotism. The confidence is given to their labour, honesty, and
patriotism joined to such a personal stake in the country as
gives them a weight and ballast which no politician in England
can possess without it.

If he was dull as a statesman he was more dull in private life,
and it may be imagined that such a woman as his wife would
find some difficulty in making his society the source of her
happiness. Their marriage, in a point of view regarding business, had been a complete success,—and a success, too, when
on the one side, that of Lady Glencora, there had been terrible
dangers of shipwreck, and when on his side also there had been
some little fears of a mishap. As regards her it has been told
how near she went to throwing herself, with all her vast wealth,
into the arms of a young man, whom no father, no guardian,
could have regarded as a well-chosen husband for any girl;—
one who as yet had shown no good qualities, who had been a
spendthrift, unprincipled, and debauched. Alas, she had loved
him! It is possible that her love and her wealth might have
turned him from evil to good. But who would have ventured to
risk her,—I will not say her and her vast inheritances,—on
such a chance? That evil, however, had been prevented, and
those about her had managed to marry her to a young man,
very steady by nature, with worldly prospects as brilliant as
her own, and with a station than which the world offers nothing

higher. His little threatened mischance,—a passing fancy for
a married lady who was too wise to receive vows which were
proffered not in the most ardent manner,—had, from special
reasons, given some little alarm to his uncle, which had just
sufficed at the time to make so very judicious a marriage doubly
pleasant to that noble duke. So that all things and all people
had conspired to shower substantial comforts on the heads of
this couple, when they were joined together, and men and
women had not yet ceased to declare how happy were both in
the accumulated gifts of fortune.

And as regards Mr. Palliser, I think that his married life,
and the wife, whom he certainly had not chosen, but who had
dropped upon him, suited him admirably. He wanted great
wealth for that position at which he aimed. He had been rich
before his marriage with his own wealth,—so rich that he
could throw thousands away if he wished it; but for him and
his career was needed that colossal wealth which would make
men talk about it,—which would necessitate an expansive expenditure, reaching far and wide, doing nothing, or less than
nothing, for his own personal comfort, but giving to him at
once that rock-like solidity which is so necessary to our great
aristocratic politicians. And his wife was, as far as he knew,
all that he desired. He had not dabbled much in the fountains
of Venus, though he had forgotten himself once, and sinned in
coveting another man's wife. But his sin then had hardly pol-
luted his natural character, and his desire had been of a kind
which was almost more gratified in its disappointment than
it would have been in its fruition. On the morning after the
lady had frowned on him he had told himself that he was very
well out of that trouble. He knew that it would never be for
him to hang up on the walls of a temple a well-worn lute as a
votive offering when leaving the pursuits of love. Idoneus puellis he never could have been. So he married Lady Glencora and
was satisfied. The story of Burgo Fitzgerald was told to him,
and he supposed that most girls had some such story to tell.
He thought little about it, and by no means understood her
when she said to him, with all the impressiveness which she

could throw into the words, 'You must know that I have really loved him.' 'You must love me now,' he had replied with a smile; and then, as regarded his mind, the thing was over. And since his marriage he had thought that things matrimonial had gone well with him, and with her too. He gave her almost unlimited power of enjoying her money, and interfered but little in her way of life. Sometimes he would say a word of caution to her with reference to those childish ways which hardly became the dull dignity of his position; and his words then would have in them something of unintentional severity, —whether instigated or not by the red-haired Radical Member of Parliament, I will not pretend to say;—but on the whole he was contented and loved his wife, as he thought, very heartily, and at least better than he loved any one else. One cause of unhappiness, or rather one doubt as to his entire good fortune, was beginning to make itself felt, as his wife had to her sorrow already discovered. He had hoped that before this he might have heard that she would give him a child. But the days were young yet for that trouble, and the care had not become a sorrow.

But this judicious arrangement as to properties, this well-ordered alliance between families, had not perhaps suited her as well as it had suited him. I think that she might have learned to forget her early lover, or to look back upon him with a soft melancholy hardly amounting to regret, had her new lord been more tender in his ways with her. I do not know that Lady Glencora's heart was made of that stern stuff which refuses to change its impressions; but it was a heart, and it required food. To love and fondle some one,—to be loved and fondled, were absolutely necessary to her happiness. She wanted the little daily assurance of her supremacy in the man's feelings, the constant touch of love, half accidental half contrived, the passing glance of the eye telling perhaps of some little joke understood only between them two rather than of love, the softness of an occasional kiss given here and there when chance might bring them together, some half-pretended interest in her little doings, a nod, a wink, a shake of the head, or even a pout. It should have been given to her to feed upon such food as this daily, and then she would have forgotten Burgo Fitzgerald. But Mr. Palliser understood none of these things; and therefore the image of Burgo Fitzgerald in all his beauty was ever before her eyes.

But not the less was Mr. Palliser a prosperous man, as to the success of whose career few who knew him had much doubt. It might be written in the book of his destiny that he would have to pass through some violent domestic trouble, some ruin in the hopes of his home, of a nature to destroy then and for ever the worldly prospects of other men. But he was one who would pass through such violence, should it come upon him, without much scathe. To lose his influence with his party would be worse to him than to lose his wife, and public disgrace would hit him harder than private dishonour.

And the present was the very moment in which success was, as was said, coming to him. He had already held laborious office under the Crown, but had never sat in the Cabinet. He had worked much harder than Cabinet Ministers generally work,—but hitherto had worked without any reward that was worth his having. For the stipend which he had received had been nothing to him,—as the great stipend which he would receive, if his hopes were true, would also be nothing to him. To have ascendancy over other men, to be known by his country-men as one of their real rulers, to have an actual and acknowledged voice in the management of nations,—those were the rewards for which he looked; and now in truth it seemed as though they were coming to him. It was all but known that the existing Chancellor of the Exchequer would separate himself from the Government, carrying various others with him, either before or immediately consequent on the meeting of Parliament;—and it was all but known, also, that Mr. Palliser would fill his place, taking that high office at once, although he had never hitherto sat in that august assembly which men call the Cabinet. He could thus afford to put up with the small everyday calamity of having a wife who loved another man better than she loved him.

The presence of the Duke of St. Bungay at Matching was assumed to be a sure sign of Mr. Palliser's coming triumph. The Duke was a statesman of a very different class, but he also had been eminently successful as an aristocratic pillar of the British Constitutional Republic. He was a minister of very many years' standing, being as used to cabinet sittings as other men are to their own arm-chairs; but he had never been a hard-working man. Though a constant politician, he had ever taken politics easy whether in office or out. The world had said before now that the Duke might be Premier, only that he would not take the trouble. He had been consulted by a very distinguished person,—so the papers had said more than once,—as to the making of Prime Ministers. His voice in council was esteemed to be very great. He was regarded as a strong rock of support to the Liberal cause, and yet nobody ever knew what he did; nor was there much record of what he said. The offices which he held, or had held, were generally those to which no very arduous duties were attached. In severe debates he never took upon himself the brunt of opposition oratory. What he said in the House was generally short and pleasant,—with some slight, drolling undercurrent of uninjurious satire running through it. But he was a walking miracle of the wisdom of common sense. He never lost his temper. He never made mistakes. He never grew either hot or cold in a cause. He was never reckless in politics, and never cowardly. He snubbed no man, and took snubbings from no man. He was a Knight of the Garter, a Lord Lieutenant of his county, and at sixty-two had his digestion unimpaired and his estate in excellent order. He was a great buyer of pictures, which, perhaps, he did not understand, and a great collector of books which certainly he never read. All the world respected him, and he was a man to whom the respect of all the world was as the breath of his nostrils.

But even he was not without his peacock on the wall, his skeleton in the closet, his thorn in his side; though the peacock did not scream loud, the skeleton was not very terrible in his anatomical arrangement, nor was the thorn likely to fester to a gangrene. The Duke was always in awe about his wife.

He was ever uneasy about his wife, but it must not be supposed that he feared the machinations of any Burgo Fitzgerald as being destructive of his domestic comfort. The Duchess was and always had been all that is proper. Ladies in high rank, when gifted with excelling beauty, have often been made the marks of undeserved calumny;—but no breath of slander had ever touched her name. I doubt if any man alive had ever had the courage even to wink at her since the Duke had first called her his own. Nor was she a spendthrift, or a gambler. She was not fast in her tastes, or given to any pursuit that was objectionable. She was simply a fool, and as a fool was ever fearing that she was the mark of ridicule. In all such miseries she would complain sorrowfully, piteously, and occasionally very angrily, to her dear Duke and protector; till sometimes her dear Duke did not quite know what to do with her or how to protect her. It did not suit him, a Knight of the Garter and a Duke of St. Bungay, to beg mercy for that poor wife of his from such a one as Mrs. Conway Sparkes; nor would it be more in his way to lodge a formal complaint against that lady before his host or hostess,—as one boy at school may sometimes do as regards another. 'If you don't like the people, my dear, we will go away,' he said to her late on that evening of which we have spoken. 'No,' she replied, 'I do not wish to go away. I have said that we would stay till December, and Longroyston won't be ready before that. But I think that something ought to be done to silence that woman.' And the accent came strong upon 'something,' and then again with terrific violence upon 'woman.'

The Duke did not know how to silence Mrs. Conway Sparkes. It was a great principle of his life never to be angry with any one. How could he get at Mrs. Conway Sparkes? 'I don't think she is worth your attention,' said the husband. 'That's all very well, Duke,' said the wife, 'and perhaps she is not. But I find her in this house, and I don't like to be laughed at. I think Lady Glencora should make her know her place.'

'Lady Glencora is very young, my dear.'

'I don't know about being so very young,' said the Duchess,

whose ear had perhaps caught some little hint of poor Lady Glencora's almost unintentional mimicry. Now as appeals of this kind were being made frequently to the Duke, and as he was often driven to say some word, of which he himself hardly approved, to some one in protection of his Duchess, he was aware that the matter was an annoyance, and at times almost wished that her Grace was at—Longroyston.

And there was a third politician staying at Matching Priory who had never yet risen to the rank of a statesman, but who had his hopes. This was Mr. Bott, the member for St. Helens,* whom Lady Glencora had described as a man who stood about, with red hair,—and perhaps told tales of her to her husband. Mr. Bott was a person who certainly had had some success in life and who had won it for himself. He was not very young, being at this time only just on the right side of fifty. He was now enjoying his second session in Parliament, having been returned as a pledged disciple of the Manchester school.* Nor had he apparently been false to his pledges. At St. Helens he was still held to be a good man and true. But they who sat on the same side with him in the House and watched his political manœuvres, knew that he was striving hard to get his finger into the public pie. He was not a rich man, though he had made calico and had got into Parliament. And though he claimed to be a thoroughgoing Radical, he was a man who liked to live with aristocrats, and was fond of listening to the whispers of such as the Duke of St. Bungay or Mr. Palliser. It was supposed that he did understand something of finance. He was at any rate great in figures; and as he was possessed of much industry, and was obedient withal, he was a man who might make himself useful to a Chancellor of the Exchequer ambitious of changes.

There are men who get into such houses as Matching Priory and whose presence there is a mystery to many;—as to whom the ladies of the house never quite understand why they are entertaining such a guest. 'And Mr. Bott is coming,' Mr. Palliser had said to his wife. 'Mr. Bott!' Lady Glencora had answered. 'Goodness me! who is Mr. Bott?' 'He is member for St. Helens,' said Mr. Palliser. 'A very serviceable man in his way.' 'And what am I to do with him?' asked Lady Glencora. 'I don't know that you can do anything with him. He is a man who has a great deal of business, and I dare say he will spend most of his time in the library.' So Mr. Bott arrived. But though a huge pile of letters and papers came to him every morning by post, he unfortunately did not seem to spend much of his time in the library. Perhaps he had not found the clue to that lost apartment. Twice he went out shooting, but as on the first day he shot the keeper, and on the second very nearly shot the Duke, he gave that up. Hunting he declined, though much pressed to make an essay in that art by Jeffrey Palliser. He seemed to spend his time, as Lady Glencora said, in standing about,—except at certain times when he was closeted with Mr. Palliser, and when, it may be presumed, he made himself useful. On such days he would be seen at the hour of lunch with fingers much stained with ink, and it was generally supposed that on those occasions he had been counting up taxes and calculating the effect of great financial changes. He was a tall, wiry, strong man, with a bald head and bristly red beard, which, however, was cut off from his upper and under lip. This was unfortunate, as had he hidden his mouth he would not have been in so marked a degree an ugly man. His upper lip was very long, and his mouth was mean. But he had found that without the help of a razor to these parts he could not manage his soup to his satisfaction, and preferring cleanliness to beauty had shaved himself accordingly.

'I shouldn't dislike Mr. Bott so much,' Lady Glencora said to her husband, 'if he didn't rub his hands and smile so often, and seem to be going to say something when he really is not going to say anything.'

'I don't think you need trouble yourself about him, my dear,' Mr. Palliser had answered.

'But when he looks at me in that way, I can't help stopping, as I think he is going to speak; and then he always says, "Can I do anything for you, Lady Glen-cowrer?"'

She instantly saw that her husband did not like this. 'Don't be angry with me, dear,' she said. 'You must admit that he is rather a bore.'

'I am not at all angry, Glencora,' said the husband; 'and if you insist upon it, I will see that he leaves;—and in such case will of course never ask him again. But that might be prejudicial to me, as he is a man whom I trust in politics, and who may perhaps be serviceable to me.'

Of course Lady Glencora declared that Mr. Bott might remain as long as he and her husband desired, and of course she mentioned his name no more to Mr. Palliser; but from that time forth she regarded Mr. Bott as an enemy, and felt also that Mr. Bott regarded her in the same light.

When it was known among outside politicians that the Duke of St. Bungay was staying at Matching Priory, outside politicians became more sure than ever that Mr. Palliser would be the new Chancellor of the Exchequer. The old minister and the young minister were of course arranging matters together. But I doubt whether Mr. Palliser and the Duke ever spoke on any such topic during the entire visit. Though Mr. Bott was occasionally closeted with Mr. Palliser, the Duke never troubled himself with such closetings. He went out shooting—on his pony, read his newspaper, wrote his notes, and looked with the eye of a connoisseur over all Mr. Palliser's farming apparatus. 'You seem to have a good man, I should say,' said the Duke. 'What! Hubbings? Yes;—he was a legacy from my uncle when he gave me up the Priory.' 'A very good man, I should say. Of course he won't make it pay; but he'll make it look as though it did;—which is the next best thing. I could never get rent out of land that I farmed myself,—never.' 'I suppose not,' said Mr. Palliser, who did not care much about it. The Duke would have talked to him by the hour together about farming had Mr. Palliser been so minded; but he talked to him very little about politics. Nor during the whole time of his stay at Matching did the Duke make any other allusion to Mr. Palliser's hopes as regarded the ministry, than that in which he had told Lady Glencora at the dinner-table that her husband's ambition was the highest by which any man could be moved.

But Mr. Bott was sometimes honoured by a few words with the Duke.

'We shall muster pretty strong, your Grace,' Mr. Bott had said to him one day before dinner.

'That depends on how the changes go,' said the Duke.

'I suppose there will be a change?'

'Oh yes; there'll be a change,—certainly, I should say. And it will be in your direction.'

'And in Palliser's?'

'Yes; I should think so;—that is, if it suits him. By-the-by, Mr. Bott——' Then there was a little whispered communication, in which perhaps Mr. Bott was undertaking some commission of that nature which Lady Glencora had called 'telling.'

CHAPTER XXV

In which much of the History of the Pallisers is told

AT the end of ten days Alice found herself quite comfortable at Matching Priory. She had now promised to remain there till the second week of December, at which time she was to go to Vavasor Hall,—there to meet her father and Kate. The Pallisers were to pass their Christmas with the Duke of Omnium in Barsetshire. 'We always are to do that,' said Glencora. 'It is the state occasion at Gatherum Castle, but it only lasts for one week. Then we go somewhere else. Oh dear!'

'Why do you say "oh dear"?'

'Because—; I don't think I mean to tell you.'

'Then I'm sure I won't ask.'

'That's so like you, Alice. But I can be as firm as you, and I'm sure I won't tell you unless you do ask.' But Alice did not ask, and it was not long before Lady Glencora's firmness gave way.

But, as I have said, Alice had become quite comfortable at Matching Priory. Perhaps she was already growing upwards towards the light. At any rate she could listen with pleasure to the few words the Duke would say to her. She could even chat a little to the Duchess,—so that her Grace had observed to Lady Glencora that 'her cousin was a very nice person,— a very nice person indeed. What a pity it was that she had been so ill-treated by that gentleman in Oxfordshire?' Lady Glencora had to explain that the gentleman lived in Cambridgeshire, and that he, at any rate, had not treated anybody ill. 'Do you mean that she—jilted him?' said the Duchess, almost whistling, and opening her eyes very wide. 'Dear me, I'm sorry for that. I shouldn't have thought it.' And when she next spoke to Alice she assumed rather a severe tone of emphasis;—but this was soon abandoned when Alice listened to her with complacency.

Alice also had learned to ride,—or rather had resumed her riding, which for years had been abandoned. Jeffrey Palliser had been her squire, and she had become intimate with him so as to learn to quarrel with him and to like him,—to such an extent that Lady Glencora had laughingly told her that she was going to do more.

'I rather think not,' said Alice.

'But what has thinking to do with it? Who ever thinks about it?'

'I don't just at present,—at any rate.'

'Upon my word it would be very nice;—and then perhaps some day you'd be the Duchess.'

'Glencora, don't talk such nonsense.'

'Those are the speculations which people make. Only I should spite you by killing myself, so that he might marry again.'

'How can you say such horrid things?'

'I think I shall,—some day. What right have I to stand in his way? He spoke to me the other day about Jeffrey's altered position, and I knew what he meant;—or rather what he didn't mean to say, but what he thought. But I shan't kill myself.'

'I should think not.'

'I only know one other way,' said Lady Glencora.

'You are thinking of things which should never be in your thoughts,' said Alice vehemently. 'Have you no trust in God's providence? Cannot you accept what has been done for you?'

Mr. Bott had gone away, much to Lady Glencora's delight, but had unfortunately come back again. On his return Alice heard more of the feud between the Duchess and Mrs. Conway Sparkes. 'I did not tell you,' said Lady Glencora to her friend; —'I did not tell you before he went that I was right about his tale-bearing.'

'And did he bear tales?'

'Yes; I did get the scolding, and I know very well that it came through him, though Mr. Palliser did not say so. But he told me that the Duchess had felt herself hurt by that other woman's way of talking.'

'But it was not your fault.'

'No; that's what I said. It was he who desired me to ask Mrs. Conway Sparkes to come here. I didn't want her. She goes everywhere, and it is thought a catch to get her; but if she had been drowned in the Red Sea I shouldn't have minded. When I told him that, he said it was nonsense,—which of course it was; and then he said I ought to make her hold her tongue. Of course I said I couldn't. Mrs. Conway Sparkes wouldn't care for me. If she quizzed me, myself, I told him that I could take care of myself, though she were ten times Mrs. Conway Sparkes, and had written finer poetry than Tennyson.'

'It is fine;—some of it,' said Alice.

'Oh, I dare say! I know a great deal of it by heart, only I wouldn't give her the pleasure of supposing that I have ever thought so much about her poetry. And then I told him that I couldn't take care of the Duchess;—and he told me that I was a child.'

'He only meant that in love.'

'I am a child; I know that. Why didn't he marry some strong-minded, ferocious woman that could keep his house in order, and frown Mrs. Sparkes out of her impudence? It wasn't my fault.'

'You didn't tell him that.'

'But I did. Then he kissed me, and said it was all right, and told me that I should grow older. "And Mrs. Sparkes will grow more impudent," I said, "and the Duchess more silly." And after that I went away. Now this horrid Mr. Bott has come back again, and only that it would be mean in me to condescend so far, I would punish him. He grins and smiles at me, and rubs his big hands more than ever, because he feels that he has behaved badly. Is it not horrid to have to live in the house with such people?'

'I don't think you need mind him much.'

'Yes; but I am the mistress here, and am told that I am to entertain the people. Fancy entertaining the Duchess of St. Bungay and Mr. Bott!'

Alice had now become so intimate with Lady Glencora that she did not scruple to read her wise lectures,—telling her that she allowed herself to think too much of little things,—and too much also of some big things. 'As regards Mr. Bott,' said Alice, 'I think you should bear it as though there were no such person.'

'But that would be pretence,—especially to you.'

'No; it would not be pretence; it would be the reticence which all women should practise,—and you, in your position, more almost than any other woman.' Then Lady Glencora pouted, told Alice that it was a pity she had not married Mr. Palliser, and left her.

That evening,—the evening of Mr. Bott's return to Matching, that gentleman found a place near to Alice in the drawing-room. He had often come up to her, rubbing his hands together, and saying little words, as though there was some reason from their positions that they two should be friends. Alice had perceived this, and had endeavoured with all her force to shake him off; but he was a man, who if he understood a hint, never took it. A cold shoulder was nothing to him, if he wanted to gain the person who showed it him. His code of perseverance taught him that it was a virtue to overcome cold shoulders. The man or woman who received his first overtures with grace would probably be one on whom it would be better that he should look down and waste no further time; whereas he or she who could afford to treat him with disdain would no doubt be worth gaining. Such men as Mr. Bott are ever gracious to cold shoulders. The colder the shoulders, the more gracious are the Mr. Botts.

'What a delightful person is our dear friend, Lady Glencora!' said Mr. Bott, having caught Alice in a position from which she could not readily escape.

Alice had half a mind to differ, or to make any remark that might rid her from Mr. Bott. But she did not dare to say a word that might seem to have been said playfully. 'Yes, indeed,' she replied. 'How very cold it is to-night!' She was angry with herself for her own stupidity as soon as the phrase was out of her mouth, and then she almost laughed as she thought of the Duchess and the hot-water pipes at Longroyston.

'Yes, it is cold. You and her ladyship are great friends, I believe, Miss Vavasor.'

'She is my cousin,' said Alice.

'Ah! yes; that is so pleasant. I have reason to know that Mr. Palliser is very much gratified that you should be so much with her.'

This was unbearable. Alice could not quite assume sufficient courage to get up from her chair and walk away from him, and yet she felt that she must escape further conversation. 'I don't know that I am very much with her, and if I were I can't think it would make any difference to Mr. Palliser.'

But Mr. Bott was not a man to be put down when he had a purpose in hand. 'I can assure you that those are his sentiments. Of course we all know that dear Lady Glencora is young. She is very young.'

'Mr. Bott, I really would rather not talk about my cousin.'

'But, dear Miss Vavasor;—when we both have her welfare in view——?'

'I haven't her welfare in view, Mr. Bott; not in the least. There is no reason why I should. You must excuse me if I say I cannot talk about her welfare with a perfect stranger.' Then she did get up, and went away from the Member of Parliament, leaving him rather astonished at her audacity. But he was a constant man, and his inner resolve was simply to the effect that he would try it again.

I wonder whether Jeffrey Palliser did think much of the

difference between his present position and that which would
have been his had Lady Glencora been the happy possessor of
a cradle upstairs with a boy in it. I suppose he must have done
so. It is hardly possible that any man should not be alive to
the importance of such a chance. His own present position was
one of the most unfortunate which can fall to the lot of a man.
His father, the Duke's youngest brother, had left him about
six hundred a year, and had left him also a taste for living with
people of six thousand. The propriety of earning his bread had
never been put before him. His father had been in Parliament,
and had been the most favoured son of the old Duke, who for
some years before his death had never spoken to him who now
reigned over the house of the Pallisers. Jeffrey's father had
been brought up at Matching Priory as scions of ducal houses
are brought up, and on the old man's death had been possessed
of means sufficient to go on in the same path, though with
difficulty. His brother had done something for him, and at
various times he had held some place near the throne. But on
his death, when the property left behind him was divided between his son and three daughters, Jeffrey Palliser became
possessed of the income above stated. Of course he could live
on it,—and as during the winter months of the year a home
was found for him free of cost, he could keep hunters, and live
as rich men live. But he was a poor, embarrassed man, without prospects,—until this fine ducal prospect became opened
to him by the want of that cradle at Matching Priory.

But the prospect was no doubt very distant. Lady Glencora
might yet have as many sons as Hecuba.* Or she might die, and
some other more fortunate lady might become the mother of
his cousin's heir. Or the Duke might marry and have a son.
And, moreover, his cousin was only one year older than himself, and the great prize, if it came his way, might not come for
forty years as yet. Nevertheless his hand might now be acceptable in quarters where it would certainly be rejected had
Lady Glencora possessed that cradle upstairs. We cannot but
suppose that he must have made some calculations of this
nature.

'It is a pity you should do nothing all your life,' his cousin Plantagenet said to him one morning just at this time. Jeffrey had sought the interview in his cousin's room, and I fear had done so with some slight request for ready money.

'What am I to do?' said Jeffrey.

'At any rate you might marry.'

'Oh, yes;—I could marry. There's no man so poor but what he can do that. The question would be how I might like the subsequent starvation.'

'I don't see that you need starve. Though your own fortune is small, it is something,—and many girls have fortunes of their own.'

Jeffrey thought of Lady Glencora, but he made no allusion to her in speech. 'I don't think I'm very good at that kind of thing,' he said. 'When the father and mother came to ask of my house and my home I should break down. I don't say it as praising myself;—indeed, quite the reverse; but I fear I have not a mercenary tendency.'

'That's nonsense.'

'Oh, yes; quite so. I admit that.'

'Men must have mercenary tendencies or they would not have bread. The man who ploughs that he may live does so because he, luckily, has a mercenary tendency.'

'Just so. But you see I am less lucky than the ploughman.'

'There is no vulgar error so vulgar,—that is to say, common or erroneous,—as that by which men have been taught to say that mercenary tendencies are bad. A desire for wealth is the source of all progress.* Civilization comes from what men call greed. Let your mercenary tendencies be combined with honesty and they cannot take you astray.' This the future Chancellor of the Exchequer said with much of that air and tone of wisdom which a Chancellor of the Exchequer ought to possess.

'But I haven't got any such tendencies,' said Jeffrey.

'Would you like to occupy a farm in Scotland?' said Plantagenet Palliser.

'And pay rent?'

'You would have to pay rent of course.'

'Thank you, no. It would be dishonest, as I know I should never pay it.'

'You are too old, I fear, for the public service.'

'You mean a desk in the Treasury,—with a hundred a year. Yes; I think I am too old.'

'But have you no plan of your own?'

'Not much of one. Sometimes I have thought I would go to New Zealand.'

'You would have to be a farmer there.'

'No;—I shouldn't do that. I should get up an opposition to the Government and that sort of thing, and then they would buy me off and give me a place.'

'That does very well here, Jeffrey, if a man can get into Parliament and has capital enough to wait; but I don't think it would do out there. Would you like to go into Parliament?'

'What; here? Of course I should. Only I should be sure to get terribly into debt. I don't owe very much, now,—not to speak of,—except what I owe you.'

'You owe nothing to me,' said Plantagenet, with some little touch of magniloquence in his tone. 'No; don't speak of it. I have no brother, and between you and me it means nothing. You see, Jeffrey, it may be that I shall have to look to you as my—my—my heir, in short.' Hereupon Jeffrey muttered something as to the small probability of such necessity, and as to the great remoteness of any result even if it were so.

'That's all true,' said the elder heir of the Pallisers, 'but still———. In short, I wish you would do something. Do think about it; and then some day speak to me again.'

Jeffrey, as he left his cousin with a cheque for 500*l.* in his waistcoat pocket, thought that the interview which had at one time taken important dimensions, had not been concluded altogether satisfactorily. A seat in Paliament! Yes, indeed! If his cousin would so far use his political, monetary, or ducal interest as to do that for him;—as to give him something of the status properly belonging to the younger son of the House, then indeed life would have some charms for him! But as for the farm in Scotland, or a desk at an office in London,—his own

New Zealand plan would be better than those. And then as he went along of course he bethought himself that it might be his lot yet to die, and at least to be buried, in the purple, as a Duke of Omnium. If so, certainly it would be his duty to prepare another heir, and leave a duke behind him,—if it were possible.

'Are you going to ride with us after lunch?' said Lady Glencora to him as he strolled into the drawing-room.

'No,' said Jeffrey; 'I'm going to study.'

'To do what?' said Lady Glencora.

'To study;—or rather I shall spend to-day in sitting down and considering what I will study. My cousin has just been telling me that I ought to do something.'

'So you ought,' said Iphigenia energetically from her writing-desk.

'But he didn't seem to have any clear opinion what it ought to be. You see there can't be two Chancellors of the Exchequer at the same time. Mrs. Sparkes, what ought a young man like me to set about doing?'

'Go into Parliament, I should say,' said Mrs. Sparkes.

'Ah, yes; exactly. He had some notion of that kind, too, but he didn't name any particular place. I think I'll try the City of London. They've four there, and of course the chance of getting in would thereby be doubled.'

'I thought that commercial men were generally preferred in the City,' said the Duchess, taking a strong and good-natured interest in the matter.

'Mr. Palliser means to make a fortune in trade as a preliminary,' said Mrs. Sparkes.

'I don't think he meant anything of the kind,' said the Duchess.

'At any rate I have got to do something, so I can't go and ride,' said Jeffrey.

'And you ought to do something,' said Iphigenia from her desk.

Twice during this little conversation Lady Glencora had looked up, catching Alice's eye, and Alice had well known

what she had meant. 'You see,' the glance had said, 'Plantagenet is beginning to take an interest in his cousin, and you
know why. The man who is to be the father of the future dukes
must not be allowed to fritter away his time in obscurity. Had
I that cradle upstairs Jeffrey might be as idle as he pleased.'
Alice understood it well.

Of course Jeffrey did join the riding party. 'What is a man
like to me to do who wants to do something?' he said to Alice.
Alice was quite aware that Lady Glencora had contrived some
little scheme that Mr. Palliser should be riding next to her.
She liked Mr. Palliser, and therefore had no objection; but she
declared to herself that her cousin was a goose for her pains.

'Mrs. Sparkes says you ought to go into Parliament.'

'Yes;—and the dear Duchess would perhaps suggest a house
in Belgrave Square. I want to hear your advice now.'

'I can only say ditto to Miss Palliser.'

'What! Iphy? About procrastination? But you see the more
of my time he steals the better it is for me.'

'That's the evil you have got to cure.'

'My cousin Plantagenet suggested—marriage.'

'A very good thing too, I'm sure,' said Alice; 'only it depends something on the sort of wife you get.'

'You mean, of course, how much money she has.'

'Not altogether.'

'Looking at it from my cousin's point of view, I suppose
that it is the only important point. Who are there coming up
this year,—in the way of heiresses?'

'Upon my word I don't know. In the first place, how much
money makes an heiress?'

'For such a fellow as me, I suppose ten thousand pounds
ought to do.'

'That's not much,' said Alice, who had exactly that amount
of her own.

'No——; perhaps that's too moderate. But the lower one
went in the money speculation, the greater would be the number to choose from, and the better the chance of getting something decent in the woman herself. I have something of my

own,—not much you know; so with the lady's ten thousand pounds we might be able to live,—in some second-rate French town perhaps.'

'But I don't see what you would gain by that.'

'My people here would have got rid of me. That seems to be the great thing. If you hear of any girl with about that sum, moderately good-looking, not too young so that she might know something of the world, decently born, and able to read and write, perhaps you will bear me in mind.'

'Yes, I will,' said Alice, who was quite aware that he had made an accurate picture of her own position. 'When I meet such a one, I will send for you at once.'

'You know no such person now?'

'Well, no; not just at present.'

'I declare I don't think he could do anything better,' her cousin said to her that night. Lady Glencora was now in the habit of having Alice with her in what she called her dressing-room every evening, and then they would sit till the small hours came upon them. Mr. Palliser always burnt the midnight oil and came to bed with the owls. They would often talk of him and his prospects till Alice had perhaps inspired his wife with more of interest in him and them than she had before felt. And Alice had managed generally to drive her friend away from those topics which were so dangerous,—those allusions to her childlessness, and those hints that Burgo Fitzgerald was still in her thoughts. And sometimes, of course, they had spoken of Alice's own prospects, till she got into a way of telling her cousin freely all that she felt. On such occasions Lady Glencora would always tell her that she had been right;—if she did not love the man. 'Though your finger were put out for the ring,' said Lady Glencora on one such occasion, 'you should go back, if you did not love him.'

'But I did love him,' said Alice.

'Then I don't understand it,' said Lady Glencora; and, in truth, close as was their intimacy, they did not perfectly understand each other.

But on this occasion they were speaking of Jeffrey Palliser.

'I declare I don't think he could do any better,' said Lady Glencora.

'If you talk such nonsense, I will not stay,' said Alice.

'But why should it be nonsense? You would be very comfortable with your joint incomes. He is one of the best fellows in the world. It is clear that he likes you; and then we should be so near to each other. I am sure Mr. Palliser would do something for him if he married,—and especially if I asked him.'

'I only know of two things against it.'

'And what are they?'

'That he would not take me for his wife, and that I would not take him for my husband.'

'Why not? What do you dislike in him?'

'I don't dislike him at all. I like him very much indeed. But one can't marry all the people one likes.'

'But what reason is there why you shouldn't marry him?'

'This chiefly,' said Alice, after a pause; 'that I have just separated myself from a man whom I certainly did love truly, and that I cannot transfer my affections quite so quickly as that.'

As soon as the words were out of her mouth she knew that they should not have been spoken. It was exactly what Glencora had done. She had loved a man and had separated herself from him and had married another, all within a month or two. Lady Glencora first became red as fire over her whole face and shoulders, and Alice afterwards did the same as she looked up, as though searching in her cousin's eyes for pardon.

'It is an unmaidenly thing to do, certainly,' said Lady Glencora very slowly, and in her lowest voice. 'Nay, it is unwomanly; but one may be driven. One may be so driven that all gentleness of womanhood is driven out of one.'

'Oh, Glencora!'

'I did not propose that you should do it as a sudden thing.'

'Glencora!'

'I did do it suddenly. I know it. I did it like a beast that is driven as its owner chooses. I know it. I was a beast. Oh, Alice, if you knew how I hate myself!'

'But I love you with all my heart,' said Alice. 'Glencora, I have learned to love you so dearly!'

'Then you are the only being that does. He can't love me. How is it possible? You,—and perhaps another.'

'There are many who love you. He loves you. Mr. Palliser loves you.'

'It is impossible. I have never said a word to him that could make him love me. I have never done a thing for him that can make him love me. The mother of his child he might have loved, because of that. Why should he love me? We were told to marry each other and did it. When could he have learned to love me? But, Alice, he requires no loving, either to take it or to give it. I wish it were so with me.'

Alice said what she could to comfort her, but her words were but of little avail as regarded those marriage sorrows.

'Forgive you!' at last Glencora said. 'What have I to forgive? You don't suppose I do not know it all, and think of it all without the chance of some stray word like that! Forgive you! I am so grateful that you love me! Some one's love I must have found,—or I could not have remained here.'

CHAPTER XXVI

Lady Midlothian

A WEEK or ten days after this, Alice, when she came down to the breakfast-parlour one morning, found herself alone with Mr. Bott. It was the fashion at Matching Priory for people to assemble rather late in the day. The nominal hour for breakfast was ten, and none of the ladies of the party were ever seen before that. Some of the gentlemen would breakfast earlier, especially on hunting mornings; and on some occasions the ladies, when they came together, would find themselves altogether deserted by their husbands and brothers. On this day it was fated that Mr. Bott alone should represent the sterner sex, and when Alice entered the room he was standing on the rug with his back to the fire, waiting till the appearance of some other guest should give him the sanction necessary for the commencement of his morning meal. Alice, when she saw him, would have retreated had it been possible, for she had learned to dislike him greatly, and was, indeed, almost afraid of him; but she could not do so without making her flight too conspicuous.

'Do you intend to prolong your stay here, Miss Vavasor?' said Mr. Bott, taking advantage of the first moment at which she looked up from a letter which she was reading.

'For a few more days, I think,' said Alice.

'Ah!—I'm glad of that. Mr. Palliser has pressed me so much to remain till he goes to the Duke's, that I cannot get away sooner. As I am an unmarried man myself, I can employ my time as well in one place as in another;—at this time of the year, at least.'

'You must find that very convenient,' said Alice.

'Yes, it is convenient. You see in my position,—Parliamentary position, I mean,—I am obliged, as a public man, to act in concert with others. A public man can be of no service unless he is prepared to do that. We must give and take, you know, Miss Vavasor.'

As Miss Vavasor made no remark in answer to this, Mr. Bott continued—'I always say to the men of my party,—of course I regard myself as belonging to the extreme Radicals.'

'Oh, indeed!' said Alice.

'Yes. I came into Parliament on that understanding; and I have never seen any occasion as yet to change any political opinion that I have expressed. But I always say to the gentlemen with whom I act, that nothing can be done if we don't give and take. I don't mind saying to you, Miss Vavasor, that I look upon our friend, Mr. Palliser, as the most rising public man in the country. I do, indeed.'

'I am happy to hear you say so,' said his victim, who found herself driven to make some remark.

'And I, as an extreme Radical, do not think I can serve my party better than by keeping in the same boat with him, as long as it will hold the two. "He'll make a Government hack of you," a friend of mine said to me the other day. "And I'll make a Manchester school Prime Minister of him," I replied. I rather think I know what I'm about, Miss Vavasor.'

'No doubt,' said Alice.

'And so does he;—and so does he. Mr. Palliser is not the man to be led by the nose by any one. But it's a fair system of give and take. You can't get on in politics without it. What a charming woman is your relative, Lady Glencowrer! I remember well what you said to me the other evening.'

'Do you?' said Alice.

'And I quite agree with you that confidential intercourse regarding dear friends should not be lightly made.'

'Certainly not,' said Alice.

'But there are occasions, Miss Vavasor; there are occasions when the ordinary laws by which we govern our social conduct must be made somewhat elastic.'

'I don't think this one of them, Mr. Bott.'

'Is it not? Just listen to me for one moment, Miss Vavasor. Our friend, Mr. Palliser, I am proud to say, relies much upon my humble friendship. Our first connection has, of course, been political; but it has extended beyond that, and has become pleasantly social;—I may say, very pleasantly social.'

'What a taste Mr. Palliser must have!' Alice thought to herself.

'But I need not tell you that Lady Glencowrer is—very young; we may say, very young indeed.'

'Mr. Bott, I will not talk to you about Lady Glencora Palliser.'

This Alice said in a determined voice, and with all the power of resistance at her command. She frowned too, and looked savagely at Mr. Bott. But he was a man of considerable courage, and knew how to bear such opposition without flinching.

'When I tell you, Miss Vavasor, that I speak solely with a view to her domestic happiness!'

'I don't think that she wishes to have any such guardian of her happiness.'

'But if he wishes it, Miss Vavasor! Now I have the means

of knowing that he has the greatest reliance on your judgment.'

Hereupon Alice got up with the intention of leaving the room, but she was met at the door by Mrs. Conway Sparkes.

'Are you running from your breakfast, Miss Vavasor?' said she.

'No, Mrs. Sparkes; I am running from Mr. Bott,' said Alice, who was almost beside herself with anger.

'Mr. Bott, what is this?' said Mrs. Sparkes. 'Ha, ha, ha,' laughed Mr. Bott.

Alice returned to the room, and Mrs. Sparkes immediately saw that she had in truth been running from Mr. Bott. 'I hope I shall be able to keep the peace,' said she. 'I trust his offence was not one that requires special punishment.'

'Ha, ha, ha,' again laughed Mr. Bott, who rather liked his position.

Alice was very angry with herself, feeling that she had told more of the truth to Mrs. Sparkes than she should have done, unless she was prepared to tell the whole. As it was, she wanted to say something, and did not know what to say; but her confusion was at once stopped by the entrance of Lady Glencora.

'Mrs. Sparkes, good morning,' said Lady Glencora. 'I hope nobody has waited breakfast. Good morning, Mr. Bott. Oh, Alice!'

'What is the matter?' said Alice, going up to her.

'Oh, Alice; such a blow!' But Alice could see that her cousin was not quite in earnest;—that the new trouble, though it might be vexatious, was no great calamity. 'Come here,' said Lady Glencora; and they both went into an embrasure of the window. 'Now I shall have to put your confidence in me to the test. This letter is from,—whom do you think?'

'How can I guess?'

'From Lady Midlothian! and she's coming here on Monday, on her road to London. Unless you tell me that you are quite sure this is as unexpected by me as by you, I will never speak to you again.'

'I am quite sure of that.'

'Ah! then we can consult. But first we'll go and have some breakfast.' Then more ladies swarmed into the room,—the Duchess and her daughter, and the two Miss Pallisers, and others; and Mr. Bott had his hands full in attending,—or rather in offering to attend, to their little wants.

The morning was nearly gone before Alice and her cousin had any further opportunity of discussing in private the approach of Lady Midlothian; but Mr. Palliser had come in among them, and had been told of the good thing which was in store for him. 'We shall be delighted to see Lady Midlothian,' said Mr. Palliser.

'But there is somebody here who will not be at all delighted to see her,' said Lady Glencora to her husband.

'Is there, indeed?' said he. 'Who is that?'

'Her most undutiful cousin, Alice Vavasor. But, Alice, Mr. Palliser knows nothing about it, and it is too long to explain.'

'I am extremely sorry—' began Mr. Palliser.

'I can assure you it does not signify in the least,' said Alice. 'It will only be taking me away three days earlier.'

Upon hearing this Mr. Palliser looked very serious. What quarrel could Miss Vavasor have had with Lady Midlothian which should make it impossible for them to be visitors at the same house?

'It will do no such thing,' said Lady Glencora. 'Do you mean to say that you are coward enough to run away from her?'

'I'm afraid, Miss Vavasor, that we can hardly bid her not come,' said Mr. Palliser. In answer to this, Alice protested that she would not for worlds have been the means of keeping Lady Midlothian away from Matching. 'I should tell you, Mr. Palliser, that I have never seen Lady Midlothian, though she is my far-away cousin. Nor have I ever quarrelled with her. But she has given me advice by letter, and I did not answer her because I thought she had no business to interfere. I shall go away, not because I am afraid of her, but because, after what has passed, our meeting would be unpleasant to her.'

'You could tell her that Miss Vavasor is here,' said Mr. Palliser. 'And then she need not come unless she pleased.'

The matter was so managed at last that Alice found herself

unable to leave Matching without making more of Lady Midlothian's coming than it was worth. It would undoubtedly be very disagreeable,—this unexpected meeting with her relative; but, as Lady Glencora said, Lady Midlothian would not eat her. In truth, she felt ashamed of herself in that she was afraid of her relative. No doubt she was afraid of her. So much she was forced to admit to herself. But she resolved at last that she would not let her fear drive her out of the house.

'Is Mr. Bott an admirer of your cousin?' Mrs. Sparkes said that evening to Lady Glencora.

'A very distant one, I should think,' said Lady Glencora.

'Goodness gracious!' exclaimed an old lady who had been rather awed by Alice's intimacy and cousinship with Lady Glencora; 'it's the very last thing I should have dreamt of.'

'But I didn't dream it, first or last,' said Mrs. Sparkes.

'Why do you ask?' said Lady Glencora.

'Don't suppose that I am asking whether Miss Vavasor is an admirer of his,' said Mrs. Sparkes. 'I have no suspicion of that nature. I rather think that when he plays Bacchus she plays Ariadne, with the full intention of flying from him in earnest.'

'Is Mr. Bott inclined to play Bacchus?' asked Lady Glencora.

'I rather thought he was this morning. If you observe, he has something of a godlike and triumphant air about him.'

'I don't think his godship will triumph there,' said Lady Glencora.

'I really think she would be throwing herself very much away,' said the old lady.

'Miss Vavasor is not at all disposed to do that,' said Mrs. Sparkes. Then that conversation was allowed to drop.

On the following Monday, Lady Midlothian arrived. The carriage was sent to meet her at the station about three o'clock in the afternoon, and Alice had to choose whether she would undergo her first introduction immediately on her relative's arrival, or whether she would keep herself out of the way till she should meet her in the drawing-room before dinner.

'I shall receive her when she comes,' said Lady Glencora, 'and of course will tell her that you are here.'

'Yes, that will be best; and——; dear me, I declare I don't know how to manage it.'

'I'll bring her to you in my room if you like it.'

'No; that would be too solemn,' said Alice. 'That would make her understand that I thought a great deal about her.'

'Then we'll let things take their chance, and you shall come across her just as you would any other stranger.' It was settled at last that this would be the better course, but that Lady Midlothian was to be informed of Alice's presence at the Priory as soon as she should arrive.

Alice was in her own room when the carriage in which sat the unwelcome old lady was driven up to the hall-door. She heard the wheels plainly, and knew well that her enemy was within the house. She had striven hard all the morning to make herself feel indifferent to this arrival, but had not succeeded; and was angry with herself at finding that she sat up stairs with an anxious heart, because she knew that her cousin was in the room down stairs. What was Lady Midlothian to her that she should be afraid of her? And yet she was very much afraid of Lady Midlothian. She questioned herself on the subject over and over again, and found herself bound to admit that such was the fact. At last, about five o'clock, having reasoned much with herself, and rebuked herself for her own timidity, she descended into the drawing-room,—Lady Glencora having promised that she would at that hour be there,—and on opening the door became immediately conscious that she was in the presence of her august relative. There sat Lady Midlothian in a great chair opposite the fire, and Lady Glencora sat near to her on a stool. One of the Miss Pallisers was reading in a further part of the room, and there was no one else present in the chamber.

The Countess of Midlothian was a very little woman, between sixty and seventy years of age, who must have been very pretty in her youth. At present she made no pretension either to youth or beauty,—as some ladies above sixty will still do,—but sat confessedly an old woman in all her external relations. She wore a round bonnet which came much over her face,—being accustomed to continue the use of her bonnet till dinner time when once she had been forced by circumstances to put it on. She wore a short cloak which fitted close to her person, and, though she occupied a great arm-chair, sat perfectly upright, looking at the fire. Very small she was, but she carried in her grey eyes and sharp-cut features a certain look of importance which saved her from being considered as small in importance. Alice, as soon as she saw her, knew that she was a lady over whom no easy victory could be obtained.

'Here is Alice,' said Lady Glencora, rising as her cousin entered the room. 'Alice, let me introduce you to Lady Midlothian.'

Alice, as she came forward, was able to assume an easy demeanour, even though her heart within was failing her. She put out her hand, leaving it to the elder lady to speak the first words of greeting.

'I am glad at last to be able to make your acquaintance, my dear,' said Lady Midlothian; 'very glad.' But still Alice did not speak. 'Your aunt, Lady Macleod, is one of my oldest friends, and I have heard her speak of you very often.'

'And Lady Macleod has often spoken to me of your ladyship,' said Alice.

'Then we know each other's names,' said the Countess; 'and it will be well that we should be acquainted with each other's persons. I am becoming an old woman, and if I did not learn to know you now, or very shortly, I might never do so.'

Alice could not help thinking that even under those circumstances neither might have had, so far as that was concerned, much cause of sorrow, but she did not say so. She was thinking altogether of Lady Midlothian's letter to her, and trying to calculate whether or no it would be well for her to rush away at once to the subject. That Lady Midlothian would mention the letter, Alice felt well assured; and when could it be better mentioned than now, in Glencora's presence,—when no other person was near them to listen to her? 'You are very kind,' said Alice.

'I would wish to be so,' said Lady Midlothian. 'Blood is thicker than water, my dear; and I know no earthly ties that can bind people together if those of family connection will not do so. Your mother, when she and I were young, was my dearest friend.'

'I never knew my mother,' said Alice,—feeling, however, as she spoke, that the strength of her resistance to the old woman was beginning to give way.

'No, my dear, you never did;—and that is to my thinking another reason why they who loved her should love you. But Lady Macleod is your nearest relative,—on your mother's side, I mean,—and she has done her duty by you well.'

'Indeed she has, Lady Midlothian.'

'She has, and others, therefore, have been the less called upon to interfere. I only say this, my dear, in my own vindication,—feeling, perhaps, that my conduct needs some excuse.'

'I'm sure Alice does not think that,' said Lady Glencora.

'It is what I think rather than what Alice thinks that concerns my own shortcomings,' said Lady Midlothian, with a smile which was intended to be pleasant. 'But I have wished to make up for former lost opportunities.' Alice knew that she was about to refer to her letter, and trembled. 'I am very anxious now to be reckoned one of Alice Vavasor's friends, if she will allow me to become so.'

'I can only be too proud,—if——'

'If what, my dear?' said the old lady. I believe that she meant to be gracious, but there was something in her manner, or, perhaps, rather in her voice, so repellent, that Alice felt that they could hardly become true friends. 'If what, my dear?'

'Alice means——' began Lady Glencora.

'Let Alice say what she means herself,' said Lady Midlothian.

'I hardly know how to say what I do mean,' said Alice, whose spirit within her was rising higher as the occasion for using it came upon her. 'I am assured that you and I, Lady Midlothian, differ very much as to a certain matter; and as it is one in which I must be guided by my own opinion, and not that of any other person, perhaps——'

'You mean about Mr. Grey?'

'Yes,' said Alice; 'I mean about Mr. Grey.'

'I think so much about that matter, and your happiness as therein concerned, that when I heard that you were here I was determined to take Matching in my way to London, so that I might have an opportunity of speaking to you.'

'Then you knew that Alice was here,' said Lady Glencora.

'Of course I did. I suppose you have heard all the history, Glencora?'

Lady Glencora was forced to acknowledge that she had heard the history,—'the history' being poor Alice's treatment of Mr. Grey.

'And what do you think of it?' Both Alice and her hostess looked round to the further end of the room in which Miss Palliser was reading, intending thus to indicate that that lady knew as yet none of the circumstances, and that there could be no good reason why she should be instructed in them at this moment. 'Perhaps another time and another place may be better,' said Lady Midlothian; 'but as I must go the day after to-morrow,—indeed, I thought of going to-morrow.'

'Oh, Lady Midlothian!' exclaimed Lady Glencora.

'You must regard this as merely a passing visit, made upon business. But, as I was saying, when shall I get an opportunity of speaking to Alice where we need not be interrupted?'

Lady Glencora suggested her room up stairs, and offered the use of it then, or on that night when the world should be about to go to bed. But the idea of this premeditated lecture was terrible to Alice, and she determined that she would not endure it.

'Lady Midlothian, it would really be of no use.'

'Of no use, my dear!'

'No, indeed. I did get your letter, you know.'

'And as you have not answered it, I have come all this way to see you.'

'I shall be so sorry if I give offence, but it is a subject which I cannot bring myself to discuss'—she was going to say with a stranger, but she was able to check herself before the offensive word was uttered,—'which I cannot bring myself to discuss with any one.'

'But you don't mean to say that you won't see me?'

'I will not talk upon that matter,' said Alice. 'I will not do it even with Lady Macleod.'

'No,' said Lady Midlothian, and her sharp grey eyes now began to kindle with anger; 'and therefore it is so very necessary that other friends should interfere.'

'But I will endure no interference,' said Alice, 'either from persons who are friends or who are not friends.' And as she spoke she rose from her chair. 'You must forgive me, Lady Midlothian, if I say that I can have no conversation with you on this matter.' Then she walked out of the room, leaving the Countess and Lady Glencora together. As she went Miss Palliser lifted her eyes from her book, and knew that there had been a quarrel, but I doubt if she had heard any of the words which had been spoken.

'The most self-willed young woman I ever met in my life,' said Lady Midlothian, as soon as Alice was gone.

'I knew very well how it would be,' said Lady Glencora.

'But it is quite frightful, my dear. She has been engaged, with the consent of all her friends, to this young man.'

'I know all about it.'

'But you must think she is very wrong.'

'I don't quite understand her, but I suppose she fears they would not be happy together.'

'Understand her! I should think not; nobody can understand her. A young woman to become engaged to a gentleman in that way,—before all the world, as one may say;—to go to his house, as I am told, and talk to the servants, and give orders about the furniture, and then turn round and simply say that she has changed her mind! She hasn't given the slightest reason to my knowledge.' And Lady Midlothian, as she insisted on the absolute iniquity of Alice's proceedings, almost startled Lady Glencora by the eagerness of her countenance. Lady Midlothian had been one of those who, even now not quite two years ago, had assisted in obtaining the submission of Lady Glencora herself. Lady Midlothian seemed on the present occasion to remember nothing of this, but Lady Glencora remembered it very exactly. 'I shall not give it up,' continued Lady Midlothian. 'I have the greatest possible objection to her father, who contrived to connect himself with our family in a most shameful manner, without the slightest encouragement. I don't think I have spoken to him since, but I shall see him now and tell him my opinion.'

Alice held her ground, and avoided all further conversation with Lady Midlothian. A message came to her through Lady Glencora imploring her to give way, but she was quite firm.

'Good-bye to you,' Lady Midlothian said to her as she went. 'Even yet I hope that things may go right, and if so you will find that I can forget and forgive.'

'If perseverance merits success,' said Lady Glencora to Alice, 'she ought to succeed.' 'But she won't succeed,' said Alice.

CHAPTER XXVII

The Priory Ruins

LADY MIDLOTHIAN went away on her road to London on the Wednesday morning, and Alice was to follow her on the next day. It was now December, and the weather was very clear and frosty, but at night there was bright moonlight. On this special night the moon would be full, and Lady Glencora had declared that she and Alice would go out amidst the ruins. It was no secret engagement, having been canvassed in public, and having been met with considerable discouragement by some of the party. Mr. Palliser had remarked that the night air would be very cold, and Mr. Bott had suggested all manner of evil consequences. Had Mr. Palliser alone objected, Lady Glencora might have given way, but Mr. Bott's word riveted her purpose.

'We are not going to be frightened,' Lady Glencora said.

'People do not generally walk out at night in December,' Mr. Palliser observed.

'That's just the reason why we want to do it,' said Lady Glencora. 'But we shall wrap ourselves up, and nobody need be afraid. Jeffrey, we shall expect you to stand sentinel at the old gate, and guard us from the ghosts.'

Jeffrey Palliser, bargaining that he might be allowed a cigar, promised that he would do as he was bidden.

The party at Matching Priory had by this time become very small. There were indeed no guests left, not counting those of the Palliser family, excepting Miss Vavasor, Mr. Bott, and an old lady who had been a great friend of Mr. Palliser's mother. It was past ten in the evening when Lady Glencora declared that the time had arrived for them to carry out their purpose. She invited the two Miss Pallisers to join her, but they declined, urging their fear of the night air, and showing by their manner that they thought the proposition a very imprudent one. Mr. Bott offered to accompany them, but Lady Glencora declined his attendance very stoutly.

'No, indeed, Mr. Bott; you were one of those who preached a sermon against my dissipation in the morning, and I'm not going to allow you to join it, now the time for its enjoyment has come.'

'My dear Lady Glencora, if I were you, indeed I wouldn't,' said the old lady, looking round towards Mr. Palliser.

'My dear Mrs. Marsham, if you were me, indeed you would,' and Lady Glencora also looked at her husband.

'I think it a foolish thing to do,' said Mr. Palliser, sternly.

'If you forbid it, of course we won't go,' said Lady Glencora.

'Forbid it:—no; I shall not forbid it.'

'Allons donc,' said Lady Glencora.

She and Alice were already muffled in cloaks and thick shawls, and Alice now followed her out of the room. There was a door which opened from the billiard-room out on to the grand terrace, which ran in front of the house, and here they found Jeffrey Palliser already armed with his cigar. Alice, to tell the truth, would much have preferred to abandon the expedition, but she had felt that it would be cowardly in her to desert Lady Glencora. There had not arisen any very close intimacy between her and Mr. Palliser, but she entertained a certain feeling that Mr. Palliser trusted her, and liked her to be with his wife. She would have wished to justify this supposed confidence, and was almost sure that Mr. Palliser expected her to do so in this instance. She did say a word or two to her cousin upstairs, urging that perhaps her husband would not like it.

'Let him say so plainly,' said Lady Glencora, 'and I'll give it up instantly. But I'm not going to be lectured out of my purposes secondhand by Mr. Bott or old Mother Marsham. I understand all these people, my dear. And if you throw me over, Alice, I'll never forgive you,' Lady Glencora added.

After this Alice resolved that she would not throw her friend over. She was afraid to do so. But she was also becoming a little afraid of her friend,—afraid that she would be driven some day either to throw her over, or to say words to her that would be very unpalatable.

'Now, Jeffrey,' said Lady Glencora, as they walked abreast along the broad terrace towards the ruins, 'when we get under the old gateway you must let me and Alice go round the dormitory and the chapel alone. Then we'll come back by the cloisters, and we'll take another turn outside with you. The outside is the finest by this light,—only I want to show Alice something by ourselves.'

'You're not afraid, I know, and if Miss Vavasor is not——'

'Miss Vavasor,—who, I think, would have allowed you to call her by her other name on such an occasion as this,—is never afraid.'

'Glencora, how dare you say so?' said Alice. 'I really think we had better go back.'

She felt herself to be very angry with her cousin. She almost began to fear that she had mistaken her, and had thought better of her than she had deserved. What she had now said struck Alice as being vulgar,—as being premeditated vulgarity, and her annoyance was excessive. Of course Mr. Palliser would think that she was a consenting party to the proposition made to him.

'Go back!' said Glencora. 'No, indeed. We'll go on, and leave him here. Then he can call nobody anything. Don't be angry with me,' she said, as soon as they were out of hearing. 'The truth is this;—if you choose to have him for your husband, you may.'

'But I do not choose.'

'Then there can be no harm done, and I will tell him so. But, Alice,—think of this. Whom will you meet that would suit you better? And you need not decide now. You need not say a word, but leave me to tell him, that if it is to be thought of at all, it cannot be thought of till he meets you in London. Trust me, you will be safe with me.'

'You shall tell him nothing of the kind,' said Alice. 'I believe you to be joking throughout, and I think the joke is a bad one.'

'No; there you wrong me. Indeed I am not joking. I know that in what I am saying I am telling you the simple truth. He has said enough to me to justify me in saying so. Alice, think of it all. It would reconcile me to much, and it would be something to be the mother of the future Duke of Omnium.'

'To me it would be nothing,' said Alice; 'less than nothing. I mean to say that the temptation is one so easily resisted that it acts in the other way. Don't say anything more about it, Glencora.'

'If you don't wish it, I will not.'

'No;—I do not wish it. I don't think I ever saw moonlight so bright as this. Look at the lines of that window against the light. They are clearer than you ever see them in the day.'

They were now standing just within the gateway of the old cruciform chapel, having entered the transept from a ruined passage which was supposed to have connected the church with the dormitory. The church was altogether roofless, but the entire walls were standing. The small clerestory windows* of the nave were perfect, and the large windows of the two transepts and of the west end were nearly so. Of the opposite window, which had formed the back of the choir, very little remained. The top of it, with all its tracery, was gone, and three broken upright mullions of uneven heights alone remained. This was all that remained of the old window, but a transom or cross-bar of stone had been added to protect the

carved stone-work of the sides, and save the form of the aperture from further ruin. That this transom was modern was to
be seen from the magnificent height and light grace of the
workmanship in the other windows, in which the long slender
mullions rose from the lower stage or foundation of the whole
up into the middle tracery of the arch without protection or
support, and then lost themselves among the curves, not running up into the roof or soppit, and there holding on as though
unable to stand alone. Such weakness as that had not as yet
shown itself in English church architecture when Matching
Priory was built.

'Is it not beautiful!' said Glencora. 'I do love it so! And
there is a peculiar feeling of cold about the chill of the moon,
different from any other cold. It makes you wrap yourself up
tight, but it does not make your teeth chatter; and it seems to
go into your senses rather than into your bones. But I suppose
that's nonsense,' she added, after a pause.

'Not more so than what people are supposed to talk by
moonlight.'

'That's unkind. I'd like what I say on such an occasion to
be more poetical or else more nonsensical than what other
people say under the same circumstances. And now I'll tell
you why I always think of you when I come here by moonlight.'

'But I suppose you don't often come.'

'Yes, I do; that is to say, I did come very often when we
had the full moon in August. The weather wasn't like this, and
I used to run out through the open windows and nobody knew
where I was gone. I made him come once, but he didn't seem
to care about it. I told him that part of the refectory wall was
falling; so he looked at that, and had a mason sent the next
day. If anything is out of order he has it put to rights at once.
There would have been no ruins if all the Pallisers had been
like him.'

'So much the better for the world.'

'No;—I say no. Things may live too long. But now I'm
going to tell you. Do you remember that night I brought you

home from the play to Queen Anne Street?' 'Indeed I do,—very well.'

Alice had occasion to remember it, for it had been in the carriage on that evening that she had positively refused to give any aid to her cousin in that matter relating to Burgo Fitzgerald.

'And do you remember how the moon shone then?'

'Yes, I think I do.'

'I know I do. As we came round the corner out of Cavendish Square he was standing there,—and a friend of yours was standing with him.'

'What friend of mine?'

'Never mind that; it does not matter now.'

'Do you mean my cousin George?'

'Yes, I do mean your cousin; and oh, Alice! dear Alice! I don't know why I should love you, for if you had not been hardhearted that night,—stony cruel in your hard propriety, I should have gone with him then, and all this icy coldness would have been prevented.'

She was standing quite close to Alice, and as she spoke she shook with shivering and wrapped her furs closer and still closer about her.

'You are very cold,' said Alice. 'We had better go in.'

'No, I am not cold,—not in that way. I won't go in yet. Jeffrey will come to us directly. Yes:—we should have escaped that night if you would have allowed him to come into your house. Ah, well! we didn't, and there's an end of it.'

'But, Glencora,—you cannot regret it.'

'Not regret it! Alice, where can your heart be? Or have you a heart? Not regret it! I would give everything I have in the world to have been true to him. They told me that he would spend my money. Though he should have spent every farthing of it, I regret it; though he should have made me a beggar, I regret it. They told me that he would ill-use me, and desert me,—perhaps beat me. I do not believe it; but even though that should have been so, I regret it. It is better to have a false husband than to be a false wife.'

'Glencora, do not speak like that. Do not try to make me think that anything could tempt you to be false to your vows.'

'Tempt me to be false! Why, child, it has been all false throughout. I never loved him. How can you talk in that way, when you know that I never loved him? They browbeat me and frightened me till I did as I was told;—and now;—what am I now?'

'You are his honest wife. Glencora, listen to me.' And Alice took hold of her arm.

'No,' she said, 'no; I am not honest. By law I am his wife; but the laws are liars! I am not his wife. I will not say the thing that I am. When I went to him at the altar, I knew that I did not love the man that was to be my husband. But him,—Burgo,—I love him with all my heart and soul. I could stoop at his feet and clean his shoes for him, and think it no disgrace!'

'Oh, Cora, my friend, do not say such words as those! Remember what you owe your husband and yourself, and come away.'

'I do know what I owe him, and I will pay it him. Alice, if I had a child I think I would be true to him. Think! I know I would;—though I had no hour of happiness left to me in my life. But what now is the only honest thing that I can do? Why, leave him;—so leave him that he may have another wife and be the father of a child. What injury shall I do him by leaving him? He does not love me; you know yourself that he does not love me.'

'I know that he does.'

'Alice, that is untrue. He does not; and you have seen clearly that it is so. It may be that he can love no woman. But another woman would give him a son, and he would be happy. I tell you that every day and every night,—every hour of every day and of every night,—I am thinking of the man I love. I have nothing else to think of. I have no occupation,—no friends,—no one to whom I care to say a word. But I am always talking to Burgo in my thoughts; and he listens to me. I dream that his arm is round me——'

'Oh, Glencora!'

'Well!—Do you begrudge me that I should tell you the truth? You have said that you would be my friend, and you must bear the burden of my friendship. And now,—this is what I want to tell you.—Immediately after Christmas, we are to go to Monkshade, and he will be there. Lady Monk is his aunt.'

'You must not go. No power should take you there.'

'That is easily said, child; but all the same I must go. I told Mr. Palliser that he would be there, and he said it did not signify. He actually said that it did not signify. I wonder whether he understands what it is for people to love each other;—whether he has ever thought about it.'

'You must tell him plainly that you will not go.'

'I did. I told him plainly as words could tell him. "Glencora," he said,—and you know the way he looks when he means to be lord and master, and put on the very husband indeed,—"This is an annoyance which you must bear and overcome. It suits me that we should go to Monkshade, and it does not suit me that there should be any one whom you are afraid to meet." Could I tell him that he would lose his wife if I did go? Could I threaten him that I would throw myself into Burgo's arms if that opportunity were given to me? You are very wise, and very prudent. What would you have had me say?'

'I would have you now tell him everything, rather than go to that house.'

'Alice, look here. I know what I am, and what I am like to become. I loathe myself, and I loathe the thing that I am thinking of. I could have clung to the outside of a man's body, to his very trappings, and loved him ten times better than myself!—ay, even though he had ill-treated me,—if I had been allowed to choose a husband for myself. Burgo would have spent my money,—all that it would have been possible for me to give him. But there would have been something left, and I think that by that time I could have won even him to care for me. But with that man——! Alice, you are very wise. What am I to do?'

Alice had no doubt as to what her cousin should do. She should be true to her marriage-vow, whether that vow when made were true or false. She should be true to it as far as truth would now carry her. And in order that she might be true, she should tell her husband as much as might be necessary to induce him to spare her the threatened visit to Monkshade. All that she said to Lady Glencora, as they walked slowly across the chapel. But Lady Glencora was more occupied with her own thoughts than with her friend's advice. 'Here's Jeffrey!' she said. 'What an unconscionable time we have kept him!'

'Don't mention it,' he said. 'And I shouldn't have come to you now, only that I thought I should find you both freezing into marble.'

'We are not such cold-blooded creatures as that,—are we, Alice?' said Lady Glencora. 'And now we'll go round the outside; only we must not stay long, or we shall frighten those two delicious old duennas, Mrs. Marsham and Mr. Bott.'

These last words were said as it were in a whisper to Alice; but they were so whispered that there was no real attempt to keep them from the ears of Mr. Jeffrey Palliser. Glencora, Alice thought, should not have allowed the word duenna to have passed her lips in speaking to any one; but, above all, she should not have done so in the hearing of Mr. Palliser's cousin.

They walked all round the ruin, on a raised gravel-path which had been made there; and Alice, who could hardly bring herself to speak,—so full was her mind of that which had just been said to her,—was surprised to find that Glencora could go on, in her usual light humour, chatting as though there were no weight within her to depress her spirits.

CHAPTER XXVIII

Alice leaves the Priory

As they came in at the billiard-room door, Mr. Palliser was there to meet them. 'You must be very cold,' he said to Glencora, who entered first. 'No, indeed,' said Glencora;— but her teeth were chattering, and her whole appearance gave the lie to her words. 'Jeffrey,' said Mr. Palliser, turning to his cousin, 'I am angry with you. You, at least, should have known better than to have allowed her to remain so long.' Then Mr. Palliser turned away, and walked his wife off, taking no notice whatsoever of Miss Vavasor.

Alice felt the slight, and understood it all. He had told her plainly enough, though not in words, that he had trusted his wife with her, and that she had betrayed the trust. She might have brought Glencora in within five or six minutes, instead of allowing her to remain out there in the freezing night air for nearly three-quarters of an hour. That was the accusation which Mr. Palliser made against her, and he made it with the utmost severity. He asked no question of her whether she were cold. He spoke no word to her, nor did he even look at her. She might get herself away to her bedroom as she pleased. Alice understood all this completely, and though she knew that she had not deserved such severity, she was not inclined to resent it. There was so much in Mr. Palliser's position that was to be pitied, that Alice could not find it in her heart to be angry with him.

'He is provoked with us, now,' said Jeffrey Palliser, standing with her for a moment in the billiard-room, as he handed her a candle.

'He is afraid that she will have caught cold.'

'Yes; and he thinks it wrong that she should remain out at night so long. You can easily understand, Miss Vavasor, that he has not much sympathy for romance.'

'I dare say he is right,' said Alice, not exactly knowing what to say, and not being able to forget what had been said about herself and Jeffrey Palliser when they first left the house. 'Romance usually means nonsense, I believe.'

'That is not Glencora's doctrine.'

'No; but she is younger than I am. My feet are very cold, Mr. Palliser, and I think I will go up to my room.'

'Good night,' said Jeffrey, offering her his hand. 'I think it so hard that you should have incurred his displeasure.'

'It will not hurt me,' said Alice, smiling.

'No;—but he does not forget.'

'Even that will not hurt me. Good night, Mr. Palliser.'

'As it is the last night, may I say "good night, Alice"? I shall be away to-morrow before you are up.'

He still held her hand; but it had not been in his for half a minute, and she had thought nothing of that, nor did she draw it away even now suddenly. 'No,' said she, 'Glencora was very wrong there,—doing an injury without meaning it to both of us. There can be no possible reason why you should call me otherwise than is customary.'

'Can there never be a reason?'

'No, Mr. Palliser. Good night;—and if I am not to see you to-morrow morning, good-bye.'

'You will certainly not see me to-morrow morning.'

'Good-bye. Had it not been for this folly of Glencora's, our acquaintance would have been very pleasant.'

'To me it has been very pleasant. Good night.'

Then she left him, and went up alone to her own room. Whether or no other guests were still left in the drawing-room she did not know; but she had seen that Mr. Palliser took his wife up stairs, and therefore she considered herself right in presuming that the party was broken up for the night. Mr. Palliser,—Plantagenet Palliser, according to all rules of courtesy should have said a word to her as he went; but, as I have said before, Alice was disposed to overlook his want of civility on this occasion. So she went up alone to her room, and was very glad to find herself able to get close to a good fire. She was, in truth, very cold—cold to her bones, in spite of what

Lady Glencora had said on behalf of the moonlight. They two had been standing all but still during the greater part of the time that they had been talking, and Alice, as she sat herself down, found that her feet were numbed with the damp that had penetrated through her boots. Certainly Mr. Palliser had reason to be angry that his wife should have remained out in the night air so long,—though perhaps not with Alice.

And then she began to think of what had been told her, and to try to think of what, under such circumstances, it behoved her to do. She could not doubt that Lady Glencora had intended to declare that, if opportunity offered itself, she would leave her husband, and put herself under the protection of Mr. Fitzgerald; and Alice, moreover, had become painfully conscious that the poor deluded unreasoning creature had taught herself to think that she might excuse herself for this sin to her own conscience by the fact that she was childless, and that she might thus give to the man who had married her an opportunity of seeking another wife who might give him an heir. Alice well knew how insufficient such an excuse would be even to the wretched woman who had framed it for herself. But still it would operate,—manifestly had already operated, on her mind, teaching her to hope that good might come out of evil. Alice, who was perfectly clearsighted as regarded her cousin, however much impaired her vision might have been with reference to herself, saw nothing but absolute ruin, ruin of the worst and most intolerable description, in the plan which Lady Glencora seemed to have formed. To her it was black as the depths of hell; and she knew that to Glencora also it was black. 'I loathe myself,' Glencora had said, 'and the thing that I am thinking of.'

What was Alice to do under these circumstances? Mr. Palliser, she was aware, had quarrelled with her: for in his silent way he had first shown that he had trusted her as his wife's friend; and then, on this evening, he had shown that he had ceased to trust her. But she cared little for this. If she told him that she wished to speak to him, he would listen, let his opinion of her be what it might; and having listened he would surely act in some way that would serve to save his wife. What Mr. Palliser might think of herself, Alice cared but little.

But then there came to her an idea,—an idea that was in every respect feminine,—that in such a matter she had no right to betray her friend. When one woman tells the story of her love to another woman, the confidant always feels that she will be a traitor if she reveals the secret. Had Lady Glencora made Alice believe that she meditated murder, or robbery, Alice would have had no difficulty in telling the tale, and thus preventing the crime. But now she hesitated, feeling that she would disgrace herself by betraying her friend. And, after all, was it not more than probable that Glencora had no intention of carrying out a threat the very thought of which must be terrible to herself?

As she was thinking of all this, sitting in her dressing-gown close over the fire, there came a loud knock at the door, which, as she had turned the key, she was forced to answer in person. She opened the door, and there was Iphigenia Palliser, Jeffrey's cousin, and Mr. Palliser's cousin. 'Miss Vavasor,' she said, 'I know that I am taking a great liberty, but may I come into your room for a few minutes? I so much wish to speak to you!' Alice of course bade her enter, and placed a chair for her by the fire.

Alice Vavasor had made very little intimacy with either of the two Miss Pallisers. It had seemed to herself as though there had been two parties in the house, and that she had belonged to the one which was headed by the wife, whereas the Miss Pallisers had been naturally attached to that of the husband. These ladies, as she had already seen, almost idolized their cousin; and though Plantagenet Palliser had till lately treated Alice with the greatest personal courtesy, there had been no intimacy of friendship between them, and consequently none between her and his special adherents. Nor was either of these ladies prone to sudden friendship with such a one as Alice Vavasor. A sudden friendship with a snuffy president of a foreign learned society, with some personally unknown lady employed on female emigration,* was very much in their way. But Alice had not shown herself to be useful or learned, and her special intimacy with Lady Glencora had marked her out as in some sort separated from them and their ways.

'I know that I am intruding,' said Miss Palliser, as though she were almost afraid of Alice.

'Oh dear, no,' said Alice. 'If I can do anything for you I shall be very happy.'

'You are going to-morrow, and if I did not speak to you now I should have no other opportunity. Glencora seems to be very much attached to you, and we all thought it so good a thing that she should have such a friend.'

'I hope you have not all changed your minds,' said Alice, with a faint smile, thinking as she spoke that the 'all' must have been specially intended to include the master of the house.

'Oh, no;—by no means. I did not mean that. My cousin, Mr. Palliser, I mean, liked you so much when you came.'

'And he does not like me quite so much now, because I went out in the moonlight with his wife. Isn't that it?'

'Well;—no, Miss Vavasor. I had not intended to mention that at all. I had not indeed. I have seen him certainly since you came in,—just for a minute, and he is vexed. But it is not about that that I would speak to you.'

'I saw plainly enough that he was angry with me.'

'He thought you would have brought her in earlier.'

'And why should he think that I can manage his wife? She was the mistress out there as she is in here. Mr. Palliser has been unreasonable. Not that it signifies.'

'I don't think he has been unreasonable; I don't, indeed, Miss Vavasor. He has certainly been vexed. Sometimes he has much to vex him. You see, Glencora is very young.'

Mr. Bott also had declared that Lady Glencora was very young. It was probable, therefore, that that special phrase had been used in some discussion among Mr. Palliser's party as to Glencora's foibles. So thought Alice as the remembrance of the word came upon her.

'She is not younger than when Mr. Palliser married her,' Alice said.

'You mean that if a man marries a young wife he must put up with the trouble. That is a matter of course. But their ages, in truth, are very suitable. My cousin himself is not yet thirty. When I say that Glencora is young——'

'You mean that she is younger in spirit, and perhaps in conduct, than he had expected to find her.'

'But you are not to suppose that he complains, Miss Vavasor. He is much too proud for that.'

'I should hope so,' said Alice, thinking of Mr. Bott.

'I hardly know how to explain to you what I wish to say, or how far I may be justified in supposing that you will believe me to be acting solely on Glencora's behalf. I think you have some influence with her;—and I know no one else that has any.'

'My friendship with her is not of very long date, Miss Palliser.'

'I know it, but still there is the fact. Am I not right in supposing——'

'In supposing what?'

'In supposing that you had heard the name of Mr. Fitzgerald as connected with Glencora's before her marriage with my cousin?'

Alice paused a moment before she answered.

'Yes, I had,' she then said.

'And I think you were agreed, with her other relations, that such a marriage would have been very dreadful.'

'I never spoke of the matter in the presence of any relatives of Glencora's. You must understand, Miss Palliser, that though I am her far-away cousin, I do not even know her nearest connections. I never saw Lady Midlothian till she came here the other day.'

'But you advised her to abandon Mr. Fitzgerald.'

'Never!'

'I know she was much with you, just at that time.'

'I used to see her, certainly.'

Then there was a pause, and Miss Palliser, in truth, scarcely knew how to go on. There had been a hardness about Alice which her visitor had not expected,—an unwillingness to speak or even to listen, which made Miss Palliser almost wish that she were out of the room. She had, however, mentioned Burgo Fitzgerald's name, and out of the room now she could not go without explaining why she had done so. But at this point Alice came suddenly to her assistance.

'Just then she was often with me,' said Alice, continuing her reply; 'and there was much talk between us about Mr. Fitzgerald. What was my advice then can be of little matter; but in this we shall be both agreed, Miss Palliser, that Glencora now should certainly not be called upon to be in his company.'

'She has told you, then?'

'Yes;—she has told me.'

'That he is to be at Lady Monk's?'

'She has told me that Mr. Palliser expects her to meet him at the place to which they are going when they leave the Duke's, and that she thinks it hard that she should be subjected to such a trial.'

'It should be no trial, Miss Vavasor.'

'How can it be otherwise? Come, Miss Palliser; if you are her friend, be fair to her.'

'I am her friend;—but I am, above everything, my cousin's friend. He has told me that she has complained of having to meet this man. He declares that it should be nothing to her, and that the fear is an idle folly. It should be nothing to her, but still the fear may not be idle. Is there any reason,—any real reason,—why she should not go? Miss Vavasor, I conjure you to tell me,—even though in doing so you must cast so deep reproach upon her name! Anything will be better than utter disgrace and sin!'

'I conceive that I cast no reproach upon her in saying that there is great reason why she should not go to Monk-shade.'

'You think there is absolute ground for interference? I must tell him, you know, openly what he would have to fear.'

'I think,—nay, Miss Palliser, I know,—that there is ample reason why you should save her from being taken to Monkshade, if you have the power to do so.'

'I can only do it, or attempt to do it, by telling him just what you tell me.'

'Then tell him. You must have thought of that, I suppose, before you came to me.'

'Yes;—yes, Miss Vavasor. I had thought of it. No doubt I had thought of it. But I had believed all through that you would assure me that there was no danger. I believed that you would have said that she was innocent.'

'And she is innocent,' said Alice, rising from her chair, as though she might thus give emphasis to words which she hardly dared to speak above a whisper. 'She is innocent. Who accuses her of guilt? You ask me a question on his behalf——'

'On hers—and on his, Miss Vavasor.'

'A question which I feel myself bound to answer truly,—to answer with reference to the welfare of them both; but I will not have it said that I accuse her. She had been attached to Mr. Fitzgerald when your cousin married her. He knew that this had been the case. She told him the whole truth. In a worldly point of view her marriage with Mr. Fitzgerald would probably have been very imprudent.'

'It would have been utterly ruinous.'

'Perhaps so; I say nothing about that. But as it turned out, she gave up her own wishes and married your cousin.'

'I don't know about her own wishes, Miss Vavasor.'

'It is what she did. She would have married Mr. Fitzgerald, had she not been hindered by the advice of those around her. It cannot be supposed that she has forgotten him in so short a time. There can be no guilt in her remembrance.'

'There is guilt in loving any other than her husband.'

'Then, Miss Palliser, it was her marriage that was guilty, and not her love. But all that is done and past. It should be your cousin's object to teach her to forget Mr. Fitzgerald, and he will not do that by taking her to a house where that gentleman is staying.'

'She has said so much to you herself?'

'I do not know that I need declare to you what she has said herself. You have asked me a question, and I have answered it, and I am thankful to you for having asked it. What object can either of us have but to assist her in her position?'

'And to save him from dishonour. I had so hoped that this was simply a childish dread on her part.'

'It is not so. It is no childish dread. If you have the power to prevent her going to Lady Monk's, I implore you to use it. Indeed, I will ask you to promise me that you will do so.'

'After what you have said, I have no alternative.'

'Exactly. There is no alternative. Either for his sake or for hers, there is none.'

Thereupon Miss Palliser got up, and wishing her companion good night, took her departure. Throughout the interview there had been no cordiality of feeling between them. There was no pretence of friendship, even as they were parting. They acknowledged that their objects were different. That of Alice was to save Lady Glencora from ruin. That of Miss Palliser was to save her cousin from disgrace,—with perhaps some further honest desire to prevent sorrow and sin. One loved Lady Glencora, and the other clearly did not love her. But, nevertheless, Alice felt that Miss Palliser, in coming to her, had acted well, and that to herself this coming had afforded immense relief. Some step would now be taken to prevent that meeting which she had so deprecated, and it would be taken without any great violation of confidence on her part. She had said nothing as to which Lady Glencora could feel herself aggrieved.

On the next morning she was down in the breakfast-room soon after nine, and had not been in the room many minutes before Mr. Palliser entered. 'The carriage is ordered for you at a quarter before ten,' he said, 'and I have come down to give you your breakfast.' There was a smile on his face as he spoke, and Alice could see that he intended to make himself pleasant.

'Will you allow me to give you yours instead?' said she.

But as it happened, no giving on either side was needed, as Alice's breakfast was brought to her separately.

'Glencora bids me say that she will be down immediately,' said Mr. Palliser.

Alice then made some inquiry with reference to the effects of last night's imprudence, which received only a half-pronounced reply. Mr. Palliser was willing to be gracious, but did not intend to be understood as having forgiven the offence. The Miss Pallisers then came in together, and after them Mr. Bott, closely followed by Mrs. Marsham, and all of them made inquiries after Lady Glencora, as though it was to be supposed that she might probably be in a perilous state after what she had undergone on the previous evening. Mr. Bott was particularly anxious. 'The frost was so uncommonly severe,' said he, 'that any delicate person like Lady Glencowrer must have suffered in remaining out so long.'

The insinuation that Alice was not a delicate person, and that, as regarded her, the severity of the frost was of no moment, was very open, and was duly appreciated. Mr. Bott was aware that his great patron had in some sort changed his opinion about Miss Vavasor, and he was of course disposed to change his own. A fortnight since Alice might have been as delicate as she pleased in Mr. Bott's estimation.

'I hope you do not consider Lady Glencora delicate,' said Alice to Mr. Palliser.

'She is not robust,' said the husband.

'By no means,' said Mrs. Marsham.

'Indeed, no,' said Mr. Bott.

Alice knew that she was being accused of being robust herself; but she bore it in silence. Ploughboys and milkmaids are robust, and the accusation was a heavy one. Alice, however, thought that she would not have minded it, if she could have allowed herself to reply; but this at the moment of her going away she could not do.

'I think she is as strong as the rest of us,' said Iphigenia Palliser, who felt that after last night she owed something to Miss Vavasor.

'As some of us,' said Mr. Bott, determined to persevere in his accusation.

At this moment Lady Glencora entered, and encountered the eager inquiries of her two duennas. These, however, she quickly put aside, and made her way up to Alice. 'The last morning has come, then,' she said.

'Yes, indeed,' said Alice. 'Mr. Palliser must have thought that I was never going.'

'On the other hand,' said he, 'I have felt much obliged to you for staying.' But he said it coldly; and Alice began to wish that she had never seen Matching Priory.

'Obliged!' exclaimed Lady Glencora. 'I can't tell you how much obliged I am. Oh, Alice, I wish you were going to stay with us!'

'We are leaving this in a week's time,' said Mr. Palliser.

'Of course we are,' said Lady Glencora. 'With all my heart I wish we were not. Dear Alice! I suppose we shall not meet till we are all in town.'

'You will let me know when you come up,' said Alice.

'I will send to you instantly; and, Alice, I will write to you from Gatherum,—or from Monkshade.'

Alice could not help looking round and catching Miss Palliser's eye. Miss Palliser was standing with her foot on the fender, but was so placed that she could see Alice. She made a slight sign with her head, as much as to say that Lady Glencora must have no opportunity of writing from that latter place; but she said nothing.

Then the carriage was announced, and Mr. Palliser took Alice out on his arm. 'Don't come to the door, Glencora,' he said. 'I especially wish you not to do so.' The two cousins then kissed each other, and Alice went away to the carriage.

'Good-bye, Miss Vavasor,' said Mr. Palliser; but he expressed no wish that he might see her again as his guest at Matching Priory.

Alice, as she was driven in solitary grandeur to the railway station, could not but wish that she had never gone there.

CHAPTER XXIX

Burgo Fitzgerald

O<small>N</small> the night before Christmas Eve two men were sitting
together in George Vavasor's rooms in Cecil Street. It
was past twelve o'clock, and they were both smoking; there
were square bottles on the table containing spirits, with hot
water and cold water in jugs, and one of the two men was
using, and had been using, these materials for enjoyment.
Vavasor had not been drinking, nor did it appear as though he
intended to begin. There was a little weak brandy and water
in a glass by his side, but there it had remained untouched for
the last twenty minutes. His companion, however, had twice
in that time replenished his beaker, and was now puffing out
the smoke of his pipe with the fury of a steamer's funnel when
she has not yet burned the black off her last instalment of fresh
coals. This man was Burgo Fitzgerald. He was as handsome
as ever;—a man whom neither man nor woman could help
regarding as a thing beautiful to behold;—but not the less was
there in his eyes and cheeks a look of haggard dissipation,—
of riotous living, which had become wearisome, by its continuance, even to himself,—that told to all who saw him much

of the history of his life. Most men who drink at nights, and are out till cockcrow doing deeds of darkness, become red in their faces, have pimpled cheeks and watery eyes, and are bloated and not comfortable to be seen. It is a kind dispensation of Providence who thus affords to such sinners a visible sign, to be seen day by day, of the injury which is being done. The first approach of a carbuncle on the nose, about the age of thirty, has stopped many a man from drinking. No one likes to have carbuncles on his nose, or to appear before his female friends with eyes which look as though they were swimming in grog. But to Burgo Fitzgerald Providence in her anger had not afforded this protection. He became at times pale, sallow, worn, and haggard. He grew thin, and still thinner. At times he had been ill to death's door. Among his intimate friends there were those who heard him declare frequently that his liver had become useless to him; and that, as for gastric juices, he had none left to him. But still his beauty remained. The perfect form of his almost godlike face was the same as ever, and the brightness of his bright blue eye was never quenched.

On the present occasion he had come to Vavasor's room with the object of asking from him certain assistance, and perhaps also some amount of advice. But as regarded the latter article he was, I think, in the state of most men when they seek for counsellors who shall counsel them to do evil. Advice administered in accordance with his own views would give him comfortable encouragement, but advice on the other side he was prepared to disregard altogether. These two men had known each other long, and a close intimacy had existed between them in the days past, previous to Lady Glencora's engagement with Mr. Palliser. When Lady Glencora endeavoured, vainly as we know, to obtain aid from Alice Vavasor, Burgo had been instigated to believe that Alice's cousin might assist him. Any such assistance George Vavasor would have been quite ready to give. Some pecuniary assistance he had given, he at that time having been in good funds. Perhaps he had for a moment induced Burgo to think that he could obtain for the pair the use of the house in Queen Anne Street as a point at which they might meet, and from whence they might start on their journey of love. All that was over. Those hopes had been frustrated, and Lady Glencora M'Cluskie had become Lady Glencora Palliser and not Lady Glencora Fitzgerald. But now other hopes had sprung up, and Burgo was again looking to his friend for assistance.

'I believe she would,' Burgo said, as he lifted the glass to his mouth. 'It's a thing of that sort that a man can only believe,—perhaps only hope,—till he has tried. I know that she is not happy with him, and I have made up my mind that I will at least ask her.'

'But he would have her fortune all the same?'

'I don't know how that would be. I haven't inquired, and I don't mean to inquire. Of course I don't expect you or any one else to believe me, but her money has no bearing on the question now. Heaven knows I want money bad enough, but I wouldn't take away another man's wife for money.'

'You don't mean to say you think it would be wicked. I supposed you to be above those prejudices.'

'It's all very well for you to chaff.'

'It's no chaff at all. I tell you fairly I wouldn't run away with any man's wife. I have an old-fashioned idea that when a man has got a wife he ought to be allowed to keep her. Public opinion, I know, is against me.'

'I think he ran away with my wife,' said Burgo, with emphasis; 'that's the way I look at it. She was engaged to me first; and she really loved me, while she never cared for him.'

'Nevertheless, marriage is marriage, and the law is against you. But if I did go in for such a troublesome job at all, I certainly should keep an eye upon the money.'

'It can make no difference.'

'It did make a difference, I suppose, when you first thought of marrying her?'

'Of course it did. My people brought us together because she had a large fortune and I had none. There's no doubt in the world about that. And I'll tell you what; I believe that old

301

harridan of an aunt of mine is willing to do the same thing now again. Of course she doesn't say as much. She wouldn't dare do that, but I do believe she means it. I wonder where she expects to go to!'

'That's grateful on your part.'

'Upon my soul I hate her. I do indeed. It isn't love for me now so much as downright malice against Palliser, because he baulked her project before. She is a wicked old woman. Some of us fellows are wicked enough—you and I for instance——'

'Thank you. I don't know, however, that I am qualified to run in a curricle*with you.'

'But we are angels to such an old she-devil as that. You may believe me or not, as you like.—I dare say you won't believe me.'

'I'll say I do, at any rate.'

'The truth is, I want to get her, partly because I love her; but chiefly because I do believe in my heart that she loves me.'

'It's for her sake then! You are ready to sacrifice yourself to do her a good turn.'

'As for sacrificing myself, that's done. I'm a man utterly ruined and would cut my throat to-morrow for the sake of my relations, if I cared enough about them. I know my own condition pretty well. I have made a shipwreck of everything, and have now only got to go down among the breakers.'

'Only you would like to take Lady Glencora with you.'

'No, by heavens! But sometimes, when I do think about it at all,—which I do as seldom as I can,—it seems to me that I might still become a different fellow if it were possible for me to marry her.'

'Had you married her when she was free to marry any one and when her money was her own, it might have been so.'

'I think it would be quite as much so now. I do, indeed. If I could get her once, say to Italy, or perhaps to Greece, I think I could treat her well, and live with her quietly. I know that I would try.'

'Without the assistance of brandy and cigars?'

'Yes.'

'And without any money?'

'With only a little. I know you'll laugh at me; but I make pictures to myself of a sort of life which I think would suit us, and be very different from this hideous way of living, with which I have become so sick that I loathe it.'

'Something like Juan and Haidee, with Planty Pall coming after you, like old Lambro.'*By the nickname of Planty Pall George Vavasor intended to designate Lady Glencora's present husband.

'He'd get a divorce, of course, and then we should be married. I really don't think he'd dislike it, when it was all done. They tell me he doesn't care for her.'

'You have seen her since her marriage?'

'Yes; twice.'

'And have spoken to her?'

'Once only,—so as to be able to do more than ask her if she were well. Once, for about two minutes, I did speak to her.'

'And what did she say?'

'She said it would be better that we should not meet. When she said that, I knew that she was still fond of me. I could have fallen at her feet that moment, only the room was full of people. I do think that she is fond of me.'

Vavasor paused a few minutes. 'I dare say she is fond of you,' he then said; 'but whether she has pluck for such a thing as this, is more than I can say. Probably she has not. And if she has, probably you would fail in carrying out your plan.'

'I must get a little money first,' said Burgo.

'And that's an operation which no doubt you find more difficult every day, as you grow older.'

'It seems to be much the same sort of thing. I went to Magruin this morning.'

'He's the fellow that lives out near Gray's Inn Lane?'

'Just beyond the Foundling Hospital.* I went to him, and he was quite civil about it. He says I owe him over three thousand pounds, but that doesn't seem to make any difference.'

'How much did you ever have from him?'

'I don't recollect that I ever absolutely had any money. He

got a bill of mine from a tailor who went to smash,* and he kept on renewing that till it grew to be ever so many bills. I think he did once let me have twenty-four pounds,—but certainly never more than that.'

'And he says he'll give you money now? I suppose you told him why you wanted it.'

'I didn't name her,—but I told him what would make him understand that I hoped to get off with a lady who had a lot of tin. I asked him for two hundred and fifty. He says he'll let me have one hundred and fifty on a bill at two months for five hundred,*—with your name to it.'

'With my name to it! That's kind on his part,—and on yours too.'

'Of course I can't take it up at the end of two months.'

'I dare say not,' said Vavasor.

'But he won't come upon you then,—nor for a year or more afterwards. I did pay you what you lent me before.'

'Yes, you did. I always thought that to be a special compliment on your part.'

'And you'll find I'll pull you through now in some way. If I don't succeed in this I shall go off the hooks altogether soon; and if I were dead my people would pay my debts then.'

Before the evening was over Vavasor promised the assistance asked of him. He knew that he was lending his name to a man who was utterly ruined, and putting it into the hands of another man who was absolutely without conscience in the use he would make of it. He knew that he was creating for himself trouble, and in all probability loss, which he was ill able to bear. But the thing was one which came within the pale of his laws. Such assistance as that he might ask of others, and had asked and received before now. It was a reckless deed on his part, but then all his doings were reckless. It was consonant with his mode of life.

'I thought you would, old fellow,' said Burgo, as he got up to go away. 'Perhaps, you know, I shall pull through in this; and perhaps, after all, some part of her fortune will come with her. If so you'll be all right.'

'Perhaps I may. But look here, Burgo,—don't you give that fellow up the bill till you've got the money into your fist.'

'You may be quite easy about that. I know their tricks. He and I will go to the bank together, and we shall squabble there at the door about four or five odd sovereigns,—and at last I shall have to give him up two or three. Beastly old robber! I declare I think he's worse than I am myself.' Then Burgo Fitzgerald took a little more brandy and water and went away.

He was living at this time in the house of one of his relatives in Cavendish Square, north of Oxford Street. His uncles and his aunts, and all those who were his natural friends, had clung to him with a tenacity that was surprising; for he had never been true to any of them, and did not even pretend to like them. His father, with whom for many years he had not been on speaking terms, was now dead; but he had sisters whose husbands would still open their houses to him, either in London or in the country;—would open their houses to him, and lend him their horses, and provide him with every luxury which the rich enjoy,—except ready money. When the uttermost stress of pecuniary embarrassment would come upon him, they would pay something to stave off the immediate evil. And so Burgo went on. Nobody now thought of saying much to reproach him. It was known to be waste of words, and trouble in vain. They were still fond of him because he was beautiful and never vain of his beauty;—because in the midst of his recklessness there was always about him a certain kindliness which made him pleasant to those around him. He was soft and gracious with children, and would be very courteous to his lady cousins. They knew that as a man he was worthless, but nevertheless they loved him. I think the secret of it was chiefly in this,—that he seemed to think so little of himself.

But now as he walked home in the middle of the night from Cecil Street to Cavendish Square he did think much of himself. Indeed such self-thoughts come naturally to all men, be their outward conduct ever so reckless. Every man to himself is the centre of the whole world;—the axle on which it all turns. All knowledge is but his own perception of the things around him.

All love, and care for others, and solicitude for the world's welfare, are but his own feelings as to the world's wants and the world's merits.

He had played his part as a centre of all things very badly. Of that he was very well aware. He had sense enough to know that it should be a man's lot to earn his bread after some fashion, and he often told himself that never as yet had he earned so much as a penny roll. He had learned to comprehend that the world's progress depends on the way in which men do their duty by each other,—that the progress of one generation depends on the discharge of such duties by that which preceded it;—and he knew that he, in his generation, had done nothing to promote such progress. He thoroughly despised himself,— if there might be any good in that! But on such occasions as these, when the wine he had drunk was sufficient only to drive away from him the numbness of despair, when he was all alone with the cold night air upon his face, when the stars were bright above him and the world around him was almost quiet, he would still ask himself whether there might not yet be, even for him, some hope of a redemption,—some chance of a better life in store for him. He was still young,—wanting some years of thirty. Could there be, even for him, some mode of extrication from his misery?'

We know what was the mode which now, at this moment, was suggesting itself to him. He was proposing to himself, as the best thing that he could do, to take away another man's wife and make himself happy with her! What he had said to Vavasor as to disregarding Lady Glencora's money had been perfectly true. That in the event of her going off with him, some portion of her enormous wealth would still cling to her, he did believe. Seeing that she had no children he could not understand where else it should all go. But he thought of this as it regarded her, not as it regarded him. When he had before made his suit to her,—a suit which was then honourable, how-ever disadvantageous it might have seemed to be to her,—he had made in his mind certain calculations as to the good things which would result to him if he were successful. He would keep hounds, and have three or four horses every day for his own riding, and he would have no more interviews with Magruin, waiting in that rogue's dingy back parlour for many a weary wretched half-hour, till the rogue should be pleased to show himself. So far he had been mercenary; but he had learned to love the girl, and to care more for her than for her money, and when the day of disappointment came upon him,—the day on which she had told him that all between them was to be over for ever,—he had, for a few hours, felt the loss of his love more than the loss of his money.

Then he had had no further hope. No such idea as that which now filled his mind had then come upon him. The girl had gone from him and married another man, and there was an end of it. But by degrees tidings had reached him that she was not happy,—reaching him through the mouths of people who were glad to exaggerate all that they had heard. A whole tribe of his female relatives had been anxious to promote his marriage with Lady Glencora M'Cluskie, declaring that, after all that was come and gone, Burgo would come forth from his troubles as a man of great wealth. So great was the wealth of the heiress that it might withstand even his propensities for spending. That whole tribe had been bitterly disappointed; and when they heard that Mr. Palliser's marriage had given him no child, and that Lady Glencora was unhappy,—they made their remarks in triumph rather than in sorrow. I will not say that they looked forward approvingly to such a step as that which Burgo now wished to take,—though as regarded his aunt, Lady Monk, he himself had accused her; but they whispered that such things had been done and must be expected, when marriages were made up as had been that marriage between Mr. Palliser and his bride.

As he walked on, thinking of his project, he strove hard to cheat himself into a belief that he would do a good thing in carrying Lady Glencora away from her husband. Bad as had been his life he had never before done aught so bad as that. The more fixed his intention became, the more thoroughly he came to perceive how great and grievous was the crime which he contemplated. To elope with another man's wife no longer appeared to him to be a joke at which such men as he might smile. But he tried to think that in this case there would be special circumstances which would almost justify him, and also her. They had loved each other and had sworn to love each other with constancy. There had been no change in the feelings or even in the wishes of either of them. But cold people had come between them with cold calculations, and had separated them. She had been, he told himself, made to marry a man she did not love. If they two loved each other truly, would it not still be better that they should come together? Would not the sin be forgiven on account of the injustice which had been done to them? Had Mr. Palliser a right to expect more from a wife who had been made to marry him without loving him? Then he reverted to those dreams of a life of love, in some sunny country, of which he had spoken to Vavasor, and he strove to nourish them. Vavasor had laughed at him, talking of Juan and Haidee. But Vavasor, he said to himself, was a hard cold man, who had no touch of romance in his character. He would not be laughed out of his plan by such as he,—nor would he be frightened by the threat of any Lambro who might come after him, whether he might come in the guise of indignant uncle or injured husband.

He had crossed from Regent Street through Hanover Square, and as he came out by the iron gates into Oxford Street, a poor wretched girl, lightly clad in thin raiment, into whose bones the sharp freezing air was penetrating, asked him for money. Would he give her something to get drink, so that for a moment she might feel the warmth of her life renewed? Such midnight petitions were common enough in his ears, and he was passing on without thinking of her. But she was urgent, and took hold of him. 'For love of God,' she said, 'if it's only a penny to get a glass of gin! Feel my hand,—how cold it is.' And she strove to put it up against his face.

He looked round at her and saw that she was very young,—sixteen, perhaps, at the most, and that she had once,—nay very lately,—been exquisitely pretty. There still lingered about her eyes some remains of that look of perfect innocency and pure faith which had been hers not more than twelve months since. And now, at midnight, in the middle of the streets, she was praying for a pennyworth of gin, as the only comfort she knew, or could expect!

'You are cold!' said he, trying to speak to her cheerily.

'Cold!' said she, repeating the word, and striving to wrap herself closer in her rags, as she shivered—'Oh God! if you knew what it was to be as cold as I am! I have nothing in the world,—not one penny,—not a hole to lie in!'

'We are alike then,' said Burgo, with a slight low laugh. 'I also have nothing. You cannot be poorer than I am.'

'You poor!' she said. And then she looked up into his face. 'Gracious; how beautiful you are! Such as you are never poor.'

He laughed again,—in a different tone. He always laughed when any one told him of his beauty. 'I am a deal poorer than you, my girl,' he said. 'You have nothing. I have thirty thousand pounds worse than nothing. But come along, and I will get you something to eat.'

'Will you?' said she, eagerly. Then looking up at him again, she exclaimed—'Oh, you are so handsome!'

He took her to a public-house and gave her bread and meat and beer, and stood by her while she ate it. She was shy with him then, and would fain have taken it to a corner by herself, had he allowed her. He perceived this, and turned his back to her, but still spoke to her a word or two as she ate. The woman at the bar who served him looked at him wonderingly, staring into his face; and the pot-boy woke himself thoroughly that he might look at Burgo; and the waterman from the cab-stand stared at him; and women who came in for gin looked almost lovingly up into his eyes. He regarded them all not at all, showing no feeling of disgrace at his position, and no desire to carry himself as a ruffler.* He quietly paid what was due when the girl had finished her meal, and then walked with her out of the shop. 'And now,' said he, 'what must I do with you? If I give you a shilling can you get a bed?' She told him that she could get a bed for sixpence. 'Then keep the other sixpence for your breakfast,' said he. 'But you must promise me that you will buy no gin to-night.' She promised him, and then he gave her his hand as he wished her good night;—his hand, which it had been the dearest wish of Lady Glencora to call her own. She took it and pressed it to her lips. 'I wish I might once see you again,' she said, 'because you are so good and so beautiful.' He laughed again cheerily, and walked on, crossing the street towards Cavendish Square. She stood looking at him till he was out of sight, and then as she moved away,—let us hope to the bed which his bounty had provided, and not to a gin-shop,—she exclaimed to herself again and again—'Gracious, how beautiful he was!' 'He's a good un,' the woman at the public-house had said as soon as he left it; 'but, my! did you ever see a man's face handsome as that fellow's?'

Poor Burgo! All who had seen him since life had begun with him had loved him and striven to cherish him. And with it all, to what a state had he come! Poor Burgo! had his eyes been less brightly blue, and his face less godlike in form, it may be that things would have gone better with him. A sweeter-tempered man than he never lived,—nor one who was of a kinder nature. At this moment he had barely money about him to take him down to his aunt's house at Monkshade, and as he had promised to be there before Christmas Day, he was bound to start on the next morning, before help from Mr. Magruin was possible. Nevertheless, out of his very narrow funds he had given half a crown to comfort the poor creature who had spoken to him in the street.

CHAPTER XXX

Containing a Love-letter

VAVASOR, as he sat alone in his room, after Fitzgerald had left him, began to think of the days in which he had before wished to assist his friend in his views with reference to Lady Glencora;—or rather he began to think of Alice's behaviour then, and of Alice's words. Alice had steadfastly refused to give any aid. No less likely assistant for such a purpose could have been selected. But she had been very earnest in declaring that it was Glencora's duty to stand by her promise to Burgo. 'He is a desperate spendthrift,' Kate Vavasor had said to her. 'Then let her teach him to be otherwise,' Alice had answered. 'That might have been a good reason for refusing his offer when he first made it; but it can be no excuse for untruth, now that she has told him that she loves him!' 'If a woman,' she had said again, 'won't venture her fortune for the man she loves, her love is not worth having.' All this George Vavasor remembered now; and as he remembered it he asked himself whether the woman that had once loved him would venture her fortune for him still.

Though his sister had pressed him on the subject with all the vehemence that she could use, he had hardly hitherto made up his mind that he really desired to marry Alice. There had grown upon him lately certain Bohemian propensities,—a love of absolute independence in his thoughts as well as actions,— which were antagonistic to marriage. He was almost inclined to think that marriage was an old-fashioned custom, fitted indeed well enough for the usual dull life of the world at large,— as many men both in heathen and in Christian ages have taught themselves to think of religion,—but which was not adapted to his advanced intelligence. If he loved any woman he loved his cousin Alice. If he thoroughly respected any woman he respected her. But that idea of tying himself down to a household was in itself distasteful to him. 'It is a thing terrible to think of,' he once said to a congenial friend in these days of his life, 'that a man should give permission to a priest to tie him to another human being like a Siamese twin, so that all power of separate and solitary action should be taken from him for ever! The beasts of the field do not treat each other so badly. They neither drink themselves drunk, nor eat themselves stupid;— nor do they bind themselves together in a union which both would have to hate.' In this way George Vavasor, trying to imitate the wisdom of the brutes, had taught himself some theories of a peculiar nature. But, nevertheless, as he thought of Alice Vavasor on this occasion, he began to feel that if a

Siamese twin were necessary for him, she of all others was the woman to whom he would wish to be so bound.

And if he did it at all, he must do it now. Under the joint instigation of himself and his sister,—as he thought, and perhaps not altogether without reason,—she had broken her engagement with Mr. Grey. That she would renew it again if left to herself, he believed probable. And then, despite that advanced intelligence which had taught him to regard all forms and ceremonies with the eye of a philosopher, he had still enough of human frailty about him to feel keenly alive to the pleasure of taking from John Grey the prize which John Grey had so nearly taken from him. If Alice could have been taught to think as he did as to the absurdity of those indissoluble ties, that would have been better. But nothing would have been more impossible than the teaching of such a lesson to his cousin Alice. George Vavasor was a man of courage, and dared do most things;—but he would not have dared to commence the teaching of such a lesson to her.

And now, at this moment, what was his outlook into life generally? He had very high ambition, and a fair hope of gratifying it if he could only provide that things should go well with him for a year or so. He was still a poor man, having been once nearly a rich man; but still so much of the result of his nearly acquired riches remained to him, that on the strength of them he might probably find his way into Parliament. He had paid the cost of the last attempt, and might, in a great degree, carry on this present attempt on credit. If he succeeded there would be open to him a mode of life, agreeable in itself, and honourable among men. But how was he to bear the cost of this for the next year, or the next two years? His grandfather was still alive, and would probably live over that period. If he married Alice he would do so with no idea of cheating her out of her money. She should learn,—nay, she had already learned from his own lips,—how perilous was his enterprise. But he knew her to be a woman who would boldly risk all in money, though no consideration would induce her to stir a hair's breadth towards danger in reputation. Towards teaching her that doctrine at which I have hinted, he would not have dared to make an attempt; but he felt that he should have no repugnance to telling her that he wanted to spend all her money in the first year or two of their married life!

He was still in his arm-chair, thinking of all this, with that small untasted modicum of brandy and water beside him, when he heard some distant Lambeth clock strike three from over the river. Then he rose from his seat, and taking the candles in his hand, sat himself down at a writing-desk on the other side of the room. 'I needn't send it when it's written,' he said to himself, 'and the chances are that I won't.' Then he took his paper, and wrote as follows:—

'DEAR ALICE,

'The time was when the privilege was mine of beginning my letters to you with a warmer show of love than the above word contains,—when I might and did call you dearest; but I lost that privilege through my own folly, and since that it has been accorded to another. But you have found,—with a thorough honesty of purpose than which I know nothing greater,—that it has behoved you to withdraw that privilege also. I need hardly say that I should not have written as I now write, had you not found it expedient to do as you have done.

'I now once again ask you to be my wife. In spite of all that passed in those old days,—of all the selfish folly of which I was then guilty, I think you know, and at the time knew, that I ever loved you. I claim to say for myself that my love to you was true from first to last, and I claim from you belief for that statement. Indeed I do not think that you ever doubted my love.

'Nevertheless, when you told me that I might no longer hope to make you my wife, I had no word of remonstrance that I could utter. You acted as any woman would act whom love had not made a fool. Then came the episode of Mr. Grey; and bitter as have been my feelings whilst that engagement lasted, I never made any attempt to come between you and the life you had chosen. In saying this I do not forget the words which

313

I spoke last summer at Basle, when, as far as I knew, you still intended that he should be your husband. But what I said then was nothing to that which, with much violence, I refrained from saying. Whether you remember those few words I cannot tell; but certainly you would not have remembered them, —would not even have noticed them,—had your heart been at Nethercoats.

'But all this is nothing. You are now again a free woman; and once again I ask you to be my wife. We are both older than we were when we loved before, and will both be prone to think of marriage in a somewhat different light. Then personal love for each other was most in our thoughts. God forbid that it should not be much in our thoughts now! Perhaps I am deceiving myself in saying that it is not even now stronger in mine than any other consideration. But we have both reached that time of life, when it is probable that in any proposition of marriage we should think more of our adaptability to each other than we did before. For myself I know that there is much in my character and disposition to make me unfit to marry a woman of the common stamp. You know my mode of life, and what are my hopes and my chances of success. I run great risk of failing. It may be that I shall encounter ruin where I look for reputation and a career of honour. The chances are perhaps more in favour of ruin than of success. But, whatever may be the chances, I shall go on as long as any means of carrying on the fight are at my disposal. If you were my wife tomorrow I should expect to use your money, if it were needed, in struggling to obtain a seat in Parliament and a hearing there. I will hardly stoop to tell you that I do not ask you to be my wife for the sake of this aid;—but if you were to become my wife I should expect all your co-operation;—with your money, possibly, but certainly with your warmest spirit.

'And now, once again, Alice,—dearest Alice, will you be my wife? I have been punished, and I have kissed the rod,— as I never kissed any other rod. You cannot accuse my love. Since the time in which I might sit with my arm round your waist, I have sat with it round no other waist. Since your lips were mine, no other lips have been dear to me. Since you were my counsellor, I have had no other counsellor,—unless it be poor Kate, whose wish that we may at length be married is second in earnestness only to my own. Nor do I think you will doubt my repentance. Such repentance indeed claims no merit, as it has been the natural result of the loss which I have suffered. Providence has hitherto been very good to me in not having made that loss irremediable by your marriage with Mr. Grey. I wish you now to consider the matter well, and to tell me whether you can pardon me and still love me. Do I flatter myself when I feel that I doubt your pardon almost more than I doubt your love?

'Think of this thing in all its bearings before you answer me. I am so anxious that you should think of it that I will not expect your reply till this day week. It can hardly be your desire to go through life unmarried. I should say that it must be essential to your ambition that you should join your lot to that of some man the nature of whose aspirations would be like to your own. It is because this was not so as regarded him whose suit you had accepted, that you found yourself at last obliged to part from him. May I not say that with us there would be no such difference? It is because I believe that in this respect we are fitted for each other, as man and woman seldom are fitted, that I once again ask you to be my wife.

'This will reach you at Vavasor, where you will now be with the old squire and Kate. I have told her nothing of my purpose in writing this letter. If it should be that your answer is such as I desire, I should use the opportunity of our re-engagement to endeavour to be reconciled to my grandfather. He has misunderstood me and has ill-used me. But I am ready to forgive that, if he will allow me to do so. In such case you and Kate would arrange that, and I would, if possible, go down to Vavasor while you are there. But I am galloping on a-head foolishly in thinking of this, and am counting up my wealth while the crockery in my basket is so very fragile. One word from you will decide whether or no I shall ever bring it into market.

'If that word is to be adverse do not say anything of a meeting between me and the Squire. Under such circumstances it would be impossible. But, oh, Alice! do not let it be adverse. I think you love me. Your woman's pride towards me has been great and good and womanly; but it has had its way; and, if you love me, might now be taught to succumb.

'Dear Alice, will you be my wife?

'Yours, in any event, most affectionately,

'GEORGE VAVASOR.'

Vavasor, when he had finished his letter, went back to his seat over the fire, and there he sat with it close at his hand for nearly an hour. Once or twice he took it up with fingers almost itching to throw it into the fire. He took it up and held the corners between his forefinger and thumb, throwing forward his hand towards the flame, as though willing that the letter should escape from him and perish if chance should so decide. But chance did not so decide, and the letter was put back upon the table at his elbow. Then when the hour was nearly over he read it again. 'I'll bet two to one that she gives way,' he said to himself, as he put the sheet of paper back into the envelope. 'Women are such out-and-out fools.' Then he took his candle, and, carrying his letter with him, went into his bedroom.

The next morning was the morning of Christmas Eve. At about nine o'clock a boy came into his room who was accustomed to call for orders for the day. 'Jem,' he said to the boy, 'there's half a crown lying there on the looking-glass.' Jem looked and acknowledged the presence of the half-crown. 'Is it a head or a tail, Jem?' asked the boy's master. Jem scrutinized the coin, and declared that the uppermost surface showed a tail. 'Then take that letter and post it,' said George Vavasor. Whereupon Jem, asking no question, and thinking but little of the circumstances under which the command was given, did take the letter and did post it. In due accordance with postal regulations it reached Vavasor Hall and was delivered to Alice on the Christmas morning.

A merry Christmas did not fall to the lot of George Vavasor on the present occasion. An early Christmas-box he did receive in the shape of a very hurried note from his friend Burgo. 'This will be brought to you by Stickling,' the note said; but who Stickling was Vavasor did not know. 'I send the bill. Couldn't you get the money and send it me, as I don't want to go up to town again before the thing comes off? You're a trump; and will do the best you can. Don't let that rogue off for less than a hundred and twenty.—Yours, B. F.' Vavasor, therefore, having nothing better to do, spent his Christmas morning in calling on Mr. Magruin.

'Oh, Mr. Vavasor,' said Magruin; 'really this is no morning for business!'

'Time and tide wait for no man, Mr. Magruin, and my friend wants his money to-morrow.'

'Oh, Mr. Vavasor,—to-morrow!'

'Yes, to-morrow. If time and tide won't wait, neither will love. Come, Mr. Magruin, out with your cheque-book, and don't let's have any nonsense.'

'But is the lady sure, Mr. Vavasor?' asked Mr. Magruin, anxiously.

'Ladies never are sure,' said Vavasor; 'hardly more sure than bills made over to money-lenders. I'm not going to wait here all day. Are you going to give him the money?'

'Christmas-day, Mr. Vavasor! There's no getting money in the city to-day.'

But Vavasor before he left did get the money from Mr. Magruin,—122*l*. 10*s*.—for which an acceptance at two months for 500*l*. was given in exchange,—and carried it off in triumph. 'Do tell him to be punctual,' said Mr. Magruin, when Vavasor took his leave. 'I do so like young men to be punctual. But I really think Mr. Fitzgerald is the most unpunctual young man I ever did know yet.'

'I think he is,' said George Vavasor, as he went away.

He ate his Christmas dinner in absolute solitude at an eating-house near his lodgings. It may be supposed that no man dares to dine at his club on a Christmas Day. He at any rate did not so dare;—and after dinner he wandered about through the streets, wondering within his mind how he would endure the restraints of married life. And the same dull monotony of his days was continued for a week, during which he waited, not impatiently, for an answer to his letter. And before the end of the week the answer came.

CHAPTER XXXI

Among the Fells

ALICE came down to breakfast on that Christmas morning at Vavasor Hall without making any sign as to the letter she had received. The party there consisted of her grandfather, her father, her cousin Kate, and herself. They all made their Christmas salutations as is usual, and Alice received and made hers as did the others, without showing that anything had occurred to disturb her tranquillity. Kate remarked that she had heard that morning from Aunt Greenow, and promised to show Alice the letter after breakfast. But Alice said no word of her own letter.

'Why didn't your aunt come here to eat her Christmas dinner?' said the Squire.

'Perhaps, sir, because you didn't ask her,' said Kate, standing close to her grandfather,—for the old man was somewhat deaf.

'And why didn't you ask her;—that is, if she stands upon asking to come to her old home?'

'Nay, sir, but I couldn't do that without your bidding. We Vavasors are not always fond of meeting each other.'

'Hold your tongue, Kate. I know what you mean, and you should be the last to speak of it. Alice, my dear, come and sit next to me. I am much obliged to you for coming down all this way to see your old grandfather at Christmas. I am indeed. I only wish you had brought better news about your sweetheart.'

'She'll think better of it before long, sir,' said her father.

'Papa, you shouldn't say that. You would not wish me to marry against my own judgment.'

'I don't know much about ladies' judgments,' said the old man. 'It does seem to me that when a lady makes a promise she ought to keep it.'

'According to that,' said Kate, 'if I were engaged to a man, and found that he was a murderer, I still ought to marry him.'

'But Mr. Grey is not a murderer,' said the Squire.

'Pray,—pray, don't talk about it,' said Alice. 'If you do I really cannot sit and hear it.'

'I have given over saying anything on the subject,' said John Vavasor, speaking as though he had already expended upon it a vast amount of paternal eloquence. He had, however, never said more than has been recorded in these pages. Alice, during this conversation, sat with her cousin's letter in her pocket, and as yet had not even begun to think what should be the nature of her reply.

The Squire of Vavasor Hall was a stout old man, with a red face and gray eyes, which looked fiercely at you, and with long gray hair, and a rough gray beard, which gave him something of the appearance of an old lion. He was passionate, unreasoning, and specially impatient of all opposition; but he was affectionate, prone to forgive when asked to do so, unselfish, and hospitable. He was, moreover, guided strictly by rules, which he believed to be rules of right. His grandson George had offended him very deeply,—had offended him and never asked his pardon. He was determined that such pardon should never be given, unless it were asked for with almost bended knees; but, nevertheless, this grandson should be his heir. That was his present intention. The right of primogeniture could not, in accordance with his theory, be abrogated by the fact that it was, in George Vavasor's case, protected by no law. The Squire could leave Vavasor Hall to whom he pleased, but he could not have hoped to rest quietly in his grave should it be found that he had left it to any one but the eldest son of his own eldest son. Though violent, and even stern, he was more prone to love than to anger; and though none of those around him dared to speak to him of his grandson, yet he longed in his heart for some opportunity of being reconciled to him.

The whole party went to church on this Christmas morning. The small parish church of Vavasor, an unpretending wooden structure, with a single bell which might be heard tinkling for a mile or two over the fells, stood all alone about half a mile from the Squire's gate. Vavasor was a parish situated on the intermediate ground between the mountains of the lake country and the plains. Its land was unproductive, ill-drained, and poor, and yet it possessed little or none of the beauty which tourists go to see. It was all amidst the fells, and very dreary. There were long skirtings of dark pines around a portion of the Squire's property, and at the back of the house there was a thick wood of firs running up to the top of what was there called the Beacon Hill.* Through this there was a wild steep walk which came out upon the moorland, and from thence there was a track across the mountain to Hawes Water and Naddale,* and on over many miles to the further beauties of Bowness and Windermere.* They who knew the country, and whose legs were of use to them, could find some of the grandest scenery in England within reach of a walk from Vavasor Hall; but to others the place was very desolate. For myself, I can find I know not what of charm in wandering over open, unadorned moorland. It must be more in the softness of the grass to the feet, and the freshness of the air to the lungs, than in anything that meets the eye. You might walk for miles and miles to the north-east, or east, or south-east of Vavasor without meeting any object to arrest the view. The great road from Lancaster to Carlisle*crossed the outskirt of the small parish about a mile from the church, and beyond that the fell seemed to be interminable. Towards the north it rose, and towards the south it fell, and it rose and fell very gradually. Here and there some slight appearance of a valley might be traced which had been formed by the action of the waters; but such breakings of ground were inconsiderable, and did not suffice to interrupt the stern sameness of the everlasting moorland.

The daily life at Vavasor was melancholy enough for such a one as the Squire's son, who regarded London as the only place on the earth's surface in which a man could live with comfort. The moors offered no charms to him. Nor did he much appreciate the homely comforts of the Hall; for the house, though warm, was old fashioned and small, and the Squire's cook was nearly as old as the Squire himself. John Vavasor's visits to Vavasor were always visits of duty rather than of pleasure. But it was not so with Alice. She could be very happy there with Kate; for, like herself, Kate was a good walker and loved the mountains. Their regard for each other had grown and become strong because they had gone together o'er river and moor, and because they had together disregarded those impediments of mud and wet which frighten so many girls away from the beauties of nature.

On this Christmas Day they all went to church, the Squire being accompanied by Alice in a vehicle which in Ireland is called an inside jaunting-car,* and which is perhaps the most uncomfortable kind of vehicle yet invented; while John Vavasor walked with his niece. But the girls had arranged that immediately after church they would start for a walk up the Beacon Hill, across the fells, towards Hawes Water. They always dined at the Hall at the vexatious hour of five; but as their church service, with the sacrament included, would be completed soon after twelve, and as lunch was a meal which the Squire did not himself attend, they could have full four hours for their excursion. This had all been planned before Alice received her letter; but there was nothing in that to make her change her mind about the walk.

'Alice, my dear,' said the old man to her when they were together in the jaunting-car, 'you ought to get married.' The Squire was hard of hearing, and under any circumstances an inside jaunting-car is a bad place for conversation, as your teeth are nearly shaken out of your head by every movement which the horse makes. Alice therefore said nothing, but smiled faintly, in reply to her grandfather. On returning from church he insisted that Alice should again accompany him, telling her specially that he desired to speak to her. 'My dear child,' he said, 'I have been thinking a great deal about you, and you ought to get married.'

'Well, sir, perhaps I shall some day.'

'Not if you quarrel with all your suitors,' said the old man. 'You quarrelled with your cousin George, and now you have quarrelled with Mr. Grey. You'll never get married, my dear, if you go on in that way.'

'Why should I be married more than Kate?'

'Oh, Kate! I don't know that anybody wants to marry Kate. I wish you'd think of what I say. If you don't get married before long, perhaps you'll never get married at all. Gentlemen won't stand that kind of thing for ever.'

The two girls took a slice of cake, each in her hand, and started on their walk. 'We shan't be able to get to the lake,' said Kate.

'No,' said Alice; 'but we can go as far as the big stone on Swindale Fell,* where we can sit down and see it.'

'Do you remember the last time we sat there?' said Kate. 'It is nearly three years ago, and it was then that you told me that all was to be over between you and George. Do you remember what a fool I was, and how I screamed in my sorrow? I sometimes wonder at myself and my own folly. How is it that I can never get up any interest about my own belongings? And then we got soaking wet through coming home.'

'I remember that very well.'

'And how dark it was! That was in September, but we had dined early. If we go as far as Swindale we shall have it very dark coming home to-day;—but I don't mind that through the Beacon Wood, because I know my way so well. You won't be afraid of half an hour's dark?'

'Oh, no,' said Alice.

'Yes; I do remember that day. Well; it's all for the best, I suppose. And now I must read you my aunt's letter.' Then, while they were still in the wood, Kate took out the letter from her aunt and read it, while they still walked slowly up the hill. It seemed that hitherto neither of her two suitors had brought the widow to terms. Indeed, she continued to write of Mr. Cheesacre as though that gentleman were inconsolable for the loss of Kate, and gave her niece much serious advice as to the expedience of returning to Norfolk, in order that she might secure so eligible a husband. 'You must understand all the time, Alice,' said Kate, pausing as she read the letter, 'that the dear man has never given me the slightest ground for the faintest hope, and that I know to a certainty that he makes an offer to her twice a week,—that is, on every market day. You can't enjoy half the joke if you won't bear that in mind.' Alice promised that she would bear it all in mind, and then Kate went on with her reading. Poor Bellfield was working very hard at his drill, Mrs. Greenow went on to say; so hard that sometimes she really thought the fatigue would be too much for his strength. He would come in sometimes of an evening and just take a cup of tea;—generally on Mondays and Thursdays. 'These are not market days at Norwich,' said Kate; 'and thus unpleasant meetings are avoided.' 'He comes in,' said Mrs. Greenow, 'and takes a little tea; and sometimes I think that he will faint at my feet.' 'That he kneels there on every occasion,' said Kate, 'and repeats his offer also twice a week, I have not the least doubt in the world.'

'And will she accept him at last?'

'Really I don't know what to think of it. Sometimes I fancy that she likes the fun of the thing, but that she is too wide-awake to put herself into any man's power. I have no doubt she lends him money, because he wants it sadly and she is very generous. She gives him money, I feel sure, but takes his receipt on stamped paper for every shilling. That's her character all over.'

The letter then went on to say that the writer had made up her mind to remain at Norwich certainly through the winter and spring, and that she was anxiously desirous that her dear Kate should go back to her. 'Come and have one other look at Oileymead,' said the letter, 'and then, if you make up your mind that you don't like it or him, I won't ask you to think of them ever again. I believe him to be a very honest fellow.'

'Did you ever know such a woman?' said Kate; 'with all her
faults I believe she would go through fire and water to servĕ
me. I think she'd lend me money without any stamped paper.'
Then Aunt Greenow's letter was put up, and the two girls had
come out upon the open fell.

It was a delicious afternoon for a winter's walk. The air was
clear and cold, but not actually frosty. The ground beneath
their feet was dry, and the sky, though not bright, had that
appearance of enduring weather which gives no foreboding of
rain. There is a special winter's light, which is very clear
though devoid of all brilliancy,—through which every object
strikes upon the eye with well-marked lines, and under which
almost all forms of nature seem graceful to the sight if not
actually beautiful. But there is a certain melancholy which ever
accompanies it. It is the light of the afternoon, and gives token
of the speedy coming of the early twilight. It tells of the shortness of the day, and contains even in its clearness a promise of
the gloom of night. It is absolute light, but it seems to contain
the darkness which is to follow it. I do not know that it is ever
to be seen and felt so plainly as on the wide moorland, where
the eye stretches away over miles, and sees at the world's
end the faint low lines of distant clouds settling themselves upon
the horizon. Such was the light of this Christmas afternoon,
and both the girls had felt the effects of it before they reached
the big stone on Swindale Fell, from which they intended to
look down upon the loveliness of Hawes Water. As they went
up through the wood there had been some laughter between
them over Aunt Greenow's letter; and they had discussed
almost with mirth the merits of Oileymead and Mr. Cheesacre;
but as they got further on to the fell, and as the half-melancholy
wildness of the place struck them, their words became less
light, and after a while they almost ceased to speak.

Alice had still her letter in her pocket. She had placed it
there when she came down to breakfast, and had carried it with
her since. She had come to no resolution as yet as to her answer
to it, nor had she resolved whether or no she would show it to
Kate. Kate had ever been regarded by her as her steadfast

friend. In all these affairs she had spoken openly to Kate. We know that Kate had in part betrayed her, but Alice suspected no such treason. She had often quarrelled with Kate; but she had quarrelled with her not on account of any sin against the faith of their friendship. She believed in her cousin perfectly, though she found herself often called upon to disagree with her almost violently. Why should she not show this letter to Kate, and discuss it in all its bearings before she replied to it? This was in her mind as she walked silently along over the fell.

The reader will surmise from this that she was already half inclined to give way, and to join her lot to that of her cousin George. Alas, yes! The reader will be right in his surmise. And yet it was not her love for the man that prompted her to run so terrible a risk. Had it been so, I think that it would be easier to forgive her. She was beginning to think that love,—the love of which she had once thought so much,—did not matter. Of what use was it, and to what had it led? What had love done for her friend Glencora? What had love done for her? Had she not loved John Grey, and had she not felt that with all her love life with him would have been distasteful to her? It would have been impossible for her to marry a man whom personally she disliked;—but she liked her cousin George,—well enough, as she said to herself almost indifferently.

Upon the whole it was a grievous task to her in these days, —this having to do something with her life. Was it not all vain and futile? As for that girl's dream of the joys of love which she had once dreamed,—that had gone from her slumbers, never to return. How might she best make herself useful, —useful in some sort that might gratify her ambition;—that was now the question which seemed to her to be of most importance.

Her cousin's letter to her had been very crafty. He had studied the whole of her character accurately as he wrote it. When he had sat down to write it he had been indifferent to the result; but he had written it with that care to attain success which a man uses when he is anxious not to fail in an attempt.

Whether or no he cared to marry his cousin was a point so little interesting to him that chance might decide it for him; but when chance had decided that he did wish it, it was necessary for his honour that he should have that for which he condescended to ask.

His letter to her had been clever and very crafty. 'At any rate he does me justice,' she said to herself, when she read those words about her money, and the use which he proposed to make of it. 'He is welcome to it all if it will help him in his career, whether he has it as my friend or as my husband.' Then she thought of Kate's promise of her little mite, and declared to herself that she would not be less noble than her cousin Kate. And would it not be well that she should be the means of reconciling George to his grandfather? George was the representative of the family,—of a family so old that no one now knew which had first taken the ancient titular name of some old Saxon landowner,—the parish, or the man. There had been in old days some worthy Vavaseurs,* as Chaucer calls them, whose rank and bearing had been adopted on that moorland side. Of these things Alice thought much, and felt that it should be her duty so to act, that future Vavasors might at any rate not be less in the world than they who had passed away. In a few years at furthest, George Vavasor must be Vavasor of Vavasor. Would it not be right that she should help him to make that position honourable?

They walked on, exchanging now and again a word or two, till the distant Cumberland mountains began to form themselves in groups of beauty before their eyes. 'There's Helvellyn at last,' said Kate. 'I'm always happy when I see that.' 'And isn't that Kidsty Pyk?' asked Alice. 'No; you don't see Kidsty yet. But you will when you get up to the bank there. That's Scaw Fell*on the left;—the round distant top. I can distinguish it, though I doubt whether you can.' Then they went on again, and were soon at the bank from whence the sharp top of the mountain which Alice had named was visible. 'And now we are on Swindale, and in five minutes we shall get to the stone.'

In less than five minutes they were there; and then, but not till then, the beauty of the little lake, lying down below them in the quiet bosom of the hills, disclosed itself. A lake should, I think, be small, and should be seen from above, to be seen in all its glory. The distance should be such that the shadows of the mountains on its surface may just be traced, and that some faint idea of the ripple on the waters may be present to the eye. And the form of the lake should be irregular, curving round from its base among the lower hills, deeper and still deeper into some close nook up among the mountains from which its head waters spring. It is thus that a lake should be seen, and it was thus that Hawes Water*was seen by them from the flat stone on the side of Swindale Fell. The basin of the lake has formed itself into the shape of the figure of 3, and the top section of the figure lies embosomed among the very wildest of the Westmoreland mountains. Altogether it is not above three miles long, and every point of it was to be seen from the spot on which the girls sat themselves down. The water beneath was still as death, and as dark,—and looked almost as cold. But the slow clouds were passing over it, and the shades of darkness on its surface changed themselves with gradual changes. And though no movement was visible, there was ever and again in places a slight sheen upon the lake, which indicated the ripple made by the breeze.

'I'm so glad I've come here,' said Alice, seating herself. 'I cannot bear the idea of coming to Vavasor without seeing one of the lakes at least.'

'We'll get over to Windermere one day,' said Kate.

'I don't think we shall. I don't think it possible that I should stay long. Kate, I've got a letter to show you.' And there was that in the tone of her voice which instantly put Kate upon her mettle.

Kate seated herself also, and put up her hand for the letter. 'Is it from Mr. Grey?' she asked.

'No,' said Alice; 'it is not from Mr. Grey.' And she gave her companion the paper. Kate before she had touched it had seen that it was from her brother George; and as she opened it looked anxiously into Alice's face. 'Has he offended you?' Kate asked.

'Read it,' said Alice, 'and then we'll talk of it afterwards,—as we go home.' Then she got up from the stone and walked a step or two towards the brow of the fell, and stood there looking down upon the lake, while Kate read the letter. 'Well!' she said, when she returned to her place.

'Well,' said Kate. 'Alice, Alice, it will, indeed, be well if you listen to him. Oh, Alice, may I hope? Alice, my own Alice, my darling, my friend! Say that it shall be so.' And Kate knelt at her friend's feet upon the heather, and looked up into her face with eyes full of tears. What shall we say of a woman who could be as false as she had been and yet could be so true?

Alice made no immediate answer, but still continued to gaze down over her friend upon the lake. 'Alice,' continued Kate, 'I did not think I should be made so happy this Christmas Day. You could not have the heart to bring me here and show me his letter in this way, and bid me read it so calmly, and then tell me that it is all for nothing. No; you could not do that? Alice, I am so happy. I will so love this place. I hated it before.' And then she put her face down upon the boulder-stone and kissed it. Still Alice said nothing, but she began to feel that she had gone further than she had intended. It was almost impossible for her now to say that her answer to George must be a refusal.

Then Kate again went on speaking. 'But is it not a beautiful letter? Say, Alice,—is it not a letter of which if he were your brother you would feel proud if another girl had shown it to you? I do feel proud of him. I know that he is a man with a manly heart and manly courage, who will yet do manly things. Here out on the mountain, with nobody near us, with Nature all round us, I ask you on your solemn word as a woman, do you love him?'

'Love him!' said Alice.

'Yes;—love him: as a woman should love her husband. Is not your heart his? Alice, there need be no lies now. If it be so, it should be your glory to say so, here, to me, as you hold that letter in your hand.'

'I can have no such glory, Kate. I have ever loved my cousin; —but not so passionately as you seem to think.'

'Then there can be no passion in you.'

'Perhaps not, Kate. I would sometimes hope that it is so. But come; we shall be late; and you will be cold sitting there.'

'I would sit here all night to be sure that your answer would be as I would have it. But, Alice, at any rate you shall tell me before I move what your answer is to be. I know you will not refuse him; but make me happy by saying so with your own lips.'

'I cannot tell you before you move, Kate.'

'And why not?'

'Because I have not as yet resolved.'

'Ah, that is impossible. That is quite impossible. On such a subject and under such circumstances a woman must resolve at the first moment. You had resolved, I know, before you had half read the letter;—though, perhaps, it may not suit you to say so.'

'You are quite mistaken. Come along and let us walk, and I will tell you all.' Then Kate arose, and they turned their back to the lake, and began to make their way homewards. 'I have not made up my mind as to what answer I will give him; but I have shown you his letter in order that I might have some one with whom I might speak openly. I knew well how it would be, and that you would strive to hurry me into an immediate promise.'

'No;—no; I want nothing of the kind.'

'But yet I could not deny myself the comfort of your friendship.'

'No, Alice, I will not hurry you. I will do nothing that you do not wish. But you cannot be surprised that I should be very eager. Has it not been the longing of all my life? Have I not passed my time plotting and planning and thinking of it till I have had time to think of nothing else? Do you not know what I suffered when, through George's fault, the engagement was broken off? Was it not martyrdom to me,—that horrid time in which your Crichton*from Cambridgeshire was in the ascendant? Did I not suffer the tortures of purgatory while that went on;—and yet, on the whole, did I not bear them with patience? And, now, can you be surprised that I am wild with joy when I begin to see that everything will be as I wish;—for it will be as I wish, Alice. It may be that you have not resolved to accept him. But you would have resolved to refuse him instantly had that been your destined answer to his letter.' There was but little more said between them on the subject as they were passing over the fell, but when they were going down the path through the Beacon Wood, Kate again spoke: 'You will not answer him without speaking to me first?' said Kate.

'I will, at any rate, not send my answer without telling you,' said Alice.

'And you will let me see it?'

'Nay,' said Alice; 'I will not promise that. But if it is unfavourable I will show it you.'

'Then I shall never see it,' said Kate, laughing. 'But that is quite enough for me. I by no means wish to criticise the love-sweet words in which you tell him that his offences are all forgiven. I know how sweet they will be. Oh, heavens! how I envy him!'

Then they were at home; and the old man met them at the front door, glowering at them angrily from out his old leonine eyes, because the roast beef was already roasted. He had his great uncouth silver watch in his hand, which was always a quarter of an hour too fast, and he pointed at it fiercely, showing them the minute hand at ten minutes past the hour.

'But, grandpapa, you are always too fast,' said Kate.

'And you are always too slow, miss,' said the hungry old Squire.

'Indeed it is not five yet. Is it, Alice?'

'And how long are you going to be dressing?'

'Not ten minutes;—are we, Alice? And, grandpapa, pray don't wait.'

'Don't wait! That's what they always say,' he muttered,

peevishly. 'As if one would be any better waiting for them after the meat is on the table.' But neither Kate nor Alice heard this, as they were already in their rooms.

Nothing more was said that evening between Alice and Kate about the letter; but Kate, as she wished her cousin good night inside her bedroom door, spoke to her just one word—'Pray for him to-night,' she said, 'as you pray for those you love best.' Alice made no answer, but we may believe that she did as she was desired to do.

CHAPTER XXXII

Containing an Answer to the Love-letter

ALICE had had a week allowed to her to write her answer; but she sent it off before the full week was past. 'Why should I keep him in suspense?' she said. 'If it is to be so, there can be no good in not saying so at once.' Then she thought, also, that if this were to be her destiny it might be well for Mr. Grey that all his doubts on the matter should be dispelled. She had treated him badly,—very badly. She had so injured him that the remembrance of the injury must always be a source of misery to her; but she owed to him above everything to let him know what were her intentions as soon as they were set-tled. She tried to console herself by thinking that the wound to him would be easy of cure. 'He also is not passionate,' she said. But in so saying she deceived herself. He was a man in whom Love could be very passionate;—and was, moreover, one in whom Love could hardly be renewed.

Each morning Kate asked her whether her answer was writ-ten; and on the third day after Christmas, just before dinner, Alice said that she had written it, and that it was gone.

'But it isn't post-day,' said Kate;—for the post illuminated Vavasor but three days a week.

'I have given a boy sixpence to take it to Shap,'*said Alice blushing.

'And what have you said?' asked Kate, taking hold of the other's arm.

'I have kept my promise,' said Alice; 'and do you keep yours by asking no further questions.'

'My sister,—my own sister,' said Kate. And then, as Alice met her embrace, there was no longer any doubt as to the nature of the reply.

After this there was of course much close discussion between them as to what other steps should now be taken. Kate wanted her cousin to write immediately to Mr. Grey, and was somewhat frightened when Alice declined to do so till she had received a further letter from George. 'You have not proposed any horrid stipulations to him?' exclaimed Kate.

'I don't know what you may call horrid stipulations,' said Alice, gravely. 'My conditions have not been very hard, and I do not think you would have disapproved them.'

'But he!—He is so impetuous! Will he disapprove them?'

'I have told him.—But, Kate, this is just what I did not mean to tell you.'

'Why should there be secrets between us?' said Kate.

'There shall be none, then. I have told him that I cannot bring myself to marry him instantly;—that he must allow me twelve months to wear off, if I can in that time, much of sadness and of self-reproach which has fallen to my lot.'

'Twelve months, Alice?'

'Listen to me. I have said so. But I have told him also that if he wishes it still, I will at once tell papa and grandpapa that I hold myself as engaged to him, so that he may know that I bind myself to him as far as it is possible that I should do so. And I have added something else, Kate,' she continued to say after a slight pause,—'something else which I can tell you, though I could tell it to no other person. I can tell you because you would do, and will do the same. I have told him that any portion of my money is at his service which may be needed for his purposes before that twelve months is over.'

'Oh, Alice! No;—no. You shall not do that. It is too generous.' And Kate perhaps felt at the moment that her brother was a man to whom such an offer could hardly be made with safety.

'But I have done it. Mercury, with sixpence in his pocket, is already posting my generosity at Shap. And, to tell the truth, Kate, it is no more than fair. He has honestly told me that while the old Squire lives he will want my money to assist him in a career of which I do much more than approve. It has been my earnest wish to see him in Parliament. It will now be the most earnest desire of my heart;—the one thing as to which I shall feel an intense anxiety. How then can I have the face to bid him wait twelve months for that which is specially needed in six months' time? It would be like the workhouses which are so long in giving bread, that in the mean time the wretches starve.'

'But the wretch shan't starve,' said Kate. 'My money, small as it is, will carry him over this bout. I have told him that he shall have it, and that I expect him to spend it. Moreover, I have no doubt that Aunt Greenow would lend me what he wants.'

'But I should not wish him to borrow from Aunt Greenow. She would advance him the money, as you say, upon stamped paper, and then talk of it.'

'He shall have mine,' said Kate.

'And who are you?' said Alice, laughing. 'You are not going to be his wife?'

'He shall not touch your money till you are his wife,' said Kate, very seriously. 'I wish you would consent to change your mind about this stupid tedious year, and then you might do as you pleased. I have no doubt such a settlement might be made as to the property here, when my grandfather hears of it, as would make you ultimately safe.'

'And do you think I care to be ultimately safe, as you call it? Kate, my dear, you do not understand me.'

'I suppose not. And yet I thought that I had known something about you.'

'It is because I do not care for the safety of which you speak that I am now going to become your brother's wife. Do you suppose that I do not see that I must run much risk?'

'You prefer the excitement of London to the tranquillity, may I say, of Cambridgeshire.'

'Exactly;—and therefore I have told George that he shall have my money whenever he wants it.'

Kate was very persistent in her objection to this scheme till George's answer came. His answer to Alice was accompanied by a letter to his sister, and after that Kate said nothing more about the money question. She said no more then; but it must not therefore be supposed that she was less determined than she had been that no part of Alice's fortune should be sacrificed to her brother's wants;—at any rate before Alice should become her brother's wife. But her brother's letter for the moment stopped her mouth. It would be necessary that she should speak to him before she again spoke to Alice.

In what words Alice had written her assent it will be necessary that the reader should know, in order that something may be understood of the struggle which she made upon the occasion; but they shall be given presently, when I come to speak of George Vavasor's position as he received them. George's reply was very short and apparently very frank. He deprecated the delay of twelve months, and still hoped to be able to induce her to be more lenient to him. He advised her to write to Mr. Grey at once,—and as regarded the Squire he gave her carte blanche to act as she pleased. If the Squire required any kind of apology, expression of sorrow,—any asking for pardon, or such like, he, George, would, under the circumstances as they now existed, comply with the requisition most willingly. He would regard it as a simple form, made necessary by his coming marriage. As to Alice's money, he thanked her heartily for her confidence. If the nature of his coming contest at Chelsea should make it necessary, he would use her offer as frankly as it had been made. Such was his letter to Alice. What was contained in his letter to Kate, Alice never knew.

Then came the business of telling this new love tale,—the third which poor Alice had been forced to tell her father and grandfather;—and a grievous task it was. In this matter she feared her father much more than her grandfather, and therefore she resolved to tell her grandfather first;—or, rather, she determined that she would tell the Squire, and that in the mean time Kate should talk to her father.

'Grandpapa,' she said to him the morning after she had received her cousin's second letter.—The old man was in the habit of breakfasting alone in a closet of his own, which was called his dressing-room, but in which he kept no appurtenances for dressing, but in lieu of them a large collection of old spuds* and sticks and horse's-bits. There was a broken spade here, and a hoe or two; and a small table in the corner was covered with the debris of tradesmen's bills from Penrith, and dirty scraps which he was wont to call his farm accounts,—'Grandpapa,' said Alice, rushing away at once into the middle of her subject, 'you told me the other day that you thought I ought to be——married.'

'Did I, my dear? Well, yes; so I did. And so you ought;—I mean to that Mr. Grey.'

'That is impossible, sir.'

'Then what's the use of your coming and talking to me about it?'

This made Alice's task not very easy; but, nevertheless, she persevered. 'I am come, grandpapa, to tell you of another engagement.'

'Another!' said he. And by the tone of his voice he accused his granddaughter of having a larger number of favoured suitors than ought to fall to the lot of any young lady. It was very hard upon her, but still she went on.

'You know,' said she, 'that some years ago I was to have been married to my cousin George;'—and then she paused.

'Well,' said the old man.

'And I remember you told me then that you were much pleased.'

'So I was. George was doing well then; or,—which is more likely,—had made us believe that he was doing well. Have you made it up with him again?'

'Yes, sir.'

'And that's the meaning of your jilting Mr. Grey, is it?'

Poor Alice! It is hard to explain how heavy a blow fell upon her from the open utterance of that word! Of all words in the language it was the one which she now most dreaded. She had called herself a jilt, with that inaudible voice which one uses in making self-accusations;—but hitherto no lips had pronounced the odious word to her ears. Poor Alice! She was a jilt; and perhaps it may have been well that the old man should tell her so.

'Grandpapa!' she said; and there was that in the tone of her voice which somewhat softened the Squire's heart.

'Well, my dear, I don't want to be ill-natured. So you are going at last to marry George, are you? I hope he'll treat you well; that's all. Does your father approve of it?'

'I have told you first, sir;—because I wish to obtain your consent to seeing George again here as your grandson.'

'Never,' said the old man, snarling;—'never!'

'If he has been wrong, he will beg your pardon.'

'If he has been wrong! Didn't he want to squander every shilling of the property,—property which has never belonged to him;—property which I could give to Tom, Dick, or Harry to-morrow, if I liked?—If he has been wrong!'

'I am not defending him, sir;—but I thought that, perhaps, on such an occasion as this——'

'A Tom Fool's occasion! You've got money of your own. He'll spend all that now.'

'He will be less likely to do so if you will recognize him as your heir. Pray believe, sir, that he is not the sort of man that he was.'

'He must be a very clever sort of a man, I think, when he has talked you out of such a husband as John Grey. It's astounding to me,—with that ugly mug of his! Well, my dear, if your father approves of it, and if George will ask my pardon,—but I don't think he ever will——'

'He will, sir. I am his messenger for as much as that.'

'Oh, you are, are you? Then you may also be my messenger to him, and tell him that, for your sake, I will let him come back here. I know he'll insult me the first day; but I'll try and put up with it,—for your sake, my dear. Of course I must know what your father thinks about it.'

It may be imagined that Kate's success was even less than that which Alice achieved. 'I knew it would be so,' said John Vavasor, when his niece first told him;—and as he spoke he struck his hand upon the table. 'I knew all along how it would be.'

'And why should it not be so, Uncle John?'

'He is your brother, and I will not tell you why.'

'You think that he is a spendthrift?'

'I think that he is as unsafe a man as ever I knew to be intrusted with the happiness of any young woman. That is all.'

'You are hard upon him, uncle.'

'Perhaps so. Tell Alice this from me,—that as I have never yet been able to get her to think anything of my opinion, I do not at all expect that I shall be able to induce her to do so now. I will not even make the attempt. As my son-in-law I will not receive George Vavasor. Tell Alice that.'

Alice was told her father's message; but Kate in telling it felt no deep regret. She well knew that Alice would not be turned back from her present intention by her father's wishes. Nor would it have been very reasonable that she should. Her father had for many years relieved himself from the burden of a father's cares, and now had hardly the right to claim a father's privileges.

We will now go once again to George Vavasor's room in Cecil Street, in which he received Alice's letter. He was dressing when it was first brought to him; and when he recognized the handwriting he put it down on his toilet table unopened. He put it down, and went on brushing his hair, as though he were determined to prove to himself that he was indifferent as to the tidings which it might contain. He went on brushing his hair, and cleaning his teeth, and tying his cravat carefully over his turned-down collar, while the unopened letter lay close to his hand. Of course he was thinking of it,—of course he was anxious,—of course his eye went to it from moment to moment. But he carried it with him into the sitting-room still unopened, and so it remained until after the girl had brought him his tea and his toast. 'And now,' said he, as he threw himself into his arm-chair, 'let us see what the girl of my heart says to me.' The girl of his heart said to him as follows:—

'My dear George,

'I feel great difficulty in answering your letter. Could I have my own way, I should make no answer to it at present, but leave it for the next six months, so that then such answer might hereafter be made as circumstances should seem to require. This will be little flattering to you, but it is less flattering to myself. Whatever answer I may make, how can anything in this affair be flattering either to you or to me? We have been like children who have quarrelled over our game of play, till now, at the close of our little day of pleasure, we are fain to meet each other in tears, and acknowledge that we have looked for delights where no delights were to be found.

'Kate, who is here, talks to me of passionate love. There is no such passion left to me;—nor, as I think, to you either. It would not now be possible that you and I should come together on such terms as that. We could not stand up together as man and wife with any hope of a happy marriage, unless we had both agreed that such happiness might be had without passionate love.

'You will see from all this that I do not refuse your offer. Without passion, I have for you a warm affection, which enables me to take a livelier interest in your career than in any other of the matters which are around me. Of course, if I become your wife that interest will be still closer and dearer, and I do feel that I can take in it that concern which a wife should have in her husband's affairs.

'If it suits you, I will become your wife;—but it cannot be quite at once. I have suffered much from the past conflicts of my life, and there has been very much with which I must reproach myself. I know that I have behaved badly. Sometimes I have to undergo the doubly bitter self-accusation of having behaved in a manner which the world will call unfeminine. You must understand that I have not passed through this unscathed, and I must beg you to allow me some time for a cure. A perfect cure I may never expect, but I think that in twelve months from this time I may so far have recovered my usual spirit and ease of mind as to enable me to devote myself to your happiness. Dear George, if you will accept me under such circumstances, I will be your wife, and will endeavour to do my duty by you faithfully.

'I have said that even now, as your cousin, I take a lively interest in your career,—of course I mean your career as a politician,—and especially in your hopes of entering Parliament. I understand, accurately as I think, what you have said about my fortune, and I perfectly appreciate your truth and frankness. If I had nothing of my own you, in your circumstances, could not possibly take me as your wife. I know, moreover, that your need of assistance from my means is immediate rather than prospective. My money may be absolutely necessary to you within this year, during which, as I tell you most truly, I cannot bring myself to become a married woman. But my money shall be less cross-grained than myself. You will take it as frankly as I mean it when I say, that whatever you want for your political purposes shall be forthcoming at your slightest wish. Dear George, let me have the honour and glory of marrying a man who has gained a seat in the Parliament of Great Britain! Of all positions which a man may attain that, to me, is the grandest.

'I shall wait for a further letter from you before I speak either to my father or to my grandfather. If you can tell me that you accede to my views, I will at once try to bring about a reconciliation between you and the Squire. I think that that will be almost easier than inducing my father to look with favour upon our marriage. But I need hardly say that should either one or the other oppose it,—or should both do so,—that would not turn me from my purpose.

'I also wait for your answer to write a last line to Mr. Grey.

'Your affectionate cousin,

'ALICE VAVASOR.'

339

George Vavasor when he had read the letter threw it carelessly from him on to the breakfast table, and began to munch his toast. He threw it carelessly from him, as though taking a certain pride in his carelessness. 'Very well,' said he; 'so be it. It is probably the best thing that I could do, whatever the effect may be on her.' Then he took up his newspaper. But before the day was over he had made many plans,—plans made almost unconsciously,—as to the benefit which might accrue to him from the offer which she had made of her money. And before night he had written that reply to her of which we have heard the contents; and had written also to his sister Kate a letter, of which Kate had kept the contents to herself.

CHAPTER XXXIII

Monkshade

WHEN the first of the new year came round Lady Glencora was not keeping her appointment at Lady Monk's house. She went to Gatherum Castle, and let us hope that she enjoyed the magnificent Christmas hospitality of the Duke; but when the time came for moving on to Monkshade, she was indisposed, and Mr. Palliser went thither alone. Lady Glencora returned to Matching and remained at home, while her husband was away, in company with the two Miss Pallisers.

When the tidings reached Monkshade that Lady Glencora was not to be expected, Burgo Fitzgerald was already there, armed with such pecuniary assistance as George Vavasor had been able to wrench out of the hands of Mr. Magruin. 'Burgo,' said his aunt, catching him one morning near his bedroom door as he was about to go down stairs in hunting trim, 'Burgo, your old flame, Lady Glencora, is not coming here.'

'Lady Glencora not coming!' said Burgo, betraying by his look and the tone of his voice too clearly that this change in the purpose of a married lady was to him of more importance than it should have been. Such betrayal, however, to Lady Monk was not perhaps matter of much moment.

'No; she is not coming. It can't be matter of any moment to you now.'

'But, by heavens, it is,' said he, putting his hand up to his forehead, and leaning back against the wall of the passage as though in despair. 'It is matter of moment to me. I am the most unfortunate devil that ever lived.'

'Fie, Burgo, fie! You must not speak in that way of a married woman. I begin to think it is better that she should not come.' At this moment another man booted and spurred came down the passage, upon whom Lady Monk smiled sweetly, speaking some pretty little word as he passed. Burgo spoke never a word, but still stood leaning against the wall, with his hand to his forehead, showing that he had heard something which had moved him greatly. 'Come back into your room, Burgo,' said his aunt; and they both went in at the door that was nearest to them, for Lady Monk had been on the look-out for him, and had caught him as soon as he appeared in the passage. 'If this does annoy you, you should keep it to yourself! What will people say?'

'How can I help what they say?'

'But you would not wish to injure her, I suppose? I thought

it best to tell you, for fear you should show any special sign of surprise if you heard of it first in public. It is very weak in you to allow yourself to feel that sort of regard for a married woman. If you cannot constrain yourself I shall be afraid to let you meet her in Brook Street.'

Burgo looked for a moment into his aunt's face without answering her, and then turned away towards the door. 'You can do as you please about that,' said he; 'but you know as well as I do what I have made up my mind to do.'

'Nonsense, Burgo; I know nothing of the kind. But do you go down stairs to breakfast, and don't look like that when you go among the people there.'

Lady Monk was a woman now about fifty years of age, who had been a great beauty, and who was still handsome in her advanced age. Her figure was very good. She was tall and of fine proportion, though by no means verging to that state of body which our excellent American friend and critic Mr. Hawthorne has described as beefy*and has declared to be the general condition of English ladies of Lady Monk's age. Lady Monk was not beefy. She was a comely, handsome, upright dame,— one of whom, as regards her outward appearance, England might be proud,—and of whom Sir Cosmo Monk was very proud. She had come of the family of the Worcestershire Fitzgeralds, of whom it used to be said that there never was one who was not beautiful and worthless. Looking at Lady Monk you would hardly think that she could be a worthless woman; but there were one or two who professed to know her, and who declared that she was a true scion of the family to which she belonged;—that even her husband's ample fortune had suffered from her extravagance, that she had quarrelled with her only son, and had succeeded in marrying her daughter to the greatest fool in the peerage. She had striven very hard to bring about a marriage between her nephew and the great heiress, and was a woman not likely to pardon those who had foiled her.

At this moment Burgo felt very certain that his aunt was aware of his purpose, and could not forgive her for pretending to be innocent of it. In this he was most ungrateful, as well as unreasonable,—and very indiscreet also. Had he been a man who ever reflected he must have known that such a woman as his aunt could only assist him as long as she might be presumed to be ignorant of his intention. But Burgo never reflected. The Fitzgeralds never reflected till they were nearer forty than thirty, and then people began to think worse of them than they had thought before.

When Burgo reached the dining-room there were many men there, but no ladies. Sir Cosmo Monk, a fine bald-headed hale man of about sixty, was standing up at the sideboard, cutting a huge game pie. He was a man also who did not reflect much, but who contrived to keep straight in his course through the world without much reflection. 'Palliser is coming without her,' he said in his loud clear voice, thinking nothing of his wife's nephew. 'She's ill, she says.'

'I'm sorry for it,' said one man. 'She's a deal the better fellow of the two.'

'She has twice more go in her than Planty Pall,' said another.

'Planty is no fool, I can tell you,' said Sir Cosmo, coming to the table with his plate full of pie. 'We think he's about the most rising man we have.' Sir Cosmo was the member for his county, and was a Liberal. He had once, when a much younger man, been at the Treasury, and had since always spoken of the Whig Government as though he himself were in some sort a part of it.

'Burgo, do you hear that? Palliser is coming without his wife,' said one man,—a very young man, who hardly knew what had been the circumstances of the case. The others, when they saw Burgo enter, had been silent on the subject of Lady Glencora.

'I have heard,—and be d—d to him,' said Burgo. Then there was suddenly a silence in the room, and everyone seemed to attend assiduously to his breakfast. It was very terrible, this clear expression of a guilty meaning with reference to the wife of another man! Burgo regarded neither his plate nor his cup, but thrusting his hands into his breeches pockets, sat back in his chair with the blackness as of a thunder cloud upon his brow.

'Burgo, you had better eat your breakfast,' said Sir Cosmo.

'I don't want any breakfast.' He took, however, a bit of toast, and crumbling it up in his hand as he put a morsel into his mouth, went away to the sideboard and filled for himself a glass of cherry brandy.

'If you don't eat any breakfast the less of that you take the better,' said Sir Cosmo.

'I'm all right now,' said he, and coming back to the table, went through some form of making a meal with a roll and a cup of tea.

They who were then present used afterwards to say that they should never forget that breakfast. There had been something, they declared, in the tone of Burgo's voice when he uttered his curse against Mr. Palliser, which had struck them all with dread. There had, too, they said, been a blackness in his face, so terrible to be seen, that it had taken from them all the power of conversation. Sir Cosmo, when he had broken the ominous silence, had done so with a manifest struggle. The loud clatter of glasses with which Burgo had swallowed his dram, as though resolved to show that he was regardless who might know that he was drinking, added to the feeling. It may easily be understood that there was no further word spoken at that breakfast-table about Planty Pall or his wife.

On that day Burgo Fitzgerald startled all those who saw him by the mad way in which he rode. Early in the day there was no excuse for any such rashness. The hounds went from wood to wood, and men went in troops along the forest sides as they do on such occasions. But Burgo was seen to cram his horse at impracticable places, and to ride at gates and rails as though resolved to do himself and his uncle's steed a mischief. This was so apparent that some friend spoke to Sir Cosmo Monk about it. 'I can do nothing,' said Sir Cosmo. 'He is a man whom no one's words will control. Something has ruffled him this morning, and he must run his chance till he becomes quiet.' In the afternoon there was a good run, and Burgo again rode as hard as he could make his horse carry him;—but then there was the usual excuse for hard riding; and such riding in a straight run is not dangerous, as it is when the circumstances of the occasion do not warrant it. But, be that as it may, Burgo went on to the end of the day without accident, and as he went home, assured Sir Cosmo, in a voice which was almost cheery, that his mare Spinster was by far the best thing in the Monkshade stables. Indeed Spinster made quite a character that day, and was sold at the end of the season for three hundred guineas on the strength of it. I am, however, inclined to believe that there was nothing particular about the mare. Horses always catch the temperament of their riders, and when a man wishes to break his neck, he will generally find a horse willing to assist him in appearance, but able to save him in the performance. Burgo, at any rate, did not break his neck, and appeared at the dinner-table in a better humour than that which he had displayed in the morning.

On the day appointed, Mr. Palliser reached Monkshade. He was, in a manner, canvassing for the support of the Liberal party, and it would not have suited him to show any indifference to the invitation of so influential a man as Sir Cosmo. Sir Cosmo had a little party of his own in the House, consisting of four or five other respectable country gentlemen, who troubled themselves little with thinking, and who mostly had bald heads. Sir Cosmo was a man with whom it was quite necessary that such an aspirant as Mr. Palliser should stand well, and therefore Mr. Palliser came to Monkshade, although Lady Glencora was unable to accompany him.

'We are so sorry,' said Lady Monk. 'We have been looking forward to having Lady Glencora with us beyond everything.'

Mr. Palliser declared that Lady Glencora herself was overwhelmed with grief in that she should have been debarred from making this special visit. She had, however, been so unwell at Gatherum, the anxious husband declared, as to make it unsafe for her to go again away from home.

'I hope it is nothing serious,' said Lady Monk, with a look of grief so well arranged that any stranger would have thought that all the Pallisers must have been very dear to her heart. Then Mr. Palliser went on to explain that Lady Glencora had unfortunately been foolish. During one of those nights of hard frost she had gone out among the ruins at Matching to show them by moonlight to a friend. The friend had thoughtlessly, foolishly, and in a manner which Mr. Palliser declared to be very reprehensible, allowed Lady Glencora to remain among the ruins till she had caught cold.

'How very wrong!' said Lady Monk with considerable emphasis.

'It was very wrong,' said Mr. Palliser, speaking of poor Alice almost maliciously. 'However, she caught a cold which, unfortunately, has become worse at my uncle's, and so I was obliged to take her home.'

Lady Monk perceived that Mr. Palliser had in truth left his wife behind because he believed her to be ill, and not because he was afraid of Burgo Fitzgerald. So accomplished a woman as Lady Monk felt no doubt that the wife's absence was caused by fear of the lover, and not by any cold caught in viewing ruins by moonlight. She was not to be deceived in such a matter. But she became aware that Mr. Palliser had been deceived. As she was right in this we must go back for a moment, and say a word of things as they went on at Matching after Alice Vavasor had left that place.

Alice had told Miss Palliser that steps ought to be taken, whatever might be their cost, to save Lady Glencora from the peril of a visit to Monkshade. To this Miss Palliser had assented, and, when she left Alice, was determined to tell Mr. Palliser the whole story. But when the time for doing so had come, her courage failed her. She could not find words in which to warn the husband that his wife would not be safe in the company of her old lover. The task with Lady Glencora herself, bad as that would be, might be easier, and this task she at last undertook,—not without success.

'Glencora,' she said, when she found a fitting opportunity, 'you won't be angry, I hope, if I say a word to you?'

'That depends very much upon what the word is,' said Lady

Glencora. And here it must be acknowledged that Mr. Palliser's wife had not done much to ingratiate herself with Mr. Palliser's cousins;—not perhaps so much as she should have done, seeing that she found them in her husband's house. She had taught herself to think that they were hard, stiff, and too proud of bearing the name of Palliser. Perhaps some little attempt may have been made by one or both of them to teach her something, and it need hardly be said that such an attempt on the part of a husband's unmarried female relations would not be forgiven by a young bride. She had undoubtedly been ungracious, and of this Miss Palliser was well aware.

'Well,—the word shall be as little unpleasant as I can make it,' said Miss Palliser, already appreciating fully the difficulty of her task.

'But why say anything that is unpleasant? However, if it is to be said, let us have it over at once.'

'You are going to Monkshade, I believe, with Plantagenet.'

'Well;—and what of that?'

'Dear Glencora, I think you had better not go. Do you not think so yourself?'

'Who has been talking to you?' said Lady Glencora, turning upon her very sharply.

'Nobody has been talking to me;—not in the sense you mean.'

'Plantagenet has spoken to you?'

'Not a word,' said Miss Palliser. 'You may be sure that he would not utter a word on such a subject to anyone unless it were to yourself. But, dear Glencora, you should not go there; —I mean it in all kindness and love,—I do indeed.' Saying this she offered her hand to Glencora, and Glencora took it.

'Perhaps you do,' said she in a low voice.

'Indeed I do. The world is so hard and cruel in what it says.'

'I do not care two straws for what the world says.'

'But he might care.'

'It is not my fault. I do not want to go to Monkshade. Lady Monk was my friend once, but I do not care if I never see her again. I did not arrange this visit. It was Plantagenet who did it.'

'But he will not take you there if you say you do not wish it.'

'I have said so, and he told me that I must go. You will hardly believe me,—but I condescended even to tell him why I thought it better to remain away. He told me, in answer, that it was a silly folly which I must live down, and that it did not become me to be afraid of any man.'

'Of course you are not afraid, but——'

'I am afraid. That is just the truth. I am afraid;—but what can I do more than I have done?'

This was very terrible to Miss Palliser. She had not thought that Lady Glencora would say so much, and she felt a true regret in having been made to hear words which so nearly amounted to a confession. But for this there was no help now. There were not many more words between them, and we already know the result of the conversation. Lady Glencora became so ill from the effects of her imprudent lingering among the ruins that she was unable to go to Monkshade.

Mr. Palliser remained three days at Monkshade, and cemented his political alliance with Sir Cosmo much in the same way as he had before done with the Duke of St. Bungay. There was little or nothing said about politics, and certainly not a word that could be taken as any definite party understanding between the men; but they sat at dinner together at the same table, drank a glass of wine or two out of the same decanters, and dropped a chance word now and again about the next session of Parliament. I do not know that anything more had been expected either by Mr. Palliser or by Sir Cosmo; but it seemed to be understood when Mr. Palliser went away that Sir Cosmo was of opinion that that young scion of a ducal house ought to become the future Chancellor of the Exchequer in the Whig Government.

'I can't see that there's so much in him,' said one young member of Parliament to Sir Cosmo.

'I rather think that there is, all the same,' said the baronet. 'There's a good deal in him, I believe! I dare say he's not very bright, but I don't know that we want brightness. A bright financier is the most dangerous man in the world. We've had enough of that already. Give me sound common sense, with just enough of the gab in a man to enable him to say what he's got to say! We don't want more than that now-a-days.' From which it became evident that Sir Cosmo was satisfied with the new political candidate for high place.

Lady Monk took an occasion to introduce Mr. Palliser to Burgo Fitzgerald; with what object it is difficult to say, unless she was anxious to make mischief between the men. Burgo scowled at him; but Mr. Palliser did not notice the scowl, and put out his hand to his late rival most affably. Burgo was forced to take it, and as he did so made a little speech. 'I'm sorry that we have not the pleasure of seeing Lady Glencora with you,' said he.

'She is unfortunately indisposed,' said Mr. Palliser.

'I am sorry for it,' said Burgo—'very sorry indeed.' Then he turned his back and walked away. The few words he had spoken, and the manner in which he had carried himself, had been such as to make all those around them notice it. Each of them knew that Lady Glencora's name should not have been in Burgo's mouth, and all felt a fear not easily to be defined that something terrible would come of it. But Mr. Palliser himself did not seem to notice anything, or to fear anything; and nothing terrible did come of it during that visit of his to Monkshade.

CHAPTER XXXIV

Mr. Vavasor speaks to his Daughter

ALICE VAVASOR returned to London with her father, leaving Kate at Vavasor Hall with her grandfather. The journey was not a pleasant one. Mr. Vavasor knew that it was his duty to do something,—to take some steps with the view of preventing the marriage which his daughter meditated; but he did not know what that something should be, and he did know that, whatever it might be, the doing of it would be thoroughly disagreeable. When they started from Vavasor he had as yet hardly spoken to her a word upon the subject. 'I cannot congratulate you,' he had simply said. 'I hope the time may come, papa, when you will,' Alice had answered; and that had been all.

The Squire had promised that he would consent to a reconciliation with his grandson, if Alice's father would express himself satisfied with the proposed marriage. John Vavasor had certainly expressed nothing of the kind. 'I think so badly of him,' he had said, speaking to the old man of George, 'that I would rather know that almost any other calamity was to befall her, than that she should be united to him.' Then the Squire, with his usual obstinacy, had taken up the cudgels on behalf of his grandson; and had tried to prove that the match after all would not be so bad in its results as his son seemed to expect. 'It would do very well for the property,' he said. 'I would settle the estate on their eldest son, so that he could not touch it; and I don't see why he shouldn't reform as well as another.' John Vavasor had then declared that George was thoroughly bad, that he was an adventurer; that he believed him to be a ruined man, and that he would never reform. The Squire upon this had waxed angry, and in this way George obtained aid and assistance down at the old house, which he certainly had no right to expect. When Alice wished her grandfather good-bye the old man gave her a message to his grandson. 'You may tell him,' said he, 'that I will never see him again unless he begs my pardon for his personal bad conduct to me, but that if he marries you, I will take care that the property is properly settled upon his child and yours. I shall always be glad to see you, my dear; and for your sake, I will see him if he will humble himself to me.' There was no word spoken then about her father's consent; and Alice, when she left Vavasor, felt that the Squire was rather her friend than her enemy in regard to this thing which she contemplated. That her father was and would be an uncompromising enemy to her,—uncompromising though probably not energetical,—she was well aware; and, therefore, the journey up to London was not comfortable.

Alice had resolved, with great pain to herself, that in this matter she owed her father no obedience. 'There cannot be obedience on one side,' she said to herself, 'without protection and support on the other.' Now it was quite true that John Vavasor had done little in the way of supporting or protecting his daughter. Early in life, before she had resided under the same roof with him in London, he had, as it were, washed his hands of all solicitude regarding her; and having no other ties of family, had fallen into habits of life which made it almost impossible for him to live with her as any other father would live with his child. Then, when there first sprang up between them that manner of sharing the same house without any joining together of their habits of life, he had excused himself to himself by saying that Alice was unlike other girls, and that she required no protection. Her fortune was her own, and at her own disposal. Her character was such that she showed no inclination to throw the burden of such disposal on her father's shoulders. She was steady, too, and given to no pursuits which made it necessary that he should watch closely over her. She was a girl, he thought, who could do as well without surveillance as with it,—as well, or perhaps better. So it had come to pass that Alice had been the free mistress of her own actions, and had been left to make the most she could of her own hours. It cannot be supposed that she had eaten her lonely dinners in Queen Anne Street night after night, week after week, month after month, without telling herself that her father was neglecting her. She could not perceive that he spent every evening in society, but never an evening in her society, without feeling that the tie between her and him was not the strong bond which usually binds a father to his child. She was well aware that she had been ill-used in being thus left desolate in her home. She had uttered no word of complaint; but she had learned, without being aware that she was doing so, to entertain a firm resolve that her father should not guide her in her path through life. In that affair of John Grey they had both for a time thought alike, and Mr. Vavasor had believed that his theory with reference to Alice had been quite correct. She had

351

been left to herself, and was going to dispose of herself in a way than which nothing could be more eligible. But evil days were now coming, and Mr. Vavasor, as he travelled up to London, with his daughter seated opposite to him in the railway carriage, felt that now, at last, he must interfere. In part of the journey they had the carriage to themselves, and Mr. Vavasor thought that he would begin what he had to say; but he put it off till others joined them, and then there was no further opportunity for such conversation as that which would be necessary between them. They reached home about eight in the evening, having dined on the road. 'She will be tired to-night,' he said to himself, as he went off to his club, 'and I will speak to her to-morrow.' Alice specially felt his going on this evening. When two persons have had together the tedium of such a journey as that from Westmoreland up to London, there should be some feeling between them to bind them together while enjoying the comfort of the evening. Had he stayed and sat with her at her tea-table, Alice would at any rate have endeavoured to be soft with him in any discussion that might have been raised; but he went away from her at once, leaving her to think alone over the perils of the life before her. 'I want to speak to you after breakfast to-morrow,' he said as he went out. Alice answered that she should be there, —as a matter of course. She scorned to tell him that she was always there,—always alone at home. She had never uttered a word of complaint, and she would not begin now.

The discussion after breakfast the next day was commenced with formal and almost ceremonial preparation. The father and daughter breakfasted together, with the knowledge that the discussion was coming. It did not give to either of them a good appetite, and very little was said at table.

'Will you come upstairs?' said Alice, when she perceived that her father had finished his tea.

'Perhaps that will be best,' said he. Then he followed her into the drawing-room in which the fire had just been lit.

'Alice,' said he, 'I must speak to you about this engagement of yours.'

'Won't you sit down, papa? It does look so dreadful, your standing up over one in that way.' He had placed himself on the rug with his back to the incipient fire, but now, at her request, he sat himself down opposite to her.

'I was greatly grieved when I heard of this at Vavasor.'

'I am sorry that you should be grieved, papa.'

'I was grieved. I must confess that I never could understand why you treated Mr. Grey as you have done.'

'Oh, papa, that's done and past. Pray let that be among the bygones.'

'Does he know yet of your engagement with your cousin?'

'He will know it by this time to-morrow.'

'Then I beg of you, as a great favour, to postpone your letter to him.' To this Alice made no answer. 'I have not troubled you with many such requests, Alice. Will you tell me that this one shall be granted?'

'I think that I owe it to him as an imperative duty to let him know the truth.'

'But you may change your mind again.' Alice found that this was hard to bear and hard to answer; but there was a certain amount of truth in the grievous reproach conveyed in her father's words, which made her bow her neck to it. 'I have no right to say that it is impossible,' she replied, in words that were barely audible.

'No;—exactly so,' said her father. 'And therefore it will be better that you should postpone any such communication.'

'For how long do you mean?'

'Till you and I shall have agreed together that he should be told.'

'No, papa; I will not consent to that. I consider myself bound to let him know the truth without delay. I have done him a great injury, and I must put an end to that as soon as possible.'

'You have done him an injury certainly, my dear;—a very great injury,' said Mr. Vavasor, going away from his object about the proposed letter; 'and I believe he will feel it as such to the last day of his life, if this goes on.'

'I hope not. I believe that it will not be so. I feel sure that it will not be so.'

'But of course what I am thinking of now is your welfare,—not his. When you simply told me that you intended to——.' Alice winced, for she feared to hear from her father that odious word which her grandfather had used to her; and indeed the word had been on her father's lips, but he had refrained and spared her—'that you intended to break your engagement with Mr. Grey,' he continued, 'I said little or nothing to you. I would not ask you to marry any man, even though you had yourself promised to marry him. But when you tell me that you are engaged to your cousin George, the matter is very different. I do not think well of your cousin. Indeed I think anything but well of him. It is my duty to tell you that the world speaks very ill of him.' He paused, but Alice remained silent. 'When you were about to travel with him,' he continued, 'I ought perhaps to have told you the same. But I did not wish to pain you or his sister; and, moreover, I have heard worse of him since then,—much worse than I had heard before.'

'As you did not tell me before, I think you might spare me now,' said Alice.

'No, my dear; I cannot allow you to sacrifice yourself without telling you that you are doing so. If it were not for your money he would never think of marrying you.'

'Of that I am well aware,' said Alice. 'He has told me so himself very plainly.'

'And yet you will marry him?'

'Certainly I will. It seems to me, papa, that there is a great deal of false feeling about this matter of money in marriage,—or rather, perhaps, a great deal of pretended feeling. Why should I be angry with a man for wishing to get that for which every man is struggling? At this point of George's career the use of money is essential to him. He could not marry without it.'

'You had better then give him your money without yourself,' said her father, speaking in irony.

'That is just what I mean to do, papa,' said Alice.

'What!' said Mr. Vavasor, jumping up from his seat. 'You mean to give him your money before you marry him?'

'Certainly I do;—if he should want it;—or, I should rather say, as much as he may want of it.'

'Heavens and earth!' exclaimed Mr. Vavasor. 'Alice, you must be mad.'

'To part with my money to my friend?' said she. 'It is a kind of madness of which I need not at any rate be ashamed.'

'Tell me this, Alice; has he got any of it as yet?'

'Not a shilling. Papa, pray do not look at me like that. If I had no thought of marrying him you would not call me mad because I lent to my cousin what money he might need.'

'I should only say that so much of your fortune was thrown away, and if it were not much that would be an end of it. I would sooner see you surrender to him the half of all you have, without any engagement to marry him, than know that he had received a shilling from you under such a promise.'

'You are prejudiced against him, sir.'

'Was it prejudice that made you reject him once before? Did you condemn him then through prejudice? Had you not ascertained that he was altogether unworthy of you?'

'We were both younger, then,' said Alice, speaking very softly, but very seriously. 'We were both much younger then, and looked at life with other eyes than those which we now use. For myself I expected much then, which I now seem hardly to regard at all; and as for him, he was then attached to pleasures to which I believe he has now learned to be indifferent.'

'Psha!' ejaculated the father.

'I can only speak as I believe,' continued Alice. 'And I think I may perhaps know more of his manner of life than you do, papa. But I am prepared to run risks now which I feared before. Even though he were all that you think him to be, I would still endeavour to do my duty to him, and to bring him to other things.'

'What is it you expect to get by marrying him?' asked Mr. Vavasor.

'A husband whose mode of thinking is congenial to my own,'

answered Alice. 'A husband who proposes to himself a career in life with which I can sympathize. I think that I may perhaps help my cousin in the career which he has chosen, and that alone is a great reason why I should attempt to do so.'

'With your money?' said Mr. Vavasor with a sneer.

'Partly with my money,' said Alice, disdaining to answer the sneer. 'Though it were only with my money, even that would be something.'

'Well, Alice, as your father, I can only implore you to pause before you commit yourself to his hands. If he demands money from you, and you are minded to give it to him, let him have it in moderation. Anything will be better than marrying him. I know that I cannot hinder you; you are as much your own mistress as I am my own master,—or rather a great deal more, as my income depends on my going to that horrid place in Chancery Lane. But yet I suppose you must think something of your father's wishes and your father's opinion. It will not be pleasant for you to stand at the altar without my being there near you.'

To this Alice made no answer; but she told herself that it had not been pleasant to her to have stood at so many places during the last four years,—and to have found herself so often alone,—without her father being near to her. That had been his fault, and it was not now in her power to remedy the ill-effects of it.

'Has any day been fixed between you and him?' he asked.

'No, papa.'

'Nothing has been said about that?'

'Yes; something has been said. I have told him that it cannot be for a year yet. It is because I told him that, that I told him also that he should have my money when he wanted it.'

'Not all of it?' said Mr. Vavasor.

'I don't suppose he will need it all. He intends to stand again for Chelsea, and it is the great expense of the election which makes him want money. You are not to suppose that he has asked me for it. When I made him understand that I did not wish to marry quite yet, I offered him the use of that which would be ultimately his own.'

'And he has accepted it?'

'He answered me just as I had intended,—that when the need came he would take me at my word.'

'Then, Alice, I will tell you what is my belief. He will drain you of every shilling of your money, and when that is gone, there will be no more heard of the marriage. We must take a small house in some cheap part of the town and live on my income as best we may. I shall go and insure my life, so that you may not absolutely starve when I die.' Having said this, Mr. Vavasor went away, not immediately to the insurance office, as his words seemed to imply, but to his club where he sat alone, reading the newspaper, very gloomily, till the time came for his afternoon rubber of whist, and the club dinner bill for the day was brought under his eye.

Alice had no such consolations in her solitude. She had fought her battle with her father tolerably well, but she was now called upon to fight a battle with herself, which was one much more difficult to win. Was her cousin, her betrothed as she now must regard him, the worthless, heartless, mercenary rascal which her father painted him? There had certainly been a time, and that not very long distant, in which Alice herself had been almost constrained so to regard him. Since that any change for the better in her opinion of him had been grounded on evidence given either by himself or by his sister Kate. He had done nothing to inspire her with any confidence, unless his reckless daring in coming forward to contest a seat in Parliament could be regarded as a doing of something. And he had owned himself to be a man almost penniless; he had spoken of himself as being utterly reckless,—as being one whose standing in the world was and must continue to be a perch on the edge of a precipice, from which any accident might knock him headlong. Alice believed in her heart that this last profession or trade to which he had applied himself, was becoming as nothing to him,—that he received from it no certain income;— no income that a man could make to appear respectable to fathers or guardians when seeking a girl in marriage. Her father declared that all men spoke badly of him. Alice knew her father to be an idle man, a man given to pleasure, to be one who thought by far too much of the good things of the world; but she had never found him to be either false or malicious. His unwonted energy in this matter was in itself evidence that he believed himself to be right in what he said.

To tell the truth, Alice was frightened at what she had done, and almost repented of it already. Her acceptance of her cousin's offer had not come of love;—nor had it, in truth, come chiefly of ambition. She had not so much asked herself why she should do this thing, as why she should not do it,—seeing that it was required of her by her friend. What after all did it matter? That was her argument with herself. It cannot be supposed that she looked back on the past events of her life with any self-satisfaction. There was no self-satisfaction, but in truth there was more self-reproach than she deserved. As a girl she had loved her cousin George passionately, and that love had failed her. She did not tell herself that she had been wrong when she gave him up, but she thought herself to have been most unfortunate in the one necessity. After such an experience as that, would it not have been better for her to have remained without further thought of marriage?

Then came that terrible episode in her life for which she never could forgive herself. She had accepted Mr. Grey because she liked him and honoured him. 'And I did love him,' she said to herself, now on this morning. Poor, wretched, heart-wrung woman! As she sat there thinking of it all in her solitude she was to be pitied at any rate, if not to be forgiven. Now, as she thought of Nethercoats, with its quiet life, its gardens, its books, and the peaceful affectionate ascendancy of him who would have been her lord and master, her feelings were very different from those which had induced her to resolve that she would not stoop to put her neck beneath that yoke. Would it not have been well for her to have a master who by his wisdom and strength could save her from such wretched doubtings as these? But she had refused to bend, and then she had found herself desolate and alone in the world.

'If I can do him good why should I not marry him?' In that feeling had been the chief argument which had induced her to return such an answer as she had sent to her cousin, 'For myself, what does it matter? As to this life of mine and all that belongs to it, why should I regard it otherwise than to make it of some service to some one who is dear to me?' He had been ever dear to her from her earliest years. She believed in his intellect, even if she could not believe in his conduct. Kate, her friend, longed for this thing. As for that dream of love, it meant nothing; and as for those arguments of prudence,—that cold calculation about her money, which all people seemed to expect from her,—she would throw it to the winds. What if she were ruined! There was always the other chance. She might save him from ruin, and help him to honour and fortune.

But then, when the word was once past her lips, there returned to her that true woman's feeling which made her plead for a long day,—which made her feel that that long day would be all too short,—which made her already dread the coming of the end of the year. She had said that she would become George Vavasor's wife, but she wished that the saying so might be the end of it. When he came to her to embrace her how should she receive him? The memory of John Grey's last kiss still lingered on her lips. She had told herself that she scorned the delights of love; if it were so, was she not bound to keep herself far from them; if it were so,—would not her cousin's kiss pollute her?

'It may be as my father says,' she thought. 'It may be that he wants my money only; if so, let him have it. Surely when the year is over I shall know.' Then a plan formed itself in her head, which she did not make willingly, with any voluntary action of her mind,—but which came upon her as plans do come,—and recommended itself to her in despite of herself. He should have her money as he might call for it,—all of it excepting some small portion of her income, which might suffice to keep her from burdening her father. Then, if he were contented, he should go free, without reproach, and there should be an end of all question of marriage for her.

As she thought of this, and matured it in her mind, the door opened, and the servant announced her cousin George.

CHAPTER XXXV

Passion versus Prudence

IT had not occurred to Alice that her accepted lover would come to her so soon. She had not told him expressly of the day on which she would return, and had not reflected that Kate would certainly inform him. She had been thinking so much of the distant perils of this engagement, that this peril, so sure to come upon her before many days or hours could pass by, had been forgotten. When the name struck her ear, and George's step was heard outside on the landing-place, she felt the blood rush violently to her heart, and she jumped up from her seat panic-stricken and in utter dismay. How should she receive him? And then again, with what form of affection would she be accosted by him? But he was there in the room with her before she had had a moment allowed to her for thought.

She hardly ventured to look up at him; but, nevertheless, she became aware that there was something in his appearance and dress brighter, more lover-like, perhaps newer, than was usual with him. This in itself was an affliction to her. He ought to have understood that such an engagement as theirs not only did not require, but absolutely forbade, any such symptom of young love as this. Even when their marriage came, if it must come, it should come without any customary sign of smartness, without any outward mark of exaltation. It would have been very good in him to have remained away from her for weeks and months; but to come upon her thus, on the first morning of her return, was a cruelty not to be forgiven. These were the feelings with which Alice regarded her betrothed when he came to see her.

'Alice,' said he, coming up to her with his extended hand,— 'Dearest Alice!'

She gave him her hand, and muttered some word which was inaudible even to him; she gave him her hand, and immediately endeavoured to resume it, but he held it clenched within his own, and she felt that she was his prisoner. He was standing close to her now, and she could not escape from him. She was trembling with fear lest worse might betide her even than this. She had promised to marry him, and now she was covered with dismay as she felt rather than thought how very far she was from loving the man to whom she had given this promise.

'Alice,' he said, 'I am a man once again. It is only now that I can tell you what I have suffered during these last few years.' He still held her hand, but he had not as yet attempted any closer embrace. She knew that she was standing away from him awkwardly, almost showing a repugnance to him; but it was altogether beyond her power to assume an attitude of ordinary ease. 'Alice,' he continued, 'I feel that I am a strong man again, armed to meet the world at all points. Will you not let me thank you for what you have done for me?'

She must speak to him! Though the doing so should be ever so painful to her, she must say some word to him which should have in it a sound of kindness. After all, it was his undoubted right to come to her, and the footing on which he assumed to stand was simply that which she herself had given to him. It was not his fault if at this moment he inspired her with disgust rather than with love.

'I have done nothing for you, George,' she said, 'nothing at all.' Then she got her hand away from him, and retreated back to a sofa where she seated herself, leaving him still standing in the space before the fire. 'That you may do much for yourself is my greatest hope. If I can help you, I will do so most heartily.' Then she became thoroughly ashamed of her words, feeling that she was at once offering to him the use of her purse.

'Of course you will help me,' he said. 'I am full of plans, all of which you must share with me. But now, at this moment, my one great plan is that in which you have already consented to be my partner. Alice, you are my wife now. Tell me that it will make you happy to call me your husband.'

Not for worlds could she have said so at this moment. It was ill-judged in him to press her thus. He should already have seen, with half an eye, that no such triumph as that which he now demanded could be his on this occasion. He had had his triumph when, in the solitude of his own room, with quiet sarcasm he had thrown on one side of him the letter in which she had accepted him, as though the matter had been one almost indifferent to him. He had no right to expect the double triumph. Then he had frankly told himself that her money would be useful to him. He should have been contented with that conviction, and not have required her also to speak to him soft winning words of love.

'That must be still distant, George,' she said. 'I have suffered so much!'

'And it has been my fault that you have suffered; I know that. These years of misery have been my doing.' It was, however, the year of coming misery that was the most to be dreaded.

'I do not say that,' she replied, 'nor have I ever thought it. I have myself and myself only to blame.' Here he altogether misunderstood her, believing her to mean that the fault for which she blamed herself had been committed in separating herself from him on that former occasion.

'Alice, dear, let bygones be bygones.'

'Bygones will not be bygones. It may be well for people to say so, but it is never true. One might as well say so to one's body as to one's heart. But the hairs will grow gray, and the heart will grow cold.'

'I do not see that one follows upon the other,' said George. 'My hair is growing very gray;'—and to show that it was so, he lifted the dark lock from the side of his forehead, and displayed the incipient grizzling of the hair from behind. 'If gray hairs make an old man, Alice, you will marry an old husband; but even you shall not be allowed to say that my heart is old.'

That word 'husband', which her cousin had twice used, was painful to Alice's ear. She shrunk from it with palpable bodily suffering. Marry an old husband! His age was nothing to the purpose, though he had been as old as Enoch.* But she was again obliged to answer him. 'I spoke of my own heart,' said she. 'I sometimes feel that it has grown very old.'

362

'Alice, that is hardly cheering to me.'

'You have come to me too quickly, George, and do not reflect how much there is that I must remember. You have said that bygones should be bygones. Let them be so, at any rate as far as words are concerned. Give me a few months in which I may learn,—not to forget them, for that will be impossible,—but to abstain from speaking of them.'

There was something in her look as she spoke, and in the tone of her voice, that was very sad. It struck him forcibly, but it struck him with anger rather than with sadness. Doubtless her money had been his chief object when he offered to renew his engagement with her. Doubtless he would have made no such offer had she been penniless, or even had his own need been less pressing. But, nevertheless, he desired something more than money. The triumph of being preferred to John Grey,—of having John Grey sent altogether adrift, in order that his old love might be recovered, would have been too costly a luxury for him to seek, had he not in seeking it been able to combine prudence with the luxury. But though his prudence had been undoubted, he desired the luxury also. It was on a calculation of the combined advantage that he had made his second offer to his cousin. As he would by no means have consented to proceed with the arrangement without the benefit of his cousin's money, so also did he feel unwilling to dispense with some expression of her love for him, which would be to him triumphant. Hitherto in their present interview there had certainly been no expression of her love.

'Alice,' he said, 'your greeting to me is hardly all that I had hoped.'

'Is it not?' said she. 'Indeed, George, I am sorry that you should be disappointed; but what can I say? You would not have me affect a lightness of spirit which I do not feel?'

'If you wish,' said he, very slowly,—'if you wish to retract your letter to me, you now have my leave to do so.'

What an opportunity was this of escape! But she had not the courage to accept it. What girl, under such circumstances, would have had such courage? How often are offers made to us which we would almost give our eyes to accept, but dare not accept because we fear the countenance of the offerer? 'I do not wish to retract my letter,' said she, speaking as slowly as he had spoken; 'but I wish to be left awhile, that I may recover my strength of mind. Have you not heard doctors say, that muscles which have been strained, should be allowed rest, or they will never entirely renew their tension? It is so with me now; if I could be quiet for a few months, I think I could learn to face the future with a better courage.'

'And is that all that you can say to me, Alice?'

'What would you have me say?'

'I would fain hear one word of love from you; is that un-reasonable? I would wish to know from your own lips that you have satisfaction in the renewed prospect of our union; is that too ambitious? It might have been that I was over-bold in pressing my suit upon you again; but as you accepted it, have I not a right to expect that you should show me that you have been happy in accepting it?'

But she had not been happy in accepting it. She was not happy now that she had accepted it. She could not show to him any sign of such joy as that which he desired to see. And now, at this moment, she feared with an excessive fear that there would come some demand for an outward demonstration of love, such as he in his position might have a right to make. She seemed to be aware that this might be prevented only by such demeanour on her part as that which she had practised, and she could not, therefore, be stirred to the expression of any word of affection. She listened to his appeal, and when it was finished she made no reply. If he chose to take her in dudgeon, he must do so. She would make for him any sacrifice that was possible to her, but this sacrifice was not possible.

'And you have not a word to say to me?' he asked. She looked up at him, and saw that the cicatrice on his face was becoming ominous; his eyes were bent upon her with all their forbidding brilliance, and he was assuming that look of angry audacity which was so peculiar to him, and which had so often cowed those with whom he was brought in contact.

'No other word, at present, George; I have told you that I am not at ease. Why do you press me now?'

He had her letter to him in the breast-pocket of his coat, and his hand was on it, that he might fling it back to her, and tell her that he would not hold her to be his promised wife under such circumstances as these. The anger which would have induced him to do so was the better part of his nature. Three or four years since, this better part would have prevailed, and he would have given way to his rage. But now, as his fingers played upon the paper, he remembered that her money was absolutely essential to him,—that some of it was needed by him almost instantly,—that on this very morning he was bound to go where money would be demanded from him, and that his hopes with regard to Chelsea could not be maintained unless he was able to make some substantial promise of providing funds. His sister Kate's fortune was just two thousand pounds. That, and no more, was now the capital at his command, if he should abandon this other source of aid. Even that must go, if all other sources should fail him; but he would fain have that untouched, if it were possible. Oh, that that old man in Westmoreland would die and be gathered to his fathers, now that he was full of years and ripe for the sickle! But there was no sign of death about the old man. So his fingers released their hold on the letter, and he stood looking at her in his anger.

'You wish me then to go from you?' he said.

'Do not be angry with me, George!'

'Angry! I have no right to be angry. But, by heaven, I am wrong there. I have the right, and I am angry. I think you owed it me to give me some warmer welcome. Is it to be thus with us always for the next accursed year?'

'Oh, George!'

'To me it will be accursed. But is it to be thus between us always? Alice, I have loved you above all women. I may say that I have never loved any woman but you; and yet I am sometimes driven to doubt whether you have a heart in you capable of love. After all that has passed, all your old protestations, all my repentance, and your proffer of forgiveness, you should have received me with open arms. I suppose I may go now, and feel that I have been kicked out of your house like a dog.'

'If you speak to me like that, and look at me like that, how can I answer you?'

'I want no answer. I wanted you to put your hand in mine, to kiss me, and to tell me that you are once more my own. Alice, think better of it; kiss me, and let me feel my arm once more round your waist.'

She shuddered as she sat, still silent, on her seat, and he saw that she shuddered. With all his desire for her money,—his instant need of it,—this was too much for him; and he turned upon his heel, and left the room without another word. She heard his quick step as he hurried down the stairs, but she did not rise to arrest him. She heard the door slam as he left the house, but still she did not move from her seat. Her immediate desire had been that he should go,—and now he was gone. There was in that a relief which almost comforted her. And this was the man from whom, within the last few days, she had accepted an offer of marriage.

George, when he left the house, walked hurriedly into Cavendish Square, and down along the east side, till he made his way out along Princes Street, into the Circus in Oxford Street. Close to him there, in Great Marlborough Street, was the house of his parliamentary attorney, Mr. Scruby, on whom he was bound to call on that morning. As he had walked away from Queen Anne Street, he had thought of nothing but that too visible shudder which his cousin Alice had been unable to repress. He had been feeding on his anger, and indulging it, telling himself at one moment that he would let her and her money go from him whither they list,—and making inward threats in the next that the time should come in which he would punish her for this ill-usage. But there was the necessity of resolving what he would say to Mr. Scruby. To Mr. Scruby was still due some trifle on the cost of the last election; but even if this were paid, Mr. Scruby would make no heavy advance towards the expense of the next election. Whoever

might come out at the end of such affairs without a satisfactory
settlement of his little bill, as had for a while been the case with
Mr. Grimes, from the Handsome Man,—and as, indeed, still
was the case with him, as that note of hand at three months'
date was not yet paid,—Mr. Scruby seldom allowed himself to
suffer. It was true that the election would not take place till the
summer; but there were preliminary expenses which needed
ready money. Metropolitan voters, as Mr. Scruby often declared, required to be kept in good-humour,—so that Mr.
Scruby wanted the present payment of some five hundred
pounds, and a well-grounded assurance that he would be put
in full funds by the beginning of next June. Even Mr. Scruby
might not be true as perfect steel, if he thought that his candidate at the last moment would not come forth properly prepared. Other candidates, with money in their pockets, might
find their way into Mr. Scruby's offices. As George Vavasor
crossed Regent Street, he gulped down his anger, and applied
his mind to business. Should he prepare himself to give orders
that Kate's little property should be sold out, or would he
resolve to use his cousin's money? That his cousin's money
would still be at his disposal, in spite of the stormy mood in
which he had retreated from her presence, he felt sure; but the
asking for it on his part would be unpleasant. That duty he
must entrust to Kate. But as he reached Mr. Scruby's door, he
had decided that for such purposes as those now in hand, it was
preferable that he should use his wife's fortune! It was thus
that in his own mind he worded the phrase, and made for himself an excuse. Yes;—he would use his wife's fortune, and
explain to Mr. Scruby that he would be justified in doing so
by the fact that his own heritage would be settled on her at
her marriage. I do not suppose that he altogether liked it. He
was not, at any rate as yet, an altogether heartless swindler.
He could not take his cousin's money without meaning,—
without thinking that he meant, to repay her in full all that he
took. Her behaviour to him this very morning had no doubt
made the affair more difficult to his mind, and more unpleasant
than it would have been had she smiled on him; but even as it

was, he managed to assure himself that he was doing her no wrong, and with this self-assurance he entered Mr. Scruby's office.

The clerks in the outer office were very civil to him, and undertook to promise him that he should not be kept waiting an instant. There were four gentlemen in the little parlour, they said, waiting to see Mr. Scruby, but there they should remain till Mr. Vavasor's interview was over. One gentleman, as it seemed, was even turned out to make way for him; for as George was ushered into the lawyer's room, a little man, looking very meek, was hurried away from it.

'You can wait, Smithers,' said Mr. Scruby, speaking from within. 'I shan't be very long.' Vavasor apologized to his agent for the injury he was doing Smithers; but Mr. Scruby explained that he was only a poor devil of a printer, looking for payment of his little account. He had printed and posted 30,000 placards for one of the late Marylebone candidates, and found some difficulty in getting his money. 'You see, when they're in a small way of business, it ruins them,' said Scruby. 'Now that poor devil,—he hasn't had a shilling of his money yet, and the greater part has been paid out of his pocket to the posters. It is hard.'

It comforted Vavasor when he thus heard that there were others who were more backward in their payments, even than himself, and made him reflect that a longer credit than had yet been achieved by him, might perhaps be within his reach. 'It is astonishing how much a man may get done for him,' said he, 'without paying anything for years.'

'Yes; that's true. So he may, if he knows how to go about it. But when he does pay, Mr. Vavasor, he does it through the nose;—cent. per cent., and worse, for all his former shortcomings.'

'How many there are who never pay at all,' said George.

'Yes, Mr. Vavasor;—that's true, too. But see what a life they lead. It isn't a pleasant thing to be afraid of coming into your agent's office; not what you would like, Mr. Vavasor;—not if I know you.'

'I never was afraid of meeting anyone yet,' said Vavasor; 'but I don't know what I may come to.'

'Nor never will, I'll go bail. But, Lord love you, I could tell you such tales! I've had Members of Parliament, past, present, and future, almost down on their knees to me in this little room. It's about a month or six weeks before the elections come on when they're at their worst. There is so much you see, Mr. Vavasor, for which a gentleman must pay ready money. It isn't like a business in which a lawyer is supposed to find the capital. If I had money enough to pay out of my own pocket all the cost of all the metropolitan gentlemen for whom I act, why, I could live on the interest without any trouble, and go into Parliament myself like a man.'

George Vavasor perfectly understood that Mr. Scruby was explaining to him, with what best attempt at delicacy he could make, that funds for the expense of the Chelsea election were not to be forthcoming from the Great Marlborough Street establishment.

'I suppose so,' said he. 'But you do it sometimes.'

'Never, Mr. Vavasor,' said Mr. Scruby, very solemnly. 'As a rule, never. I may advance the money, on interest, of course, when I receive a guarantee from the candidate's father, or from six or seven among the committee, who must all be very substantial,—very substantial indeed. But in a general way I don't do it. It isn't my place.'

'I thought you did;—but at any rate I don't want you to do it for me.'

'I'm quite sure you don't,' said Mr. Scruby, with a brighter tone of voice than that he had just been using. 'I never thought you did, Mr. Vavasor. Lord bless you, Mr. Vavasor, I know the difference between gentlemen as soon as I see them.'

Then they went to business, and Vavasor became aware that it would be thought convenient that he should lodge with Mr. Scruby, to his own account, a sum not less than six hundred pounds within the next week, and it would be also necessary that he should provide for taking up that bill, amounting to ninety-two pounds, which he had given to the landlord of the

Handsome Man. In short, it would be well that he should borrow a thousand pounds from Alice, and as he did not wish that the family attorney of the Vavasors should be employed to raise it, he communicated to Mr. Scruby as much of his plans as was necessary,—feeling more hesitation in doing it than might have been expected from him. When he had done so, he was very intent on explaining also that the money taken from his cousin, and future bride, would be repaid to her out of the property in Westmoreland, which was,—did he say settled on himself? I am afraid he did.

'Yes, yes;—a family arrangement,' said Mr. Scruby, as he congratulated him on his proposed marriage. Mr. Scruby did not care a straw from what source the necessary funds might be drawn.

CHAPTER XXXVI

John Grey goes a Second Time to London

EARLY in that conversation which Mr. Vavasor had with his daughter, and which was recorded a few pages back, he implored her to pause a while before she informed Mr. Grey of her engagement with her cousin. Nothing, however, on that point had been settled between them. Mr. Vavasor had wished her to say that she would not write till he should have assented to her doing so. She had declined to bind herself in this way, and then they had gone off to other things;—to George Vavasor's character and the disposition of her money. Alice, however, had felt herself bound not to write to Mr. Grey quite at once. Indeed, when her cousin left her she had no appetite for writing such a letter as hers was to be. A day or two passed by her in this way, and nothing more was said by her or her father. It was now the middle of January, and the reader may remember that Mr. Grey had promised that he would come to her in London in that month, as soon as he should know that she had returned from Westmoreland. She must at any rate do something to prevent that visit. Mr. Grey would not come without giving her notice. She knew enough of the habits of the man to be sure of that. But she desired that her letter to him should be in time to prevent his to her; so when those few days were gone, she sat down to write without speaking to her father again upon the subject.

It was a terrible job;—perhaps the most difficult of all the difficult tasks which her adverse fate had imposed upon her. She found when she did attempt it, that she could have done it better if she had done it at the moment when she was writing the other letter to her cousin George. Then Kate had been near her, and she had been comforted by Kate's affectionate happiness. She had been strengthened at that moment by a feeling that she was doing the best in her power, if not for herself, at any rate for others. All that comfort and all that strength had left her now. The atmosphere of the fells had buoyed her up, and now the thick air of London depressed her. She sat for hours with the pen in her hand, and could not write the letter. She let a day go by and a night, and still it was not written. She hardly knew herself in her unnatural weakness. As the mental photographs of the two men forced themselves upon her, she could not force herself to forget those words— 'Look here, upon this picture—and on this.'*How was it that she now knew how great was the difference between the two men, how immense the pre-eminence of him whom she had rejected;—and that she had not before been able to see this on any of those many previous occasions on which she had compared the two together? As she thought of her cousin George's face when he left her room a few days since, and remembered Mr. Grey's countenance when last he held her hand at Cheltenham, the quiet dignity of his beauty which would submit to show no consciousness of injury, she could not but tell herself that when Paradise had been opened to her, she had declared herself to be fit only for Pandemonium.* In that was her chief misery; that now,—now when it was too late,—she could look at it aright.

But the letter must be written, and on the second day she declared to herself that she would not rise from her chair till it was done. The letter was written on that day and was posted. I will now ask the reader to go down with me to Nethercoats that we may be present with John Grey when he received it. He was sitting at breakfast in his study there, and opposite to him, lounging in an arm-chair, with a Quarterly*in his hand, was the most intimate of his friends, Frank Seward, a fellow of the college to which they had both belonged. Mr. Seward was a clergyman, and the tutor of his college, and a man who worked very hard at Cambridge. In the days of his leisure he spent much of his time at Nethercoats, and he was the only man to whom Grey had told anything of his love for Alice and of his disappointment. Even to Seward he had not told the whole story. He had at first informed his friend that he was engaged to be married, and as he had told this as no secret,—having even said that he hated secrets on such matters,—the engagement had been mentioned in the common room of their college, and men at Cambridge knew that Mr. Grey was going to take to himself a wife. Then Mr. Seward had been told that trouble had come, and that it was not improbable that there would be no such marriage. Even when saying this Mr. Grey told none of the particulars, though he owned to his friend that a heavy blow had struck him. His intimacy with Seward was of that thorough kind which is engendered only out of such young and lasting friendship as had existed between them; but even to such a friend as this Mr. Grey could not open his whole heart. It was only to a friend who should also be his wife that he could do that,—as he himself thoroughly understood. He had felt that such a friend was wanting to him, and he had made the attempt.

'Don't speak of this as yet,' he had said to Mr. Seward. 'Of course when the matter is settled, those few people who know me must know it. But perhaps there may be a doubt as yet, and as long as there is a doubt, it is better that it should not be discussed.'

He had said no more than this,—had imputed no blame to Alice,—had told none of the circumstances; but Seward had known that the girl had jilted his friend, and had made up his mind that she must be heartless and false. He had known also that his friend would never look for any other such companion for his home.

Letters were brought to each of them on this morning, and Seward's attention was of course occupied by those which he received. Grey, as soon as the envelopes had touched his hand, became aware that one of them was from Alice, and this he at once opened. He did it very calmly, but without any of that bravado of indifference with which George Vavasor had received Alice's letter from Westmoreland. 'It is right that I should tell you at once,' said Alice, rushing into the middle of her subject without even the formality of the customary address—'It is right that I should tell you at once that—.' Oh, the difficulty which she had encountered when her words had carried her as far as this!—'that my cousin, George Vavasor, has repeated to me his offer of marriage, and that I have accepted it. I tell you, chiefly in order that I may save you from the trouble which you purposed to take when I last saw you at Cheltenham. I will not tell you any of the circumstances of this engagement, because I have no right to presume that you will care to hear them. I hardly dare to ask you to believe of me that in all that I have done, I have endeavoured to act with truth and honesty. That I have been very ignorant, fool-ish,—what you will that is bad, I know well; otherwise there could not have been so much in the last few years of my life on which I am utterly ashamed to look back. For the injury that I have done you, I can only express deep contrition. I do not dare to ask you to forgive me.—ALICE VAVASOR.' She had tormented herself in writing this,—had so nearly driven her-self distracted with attempts which she had destroyed, that she would not even read over to herself these last words. 'He'll know it, and that is all that is necessary,' she said to her-self as she sent the letter away from her.

Mr. Grey read it twice over, leaving the other letters un-noticed on the table by his tea-cup. He read it twice over, and the work of reading it was one to him of intense agony. Hither-to he had fed himself with hope. That Alice should have been brought to think of her engagement with him in a spirit of doubt, and with a mind so troubled that she had been inclined to attempt an escape from it, had been very grievous to him; but it had been in his mind a fantasy, a morbid fear of himself, which might be cured by time. He, at any rate, would give all his energies towards achieving such a cure. There had been one thing, however, which he most feared;—which he had chiefly feared, though he had forbidden himself to think that it could be probable, and this thing had now happened.

He had ever disliked and feared George Vavasor;—not from any effect which the man had upon himself, for as we know his acquaintance with Vavasor was of the slightest;—but he had feared and disliked his influence upon Alice. He had also feared the influence of her cousin Kate. To have cautioned Alice against her cousins would have been to him impossible. It was not his nature to express suspicion to one he loved. Is the tone of that letter remembered in which he had answered Alice when she informed him that her cousin George was to go with Kate and her to Switzerland? He had written, with a pleasant joke, words which Alice had been able to read with some little feeling of triumph to her two friends. He had not so written because he liked what he knew of the man. He disliked all that he knew of him. But it had not been possible for him to show that he distrusted the prudence of her, whom, as his future wife, he was prepared to trust in all things.

I have said that he read Alice's letter with an agony of sorrow; as he sat with it in his hand he suffered as, probably, he had never suffered before. But there was nothing in his countenance to show that he was in pain. Seward had received some long epistle, crossed from end to end,—indicative, I should say, of a not far distant termination to that college tutorship*—and was reading it with placid contentment. It did not occur to him to look across at Grey, but had he done so, I doubt whether he would have seen anything to attract his attention. But Grey, though he was wounded, would not allow himself to be dismayed. There was less hope now than before, but there might still be hope;—hope for her, even though there might be none for him. Tidings had reached his ears also as to George Vavasor, which had taught him to believe that the man was needy, reckless, and on the brink of ruin. Such a marriage to Alice Vavasor would be altogether ruinous. Whatever might be his own ultimate fate he would still seek to save her from that. Her cousin, doubtless, wanted her money. Might it not be possible that he would be satisfied with her money, and that thus the woman might be saved?

'Seward,' he said at last, addressing his friend, who had not yet come to the end of the last crossed page.

'Is there anything wrong?' said Seward.

'Well;—yes; there is something a little wrong. I fear I must leave you, and go up to town to-day.'

'Nobody ill, I hope?'

'No;—nobody is ill. But I must go up to London. Mrs. Bole will take care of you, and you must not be angry with me for leaving you.'

Seward assured him that he would not be in the least angry, and that he was thoroughly conversant with the capabilities and good intentions of Mrs. Bole the housekeeper; but added, that as he was so near his own college, he would of course go back to Cambridge. He longed to say some word as to the purpose of Grey's threatened journey; to make some inquiry as to this new trouble; but he knew that Grey was a man who did not well bear close inquiries, and he was silent.

'Why not stay here?' said Grey, after a minute's pause. 'I wish you would, old fellow; I do, indeed.' There was a tone of special affection in his voice which struck Seward at once. 'If I can be of the slightest service or comfort to you, I will of course.'

Grey again sat silent for a little while. 'I wish you would; I do, indeed.'

'Then I will.' And again there was a pause.

'I have got a letter here from—Miss Vavasor,' said Grey.

'May I hope that——'

'No;—it does not bring good news to me. I do not know that I can tell it you all. I would if I could, but the whole story

375

is one not to be told in a hurry. I should leave false impressions. There are things which a man cannot tell.'

'Indeed there are,' said Seward.

'I wish with all my heart that you knew it all as I know it; but that is impossible. There are things which happen in a day which it would take a lifetime to explain.' Then there was another pause. 'I have heard bad news this morning, and I must go up to London at once. I shall go into Ely so as to be there by twelve; and if you will, you shall drive me over. I may be back in a day; certainly in less than a week; but it will be a comfort to me to know that I shall find you here.'

The matter was so arranged, and at eleven they started. During the first two miles not a word was spoken between them. 'Seward,' Grey said at last, 'if I fail in what I am going to attempt, it is probable that you will never hear Alice Vavasor's name mentioned by me again; but I want you always to bear this in mind;—that at no moment has my opinion of her ever been changed, nor must you in such case imagine from my silence that it has changed. Do you understand me?'

'I think I do.'

'To my thinking she is the finest of God's creatures that I have known. It may be that in her future life she will be severed from me altogether; but I shall not, therefore, think the less well of her; and I wish that you, as my friend, should know that I so esteem her, even though her name should never be mentioned between us.' Seward, in some few words, assured him that it should be so, and then they finished their journey in silence.

From the station at Ely, Grey sent a message by the wires up to John Vavasor, saying that he would call on him that afternoon at his office in Chancery Lane. The chances were always much against finding Mr. Vavasor at his office; but on this occasion the telegram did reach him there, and he remained till the unaccustomed hour of half-past four to meet the man who was to have been his son-in-law.

'Have you heard from her?' he asked as soon as Grey entered the dingy little room, not in Chancery Lane, but in its neighbourhood, which was allocated to him for his signing purposes.

'Yes,'—said Grey; 'she has written to me.'

'And told you about her cousin George. I tried to hinder her from writing, but she is very wilful.'

'Why should you have hindered her? If the thing was to be told, it is better that it should be done at once.'

'But I hoped that there might be an escape. I don't know what you think of all this, Grey, but to me it is the bitterest misfortune that I have known. And I've had some bitter things, too,' he added,—thinking of that period of his life, when the work of which he was ashamed was first ordained as his future task.

'What is the escape that you hoped?' asked Grey.

'I hardly know. The whole thing seems to me to be so mad, that I partly trusted that she would see the madness of it. I am not sure whether you know anything of my nephew George?' asked Mr. Vavasor.

'Very little,' said Grey.

'I believe him to be utterly an adventurer,—a man without means and without principle,—upon the whole about as bad a man as you may meet. I give you my word, Grey, that I don't think I know a worse man. He's going to marry her for her money; then he will beggar her, after that he'll ill-treat her, and yet what can I do?'

'Prevent the marriage.'

'But how, my dear fellow? Prevent it! It's all very well to say that, and it's the very thing I want to do. But how am I to prevent it? She's as much her own master as you are yours. She can give him every shilling of her fortune to-morrow. How am I to prevent her from marrying him?'

'Let her give him every shilling of her fortune to-morrow,' said Grey.

'And what is she to do then?' asked Mr. Vavasor.

'Then—then,—then,—then let her come to me,' said John Grey; and as he spoke there was the fragment of a tear in his eye, and the hint of quiver in his voice.

Even the worldly, worn-out, unsympathetic nature of John Vavasor was struck, and, as it were, warmed by this.

'God bless you; God bless you, my dear fellow. I heartily wish for her sake that I could look forward to any such an end to this affair.'

'And why not look forward to it? You say that he merely wants her money. As he wants it let him have it!'

'But Grey, you do not know Alice; you do not understand my girl. When she had lost her fortune nothing would induce her to become your wife.'

'Leave that to follow as it may,' said John Grey. 'Our first object must be to sever her from a man, who is, as you say, himself on the verge of ruin; and who would certainly make her wretched. I am here now, not because I wish her to be my own wife, but because I wish that she should not become the wife of such a one as your nephew. If I were you I would let him have her money.'

'If you were I, you would have nothing more to do with it than the man that is as yet unborn. I know that she will give him her money because she has said so; but I have no power as to her giving it or as to her withholding it. That's the hardship of my position;—but it is of no use to think of that now.'

John Grey certainly did not think about it. He knew well that Alice was independent, and that she was not inclined to give up that independence to anyone. He had not expected that her father would be able to do much towards hindering his daughter from becoming the wife of George Vavasor, but he had wished that he himself and her father should be in accord in their views, and he found that this was so. When he left Mr. Vavasor's room nothing had been said about the period of the marriage. Grey thought it improbable that Alice would find herself able to give herself in marriage to her cousin immediately,—so soon after her breach with him; but as to this he had no assurance, and he determined to have the facts from her own lips, if she would see him. So he wrote to her, naming a day on which he would call upon her early in the morning;

and having received from her no prohibition, he was in Queen Anne Street at the hour appointed.

He had conceived a scheme which he had not made known to Mr. Vavasor, and as to the practicability of which he had much doubt; but which, nevertheless, he was resolved to try if he should find the attempt possible. He himself would buy off George Vavasor. He had ever been a prudent man, and he had money at command. If Vavasor was such a man as they, who knew him best, represented him, such a purchase might be possible. But then, before this was attempted, he must be quite sure that he knew his man, and he must satisfy himself also that in doing so he would not, in truth, add to Alice's misery. He could hardly bring himself to think it possible that she did, in truth, love her cousin with passionate love. It seemed to him, as he remembered what Alice had been to himself, that this must be impossible. But if it were so, that of course must put an end to his interference. He thought that if he saw her he might learn all this, and therefore he went to Queen Anne Street.

'Of course he must come if he will,' she said to herself when she received his note. 'It can make no matter. He will say nothing half so hard to me as what I say to myself all day long.' But when the morning came, and the hour came, and the knock at the door for which her ears were on the alert, her heart misgave her, and she felt that the present moment of her punishment, though not the heaviest, would still be hard to bear.

He came slowly up stairs,—his step was ever slow,—and gently opened the door for himself. Then, before he even looked at her, he closed it again. I do not know how to explain that it was so; but it was this perfect command of himself at all seasons which had in part made Alice afraid of him, and drove her to believe that they were not fitted for each other. She, when he thus turned for a moment from her, and then walked slowly towards her, stood with both her hands leaning on the centre table of the room, and with her eyes fixed upon its surface.

'Alice,' he said, walking up to her very slowly.

Her whole frame shuddered as she heard the sweetness of

his voice. Had I not better tell the truth of her at once? Oh, if she could only have been his again! What madness during these last six months had driven her to such a plight as this! The old love came back upon her. Nay; it had never gone. But that trust in his love returned to her,—that trust which told her that such love and such worth would have sufficed to make her happy. But this confidence in him was worthless now! Even though he should desire it, she could not change again.

'Alice,' he said again. And then, as slowly she looked up at him, he asked her for her hand. 'You may give it me,' he said, 'as to an old friend.' She put her hand in his hand, and then, withdrawing it, felt that she must never trust herself to do so again.

'Alice,' he continued, 'I do not expect you to say much to me; but there is a question or two which I think you will answer. Has a day been fixed for this marriage?'

'No,' she said.

'Will it be in a month?'

'Oh, no;—not for a year,' she replied hurriedly;—and he knew at once by her voice that she already dreaded this new wedlock. Whatever of anger he might before have felt for her was banished. She had brought herself by her ill-judgment,—by her ignorance, as she had confessed,—to a sad pass; but he believed that she was still worthy of his love.

'And now one other question, Alice;—but if you are silent, I will not ask it again. Can you tell me why you have again accepted your cousin's offer?'

'Because—,' she said very quickly, looking up as though she were about to speak with all her old courage. 'But you would never understand me,' she said,—'and there can be no reason why I should dare to hope that you should ever think well of me again.'

He knew that there was no love,—no love for that man to whom she had pledged her hand. He did not know, on the other hand, how strong, how unchanged, how true was her love for himself. Indeed, of himself he was thinking not at all. He desired to learn whether she would suffer, if by any scheme he might succeed in breaking off this marriage. When he had asked her whether she were to be married at once, she had shuddered at the thought. When he asked her why she had accepted her cousin, she had faltered, and hinted at some excuse which he might fail to understand. Had she loved George Vavasor, he could have understood that well enough.

'Alice,' he said, speaking still very slowly, 'nothing has ever yet been done which need to a certainty separate you and me. I am a persistent man, and I do not even yet give up all hope. A year is a long time. As you say yourself, I do not as yet quite understand you. But, Alice,—and I think that the position in which we stood a few months since justifies me in saying so without offence,—I love you now as well as ever, and should things change with you, I cannot tell you with how much joy and eagerness I should take you back to my bosom. My heart is yours now as it has been since I knew you.'

Then he again just touched her hand, and left her before she had been able to answer a word.

CHAPTER XXXVII

Mr. Tombe's Advice

ALICE sat alone for an hour without moving when John Grey had left her, and the last words which he had uttered were sounding in her ears all the time, 'My heart is still yours, as it has been since I knew you.' There had been something in his words which had soothed her spirits, and had, for the moment, almost comforted her. At any rate, he did not despise her. He could not have spoken such words as these to her had he not still held her high in his esteem. Nay;—had he not even declared that he would yet take her as his own if she would come to him? 'I cannot tell you with how much joy I would take you back to my bosom!' Ah! that might never be. But yet the assurance had been sweet to her;—dangerously sweet, as she soon told herself. She knew that she had lost her Eden, but it was something to her that the master of the garden had not

himself driven her forth. She sat there, thinking of her fate, as
though it belonged to some other one,—not to herself; as
though it were a tale that she had read. Herself she had shipwrecked altogether; but though she might sink, she had not
been thrust from the ship by hands which she loved.

But would it not have been better that he should have scorned
her and reviled her? Had he been able to do so, he at least
would have escaped the grief of disappointed love. Had he
learned to despise her, he would have ceased to regret her.
She had no right to feel consolation in the fact that his sufferings were equal to her own. But when she thought of this, she
told herself that it could not be that it was so. He was a man,
she said, not passionate by nature. Alas! it was the mistake
she had ever made when summing up the items of his character! He might be persistent, she thought, in still striving to
do that upon which he had once resolved. He had said so, and
that which he said was always true to the letter. But, nevertheless, when this thing which he still chose to pursue should
have been put absolutely beyond his reach, he would not allow
his calm bosom to be harassed by a vain regret. He was a man
too whole at every point,—so Alice told herself,—to allow his
happiness to be marred by such an accident.

But must the accident occur? Was there no chance that he
might be saved, even from such trouble as might follow upon
such a loss? Could it not be possible that he might be gratified,
—since it would gratify him,—and that she might be saved!
Over and over again she considered this,—but always as though
it were another woman whom she would fain save, and not
herself.

But she knew that her own fate was fixed. She had been mad
when she had done the thing, but the thing was not on that
account the less done. She had been mad when she had trusted
herself abroad with two persons, both of whom, as she had
well known, were intent on wrenching her happiness from out
of her grasp. She had been mad when she had told herself,
whilst walking over the Westmoreland fells, that after all she
might as well marry her cousin, since that other marriage was

then beyond her reach! Her two cousins had succeeded in blighting all the hopes of her life;—but what could she now think of herself in that she had been so weak as to submit to such usage from their hands? Alas!—she told herself, admitting in her misery all her weakness,—alas, she had had no mother. She had gloried in her independence, and this had come of it! She had scorned the prudence of Lady Macleod, and her scorn had brought her to this pass!

Was she to give herself bodily,—body and soul, as she said aloud in her solitary agony,—to a man whom she did not love? Must she submit to his caresses,—lie on his bosom,—turn herself warmly to his kisses? 'No,' she said, 'no,'—speaking audibly, as she walked about the room; 'no;—it was not in my bargain; I never meant it.' But if so what had she meant;—what had been her dream? Of what marriage had she thought, when she was writing that letter back to George Vavasor? How am I to analyze her mind, and make her thoughts and feelings intelligible to those who may care to trouble themselves with the study? Any sacrifice she would make for her cousin which one friend could make for another. She would fight his battles with her money, with her words, with her sympathy. She would sit with him if he needed it, and speak comfort to him by the hour. His disgrace should be her disgrace;—his glory her glory;—his pursuits her pursuits. Was not that the marriage to which she had consented? But he had come to her and asked her for a kiss, and she had shuddered before him, when he made the demand. Then that other one had come and had touched her hand, and the fibres of her body had seemed to melt within her at the touch, so that she could have fallen at his feet.

She had done very wrong. She knew that she had done wrong. She knew that she had sinned with that sin which specially disgraces a woman. She had said that she would become the wife of a man to whom she could not cleave with a wife's love; and, mad with a vile ambition, she had given up the man for whose modest love her heart was longing. She had thrown off from her that wondrous aroma of precious delicacy, which is the greatest treasure of womanhood. She had sinned against her sex; and, in an agony of despair, as she crouched down upon the floor with her head against her chair, she told herself that there was no pardon for her. She understood it now, and knew that she could not forgive herself.

But can you forgive her, delicate reader? Or am I asking the question too early in my story? For myself, I have forgiven her. The story of the struggle has been present to my mind for many years,*—and I have learned to think that even this offence against womanhood may, with deep repentance, be forgiven. And you also must forgive her before we close the book, or else my story will have been told amiss.

But let us own that she had sinned,—almost damnably, almost past forgiveness. What;—think that she knew what love meant, and not know which of two she loved! What;—doubt, of two men for whose arms she longed; of which the kisses would be sweet to bear; on which side lay the modesty of her maiden love! Faugh! She had submitted to pollution of heart and feeling before she had brought herself to such a pass as this. Come;—let us see if it be possible that she may be cleansed by the fire of her sorrow.

'What am I to do?' She passed that whole day in asking herself that question. She was herself astounded at the rapidity with which the conviction had forced itself upon her that a marriage with her cousin would be to her almost impossible; and could she permit it to be said of her that she had thrice in her career jilted a promised suitor,—that three times she would go back from her word because her fancy had changed? Where could she find the courage to tell her father, to tell Kate, to tell even George himself, that her purpose was again altered? But she had a year at her disposal. If only during that year he would take her money and squander it, and then require nothing further of her hands, might she not thus escape the doom before her? Might it not be possible that the refusal should this time come from him? But she succeeded in making one resolve. She thought at least that she succeeded. Come what come might, she would never stand with him at the altar. While there was a cliff from which she might fall, water that would cover her, a death-dealing grain that might be mixed in her cup, she could not submit herself to be George Vavasor's wife. To no ear could she tell of this resolve. To no friend could she hint her purpose. She owed her money to the man after what had passed between them. It was his right to count upon such assistance as that would give him, and he should have it. Only as his betrothed she could give it him, for she understood well that if there were any breach between them, his accepting of such aid would be impossible. He should have her money, and then, when the day came, some escape should be found.

In the afternoon her father came to her, and it may be as well to explain that Mr. Grey had seen him again that day. Mr. Grey, when he left Queen Anne Street, had gone to his lawyer, and from thence had made his way to Mr. Vavasor. It was between five and six when Mr. Vavasor came back to his house, and he then found his daughter sitting over the drawing-room fire, without lights, in the gloom of the evening. Mr. Vavasor had returned with Grey to the lawyer's chambers, and had from thence come direct to his own house. He had been startled at the precision with which all the circumstances of his daughter's position had been explained to a mild-eyed old gentleman, with a bald head, who carried on his business in a narrow, dark, clean street, behind Doctors' Commons.* Mr. Tombe was his name. 'No;' Mr. Grey had said, when Mr. Vavasor had asked as to the peculiar nature of Mr. Tombe's business; 'he is not specially an ecclesiastical lawyer. He had a partner at Ely, and was always employed by my father, and by most of the clergy there.' Mr. Tombe had evinced no surprise, no dismay, and certainly no mock delicacy, when the whole affair was under discussion. George Vavasor was to get present moneys, but,—if it could be so arranged—from John Grey's stores rather than from those belonging to Alice. Mr. Tombe could probably arrange that with Mr. Vavasor's lawyer, who would no doubt be able to make difficulty as to raising ready money. Mr. Tombe would be able to raise ready money without difficulty. And then, at last, George Vavasor was to be made to surrender his bride, taking or having taken the price of his bargain. John Vavasor sat by in silence as the arrangement was being made, not knowing how to speak. He had no money with which to give assistance. 'I wish you to understand from the lady's father,' Grey said to the lawyer, 'that the marriage would be regarded by him with as much dismay as by myself.'

'Certainly;—it would be ruinous,' Mr. Vavasor had answered.

'And you see, Mr. Tombe,' Mr. Grey went on, 'we only wish to try the man. If he be not such as we believe him to be, he can prove it by his conduct. If he is worthy of her, he can then take her.'

'You merely wish to open her eyes, Mr. Grey,' said the mild-eyed lawyer.

'I wish that he should have what money he wants, and then we shall find what it is he really wishes.'

'Yes; we shall know our man,' said the lawyer. 'He shall have the money, Mr. Grey,' and so the interview had been ended.

Mr. Vavasor, when he entered the drawing-room, addressed his daughter in a cheery voice. 'What; all in the dark?'

'Yes, papa. Why should I have candles when I am doing nothing? I did not expect you.'

'No; I suppose not. I came here because I want to say a few words to you about business.'

'What business, papa?' Alice well understood the tone of her father's voice. He was desirous of propitiating her; but was at the same time desirous of carrying some point in which he thought it probable that she would oppose him.

'Well; my love, if I understood you rightly, your cousin George wants some money.'

'I did not say that he wants it now; but I think he will want it before the time for the election comes.'

'If so, he will want it at once. He has not asked you for it yet?'

'No; he has merely said that should he be in need he would take me at my word.'

'I think there is no doubt that he wants it. Indeed, I believe that he is almost entirely without present means of his own.'

'I can hardly think so; but I have no knowledge about it. I can only say that he has not asked me yet, and that I should wish to oblige him whenever he may do so.'

'To what extent, Alice?'

'I don't know what I have. I get about four hundred a year, but I do not know what it is worth, or how far it can all be turned into money. I should wish to keep a hundred a year, and let him have the rest.'

'What; eight thousand pounds!' said the father, who in spite of his wish not to oppose her, could not but express his dismay.

'I do not imagine that he will want so much; but if he should, I wish that he should have it.'

'Heaven and earth!' said John Vavasor. 'Of course we should have to give up the house.' He could not suppress his trouble, or refrain from bursting out in agony at the prospect of such a loss.

'But he has asked me for nothing yet, papa.'

'No, exactly; and perhaps he may not; but I wish to know what to do when the demand is made. I am not going to oppose you now; your money is your own, and you have a right to do with it as you please;—but would you gratify me in one thing?'

'What is it, papa?'

'When he does apply, let the amount be raised through me?'

'How through you?'

'Come to me; I mean, so that I may see the lawyer, and have the arrangements made.' Then he explained to her that in dealing with large sums of money, it could not be right that she should do so without his knowledge, even though the property was her own. 'I will promise you that I will not oppose your wishes,' he said. Then Alice undertook that when such case should arise the money should be raised through his means.

The day but one following this she received a letter from Lady Glencora, who was still at Matching Priory. It was a light-spirited, chatty, amusing letter, intended to be happy in its tone,—intended to have a flavour of happiness, but just failing through the too apparent meaning of a word here and there. 'You will see that I am at Matching,' the letter said, 'whereas you will remember that I was to have been at Monkshade. I escaped at last by a violent effort, and am now passing my time innocently,—I fear not so profitably as she would induce me to do,—with Iphy Palliser. You remember Iphy. She is a good creature, and would fain turn even me to profit, if it were possible. I own that I am thinking of them all at Monkshade, and am in truth delighted that I am not there. My absence is entirely laid upon your shoulders. That wicked evening amidst the ruins! Poor ruins. I go there alone sometimes and fancy that I hear such voices from the walls, and see such faces through the broken windows! All the old Pallisers come and frown at me, and tell me that I am not good enough to belong to them. There is a particular window to which Sir Guy comes and makes faces at me. I told Iphy the other day, and she answered me very gravely, that I might, if I chose, make myself good enough for the Pallisers. Even for the Pallisers! Isn't that beautiful?'

Then Lady Glencora went on to say, that her husband intended to come up to London early in the session, and that she would accompany him. 'That is,' added Lady Glencora, 'if I am still good enough for the Pallisers at that time.'

CHAPTER XXXVIII

The Inn at Shap

WHEN George Vavasor left Mr. Scruby's office—the attentive reader will remember that he did call upon Mr. Scruby, the Parliamentary lawyer, and there recognised the necessity of putting himself in possession of a small sum of money with as little delay as possible;—when he left the attorney's office, he was well aware that the work to be done was still before him. And he knew also that the job to be undertaken was a very disagreeable job. He did not like the task of borrowing his cousin Alice's money.

We all of us know that swindlers and rogues do very dirty tricks, and we are apt to picture to ourselves a certain amount of gusto and delight on the part of the swindlers in the doing of them. In this, I think we are wrong. The poor, broken, semi-genteel beggar, who borrows half-sovereigns apiece from all his old acquaintances, knowing that they know that he will never repay them, suffers a separate little agony with each petition that he makes. He does not enjoy pleasant sailing in this journey which he is making. To be refused is painful to him. To get his half-sovereign with scorn is painful. To get it with apparent confidence in his honour is almost more painful. 'D— it,' he says to himself on such rare occasions, 'I will pay that fellow;' and yet, as he says it, he knows that he never will pay even that fellow. It is a comfortless unsatisfying trade, that of living upon other people's money.

How was George Vavasor to make his first step towards getting his hand into his cousin's purse? He had gone to her asking for her love, and she had shuddered when he asked her. That had been the commencement of their life under their new engagement. He knew very well that the money would be forthcoming when he demanded it,—but under their present joint circumstances, how was he to make the demand? If he wrote to her, should he simply ask for money, and make no allusion to his love? If he went to her in person, should he make his visit a mere visit of business,—as he might call on his banker?

He resolved at last that Kate should do the work for him. Indeed, he had felt all along that it would be well that Kate should act as ambassador between him and Alice in money matters, as she had long done in other things. He could talk to Kate as he could not talk to Alice;—and then, between the women, those hard money necessities would be softened down by a romantic phraseology which he would not himself know how to use with any effect. He made up his mind to see Kate, and with this view he went down to Westmoreland; and took himself to a small wayside inn at Shap among the fells, which had been known to him of old. He gave his sister notice that he would be there, and begged her to come over to him as early as she might find it possible on the morning after his arrival. He himself reached the place late in the evening by train from London. There is a station at Shap, by which the railway company no doubt conceives that it has conferred on that somewhat rough and remote locality all the advantages of a refined civilization; but I doubt whether the Shappites have been thankful for the favour. The landlord at the inn, for one, is not thankful. Shap had been a place owing all such life as it had possessed to coaching and posting. It had been a stage on the high road from Lancaster to Carlisle, and though it lay high and bleak among the fells, and was a cold, windy, thinly-populated place,—filling all travellers with thankfulness that they had not been made Shappites, nevertheless, it had had its glory in its coaching and posting. I have no doubt that there are men and women who look back with a fond regret to the palmy days of Shap.

Vavasor reached the little Inn about nine in the evening on a night that was pitchy dark, and in a wind which made it necessary for him to hold his hat on to his head. 'What a beastly country to live in,' he said to himself, resolving that he would certainly sell Vavasor Hall in spite of all family associations, if ever the power to do so should be his. 'What trash it is,' he said, 'hanging on to such a place as that without the means of living like a gentleman, simply because one's ancestors have done so.' And then he expressed a doubt to himself whether all the world contained a more ignorant, opinionated, useless old man than his grandfather,—or, in short, a greater fool.

'Well, Mr. George,' said the landlord as soon as he saw him, 'a sight of you's guid for sair een. It's o'er lang since you've been doon amang the fells.' But George did not want to converse with the innkeeper, or to explain how it was that he did not visit Vavasor Hall. The innkeeper, no doubt, knew all about it,—knew that the grandfather had quarrelled with his grandson, and knew the reason why; but George, if he suspected such knowledge, did not choose to refer to it. So he simply grunted something in reply, and getting himself in before a spark of fire which hardly was burning in a public room with a sandy floor, begged that the little sitting-room up-stairs might be got ready for him. There he passed the evening in solitude, giving no encouragement to the landlord, who, nevertheless, looked him up three or four times,—till at last George said that his head ached, and that he would wish to be alone. 'He was always one of them cankery chiels*as never have a kindly word for man nor beast,' said the landlord. 'Seems as though that raw slash in his face had gone right through into his heart.' After that George was left alone, and sat thinking whether it would not be better to ask Alice for two thousand pounds at once,—so as to save him from the disagreeable necessity of a second borrowing before their marriage. He was very uneasy in his mind. He had flattered himself through it all that his cousin had loved him. He had felt sure that such was the case while they were together in Switzerland. When she had determined to give up John Grey, of course he had told himself the same thing. When she had at once answered his first subsequent overture with an assent, he had of course been certain that it was so. Dark, selfish, and even dishonest as he was, he had, nevertheless, enjoyed something of a lover's true pleasure in believing that Alice had still loved him through all their mischances. But his joy had in a moment been turned into gall during that interview in Queen Anne Street. He had read the truth at a glance. A man must be very vain, or else very little used to such matters, who at George Vavasor's age cannot understand the feelings with which a woman receives him. When Alice contrived as she had done to escape the embrace he was so well justified in asking, he knew the whole truth. He was sore at heart, and very angry withal. He could have readily spurned her from him, and rejected her who had once rejected him. He would have done so had not his need for her money restrained him. He was not a man who could deceive himself in such matters. He knew that this was so, and he told himself that he was a rascal.

Vavasor Hall was, by the road, about five miles from Shap, and it was not altogether an easy task for Kate to get over to the village without informing her grandfather that the visit was to be made, and what was its purport. She could, indeed, walk, and the walk would not be so long as that she had taken with Alice to Swindale fell;—but walking to an inn on a high road, is not the same thing as walking to a point on a hill side over a lake. Had she been dirty, draggled, and wet through on Swindale fell, it would have simply been matter for mirth; but her brother, she knew, would not have liked to see her enter the Lowther Arms at Shap in such a condition. It, therefore, became necessary that she should ask her grandfather to lend her the jaunting-car.

'Where do you want to go?' he asked sharply. In such establishments as that at Vavasor Hall the family horse is generally used for double duties. Though he draws the lady of the house one day, he is not too proud to draw manure on the next. And it will always be found that the master of the house gives a great preference to the manure over the lady. The Squire at Vavasor had come to do so to such an extent that he regarded any application for the animal's services as an encroachment.

'Only to Shap, grandpapa.'

'To Shap! what on earth can take you to Shap? There are no shops at Shap.'

'I am not going to do shopping, I want to see some one there.'

'Whom can you want to see at Shap?'

Then it occurred to Kate on the spur of the moment that she might as well tell her grandfather the fact. 'My brother has come down,' she said; 'and is at the inn there. I had not intended to tell you, as I did not wish to mention his name till you had consented to receive him here.'

'And he expects to come here now;—does he?' said the Squire.

'Oh, no, sir. I think he has no expectation of the kind. He has come down simply to see me;—about business I believe.'

'Business! what business? I suppose he wants to get your money from you?'

'I think it is with reference to his marriage. I think he wants me to use my influence with Alice that it may not be delayed.'

'Look here, Kate; if ever you lend him your money, or any of it,—that is, of the principal I mean,—I will never speak to him again under any circumstance. And more than that! Look here, Kate. In spite of all that has passed and gone, the property will become his for his life when I die,—unless I change my will. If he gets your money from you, I will change it, and he shall not be a shilling richer at my death than he is now. You can have the horse to go to Shap.'

What unlucky chance had it been which had put this idea into the old Squire's head on this especial morning? Kate had resolved that she would entreat her brother to make use of her little fortune. She feared that he was now coming with some reference to his cousin's money,—that something was to be done to enable him to avail himself of his cousin's offer; and Kate, almost blushing in the solitude of her chamber at the thought, was determined that her brother must be saved from such temptation. She knew that money was necessary to him. She knew that he could not stand a second contest without assistance. With all their confidences, he had never told her much of his pecuniary circumstances in the world, but she was almost sure that he was a poor man. He had said as much as that to her, and in his letter desiring her to come to him at Shap, he had inserted a word or two purposely intended to prepare her mind for monetary considerations.

As she was jogged along over the rough road to Shap, she made up her mind that Aunt Greenow would be the proper person to defray the expense of the coming election. To give Kate her due, she would have given up every shilling of her own money without a moment's hesitation, or any feeling that her brother would be wrong to accept it. Nor would she, perhaps, have been unalterably opposed to his taking Alice's money, had Alice simply been his cousin. She felt that as Vavasors they were bound to stand by the future head of the family in an attempt which was to be made, as she felt, for the general Vavasor interest. But she could not endure to think that her

brother should take the money of the girl whom he was engaged to marry. Aunt Greenow's money she thought was fair
game. Aunt Greenow herself had made various liberal offers
to herself which Kate had declined, not caring to be under
pecuniary obligations even to Aunt Greenow without necessity; but she felt that for such a purpose as her brother's contest, she need not hesitate to ask for assistance, and she thought
also that such assistance would be forthcoming.

'Grandpapa knows that you are here, George,' said Kate,
when their first greeting was over.

'The deuce he does! and why did you tell him?'

'I could not get the car to come in without letting him know
why I wanted it.'

'What nonsense! as if you couldn't have made any excuse!
I was particularly anxious that he should not guess that I am
here.'

'I don't see that it can make any difference, George.'

'But I see that it can,—a very great difference. It may prevent my ever being able to get near him again before he dies.
What did he say about my coming?'

'He didn't say much.'

'He made no offer as to my going there?'

'No.'

'I should not have gone if he had. I don't know now that I
ever shall go. To be there to do any good,—so as to make him
alter his will, and leave me in the position which I have a right
to expect, would take more time than the whole property is
worth. And he would endeavour to tie me down in some way
I could not stand;—perhaps ask me to give up my notion of
going into Parliament.'

'He might ask you, but he would not make it ground for
another quarrel, if you refused.'

'He is so unreasonable and ignorant that I am better away
from him. But, Kate, you have not congratulated me on my
matrimonial prospects.'

'Indeed I did, George, when I wrote to you.'

'Did you? well; I had forgotten. I don't know that any very

strong congratulatory tone is necessary. As things go, perhaps it may be as well for all of us, and that's about the best that can be said for it.'

'Oh, George!'

'You see I'm not romantic, Kate, as you are. Half a dozen children with a small income do not generally present themselves as being desirable to men who wish to push their way in the world.'

'You know you have always longed to make her your wife.'

'I don't know anything of the kind. You have always been under a match-making hallucination on that point. But in this case you have been so far successful, and are entitled to your triumph.'

'I don't want any triumph; you ought to know that.'

'But I'll tell you what I do want, Kate. I want some money.' Then he paused, but as she did not answer immediately, he was obliged to go on speaking. 'I'm not at all sure that I have not been wrong in making this attempt to get into Parliament,— that I'm not struggling to pick fruit which is above my reach.'

'Don't say that, George.'

'Ah, but I can't help feeling it. I need hardly tell you that I am ready to risk anything of my own. If I know myself I would toss up to-morrow, or for the matter of that to-day, between the gallows and a seat in the House. But I cannot go on with this contest by risking what is merely my own. Money, for immediate use, I have none left, and my neck, though I were ever so willing to risk it, is of no service.'

'Whatever I have can be yours to-morrow,' said Kate in a hesitating voice, which too plainly pronounced her misery as she made the offer. She could not refrain herself from making it. Though her grandfather's threat was ringing in her ears,— though she knew that she might be ruining her brother by proposing such a loan, she had no alternative. When her brother told her of his want of money, she could not abstain from tendering to him the use of what was her own.

'No;' said he. 'I shall not take your money.'

'You would not scruple, if you knew how welcome you are.'

'At any rate, I shall not take it. I should not think it right. All that you have would only just suffice for my present wants, and I should not choose to make you a beggar. There would, moreover, be a difficulty about readjusting the payment.'*

'There would be no difficulty, because no one need be consulted but us two.'

'I should not think it right, and therefore let there be an end of it,' said George in a tone of voice which had in it something of magniloquence.

'What is it you wish, then?' said Kate, who knew too well what he did wish.

'I will explain to you. When Alice and I are married, of course there will be a settlement made on her, and as we are both the grandchildren of the old Squire I shall propose that the Vavasor property shall be hers for life in the event of her outliving me.'

'Well,' said Kate.

'And if this be done, there can be no harm in my forestalling some of her property, which, under the circumstances of such a settlement, would of course become mine when we are married.'

'But the Squire might leave the property to whom he pleases.'

'We know very well that he won't, at any rate, leave it out of the family. In fact, he would only be too glad to consent to such an agreement as that I have proposed, because he would thereby rob me of all power in the matter.'

'But that could not be done till you are married.'

'Look here, Kate;—don't you make difficulties.' And now, as he looked at her, the cicature on his face seemed to open and yawn at her. 'If you mean to say that you won't help me, do say so, and I will go back to London.'

'I would do anything in my power to help you,—that was not wrong!'

'Yes; anybody could say as much as that. That is not much of an offer if you are to keep to yourself the power of deciding what is wrong. Will you write to Alice,—or better still, go to her, and explain that I want the money.'

'How can I go to London now?'

'You can do it very well, if you choose. But if that be too much, then write to her. It will come much better from you than from me; write to her, and explain that I must pay in advance the expenses of this contest, and that I cannot look for success unless I do so. I did not think that the demand would come so quick on me; but they know that I am not a man of capital, and therefore I cannot expect them to carry on the fight for me, unless they know that the money is sure. Scruby has been bitten two or three times by these metropolitan fellows, and he is determined that he will not be bitten again.' Then he paused for Kate to speak.

'George,' she said, slowly.

'Well.'

'I wish you would try any other scheme but that.'

'There is no other scheme! That's so like a woman;—to quarrel with the only plan that is practicable.'

'I do not think you ought to take Alice's money.'

'My dear Kate, you must allow me to be the best judge of what I ought to do, and what I ought not to do. Alice herself understands the matter perfectly. She knows that I cannot obtain this position, which is as desirable for her as it is for me——'

'And for me as much as for either,' said Kate, interrupting him.

'Very well. Alice, I say, knows that I cannot do this without money, and has offered the assistance which I want. I would rather that you should tell her how much I want, and that I want it now, than that I should do so. That is all. If you are half the woman that I take you to be, you will understand this well enough.'

Kate did understand it well enough. She was quite awake to the fact that her brother was ashamed of the thing he was about to do,—so much ashamed of it that he was desirous of using her voice instead of his own. 'I want you to write to her quite at once,' he continued; 'since you seem to think that it is not worth while to take the trouble of a journey to London.'

'There is no question about the trouble,' said Kate. 'I would walk to London to get the money for you, if that were all.'

'Do you think that Alice will refuse to lend it me?' said he, looking into her face.

'I am sure that she would not, but I think that you ought not to take it from her. There seems to me to be something sacred about property that belongs to the girl you are going to marry.'

'If there is anything on earth I hate,' said George, walking about the room, 'it is romance. If you keep it for reading in your bed-room, it's all very well for those who like it, but when it comes to be mixed up with one's business it plays the devil. If you would only sift what you have said, you would see what nonsense it is. Alice and I are to be man and wife. All our interests, and all our money, and our station in life, whatever it may be, are to be joint property. And yet she is the last person in the world to whom I ought to go for money to improve her prospects as well as my own. That's what you call delicacy. I call it infernal nonsense.'

'I'll tell you what I'll do, George. I'll ask Aunt Greenow to lend you the money,—or to lend it to me.'

'I don't believe she'd give me a shilling. Moreover, I want it quite immediately, and the time taken up in letter-writing and negotiations would be fatal to me. If you won't apply to Alice, I must. I want you to tell me whether you will oblige me in this matter.'

Kate was still hesitating as to her answer, when there came a knock at the door, and a little crumpled note was brought up to her. A boy had just come with it across the fell from Vavasor Hall, and Kate, as soon as she saw her name on the outside, knew that it was from her grandfather. It was as follows:—

'If George wishes to come to the Hall, let him come. If he chooses to tell me that he regrets his conduct to me, I will see him.'

'What is it?' said George. Then Kate put the note into her brother's hand.

'I'll do nothing of the kind,' he said. 'What good should I get by going to the old man's house?'

'Every good,' said Kate. 'If you don't go now you never can do so.'

'Never till it's my own,' said George.

'If you show him that you are determined to be at variance with him, it never will be your own;—unless, indeed, it should some day come to you as part of Alice's fortune. Think of it, George; you would not like to receive everything from her.'

He walked about the room, muttering maledictions between his teeth, and balancing, as best he was able at such a moment, his pride against his profit. 'You haven't answered my question,' said he. 'If I go to the Hall, will you write to Alice?'

'No, George; I cannot write to Alice asking her for the money.'

'You won't?'

'I could not bring myself to do it.'

'Then, Kate, you and my grandfather may work together for the future. You may get him to leave you the place if you have skill enough.'

'That is as undeserved a reproach as any woman ever encountered,' said Kate, standing her ground boldly before him. 'If you have either heart or conscience, you will feel that it is so.'

'I'm not much troubled with either one or the other, I fancy. Things are being brought to such a pass with me, that I am better without them.'

'Will you take my money, George; just for the present?'

'No. I haven't much conscience; but I have a little left.'

'Will you let me write to Mrs. Greenow?'

'I have not the slightest objection; but it will be of no use whatsoever.'

'I will do so, at any rate. And now will you come to the Hall?'

'To beg that old fool's pardon? No; I won't. In the mood I am in at present, I couldn't do it. I should only anger him worse than ever. Tell him that I've business which calls me back to London at once.'

'It is a thousand pities.'

'It can't be helped.'

'It may make so great a difference to you for your whole life!' urged Kate.

'I'll tell you what I'll do,' said George. 'I'll go to Vavasor and put up with the old Squire's insolence, if you'll make this application for me to Alice.' I wonder whether it occurred to him that his sister desired his presence at the Hall solely on his own behalf. The same idea certainly did not occur to Kate. She hesitated, feeling that she would almost do anything to achieve a reconciliation between her grandfather and her brother.

'But you'll let me write to Aunt Greenow first?' said she. 'It will take only two days,—or at the most three.'

To this George consented as though he were yielding a great deal; and Kate, with a sore conscience, with a full knowledge that she was undertaking to do wrong, promised that she would apply to Alice for her money, if sufficient funds should not be forthcoming from Mrs. Greenow. Thereupon, George graciously consented to proceed to his bedroom, and put together his clothes with a view to his visit to the Hall.

'I thank Providence, Kate, that circumstances make it impossible for me to stay above two days. I have not linen to last me longer.'

'We'll manage that for you at the Hall.'

'Indeed you won't do anything of the kind. And look, Kate, when I make that excuse don't you offer to do so. I will stay there over to-morrow night, and shall go into Kendal early, so as to catch the express train up on Thursday morning. Don't you throw me over by any counter proposition.'

Then they started together in the car, and very few words were said till they reached the old lodge, which stood at the entrance to the place. 'Eh, Mr. George; be that you?' said the old woman, who came out to swing back for them the broken gate. 'A sight of you is good for sair een.' It was the same welcome that the innkeeper had given him, and equally sincere.

George had never made himself popular about the place, but he was the heir.

'I suppose you had better go into the drawing-room,' said Kate; 'while I go to my grandfather. You won't find a fire there.'

'Manage it how you please; but don't keep me in the cold very long. Heavens, what a country house! The middle of January, and no fires in the rooms.'

'And remember, George, when you see him you must say that you regret that you ever displeased him. Now that you are here, don't let there be any further misunderstanding.'

'I think it very probable that there will be,' said George. 'I only hope he'll let me have the old horse to take me back to Shap if there is. There he is at the front door, so I shan't have to go into the room without a fire.'

The old man was standing at the Hall steps when the car drove up, as though to welcome his grandson. He put out his hand to help Kate down the steps, keeping his eye all the time on George's face.

'So you've come back,' the Squire said to him.

'Yes, sir;—I've come back,—like the prodigal son in the parable.'

'The prodigal son was contrite. I hope you are so.'

'Pretty well for that, sir. I'm sorry there has been any quarrel, and all that, you know.'

'Go in,' said the Squire, very angrily. 'Go in. To expect anything gracious from you would be to expect pearls from swine. Go in.'

George went in, shrugging his shoulders as his eyes met his sister's. It was in this fashion that the reconciliation took place between Squire Vavasor and his heir.

CHAPTER XXXIX

Mr. Cheesacre's Hospitality

As the winter wore itself away, Mr. Cheesacre, happy as he was amidst the sports of Norfolk, and prosperous as he might be with the augean*spoils of Oileymead, fretted himself with an intense anxiety to bring to a close that affair which he had on his hands with the widow Greenow. There were two special dangers which disturbed him. She would give herself and all her money to that adventurer, Bellfield; or else she would spend her own money so fast before he got hold upon it, that the prize would be greatly damaged. 'I'm —— if she hasn't been and set up a carriage!' he said to himself one day, as, standing on the pavement of Tombland,* in Norwich, he saw Mrs. Greenow issue forth from the Close in a private brougham,* accompanied by one of the Fairstairs girls. 'She's been and set up her carriage as sure as my name's Cheesacre!'

Whatever reason he might have to fear the former danger, we may declare that he had none whatever as to the latter. Mrs. Greenow knew what she was doing with her money as well as any lady in England. The private carriage was only a hired brougham taken by the month, and as to that boy in buttons whom she had lately established, why should she not keep a young servant, and call him a page, if it gave her any comfort to do so? If Mr. Cheesacre had also known that she had lent the Fairstairs family fifty pounds to help them through with some difficulty which Joe had encountered with the Norwich tradespeople, he would have been beside himself with dismay. He desired to obtain the prize unmutilated,—in all its fair proportions. Any such clippings he regarded as robberies against himself.

But he feared Bellfield more than he feared the brougham. That all is fair in love and war was no doubt, at this period, Captain Bellfield's maxim, and we can only trust that he found in it some consolation, or ease to his conscience, in regard to the monstrous lies which he told his friend. In war, no doubt, all stratagems are fair. The one general is quite justified in making the other believe that he is far to the right, when in truth he is turning his enemy's left flank. If successful, he will be put upon a pedestal for his clever deceit, and crowned with laurels because of his lie. If Bellfield could only be successful, and achieve for himself the mastery over those forty thousand pounds, the world would forgive him and place, on his brow also, some not uncomfortable crown. In the mean time, his stratagems were as deep and his lies as profound as those of any general.

It must not be supposed that Cheesacre ever believed him. In the first place, he knew that Bellfield was not a man to be believed in any way. Had he not been living on lies for the last ten years? But then a man may lie in such a way as to deceive, though no one believe him. Mr. Cheesacre was kept in an agony of doubt while Captain Bellfield occupied his lodgings in Norwich. He fee'd Jeannette liberally. He even fee'd Charlie Fairstairs,—Miss Fairstairs I mean,—with gloves, and chickens from Oileymead, so that he might know whether that kite fluttered about his dovecote, and of what nature were the flutterings. He went even further than this, and fee'd the Captain himself,—binding him down not to flutter as value given in return for such fees. He attempted even to fee the widow,— cautioning her against the fluttering, as he tendered to her, on his knees, a brooch as big as a breast-plate. She waved aside the breast-plate, declaring that the mourning ring which contained poor Greenow's final grey lock of hair, was the last article from a jeweller's shop which should ever find a place about her person. At the same time she declared that Captain Bellfield was nothing to her; Mr. Cheesacre need have no fears in that quarter. But then, she added, neither was he to have any hope. Her affections were all buried under the cold sod. This was harassing. Nevertheless, though no absolute satisfaction was to be attained in the wooing of Mrs. Greenow, there was a pleasantness in the occupation which ought to have reconciled her suitors to their destiny. With most ladies, when a gentleman has been on his knees before one of them in the

morning, with outspoken protestations of love, with clearly
defined proffers of marriage, with a minute inventory of the
offerer's worldly wealth,—down even to the 'mahogany-furnitured' bed-chambers, as was the case with Mr. Cheesacre, and
when all these overtures have been peremptorily declined,—
a gentleman in such a case, I say, would generally feel some
awkwardness in sitting down to tea with the lady at the close
of such a performance. But with Mrs. Greenow there was no
such awkwardness. After an hour's work of the nature above
described she would play the hostess with a genial hospitality,
that eased off all the annoyance of disappointment; and then
at the end of the evening, she would accept a squeeze of the
hand, a good, palpable, long-protracted squeeze, with that sort
of 'don't;—have done now,' by which Irish young ladies allure
their lovers.* Mr. Cheesacre, on such occasions, would leave the
Close, swearing that she should be his on the next market-day,
—or at any rate, on the next Saturday. Then, on the Monday, tidings would reach him that Bellfield had passed all Sunday afternoon with his lady-love,—Bellfield, to whom he had
lent five pound on purpose that he might be enabled to spend
that very Sunday with some officers of the Suffolk volunteers
at Ipswich. And hearing this, he would walk out among those
rich heaps, at the back of his farmyard, uttering deep curses
against the falsehood of men and the fickleness of women.

Driven to despair, he at last resolved to ask Bellfield to come
to Oileymead for a month. That drilling at Norwich, or the
part of it which was supposed to be profitable, was wearing itself out. Funds were low with the Captain,—as he did not
scruple to tell his friend Cheesacre, and he accepted the invitation. 'I'll mount you with the harriers, old fellow,' Cheesacre
had said; 'and give you a little shooting. Only I won't have
you go out when I'm not with you.' Bellfield agreed. Each of
them understood the nature of the bargain; though Bellfield,
I think, had somewhat the clearer understanding in the matter.
He would not be so near the widow as he had been at Norwich,
but he would not be less near than his kind host. And his host
would no doubt watch him closely;—but then he also could

watch his host. There was a railway station not two miles from Oileymead, and the journey thence into Norwich was one of half an hour. Mr. Cheesacre would doubtless be very jealous of such journeys, but with all his jealousy he could not prevent them. And then, in regard to this arrangement, Mr. Cheesacre paid the piper, whereas Captain Bellfield paid nothing. Would it not be sweet to him if he could carry off his friend's prize from under the very eaves of his friend's house?

And Mrs. Greenow also understood the arrangement. 'Going to Oileymead; are you?' she said when Captain Bellfield came to tell her of his departure. Charlie Fairstairs was with her, so that the Captain could not utilize the moment in any special way. 'It's quite delightful,' continued the widow, 'to see how fond you two gentlemen are of each other.'

'I think gentlemen always like to go best to gentlemen's houses where there are no ladies,' said Charlie Fairstairs, whose career in life had not as yet been satisfactory to her.

'As for that,' said Bellfield, 'I wish with all my heart that dear old Cheesy would get a wife. He wants a wife badly, if ever a man did, with all that house full of blankets and crockery. Why don't you set your cap at him, Miss Fairstairs?'

'What;—at a farmer!' said Charlie who was particularly anxious that her dear friend, Mrs. Greenow, should not marry Mr. Cheesacre, and who weakly thought to belittle him accordingly.

'Give him my kind love,' said Mrs. Greenow, thereby resenting the impotent interference. 'And look here, Captain Bellfield, suppose you both dine with me next Saturday. He always comes in on Saturday, and you might as well come too.'

Captain Bellfield declared that he would only be too happy.

'And Charlie shall come to set her cap at Mr. Cheesacre,' said the widow, turning a soft and gracious eye on the Captain.

'I shall be happy to come,'—said Charlie, quite delighted; 'but not with that object. Mr. Cheesacre is very respectable, I'm sure.' Charlie's mother had been the daughter of a small squire who had let his land to tenants, and she was, therefore, justified by circumstances in looking down upon a farmer.

The matter was so settled,—pending the consent of Mr. Cheesacre; and Bellfield went out to Oileymead. He knew the ways of the house, and was not surprised to find himself left alone till after dusk; nor was he much surprised when he learned that he was not put into one of the mahogany-furnitured chambers, but into a back room looking over the farmyard in which there was no fire-place. The Captain had already endured some of the evils of poverty, and could have put up with this easily had nothing been said about it. As it was, Cheesacre brought the matter forward, and apologized, and made the thing difficult.

'You see, old fellow,' he said, 'there are the rooms, and of course they're empty. But it's such a bore hauling out all the things and putting up the curtains. You'll be very snug where you are.'

'I shall do very well,' said Bellfield rather sulkily.

'Of course you'll do very well. It's the warmest room in the house in one way.' He did not say in what way. Perhaps the near neighbourhood of the stables may have had a warming effect.

Bellfield did not like it; but what is a poor man to do under such circumstances? So he went up-stairs and washed his hands before dinner in the room without a fire-place, flattering himself that he would yet be even with his friend Cheesacre.

They dined together not in the best humour, and after dinner they sat down to enjoy themselves with pipes and brandy and water. Bellfield, having a taste for everything that was expensive, would have preferred cigars; but his friend put none upon the table. Mr. Cheesacre, though he could spend his money liberally when occasion required such spending, knew well the value of domestic economy. He wasn't going to put himself out, as he called it, for Bellfield! What was good enough for himself was good enough for Bellfield. 'A beggar, you know; just a regular beggar!' as he was betrayed into saying to Mrs. Greenow on some occasion just at this period. 'Poor fellow! He only wants money to make him almost perfect,' Mrs. Greenow had answered;—and Mr. Cheesacre had felt that he had made a mistake.

Both the men became talkative, if not good-humoured, under the effects of the brandy and water, and the Captain then communicated Mrs. Greenow's invitation to Mr. Cheesacre. He had had his doubts as to the propriety of doing so,—thinking that perhaps it might be to his advantage to forget the message. But he reflected that he was at any rate a match for Cheesacre when they were present together, and finally came to the conclusion that the message should be delivered. 'I had to go and just wish her good-bye, you know,' he said apologetically, as he finished his little speech.

'I don't see that at all,' said Cheesacre.

'Why, my dear fellow, how foolishly jealous you are. If I were to be downright uncivil to her, as you would have me be, it would only call attention to the thing.'

'I'm not a bit jealous. A man who sits upon his own ground as I do hasn't any occasion to be jealous.'

'I don't know what your own ground has to do with it,—but we'll let that pass.'

'I think it has a great deal to do with it. If a man does intend to marry he ought to have things comfortable about him; unless he wants to live on his wife, which I look upon as about the meanest thing a man can do. By George, I'd sooner break stones than that.'

This was hard for any captain to bear,—even for Captain Bellfield; but he did bear it,—looking forward to revenge.

'There's no pleasing you, I know,' said he. 'But there's the fact. I went to say good-bye to her, and she asked me to give you that message. Shall we go or not?'

Cheesacre sat for some time silent, blowing out huge clouds of smoke while he meditated a little plan. 'I'll tell you what it is, Bellfield,' he said at last. 'She's nothing to you, and if you won't mind it, I'll go. Mrs. Jones shall get you anything you like for dinner,—and,—and—I'll stand you a bottle of the 34 port!'

But Captain Bellfield was not going to put up with this. He had not sold himself altogether to work Mr. Cheesacre's will. 'No, old fellow,' said he; 'that cock won't fight. She has asked me to dine with her on Saturday, and I mean to go. I don't intend that she shall think that I'm afraid of her,—or of you either.'

'You don't;—don't you?'

'No, I don't,' said the Captain stoutly.

'I wish you'd pay me some of that money you owe me,' said Cheesacre.

'So I will,—when I've married the widow. Ha,—ha,—ha.'

Cheesacre longed to turn him out of the house. Words to bid him go, were, so to say, upon his tongue. But the man would only have taken himself to Norwich, and would have gone without any embargo upon his suit; all their treaties would then be at an end. 'She knows a trick worth two of that,' said Cheesacre at last.

'I dare say she does; and if so, why shouldn't I go and dine with her next Saturday?'

'I'll tell you why,—because you're in my way. The deuce is in it if I haven't made the whole thing clear enough. I've told you all my plans because I thought you were my friend, and I've paid you well to help me, too; and yet it seems to me you'd do anything in your power to throw me over,—only you can't.'

'What an ass you are,' said the Captain after a pause; 'just you listen to me. That scraggy young woman, Charlie Fair-stairs, is to be there of course.'

'How do you know?'

'I tell you that I do know. She was present when the whole thing was arranged, and I heard her asked, and heard her say that she would come;—and for the matter of that I heard her declare that she wouldn't set her cap at you, because you're a farmer.'

'Upon my word she's kind. Upon my word she is,' said Cheesacre, getting very angry and very red. 'Charlie Fair-stairs, indeed! I wouldn't pick her out of a gutter with a pair of tongs. She ain't good enough for my bailiff, let alone me.'

'But somebody must take her in hand on Saturday, if you're to do any good,' said the crafty Bellfield.

'What the deuce does she have that nasty creature there for?' said Cheesacre, who thought it very hard that everything should not be arranged exactly as he would desire.

'She wants a companion, of course. You can get rid of Charlie, you know, when you make her Mrs. Cheesacre.'

'Get rid of her! You don't suppose she'll ever put her foot in this house. Not if I know it. I've detested that woman for the last ten years.' Cheesacre could forgive no word of slight respecting his social position, and the idea of Miss Fairstairs having pretended to look down upon him, galled him to the quick.

'You'll have to dine with her at any rate,' said Bellfield, 'and I always think that four are better company than three on such occasions.'

Mr. Cheesacre grunted an unwilling assent, and after this it was looked upon as an arranged thing that they two should go into Norwich on the Saturday together, and that they should both dine with the widow. Indeed, Mrs. Greenow got two notes, one from each of them, accepting the invitation. Cheesacre wrote in the singular number, altogether ignoring Captain Bellfield, as he might have ignored his footman had he intended to take one. The Captain condescended to use the plural pronoun. 'We shall be so happy to come,' said he. 'Dear old Cheesy is out of his little wits with delight,' he added, 'and has already begun to polish off the effects of the farmyard.'

'Effects of the farmyard,' said Mrs. Greenow aloud, in Jeannette's hearing, when she received the note. 'It would be well for Captain Bellfield if he had a few such effects himself.'

'You can give him enough, ma'am,' said Jeannette, 'to make him a better man than Mr. Cheesacre any day. And for a gentleman——; of course I say nothing, but if I was a lady, I know which should be the man for me.'

CHAPTER XL

Mrs. Greenow's Little Dinner in the Close

How deep and cunning are the wiles of love! When that Saturday morning arrived not a word was said by Cheesacre to his rival as to his plans for the day. 'You'll take the dog-cart in?' Captain Bellfield had asked overnight. 'I don't know what I shall do as yet,' replied he who was master of the house, of the dog-cart, and, as he fondly thought, of the situation. But Bellfield knew that Cheesacre must take the dog-cart, and was contented. His friend would leave him behind, if it were possible, but Bellfield would take care that it should not be possible.

Before breakfast Mr. Cheesacre surreptitiously carried out into the yard a bag containing all his apparatus for dressing,—his marrow oil for his hair, his shirt with the wondrous worked front upon an under-stratum of pink to give it colour, his shiny boots, and all the rest of the paraphernalia. When dining in Norwich on ordinary occasions, he simply washed his hands there, trusting to the chambermaid at the inn to find him a comb; and now he came down with his bag surreptitiously, and hid it away in the back of the dog-cart with secret, but alas, not unobserved hands, hoping that Bellfield would forget his toilet. But when did such a Captain ever forget his outward man? Cheesacre, as he returned through the kitchen from the yard into the front hall, perceived another bag lying near the door, apparently filled almost as well as his own.

'What the deuce are you going to do with all this luggage?' said he, giving the bag a kick.

'Put it where I saw you putting yours when I opened my window just now,' said Bellfield.

'D—— the window,' exclaimed Cheesacre, and then they sat down to breakfast. 'How you do hack that ham about,' he said. 'If you ever cured hams yourself you'd be more particular in cutting them.' This was very bad. Even Bellfield could not bear it with equanimity, and feeling unable to eat the ham under such circumstances, made his breakfast with a couple of fresh eggs. 'If you didn't mean to eat the meat, why the mischief did you cut it?' said Cheesacre.

'Upon my word, Cheesacre, you're too bad;—upon my word you are,' said Bellfield, almost sobbing.

'What's the matter now?' said the other.

'Who wants your ham?'

'You do, I suppose, or you wouldn't cut it.'

'No, I don't;—nor anything else either that you've got. It isn't fair to ask a fellow into your house, and then say such things to him as that. And it isn't what I've been accustomed to either; I can tell you that, Mr. Cheesacre.'

'Oh, bother!'

'It's all very well to say bother, but I choose to be treated like a gentleman wherever I go. You and I have known each other a long time, and I'd put up with more from you than from anyone else; but——.'

'Can you pay me the money that you owe me, Bellfield?' said Cheesacre, looking hard at him.

'No, I can't,' said Bellfield; 'not immediately.'

'Then eat your breakfast, and hold your tongue.'

After that Captain Bellfield did eat his breakfast,—leaving the ham however untouched, and did hold his tongue, vowing vengeance in his heart. But the two men went into Norwich more amicably together than they would have done had there been no words between them. Cheesacre felt that he had trespassed a little, and therefore offered the Captain a cigar as he seated himself in the cart. Bellfield accepted the offering, and smoked the weed of peace.

'Now,' said Cheesacre, as he drove into the 'Swan' yard, 'what do you mean to do with yourself all day?'

'I shall go down to the quarters, and look the fellows up.'

'All right. But mind this, Bellfield;—it's an understood thing, that you're not to be in the Close before four?'

'I won't be in the Close before four!'

'Very well. That's understood. If you deceive me, I'll not drive you back to Oileymead to-night.'

In this instance Captain Bellfield had no intention to deceive. He did not think it probable that he could do himself any good by philandering about the widow early in the day. She would be engaged with her dinner and with an early toilet. Captain Bellfield, moreover, had learned from experience that the first comer has not always an advantage in ladies' society. The mind of a woman is greedy after novelty, and it is upon the stranger, or upon the most strange of her slaves around her, that she often smiles the sweetest. The cathedral clock, therefore, had struck four before Captain Bellfield rang Mrs. Greenow's bell, and then, when he was shown into the drawing-room, he found Cheesacre there alone, redolent with the marrow oil, and beautiful with the pink bosom.

'Haven't you seen her yet?' asked the Captain almost in a whisper.

'No,' said Cheesacre sulkily.

'Nor yet Charlie Fairstairs?'

'I've seen nobody,' said Cheesacre.

But at this moment he was compelled to swallow his anger, as Mrs. Greenow, accompanied by her lady guest, came into the room. 'Whoever would have expected two gentlemen to be so punctual,' said she, 'especially on market-day!'

'Market-day makes no difference when I come to see you,' said Cheesacre, putting his best foot forward, while Captain Bellfield contented himself with saying something civil to Charlie. He would bide his time and ride a waiting race.

The widow was almost gorgeous in her weeds. I believe that she had not sinned in her dress against any of those canons which the semi-ecclesiastical authorities on widowhood have laid down as to the outward garments fitted for gentlemen's relicts. The materials were those which are devoted to the deepest conjugal grief. As regarded every item of the written law her suttee worship was carried out to the letter. There was the widow's cap, generally so hideous, so well known to the eyes of all men, so odious to womanhood. Let us hope that such headgear may have some assuaging effect on the departed spirits of husbands. There was the dress of deep, clinging, melancholy crape,—of crape which becomes so brown and so rusty, and which makes the six months' widow seem so much more afflicted a creature than she whose husband is just gone, and whose crape is therefore new. There were the trailing weepers, and the widow's kerchief pinned close round her neck and somewhat tightly over her bosom. But there was that of genius about Mrs. Greenow, that she had turned every seeming disadvantage to some special profit, and had so dressed herself that though she had obeyed the law to the letter, she had thrown the spirit of it to the winds. Her cap sat jauntily on her head, and showed just so much of her rich brown hair as to give her the appearance of youth which she desired. Cheesacre had blamed her in his heart for her private carriage, but she spent more money, I think, on new crape than she did on her brougham. It never became brown and rusty with her, or formed itself into old lumpy folds, or shaped itself round her like a grave cloth. The written law had not interdicted crinoline, and she loomed as large with weeds, which with her were not sombre, as she would do with her silks when the period of her probation should be over. Her weepers were bright with newness, and she would waft them aside from her shoulder with an air which turned even them into auxiliaries. Her kerchief was fastened close round her neck and close over her bosom; but Jeannette well knew what she was doing as she fastened it,—and so did Jeannette's mistress.

Mrs. Greenow would still talk much about her husband, declaring that her loss was as fresh to her wounded heart, as though he, on whom all her happiness had rested, had left her only yesterday; but yet she mistook her dates, frequently referring to the melancholy circumstance, as having taken place fifteen months ago. In truth, however, Mr. Greenow had been alive within the last nine months,—as everybody around her knew. But if she chose to forget the exact day, why should her friends or dependents remind her of it? No friend or dependent did remind her of it, and Charlie Fairstairs spoke of the fifteen months with bold confidence,—false-tongued little parasite that she was.

'Looking well?' said the widow, in answer to some out-spoken compliment from Mr. Cheesacre. 'Yes, I'm well enough in health, and I suppose I ought to be thankful that it is so. But if you had buried a wife whom you had loved within the last eighteen months, you would have become as indifferent as I am to all that kind of thing.'

'I never was married yet,' said Mr. Cheesacre.

'And therefore you know nothing about it. Everything in the world is gay and fresh to you. If I were you, Mr. Chees-acre, I would not run the risk. It is hardly worth a woman's while, and I suppose not a man's. The sufferings are too great!' Whereupon she pressed her handkerchief to her eyes.

'But I mean to try all the same,' said Cheesacre, looking the lover all over as he gazed into the fair one's face.

'I hope that you may be successful, Mr. Cheesacre, and that she may not be torn away from you early in life. Is dinner ready, Jeannette? That's well. Mr. Cheesacre, will you give your arm to Miss Fairstairs?'

There was no doubt as to Mrs. Greenow's correctness. As Captain Bellfield held, or had held, her Majesty's commission, he was clearly entitled to take the mistress of the festival down to dinner. But Cheesacre would not look at it in this light. He would only remember that he had paid for the Captain's food for some time past, that the Captain had been brought into Norwich in his gig, that the Captain owed him money, and ought, so to say, to be regarded as his property on the occasion. 'I pay my way, and that ought to give a man higher station than being a beggarly captain,—which I don't believe he is, if all the truth was known.' It was thus that he took an occasion to express himself to Miss Fairstairs on that very evening. 'Military rank is always recognized,' Miss Fairstairs had replied, taking Mr. Cheesacre's remarks as a direct slight upon herself. He had taken her down to dinner, and had then come to her complaining that he had been injured in being called upon to do so! 'If you were a magistrate, Mr. Cheesacre, you would have rank; but I believe you are not.' Charlie Fair-stairs knew well what she was about. Mr. Cheesacre had striven much to get his name put upon the commission of the peace, but had failed. 'Nasty, scraggy old cat,' Cheesacre said to himself, as he turned away from her.

But Bellfield gained little by taking the widow down. He and Cheesacre were placed at the top and bottom of the table, so that they might do the work of carving; and the ladies sat at the sides. Mrs. Greenow's hospitality was very good. The dinner was exactly what a dinner ought to be for four persons. There was soup, fish, a cutlet, a roast fowl, and some game. Jeannette waited at table nimbly, and the thing could not have been done better. Mrs. Greenow's appetite was not injured by her grief, and she so far repressed for the time all remembrance of her sorrow as to enable her to play the kind hostess to perfection. Under her immediate eye Cheesacre was forced into apparent cordiality with his friend Bellfield, and the Captain himself took the good things which the gods provided with thankful good-humour.

Nothing, however, was done at the dinner-table. No work got itself accomplished. The widow was so accurately fair in the adjustment of her favours, that even Jeannette could not perceive to which of the two she turned with the amplest smile. She talked herself and made others talk, till Cheesacre became almost comfortable, in spite of his jealousy. 'And now,' she said, as she got up to leave the room, when she had taken her own glass of wine, 'We will allow these two gentlemen just half an hour, eh, Charlie? and then we shall expect them up-stairs.'

'Ten minutes will be enough for us here,' said Cheesacre, who was in a hurry to utilize his time.

'Half an hour,' said Mrs. Greenow, not without some little tone of command in her voice. Ten minutes might be enough for Mr. Cheesacre, but ten minutes was not enough for her.

Bellfield had opened the door, and it was upon him that the widow's eye glanced as she left the room. Cheesacre saw it, and resolved to resent the injury. 'I'll tell you what it is, Bellfield,' he said, as he sat down moodily over the fire, 'I won't have you coming here at all, till this matter is settled.'

'Till what matter is settled?' said Bellfield, filling his glass.

'You know what matter I mean.'

'You take such a deuce of a time about it.'

'No, I don't. I take as little time as anybody could. That other fellow has only been dead about nine months, and I've got the thing in excellent training already.'

'And what harm do I do?'

'You disturb me, and you disturb her. You do it on purpose. Do you suppose I can't see? I'll tell you what, now; if you'll go clean out of Norwich for a month, I'll lend you two hundred pounds on the day she becomes Mrs. Cheesacre.'

'And where am I to go to?'

'You may stay at Oileymead if you like;—that is, on condition that you do stay there.'

'And be told that I hack the ham because it's not my own. Shall I tell you a piece of my mind, Cheesacre?'

'What do you mean?'

'That woman has no more idea of marrying you than she has of marrying the Bishop. Won't you fill your glass, old fellow? I know where the tap is if you want another bottle. You may as well give it up, and spend no more money in pink fronts and polished boots on her account. You're a podgy man, you see, and Mrs. Greenow doesn't like podgy men.'

Cheesacre sat looking at him with his mouth open, dumb with surprise, and almost paralysed with impotent anger. What had happened during the last few hours to change so entirely the tone of his dependent Captain? Could it be that Bellfield had been there during the morning, and that she had accepted him?

'You are very podgy, Cheesacre,' Bellfield continued, 'and then you so often smell of the farm-yard; and you talk too much of your money and your property. You'd have had a better chance if you had openly talked to her of hers,—as I have done. As it is, you haven't any chance at all.'

Bellfield, as he thus spoke to the man opposite to him, went on drinking his wine comfortably, and seemed to be chuckling with glee. Cheesacre was so astounded, so lost in amazement that the creature whom he had fed,—whom he had bribed with money out of his own pocket, should thus turn against him, that for a while he could not collect his thoughts or find voice wherewith to make any answer. It occurred to him immediately that Bellfield was even now, at this very time, staying at his house,—that he, Cheesacre, was expected to drive him, Bellfield, back to Oileymead, to his own Oileymead, on this very evening; and as he thought of this he almost fancied that he must be in a dream. He shook himself, and looked again, and there sat Bellfield, eyeing him through the bright colour of a glass of port.

'Now I've told you a bit of my mind, Cheesy, my boy,' continued Bellfield, 'and you'll save yourself a deal of trouble and annoyance if you'll believe what I say. She don't mean to marry you. It's most probable that she'll marry me; but, at any rate, she won't marry you.'

'Do you mean to pay me my money, sir?' said Cheesacre, at last, finding his readiest means of attack in that quarter.

'Yes, I do.'

'But when?'

'When I've married Mrs. Greenow,—and, therefore, I expect your assistance in that little scheme. Let us drink her health. We shall always be delighted to see you at our house, Cheesy, my boy, and you shall be allowed to hack the hams just as much as you please.'

'You shall be made to pay for this,' said Cheesacre, gasping with anger;—gasping almost more with dismay than he did with anger.

'All right, old fellow; I'll pay for it,—with the widow's money. Come; our half-hour is nearly over; shall we go upstairs?'

'I'll expose you.'

'Don't now;—don't be ill-natured.'

'Will you tell me where you mean to sleep tonight, Captain Bellfield?'

'If I sleep at Oileymead it will only be on condition that I have one of the mahogany-furnitured bedrooms.'

'You'll never put your foot in that house again. You're a rascal, sir.'

'Come, come, Cheesy, it won't do for us to quarrel in a lady's house. It wouldn't be the thing at all. You're not drinking your wine. You might as well take another glass, and then we'll go up-stairs.'

'You've left your traps at Oileymead, and not one of them you shall have till you've paid me every shilling you owe me. I don't believe you've a shirt in the world beyond what you've got there.'

'It's lucky I brought one in to change; wasn't it, Cheesy? I shouldn't have thought of it only for the hint you gave me. I might as well ring the bell for Jeannette to put away the wine, if you won't take any more.' Then he rang the bell, and when Jeannette came he skipped lightly up-stairs into the drawing-room.

'Was he here before to-day?' said Cheesacre, nodding his head at the door-way through which Bellfield had passed.

'Who? The Captain? Oh dear no. The Captain don't come here much now;—not to say often, by no means.'

'He's a confounded rascal.'

'Oh, Mr. Cheesacre!' said Jeannette.

'He is;—and I ain't sure that there ain't others nearly as bad as he is.'

'If you mean me, Mr. Cheesacre, I do declare you're a wronging me; I do indeed.'

'What's the meaning of his going on in this way?'

'I don't know nothing of his ways, Mr. Cheesacre; but I've been as true to you, sir;—so I have;—as true as true.' And Jeannette put her handkerchief up to her eyes.

He moved to the door, and then a thought occurred to him. He put his hand to his trousers pocket, and turning back towards the girl, gave her half-a-crown. She curtsied as she took it, and then repeated her last words. 'Yes, Mr. Cheesacre,—as true as true.' Mr. Cheesacre said nothing further, but followed his enemy up to the drawing-room. 'What game is up now, I wonder,' said Jeannette to herself, when she was left alone. 'They two'll be cutting each other's throatses before they've done, and then my missus will take the surwiver.' But she made up her mind that Cheesacre should be the one to have his throat cut fatally, and that Bellfield should be the survivor.

Cheesacre, when he reached the drawing-room, found Bellfield sitting on the same sofa with Mrs. Greenow looking at a book of photographs which they both of them were handling together. The outside rim of her widow's frill on one occasion touched the Captain's whisker, and as it did so the Captain looked up with a gratified expression of triumph. If any gentleman has ever seen the same thing under similar circumstances, he will understand that Cheesacre must have been annoyed.

'Yes,' said Mrs. Greenow, waving her handkerchief, of which little but a two-inch-deep border seemed to be visible. Bellfield knew at once that it was not the same handkerchief which she had waved before they went down to dinner. 'Yes, —there he is. It's so like him.' And then she apostrophized the carte de visite of the departed one. 'Dear Greenow; dear husband! When my spirit is false to thee, let thine forget to visit me softly in my dreams. Thou wast unmatched among husbands. Whose tender kindness was ever equal to thine? whose sweet temper was ever so constant? whose manly care so all-sufficient?' While the words fell from her lips her little finger was touching Bellfield's little finger, as they held the book between them. Charlie Fairstairs and Mr. Cheesacre were watching her narrowly, and she knew that they were watching her. She was certainly a woman of great genius and of great courage.

Bellfield, moved by the eloquence of her words, looked with some interest at the photograph. There was represented there before him, a small, grey-looking, insignificant old man, with pig's eyes and a toothless mouth,—one who should never have been compelled to submit himself to the cruelty of the sun's portraiture!*Another widow, even if she had kept in her book the photograph of such a husband, would have scrambled it over silently,—would have been ashamed to show it. 'Have you ever seen it, Mr. Cheesacre?' asked Mrs. Greenow. 'It's so like him.'

'I saw it at Yarmouth,' said Cheesacre, very sulkily.

'That you did not,' said the lady with some dignity, and not a little of rebuke in her tone; 'simply because it never was at Yarmouth. A larger one you may have seen, which I always keep, and always shall keep, close by my bedside.'

'Not if I know it,' said Captain Bellfield to himself. Then the widow punished Mr. Cheesacre for his sullenness by whispering a few words to the Captain; and Cheesacre in his wrath turned to Charlie Fairstairs. Then it was that he spake out his mind about the Captain's rank, and was snubbed by Charlie,— as was told a page or two back.

After that, coffee was brought to them, and here again Cheesacre in his ill-humour allowed the Captain to out-manœuvre him. It was the Captain who put the sugar into the cups, and handed them round. He even handed a cup to his enemy. 'None for me, Captain Bellfield; many thanks for your politeness all the same,' said Mr. Cheesacre; and Mrs. Greenow knew from the tone of his voice that there had been a quarrel.

Cheesacre sitting then in his gloom, had resolved upon one thing,—or, I may perhaps say, upon two things. He had resolved that he would not leave the room that evening till Bellfield had left it; and that he would get a final answer from the widow, if not that night,—for he thought it very possible that they might both be sent away together,—then early after breakfast on the following morning. For the present, he had given up any idea of turning his time to good account. He was not perhaps a coward, but he had not that special courage which enables a man to fight well under adverse circumstances. He had been cowed by the unexpected impertinence of his rival,—by the insolence of a man to whom he thought that he had obtained the power of being always himself as insolent as he pleased. He could not recover his ground quickly, or carry himself before his lady's eye as though he was unconscious of the wound he had received. So he sat silent, while Bellfield was discoursing fluently. He sat in silence, comforting himself with reflections on his own wealth, and on the poverty of the other, and promising himself a rich harvest of revenge when the moment should come in which he might tell Mrs. Greenow how absolutely that man was a beggar, a swindler, and a rascal.

And he was astonished when an opportunity for doing so came very quickly. Before the neighbouring clock had done striking seven, Bellfield rose from his chair to go. He first of all spoke a word of farewell to Miss Fairstairs; then he turned to his late host; 'Good-night, Cheesacre,' he said, in the easiest tone in the world; after that he pressed the widow's hand and whispered his adieu.

'I thought you were staying at Oileymead?' said Mrs. Greenow.

'I came from there this morning,' said the Captain.

'But he isn't going back there, I can tell you,' said Mr. Cheesacre.

'Oh, indeed,' said Mrs. Greenow; 'I hope there is nothing wrong.'

'All as right as a trivet,' said the Captain; and then he was off.

'I promised mamma that I would be home by seven,' said Charlie Fairstairs, rising from her chair. It cannot be supposed that she had any wish to oblige Mr. Cheesacre, and therefore this movement on her part must be regarded simply as done in kindness to Mrs. Greenow. She might be mistaken in supposing that Mrs. Greenow would desire to be left alone with Mr. Cheesacre; but it was clear to her that in this way she could give no offence, whereas it was quite possible that she might offend by remaining. A little after seven Mr. Cheesacre found himself alone with the lady.

'I'm sorry to find,' said she, gravely, 'that you two have quarrelled.'

'Mrs. Greenow,' said he, jumping up, and becoming on a sudden full of life, 'that man is a downright swindler.'

'Oh, Mr. Cheesacre.'

'He is. He'll tell you that he was at Inkermann, but I believe he was in prison all the time.' The Captain had been arrested, I think twice, and thus Mr. Cheesacre justified to himself this assertion. 'I doubt whether he ever saw a shot fired,' he continued.

'He's none the worse for that.'

'But he tells such lies; and then he has not a penny in the world. How much do you suppose he owes me, now?'

'However much it is, I'm sure you are too much of a gentleman to say.'

'Well;—yes, I am,' said he, trying to recover himself. 'But when I asked him how he intended to pay me, what do you think he said? He said he'd pay me when he got your money.'

'My money! He couldn't have said that!'

'But he did, Mrs. Greenow; I give you my word and honour. "I'll pay you when I get the widow's money," he said.'

'You gentlemen must have a nice way of talking about me when I am absent.'

'I never said a disrespectful word about you in my life, Mrs. Greenow,—or thought one. He does;—he says horrible things.'

'What horrible things, Mr. Cheesacre?'

'Oh, I can't tell you;—but he does. What can you expect from such a man as that, who, to my knowledge, won't have a change of clothes to-morrow, except what he brought in on his back this morning? Where he's to get a bed to-night, I don't know, for I doubt whether he's got half-a-crown in the world.'

'Poor Bellfield!'

'Yes; he is poor.'

'But how gracefully he carries his poverty.'

'I should call it very disgraceful, Mrs. Greenow.' To this she made no reply, and then he thought that he might begin his work. 'Mrs. Greenow,—may I say Arabella?'

'Mr. Cheesacre!'

'But mayn't I? Come, Mrs. Greenow. You know well enough by this time what it is I mean. What's the use of shilly-shallying?'

'Shilly-shallying, Mr. Cheesacre! I never heard such language. If I bid you good-night, now, and tell you that it is time for you to go home, shall you call that shilly-shallying?'

He had made a mistake in his word and repented it. 'I beg your pardon, Mrs. Greenow; I do indeed. I didn't mean anything offensive.'

'Shilly-shallying, indeed! There's very little shall in it, I can assure you.'

The poor man was dreadfully crestfallen, so much so that the widow's heart relented, and she pardoned him. It was not in her nature to quarrel with people;—at any rate, not with her lovers. 'I beg your pardon, Mrs. Greenow,' said the culprit, humbly. 'It is granted,' said the widow; 'but never tell a lady again that she is shilly-shallying. And look here, Mr. Cheesacre, if it should ever come to pass that you are making love to a lady in earnest——'

'I couldn't be more in earnest,' said he.

'That you are making love to a lady in earnest, talk to her a little more about your passion and a little less about your purse. Now, good night.'

'But we are friends.'

'Oh yes;—as good friends as ever.'

Cheesacre, as he drove himself home in the dark, tried to console himself by thinking of the miserable plight in which Bellfield would find himself in at Norwich, with no possessions but what he had brought into the town that day in a small bag. But as he turned in at his own gate he met two figures emerging; one of them was laden with a portmanteau, and the other with a hat case.

'It's only me, Cheesy, my boy,' said Bellfield. 'I've just come down by the rail to fetch my things, and I'm going back to Norwich by the 9.20.'

'If you've stolen anything of mine I'll have you prosecuted,' roared Cheesacre, as he drove his gig up to his own door.

CAN YOU FORGIVE HER?

VOLUME II

CHAPTER XLI

A Noble Lord Dies

GEORGE VAVASOR remained about four days beneath his grandfather's roof; but he was not happy there himself, nor did he contribute to the happiness of any one else. He remained there in great discomfort so long, being unwilling to leave till an answer had been received to the request made to Aunt Greenow, in order that he might insist on Kate's performance of her promise with reference to Alice, if that answer should be unfavourable. During these five days Kate did all in her power to induce her brother to be, at any rate, kind in his manner towards his grandfather, but it was in vain. The Squire would not be the first to be gracious; and George, quite as obstinate as the old man, would take no steps in that direction till encouraged to do so by graciousness from the other side. Poor Kate entreated each of them to begin, but her entreaties were of no avail. 'He is an ill-mannered cub,' the old man said, 'and I was a fool to let him into the house. Don't mention his name to me again.' George argued the matter more at length. Kate spoke to him of his own interest in the matter, urging upon him that he might, by such conduct, drive the Squire to exclude him altogether from the property.

'He must do as he likes,' George said, sulkily.

'But for Alice's sake!' Kate answered.

'Alice would be the last to expect me to submit to unreasonable ill-usage for the sake of money. As regards myself, I confess that I'm very fond of money and am not particularly squeamish. I would do anything that a man can do to secure it. But this I can't do. I never injured him, and I never asked him to injure himself. I never attempted to borrow money from him. I have never cost him a shilling. When I was in the wine business he might have enabled me to make a large fortune simply by settling on me then the reversion of property which, when he dies, ought to be my own. He was so perversely ignorant that he would make no inquiry, but chose to think

1

that I was ruining myself, at the only time of my life when I was really doing well.'

'But he had a right to act as he pleased,' urged Kate.

'Certainly he had. But he had no right to resent my asking such a favour at his hands. He was an ignorant old fool not to do it; but I should never have quarrelled with him on that account. Nature made him a fool, and it wasn't his fault. But I can't bring myself to kneel in the dirt before him simply because I asked for what was reasonable.'

The two men said very little to each other. They were never alone together except during that half-hour after dinner in which they were supposed to drink their wine. The old Squire always took three glasses of port during this period, and expected that his grandson would take three with him. But George would drink none at all. 'I have given up drinking wine after dinner,' said he, when his grandfather pushed the bottle over to him. 'I suppose you mean that you drink nothing but claret,' said the Squire, in a tone of voice that was certainly not conciliatory. 'I mean simply what I say,' said George— 'that I have given up drinking wine after dinner.' The old man could not openly quarrel with his heir on such a point as that. Even Mr. Vavasor could not tell his grandson that he was going to the dogs because he had become temperate. But, nevertheless, there was offence in it; and when George sat perfectly silent, looking at the fire, evidently determined to make no attempt at conversation, the offence grew, and became strong. 'What the devil's the use of your sitting there if you neither drink nor talk?' said the old man. 'No use in the world, that I can see,' said George; 'if, however, I were to leave you, you would abuse me for it.' 'I don't care how soon you leave me,' said the Squire. From all which it may be seen that George Vavasor's visit to the hall of his ancestors was not satisfactory.

On the fourth day, about noon, came Aunt Greenow's reply. 'Dearest Kate,' she said, 'I am not going to do what you ask me,'—thus rushing instantly into the middle of her subject. 'You see, I don't know my nephew, and have no reason for being specially anxious that he should be in Parliament. I don't care two straws about the glory of the Vavasor family. If I had never done anything for myself, the Vavasors would have done very little for me. I don't care much about what you call "blood." I like those who like me, and whom I know. I am very fond of you, and because you have been good to me I would give you a thousand pounds if you wanted it for yourself; but I don't see why I am to give my money to those I don't know. If it is necessary to tell my nephew of this, pray tell him that I mean no offence.

'Your friend C. is still waiting—waiting—waiting, patiently; but his patience may be exhausted.

'Your affectionate aunt,
'ARABELLA GREENOW.'

'Of course she won't,' said George, as he threw back the letter to his sister. 'Why should she?'

'I had hoped she would,' said Kate.

'Why should she? What did I ever do for her? She is a sensible woman. Who is your friend C., and why is he waiting patiently?'

'He is a man who would be glad to marry her for her money, if she would take him.'

'Then what does she mean by his patience being exhausted?'

'It is her folly. She chooses to pretend to think that the man is a lover of mine.'

'Has he got any money?'

'Yes; lots of money—or money's worth.'

'And what is his name?'

'His name is Cheesacre. But pray don't trouble yourself to talk about him.'

'If he wants to marry you, and has plenty of money, why shouldn't you take him?'

'Good heavens, George! In the first place he does not want to marry me. In the next place all his heart is in his farmyard.'

'And a very good place to have it,' said George.

'Undoubtedly. But, really, you must not trouble yourself to talk about him.'

'Only this,—that I should be very glad to see you well married.'

'Should you?' said she, thinking of her close attachment to himself.

'And, now, about the money,' said George. 'You must write to Alice at once.'—'Oh, George!'

'Of course you must; you have promised. Indeed, it would have been much wiser if you had taken me at my word, and done it at once.'—'I cannot do it.'

Then the scar on his face opened itself, and his sister stood before him in fear and trembling. 'Do you mean to tell me,' said he, 'that you will go back from your word, and deceive me;—that after having kept me here by this promise, you will not do what you have said you would do?'

'Take my money now, and pay me out of hers as soon as you are married. I will be the first to claim it from her,—and from you.'

'That is nonsense.'

'Why should it be nonsense? Surely you need have no scruple with me. I should have none with you if I wanted assistance.'

'Look here, Kate; I won't have it, and there's an end of it. All that you have in the world would not pull me through this election, and therefore such a loan would be worse than useless.'

'And am I to ask her for more than two thousand pounds?'

'You are to ask her simply for one thousand. That is what I want, and must have, at present. And she knows that I want it, and that she is to supply it; only she does not know that my need is so immediate. That you must explain to her.'

'I would sooner burn my hand, George!'

'But burning your hand, unfortunately, won't do any good. Look here, Kate; I insist upon your doing this for me. If you do not, I shall do it, of course, myself; but I shall regard your refusal as an unjustifiable falsehood on your part, and shall certainly not see you afterwards. I do not wish, for reasons which you may well understand, to write to Alice myself on any subject at present. I now claim your promise to do so; and if you refuse, I shall know very well what to do.'

4

Of course she did not persist in her refusal. With a sorrowful heart, and with fingers that could hardly form the needful letters, she did write a letter to her cousin, which explained the fact—that George Vavasor immediately wanted a thousand pounds for his electioneering purposes. It was a stiff, uncomfortable letter, unnatural in its phraseology, telling its own tale of grief and shame. Alice understood very plainly all the circumstances under which it was written, but she sent back word to Kate at once, undertaking that the money should be forthcoming; and she wrote again before the end of January, saying that the sum named had been paid to George's credit at his own bankers.

Kate had taken immense pride in the renewal of the match between her brother and her cousin, and had rejoiced in it greatly as being her own work. But all that pride and joy were now over. She could no longer write triumphant notes to Alice, speaking always of George as one who was to be their joint hero, foretelling great things of his career in Parliament, and saying little soft things of his enduring love. It was no longer possible to her now to write of George at all, and it was equally impossible to Alice. Indeed, no letters passed between them, when that monetary correspondence was over, up to the end of the winter. Kate remained down in Westmoreland, wretched and ill at ease, listening to hard words spoken by her grandfather against her brother, and feeling herself unable to take her brother's part as she had been wont to do in other times.

George returned to town at the end of those four days, and found that the thousand pounds was duly placed to his credit before the end of the month. It is hardly necessary to tell the reader that this money had come from the stores of Mr. Tombe, and that Mr. Tombe duly debited Mr. Grey with the amount. Alice, in accordance with her promise, had told her father that the money was needed, and her father, in accordance with his promise, had procured it without a word of remonstrance. 'Surely I must sign some paper,' Alice had said. But she had been contented when her father told her that the lawyers would manage all that.

It was nearly the end of February when George Vavasor
made his first payment to Mr. Scruby on behalf of the coming
election; and when he called at Mr. Scruby's office with this
object, he received some intelligence which surprised him not
a little. 'You haven't heard the news,' said Scruby. 'What
news?' said George.

'The Marquis is as nearly off the hooks as a man can be.'
Mr. Scruby, as he communicated the tidings, showed clearly
by his face and voice that they were supposed to be of very
great importance; but Vavasor did not at first seem to be as
much interested in the fate of 'the Marquis' as Scruby had
intended.

'I'm very sorry for him,' said George. 'Who is the Marquis?
There'll be sure to come another, so it don't much signify.'

'There will come another, and that's just it. It's the Marquis of Bunratty; and if he drops, our young Member will go
into the Upper House.'

'What, immediately; before the end of the Session?' George,
of course, knew well enough that such would be the case, but
the effect which this event would have upon himself now struck
him suddenly.

'To be sure,' said Scruby. 'The writ*would be out immediately. I should be glad enough of it, only that I know that
Travers's people have heard of it before us, and that they are
ready to be up with their posters directly the breath is out of the
Marquis's body. We must go to work immediately; that's all.'

'It will only be for part of a Session,' said George.

'Just so,' said Mr. Scruby.

'And then there'll be the cost of another election.'

'That's true,' said Mr. Scruby; 'but in such cases we do
manage to make it come a little cheaper. If you lick Travers
now, it may be that you'll have a walk over for the next.'

'Have you seen Grimes?' asked George.

'Yes, I have; the blackguard! He is going to open his house
on Travers's side. He came to me as bold as brass, and told me
so, saying that he never liked gentlemen who kept him waiting
for his odd money. What angers me is that he ever got it.'

'We have not managed it very well, certainly,' said Vavasor, looking nastily at the attorney.

'We can't help those little accidents, Mr. Vavasor. There are worse accidents than that turn up almost daily in my business. You may think yourself almost lucky that I haven't gone over to Travers myself. He is a Liberal, you know; and it hasn't been for want of an offer, I can tell you.'

Vavasor was inclined to doubt the extent of his luck in this respect, and was almost disposed to repent of his Parliamentary ambition. He would now be called upon to spend certainly not less than three thousand pounds of his cousin's money on the chance of being able to sit in Parliament for a few months. And then, after what a fashion would he be compelled to negotiate that loan! He might, to be sure, allow the remainder of this Session to run, and stand, as he had intended, at the general election; but he knew that if he now allowed a Liberal to win the seat, the holder of the seat would be almost sure of subsequent success. He must either fight now, or give up the fight altogether; and he was a man who did not love to abandon any contest in which he had been engaged.

'Well, Squire,' said Scruby, 'how is it to be?' And Vavasor felt that he detected in the man's voice some diminution of that respect with which he had hitherto been treated as a paying candidate for a metropolitan borough.

'This lord is not dead yet,' said Vavasor.

'No; he's not dead yet, that we have heard; but it won't do for us to wait. We want every minute of time that we can get. There isn't any hope for him, I'm told. It's gout in the stomach, or dropsy at the heart, or some of those things that make a fellow safe to go.'

'It won't do to wait for the next election?'

'If you ask me, I should say certainly not. Indeed, I shouldn't wish to have to conduct it under such circumstances. I hate a fight when there's no chance of success. I grudge spending a man's money in such a case; I do indeed, Mr. Vavasor.'

'I suppose Grimes's going over won't make much difference?'

7

'The blackguard! He'll take a hundred and fifty votes, I suppose; perhaps more. But that is not much in such a constituency as the Chelsea districts. You see, Travers played mean at the last election, and that will be against him.'

'But the Conservatives will have a candidate.'

'There's no knowing; but I don't think they will. They'll try one at the general, no doubt; but if the two sitting Members can pull together, they won't have much of a chance.'

Vavasor found himself compelled to say that he would stand; and Scruby undertook to give the initiatory orders at once, not waiting even till the Marquis should be dead. 'We should have our houses open as soon as theirs,' said he. 'There's a deal in that.' So George Vavasor gave his orders. 'If the worst comes to the worst,' he said to himself, 'I can always cut my throat.'

As he walked from the attorney's office to his club he bethought himself that that might not unprobably be the necessary termination of his career. Everything was going wrong with him. His grandfather, who was eighty years of age, would not die,—appeared to have no symptoms of dying;—whereas this Marquis, who was not yet much over fifty, was rushing headlong out of the world, simply because he was the one man whose continued life at the present moment would be serviceable to George Vavasor. As he thought of his grandfather he almost broke his umbrella by the vehemence with which he struck it against the pavement. What right could an ignorant old fool like that have to live for ever, keeping possession of a property which he could not use, and ruining those who were to come after him? If now, at this moment, that wretched place down in Westmoreland could become his, he might yet ride triumphantly over his difficulties, and refrain from sullying his hands with more of his cousin's money till she should become his wife.

Even that thousand pounds had not passed through his hands without giving him much bitter suffering. As is always the case in such matters, the thing done was worse than the doing of it. He had taught himself to look at it lightly whilst it was yet unaccomplished; but he could not think of it lightly now. Kate had been right. It would have been better for him to take her money. Any money would have been better than that upon which he had laid his sacrilegious hands. If he could have cut a purse,* after the old fashion, the stain of the deed would hardly have been so deep. In these days,—for more than a month, indeed, after his return from Westmoreland,—he did not go near Queen Anne Street, trying to persuade himself that he stayed away because of her coldness to him. But, in truth, he was afraid of seeing her without speaking of her money, and afraid to see her if he were to speak of it.

'You have seen the "Globe"?'*some one said to him as he entered the club.

'No, indeed; I have seen nothing.'

'Bunratty died in Ireland this morning. I suppose you'll be up for the Chelsea districts?'

CHAPTER XLII

Parliament Meets

PARLIAMENT opened that year on the twelfth of February, and Mr. Palliser was one of the first Members of the Lower House to take his seat. It had been generally asserted through the country, during the last week, that the existing Chancellor of the Exchequer had, so to say, ceased to exist as such; that though he still existed to the outer world, drawing his salary, and doing routine work,—if a man so big can have any routine work to do,—he existed no longer in the inner world of the Cabinet. He had differed, men said, with his friend and chief, the Prime Minister, as to the expediency of repealing what were left of the direct taxes*of the country, and was prepared to launch himself into opposition with his small bodyguard of followers, with all his energy and with all his venom.

There is something very pleasant in the close, bosom friendship, and bitter, uncompromising animosity, of these human gods,—of these human beings who would be gods were they not shorn so short of their divinity in that matter of immortality. If it were so arranged that the same persons were always friends, and the same persons were always enemies, as used to be the case among the dear old heathen gods and goddesses; —if Parliament were an Olympus in which Juno and Venus* never kissed, the thing would not be nearly so interesting. But in this Olympus partners are changed, the divine bosom, now rabid with hatred against some opposing deity, suddenly becomes replete with love towards its late enemy, and exciting changes occur which give to the whole thing all the keen interest of a sensational novel. No doubt this is greatly lessened for those who come too near the scene of action. Members of Parliament, and the friends of Members of Parliament, are apt to teach themselves that it means nothing; that Lord This does not hate Mr. That, or think him a traitor to his country, or wish to crucify him; and that Sir John of the Treasury is not much in earnest when he speaks of his noble friend at the 'Foreign Office' as a god to whom no other god was ever comparable in honesty, discretion, patriotism, and genius. But the outside Briton who takes a delight in politics,—and this description should include ninety-nine educated Englishmen out of every hundred,—should not be desirous of peeping behind the scenes. No beholder at any theatre should do so. It is good to believe in these friendships and these enmities, and very pleasant to watch their changes. It is delightful when Oxford embraces Manchester,* finding that it cannot live without support in that quarter; and very delightful when the uncompromising assailant of all men in power receives the legitimate reward of his energy by being taken in among the bosoms of the blessed.

But although the outer world was so sure that the existing Chancellor of the Exchequer had ceased to exist, when the House of Commons met that gentleman took his seat on the Treasury Bench. Mr. Palliser, who had by no means given a general support to the Ministry in the last Session, took his seat on the same side of the House indeed, but low down, and near to the cross benches. Mr. Bott sat close behind him, and

10

men knew that Mr. Bott was a distinguished member of Mr. Palliser's party, whatever that party might be. Lord Cinquebars moved the Address, and I must confess that he did it very lamely. He was once accused by Mr. Maxwell, the brewer, of making a great noise in the hunting-field. The accusation could not be repeated as to his performance on this occasion, as no one could hear a word that he said. The Address was seconded by Mr. Loftus Fitzhoward, a nephew of the Duke of St. Bungay, who spoke as though he were resolved to trump poor Lord Cinquebars in every sentence which he pronounced,—as we so often hear the second clergyman from the Communion Table trumping his weary predecessor, who has just finished the Litany not in the clearest or most audible voice. Every word fell from Mr. Fitzhoward with the elaborate accuracy of a separate pistol-shot; and as he became pleased with himself in his progress, and warm with his work, he accented his words sharply, made rhetorical pauses, even moved his hands about in action, and quite disgusted his own party, who had been very well satisfied with Lord Cinquebars. There are many rocks which a young speaker in Parliament should avoid, but no rock which requires such careful avoiding as the rock of eloquence. Whatever may be his faults, let him at least avoid eloquence. He should not be inaccurate, which, however, is not much; he should not be long-winded, which is a good deal; he should not be ill-tempered, which is more; but none of these faults are so damnable as eloquence. All Mr. Fitzhoward's friends and all his enemies knew that he had had his chance, and that he had thrown it away.

In the Queen's Speech there had been some very lukewarm allusion to remission of direct taxation. This remission, which had already been carried so far, should be carried further if such further carrying were found practicable. So had said the Queen. Those words, it was known, could not have been approved of by the energetic and still existing Chancellor of the Exchequer. On this subject the mover of the Address said never a word, and the seconder only a word or two. What they had said had, of course, been laid down for them; though,

11

unfortunately, the manner of saying could not be so easily prescribed. Then there arose a great enemy, a man fluent of diction, apparently with deep malice at his heart, though at home,—as we used to say at school,—one of the most good-natured fellows in the world; one ambitious of that godship which a seat on the other side of the House bestowed, and greedy to grasp at the chances which this disagreement in the councils of the gods might give him. He was quite content, he said, to vote for the Address, as, he believed, would be all the gentlemen on his side of the House. No one could suspect them or him of giving a factious opposition to Government. Had they not borne and forborne beyond all precedent known in that House? Then he touched lightly, and almost with grace to his opponents, on many subjects, promising support, and barely hinting that they were totally and manifestly wrong in all things. But——. Then the tone of his voice changed, and the well-known look of fury was assumed upon his countenance. Then great Jove on the other side pulled his hat*over his eyes, and smiled blandly. Then members put away the papers they had been reading for a moment, and men in the gallery began to listen. But——. The long and the short of it was this; that the existing Government had come into power on the cry of a reduction of taxation, and now they were going to shirk the responsibility of their own measures. They were going to shirk the responsibility of their own election cry, although it was known that their own Chancellor of the Exchequer was prepared to carry it out to the full. He was willing to carry it out to the full were he not restrained by the timidity, false-hood, and treachery of his colleagues, of whom, of course, the most timid, the most false, and the most treacherous was—the great god Jove, who sat blandly smiling on the other side.

No one should ever go near the House of Commons who wishes to enjoy all this. It was so manifestly evident that neither Jove nor any of his satellites cared twopence for what the irate gentleman was saying; nay, it became so evident that, in spite of his assumed fury, the gentleman was not irate. He intended to communicate his look of anger to the newspaper reports of his speech; and he knew from experience that he could succeed in that. And men walked about the House in the most telling moments,—enemies shaking hands with enemies, —in a way that showed an entire absence of all good, honest hatred among them. But the gentleman went on and finished his speech, demanding at last, in direct terms, that the Treasury Jove should state plainly to the House who was to be, and who was not to be, the bearer of the purse among the gods.

Then Treasury Jove got up smiling, and thanked his enemy for the cordiality of his support. 'He had always,' he said, 'done the gentleman's party justice for their clemency, and had feared no opposition from them; and he was glad to find that he was correct in his anticipations as to the course they would pursue on the present occasion.' He went on saying a good deal about home matters, and foreign matters, proving that everything was right, just as easily as his enemy had proved that everything was wrong. On all these points he was very full, and very courteous; but when he came to the subject of taxation, he simply repeated the passage from the Queen's Speech, expressing a hope that his right honourable friend, the Chancellor of the Exchequer, would be able to satisfy the judgment of the House, and the wishes of the people. That specially personal question which had been asked he did not answer at all.

But the House was still all agog, as was the crowded gallery. The energetic and still existing Chancellor of the Exchequer was then present, divided only by one little thin Secretary of State from Jove himself. Would he get up and declare his purposes? He was a man who almost always did get up when an opportunity offered itself,—or when it did not. Some second little gun was fired off from the Opposition benches, and then there was a pause. Would the purse-bearer of Olympus rise upon his wings and speak his mind, or would he sit in silence upon his cloud? There was a general call for the purse-bearer, but he floated in silence, and was inexplicable. The purse-bearer was not to be bullied into any sudden reading of the riddle. Then there came on a general debate about money matters, in which the purse-bearer did say a few words, but he said nothing as to the great question at issue. At last up got Mr. Palliser, towards the close of the evening, and occupied a full hour in explaining what taxes the Government might remit with safety, and what they might not,—Mr. Bott, meanwhile, prompting him with figures from behind with an assiduity that was almost too persistent. According to Mr. Palliser, the words used in the Queen's Speech were not at all too cautious. The Members went out gradually, and the House became very thin during this oration; but the newspapers declared, next morning, that his speech had been the speech of the night, and that the perspicuity of Mr. Palliser pointed him out as the coming man.

He returned home to his house in Park Lane quite triumphant after his success, and found Lady Glencora, at about twelve o'clock, sitting alone. She had arrived in town on that day, having come up at her own request, instead of remaining at Matching Priory till after Easter, as he had proposed. He had wished her to stay, in order, as he had said, that there might be a home for his cousins. But she had expressed herself unwilling to remain without him, explaining that the cousins might have the home in her absence, as well as they could in her presence; and he had given way. But, in truth, she had learned to hate her cousin Iphy Palliser with a hatred that was unreasonable,—seeing that she did not also hate Alice Vavasor, who had done as much to merit her hatred as had her cousin. Lady Glencora knew by what means her absence from Monkshade had been brought about. Miss Palliser had told her all that had passed in Alice's bedroom on the last night of Alice's stay at Matching, and had, by so doing, contrived to prevent the visit. Lady Glencora understood well all that Alice had said; and yet, though she hated Miss Palliser for what had been done, she entertained no anger against Alice. Of course Alice would have prevented that visit to Monkshade if it were in her power to do so. Of course she would save her friend. It is hardly too much to say that Lady Glencora looked to Alice to save her. Nevertheless she hated Iphy Palliser for engaging

14

herself in the same business. Lady Glencora looked to Alice to save her, and yet it may be doubted whether she did, in truth, wish to be saved.

While she was at Matching, and before Mr. Palliser had returned from Monkshade, a letter reached her, by what means she had never learned. 'A letter has been placed within my writing-case,' she said to her maid, quite openly. 'Who put it there?' The maid had declared her ignorance in a manner that had satisfied Lady Glencora of her truth. 'If such a thing happens again,' said Lady Glencora, 'I shall be obliged to have the matter investigated. I cannot allow that anything should be put into my room surreptitiously.' There, then, had been an end of that, as regarded any steps taken by Lady Glencora. The letter had been from Burgo Fitzgerald, and had contained a direct proposal that she should go off with him. 'I am at Matching,' the letter said, 'at the Inn; but I do not dare to show myself, lest I should do you an injury. I walked round the house yesterday, at night, and I know that I saw your room. If I am wrong in thinking that you love me, I would not for worlds insult you by my presence; but if you love me still, I ask you to throw aside from you that fictitious marriage, and give yourself to the man whom, if you love him, you should regard as your husband.' There had been more of it, but it had been to the same effect. To Lady Glencora it had seemed to convey an assurance of devoted love,—of that love which, in former days, her friends had told her was not within the compass of Burgo's nature. He had not asked her to meet him then, but saying that he would return to Matching after Parliament was met, begged her to let him have some means of knowing whether her heart was true to him.

She told no one of the letter, but she kept it, and read it over and over again in the silence and solitude of her room. She felt that she was guilty in thus reading it,—even in keeping it from her husband's knowledge; but though conscious of this guilt, though resolute almost in its commission, still she determined not to remain at Matching after her husband's departure,—not to undergo the danger of remaining there while

15

Burgo Fitzgerald should be in the vicinity. She could not analyze her own wishes. She often told herself, as she had told Alice, that it would be better for them all that she should go away; that in throwing herself even to the dogs, if such must be the result, she would do more of good than of harm. She declared to herself, in the most passionate words she could use, that she loved this man with all her heart. She protested that the fault would not be hers, but theirs, who had forced her to marry the man she did not love. She assured herself that her husband had no affection for her, and that their marriage was in every respect prejudicial to him. She recurred over and over again, in her thoughts, to her own childlessness, and to his extreme desire for an heir. 'Though I do sacrifice myself,' she would say, 'I shall do more of good than harm, and I cannot be more wretched than I am now.' But yet she fled to London because she feared to leave herself at Matching when Burgo Fitzgerald should be there. She sent no answer to his letter. She made no preparation for going with him. She longed to see Alice, to whom alone, since her marriage, had she ever spoken of her love, and intended to tell her the whole tale of that letter. She was as one who, in madness, was resolute to throw herself from a precipice, but to whom some remnant of sanity remained which forced her to seek those who would save her from herself.

Mr. Palliser had not seen her since her arrival in London, and, of course, he took her by the hand and kissed her. But it was the embrace of a brother rather than of a lover or a husband. Lady Glencora, with her full woman's nature, understood this thoroughly, and appreciated by instinct the true bearing of every touch from his hand. 'I hope you are well?' she said.

'Oh, yes; quite well. And you? A little fatigued with your journey, I suppose?'

'No; not much.'

'Well, we have had a debate on the Address. Don't you want to know how it has gone?'

'If it has concerned you particularly, I do, of course.'

16

'Concerned me! It has concerned me certainly.'

'They haven't appointed you yet; have they?'

'No; they don't appoint people during debates, in the House of Commons. But I fear I shall never make you a politician.'

'I'm almost afraid you never will. But I'm not the less anxious for your success, since you wish it yourself. I don't understand why you should work so very hard; but, as you like it, I'm as anxious as anybody can be that you should triumph.'

'Yes; I do like it,' he said. 'A man must like something, and I don't know what there is to like better. Some people can eat and drink all day; and some people can care about a horse. I can do neither.'

And there were others, Lady Glencora thought, who could love to lie in the sun, and could look up into the eyes of women, and seek their happiness there. She was sure, at any rate, that she knew one such. But she said nothing of this.

'I spoke for a moment to Lord Brock,' said Mr. Palliser. Lord Brock was the name by which the present Jove of the Treasury was known among men.

'And what did Lord Brock say?'

'He didn't say much, but he was very cordial.'

'But I thought, Plantagenet, that he could appoint you if he pleased? Doesn't he do it all?'

'Well, in one sense, he does. But I don't suppose I shall ever make you understand.' He endeavoured, however, to do so on the present occasion, and gave her a somewhat longer lecture on the working of the British Constitution, and the manner in which British politics evolved themselves, than would have been expected from most young husbands to their young wives under similar circumstances. Lady Glencora yawned, and strove lustily, but ineffectually, to hide her yawn in her handkerchief.

'But I see you don't care a bit about it,' said he, peevishly.

'Don't be angry, Plantagenet. Indeed I do care about it, but I am so ignorant that I can't understand it all at once. I am rather tired, and I think I'll go to bed now. Shall you be late?'

'No, not very; that is, I shall be rather late. I've a lot of

17

letters I want to write to-night, as I must be at work all to-morrow. By-the-by, Mr. Bott is coming to dine here. There will be no one else.' The next day was a Wednesday, and the House would not sit in the evening.

'Mr. Bott!' said Lady Glencora, showing by her voice that she anticipated no pleasure from that gentleman's company.

'Yes, Mr. Bott. Have you any objection?'

'Oh, no. Would you like to dine alone with him?'

'Why should I dine alone with him? Why shouldn't you eat your dinner with us? I hope you are not going to become fastidious, and to turn up your nose at people. Mrs. Marsham is in town, and I dare say she'll come to you if you ask her.'

But this was too much for Lady Glencora. She was disposed to be mild, but she could not endure to have her two duennas thus brought upon her together on the first day of her arrival in London. And Mrs. Marsham would be worse than Mr. Bott. Mr. Bott would be engaged with Mr. Palliser during the greater part of the evening. 'I thought,' said she, 'of asking my cousin, Alice Vavasor, to spend the evening with me.'

'Miss Vavasor!' said the husband. 'I must say that I thought Miss Vavasor——' He was going to make some allusion to that unfortunate hour spent among the ruins, but he stopped himself.

'I hope you have nothing to say against my cousin?' said his wife. 'She is my only near relative that I really care for;—the only woman, I mean.'

'No; I don't mean to say anything against her. She's very well as a young lady, I dare say. I would sooner that you would ask Mrs. Marsham to-morrow.'

Lady Glencora was standing, waiting to go away to her own room, but it was absolutely necessary that this matter should be decided before she went. She felt that he was hard to her, and unreasonable, and that he was treating her like a child who should not be allowed her own way in anything. She had endeavoured to please him, and, having failed, was not now disposed to give way.

'As there will be no other ladies here to-morrow evening,

18

Plantagenet, and as I have not yet seen Alice since I have been in town, I wish you would let me have my way in this. Of course I cannot have very much to say to Mrs. Marsham, who is an old woman.'

'I especially want Mrs. Marsham to be your friend,' said he.

'Friendships will not come by ordering, Plantagenet,' said she.

'Very well,' said he. 'Of course, you will do as you please. I am sorry that you have refused the first favour I have asked you this year.' Then he left the room, and she went away to bed.

CHAPTER XLIII

Mrs. Marsham

BUT Lady Glencora was not brought to repentance by her husband's last words. It seemed to her to be so intolerably cruel, this demand of his, that she should be made to pass the whole of her first evening in town with an old woman for whom it was impossible that she should entertain the slightest regard, that she resolved upon rebellion. Had he positively ordered Mrs. Marsham, she would have sent for that lady, and have contented herself with enduring her presence in disdainful silence; but Mr. Palliser had not given any order. He had made a request, and a request, from its very nature, admits of no obedience. The compliance with a request must be voluntary, and she would not send for Mrs. Marsham, except upon compulsion. Had not she also made a request to him, and had not he refused it? It was his prerogative, undoubtedly, to command; but in that matter of requests she had a right to expect that her voice should be as potent as his own. She wrote a line, therefore, to Alice before she went to bed, begging her cousin to come to her early on the following day, so that they might go out together, and then afterwards dine in company with Mr. Bott.

'I know that will be an inducement to you,' Lady Glencora said, 'because your generous heart will feel of what service

19

you may be to me. Nobody else will be here,—unless, indeed, Mrs. Marsham should be asked, unknown to myself.'

Then she sat herself down to think,—to think especially about the cruelty of husbands. She had been told over and over again, in the days before her marriage, that Burgo would ill-use her if he became her husband. The Marquis of Auld Reekie had gone so far as to suggest that Burgo might probably beat her. But what hard treatment, even what beating, could be so unendurable as this total want of sympathy, as this deadness in life, which her present lot entailed upon her? As for that matter of beating, she ridiculed the idea in her very soul. She sat smiling at the absurdity of the thing as she thought of the beauty of Burgo's eyes, of the softness of his touch, of the loving, almost worshipping, tones of his voice. Would it not even be better to be beaten by him than to have politics explained to her at one o'clock at night by such a husband as Plantagenet Palliser? The British Constitution, indeed! Had she married Burgo they would have been in sunny Italy, and he would have told her some other tale than that as they sat together under the pale moonlight. She had a little water-coloured drawing called Raphael and Fornarina, and she was infantine enough to tell herself that the so-called Raphael was like her Burgo—no, not her Burgo, but the Burgo that was not hers. At any rate, all the romance of the picture she might have enjoyed had they allowed her to dispose as she had wished of her own hand. She might have sat in marble balconies, while the vines clustered over her head, and he would have been at her knee, hardly speaking to her, but making his presence felt by the halo of its divinity. He would have called upon her for no hard replies. With him near her she would have enjoyed the soft air, and would have sat happy, without trouble, lapped in the delight of loving. It was thus that Fornarina sat. And why should not such a lot have been hers? Her Raphael would have loved her, let them say what they would about his cruelty.

Poor, wretched, overburthened child, to whom the commonest lessons of life had not yet been taught, and who had now fallen into the hands of one who was so ill-fitted to teach them!

Who would not pity her? Who could say that the fault was hers? The world had laden her with wealth till she had had no limb free for its ordinary uses, and then had turned her loose to run her race!

'Have you written to your cousin?' her husband asked her the next morning. His voice, as he spoke, clearly showed that his anger was either over or suppressed.

'Yes; I have asked her to come and drive, and then to stay for dinner. I shall send the carriage for her if she can come. The man is to wait for an answer.'

'Very well,' said Mr. Palliser, mildly. And then, after a short pause, he added, 'As that is settled, perhaps you would have no objection to ask Mrs. Marsham also?'

'Won't she probably be engaged?'

'No; I think not,' said Mr. Palliser. And then he added, being ashamed of the tinge of falsehood of which he would otherwise have been guilty, 'I know she is not engaged.'

'She expects to come, then?' said Lady Glencora.

'I have not asked her, if you mean that, Glencora. Had I done so, I should have said so. I told her that I did not know what your engagements were.'

'I will write to her, if you please,' said the wife, who felt that she could hardly refuse any longer.

'Do, my dear!' said the husband. So Lady Glencora did write to Mrs. Marsham, who promised to come,—as did also Alice Vavasor.

Lady Glencora would, at any rate, have Alice to herself for some hours before dinner. At first she took comfort in that reflection; but after a while she bethought herself that she would not know what to tell Alice, or what not to tell. Did she mean to show that letter to her cousin? If she did show it, then,—so she argued with herself,—she must bring herself to endure the wretchedness of her present lot, and must give up for ever all her dreams about Raphael and Fornarina. If she did not show it,—or, at any rate, tell of it,—then it would come to pass that she would leave her husband under the protection of another man, and she would become—what she did not dare to name even to herself. She declared that so it must be. She knew that she would go with Burgo, should he ever come to her with the means of going at his and her instant command. But should she bring herself to let Alice know that such a letter had been conveyed to her, Burgo would never have such power.

I remember the story of a case of abduction in which a man was tried for his life, and was acquitted, because the lady had acquiesced in the carrying away while it was in progress. She had, as she herself declared, armed herself with a sure and certain charm or talisman against such dangers, which she kept suspended round her neck; but whilst she was in the post-chaise she opened the window and threw the charm from her, no longer desiring, as the learned counsel for the defence efficiently alleged, to be kept under the bonds of such protection. Lady Glencora's state of mind was, in its nature, nearly the same as that of the lady in the post-chaise. Whether or no she would use her charm, she had not yet decided, but the power of doing so was still hers.

Alice came, and the greeting between the cousins was very affectionate. Lady Glencora received her as though they had been playmates from early childhood; and Alice, though such impulsive love was not natural to her as to the other, could not bring herself to be cold to one who was so warm to her. Indeed, had she not promised her love in that meeting at Matching Priory in which her cousin had told her of all her wretchedness? 'I will love you!' Alice had said; and though there was much in Lady Glencora that she could not approve, —much even that she could not bring herself to like,—still she would not allow her heart to contradict her words.

They sat so long over the fire in the drawing-room that at last they agreed that the driving should be abandoned.

'What's the use of it?' said Lady Glencora. 'There's nothing to see, and the wind is as cold as charity. We are much more comfortable here; are we not?' Alice quite acquiesced in this, having no great desire to be driven through the parks in the gloom of a February afternoon.

'If I had Dandy and Flirt up here, there would be some fun in it; but Mr. Palliser doesn't wish me to drive in London.'

'I suppose it would be dangerous?'

'Not in the least. I don't think it's that he minds; but he has an idea that it looks fast.'

'So it does. If I were a man, I'm sure I shouldn't like my wife to drive horses about London.'

'And why not? Just because you'd be a tyrant,—like other husbands? What's the harm of looking fast, if one doesn't do anything improper? Poor Dandy, and dear Flirt! I'm sure they'd like it.'

'Perhaps Mr. Palliser doesn't care for that?'

'I can tell you something else he doesn't care for. He doesn't care whether Dandy's mistress likes it.'

'Don't say that, Glencora.'

'Why not say it,—to you?'

'Don't teach yourself to think it. That's what I mean. I believe he would consent to anything that he didn't think wrong.'

'Such as lectures about the British Constitution! But never mind about that, Alice. Of course the British Constitution is everything to him, and I wish I knew more about it;—that's all. But I haven't told you whom you are to meet at dinner.'

'Yes, you have—Mr. Bott.'

'But there's another guest, a Mrs. Marsham. I thought I'd got rid of her for to-day, when I wrote to you; but I hadn't. She's coming.'

'She won't hurt me at all,' said Alice.

'She will hurt me very much. She'll destroy the pleasure of our whole evening. I do believe that she hates you, and that she thinks you instigate me to all manner of iniquity. What fools they all are!'

'Who are they all, Glencora?'

'She and that man, and——. Never mind. It makes me sick when I think that they should be so blind. Alice, I hardly know how much I owe to you; I don't, indeed. Everything, I believe.' Lady Glencora, as she spoke, put her hand into her pocket, and grasped the letter which lay there.

'That's nonsense,' said Alice.

'No; it's not nonsense. Who do you think came to Matching when I was there?'

'What;—to the house?' said Alice, feeling almost certain that Mr. Fitzgerald was the person to whom Lady Glencora was alluding.

'No; not to the house.'

'If it is the person of whom I am thinking,' said Alice, solemnly, 'let me implore you not to speak of him.'

'And why should I not speak of him? Did I not speak of him before to you, and was it not for good? How are you to be my friend, if I may not speak to you of everything?'

'But you should not think of him.'

'What nonsense you talk, Alice! Not think of him! How is one to help one's thoughts? Look here.'

Her hand was on the letter, and it would have been out in a moment, and thrown upon Alice's lap, had not the servant opened the door and announced Mrs. Marsham.

'Oh, how I do wish we had gone to drive!' said Lady Glencora, in a voice which the servant certainly heard, and which Mrs. Marsham would have heard had she not been a little hard of hearing,—in her bonnet.

'How do, my dear?' said Mrs. Marsham. 'I thought I'd just come across from Norfolk Street and see you, though I am coming to dinner in the evening. It's only just a step,* you know. How d'ye do, Miss Vavasor?' and she made a salutation to Alice which was nearly as cold as it could be.

Mrs. Marsham was a woman who had many good points. She was poor, and bore her poverty without complaint. She was connected by blood and friendship with people rich and titled; but she paid to none of them egregious respect on account of their wealth or titles. She was stanch in her friendships, and stanch in her enmities. She was no fool, and knew well what was going on in the world. She could talk about the last novel, or—if need be—about the Constitution. She had been a true wife, though sometimes too strong-minded, and a painstaking mother, whose children, however, had never loved her as most mothers like to be loved.

The catalogue of her faults must be quite as long as that of her virtues. She was one of those women who are ambitious of power, and not very scrupulous as to the manner in which they obtain it. She was hardhearted, and capable of pursuing an object without much regard to the injury she might do. She would not flatter wealth or fawn before a title, but she was not above any artifice by which she might ingratiate herself with those whom it suited her purpose to conciliate. She thought evil rather than good. She was herself untrue in action, if not absolutely in word. I do not say that she would coin lies, but she would willingly leave false impressions. She had been the bosom friend, and in many things the guide in life, of Mr. Palliser's mother; and she took a special interest in Mr. Palliser's welfare. When he married, she heard the story of the loves of Burgo and Lady Glencora; and though she thought well of the money, she was not disposed to think very well of the bride. She made up her mind that the young lady would

25

want watching, and she was of opinion that no one would be so well able to watch Lady Glencora as herself. She had not plainly opened her mind on this matter to Mr. Palliser; she had not made any distinct suggestion to him that she would act as Argus*to his wife. Mr. Palliser would have rejected any such suggestion, and Mrs. Marsham knew that he would do so; but she had let a word or two drop, hinting that Lady Glencora was very young,—hinting that Lady Glencora's manners were charming in their childlike simplicity; but hinting also that precaution was, for that reason, the more necessary. Mr. Palliser, who suspected nothing as to Burgo or as to any other special peril, whose whole disposition was void of suspicion, whose dry nature realized neither the delights nor the dangers of love, acknowledged that Glencora was young. He especially wished that she should be discreet and matronly; he feared no lovers, but he feared that she might do silly things,—that she would catch cold,—and not know how to live a life becoming the wife of a Chancellor of the Exchequer. Therefore he submitted Glencora,—and, to a certain extent, himself,—into the hands of Mrs. Marsham.

Lady Glencora had not been twenty-four hours in the house with this lady before she recognized in her a duenna. In all such matters no one could be quicker than Lady Glencora. She might be very ignorant about the British Constitution, and, alas! very ignorant also as to the real elements of right and wrong in a woman's conduct, but she was no fool. She had an eye that could see, and an ear that could understand, and an abundance of that feminine instinct which teaches a woman to know her friend or her enemy at a glance, at a touch, at a word. In many things Lady Glencora was much quicker, much more clever, than her husband, though he was to be Chancellor of the Exchequer, and though she did know nothing of the Constitution. She knew, too, that he was easily to be deceived, —that though his intelligence was keen, his instincts were dull,—that he was gifted with no fineness of touch, with no subtle appreciation of the characters of men and women; and, to a certain extent, she looked down upon him for this obtusity.

He should have been aware that Burgo was a danger to be avoided; and he should have been aware also that Mrs. Marsham was a duenna not to be employed. When a woman knows that she is guarded by a watch-dog, she is bound to deceive her Cerberus; if it be possible, and is usually not ill-disposed to deceive also the owner of Cerberus. Lady Glencora felt that Mrs. Marsham was her Cerberus, and she was heartily resolved that if she was to be kept in the proper line at all, she would not be so kept by Mrs. Marsham.

Alice rose and accepted Mrs. Marsham's salutation quite as coldly as it had been given, and from that time forward those two ladies were enemies. Mrs. Marsham, groping quite in the dark, partly guessed that Alice had in some way interfered to prevent Lady Glencora's visit to Monkshade, and, though such prevention was, no doubt, good in that lady's eyes, she resented the interference. She had made up her mind that Alice was not the sort of friend that Lady Glencora should have about her. Alice recognized and accepted the feud.

'I thought I might find you at home,' said Mrs. Marsham, 'as I know you are lazy about going out in the cold,—unless it be for a foolish midnight ramble,' and Mrs. Marsham shook her head. She was a little woman, with sharp small eyes, with a permanent colour in her face, and two short, crisp, grey curls at each side of her face; always well dressed, always in good health, and, as Lady Glencora believed, altogether incapable of fatigue.

'The ramble you speak of was very wise, I think,' said Lady Glencora; 'but I never could see the use of driving about in London in the middle of winter.'

'One ought to go out of the house every day,' said Mrs. Marsham.

'I hate all those rules. Don't you, Alice?' Alice did not hate them, therefore she said nothing.

'My dear Glencora, one must live by rules in this life. You might as well say that you hated sitting down to dinner.'

'So I do, very often; almost always when there's company.'

'You'll get over that feeling after another season in town,'

27

said Mrs. Marsham, pretending to suppose that Lady Glencora alluded to some remaining timidity in receiving her own guests.

'Upon my word I don't think I shall. It's a thing that seems always to be getting more grievous, instead of less so. Mr. Bott is coming to dine here to-night.'

There was no mistaking the meaning of this. There was no pretending even to mistake it. Now, Mrs. Marsham had accepted the right hand of fellowship from Mr. Bott,—not because she especially liked him, but in compliance with the apparent necessities of Mr. Palliser's position. Mr. Bott had made good his ground about Mr. Palliser; and Mrs. Marsham, as she was not strong enough to turn him off from it, had given him the right hand of fellowship.

'Mr. Bott is a Member of Parliament, and a very serviceable friend of Mr. Palliser's,' said Mrs. Marsham.

'All the same; we do not like Mr. Bott—do we, Alice? He is Doctor Fell*to us; only I think we could tell why.'

'I certainly do not like him,' said Alice.

'It can be but of small matter to you, Miss Vavasor,' said Mrs. Marsham, 'as you will not probably have to see much of him.'

'Of the very smallest moment,' said Alice. 'He did annoy me once, but will never, I dare say, have an opportunity of doing so again.'

'I don't know what the annoyance may have been.'

'Of course you don't, Mrs. Marsham.'

'But I shouldn't have thought it likely that a person so fully employed as Mr. Bott, and employed, too, on matters of such vast importance, would have gone out of his way to annoy a young lady whom he chanced to meet for a day or two in a country-house.'

'I don't think that Alice means that he attempted to flirt with her,' said Lady Glencora, laughing. 'Fancy Mr. Bott's flirtation!'

'Perhaps he did not attempt,' said Mrs. Marsham; and the words, the tone, and the innuendo together were more than Alice was able to bear with equanimity.

'Glencora,' said she, rising from her chair, 'I think I'll leave you alone with Mrs. Marsham. I'm not disposed to discuss Mr. Bott's character, and certainly not to hear his name mentioned in disagreeable connection with my own.'

But Lady Glencora would not let her go. 'Nonsense, Alice,' she said. 'If you and I can't fight our little battles against Mr. Bott and Mrs. Marsham without running away, it is odd. There is a warfare in which they who run away never live to fight another day.'

'I hope, Glencora, you do not count me as your enemy?' said Mrs. Marsham, drawing herself up.

'But I shall,—certainly, if you attack Alice. Love me, love my dog. I beg your pardon, Alice; but what I meant was this, Mrs. Marsham; Love me, love the best friend I have in the world.'

'I did not mean to offend Miss Vavasor,' said Mrs. Marsham, looking at her very grimly. Alice merely bowed her head. She had been offended, and she would not deny it. After that, Mrs. Marsham took herself off, saying that she would be back to dinner. She was angry, but not unhappy. She thought that she could put down Miss Vavasor, and she was prepared to bear a good deal from Lady Glencora—for Mr. Palliser's sake, as she said to herself, with some attempt at a sentimental remembrance of her old friend.

'She's a nasty old cat,' said Lady Glencora, as soon as the door was closed; and she said these words with so droll a voice, with such a childlike shaking of her head, with so much comedy in her grimace, that Alice could not but laugh. 'She is,' said Lady Glencora. 'I know her, and you'll have to know her, too, before you've done with her. It won't at all do for you to run away when she spits at you. You must hold your ground, and show your claws,—and make her know that if she spits, you can scratch.'

'But I don't want to be a cat myself.'

'She'll find I'm of the genus, but of the tiger kind, if she persecutes me. Alice, there's one thing I have made up my mind about. I will not be persecuted. If my husband tells me to do anything, as long as he is my husband I'll do it; but I won't be persecuted.'

29

'You should remember that she was a very old friend of Mr. Palliser's mother.'

'I do remember; and that may be a very good reason why she should come here occasionally, or go to Matching, or to any place in which we may be living. It's a bore, of course; but it's a natural bore, and one that ought to be borne.'

'And that will be the beginning and the end of it.'

'I'm afraid not, my dear. It may be perhaps the end of it, but I fear it won't be the beginning. I won't be persecuted. If she gives me advice, I shall tell her to her face that it's not wanted; and if she insults any friend of mine, as she did you, I shall tell her that she had better stay away. She'll go and tell him, of course; but I can't help that. I've made up my mind that I won't be persecuted.'

After that, Lady Glencora felt no further inclination to show Burgo's letter to Alice on that occasion. They sat over the drawing-room fire, talking chiefly of Alice's affairs, till it was time for them to dress. But Alice, though she spoke much of Mr. Grey, said no word as to her engagement with George Vavasor. How could she speak of it, inasmuch as she had already resolved,—already almost resolved,—that that engagement also should be broken?

Alice, when she came down to the drawing-room, before dinner, found Mr. Bott there alone. She had dressed more quickly than her friend, and Mr. Palliser had not yet made his appearance.

'I did not expect the pleasure of meeting Miss Vavasor to-day,' he said, as he came up, offering his hand. She gave him her hand, and then sat down, merely muttering some word of reply.

'We spent a very pleasant month down at Matching to-gether;—didn't you think so?'

'I spent a pleasant month there certainly.'

'You left, if I remember, the morning after that late walk out among the ruins? That was unfortunate, was it not? Poor Lady Glencora! it made her very ill; so much so, that she could not go to Monkshade, as she particularly wished. It was very sad. Lady Glencora is very delicate,—very delicate, indeed.

We, who have the privilege of being near her, ought always to remember that.'

'I don't think she is at all delicate.'

'Oh! don't you? I'm afraid that's your mistake, Miss Vavasor.'

'I believe she has very good health, which is the greatest blessing in the world. By delicate I suppose you mean weak and infirm.'

'Oh, dear, no,—not in the least,—not infirm certainly! I should be very sorry to be supposed to have said that Lady Glencora is infirm. What I mean is, not robust, Miss Vavasor. Her general organization, if you understand me, is exquisitely delicate. One can see that, I think, in every glance of her eye.'

Alice was going to protest that she had never seen it at all, when Mr. Palliser entered the room along with Mrs. Marsham.

The two gentlemen shook hands, and then Mr. Palliser turned to Alice. She perceived at once by his face that she was unwelcome, and wished herself away from his house. It might be all very well for Lady Glencora to fight with Mrs. Marsham,—and with her husband, too, in regard to the Marsham persecution,—but there could be no reason why she should do so. He just touched her hand, barely closing his thumb upon her fingers, and asked her how she was. Then he turned away from her side of the fire, and began talking to Mrs. Marsham on the other. There was that in his face and in his manner which was positively offensive to her. He made no allusion to his former acquaintance with her,—spoke no word about Matching, no word about his wife, as he would naturally have done to his wife's friend. Alice felt the blood mount into her face, and regretted greatly that she had ever come among these people. Had she not long since made up her mind that she would avoid her great relations, and did not all this prove that it would have been well for her to have clung to that resolution? What was Lady Glencora to her that she should submit herself to be treated as though she were a poor companion,—a dependent, who received a salary for her attendance,—an indigent cousin, hanging on to the bounty of her rich connection? Alice was proud to a fault. She had nursed her pride till it was very faulty. All her troubles and sorrows in life had come from an overfed craving for independence. Why, then, should she submit to be treated with open want of courtesy by any man; but, of all men, why should she submit to it from such a one as Mr. Palliser,—the heir of a ducal house, rolling in wealth, and magnificent with all the magnificence of British pomp and pride? No; she would make Lady Glencora understand that the close intimacies of daily life were not possible to them!

'I declare I'm very much ashamed,' said Lady Glencora, as she entered the room. 'I shan't apologize to you, Alice, for it was you who kept me talking; but I do beg Mrs. Marsham's pardon.'

Mrs. Marsham was all smiles and forgiveness, and hoped that Lady Glencora would not make a stranger of her. Then dinner was announced, and Alice had to walk down stairs by herself. She did not care a doit*for that, but there had been a disagreeable little contest when the moment came. Lady Glencora had wished to give up Mr. Bott to her cousin, but Mr. Bott had stuck manfully to Lady Glencora's side. He hoped to take Lady Glencora down to dinner very often, and was not at all disposed to abate his privilege.

During dinner-time Alice said very little, nor was there given to her opportunity of saying much. She could not but think of the day of her first arrival at Matching Priory, when she had sat between the Duke of St. Bungay and Jeffrey Palliser, and when everybody had been so civil to her! She now occupied one side of the table by herself, away from the fire, where she felt cold and desolate in the gloom of the large half-lighted room. Mr. Palliser occupied himself with Mrs. Marsham, who talked politics to him; and Mr. Bott never lost a moment in his endeavours to say some civil word to Lady Glencora. Lady Glencora gave him no encouragement; but she hardly dared to snub him openly in her husband's immediate presence. Twenty times during dinner she said some little word to Alice, attempting at first to make the time pleasant, and then, when the matter was too far gone for that, attempting to give some

32

relief. But it was of no avail. There are moments in which conversation seems to be impossible,—in which the very gods interfere to put a seal upon the lips of the unfortunate one. It was such a moment now with Alice. She had never as yet been used to snubbing. Whatever position she had hitherto held, in that she had always stood foremost,—much more so than had been good for her. When she had gone to Matching, she had trembled for her position; but there all had gone well with her; there Lady Glencora's kindness had at first been able to secure for her a reception that had been flattering, and almost better than flattering. Jeffrey Palliser had been her friend, and would, had she so willed it, have been more than her friend. But now she felt that the halls of the Pallisers were too cold for her, and that the sooner she escaped from their gloom and hard discourtesy the better for her.

Mrs. Marsham, when the three ladies had returned to the drawing-room together, was a little triumphant. She felt that she had put Alice down; and with the energetic prudence of a good general who knows that he should follow up a victory, let the cost of doing so be what it may, she determined to keep her down. Alice had resolved that she would come as seldom as might be to Mr. Palliser's house in Park Lane. That resolution on her part was in close accordance with Mrs. Marsham's own views.

'Is Miss Vavasor going to walk home?' she asked.

'Walk home;—all along Oxford Street! Good gracious! no. Why should she walk? The carriage will take her.'

'Or a cab,' said Alice. 'I am quite used to go about London in a cab by myself.'

'I don't think they are nice for young ladies after dark,' said Mrs. Marsham. 'I was going to offer my servant to walk with her. She is an elderly woman, and would not mind it.'

'I'm sure Alice is very much obliged,' said Lady Glencora; 'but she will have the carriage.'

'You are very good-natured,' said Mrs. Marsham; 'but gentlemen do so dislike having their horses out at night.'

'No gentleman's horses will be out,' said Lady Glencora,

savagely; 'and as for mine, it's what they are there for.' It was not often that Lady Glencora made any allusion to her own property, or allowed any one near her to suppose that she remembered the fact that her husband's great wealth was, in truth, her wealth. As to many matters her mind was wrong. In some things her taste was not delicate as should be that of a woman. But, as regarded her money, no woman could have behaved with greater reticence, or a purer delicacy. But now, when she was twitted by her husband's special friend with ill-usage to her husband's horses, because she chose to send her own friend home in her own carriage, she did find it hard to bear.

'I dare say it's all right,' said Mrs. Marsham.

'It is all right,' said Lady Glencora. 'Mr. Palliser has given me my horses for my own use, to do as I like with them; and if he thinks I take them out when they ought to be left at home, he can tell me so. Nobody else has a right to do it.' Lady Glencora, by this time, was almost in a passion, and showed that she was so.

'My dear Lady Glencora, you have mistaken me,' said Mrs. Marsham; 'I did not mean anything of that kind.'

'I am so sorry,' said Alice. 'And it is such a pity as I am quite used to going about in cabs.'

'Of course you are,' said Lady Glencora. 'Why shouldn't you? I'd go home in a wheelbarrow if I couldn't walk, and had no other conveyance. That's not the question. Mrs. Marsham understands that.'

'Upon my word, I don't understand anything,' said that lady.

'I understand this,' said Lady Glencora; 'that in all such matters as that, I intend to follow my own pleasure. Come, Alice, let us have some coffee,'—and she rang the bell. 'What a fuss we have made about a stupid old carriage!'

The gentlemen did not return to the drawing-room that evening, having, no doubt, joint work to do in arranging the great financial calculations of the nation; and, at an early hour, Alice was taken home in Lady Glencora's brougham, leaving her cousin still in the hands of Mrs. Marsham.

CHAPTER XLIV

The Election for the Chelsea Districts

Mᴀʀᴄʜ came, and still the Chancellor of the Exchequer held his position. In the early days of March there was given in the House a certain parliamentary explanation on the subject, which, however, did not explain very much to any person. A statement was made which was declared by the persons making it to be altogether satisfactory, but nobody else seemed to find any satisfaction in it. The big wigs of the Cabinet had made an arrangement which, from the language used by them on this occasion, they must be supposed to have regarded as hardly less permanent than the stars; but everybody else protested that the Government was going to pieces; and Mr. Bott was heard to declare in clubs and lobbies, and wherever he could get a semi-public, political hearing, that this kind of thing wouldn't do. Lord Brock must either blow hot or cold. If he chose to lean upon Mr. Palliser, he might lean upon him, and Mr. Palliser would not be found wanting. In such case no opposition could touch Lord Brock or the Government. That was Mr. Bott's opinion. But if Lord Brock did not so choose, why, in that case, he must expect that Mr. Palliser, and Mr. Palliser's friends, would——. Mr. Bott did not say what they would do; but he was supposed by those who understood the

35

matter to hint at an Opposition lobby, and adverse divisions, and to threaten Lord Brock with the open enmity of Mr. Palliser,—and of Mr. Palliser's great follower.

'This kind of thing won't do long, you know,' repeated Mr. Bott for the second or third time, as he stood upon the rug before the fire at his club, with one or two of his young friends round him.

'I suppose not,' said Calder Jones, the hunting Member of Parliament whom we once met at Roebury. 'Planty Pall won't stand it, I should say.'

'What can he do?' asked another, an unfledged Member who was not as yet quite settled as to the leadership under which he intended to work.

'What can he do?' said Mr. Bott, who on such an occasion as this could be very great,—who, for a moment, could almost feel that he might become a leader of a party for himself, and some day institute a Bott Ministry. 'What can he do? You will very shortly see what he can do. He can make himself the master of the occasion. If Lord Brock doesn't look about him, he'll find that Mr. Palliser will be in the Cabinet without his help.'

'You don't mean to say that the Queen will send for Planty Pall!' said the young Member.

'I mean to say that the Queen will send for any one that the House of Commons may direct her to call upon,' said Mr. Bott, who conceived himself to have gauged the very depths of our glorious Constitution. 'How hard it is to make any one understand that the Queen has really nothing to do with it!'

'Come, Bott, draw it mild,' said Calder Jones, whose loyalty was shocked by the utter Manchesterialism of his political friend.

'Not if I know it,' said Mr. Bott, with something of grandeur in his tone and countenance. 'I never drew it mild yet, and I shan't begin now. All our political offences against civilization have come from men drawing it mild, as you call it. Why is it that Englishmen can't read and write as Americans do? Why can't they vote as they do even in Imperial France? Why are they serfs, less free than those whose chains were broken the other day in Russia?*Why is the Spaniard more happy, and the Italian more contented? Because men in power have been drawing it mild!' And Mr. Bott made an action with his hand as though he were drawing up beer from a patent tap.

'But you can't set aside Her Majesty like that, you know,' said the young Member, who had been presented, and whose mother's old-world notions about the throne still clung to him.

'I should be very sorry,' said Mr. Bott; 'I'm no republican.' With all his constitutional lore, Mr. Bott did not know what the word republican meant. 'I mean no disrespect to the throne. The throne in its place is very well. But the power of governing this great nation does not rest with the throne. It is contained within the four walls of the House of Commons. That is the great truth which all young Members should learn, and take to their hearts.'

'And you think Planty Pall will become Prime Minister?' said Calder Jones.

'I haven't said that; but there are more unlikely things. Among young men I know no man more likely. But I certainly think this,—that if Lord Brock doesn't take him into the Cabinet, Lord Brock won't long remain there himself.'

In the meantime the election came on in the Chelsea districts, and the whole of the south-western part of the metropolis was covered with posters bearing George Vavasor's name. 'Vote for Vavasor and the River Bank.' That was the cry with which he went to the electors; and though it must be presumed that it was understood by some portion of the Chelsea electors, it was perfectly unintelligible to the majority of those who read it. His special acquaintances and his general enemies called him Viscount Riverbank, and he was pestered on all sides by questions as to Father Thames. It was Mr. Scruby who invented the legend, and who gave George Vavasor an infinity of trouble by the invention. There was a question in those days as to embanking the river from the Houses of Parliament up to the remote desolations of further Pimlico,* and Mr. Scruby recommended the coming Member to pledge himself that he would have the work carried on even to Battersea

Bridge. 'You must have a subject,' pleaded Mr. Scruby. 'No young Member can do anything without a subject. And it should be local;—that is to say, if you have anything of a constituency. Such a subject as that, if it's well worked, may save you thousands of pounds—thousands of pounds at future elections.'

'It won't save me anything at this one, I take it.'

'But it may secure the seat, Mr. Vavasor, and afterwards make you the most popular metropolitan Member in the House; that is, with your own constituency. Only look at the money that would be spent in the districts if that were done! It would come to millions, sir!'

'But it never will be done.'

'What matters that?' and Mr. Scruby almost became eloquent as he explained the nature of a good parliamentary subject. 'You should work it up, so as to be able to discuss it at all points. Get the figures by heart, and then, as nobody else will do so, nobody can put you down. Of course it won't be done. If it were done, that would be an end of it, and your bread would be taken out of your mouth. But you can always promise it at the hustings, and can always demand it in the House. I've known men who've walked into as much as two thousand a year, permanent place, on the strength of a worse subject than that!'

Vavasor allowed Mr. Scruby to manage the matter for him, and took up the subject of the River Bank. Vavasor and the River Bank was carried about by an army of men with iron shoulder-straps, and huge pasteboards placards six feet high on the top of them. You would think, as you saw the long rows, that the men were being marshalled to their several routes; but they always kept together—four-and-twenty at the heels of each other. 'One placard at a time would strike the eye,' said Mr. Vavasor, counting the expense up to himself. 'There's no doubt of it,' said Mr. Scruby in reply. 'One placard will do that, if it's big enough; but it takes four-and-twenty to touch the imagination.' And then sides of houses were covered with that shibboleth, 'Vavasor and the River Bank': the same words repeated in columns down the whole sides of houses. Vavasor himself declared that he was ashamed to walk among his future constituents, so conspicuous had his name become. Grimes saw it, and was dismayed. At first, Grimes ridiculed the cry with all his publican's wit. 'Unless he mean to drown hisself in the Reach,* it's hard to say what he do mean by all that gammon about the River Bank,' said Grimes, as he canvassed for the other Liberal candidate. But after a while, Grimes was driven to confess that Mr. Scruby knew what he was about. 'He is a sharp 'un, that he is,' said Grimes in the inside bar of the 'Handsome Man'; and he almost regretted that he had left the leadership of Mr. Scruby, although he knew that on this occasion he would not have gotten his odd money.

George Vavasor, with much labour, actually did get up the subject of the River Bank. He got himself introduced to men belonging to the Metropolitan Board,* and went manfully into the matter of pounds, shillings, and pence. He was able even to work himself into an apparent heat when he was told that the thing was out of the question; and soon found that he had disciples who really believed in him. If he could have brought himself to believe in the thing,—if he could have been induced himself to care whether Chelsea was to be embanked or no, the work would not have been so difficult to him. In that case it would have done good to him, if to no one else. But such belief was beyond him. He had gone too far in life to be capable of believing in, or of caring for, such things. He was ambitious of having a hand in the government of his country, but he was not capable of caring even for that.

But he worked. He worked hard, and spoke vehemently, and promised the men of Chelsea, Pimlico, and Brompton that the path of London westwards had hardly commenced as yet. Sloane Street should be the new Cheapside.* Squares should arise around the Chelsea barracks, with sides open to the water, for which Belgravia would be deserted. There should be palaces there for the rich, because the rich spend their riches; but no rich man's palace should interfere with the poor man's right to the River Bank. Three millions and a half should be spent on the noble street to be constructed, the grandest pathway that the world should ever yet have seen; three millions and a half to be drawn from,—to be drawn from anywhere except from Chelsea;—from the bloated money-bags of the City Corporation, Vavasor once ventured to declare, amidst the encouraging shouts of the men of Chelsea. Mr. Scruby was forced to own that his pupil worked the subject well. 'Upon my word, that was uncommon good,' he said, almost patting Vavasor on the back, after a speech in which he had vehemently asserted that his ambition to represent the Chelsea districts had all come of his long-fixed idea that the glory of future London would be brought about by the embankment of the river at Chelsea.

But armies of men carrying big boards, and public houses open at every corner, and placards in which the letters are three feet long, cost money. Those few modest hundreds which Mr. Scruby had already received before the work began, had been paid on the supposition that the election would not take place till September. Mr. Scruby made an early request, a very early request, that a further sum of fifteen hundred pounds should be placed in his hands; and he did this in a tone which clearly signified that not a man would be sent about through the streets, or a poster put upon a wall, till this request had been conceded. Mr. Scruby was in possession of two very distinct manners of address. In his jovial moods, when he was instigating his clients to fight their battles well, it might almost be thought that he was doing it really for the love of the thing; and some clients, so thinking, had believed for a few hours that Scruby, in his jolly, passionate eagerness, would pour out his own money like dust, trusting implicitly to future days for its return. But such clients had soon encountered Mr. Scruby's other manner, and had perceived that they were mistaken.

The thing had come so suddenly upon George Vavasor that there was not time for him to carry on his further operations through his sister. Had he written to Kate,—let him have written in what language he would,—she would have first rejoined by a negative, and there would have been a correspondence before he had induced her to comply. He thought of sending for her by telegram, but even in that there would have been too much delay. He resolved, therefore, to make his application to Alice himself, and he wrote to her, explaining his condition. The election had come upon him quite suddenly, as she knew, he said. He wanted two thousand pounds instantly, and felt little scruple in asking her for it, as he was aware that the old Squire would be only too glad to saddle the property with a legacy to Alice for the repayment of this money, though he would not have advanced a shilling himself for the purpose of the election. Then he said a word or two as to his prolonged absence from Queen Anne Street. He had not been there because he had felt, from her manner when they last met, that she would for a while prefer to be left free from the unavoidable excitement of such interviews. But should he be triumphant in his present contest, he should go to her to share his triumph with her; or, should he fail, he should go to her to console him in his failure.

Within three days he heard from her, saying that the money would be at once placed to his credit. She sent him also her cordial good wishes for success in his enterprise, but beyond this her letter said nothing. There was no word of love,—no word of welcome,—no expression of a desire to see him. Vavasor, as he perceived all this in the reading of her note, felt a triumph in the possession of her money. She was ill-using him by her coldness, and there was comfort in revenge. 'It serves her right,' he said to himself. 'She should have married me at once when she said she would do so, and then it would have been my own.'

When Mr. Tombe had communicated with John Grey on the matter of this increased demand,—this demand which Mr. Tombe began to regard as carrying a love affair rather too far,—Grey had telegraphed back that Vavasor's demand for money, if made through Mr. John Vavasor, was to be honoured to the extent of five thousand pounds. Mr. Tombe raised his eyebrows, and reflected that some men were very foolish. But

41

John Grey's money matters were of such a nature as to make Mr. Tombe know that he must do as he was bidden; and the money was paid to George Vavasor's account.

He told Kate nothing of this. Why should he trouble himself to do so? Indeed, at this time he wrote no letters to his sister, though she twice sent to him, knowing what his exigencies would be, and made further tenders of her own money. He could not reply to these offers without telling her that money had been forthcoming from that other quarter, and so he left them unanswered.

In the meantime the battle went on gloriously. Mr. Travers, the other Liberal candidate, spent his money freely,—or else some other person did so on his behalf. When Mr. Scruby mentioned this last alternative to George Vavasor, George cursed his own luck in that he had never found such backers. 'I don't call a man half a Member when he's brought in like that,' said Mr. Scruby, comforting him. 'He can't do what he likes with his vote. He ain't independent. You never hear of those fellows getting anything good. Pay for the article yourself, Mr. Vavasor, and then it's your own. That's what I always say.'

Mr. Grimes went to work strenuously, almost fiercely, in the opposite interest, telling all that he knew, and perhaps more than he knew, of Vavasor's circumstances. He was at work morning, noon, and night, not only in his own neighbourhood, but among those men on the river bank of whom he had spoken so much in his interview with Vavasor in Cecil Street. The entire Vavasorian army with its placards was entirely upset on more than one occasion, and was once absolutely driven ignominiously into the river mud. And all this was done under the direction of Mr. Grimes. Vavasor himself was pelted with offal from the sinking tide, so that the very name of the River Bank became odious to him. He was a man who did not like to have his person touched, and when they hustled him he became angry. 'Lord love you, Mr. Vavasor,' said Scruby, 'that's nothing! I've had a candidate so mauled,—it was in the Hamlets, I think,—that there wasn't a spot on him that wasn't painted with rotten eggs. The smell was something quite awful. But I brought him in, through it all.'

And Mr. Scruby at last did as much for George Vavasor as he had done for the hero of the Hamlets. At the close of the poll Vavasor's name stood at the head by a considerable majority, and Scruby comforted him by saying that Travers certainly wouldn't stand the expense of a petition,* as the seat was to be held only for a few months.

'And you've done it very cheap, Mr. Vavasor,' said Scruby, 'considering that the seat is metropolitan. I do say that you have done it cheap. Another thousand, or twelve hundred, will cover everything—say thirteen, perhaps, at the outside. And when you shall have fought the battle once again, you'll have paid your footing, and the fellows will let you in almost for nothing after that.'

A further sum of thirteen hundred pounds was wanted at once, and then the whole thing was to be repeated over again in six months' time! This was not consolatory. But, nevertheless, there was a triumph in the thing itself which George Vavasor was man enough to enjoy. It would be something to have sat in the House of Commons, though it should only have been for half a session.

CHAPTER XLV

George Vavasor takes his Seat

GEORGE VAVASOR's feeling of triumph was not unjustifiable. It is something to have sat in the House of Commons, though it has been but for one session! There is on the left-hand side of our great national hall,—on the left-hand side as one enters it, and opposite to the doors leading to the Law Courts,—a pair of gilded lamps, with a door between them, near to which a privileged old dame sells her apples and her oranges solely, as I presume, for the accommodation of the Members of the House and of the great policeman who guards the pass. Between those lamps is the entrance to the House of

Commons, and none but Members may go that way! It is the only gate before which I have ever stood filled with envy,—sorrowing to think that my steps might never pass under it. There are many portals forbidden to me, as there are many forbidden to all men; and forbidden fruit, they say, is sweet; but my lips have watered after no other fruit but that which grows so high, within the sweep of that great policeman's truncheon.

Ah, my male friend and reader, who earnest thy bread, perhaps, as a country vicar; or sittest, may-be, at some weary desk in Somerset House;* or who, perhaps, rulest the yard behind the Cheapside counter, hast thou never stood there and longed, —hast thou never confessed, when standing there, that Fate has been unkind to thee in denying thee the one thing that thou hast wanted? I have done so; and as my slow steps have led me up that more than royal staircase, to those passages and halls which require the hallowing breath of centuries to give them the glory in British eyes which they shall one day possess, I have told myself, in anger and in grief, that to die and not to have won that right of way, though but for a session,—not to have passed by the narrow entrance through those lamps,—is to die and not to have done that which it most becomes an Englishman to have achieved.*

There are, doubtless, some who came out by that road, the loss of whose society is not to be regretted. England does not choose her six hundred and fifty-four best men. One comfort's one's self, sometimes, with remembering that. The George Vavasors, the Calder Joneses, and the Botts are admitted. Dishonesty, ignorance, and vulgarity do not close the gate of that heaven against aspirants; and it is a consolation to the ambition of the poor to know that the ambition of the rich can attain that glory by the strength of its riches alone. But though England does not send thither none but her best men, the best of her Commoners do find their way there. It is the highest and most legitimate pride of an Englishman to have the letters M.P. written after his name. No selection from the alphabet, no doctorship, no fellowship, be it of ever so learned or royal a society, no knightship,—not though it be of the Garter,—confers so fair an honour. Mr. Bott was right when he declared that this country is governed from between the walls of that House, though the truth was almost defiled by the lips which uttered it. He might have added that from thence flow the waters of the world's progress,—the fullest fountain of advancing civilization.

George Vavasor, as he went in by the lamps and the apple-stall, under the guardianship of Mr. Bott, felt all the pride of which I have been speaking. He was a man quite capable of feeling such pride as it should be felt,—capable, in certain dreamy moments, of looking at the thing with pure and almost noble eyes; of understanding the ambition of serving with truth so great a nation as that which fate had made his own. Nature, I think, had so fashioned George Vavasor, that he might have been a good, and perhaps a great man; whereas Mr. Bott had been born small. Vavasor had educated himself to badness with his eyes open. He had known what was wrong, and had done it, having taught himself to think that bad things were best. But poor Mr. Bott had meant to do well, and thought that he had done very well indeed. He was a tuft-hunter and a toady, but he did not know that he was doing amiss in seeking to rise by tuft-hunting and toadying. He was both mean and vain, both a bully and a coward, and in politics, I fear, quite unscrupulous in spite of his grand dogmas; but he believed that he was progressing in public life by the proper and usual means, and was troubled by no idea that he did wrong.

Vavasor, in those dreamy moments of which I have spoken, would sometimes feel tempted to cut his throat and put an end to himself, because he knew that he had taught himself amiss. Again he would sadly ask himself whether it was yet too late; always, however, answering himself that it was too late. Even now, at this moment, as he went in between the lamps, and felt much of the honest pride of which I have spoken, he told himself that it was too late. What could he do now, hampered by such a debt as that which he owed to his cousin, and with the knowledge that it must be almost indefinitely increased, unless he meant to give up this seat in Parliament, which had cost him so dearly, almost before he had begun to enjoy it? But his courage was good, and he was able to resolve that he could go on with the business that he had in hand, and play out his game to the end. He had achieved his seat in the House of Commons, and was so far successful. Men who had ever been gracious to him were now more gracious than ever, and they who had not hitherto treated him with courtesy, now began to smile and to be very civil. It was, no doubt, a great thing to have the privilege of that entrance between the lamps.

Mr. Bott had the new Member now in hand, not because there had been any old friendship between them, but Mr. Bott was on the look-out for followers and Vavasor was on the look-out for a party. A man gets no great thanks for attaching himself to existing power. Our friend might have enrolled himself among the general supporters of the Government without attracting much attention. He would in such case have been at the bottom of a long list. But Mr. Palliser was a rising man, round whom, almost without wish of his own, a party was forming itself.* If he came into power,—as come he must, according to Mr. Bott and many others,—then they who had acknowledged the new light before its brightness had been declared, might expect their reward.

Vavasor, as he passed through the lobby to the door of the House, leaning on Mr. Bott's arm, was very silent. He had spoken but little since they had left their cab in Palace Yard, and was not very well pleased by the garrulity of his companion. He was going to sit among the first men of his nation, and to take his chance of making himself one of them. He believed in his own ability; he believed thoroughly in his own courage; but he did not believe in his own conduct. He feared that he had done,—feared still more strongly that he would be driven to do,—that which would shut men's ears against his words, and would banish him from high places. No man believes in himself who knows himself to be a rascal, however great may be his talent, or however high his pluck.

'Of course you have heard a debate?' said Mr. Bott.

'Yes,' answered Vavasor, who wished to remain silent.

'Many, probably?'

'No.'

'But you have heard debates from the gallery. Now you'll hear them from the body of the House, and you'll find how very different it is. There's no man can know what Parliament is who has never had a seat. Indeed no one can thoroughly understand the British Constitution without it. I felt, very early in life, that that should be my line; and though it's hard work and no pay, I mean to stick to it. How do, Thompson? You know Vavasor? He's just returned for the Chelsea Districts, and I'm taking him up. We shan't divide to-night; shall we? Look! there's Farringcourt just coming out; he's listened to better than any man on the House now, but he'll borrow half-a-crown from you if you'll lend him one. How d'ye do, my lord? I hope I have the pleasure of seeing you well?' and Bott bowed low to a lord who was hurrying through the lobby as fast as his shuffling feet would carry him. 'Of course you know him?'

Vavasor, however, did not know the lord in question, and was obliged to say so.

'I thought you were up to all these things?' said Bott.

'Taking the peerage generally, I am not up to it,' said Vavasor, with a curl on his lip.

'But you ought to have known him. That was Viscount Middlesex; he has got something on tonight about the Irish Church. His father is past ninety, and he's over sixty. We'll go in now; but let me give you one bit of advice, my dear fellow—don't think of speaking this session. A Member can do no good at that work till he has learned something of the forms of the House. The forms of the House are everything; upon my word they are. This is Mr. Vavasor, the new Member for the Chelsea Districts.'

Our friend was thus introduced to the doorkeeper, who smiled familiarly, and seemed to wink his eye. Then George Vavasor passed through into the House itself, under the wing of Mr. Bott.

Vavasor, as he walked up the House to the Clerk's table and took the oath and then walked down again, felt himself to be almost taken aback by the little notice which was accorded to him. It was not that he had expected to create a sensation, or that he had for a moment thought on the subject, but the thing which he was doing was so great to him, that the total indifference of those around him was a surprise to him. After he had taken his seat, a few men came up by degrees and shook hands with him; but it seemed, as they did so, merely because they were passing that way. He was anxious not to sit next to Mr. Bott, but he found himself unable to avoid this contiguity. That gentleman stuck to him pertinaciously, giving him directions which, at the spur of the moment, he hardly knew how not to obey. So he found himself sitting behind Mr. Palliser, a little to the right, while Mr. Bott occupied the ear of the rising man.

There was a debate in progress, but it seemed to Vavasor, as soon as he was able to become critical, to be but a dull affair, and yet the Chancellor of the Exchequer was on his legs, and Mr. Palliser was watching him as a cat watches a mouse. The speaker was full of figures, as becomes a Chancellor of the Exchequer; and as every new budget of them fell from him, Mr. Bott, with audible whispers, poured into the ear of his chief certain calculations of his own most of which went to prove that the financier in office was altogether wrong. Vavasor thought that he could see that Mr. Palliser was receiving more of this assistance than was palatable to him. He would listen, if he did listen, without making any sign that he heard, and would occasionally shake his head with symptoms of impatience. But Mr. Bott was a man not to be repressed by a trifle. When Mr. Palliser shook his head he became more assiduous than ever, and when Mr. Palliser slightly moved himself to the left, he boldly followed him.

No general debate arose on the subject which the Minister had in hand, and when he sat down, Mr. Palliser would not get up, though Mr. Bott counselled him to do so. The matter was over for the night, and the time had arrived for Lord

48

Middlesex. That nobleman got upon his feet, with a roll of papers in his hand, and was proceeding to address the House on certain matters of church reform, with great energy; but, alas, for him and his feelings! before his energy had got itself into full swing, the Members were swarming away through the doors like a flock of sheep. Mr. Palliser got up and went, and was followed at once by Mr. Bott, who succeeded in getting hold of his arm in the lobby. Had not Mr. Palliser been an even-tempered, calculating man, with a mind and spirit well under his command, he must have learned to hate Mr. Bott before this time. Away streamed the Members, but still the noble lord went on speaking, struggling hard to keep up his fire as though no such exodus were in process. There was but little to console him. He knew that the papers would not report one sentence in twenty of those he uttered. He knew that no one would listen to him willingly. He knew that he had worked for weeks and months to get up his facts, and he was beginning to know that he had worked in vain. As he summoned courage to look round, he began to fear that some enemy would count the House, and that all would be over. He had given heart and soul to this affair. His cry was not as Vavasor's cry about the River Bank. He believed in his own subject with a great faith, thinking that he could make men happier and better, and bring them nearer to their God. I said that he had worked for weeks and months. I might have said that he had been all his life at this work. Though he shuffled with his feet when he walked, and knocked his words together when he talked, he was an earnest man, meaning to do well, seeking no other reward for his work than the appreciation of those whom he desired to serve. But this was never to be his. For him there was in store nothing but disappointment. And yet he will work on to the end, either in this House or in the other, labouring wearily, without visible wages of any kind, and, one may say, very sadly. But when he has been taken to his long rest, men will acknowledge that he has done something, and there will be left on the minds of those who shall remember him a conviction that he served a good cause diligently, and not altogether inefficiently. Invisible are his wages, yet in some coin are they paid. Invisible is the thing he does, and yet it is done. Let us hope that some sense of this tardy appreciation may soothe his spirit beyond the grave. On the present occasion there was nothing to soothe his spirit. The Speaker sat, urbane and courteous, with his eyes turned towards the unfortunate orator; but no other ears in the House seemed to listen to him. The corps of reporters had dwindled down to two, and they used their pens very listlessly, taking down here a sentence and there a sentence, knowing that their work was naught. Vavasor sat it out to the last, as it taught him a lesson in those forms of the House which Mr. Bott had truly told him it would be well that he should learn. And at last he did learn the form of a 'count-out.'*Some one from a back seat muttered something, which the Speaker understood; and that high officer, having had his attention called to a fact of which he would never have taken cognisance without such calling, did count the House, and finding that it contained but twenty-three Members, he put an end to his own labours and to those of poor Lord Middlesex. With what feelings that noble lord must have taken himself home, and sat himself down in his study, vainly opening a book before his eyes, can we not all imagine? A man he was with ample means, with children who would do honour to his name; one whose wife believed in him, if no one else would do so; a man, let us say, with a clear conscience, to whom all good things had been given. But of whom now was he thinking with envy? Early on that same day Farringcourt had spoken in the House,—a man to whom no one would lend a shilling, whom the privilege of that House*kept out of gaol, whose word no man believed; who was wifeless, childless, and unloved. But three hundred men had hung listening upon his words. When he laughed in his speech, they laughed; when he was indignant against the Minister, they sat breathless, as the Spaniard sits in the critical moment of the bull-killing. Whichever way he turned himself, he carried them with him. Crowds of Members flocked into the House from libraries and smoking rooms when it was known that this ne'er-do-well was on his legs. The Strangers' Gallery was filled to overflowing. The reporters turned their rapid pages, working their fingers wearily till the sweat drops stood upon their brows. And as the Premier was attacked with some special impetus of redoubled irony, men declared that he would be driven to enrol the speaker among his colleagues, in spite of dishonoured bills and evil reports. A man who could shake the thunderbolts like that must be paid to shake them on the right side. It was of this man, and of his success, that Lord Middlesex was envious, as he sat, wretched and respectable, in his solitary study!

Mr. Bott had left the House with Mr. Palliser; and Vavasor, after the count-out, was able to walk home by himself, and think of the position which he had achieved. He told himself over and over again that he had done a great thing in obtaining that which he now possessed, and he endeavoured to teach himself that the price he was paying for it was not too dear. But already there had come upon him something of that feeling,—that terribly human feeling,—which deprives every prize that is gained of half its value. The mere having it robs the diamond of its purity, and mixes vile alloy with the gold. Lord Middlesex, as he had floundered on into terrible disaster, had not been a subject to envy. There had been nothing of brilliance in the debate, and the Members had loomed no larger than ordinary men at ordinary clubs. The very door-keepers had hardly treated them with respect. The great men with whose names the papers are filled had sat silent, gloomy, and apparently idle. As soon as a fair opportunity was given them they escaped out of the House, as boys might escape from school. Everybody had rejoiced in the break-up of the evening, except that one poor old lord who had worked so hard. Vavasor had spent everything that he had to become a Member of that House, and now, as he went alone to his lodgings, he could not but ask himself whether the thing purchased was worth the purchase-money.

But his courage was still high. Though he was gloomy, and almost sad, he knew that he could trust himself to fight out the battle to the last. On the morrow he would go to Queen Anne Street, and would demand sympathy there from her who had professed to sympathize with him so strongly in his political desires. With her, at any rate, the glory of his Membership would not be dimmed by any untoward knowledge of the realities. She had only seen the play acted from the boxes; and to her eyes the dresses would still be of silk velvet, and the swords of bright steel.

CHAPTER XLVI

A Love Gift

WHEN Alice heard of her cousin's success, and understood that he was actually Member of Parliament for the Chelsea Districts, she resolved that she would be triumphant. She had sacrificed nearly everything to her desire for his success in public life, and now that he had achieved the first great step towards that success, it would have been madness on her part to decline her share in the ovation. If she could not rejoice in that, what source of joy would then be left for her? She had promised to be his wife, and at present she was under the bonds of that promise. She had so promised because she had desired to identify her interests with his,—because she wished to share his risks, to assist his struggles, and to aid him in his public career. She had done all this, and he had been successful. She strove, therefore, to be triumphant on his behalf, but she knew that she was striving ineffectually. She had made a mistake, and the days were coming in which she would have to own to herself that she had done so in sackcloth, and to repent with ashes.

But yet she struggled to be triumphant. The tidings were first brought to her by her servant, and then she at once sat down to write him a word or two of congratulation. But she found the task more difficult than she had expected, and she gave it up. She had written no word to him since the day on which he had left her almost in anger, and now she did not know how she was to address him. 'I will wait till he comes,' she said, putting away from her the paper and pens. 'It will be easier to speak than to write.' But she wrote to Kate, and contrived to put some note of triumph into her letter. Kate had written to her at length, filling her sheet with a loud pæan of sincere rejoicing. To Kate, down in Westmoreland, it had seemed that her brother had already done everything. He had already tied Fortune to his chariot wheels. He had made the great leap, and had overcome the only obstacle that Fate had placed in his way. In her great joy she almost forgot whence had come the money with which the contest had been won. She was not enthusiastic in many things;—about herself she was never so; but now she was elated with an enthusiasm which seemed to know no bounds. 'I am proud,' she said, in her letter to Alice. 'No other thing that he could have done would have made me so proud of him. Had the Queen sent for him and made him an earl, it would have been as nothing to this. When I think that he has forced his way into Parliament without any great friend, with nothing to back him but his own wit'—she had, in truth, forgotten Alice's money as she wrote;—'that he has achieved his triumph in the metropolis, among the most wealthy and most fastidious of the richest city in the world, I do feel proud of my brother. And, Alice, I hope that you are proud of your lover.' Poor girl! One cannot but like her pride, nay, almost love her for it, though it was so sorely misplaced. It must be remembered that she had known nothing of Messrs. Grimes and Scruby, and the River Bank, and that the means had been wanting to her of learning the principles upon which some metropolitan elections are conducted.

'And, Alice, I hope that you are proud of your lover!' 'He is not my lover,' Alice said to herself. 'He knows that he is not. He understands it, though she may not.' And if not your lover, Alice Vavasor, what is he then to you? And what are you to him, if not his love? She was beginning to understand that she had put herself in the way of utter destruction;—that she had walked to the brink of a precipice, and that she must now topple over it. 'He is not my lover,' she said; and then she sat silent and moody, and it took her hours to get her answer written to Kate.

On the same afternoon she saw her father for a moment or two. 'So George has got himself returned,' he said, raising his eyebrows.

'Yes, he has been successful. I'm sure you must be glad, papa.'

'Upon my word, I'm not. He has bought a seat for three months; and with whose money has he purchased it?'

'Don't let us always speak of money, papa.'

'When you discuss the value of a thing just purchased, you must mention the price before you know whether the purchaser has done well or badly. They have let him in for his money because there are only a few months left before the general election. Two thousand pounds he has had, I believe?'

'And if as much more is wanted for the next election he shall have it.'

'Very well, my dear;—very well. If you choose to make a beggar of yourself, I cannot help it. Indeed, I shall not complain though he should spend all your money, if you do not marry him at last.' In answer to this, Alice said nothing. On that point her father's wishes were fast growing to be identical with her own.

'I tell you fairly what are my feelings and my wishes,' he continued. 'Nothing, in my opinion, would be so deplorable and ruinous as such a marriage. You tell me that you have made up your mind to take him, and I know well that nothing that I can say will turn you. But I believe that when he has spent all your money he will not take you, and that thus you will be saved. Thinking as I do about him, you can hardly expect that I should triumph because he has got himself into Parliament with your money!'

Then he left her, and it seemed to Alice that he had been very cruel. There had been little, she thought,—nay, nothing, —of a father's loving tenderness in his words to her. If he had spoken to her differently, might she not even now have confessed everything to him? But herein Alice accused him wrong-fully. Tenderness from him on this subject had, we may say, become impossible. She had made it impossible. Nor could he tell her the extent of his wishes without damaging his own cause. He could not let her know that all that was done was so done with the view of driving her into John Grey's arms.

But what words were those for a father to speak to a daughter! Had she brought herself to such a state that her own father desired to see her deserted and thrown aside? And was it probable that this wish of his should come to pass? As to that, Alice had already made up her mind. She thought that she had made up her mind that she would never become her cousin's wife. It needed not her father's wish to accomplish her salvation, if her salvation lay in being separated from him.

On the next morning George went to her. The reader will, perhaps, remember their last interview. He had come to her after her letter to him from Westmoreland, and had asked her to seal their reconciliation with a kiss; but she had refused him. He had offered to embrace her, and she had shuddered before him, fearing his touch, telling him by signs much more clear than any words, that she felt for him none of the love of a woman. Then he had turned from her in anger, declaring to her honestly that he was angry. Since that he had borrowed her money,—had made two separate assaults upon her purse, —and was now come to tell her of the results. How was he to address her? I beg that it may be also remembered that he was not a man to forget the treatment he had received. When he entered the room, Alice looked at him, at first, almost furtively. She was afraid of him. It must be confessed that she already feared him. Had there been in the man anything of lofty principle he might still have made her his slave, though I doubt whether he could ever again have forced her to love him. She looked at him furtively, and perceived that the gash on his face was nearly closed. The mark of existing anger was not there. He had come to her intending to be gentle, if it might be possible. He had been careful in his dress, as though he wished to try once again if the rôle of lover might be within his reach.

Alice was the first to speak. 'George, I am so glad that you have succeeded! I wish you joy with my whole heart.'

'Thanks, dearest. But before I say another word, let me acknowledge my debt. Unless you had aided me with your money, I could not have succeeded.'

'Oh, George! pray don't speak of that!'

'Let me rather speak of it at once, and have done. If you will think of it, you will know that I must speak of it sooner or later.' He smiled and looked pleasant, as he used to do in those Swiss days.

'Well, then, speak and have done.'

'I hope you have trusted me in thus giving me the command of your fortune?'

'Oh, yes.'

'I do believe that you have. I need hardly say that I could not have stood for this last election without it; and I must try to make you understand that if I had not come forward at this vacancy, I should have stood no chance for the next; otherwise, I should not have been justified in paying so dearly for a seat for one session. You can understand that; eh, Alice?'

'Yes; I think so.'

'Anybody, even your father, would tell you that; though, probably, he regards my ambition to be a Member of Parliament as a sign of downright madness. But I was obliged to stand now, if I intended to go on with it, as that old lord died so inopportunely. Well, about the money! It is quite upon the cards that I may be forced to ask for another loan when the autumn comes.'

'You shall have it, George.'

'Thanks, Alice. And now I will tell you what I propose. You know that I have been reconciled,—with a sort of reconciliation,—to my grandfather? Well, when the next affair is over, I propose to tell him exactly how you and I then stand.'

'Do not go into that now, George. It is enough for you at present to be assured that such assistance as I can give you is at your command. I want you to feel the full joy of your success, and you will do so more thoroughly if you will banish all these money troubles from your mind for a while.'

'They shall, at any rate, be banished while I am with you,' said he. 'There; let them go!' And he lifted up his right hand, and blew at the tips of his fingers. 'Let them vanish,' said he. 'It is always well to be rid of such troubles for a time.'

It is well to be rid of them at any time, or at all times, if only they can be banished without danger. But when a man has over-used his liver till it will not act for him any longer, it is not well for him to resolve that he will forget the weakness of his organ just as he sits down to dinner.

It was a pretty bit of acting, that of Vavasor's, when he blew away his cares; and, upon the whole, I do not know that he could have done better. But Alice saw through it, and he knew that she did so. The whole thing was uncomfortable to him, except the fact that he had the promise of her further moneys. But he did not intend to rest satisfied with this. He must extract from her some meed of approbation, some show of sympathy, some spark of affection, true or pretended, in order that he might at least affect to be satisfied, and be enabled to speak of the future without open embarrassment. How could even he take her money from her, unless he might presume that he stood with her upon some ground that belonged mutually to them both?

'I have already taken my seat,' said he.

'Yes; I saw that in the newspapers. My acquaintance among Members of Parliament is very small, but I see that you were introduced, as they call it, by one of the few men that I do know. Is Mr. Bott a friend of yours?'

'No,—certainly not a friend. I may probably have to act with him in public.'

'Ah, that's just what they said of Mr. Palliser when they felt ashamed of his having such a man as his guest. I think if I were in public life I should try to act with people that I could like.'

'Then you dislike Mr. Bott?'

'I do not like him, but my feelings about him are not violent.'

'He is a vulgar ass,' said George, 'with no more pretensions to rank himself a gentleman than your footman.'

'If I had one.'

'But he will get on in Parliament, to a certain extent.'

'I'm afraid I don't quite understand what are the requisites for Parliamentary success, or indeed of what it consists. Is his ambition, do you suppose, the same as yours?'

'His ambition, I take it, does not go beyond a desire to be Parliamentary flunkey to a big man,—with wages, if possible, but without, if the wages are impossible.'

'And yours?'

'Oh, as to mine;—there are some things, Alice, that a man does not tell to any one.'

'Are there? They must be very terrible things.'

'The schoolboy, when he sits down to make his rhymes, dares not say, even to his sister, that he hopes to rival Milton; but he nurses such a hope. The preacher, when he prepares his sermon, does not whisper, even to his wife, his belief that thousands may perhaps be turned to repentance by the strength of his words; but he thinks that the thousand converts are possible.'

'And you, though you will not say so, intend to rival Chatham,* and to make your thousand converts in politics.'

'I like to hear you laugh at me,—I do indeed. It does me good to hear your voice again with some touch of satire in it. It brings back the old days,—the days to which I hope we may soon revert without pain. Shall it not be so, dearest?'

Her playful manner at once deserted her. Why had he made this foolish attempt to be tender? 'I do not know,' she said gloomily.

For a few minutes he sat silent, fingering some article belonging to her which was lying on the table. It was a small steel paper-knife, of which the handle was cast and gilt; a thing of no great value, of which the price may have been five shillings. He sat with it, passing it through his fingers, while she went on with her work.

'Who gave you this paper-cutter?' he said, suddenly.

'Goodness me, why do you ask? and especially, why do you ask in that way?'

'I asked simply because if it is a present to you from any one, I will take up something else.'

'It was given me by Mr. Grey.'

He let it drop from his fingers on to the table with a noise, and then pushed it from him, so that it fell on the other side, near to where she sat.

'George,' she said, as she stooped and picked it up, 'your violence is unreasonable; pray do not repeat it.'

'I did not mean it,' he said, 'and I beg your pardon. I was simply unfortunate in the article I selected. And who gave you this?' In saying which he took up a little ivory foot-rule that was folded up so as to bring it within the compass of three inches.

'It so happens that no one gave me that; I bought it at a stupid bazaar.'

'Then this will do. You shall give it me as a present, on the renewal of our love.'

'It is too poor a thing to give,' said she, speaking still more gloomily than she had done before.

'By no means; nothing is too poor, if given in that way. Anything will do; a ribbon, a glove, a broken sixpence. Will you give me something that I may take, and, taking it, may know that your heart is given with it?'

'Take the rule, if you please,' she said.

'And about the heart?' he asked.

He should have been more of a rascal or less. Seeing how very much of a rascal he was already, I think it would have been better that he should have been more,—that he should have been able to content his spirit with the simple acquisition of her money, and that he should have been free from all those remains of a finer feeling which made him desire her love also. But it was not so. It was necessary for his comfort that she should, at any rate, say she loved him. 'Well, Alice, and what about the heart?' he asked again.

'I would so much rather talk about politics, George,' said she.

The cicatrice began to make itself very visible in his face, and the debonair manner was fast vanishing. He had fixed his eyes upon her, and had inserted his thumbs in the armholes of his waistcoat.

'Alice, that is not quite fair,' he said.

'I do not mean to be unfair.'

'I am not so sure of that. I almost think that you do mean it. You have told me that you intend to become my wife. If, after that, you wilfully make me miserable, will not that be unfair?'

'I am not making you miserable,—certainly not wilfully.'

'Did that letter which you wrote to me from Westmoreland mean anything?'

'George, do not strive to make me think that it meant too much.'

'If it did, you had better say so at once.'

But Alice, though she would have said so had she dared, made no answer to this. She sat silent, turning her face away from his gaze, longing that the meeting might be over, and feeling that she had lost her own self-respect.

'Look here, Alice,' he said, 'I find it very hard to understand you. When I look back over all that has passed between us, and to that other episode in your life, summing it all up with your conduct to me at present, I find myself at a loss to read your character.'

'I fear I cannot help you in the reading of it.'

'When you first loved me;—for you did love me. I understood that well enough. There is no young man who in early life does not read with sufficient clearness that sweetest morsel of poetry.—And when you quarrelled with me, judging somewhat harshly of my offences, I understood that also; for it is the custom of women to be hard in their judgment on such sins. When I heard that you had accepted the offer made to you by that gentleman in Cambridgeshire, I thought that I understood you still,—knowing how natural it was that you should seek some cure for your wound. I understood it, and accused my-

self, not you, in that I had driven you to so fatal a remedy.'
Here Alice turned round towards him sharply, as though she
were going to interrupt him, but she said nothing, though he
paused for her to speak; and then he went on. 'And I understood it well when I heard that this cure had been too much
for you. By heavens, yes! there was no misunderstanding that.
I meant no insult to the man when I upset his little toy just
now. I have not a word to say against him. For many women
he would make a model husband, but you are not one of them.
And when you discovered this yourself, as you did, I understood that without difficulty. Yes, by heavens! if ever woman
had been driven to a mistake, you had been driven to one
there.' Here she looked at him again, and met his eyes. She
looked at him with something of his own fierceness in her face,
as though she were preparing herself to fight with him; but
she said nothing at the moment, and then he again went on.
'And, Alice, I understood it also when you again consented to
be my wife. I thought that I still understood you then. I may
have been vain to think so, but surely it was natural. I believed
that the old love had come back upon you, and again warmed
your heart. I thought that it had been cold during our separation, and I was pleased to think so. Was that unnatural? Put
yourself in my place, and say if you would not have thought
so. I told myself that I understood you then, and I told myself
that in all that you had done you had acted as a true, and good,
and loving woman. I thought of you much, and I saw that your
conduct, as a whole, was intelligible and becoming.' The last
word grated on Alice's ears, and she showed her anger by the
motion of her foot upon the floor. Her cousin noted it all, but
went on as though he had not noted it. 'But now your present
behaviour makes all the rest a riddle. You have said that you
would be my wife, declaring thereby that you had forgiven my
offences, and, as I suppose, reassuring me of your love; and
yet you receive me with all imaginable coldness. What am I
to think of it, and in what way would you have me behave to
you? When last I was here I asked you for a kiss.' As he said
this he looked at her with all his eyes, with his mouth just

open, so as to show the edges of his white teeth, with the wound down his face all wide and purple. The last word came with a stigmatizing hiss from his lips. Though she did not essay to speak, he paused again, as if he were desirous that she might realize the full purport of such a request. I think that, in the energy of his speaking, a touch of true passion had come upon him; that he had forgotten his rascaldom, and his need of her money, and that he was punishing her with his whole power of his vengeance for the treatment which he had received from her. 'I asked you for a kiss. If you are to be my wife you can have no shame in granting me such a request. Within the last two months you have told me that you would marry me. What am I to think of such a promise if you deny me all customary signs of your affection?' Then he paused again, and she found that the time had come in which she must say something to him.

'I wonder you cannot understand,' she said, 'that I have suffered much.'

'And is that to be my answer?'

'I don't know what answer you want.'

'Come, Alice, do not be untrue; you do know what answer I want, and you know also whether my wanting it is unreasonable.'

'No one ever told me that I was untrue before,' she said.

'You do know what it is that I desire. I desire to learn that the woman who is to be my wife, in truth, loves me.'

She was standing up, and so was he also, but still she said nothing. He had in his hand the little rule which she had told him that he might take, but he held it as though in doubt what he would do with it. 'Well, Alice, am I to hear anything from you?'

'Not now, George; you are angry, and I will not speak to you in your anger.'

'Have I not cause to be angry? Do you not know that you are treating me badly?'

'I know that my head aches, and that I am very wretched. I wish you would leave me.'

'There, then, is your gift,' said he, and he threw the rule over on to the sofa behind her. 'And there is the trumpery trinket which I had hoped you would have worn for my sake.' Whereupon something which he had taken from his waistcoat-pocket was thrown violently into the fender, beneath the fire-grate. He then walked with quick steps to the door; but when his hand was on the handle, he turned. 'Alice,' he said, 'when I am gone, try to think honestly of your conduct to me.' Then he went, and she remained still, till she heard the front door close behind him.

When she was sure that he was gone, her first movement was made in search of the trinket. I fear that this was not dignified on her part; but I think that it was natural. It was not that she had any desire for the jewel, or any curiosity even to see it. She would very much have preferred that he should have brought nothing of the kind to her. But she had a feminine reluctance that anything of value should be destroyed without a purpose. So she took the shovel, and poked among the ashes, and found the ring which her cousin had thrown there. It was a valuable ring, bearing a ruby on it between two small diamonds. Such at least, she became aware, had been its bearing; but one of the side stones had been knocked out by the violence with which the ring had been flung. She searched even for this, scorching her face and eyes, but in vain. Then she made up her mind that the diamond should be lost for ever, and that it should go out among the cinders into the huge dust-heaps of the metropolis. Better that, though it was distasteful to her feminine economy, than the other alternative of setting the servants to search, and thereby telling them something of what had been done.

When her search was over, she placed the ring on the mantelpiece; but she knew that it would not do to leave it there,—so she folded it up carefully in a new sheet of note-paper, and put it in the drawer of her desk. After that she sat herself down at the table to think what she would do; but her head was, in truth, racked with pain, and on that occasion she could bring her thoughts to no conclusion.

CHAPTER XLVII

Mr. Cheesacre's Disappointment

WHEN Mrs. Greenow was left alone in her lodgings, after the little entertainment which she had given to her two lovers, she sat herself down to think seriously over her affairs. There were three paths open before her. She might take Mr. Cheesacre, or she might take Captain Bellfield—or she might decide that she would have nothing more to say to either of them in the way of courting. They were very persistent, no doubt; but she thought that she would know how to make them understand her, if she should really make up her mind that she would have neither one nor the other. She was going to leave Norwich after Easter, and they knew that such was her purpose. Something had been said of her returning to Yarmouth in the summer. She was a just woman at heart, and justice required that each of them should know what was to be his prospect if she did so return.

There was a good deal to be said on Mr. Cheesacre's behalf. Mahogany-furnitured bedrooms assist one's comfort in this life; and heaps of manure, though they are not brilliant in romance, are very efficacious in farming. Mrs. Greenow by no means despised these things; and as for the owner of them, though she saw that there was much amiss in his character, she thought that his little foibles were of such a nature that she, as his wife, or any other woman of spirit, might be able to repress them, if not to cure them. But she had already married for money once, as she told herself very plainly on this occasion, and she thought that she might now venture on a little love. Her marriage for money had been altogether successful. The nursing of old Greenow had not been very disagreeable to her, nor had it taken longer than she had anticipated. She had now got all the reward that she had ever promised herself, and she really did feel grateful to his memory. I almost think that among those plentiful tears some few drops belonged to sincerity. She was essentially a happy-tempered woman, blessed with a good digestion, who looked back upon her past life with contentment, and forward to her future life with confidence. She would not be greedy, she said to herself. She did not want more money, and therefore she would have none of Mr. Cheesacre. So far she resolved,—resolving also that, if possible, the mahogany-furnitured bedrooms should be kept in the family, and made over to her niece, Kate Vavasor.

But should she marry for love; and if so, should Captain Bellfield be the man? Strange to say, his poverty and his scampishness and his lies almost recommended him to her. At any rate, it was not of those things that she was afraid. She had a woman's true belief in her own power, and thought that she could cure them,—as far as they needed cure. As for his stories about Inkerman, and his little debts, she cared nothing about that. She also had her Inkermans, and was quite aware that she made as good use of them as the Captain did of his. And as for the debts,—what was a man to do who hadn't got any money? She also had owed for her gloves and corsets in the ante-Greenow days of her adventures. But there was this danger,— that there might be more behind of which she had never heard. Another Mrs. Bellfield was not impossible; and what, if instead of being a real captain at all, he should be a returned ticket-of-leave*man! Such things had happened. Her chief security was in this,—that Cheesacre had known the man for many years, and would certainly have told anything against him that he did know. Under all these circumstances, she could not quite make up her mind either for or against Captain Bellfield.

Between nine and ten in the evening, an hour or so after Mr. Cheesacre had left her, Jeannette brought to her some arrowroot with a little sherry in it. She usually dined early, and it was her habit to take a light repast before she retired for the night.

'Jeannette,' she said, as she stirred the lumps of white sugar in the bowl, 'I'm afraid those two gentlemen have quarrelled.'

'Oh, laws, ma'am, in course they have! How was they to help it?'

Jeannette, on these occasions, was in the habit of standing beside the chair of her mistress, and chatting with her; and then, if the chatting was much prolonged, she would gradually sink down upon the corner of a chair herself,—and then the two women would be very comfortable together over the fire, Jeannette never forgetting that she was the servant, and Mrs. Greenow never forgetting that she was the mistress.

'And why should they quarrel, Jeannette? It's very foolish.'

'I don't know about being foolish, ma'am; but it's the most natural thing in life. If I had two beaux as was a-courting me together, in course I should expect as they would punch each other's heads. There's some girls do it a purpose, because they like to see it. One at a time's what I say.'

'You're a young thing, Jeannette.'

'Well, ma'am—yes; I am young, no doubt. But I won't say but what I've had a beau, young as I look.'

'But you don't suppose that I want beaux, as you call them?'

'I don't know, ma'am, as you wants 'em exactly. That's as may be. There they are; and if they was to blow each other's brains out in the gig to-night, I shouldn't be a bit surprised for one. There's nothing won't quiet them at Oileymead to-night, if brandy-and-water don't do it.' As she said this, Jeannette slipt into her chair, and held up her hands in token of the intensity of her fears.

'Why, you silly child, they're not going home together at all. Did not the Captain go away first?'

'The Captain did go away first, certainly; but I thought perhaps it was to get his pistols and fighting things ready.'

'They won't fight, Jeannette. Gentlemen have given over fighting.'

'Have they, ma'am? That makes it much easier for ladies, no doubt. Perhaps them peaceable ways will come down to such as us in time. It'd be a comfort, I know, to them as are quiet given, like me. I hate to see men knocking each other's heads about,—I do. So Mr. Cheesacre and the Captain won't fight, ma'am?'

'Of course they won't, you little fool, you.'

'Dear, dear; I was so sure we should have had the papers all full of it,—and perhaps one of them stretched upon his bloody bier! I wonder which it would have been? I always made up my mind that the Captain wouldn't be wounded in any of his wital parts—unless it was his heart, you know, ma'am.'

'But why should they quarrel at all, Jeannette? It is the most foolish thing.'

'Well, ma'am, I don't know about that. What else is they to do? There's some things as you can cry halves about, but there's no crying halves about this.'

'About what, Jeannette?'—'Why, about you, ma'am.'

'Jeannette, I wonder how you can say such things; as if I, in my position, had ever said a word to encourage either of them. You know it's not true, Jeannette, and you shouldn't say so.' Whereupon Mrs. Greenow put her handkerchief to her eyes, and Jeannette, probably in token of contrition, put her apron to hers.

'To be sure, ma'am, no lady could have behaved better through it than you have done, and goodness knows you have been tried hard.'

'Indeed I have, Jeannette.'

'And if gentlemen will make fools of themselves, it isn't your fault; is it, ma'am?'

'But I'm so sorry that they should have quarrelled. They were such dear friends, you know;—quite all in all to each other.'

'When you've settled which it's to be, ma'am, that'll all come right again,—seeing that gentlefolks like them have given up fighting, as you say.' Then there was a little pause. 'I suppose, ma'am, it won't be Mr. Cheesacre? To be sure, he's a man as is uncommonly well-to-do in the world.'

'What's all that to me, Jeannette? I shall ever regard Mr. Cheesacre as a dear friend who has been very good to me at a time of trouble; but he'll never be more than that.'

'Then it'll be the Captain, ma'am? I'm sure, for my part, I've always thought the Captain was the nicer gentleman of the two,—and have always said so.'

'He's nothing to me, girl.'

'And as for money,—what's the good of having more than enough? If he can bring love, you can bring money; can't you, ma'am?'

'He's nothing to me, girl,' repeated Mrs. Greenow.

'But he will be?' said Jeannette, plainly asking a question.

'Well, I'm sure! What's the world come to, I wonder, when you sit yourself down there, and cross-examine your mistress in that way! Get to bed, will you? It's near ten o'clock.'

'I hope I haven't said anything amiss, ma'am;' and Jeannette rose from her seat.

'It's my fault for encouraging you,' said Mrs. Greenow. 'Go down stairs and finish your work, do; and then take yourself off to bed. Next week we shall have to be packing up, and there'll be all my things to see to before that.' So Jeannette got up and departed, and after some few further thoughts about Captain Bellfield, Mrs. Greenow herself went to her bedroom.

Mr. Cheesacre, when he drove back to Oileymead alone from Norwich, after dining with Mrs. Greenow, had kept himself hot, and almost comfortable, with passion against Bellfield;

and his heat, if not his comfort, had been sustained by his seeing the Captain, with his portmanteau, escaping just as he
reached his own homestead. But early on the following morning his mind reverted to Mrs. Greenow, and he remembered,
with anything but satisfaction, some of the hard things which
she had said to him. He had made mistakes in his manner of
wooing. He was quite aware of that now, and was determined
that they should be rectified for the future. She had rebuked
him for having said nothing about his love. He would instantly
mend that fault. And she had bidden him not to be so com-
municative about his wealth. Henceforth he would be dumb on
that subject. Nevertheless, he could not but think that the knowledge of his circumstances which the lady already possessed,
must be of service to him. 'She can't really like a poor beggarly
wretch who hasn't got a shilling,' he said to himself. He was
very far from feeling that the battle was already lost. Her last
word to him had been an assurance of her friendship; and then
why should she have been at so much trouble to tell him the
way in which he ought to address her if she were herself indifferent as to his addresses? He was, no doubt, becoming
tired of his courtship, and heartily wished that the work were
over; but he was not minded to give it up. He therefore prepared himself for another attack, and took himself into Norwich without seeking counsel from any one. He could not trust
himself to think that she could really wish to refuse him after all
the encouragement she had given him. On this occasion he put
on no pink shirt or shiny boots, being deterred from doing so
by a remembrance of Captain Bellfield's ridicule; but, nevertheless, he dressed himself with considerable care. He clothed his
nether person in knickerbockers, with tight, leathern, bright-
coloured gaiters round his legs, being conscious of certain
manly graces and symmetrical proportions which might, as he
thought, stand him in good stead. And he put on a new shoot-
ing-coat, the buttons on which were elaborate, and a wonderful
waistcoat worked over with foxes' heads. He completed his
toilet with a round, low-crowned hat, with dog's-skin gloves,
and a cutting whip. Thus armed he went forth resolved to

conquer or to die,—as far as death might result from any wound which Mrs. Greenow might be able to give him. He waited, on this occasion, for the coming of no market-day; indeed, the journey into the city was altogether special, and he was desirous that she should know that such was the case. He drove at a great pace into the inn-yard, threw his reins to the ostler, took just one glass of cherry-brandy at the bar, and then marched off across the market-place to the Close, with quiet and decisive steps.

'Is that you, Cheesacre?' said a friendly voice, in one of the narrow streets. 'Who expected to see you in Norwich on a Thursday!' It was Grimsby, the son of old Grimsby of Hatherwich, a country gentleman, and one, therefore, to whom Cheesacre would generally pay much respect; but on this occasion he did not even pull up for an instant, or moderate his pace. 'A little bit of private business,' he said, and marched onwards with his head towards the Close. 'I'm not going to be afraid of a woman—not if I know it,' he said to himself; but, nevertheless, at a certain pastrycook's, of whose shop he had knowledge, he pulled up and had another glass of cherry-brandy.

'Mrs. Greenow is at home,' he said to Jeannette, not deigning to ask any question.

'Oh, yes, sir; she is at home,' said Jeannette, conscious that some occasion had arrived; and in another second he was in the presence of his angel.

'Mr. Cheesacre, whoever expected to see you in Norwich on a Thursday?' said the lady, as she welcomed him, using almost the same words as his friend had done in the street. Why should not he come into Norwich on a Thursday, as well as any one else? Did they suppose that he was tied for ever to his ploughs and carts? He was minded to conduct himself with a little spirit on this occasion, and to improve the opinion which Mrs. Greenow had formed about him. On this account he answered her somewhat boldly.

'There's no knowing when I may be in Norwich, Mrs. Greenow, or when I mayn't. I'm one of those men of whom nobody knows anything certain, except that I pay as I go.'

Then he remembered that he was not to make any more boasts about his money, and he endeavoured to cover the error. 'There's one other thing they may all know if they please, but we won't say what that is just at present.'

'Won't you sit down, Mr. Cheesacre?'

'Well,—thank you,—I will sit down for a few minutes if you'll let me, Mrs. Greenow. Mrs. Greenow, I'm in such a state of mind that I must put an end to it, or else I shall be going mad, and doing somebody a damage.'

'Dear me! what has happened to you? You're going out shooting, presently; are you not?' and Mrs. Greenow looked down at his garments.

'No, Mrs. Greenow, I'm not going out shooting. I put on these things because I thought I might take a shot as I came along. But I couldn't bring myself to do it, and then I wouldn't take them off again. What does it matter what a man wears?'

'Not in the least, so long as he is decent.'

'I'm sure I'm always that, Mrs. Greenow.'

'Oh, dear, yes. More than that, I should say. I consider you to be rather gay in your attire.'

'I don't pretend to anything of that kind, Mrs. Greenow. I like to be nice, and all that kind of thing. There are people who think that because a man farms his own land, he must be always in the muck. It is the case, of course, with those who have to make their rent and living out of it.' Then he remembered that he was again treading on forbidden ground, and stopped himself. 'But it don't matter what a man wears if his heart isn't easy within him.'

'I don't know why you should speak in that way, Mr. Cheesacre; but it's what I have felt every hour since—since Greenow left me.'

Mr. Cheesacre was rather at a loss to know how he should begin. This allusion to the departed one did not at all assist him. He had so often told the widow that care killed a cat, and that a live dog was better than a dead lion; and had found so little efficacy in the proverbs, that he did not care to revert to them. He was aware that some more decided method of

proceeding was now required. Little hints at love-making had
been all very well in the earlier days of their acquaintance; but
there must be something more than little hints before he could
hope to bring the matter to a favourable conclusion. The widow
herself had told him that he ought to talk about love; and he
had taken two glasses of cherry-brandy, hoping that they might
enable him to do so. He had put on a coat with brilliant
buttons, and new knickerbockers, in order that he might be
master of the occasion. He was resolved to call a spade a spade,
and to speak boldly of his passion; but how was he to begin?
There was the difficulty. He was now seated in a chair, and
there he remained silent for a minute or two, while she
smoothed her eyebrows with her handkerchief after her last
slight ebullition of grief.

'Mrs. Greenow,' he exclaimed at last, jumping up before
her; 'dearest Mrs. Greenow; darling Mrs. Greenow, will you
be my wife? There! I have said it at last, and I mean it. Everything that I've got shall be yours. Of course I speak specially
of my hand and heart. As for love;—oh, Arabella, if you only
knew me! I don't think there's a man in Norfolk better able
to love a woman than I am. Ever since I first saw you at Yarmouth, I've been in love to that extent that I've not known
what I've been about. If you'll ask them at home, they'll tell
you that I've not been able to look after anything about the
place,—not as it should be done. I haven't really. I don't suppose I've opened the wages-book half a dozen times since last
July.'

'And has that been my fault, Mr. Cheesacre?'

'Upon my word, it has. I can't move about anywhere without thinking about you. My mind's made up; I won't stay at
Oileymead unless you will come and be its mistress.'

'Not stay at Oileymead?'

'No, indeed. I'll let the place, and go and travel somewheres.
What's the use of my hanging on there without the woman of
my heart? I couldn't do it, Mrs. Greenow; I couldn't, indeed.
Of course I've got everything there that money can buy,—but
it's all of no use to a man that's in love. Do you know, I've

come quite to despise money and stock, and all that sort of thing. I haven't had my banker's book home these last three months. Only think of that now.'

'But how can I help you, Mr. Cheesacre?'

'Just say one word, and the thing'll be done. Say you'll be my wife? I'll be so good to you. I will, indeed. As for your fortune, I don't care that for it! I'm not like somebody else; it's yourself I want. You shall be my pet, and my poppet, and my dearest little duck all the days of your life.'

'No, Mr. Cheesacre; it cannot be.'

'And why not? Look here, Arabella!' At these words he rose from his chair, and coming immediately before her, went down on both knees so close to her as to prevent the possibility of her escaping from him. There could be no doubt as to the efficacy of the cherry-brandy. There he was, well down on his knees; but he had not got down so low without some little cracking and straining on the part of the gaiters with which his legs were encompassed. He, in his passion, had probably omitted to notice this; but Mrs. Greenow, who was more cool in her present temperament, was painfully aware that he might not be able to rise with ease.

'Mr. Cheesacre, don't make a fool of yourself. Get up,' said she.

'Never, till you have told me that you will be mine!'

'Then you'll remain there for ever, which will be inconvenient. I won't have you take hold of my hand, Mr. Cheesacre. I tell you to have done.' Whereupon his grasp upon her hand was released; but he made no attempt to rise.

'I never saw a man look so much like a fool in my life,' said she. 'If you don't get up, I'll push you over. There; don't you hear? There's somebody coming.'

But Cheesacre, whose senses were less acute than the lady's, did not hear. 'I'll never get up,' said he, 'till you have bid me hope.'

'Bid you play the fiddle. Get away from my knees, at any rate. There;—he'll be in the room now before——'

Cheesacre now did hear a sound of steps, and the door was

opened while he made his first futile attempt to get back to a standing position. The door was opened, and Captain Bellfield entered. 'I beg ten thousand pardons,' said he; 'but as I did not see Jeannette, I ventured to come in. May I venture to congratulate my friend Cheesacre on his success?'

In the meantime Cheesacre had risen; but he had done so slowly, and with evident difficulty. 'I'll trouble you to leave the room, Captain Bellfield,' said he. 'I'm particularly engaged with Mrs. Greenow, as any gentleman might have seen.'

'There wasn't the slightest difficulty in seeing it, old fellow,' said the Captain. 'Shall I wish you joy?'

'I'll trouble you to leave the room, sir,' said Cheesacre, walking up to him.

'Certainly, if Mrs. Greenow will desire me to do so,' said the Captain.

Then Mrs. Greenow felt herself called upon to speak.

'Gentlemen, I must beg that you will not make my drawing-room a place for quarrelling. Captain Bellfield, lest there should be any misconception, I must beg you to understand that the position in which you found Mr. Cheesacre was one altogether of his own seeking. It was not with my consent that he was there.'

'I can easily believe that, Mrs. Greenow,' said the Captain.

'Who cares what you believe, sir?' said Mr. Cheesacre.

'Gentlemen! gentlemen! this is really unkind. Captain Bellfield, I think I had better ask you to withdraw.'

'By all means,' said Mr. Cheesacre.

'As it is absolutely necessary that I should give Mr. Cheesacre a definite answer after what has occurred——'

'Of course,' said Captain Bellfield, preparing to go. 'I'll take another opportunity of paying my respects to you. Perhaps I might be allowed to come this evening?'

To this Mrs. Greenow half assented with an uncertain nod, and then the Captain went. As soon as the door was closed behind his back, Mr. Cheesacre again prepared to throw himself into his former position, but to this Mrs. Greenow decidedly objected. If he were allowed to go down again, there was no knowing what force might be necessary to raise him. 'Mr. Cheesacre,' she said, 'let there be an end to this little farce between us.'

'Farce!' said he, standing with his hand on his heart, and his legs and knickerbockers well displayed.

'It is certainly either a farce or a mistake. If the latter,—and I have been at all to blame,—I ask your pardon most sincerely.'

'But you'll be Mrs. Cheesacre, won't you?'

'No, Mr. Cheesacre; no. One husband is enough for any woman, and mine lies buried at Birmingham.'

'Oh, damn it!' said he, in utter disgust at this further reference to Mr. Greenow. The expression, at such a moment, militated against courtesy; but even Mrs. Greenow herself felt that the poor man had been subjected to provocation.

'Let us part friends,' said she, offering him her hand.

But he turned his back upon her, for there was a something in his eye that he wanted to hide. I believe that he really did love her, and that at this moment he would have taken her, even though he had learned that her fortune was gone.

'Will you not give me your hand,' said she, 'in token that there is no anger between us?'

'Do think about it again—do!' said he. 'If there's anything you like to have changed, I'll change it at once. I'll give up Oileymead altogether, if you don't like being so near the farm-yard. I'll give up anything; so I will. Mrs. Greenow, if you only knew how I've set my heart upon it!' And now, though his back was turned, the whimpering of his voice told plainly that tears were in his eyes.

She was a little touched. No woman would feel disposed to marry a man simply because he cried, and perhaps few women would be less likely to give way to such tenderness than Mrs. Greenow. She understood men and women too well, and had seen too much both of the world's rough side and of its smooth side to fall into such a blunder as that; but she was touched. 'My friend,' she said, putting her hand upon his arm, 'think no more of it.'

75

'But I can't help thinking of it,' said he, almost blubbering in his earnestness.

'No, no, no,' said she, still touching him with her hand. 'Why, Mr. Cheesacre, how can you bring yourself to care for an old woman like me, when so many pretty young ladies would give their eyes to get a kind word from you?'

'I don't want any young lady,' said he.

'There's Charlie Fairstairs, who would make as good a wife as any girl I know.'

'Psha! Charlie Fairstairs, indeed!' The very idea of having such a bride palmed off upon him did something to restore him to his manly courage.

'Or my niece, Kate Vavasor, who has a nice little fortune of her own, and who is as accomplished as she is good-looking.'

'She's nothing to me, Mrs. Greenow.'

'That's because you never asked her to be anything. If I get her to come back to Yarmouth next summer, will you think about it? You want a wife, and you couldn't do better if you searched all England over. It would be so pleasant for us to be such near friends; wouldn't it?' And again she put her hand upon his arm.

'Mrs. Greenow, just at present there's only one woman in the world that I can think of.'

'And that's my niece.'

'And that's yourself. I'm a broken-hearted man,—I am, indeed. I didn't ever think I should feel so much about a thing of the kind—I didn't, really. I hardly know what to do with myself; but I suppose I'd better go back to Oileymead.' He had become so painfully unconscious of his new coat and his knickerbockers that it was impossible not to pity him. 'I shall always hate the place now,' he said,—'always.'

'That will pass away. You'd be as happy as a king there, if you'd take Kate for your queen.'

'And what'll you do, Mrs. Greenow?'

'What shall I do?'—'Yes; what will you do?'

'That is, if you marry Kate? Why, I'll come and stay with you half my time, and nurse the children, as an old grand-aunt should.'

'But about——.' Then he hesitated, and she asked him of what he was thinking.

'You don't mean to take that man Bellfield, do you?'

'Come, Mr. Cheesacre, that's rank jealousy. What right can you have to ask me whether I shall take any man or no man? The chances are that I shall remain as I am till I'm carried to my grave; but I'm not going to give any pledge about it to you or to any one.'

'You don't know that man, Mrs. Greenow; you don't, indeed. I tell it you as your friend. Does not it stand to reason, when he has got nothing in the world, that he must be a beggar? It's all very well saying that when a man is courting a lady, he shouldn't say much about his money; but you won't make me believe that any man will make a good husband who hasn't got a shilling. And for lies, there's no beating him!'

'Why, then, has he been such a friend of yours?'

'Well, because I've been foolish. I took up with him just because he looked pleasant, I suppose.'

'And you want to prevent me from doing the same thing.'

'If you were to marry him, Mrs. Greenow, it's my belief I should do him a mischief; it is, really. I don't think I could stand it;—a mean, skulking beggar! I suppose I'd better go now?'

'Certainly, if that's the way you choose to talk about my friends.'

'Friends, indeed! Well, I won't say any more at present. I suppose if I was to talk for ever it wouldn't be any good?'

'Come and talk to Kate Vavasor for ever, Mr. Cheesacre.'

To this he made no reply, but went forth from the house, and got his gig, and drove himself home to Oileymead, thinking of his disappointment with all the bitterness of a young lover. 'I didn't ever think I should ever care so much about anything,' he said, as he took himself up to bed that night.

That evening Captain Bellfield did call in the Close, as he had said he would do, but he was not admitted. 'Her mistress was very bad with a headache,' Jeannette said.

CHAPTER XLVIII

Preparations for Lady Monk's Party

Early in April, the Easter recess being all over, Lady Monk gave a grand party in London. Lady Monk's town house was in Gloucester Square. It was a large mansion, and Lady Monk's parties in London were known to be very great affairs. She usually gave two or three in the season, and spent a large portion of her time and energy in so arranging matters that her parties should be successful. As this was her special line in life, a failure would have been very distressing to her;—and we may also say very disgraceful, taking into consideration, as we should do in forming our judgment on the subject, the very large sums of Sir Cosmo's money which she spent in this way. But she seldom did fail. She knew how to select her days, so as not to fall foul of other events. It seldom happened that people could not come to her because of a division which occupied all the Members of Parliament, or that they were drawn away by the superior magnitude of some other attraction in the world of fashion. This giving of parties was her business, and she had learned it thoroughly. She worked at it harder than most men work at their trades, and let us hope that the profits were consolatory.

It was generally acknowledged to be the proper thing to go to Lady Monk's parties. There were certain people who were asked, and who went as a matter of course,—people who were by no means on intimate terms with Lady Monk, or with Sir Cosmo; but they were people to have whom was the proper thing, and they were people who understood that to go to Lady Monk's was the proper thing for them. The Duchess of St. Bungay was always there, though she hated Lady Monk, and Lady Monk always abused her; but a card was sent to the Duchess in the same way as the Lord Mayor invites a Cabinet Minister to dinner, even though the one man might believe the other to be a thief. And Mrs. Conway Sparkes was generally there; she went everywhere. Lady Monk did not at all know why Mrs. Conway Sparkes was so favoured by the world; but there was the fact, and she bowed to it. Then there were another set, the members of which were or were not invited, according to circumstances, at the time; and these were the people who were probably the most legitimate recipients of Lady Monk's hospitality. Old family friends of her husband were among the number. Let the Tuftons come in April, and perhaps again in May; then they will not feel their exclusion from that seventh heaven of glory,—the great culminating crush in July. Scores of young ladies who really loved parties belonged to this set. Their mothers and aunts knew Lady Monk's sisters and cousins. They accepted so much of Lady Monk's good things as she vouchsafed them, and were thankful. Then there was another lot, which generally became, especially on that great July occasion, the most numerous of the three. It comprised all those who made strong interest to obtain admittance within her ladyship's house,—who struggled and fought almost with tooth and nail to get invitations. Against these people Lady Monk carried on an internecine war. Had she not done so she would have been swamped by them, and her success would have been at an end; but yet she never dreamed of shutting her doors against them altogether, or of saying boldly that none such should hamper her stair-cases. She knew that she must yield, but her effort was made to yield to as few as might be possible. When she was first told by her factotum in these operations that Mr. Bott wanted to come, she positively declined to have him. When it was afterwards intimated to her that the Duchess of St. Bungay had made a point of it, she sneered at the Duchess, and did not even then yield. But when at last it was brought home to her understanding that Mr. Palliser wished it, and that Mr. Palliser probably would not come himself unless his wishes were gratified, she gave way. She was especially anxious that Lady Glencora should come to her gathering, and she knew that Lady Glencora could not be had without Mr. Palliser.

It was very much desired by her that Lady Glencora should be there. 'Burgo,' said she to her nephew, one morning, 'look here.' Burgo was at the time staying with his aunt, in Glouces-ter Square, much to the annoyance of Sir Cosmo, who had become heartily tired of his nephew. The aunt and the nephew had been closeted together more than once lately, and perhaps they understood each other better now than they had done down at Monkshade. The aunt had handed a little note to Burgo, which he read and then threw back to her. 'You see that she is not afraid of coming,' said Lady Monk.

'I suppose she doesn't think much about it,' said Burgo.

'If that's what you really believe, you'd better give it up. Nothing on earth would justify such a step on your part except a thorough conviction that she is attached to you.'

Burgo looked at the fireplace, almost savagely, and his aunt looked at him very keenly. 'Well,' she said, 'if there's to be an end of it, let there be an end of it.'

'I think I'd better hang myself,' he said.

'Burgo, I will not have you here if you talk to me in that way. I am trying to help you once again; but if you look like that, and talk like that, I will give it up.'

'I think you'd better give it up.'

'Are you becoming cowardly at last? With all your faults I never expected that of you.'

'No; I am not a coward. I'd go out and fight him at two paces' distance with the greatest pleasure in the world.'

'You know that's nonsense, Burgo. It's downright braggadocio. Men do not fight now; nor at any time would a man be called upon to fight, because you simply wanted to take his wife from him. If you had done it, indeed!'

'How am I to do it? I'd do it to-morrow if it depended on me. No one can say that I'm afraid of anybody or of anything.'

'I suppose something in the matter depends on her?'

'I believe she loves me,—if you mean that?'

'Look here, Burgo,' and the considerate aunt gave to the impoverished and ruined nephew such counsel as she, in accordance with her lights, was enabled to bestow. 'I think you were much wronged in that matter. After what had passed I thought that you had a right to claim Lady Glencora as your wife. Mr. Palliser, in my mind, behaved very wrongly in stepping in between you and—you and such a fortune as hers, in that way. He cannot expect that his wife should have any affection for him. There is nobody alive who has a greater horror of anything improper in married women than I have. I have always shown it. When Lady Madeline Madtop left her husband, I would never allow her to come inside my doors again,—though I have no doubt he ill-used her dreadfully, and there was nothing ever proved between her and Colonel Graham. One can't be too particular in such matters. But here, if you,—if you can succeed, you know, I shall always regard the Palliser episode in Lady Glencora's life as a tragical accident. I shall, indeed. Poor dear! It was done exactly as they make nuns of girls in Roman Catholic countries; and as I should think no harm of helping a nun out of her convent, so I should think no harm of helping her now. If you are to say anything to her, I think you might have an opportunity at the party.'

Burgo was still looking at the fireplace; and he sat on, looking and still looking, but he said nothing.

'You can think of what I have said, Burgo,' continued his aunt, meaning that he should get up and go. But he did not go. 'Have you anything more that you wish to say to me?' she asked.

'I've got no money,' said Burgo, still looking at the fire-place.

Lady Glencora's property was worth not less than fifty thousand a year.* He was a young man ambitious of obtaining that almost incredible amount of wealth, and who once had nearly reached it, by means of her love. His present obstacle consisted in his want of a twenty-pound note! 'I've got no money.' The words were growled out rather than spoken, and his eyes were never turned even for a moment towards his aunt's face.

'You've never got any money,' said she, speaking almost with passion.

'How can I help it? I can't make money. If I had a couple of hundred pounds, so that I could take her, I believe that she would go with me. It should not be my fault if she did not. It would have been all right if she had come to Monkshade.'

'I've got no money for you, Burgo. I have not five pounds belonging to me.'

'But you've got——?'

'What?' said Lady Monk, interrupting him sharply.

'Would Cosmo lend it me?' said he, hesitating to go on with that suggestion which he had been about to make. The Cosmo of whom he spoke was not his uncle, but his cousin. No eloquence could have induced his uncle, Sir Cosmo, to lend him another shilling. But the son of the house was a man rich with his own wealth, and Burgo had not taxed him for some years.

'I do not know,' said Lady Monk. 'I never see him. Probably not.'

'It is hard,' said Burgo. 'Fancy that a man should be ruined for two hundred pounds, just at such a moment of his life as this!' He was a man bold by nature, and he did make his proposition. 'You have jewels, aunt;—could you not raise it for me? I would redeem them with the very first money that I got.'

Lady Monk rose in a passion when the suggestion was first made, but before the interview was over she had promised that she would endeavour to do something in the way of raising money for him yet once again. He was her favourite nephew, and the same almost to her as a child of her own. With one of her own children indeed she had quarrelled, and of the other, a married daughter, she rarely saw much. Such love as she had to give she gave to Burgo, and she promised him the money though she knew that she must raise it by some villanous falsehood to her husband.

On the same morning Lady Glencora went to Queen Anne Street with the purpose of inducing Alice to go to Lady Monk's party; but Alice would not accede to the proposition, though Lady Glencora pressed it with all her eloquence. 'I don't know her,' said Alice.

'My dear,' said Lady Glencora, 'that's absurd. Half the people there won't know her.'

'But they know her set, or know her friends,—or, at any rate, will meet their own friends at her house. I should only bother you, and should not in the least gratify myself.'

'The fact is, everybody will go who can, and I should have no sort of trouble in getting a card for you. Indeed I should simply write a note and say I meant to bring you.'

'Pray don't do any such thing, for I certainly shall not go. I can't conceive why you should wish it.'

'Mr. Fitzgerald will be there,' said Lady Glencora, altering her voice altogether, and speaking in that low tone with which she used to win Alice's heart down at Matching. She was sitting close over the fire, leaning low, holding up her little hands as a screen to her face, and looking at her companion earnestly. 'I'm sure that he will be there, though nobody has told me.'

'That may be a reason for your staying away,' said Alice, slowly, 'but hardly a reason for my going with you.'

Lady Glencora would not condescend to tell her friend in so many words that she wanted her protection. She could not bring herself to say that, though she wished it to be understood. 'Ah! I thought you would have gone,' said she.

'It would be contrary to all my habits,' said Alice. 'I never go to people's houses when I don't know them. It's a kind of society which I don't like. Pray do not ask me.'

'Oh! very well. If it must be so, I won't press it.' Lady Glencora had moved the position of one of her hands so as to get it to her pocket, and there had grasped a letter, which she still carried; but when Alice said those last cold words, 'Pray do not ask me,' she released the grasp, and left the letter where it was. 'I suppose he won't bite me, at any rate,' she said, and she assumed that look of childish drollery which she would sometimes put on, almost with a grimace, but still with so much prettiness that no one who saw her would regret it.

'He certainly can't bite you, if you will not let him.'

'Do you know, Alice, though they all say that Plantagenet is one of the wisest men in London, I sometimes think that he is one of the greatest fools. Soon after we came to town I told him that we had better not go to that woman's house. Of course he understood me. He simply said that he wished that I should do so. "I hate anything out of the way," he said. "There can be no reason why my wife should not go to Lady Monk's house as well as to any other." There was an end of it, you know, as far as anything I could do was concerned. But there wasn't an end of it with him. He insists that I shall go, but he sends my duenna with me. Dear Mrs. Marsham is to be there!'

'She'll do you no harm, I suppose?'

'I'm not so sure of that, Alice. In the first place, one doesn't like to be followed everywhere by a policeman, even though one isn't going to pick a pocket. And then, the devil is so strong within me, that I should like to dodge the policeman. I can fancy a woman being driven to do wrong simply by a desire to show her policeman that she can be too many for him.'

'Glencora, you make me so wretched when you talk like that.'

'Will you go with me, then, so that I may have a policeman of my own choosing? He asked me if I would mind taking Mrs. Marsham with me in my carriage. So I up and spoke, very boldly, like the proud young porter,* and told him I would not; and when he asked why not, I said that I preferred taking a friend of my own,—a young friend, I said, and I then named you or my cousin, Lady Jane. I told him I should bring one or the other.'

'And was he angry?'

'No; he took it very quietly,—saying something, in his calm way, about hoping that I should get over a prejudice against one of his earliest and dearest friends. He twits at me because I don't understand Parliament and the British Constitution, but I know more of them than he does about a woman. You are quite sure you won't go, then?' Alice hesitated a moment. 'Do,' said Lady Glencora; and there was an amount of persuasion in her accent which should, I think, have overcome her cousin's scruples.

'It is against the whole tenor of my life's way,'* she said. 'And, Glencora, I am not happy myself. I am not fit for parties. I sometimes think that I shall never go into society again.'

'That's nonsense, you know.'

'I suppose it is, but I cannot go now. I would if I really thought——'

'Oh, very well,' said Lady Glencora, interrupting her. 'I suppose I shall get through it. If he asks me to dance, I shall stand up with him, just as though I had never seen him before.' Then she remembered the letter in her pocket,—remembered that at this moment she bore about with her a written proposition from this man to go off with him and leave her husband's house. She had intended to show it to Alice on this occasion; but as Alice had refused her request, she was glad that she had not done so. 'You'll come to me the morning after,' said Lady Glencora, as she went. This Alice promised to do; and then she was left alone.

Alice regretted,—regretted deeply that she had not consented to go with her cousin. After all, of what importance had been her objection when compared with the cause for which her presence had been desired? Doubtless she would have been uncomfortable at Lady Monk's house; but could she not have borne some hour or two of discomfort on her friend's behalf? But, in truth, it was only after Lady Glencora had left her that she began to understand the subject fully, and to feel that she might possibly have been of service in a great danger. But it was too late now. Then she strove to comfort herself with the reflection that a casual meeting at an evening party in London could not be perilous in the same degree as a prolonged sojourn together in a country-house.

CHAPTER XLIX

How Lady Glencora went to Lady Monk's Party

LADY MONK's house in Gloucester Square was admirably well adapted for the giving of parties. It was a large house, and seemed to the eyes of guests to be much larger than it was. The hall was spacious, and the stairs went up in the centre, facing you as you entered the inner hall. Round the top of the stairs there was a broad gallery, with an ornamented railing, and from this opened the doors into the three reception-rooms. There were two on the right, the larger of which looked out backwards, and these two were connected by an archway, as though made for folding-doors; but the doors, I believe, never were there. Fronting the top of the staircase there was a smaller room, looking out backwards, very prettily furnished, and much used by Lady Monk when alone. It was here that Burgo had held that conference with his aunt of which mention has been made. Below stairs there was the great dining-room, in which, on these occasions, a huge buffet was erected for refreshments,—what I may call a masculine buffet, as it was attended by butlers and men in livery,—and there was a smaller room looking out into the square, in which there was a feminine buttery for the dispensing of tea and such like smaller good things, and from which female aid could be attained for the arrangement or mending of dresses in a further sanctum within it. For such purposes as that now on foot the house was most commodious. Lady Monk, on these occasions, was moved by a noble ambition to do something different from that done by her neighbours in similar circumstances, and therefore she never came forward to receive her guests. She ensconced herself, early in the evening, in that room at the head of the stairs, and there they who chose to see her made their way up to her, and spoke their little speeches. They who thought her to be a great woman,—and many people did think her to be great,—were wont to declare that she never forgot those who did come, or those who did not. And even they who desired to describe her as little,—for even Lady Monk had enemies,—would hint that though she never came out of the room, she would rise from her chair and make a step towards the door whenever any name very high in fashionable life greeted her ears. So that a mighty Cabinet Minister, or a duchess in great repute, or any special wonder of the season, could not fail of entering her precincts and being seen there for a few moments. It would, of course, happen that the doorway of her chamber would become blocked; but there were precautions taken to avoid this inconvenience as far as possible, and one man in livery was employed to go backwards and forwards between his mistress and the outer world, so as to keep the thread of a passage open.

But though Lady Monk was in this way enabled to rest herself during her labours, there was much in her night's work which was not altogether exhilarating. Ladies would come into her small room and sit there by the hour, with whom she had not the slightest wish to hold conversation. The Duchess of St. Bungay would always be there,—so that there was a special seat in one corner of the room which was called the Duchess' stool. 'I shouldn't care a straw about her,' Lady Monk had been heard to complain, 'if she would talk to anybody. But nobody will talk to her, and then she listens to everything.'

There had been another word or two between Burgo Fitzgerald and his aunt before the evening came, a word or two in the speaking of which she had found some difficulty. She was prepared with the money,—with that two hundred pounds for which he had asked,—obtained with what wiles, and lies, and baseness of subterfuge I need not stop here to describe. But she was by no means willing to give this over into her nephew's hands without security. She was willing to advance him this money; she had been willing even to go through unusual dirt to get it for him; but she was desirous that he should have it only for a certain purpose. How could she bind him down to spend it as she would have it spent? Could she undertake to hand it to him as soon as Lady Glencora should be in his power? Even though she could have brought herself to say as much,—and I think she might almost have done so after what she had said,—she could not have carried out such a plan. In that case the want would be instant, and the action must be rapid. She therefore had no alternative but to entrust him with the bank-notes at once. 'Burgo,' she said, 'if I find that you deceive me now, I will never trust you again.' 'All right,' said Burgo, as he barely counted the money before he thrust it into his breast-pocket. 'It is lent to you for a certain purpose, should you happen to want it,' she said, solemnly. 'I do happen to want it very much,' he answered. She did not dare to say more; but as her nephew turned away from her with a step that was quite light in its gaiety, she almost felt that she was already cozened. Let Burgo's troubles be as heavy as they might be, there was something to him ecstatic in the touch of ready money which always cured them for the moment.

On the morning of Lady Monk's party a few very uncomfortable words passed between Mr. Palliser and his wife.

'Your cousin is not going, then?' said he.

'Alice is not going.'

'Then you can give Mrs. Marsham a seat in your carriage?'

'Impossible, Plantagenet. I thought I had told you that I had promised my cousin Jane.'

'But you can take three.'

'Indeed I can't,—unless you would like me to sit out with the coachman.'

There was something in this,—a tone of loudness, a touch of what he called to himself vulgarity,—which made him very angry. So he turned away from her, and looked as black as a thunder-cloud.

'You must know, Plantagenet,' she went on, 'that it is impossible for three women dressed to go out in one carriage. I am sure you wouldn't like to see me afterwards if I had been one of them.'

'You need not have said anything to Lady Jane when Miss Vavasor refused. I had asked you before that.'

'And I had told you that I liked going with young women, and not with old ones. That's the long and the short of it.'

'Glencora, I wish you would not use such expressions.'

'What! not the long and the short? It's good English. Quite as good as Mr. Bott's, when he said in the House the other night that the Government kept their accounts in a higgledy-piggledy way. You see, I have been studying the debates, and you shouldn't be angry with me.'

'I am not angry with you. You speak like a child to say so. Then, I suppose, the carriage must go for Mrs. Marsham after it has taken you?'

'It shall go before. Jane will not be in a hurry, and I am sure I shall not.'

'She will think you very uncivil; that is all. I told her that she could go with you when I heard that Miss Vavasor was not to be there.'

'Then, Plantagenet, you shouldn't have told her so, and that's the long——; but I mustn't say that. The truth is this, if you give me any orders I'll obey them,—as far as I can. If I can't I'll say so. But if I'm left to go by my own judgment, it's not fair that I should be scolded afterwards.'

'I have never scolded you.'

'Yes, you have. You have told me that I was uncivil.'

'I said that she would think you so.'

'Then, if it's only what she thinks, I don't care two straws about it. She may have the carriage to herself if she likes, but she shan't have me in it,—not unless I'm ordered to go. I don't like her, and I won't pretend to like her. My belief is that she follows me about to tell you if she thinks that I do wrong.'

'Glencora!'

'And that odious baboon with the red bristles does the same thing,—only he goes to her because he does'nt dare to go to you.'

Plantagenet Palliser was struck wild with dismay. He understood well who it was whom his wife intended to describe; but that she should have spoken of any man as a baboon with red bristles, was terrible to his mind! He was beginning to think that he hardly knew how to manage his wife. And the picture she had drawn was very distressing to him. She had no mother; neither had he; and he had wished that Mrs. Marsham should give to her some of that matronly assistance and guidance which a mother does give to her young married daughter. It was true, too, as he knew, that a word or two as to some socially domestic matters had filtered through to him from Mr. Bott, down at Matching Priory, but only in such a way as to enable him to see what counsel it was needful that he should give. As for espionage over his wife,—no man could despise it more than he did! No man would be less willing to resort to it! And now his wife was accusing him of keeping spies, both male and female.

'Glencora!' he said again; and then he stopped, not knowing what to say to her.

'Well, my dear, it's better you should know at once what I feel about it. I don't suppose I'm very good; indeed I dare say I'm bad enough, but these people about me won't make me any better. The duennas don't make the Spanish ladies worth much.'

'Duennas!' After that, Lady Glencora sat herself down, and Mr. Palliser stood for some moments looking at her.

It ended in his making her a long speech, in which he said a good deal of his own justice and forbearance, and something also of her frivolity and childishness. He told her that his only complaint of her was that she was too young, and, as he did so, she made a little grimace,—not to him, but to herself, as though saying to herself that that was all he knew about it. He did not notice it, or, if he did, his notice did not stop his eloquence. He assured her that he was far from keeping any watch over her, and declared that she had altogether mistaken Mrs. Marsham's character. Then there was another little grimace. 'There's somebody has mistaken it worse than I have,' the grimace said. Of the bristly baboon he condescended to say nothing, and he wound up by giving her a cold kiss, and saying that he would meet her at Lady Monk's.

When the evening came,—or rather the night,—the carriage went first for Mrs. Marsham, and having deposited her at Lady Monk's, went back to Park Lane for Lady Glencora. Then she had herself driven to St. James's Square, to pick up Lady Jane, so that altogether the coachman and horses did not have a good time of it. 'I wish he'd keep a separate carriage for her,' Lady Glencora said to her cousin Jane,—having perceived that her servants were not in a good humour. 'That would be expensive,' said Lady Jane. 'Yes, it would be expensive,' said Lady Glencora. She would not condescend to make any remark as to the non-importance of such expense to a man so wealthy as her husband, knowing that his wealth was, in fact, hers. Never to him or to any other,—not even to herself, —had she hinted that much was due to her because she had been magnificent as an heiress. There were many things about this woman that were not altogether what a husband might wish. She was not softly delicate in all her ways; but in disposition and temper she was altogether generous. I do not know that she was at all points a lady, but had Fate so willed it she would have been a thorough gentleman.

Mrs. Marsham was by no means satisfied with the way in which she was treated. She would not have cared to go at all to Lady Monk's party had she supposed that she would have to make her entry there alone. With Lady Glencora she would have seemed to receive some of that homage which would certainly have been paid to her companion. The carriage called, moreover, before she was fully ready, and the footman, as he stood at the door to hand her in, had been very sulky. She understood it all. She knew that Lady Glencora had positively declined her companionship; and if she resolved to be revenged, such resolution on her part was only natural. When she reached Lady Monk's house, she had to make her way up stairs all alone. The servants called her Mrs. Marsh, and under that name she got passed on into the front drawing-room. There she sat down, not having seen Lady Monk, and meditated over her injuries.

It was past eleven before Lady Glencora arrived, and Burgo Fitzgerald had begun to think that his evil stars intended that he should never see her again. He had been wickedly baulked at Monkshade, by what influence he had never yet ascertained; and now he thought that the same influence must be at work to keep her again away from his aunt's house. He had settled in his mind no accurate plan of a campaign; he had in his thoughts no fixed arrangement by which he might do the thing which he meditated. He had attempted to make some such plan; but, as is the case with all men to whom thinking is an unusual operation, concluded at last that he had better leave it to the course of events. It was, however, obviously necessary that he should see Lady Glencora before the course of events could be made to do anything for him. He had written to her, making his proposition in bold terms, and he felt that if she were utterly decided against him, her anger at his suggestion, or at least her refusal, would have been made known to him in some way. Silence did not absolutely give consent, but it seemed to show that consent was not impossible. From ten o'clock to past eleven he stood about on the staircase of his aunt's house, waiting for the name which he was desirous of hearing, and which he almost feared to hear. Men spoke to him, and women also, but he hardly answered. His aunt once called him into her room, and with a cautionary frown on her brow, bade him go and dance. 'Don't look so dreadfully pre-occupied,' she said to him in a whisper. But he shook his head at her, almost savagely, and went away, and did not dance. Dance! How was he to dance with such an enterprise as that upon his mind? Even to Burgo Fitzgerald the task of running away with another man's wife had in it something which prevented dancing. Lady Monk was older, and was able to regulate her feelings with more exactness. But Burgo, though he could not dance, went down into the dining-room and drank. He took a large beer-glass full of champagne, and soon after that another. The drink did not flush his cheeks, or make his fore-head red, or bring out the sweat-drops on his brow, as it does with some men; but it added a peculiar brightness to his blue eyes. It was by the light of his eyes that men knew when Burgo had been drinking.

At last, while he was still in the supper-room, he heard Lady Glencora's name announced. He had already seen Mr. Palliser come in and make his way upstairs some quarter of an hour before; but as to that he was indifferent. He had known that the husband was to be there. When the long-expected name reached his ears, his heart seemed to jump within him. What, on the spur of the moment, should he do? As he had resolved that he would be doing,—that something should be done, let it be what it might,—he hurried to the dining-room door, and was just in time to see and be seen as Lady Glencora was passing up the stairs. She was just above him as he got himself out into the hall, so that he could not absolutely greet her with his hand; but he looked up at her, and caught her eye. He looked up, and moved his hand to her in token of salutation. She looked down at him, and the expression of her face altered visibly as her glance met his. She barely bowed to him,— with her eyes rather than with her head, but he flattered him-self that there was, at any rate, no anger in her countenance. How beautiful he was as he gazed up at her, leaning against the wall as he stood, and watching her as she made her slow way up the stairs! She felt that his eyes were on her, and where the stairs turned she could not restrain herself from one other glance. As her eyes fell on his again, his mouth opened, and she fancied that she could hear the faint sigh that he uttered. It was a glorious mouth, such as the old sculptors gave to their marble gods! And Burgo, if it was so that he had not heart enough to love truly, could look as though he loved. It was not in him deceit,—or what men call acting. The expression came to him naturally, though it expressed so much more than there was within; as strong words come to some men who have no knowledge that they are speaking strongly. At

this moment Burgo Fitzgerald looked as though it were possible that he might die of love.

Lady Glencora was met at the top of the stairs by Lady
Monk, who came out to her, almost into the gallery, with her
sweetest smile,—so that the newly-arrived guest, of course,
entered into the small room. There sat the Duchess of St.
Bungay on her stool in the corner, and there, next to the
Duchess, but at the moment engaged in no conversation, stood
Mr. Bott. There was another lady there, who stood very high
in the world, and whom Lady Monk was very glad to welcome
—the young Marchioness of Hartletop.* She was in slight
mourning; for her father-in-law, the late Marquis, had died
not yet quite six months since. Very beautiful she was, and
one whose presence at their houses ladies and gentlemen prized
alike. She never said silly things, like the Duchess, never was
troublesome as to people's conduct to her, was always gracious, yet was never led away into intimacies, was without
peer the best-dressed woman in London, and yet gave herself
no airs;—and then she was so exquisitely beautiful. Her smile
was loveliness itself. There were, indeed, people who said that
it meant nothing; but then, what should the smile of a young
married woman mean? She had not been born in the purple,
like Lady Glencora, her father being a country clergyman who
had never reached a higher grade than that of an archdeacon;
but she knew the ways of high life, and what an exigeant husband would demand of her, much better than poor Glencora.
She would have spoken of no man as a baboon with a bristly
beard. She never talked of the long and the short of it. She did
not wander out o' nights in winter among the ruins. She made
no fast friendship with ladies whom her lord did not like. She
had once, indeed, been approached by a lover since she had
been married,—Mr. Palliser himself having been the offender,
—but she had turned the affair to infinite credit and profit, had
gained her husband's closest confidence by telling him of it all,
had yet not brought on any hostile collision, and had even dismissed her lover without annoying him. But then Lady Hartletop was a miracle of a woman!

Lady Glencora was no miracle. Though born in the purple, she was made of ordinary flesh and blood, and as she entered Lady Monk's little room, hardly knew how to recover herself sufficiently for the purposes of ordinary conversation. 'Dear Lady Glencora, do come in for a moment to my den. We were so sorry not to have you at Monkshade. We heard such terrible things about your health.' Lady Glencora said that it was only a cold,—a bad cold. 'Oh, yes; we heard,—something about moonlight and ruins. So like you, you know. I love that sort of thing, above all people; but it doesn't do; does it? Circumstances are so exacting. I think you know Lady Hartletop;— and there's the Duchess of St. Bungay. Mr. Palliser was here five minutes since.' Then Lady Monk was obliged to get to her door again, and Lady Glencora found herself standing close to Lady Hartletop.

'We saw Mr. Palliser just pass through,' said Lady Hartletop, who was able to meet and speak of the man who had dared to approach her with his love, without the slightest nervousness.

'Yes; he said he should be here,' said Lady Glencora.

'There's a great crowd,' said Lady Hartletop. 'I didn't think London was so full.'

'Very great,' said Lady Glencora, and then they had said to each other all that society required. Lady Glencora, as we know, could talk with imprudent vehemence by the hour together if she liked her companion; but the other lady seldom committed herself by more words than she had uttered now,— unless it was to her tirewoman.

'How *very* well you *are* looking!' said the Duchess. 'And I heard you had been *so* ill.' Of that midnight escapade among the ruins it was fated that Lady Glencora should never hear the last.

'How d'ye do, Lady Glencower?' sounded in her ear, and there was a great red paw stuck out for her to take. But after what had passed between Lady Glencora and her husband to-day about Mr. Bott, she was determined that she would not take Mr. Bott's hand.

'How are you, Mr. Bott?' she said. 'I think I'll look for Mr. Palliser in the back room.'

'Dear Lady Glencora,' whispered the Duchess, in an ecstasy of agony. Lady Glencora turned and bowed her head to her stout friend. 'Do let me go away with you. There's that woman, Mrs. Conway Sparkes, coming, and you know how I hate her.' She had nothing to do but to take the Duchess under her wing, and they passed into the large room together. It is, I think, more than probable that Mrs. Conway Sparkes had been brought in by Lady Monk as the only way of removing the Duchess from her stool.

Just within the dancing-room Lady Glencora found her husband, standing in a corner, looking as though he were making calculations.

'I'm going away,' said he, coming up to her. 'I only just came because I said I would. Shall you be late?'

'Oh, no; I suppose not.'

'Shall you dance?'

'Perhaps once,—just to show that I'm not an old woman.'

'Don't heat yourself. Good-bye.' Then he went, and in the crush of the doorway he passed Burgo Fitzgerald, whose eye was intently fixed upon his wife. He looked at Burgo, and some thought of that young man's former hopes flashed across his mind,—some remembrance, too, of a caution that had been whispered to him; but for no moment did a suspicion come to him that he ought to stop and watch by his wife.

CHAPTER L

How Lady Glencora came back from Lady Monk's Party

BURGO FITZGERALD remained for a minute or two leaning where we last saw him,—against the dining-room wall at the bottom of the staircase; and as he did so some thoughts that were almost solemn passed across his mind. This thing that he was about to do, or to attempt,—was it in itself a good thing, and would it be good for her whom he pretended to

love? What would be her future if she consented now to go
with him, and to divide herself from her husband? Of his own
future he thought not at all. He had never done so. Even when
he had first found himself attracted by the reputation of her
wealth, he cannot be said to have looked forward in any prudential way to coming years. His desire to put himself in possession of so magnificent a fortune had simply prompted him, as
he might have been prompted to play for a high stake at a
gaming-table. But now, during these moments, he did think
a little of her. Would she be happy, simply because he loved
her, when all women should cease to acknowledge her; when
men would regard her as one degraded and dishonoured; when
society should be closed against her; when she would be driven
to live loudly because the softness and graces of quiet life would
be denied to her? Burgo knew well what must be the nature
of such a woman's life in such circumstances. Would Glencora
be happy with him while living such a life simply because he
loved her? And, under such circumstances, was it likely that
he would continue to love her? Did he not know himself to be
the most inconstant of men, and the least trustworthy? Leaning thus against the wall at the bottom of the stairs he did ask
himself all these questions with something of true feeling about
his heart, and almost persuaded himself that he had better take
his hat and wander forth anywhere into the streets. It mattered
little what might become of himself. If he could drink himself
out of the world, it might be an end of things that would be
not altogether undesirable.

But then the remembrance of his aunt's two hundred pounds
came upon him, which money he even now had about him on
his person, and a certain idea of honour told him that he was
bound to do that for which the money had been given to him.
As to telling his aunt that he had changed his mind, and, therefore, refunding the money—no such thought as that was possible to him! To give back two hundred pounds entire,—two
hundred pounds which were already within his clutches, was
not within the compass of Burgo's generosity. Remembering
the cash, he told himself that hesitation was no longer possible

to him. So he gathered himself up, stretched his hands over his head, uttered a sigh that was audible to all around him, and took himself upstairs.

He looked in at his aunt's room, and then he saw her and was seen by her. 'Well, Burgo,' she said, with her sweetest smile, 'have you been dancing?' He turned away from her without answering her, muttering something between his teeth about a cold-blooded Jezebel,—which, if she had heard it, would have made her think him the most ungrateful of men. But she did not hear him, and smiled still as he went away, saying something to Mrs. Conway Sparkes as to the great change for the better which had taken place in her nephew's conduct.

'There's no knowing who may not reform,' said Mrs. Sparkes, with an emphasis which seemed to Lady Monk to be almost uncourteous.

Burgo made his way first into the front room and then into the larger room where the dancing was in progress, and there he saw Lady Glencora standing up in a quadrille with the Marquis of Hartletop. Lord Hartletop was a man not much more given to conversation than his wife, and Lady Glencora seemed to go through her work with very little gratification either in the dancing or in the society of her partner. She was simply standing up to dance, because, as she had told Mr. Palliser, ladies of her age generally do stand up on such occasions. Burgo watched her as she crossed and re-crossed the room, and at last she was aware of his presence. It made no change in her, except that she became even somewhat less animated than she had been before. She would not seem to see him, nor would she allow herself to be driven into a pretence of a conversation with her partner because he was there. 'I will go up to her at once, and ask her to waltz,' Burgo said to himself, as soon as the last figure of the quadrille was in action. 'Why should I not ask her as well as any other woman?' Then the music ceased, and after a minute's interval Lord Hartletop took away his partner on his arm into another room. Burgo, who had been standing near the door, followed them at once. The crowd was great, so that he could not get near them or even keep them in sight, but he was aware of the way in which they were going.

It was five minutes after this when he again saw her, and then she was seated on a cane bench in the gallery, and an old woman was standing close to her, talking to her. It was Mrs. Marsham cautioning her against some petty imprudence, and Lady Glencora was telling that lady that she needed no such advice, in words almost as curt as those I have used. Lord Hartletop had left her, feeling that, as far as that was concerned, he had done his duty for the night. Burgo knew nothing of Mrs. Marsham,—had never seen her before, and was quite unaware that she had any special connection with Mr. Palliser. It was impossible, he thought, to find Lady Glencora in a better position for his purpose, so he made his way up to her through the crowd, and muttering some slight inaudible word, offered her his hand.

'That will do very well, thank you, Mrs. Marsham,' Lady Glencora said at this moment. 'Pray, do not trouble yourself,' and then she gave her hand to Fitzgerald. Mrs. Marsham, though unknown to him, knew with quite sufficient accuracy who he was, and all his history, as far as it concerned her friend's wife. She had learned the whole story of the loves of Burgo and Lady Glencora. Though Mr. Palliser had never mentioned that man's name to her, she was well aware that her duty as a duenna would make it expedient that she should keep a doubly wary eye upon him should he come near the sheepfold. And there he was, close to them, almost leaning over them, with the hand of his late lady love,—the hand of Mr. Palliser's wife,—within his own! How Lady Glencora might have carried herself at this moment had Mrs. Marsham not been there, it is bootless now to surmise; but it may be well understood that under Mrs. Marsham's immediate eye all her resolution would be in Burgo's favour. She looked at him softly and kindly, and though she uttered no articulate word, her countenance seemed to show that the meeting was not unpleasant to her.

'Will you waltz?' said Burgo,—asking it not at all as though it were a special favour,—asking it exactly as he might have done had they been in the habit of dancing with each other every other night for the last three months.

'I don't think Lady Glencora will waltz to-night,' said Mrs. Marsham, very stiffly. She certainly did not know her business as a duenna, or else the enormity of Burgo's proposition had struck her so forcibly as to take away from her all her presence of mind. Otherwise, she must have been aware that such an answer from her would surely drive her friend's wife into open hostility.

'And why not, Mrs. Marsham?' said Lady Glencora rising from her seat. 'Why shouldn't I waltz to-night? I rather think I shall, the more especially as Mr. Fitzgerald waltzes very well.' Thereupon she put her hand upon Burgo's arm.

Mrs. Marsham made still a little effort,—a little effort that was probably involuntary. She put out her hand, and laid it on Lady Glencora's left shoulder, looking into her face as she did so with all the severity of caution of which she was mistress. Lady Glencora shook her duenna off angrily. Whether she would put her fate into the hands of this man who was now touching her, or whether she would not, she had not as yet decided; but of this she was very sure, that nothing said or done by Mrs. Marsham should have any effect in restraining her.

What could Mrs. Marsham do? Mr. Palliser was gone. Some rumour of that proposed visit to Monkshade, and the way in which it had been prevented, had reached her ear. Some whispers had come to her that Fitzgerald still dared to love, as married, the woman whom he had loved before she was married. There was a rumour about that he still had some hope. Mrs. Marsham had never believed that Mr. Palliser's wife would really be false to her vows. It was not in fear of any such catastrophe as a positive elopement that she had taken upon herself the duty of duenna. Lady Glencora would, no doubt, require to be pressed down into that decent mould which it would become the wife of a Mr. Palliser to assume as her form; and this pressing down, and this moulding, Mrs. Marsham thought that she could accomplish. It had not hither-to occurred to her that she might be required to guard Mr. Palliser from positive dishonour; but now—now she hardly

knew what to think about it. What should she do? To whom should she go? And then she saw Mr. Bott looming large before her on the top of the staircase.

In the meantime Lady Glencora went off towards the dan-cers, leaning on Burgo's arm. 'Who is that woman?' said Burgo. They were the first words he spoke to her, though since he had last seen her he had written to her that letter which even now she carried about her. His voice in her ears sounded as it used to sound when their intimacy had been close, and questions such as that he had asked were common between them. And her answer was of the same nature. 'Oh, such an odious woman!' she said. 'Her name is Mrs. Marsham; she is my bête noire.' And then they were actually dancing, whirling round the room together, before a word had been said of that which was Burgo's settled purpose, and which at some moments was her settled purpose also.

Burgo waltzed excellently, and in old days, before her marriage, Lady Glencora had been passionately fond of dancing. She seemed to give herself up to it now as though the old days had come back to her. Lady Monk, creeping to the intermediate door between her den and the dancing-room, looked in on them, and then crept back again. Mrs. Marsham and Mr. Bott standing together just inside the other door, near to the staircase, looked on also—in horror.

'He shouldn't have gone away and left her,' said Mr. Bott, almost hoarsely.

'But who could have thought it?' said Mrs. Marsham. 'I'm sure I didn't.'

'I suppose you'd better tell him?' said Mr. Bott.

'But I don't know where to find him,' said Mrs. Marsham.

'I didn't mean now at once,' said Mr. Bott;—and then he added, 'Do you think it is as bad as that?'

'I don't know what to think,' said Mrs. Marsham.

The waltzers went on till they were stopped by want of breath. 'I am so much out of practice,' said Lady Glencora; 'I didn't think—I should have been able—to dance at all.' Then she put up her face, and slightly opened her mouth, and stretched her nostrils,—as ladies do as well as horses when the running has been severe and they want air.

'You'll take another turn,' said he.

'Presently,' said she, beginning to have some thought in her mind as to whether Mrs. Marsham was watching her. Then there was a little pause, after which he spoke in an altered voice.

'Does it put you in mind of old days?' said he.

It was, of course, necessary for him that he should bring her to some thought of the truth. It was all very sweet, that dancing with her, as they used to dance, without any question as to the reason why it was so; that sudden falling into the old habits, as though everything between this night and the former nights had been a dream; but this would not further his views. The opportunity had come to him which he must use, if he intended ever to use such opportunity. There was the two hundred pounds in his pocket, which he did not intend to give back. 'Does it put you in mind of "old days?"' he said.

The words roused her from her sleep at once, and dissipated her dream. The facts all rushed upon her in an instant; the letter in her pocket; the request which she had made to Alice, that Alice might be induced to guard her from this danger; the words which her husband had spoken to her in the morning, and her anger against him in that he had subjected her to the eyes of a Mrs. Marsham; her own unsettled mind—quite unsettled whether it would be best for her to go or to stay! It all came upon her now at the first word of tenderness which Burgo spoke to her.

It has often been said of woman that she who doubts is lost, —so often that they who say it now, say it simply because others have said it before them, never thinking whether or no there be any truth in the proverb. But they who have said so, thinking of their words as they were uttered, have known but little of women. Women doubt every day, who solve their doubts at last on the right side, driven to do so, some by fear, more by conscience, but most of them by that half-prudential, half-unconscious knowledge of what is fitting, useful, and best under the circumstances, which rarely deserts either men or women till they have brought themselves to the Burgo Fitzgerald state of recklessness. Men when they have fallen even to that, will still keep up some outward show towards the world; but women in this condition defy the world, and declare themselves to be children of perdition. Lady Glencora was doubting sorely; but, though doubting, she was not as yet lost.

'Does it put you in mind of old days?' said Burgo.

She was driven to answer, and she knew that much would be decided by the way in which she might now speak. 'You must not talk of that,' she said, very softly.

'May I not?' And now his tongue was unloosed, so that he began to speak quickly. 'May I not? And why not? They were happy days,—so happy! Were not you happy when you thought——? Ah, dear! I suppose it is best not even to think of them?'

'Much the best.'

'Only it is impossible. I wish I knew the inside of your heart, Cora, so that I could see what it is that you really wish.'

In the old days he had always called her Cora, and now the name came from his lips upon her ears as a thing of custom, causing no surprise. They were standing back, behind the circle, almost in a corner, and Burgo knew well how to speak at such moments so that his words should be audible to none but her whom he addressed.

'You should not have come to me at all,' she said.

'And why not? Who has a better right to come to you? Who has ever loved you as I have done? Cora, did you get my letter?'

'Come and dance,' she said; 'I see a pair of eyes looking at us.' The pair of eyes which Lady Glencora saw were in the possession of Mr. Bott, who was standing alone, leaning against the side of the doorway, every now and then raising his heels from the ground, so that he might look down upon the sinners as from a vantage ground. He was quite alone. Mrs. Marsham had left him, and had gotten herself away in Lady Glencora's own carriage to Park Lane, in order that she might find Mr. Palliser there, if by chance he should be at home.

'Won't it be making mischief?' Mrs. Marsham had said when Mr. Bott had suggested this line of conduct.

'There'll be worse mischief if you don't,' Mr. Bott had answered. 'He can come back, and then he can do as he likes. I'll keep my eyes upon them.' And so he did keep his eyes upon them.

Again they went round the room,—or that small portion of the room which the invading crowd had left to the dancers,—as though they were enjoying themselves thoroughly, and in all innocence. But there were others besides Mr. Bott who looked on and wondered. The Duchess of St. Bungay saw it, and shook her head sorrowing,—for the Duchess was good at heart. Mrs. Conway Sparkes saw it, and drank it down with keen appetite,—as a thirsty man with a longing for wine will drink champagne,—for Mrs. Conway Sparkes was not good at heart. Lady Hartletop saw it, and just raised her eyebrows. It was nothing to her. She liked to know what was going on, as such knowledge was sometimes useful; but, as for heart,— what she had was, in such a matter, neither good nor bad. Her blood circulated with its ordinary precision, and, in that respect, no woman ever had a better heart. Lady Monk saw it, and a frown gathered on her brow. 'The fool!' she said to herself. She knew that Burgo would not help his success by drawing down the eyes of all her guests upon his attempt. In the meantime Mr. Bott stood there, mounting still higher on his toes, straightening his back against the wall.

'Did you get my letter?' Burgo said again, as soon as a moment's pause gave him breath to speak. She did not answer him. Perhaps her breath did not return to her as rapidly as his. But, of course, he knew that she had received it. She would have quickly signified to him that no letter from him had come to her hands had it not reached her. 'Let us go out upon the stairs,' he said, 'for I must speak to you. Oh, if you could know what I suffered when you did not come to Monkshade! Why did you not come?'

'I wish I had not come here,' she said.

'Because you have seen me? That, at any rate, is not kind of you.'

They were now making their way slowly down the stairs, in the crowd, towards the supper-room. All the world was now intent on food and drink, and they were only doing as others did. Lady Glencora was not thinking where she went, but, glancing upwards, as she stood for a moment wedged upon the stairs, her eyes met those of Mr. Bott. 'A man that can treat me like that deserves that I should leave him.' That was the thought that crossed her mind at the moment.

'I'll get you some champagne with water in it,' said Burgo. 'I know that is what you like.'

'Do not get me anything,' she said. They had now got into

105

the room, and had therefore escaped Mr. Bott's eyes for the moment. 'Mr. Fitzgerald,'—and now her words had become a whisper in his ear,—'do what I ask you. For the sake of the old days of which you spoke, the dear old days which can never come again——'

'By G—! they can,' said he. 'They can come back, and they shall.'

'Never. But you can still do me a kindness. Go away, and leave me. Go to the sideboard, and then do not come back. You are doing me an injury while you remain with me.'

'Cora,' he said.

But she had now recovered her presence of mind, and understood what was going on. She was no longer in a dream, but words and things bore to her again their proper meaning. 'I will not have it, Mr. Fitzgerald,' she answered, speaking almost passionately. 'I will not have it. Do as I bid you. Go and leave me, and do not return. I tell you that we are watched.' This was still true, for Mr. Bott had now again got his eyes on them, round the supper-room door. Whatever was the reward for which he was working, private secretaryship or what else, it must be owned that he worked hard for it. But there are labours which are labours of love.

'Who is watching us?' said Burgo; 'and what does it matter? If you are minded to do as I have asked you——'

'But I am not so minded. Do you not know that you insult me by proposing it?'

'Yes;—it is an insult, Cora,—unless such an offer be a joy to you. If you wish to be my wife instead of his, it is no insult.'

'How can I be that?' Her face was not turned to him, and her words were half-pronounced, and in the lowest whisper, but, nevertheless, he heard them.

'Come with me,—abroad, and you shall yet be my wife. You got my letter? Do what I asked you, then. Come with me—to-night.'

The pressing instance of the suggestion, the fixing of a present hour, startled her back to her propriety. 'Mr. Fitzgerald,' she said, 'I asked you to go and leave me. If you do not do so, I must get up and leave you. It will be much more difficult.'

'And is that to be all?'

'All;—at any rate, now.' Oh, Glencora! how could you be so weak? Why did you add that word, 'now'? In truth, she added it then, at that moment, simply feeling that she could thus best secure an immediate compliance with her request.

'I will not go,' he said, looking at her sternly, and leaning before her, with earnest face, with utter indifference as to the eyes of any that might see them. 'I will not go till you tell me that you will see me again.'

'I will,' she said in that low, all-but-unuttered whisper.

'When,—when,—when?' he asked.

Looking up again towards the doorway, in fear of Mr. Bott's eyes, she saw the face of Mr. Palliser as he entered the room. Mr. Bott had also seen him, and had tried to clutch him by the arm; but Mr. Palliser had shaken him off, apparently with indifference,—had got rid of him, as it were, without noticing him. Lady Glencora, when she saw her husband, immediately recovered her courage. She would not cower before him, or show herself ashamed of what she had done. For the matter of that, if he pressed her on the subject, she could bring herself to tell him that she loved Burgo Fitzgerald much more easily than she could whisper such a word to Burgo himself. Mr. Bott's eyes were odious to her as they watched her; but her husband's glance she could meet without quailing before it. 'Here is Mr. Palliser,' said she, speaking again in her ordinary clear-toned voice. Burgo immediately rose from his seat with a start, and turned quickly towards the door; but Lady Glencora kept her chair.

Mr. Palliser made his way as best he could through the crowd up to his wife. He, too, kept his countenance without betraying his secret. There was neither anger nor dismay in his face, nor was there any untoward hurry in his movement. Burgo stood aside as he came up, and Lady Glencora was the first to speak. 'I thought you were gone home hours ago,' she said.

'I did go home,' he answered, 'but I thought I might as well come back for you.'

'What a model of a husband! Well; I am ready. Only, what shall we do about Jane? Mr. Fitzgerald, I left a scarf in your aunt's room,—a little black and yellow scarf,—would you mind getting it for me?'

'I will fetch it,' said Mr. Palliser; 'and I will tell your cousin that the carriage shall come back for her.'

'If you will allow me——' said Burgo.

'I will do it,' said Mr. Palliser; and away he went, making his slow progress up through the crowd, ordering his carriage as he passed through the hall, and leaving Mr. Bott still watching at the door.

Lady Glencora resolved that she would say nothing to Burgo while her husband was gone. There was a touch of chivalry in his leaving them again together, which so far conquered her. He might have bade her leave the scarf, and come at once. She had seen, moreover, that he had not spoken to Mr. Bott, and was thankful to him also for that. Burgo also seemed to have become aware that his chance for that time was over. 'I will say good night,' he said. 'Good night, Mr. Fitzgerald,' she answered, giving him her hand. He pressed it for a moment, and then turned and went. When Mr. Palliser came back he was no more to be seen.

Lady Glencora was at the dining-room door when her husband returned, standing close to Mr. Bott. Mr. Bott had spoken to her, but she made no reply. He spoke again, but her face remained as immovable as though she had been deaf. 'And what shall we do about Mrs. Marsham?' she said, quite out loud, as soon as she put her hand on her husband's arm. 'I had forgotten her.'

'Mrs. Marsham has gone home,' he replied.

'Have you seen her?'

'Yes.'

'When did you see her?'

'She came to Park Lane.'

'What made her do that?'

These questions were asked and answered as he was putting her into the carriage. She got in just as she asked the last, and he, as he took his seat, did not find it necessary to answer it. But that would not serve her turn. 'What made Mrs. Marsham go to you at Park Lane after she left Lady Monk's?' she asked again. Mr. Palliser sat silent, not having made up his mind what he would say on the subject. 'I suppose she went,' continued Lady Glencora, 'to tell you that I was dancing with Mr. Fitzgerald. Was that it?'

'I think, Glencora, we had better not discuss it now.'

'I don't mean to discuss it now, or ever. If you did not wish me to see Mr. Fitzgerald you should not have sent me to Lady Monk's. But, Plantagenet, I hope you will forgive me if I say that no consideration shall induce me to receive again as a guest, in my own house, either Mrs. Marsham or Mr. Bott.'

Mr. Palliser absolutely declined to say anything on the subject on that occasion, and the evening of Lady Monk's party in this way came to an end.

CHAPTER LI

Bold Speculations on Murder

GEORGE VAVASOR was not in a very happy mood when he left Queen Anne Street, after having flung his gift ring under the grate. Indeed there was much in his condition, as connected with the house which he was leaving, which could not but make him unhappy. Alice was engaged to be his wife, and had as yet said nothing to show that she meditated any breach of that engagement, but she had treated him in a way which made him long to throw her promise in her teeth. He was a man to whom any personal slight from a woman was unendurable. To slights from men, unless they were of a nature to provoke offence, he was indifferent. There was no man living for whose liking or disliking George Vavasor cared anything. But he did care much for the good opinion, or rather for the personal favour, of any woman to whom he had endeavoured to make himself agreeable. 'I will marry you,' Alice had said to him,—not in words, but in acts and looks, which were plainer than words,—'I will marry you for certain reasons of my own, which in my present condition make it seem that that arrangement will be more convenient to me than any other that I can make; but pray understand that there is no love mixed up with this. There is another man whom I love;—only, for those reasons above hinted, I do not care to marry him.' It was thus that he read Alice's present treatment of him, and he was a man who could not endure this treatment with ease.

But though he could throw his ring under the grate in his passion, he could not so dispose of her. That he would have done so had his hands been free, we need not doubt. And he would have been clever enough to do so in some manner that would have been exquisitely painful to Alice, willing as she might be to be released from her engagement. But he could not do this to a woman whose money he had borrowed, and whose money he could not repay;—to a woman, more of whose money he intended to borrow immediately. As to that latter part of it, he did say to himself over and over again, that he would have no more of it. As he left the house in Queen Anne Street, on that occasion, he swore, that under no circumstances would he be indebted to her for another shilling. But before he had reached Great Marlborough Street, to which his steps took him, he had reminded himself that everything depended on a further advance. He was in Parliament, but Parliament would be dissolved within three months. Having sacrificed so much for his position, should he let it all fall from him now, —now, when success seemed to be within his reach? That wretched old man in Westmoreland, who seemed gifted almost with immortality,—why could he not die and surrender his paltry acres to one who could use them? He turned away from Regent Street into Hanover Square before he crossed to Great Marlborough Street, giving vent to his passion rather than arranging his thoughts. As he walked the four sides of the square he considered how good it would be if some accident should befal the old man. How he would rejoice were he to hear to-morrow that one of the trees of the 'accursed place,' had fallen on the 'obstinate old idiot,' and put an end to him! I will not say that he meditated the murder of his grandfather. There was a firm conviction on his mind, as he thought of all this, that such a deed as that would never come in his way. But he told himself, that if he chose to make the attempt, he would certainly be able to carry it through without detection. Then he remembered Rush and Palmer,*—the openly bold murderer and the secret poisoner. Both of them, in Vavasor's estimation, were great men. He had often said so in company. He had declared that the courage of Rush had never been surpassed. 'Think of him,' he would say with admiration, 'walking into a man's house, with pistols sufficient to shoot every one there, and doing it as though he were killing rats! What was Nelson at Trafalgar to that? Nelson had nothing to fear!' And of Palmer he declared that he was a man of genius as well as courage. He had 'looked the whole thing in the face,' Vavasor would say, 'and told himself that all scruples and squeamishness are bosh,—child's tales. And so they are. Who lives as though they fear either heaven or hell? And if we do live without such fear or respect, what is the use of telling lies to ourselves? To throw it all to the dogs, as Palmer did, is more manly.' 'And be hanged,' some hearer of George's doctrine replied. 'Yes, and be hanged,—if such is your destiny. But you hear of the one who is hanged, but hear nothing of the twenty who are not.'

Vavasor walked round Hanover Square, nursing his hatred against the old Squire. He did not tell himself that he would like to murder his grandfather. But he suggested to himself, that if he desired to do so, he would have courage enough to make his way into the old man's room, and strangle him; and he explained to himself how he would be able to get down into Westmoreland without the world knowing that he had been there,—how he would find an entrance into the house by a window with which he was acquainted,—how he could cause the man to die as though, those around him should think, it was apoplexy,—he, George Vavasor, having read something on that subject lately. All this he considered very fully, walking rapidly round Hanover Square more than once or twice. If he were to become an active student in the Rush or Palmer school, he would so study the matter that he would not be the one that should be hung. He thought that he could, so far, trust his own ingenuity. But yet he did not meditate murder. 'Beastly old idiot!' he said to himself, 'he must have his chance as other men have, I suppose.' And then he went across Regent Street to Mr. Scruby's office in Great Marlborough Street, not having, as yet, come to any positive conclusion as to what he would do in reference to Alice's money.

But he soon found himself talking to Mr. Scruby as though there were no doubts as to the forthcoming funds for the next election. And Mr. Scruby talked to him very plainly, as though those funds must be forthcoming before long. 'A stitch in time saves nine,' said Mr. Scruby, meaning to insinuate that a pound in time might have the same effect. 'And I'll tell you what, Mr. Vavasor,—of course I've my outstanding bills for the last affair. That's no fault of yours, for the things came so sharp one on another that my fellows haven't had time to make it out. But if you'll put me in funds for what I must be out of pocket in June——'

'Will it be so soon as June?'

'They are talking of June. Why, then, I'll lump the two bills together when it's all over.'

In their discussion respecting money Mr. Scruby injudiciously mentioned the name of Mr. Tombe. No precise caution had been given to him, but he had become aware that the matter was being managed through an agency that was not recognized by his client; and as that agency was simply a vehicle of money which found its way into Mr. Scruby's pocket, he should have held his tongue. But Mr. Tombe's name escaped from him, and Vavasor immediately questioned him. Scruby, who did not often make such blunders, readily excused himself, shaking his head, and declaring that the name had fallen from his lips instead of that of another man. Vavasor accepted the excuse without further notice, and nothing more was said about Mr. Tombe while he was in Mr. Scruby's office. But he had not heard the name in vain, and had unfortunately heard it before. Mr. Tombe was a remarkable man in his way. He wore powder to his hair,—was very polite in his bearing, —was somewhat asthmatic, and wheezed in his talking,—and was, moreover, the most obedient of men, though it was said of him that he managed the whole income of the Ely Chapter just as he pleased. Being in these ways a man of note, John Grey had spoken of him to Alice, and his name had filtered through Alice and her cousin Kate to George Vavasor. George seldom forgot things or names, and when he heard Mr. Tombe's name mentioned in connection with his own money matters, he remembered that Mr. Tombe was John Grey's lawyer.

As soon as he could escape out into the street he endeavoured to put all these things together, and after awhile resolved that he would go to Mr. Tombe. What if there should be an understanding between John Grey and Alice, and Mr. Tombe should be arranging his money matters for him! Would not anything be better than this,—even that little tragedy down in Westmoreland, for which his ingenuity and courage would be required? He could endure to borrow money from Alice. He might even endure it still,—though that was very difficult after her treatment of him; but he could not endure to be the recipient of John Grey's money. By heavens, no! And as he got into a cab, and had himself driven off to the neighbourhood of Doctors' Commons, he gave himself credit for much fine manly feeling. Mr. Tombe's chambers were found without difficulty, and, as it happened, Mr. Tombe was there.

The lawyer rose from his chair as Vavasor entered, and bowed his powdered head very meekly as he asked his visitor to sit down. 'Mr. Vavasor;—oh, yes. He had heard the name. Yes; he was in the habit of acting for his very old friend Mr. John Grey. He had acted for Mr. John Grey, and for Mr. John Grey's father,—he or his partner,—he believed he might say, for about half a century. There could not be a nicer gentleman

113

than Mr. John Grey;—and such a pretty child as he used to be!' At every new sentence Mr. Tombe caught his poor asthmatic breath, and bowed his meek old head, and rubbed his hands together as though he hardly dared to keep his seat in Vavasor's presence without the support of some such motion; and wheezed apologetically, and seemed to ask pardon of his visitor for not knowing intuitively what was the nature of that visitor's business. But he was a sly old fox, was Mr. Tombe, and was considering all this time how much it would be well that he should tell Mr. Vavasor, and how much it would be well that he should conceal. 'The fat had got into the fire,' as he told his old wife when he got home that evening. He told his old wife everything, and I don't know that any of his clients were the worse for his doing so. But while he was wheezing, and coughing, and apologizing, he made up his mind that if George Vavasor were to ask him certain questions, it would be best that he should answer them truly. If Vavasor did ask those questions, he would probably do so upon certain knowledge, and if so, why, in that case, lying would be of no use. Lying would not put the fat back into the frying-pan. And even though such questions might be asked without any absolute knowledge, they would, at any rate, show that the questioner had the means of ascertaining the truth. He would tell as little as he could; but he decided during his last wheeze, that he could not lie in the matter with any chance of benefiting his client. 'The prettiest child I ever saw, Mr. Vavasor!' said Mr. Tombe, and then he coughed violently. Some people who knew Mr. Tombe declared that he nursed his cough.

'I dare say,' said George.

'Yes, indeed,—ugh—ugh—ugh.'

'Can you tell me, Mr. Tombe, whether either you or he have anything to do with the payment of certain sums to my credit at Messrs. Hock and Block's?'

'Messrs. Hock and Block's, the bankers,—in Lom—bard Street?' said Mr. Tombe, taking a little more time.

'Yes; I bank there,' said Vavasor, sharply.

'A most respectable house.'

'Has any money been paid there to my credit, by you, Mr. Tombe?'

'May I ask why you put the question to me, Mr. Vavasor?'

'Well, I don't think you may. That is to say, my reason for asking it can have nothing to do with yours for replying to it. If you have had no hand in any such payment, there is an end of it, and I need not take up your time by saying anything more on the subject.'

'I am not prepared to go that length, Mr. Vavasor,—not altogether to go that length,—ugh—ugh—ugh.'

'Then, will you tell me what you have done in the matter?'

'Well,—upon my word, you've taken me a little by surprise. Let me see. Pinkle,—Pinkle.' Pinkle was a clerk who sat in an inner room, and Mr. Tombe's effort to call him seemed to be most ineffectual. But Pinkle understood the sound, and came. 'Pinkle, didn't we pay some money into Hock and Block's a few weeks since, to the credit of Mr. George Vavasor?'

'Did we, sir?' said Pinkle, who probably knew that his employer was an old fox, and who, perhaps, had caught something of the fox nature himself.

'I think we did. Just look, Pinkle;—and, Pinkle,—see the date, and let me know all about it. It's fine bright weather for this time of year, Mr. Vavasor; but these easterly winds!—ugh—ugh—ugh!'

Vavasor found himself sitting for an apparently interminable number of minutes in Mr. Tombe's dingy chamber, and was coughed at, and wheezed at, till he begun to be tired of his position; moreover, when tired, he showed his impatience. 'Perhaps you'll let us write you a line when we have looked into the matter?' suggested Mr. Tombe.

'I'd rather know at once,' said Vavasor. 'I don't suppose it can take you very long to find out whether you have paid money to my account, by order of Mr. Grey. At any rate, I must know before I go away.'

'Pinkle, Pinkle!' screamed the old man through his coughing; and again Pinkle came. 'Well, Pinkle, was anything of

115

the kind done, or is my memory deceiving me?' Mr. Tombe was, no doubt, lying shamefully, for, of course, he remembered all about it; and, indeed, George Vavasor had learned already quite enough for his own purposes.

'I was going to look,' said Pinkle; and Pinkle again went away.

'I'm sorry to give your clerk so much trouble,' said Vavasor, in an angry voice; 'and I think it must be unnecessary. Surely you know whether Mr. Grey has commissioned you to pay money for me?'

'We have so many things to do, Mr. Vavasor; and so many clients. We have, indeed. You see, it isn't only one gentleman's affairs. But I think there was something done. I do, indeed.'

'What is Mr. John Grey's address?' asked Vavasor, very sharply.

'Number 5, Suffolk Street, Pall Mall East,' said Mr. Tombe. Herein Mr. Tombe somewhat committed himself. His client, Mr. Grey, was, in fact, in town, but Vavasor had not known or imagined that such was the case. Had Mr. Tombe given the usual address of Nethercoats, nothing further would have been demanded from him on that subject. But he had foolishly presumed that the question had been based on special information as to his client's visit to London, and he had told the plain truth in a very simple way.

'Number 5, Suffolk Street,' said Vavasor, writing down the address. 'Perhaps it will be better that I should go to him, as you do not seem inclined to give me any information.' Then he took up his hat, and hardly bowing to Mr. Tombe, left the chambers. Mr. Tombe, as he did so, rose from his chair, and bent his head meekly down upon the table.

'Pinkle, Pinkle,' wheezed Mr. Tombe. 'Never mind; never mind.' Pinkle didn't mind; and we may say that he had not minded; for up to that moment he had taken no steps towards a performance of the order which had been given him.

CHAPTER LII

What occurred in Suffolk Street, Pall Mall

M R. TOMBE had gained nothing for the cause by his crafty silence. George Vavasor felt perfectly certain, as he walked out from the little street which runs at the back of Doctors' Commons, that the money which he had been using had come, in some shape, through the hands of John Grey. He did not care much to calculate whether the payments had been made from the personal funds of his rival, or whether that rival had been employed to dispense Alice's fortune. Under either view of the case his position was sufficiently bitter. The truth never for a moment occurred to him. He never dreamed that there might be a conspiracy in the matter, of which Alice was as ignorant as he himself had been. He never reflected that his uncle John, together with John, the lover, whom he so hated, might be the conspirators. To him it seemed to be certain that Alice and Mr. Grey were in league;—and if they were in league, what must he think of Alice, and of her engagement with himself!

There are men who rarely think well of women,—who hardly think well of any woman. They put their mothers and sisters into the background,—as though they belonged to some sex or race apart,—and then declare to themselves and to their friends that all women are false,—that no woman can be trusted unless her ugliness protect her; and that every woman may be attacked as fairly as may game in a cover, or deer on a mountain. What man does not know men who have so thought? I cannot say that such had been Vavasor's creed,—not entirely such. There had been periods of his life when he had believed implicitly in his cousin Alice;—but then there had been other moments in which he had ridiculed himself for his Quixotism in believing in any woman. And as he had grown older the moments of his Quixotism had become more rare. There would have been no such Quixotism left with him now, had not the various circumstances which I have attempted to describe,

117

filled him, during the last twelve months, with a renewed desire to marry his cousin. Every man tries to believe in the honesty of his future wife; and, therefore, Vavasor had tried, and had, in his way, believed. He had flattered himself, too, that Alice's heart had, in truth, been more prone to him than to that other suitor. Grey, as he thought, had been accepted by her cold prudence; but he thought, also, that she had found her prudence to be too cold, and had therefore returned where she had truly loved. Vavasor, though he did not love much himself, was willing enough to be the object of love.

This idea of his, however, had been greatly shaken by Alice's treatment of himself personally; but still he had not, hitherto, believed that she was false to him. Now, what could he believe of her? What was there within the compass of such a one to believe? As he walked out into St. Paul's Churchyard he called her by every name which is most offensive to a woman's ears. He hated her at this moment with even a more bitter hatred than that which he felt towards John Grey. She must have deceived him with unparalleled hypocrisy, and lied to him and to his sister Kate as hardly any woman had ever lied before. Or could it be that Kate, also, was lying to him? If so, Kate also should be included in the punishment.

But why should they have conspired to feed him with these moneys? There had been no deceit, at any rate, in reference to the pounds sterling which Scruby had already swallowed. They had been supplied, whatever had been the motives of the suppliers; and he had no doubt that more would be supplied if he would only keep himself quiet. He was still walking westward as he thought of this, down Ludgate Hill, on his direct line towards Suffolk Street; and he tried to persuade himself that it would be well that he should hide his wrath till after provision should have been made for this other election. They were his enemies,—Alice and Mr. Grey,—and why should he keep any terms with his enemies? It was still a trouble to him to think that he should have been in any way beholden to John Grey; but the terrible thing had been done; the evil had occurred. What would he gain by staying his hand now? Still, however, he walked on quickly along Fleet Street, and along the Strand, and was already crossing under the Picture Galleries*towards Pall Mall East before he had definitely decided what steps he would take on this very day. Exactly at the corner of Suffolk Street he met John Grey.

'Mr. Grey,' he said, stopping himself suddenly, 'I was this moment going to call on you at your lodgings.'

'At my lodgings, were you? Shall I return with you?'

'If you please,' said Vavasor, leading the way up Suffolk Street. There had been no other greeting than this between them. Mr. Grey himself, though a man very courteous in his general demeanour, would probably have passed Vavasor in the street with no more than the barest salutation. Situated as they were towards each other there could hardly be any show of friendship between them; but when Vavasor had spoken to him, he had dressed his face in that guise of civility which men always use who do not intend to be offensive;—but Vavasor dressed his as men dress theirs who do mean to be offensive; and Mr. Grey had thoroughly appreciated the dressing.

'If you will allow me, I have the key,' said Grey. Then they both entered the house, and Vavasor followed his host up stairs. Mr. Grey, as he went up, felt almost angry with himself in having admitted his enemy into his lodgings. He was sure that no good could come of it, and remembered, when it was too late, that he might easily have saved himself from giving the invitation while he was still in the street. There they were, however, together in the sitting-room, and Grey had nothing to do but to listen. 'Will you take a chair, Mr. Vavasor?' he said. 'No,' said Vavasor; 'I will stand up.' And he stood up, holding his hat behind his back with his left hand, with his right leg forward, and the thumb of his right hand in his waistcoat-pocket. He looked full into Grey's face, and Grey looked full into his; and as he looked the great cicatrice seemed to open itself and to become purple with fresh blood stains.

'I have come here from Mr. Tombe's office in the City,' said Vavasor, 'to ask you of what nature has been the interference which you have taken in my money matters?'

This was a question which Mr. Grey could not answer very quickly. In the first place it was altogether unexpected; in the next place he did not know what Mr. Tombe had told, and what he had not told; and then, before he replied, he must think how much of the truth he was bound to tell in answer to a question so put to him.

'Do you say that you have come from Mr. Tombe?' he asked.

'I think you heard me say so. I have come here direct from Mr. Tombe's chambers. He is your lawyer, I believe?'

'He is so.'

'And I have come from him to ask you what interference you have lately taken in my money matters. When you have answered that, I shall have other questions to ask you.'

'But, Mr. Vavasor, has it occurred to you that I may not be disposed to answer questions so asked?'

'It has not occurred to me to think that you will prevaricate. If there has been no such interference, I will ask your pardon, and go away; but if there has been such interference on your part, I have a right to demand that you shall explain to me its nature.'

Grey had now made up his mind that it would be better that he should tell the whole story,—better not only for himself, but for all the Vavasors, including this angry man himself. The angry man evidently knew something, and it would be better that he should know the truth. 'There has been such interference, Mr. Vavasor, if you choose to call it so. Money, to the extent of two thousand pounds, I think, has by my directions been paid to your credit by Mr. Tombe.'

'Well,' said Vavasor, taking his right hand away from his waistcoat, and tapping the round table with his fingers impatiently.

'I hardly know how to explain all the circumstances under which this has been done.'

'I dare say not; but, nevertheless, you must explain them.'

Grey was a man tranquil in temperament, very little prone to quarrelling, with perhaps an exaggerated idea of the evil

120

results of a row,—a man who would take infinite trouble to avoid any such scene as that which now seemed to be imminent; but he was a man whose courage was quite as high as that of his opponent. To bully or to be bullied were alike contrary to his nature. It was clear enough now that Vavasor intended to bully him, and he made up his mind at once that if the quarrel were forced upon him it should find him ready to take his own part. 'My difficulty in explaining it comes from consideration for you,' he said.

'Then I beg that your difficulty will cease, and that you will have no consideration for me. We are so circumstanced towards each other that any consideration must be humbug and nonsense. At any rate, I intend to have none for you. Now, let me know why you have meddled with my matters.'

'I think I might, perhaps, better refer you to your uncle.'

'No, sir; Mr. Tombe is not my uncle's lawyer. My uncle never heard his name, unless he heard of it from you.'

'But it was by agreement with your uncle that I commissioned Mr. Tombe to raise for you the money you were desirous of borrowing from your cousin. We thought it better that her fortune should not be for the moment disturbed.'

'But what had you to do with it? Why should you have done it? In the first place, I don't believe your story; it is altogether improbable. But why should he come to you of all men to raise money on his daughter's behalf?'

'Unless you can behave yourself with more discretion, Mr. Vavasor, you must leave the room,' said Mr. Grey. Then, as Vavasor simply sneered at him, but spoke nothing, he went on. 'It was I who suggested to your uncle that this arrangement should be made. I did not wish to see Miss Vavasor's fortune squandered.'

'And what was her fortune to you, sir? Are you aware that she is engaged to me as my wife? I ask you, sir, whether you are aware that Miss Vavasor is to be my wife?'

'I must altogether decline to discuss with you Miss Vavasor's present or future position.'

'By heavens, then, you shall hear me discuss it! She was

121

engaged to you, and she has given you your dismissal. If you had understood anything of the conduct which is usual among gentlemen, or if you had had any particle of pride in you, sir, you would have left her and never mentioned her name again. I now find you meddling with her money matters, so as to get a hold upon her fortune.'

'I have no hold upon her fortune.'

'Yes, sir, you have. You do not advance two thousand pounds without knowing that you have security. She has rejected you; and in order that you may be revenged, or that you may have some further hold upon her,—that she may be in some sort within your power, you have contrived this rascally petti- fogging way of obtaining power over her income. The money shall be repaid at once, with any interest that can be due; and if I find you interfering again, I will expose you.'

'Mr. Vavasor,' said Grey very slowly, in a low tone of voice, but with something in his eye which would have told any by- stander that he was much in earnest, 'you have used words in your anger which I cannot allow to pass. You must recall them.'

'What were the words? I said that you were a pettifogging rascal. I now repeat them.' As he spoke he put on his hat, so as to leave both his hands ready for action if action should be required.

Grey was much the larger man and much the stronger. It may be doubted whether he knew himself the extent of his own strength, but such as it was he resolved that he must now use it. 'There is no help for it,' he said, as he also prepared for action. The first thing he did was to open the door, and as he did so he became conscious that his mouth was full of blood from a sharp blow upon his face. Vavasor had struck him with his fist, and had cut his lip against his teeth. Then there came a scramble, and Grey was soon aware that he had his opponent in his hands. I doubt whether he had attempted to strike a blow, or whether he had so much as clenched his fist. Vavasor had struck him repeatedly, but the blows had fallen on his body or his head, and he was unconscious of them. He had but one object now in his mind, and that object was the kicking his assailant down the stairs. Then came a scramble, as I have said, and Grey had a hold of the smaller man by the nape of his neck. So holding him he forced him back through the door on to the landing, and then succeeded in pushing him down the first flight of steps. Grey kicked at him as he went, but the kick was impotent. He had, however, been so far successful that he had thrust his enemy out of the room, and had the satisfaction of seeing him sprawling on the landing-place.

Vavasor, when he raised himself, prepared to make another rush at the room, but before he could do so a man from below, hearing the noise, had come upon him and interrupted him. 'Mr. Jones,' said Grey, speaking from above, 'if that gentleman does not leave the house, I must get you to search for a policeman.'

Vavasor, though the lodging-house man had hold of the collar of his coat, made no attempt to turn upon his new enemy. When two dogs are fighting, any bystander may attempt to separate them with impunity. The brutes are so anxious to tear each other that they have no energies left for other purposes. It never occurs to them to turn their teeth upon the new comers in the quarrel. So it was with George Vavasor. Jones was sufficient to prevent his further attack upon the foe up stairs, and therefore he had no alternative but to relinquish the fight.

'What's it all about, sir?' said Jones, who kept a tailor's establishment, and, as a tailor, was something of a fighting man himself. Of all tradesmen in London the tailors are, no doubt, the most combative,—as might be expected from the necessity which lies upon them of living down the general bad character in this respect which the world has wrongly given them. 'What's it all about, sir?' said Jones, still holding Vavasor by his coat.

'That man has ill-used me, and I've punished him; that's all.'

'I don't know much about punishing,' said the tailor. 'It seems to me he pitched you down pretty clean out of the room above. I think the best thing you can do now is to walk yourself off.'

It was the only thing that Vavasor could do, and he did walk himself off. He walked himself off, and went home to his own lodgings in Cecil Street, that he might smooth his feathers after the late encounter before he went down to Westminster to take his seat in the House of Commons. I do not think that he was comfortable when he got there, or that he felt himself very well able to fight another battle that night on behalf of the River Bank. He had not been hurt, but he had been worsted. Grey had probably received more personal damage than had fallen to his share; but Grey had succeeded in expelling him from the room, and he knew that he had been found prostrate on the landing-place when the tailor first saw him.

But he might probably have got over the annoyance of this feeling had he not been overwhelmed by a consciousness that everything was going badly with him. He was already beginning to hate his seat in Parliament. What good had it done for him, or was it likely to do for him? He found himself to be associated there with Mr. Bott, and a few others of the same class,—men whom he despised; and even they did not admit him among them without a certain show of superiority on their part. Who has not ascertained by his own experience the different lights through which the same events may be seen, according to the success, or want of success, which pervades the atmosphere at the moment? At the present time everything was unsuccessful with George Vavasor; and though he told himself, almost from hour to hour, that he would go on with the thing which he had begun,—that he would persevere in Parliament till he had obtained a hearing there and created for himself success, he could not himself believe in the promises which he had made to himself. He had looked forward to his entrance into that Chamber as the hour of his triumph; but he had entered it with Mr. Bott, and there had been no triumph to him in doing so. He had sworn to himself that when there he would find men to hear him. Hitherto, indeed, he could not accuse himself of having missed his opportunities; his election had been so recent that he could hardly yet have made the attempt. But he had been there long enough to learn to fancy that there was no glory in attempting. This art of speaking in Parliament, which had appeared to him to be so grand, seemed already to be a humdrum, homely, dull affair. No one seemed to listen much to what was said. To such as himself,—Members without an acquired name,—men did not seem to listen at all. Mr. Palliser had once, in his hearing, spoken for two hours together, and all the House had treated his speech with respect,—had declared that it was useful, solid, conscientious, and what not; but more than half the House had been asleep more than half the time that he was on his legs. Vavasor had not as yet commenced his career as an orator; but night after night, as he sat there, the chance of commencing it with brilliance seemed to be further from him, and still further. Two thousand pounds of his own money, and two thousand more of Alice's money,—or of Mr. Grey's,—he had already spent to make his way into that assembly. He must spend, at any rate, two thousand more if he intended that his career should be prolonged beyond a three months' sitting;—and how was he to get this further sum after what had taken place to-day?

He would get it. That was his resolve as he walked in by the apple-woman's stall, under the shadow of the great policeman, and between the two august lamps. He would get it;—as long as Alice had a pound over which he could obtain mastery by any act or violence within his compass. He would get it; even though it should come through the hands of John Grey and Mr. Tombe. He would get it; though in doing so he might destroy his cousin Alice and ruin his sister Kate. He had gone too far to stick at any scruples. Had he not often declared how great had been that murderer who had been able to divest himself of all such scruples,—who had scoured his bosom free from all fears of the hereafter, and, as regarded the present, had dared to trust for everything to success? He would go to Alice and demand the money from her with threats, and with that violence in his eyes which he knew so well how to assume. He believed that when he so demanded it, the money would be forthcoming so as to satisfy, at any rate, his present emergencies.

125

That wretched old man in Westmoreland! If he would but die, there might yet be a hope remaining of permanent success! Even though the estate might be entailed so as to give him no more than a life-interest, still money might be raised on it. His life-interest in it would be worth ten or twelve years' purchase. He had an idea that his grandfather had not as yet made any such will when he left the place in Westmoreland. What a boon it would be if death could be made to overtake the old man before he did so! On this very night he walked about the lobbies of the House, thinking of all this. He went by himself from room to room, roaming along passages, sitting now for ten minutes in the gallery, and then again for a short space in the body of the House,—till he would get up and wander again out into the lobby, impatient of the neighbourhood of Mr. Bott. Certainly just at this time he felt no desire to bring before the House the subject of the River Embankment.

Nor was Mr. Grey much happier when he was left alone, than was his assailant. To give Vavasor his due, the memory of the affray itself did not long trouble him much. The success between the combatants had been nearly equal, and he had, at any rate, spoken his mind freely. His misery had come from other sources. But the reflection that he had been concerned in a row was in itself enough to make John Grey wretched for the time. Such a misfortune had never hitherto befallen him. In all his dealings with men words had been sufficient, and generally words of courtesy had sufficed. To have been personally engaged in a fighting scramble with such a man as George Vavasor was to him terrible. When ordering that his money might be expended with the possible object of saving Alice from her cousin, he had never felt a moment's regret; he had never thought that he was doing more than circumstances fairly demanded of him. But now he was almost driven to utter a reproach. 'Oh, Alice! Alice! that this thing should have come upon me through thy fault!'

When Vavasor was led away down stairs by the tailor, and Grey found that no more actual fighting would be required of him, he retired into his bedroom, that he might wash his mouth and free himself from the stains of the combat. He had heard the front door closed, and knew that the miscreant was gone,—the miscreant who had disturbed his quiet. Then he began to think what was the accusation with which Vavasor had charged him. He had been told that he had advanced money on behalf of Alice, in order that he might obtain some power over Alice's fortune, and thus revenge himself upon Alice for her treatment of him. Nothing could be more damnably false than this accusation. Of that he was well aware. But were not the circumstances of a nature to make it appear that the accusation was true? Security for the money advanced by him, of course, he had none;—of course he had desired none;—of course the money had been given out of his own pocket with the sole object of saving Alice, if that might be possible; but of all those who might hear of this affair, how many would know or even guess the truth?

While he was in this wretched state of mind, washing his mouth, and disturbing his spirit, Mr. Jones, his landlord, came up to him. Mr. Jones had known him for some years, and entertained a most profound respect for his character. A rather sporting man than otherwise was Mr. Jones. His father had been a tradesman at Cambridge, and in this way Jones had become known to Mr. Grey. But though given to sport, by which he meant modern prize-fighting and the Epsom course on the Derby day, Mr. Jones was a man who dearly loved respectable customers and respectable lodgers. Mr. Grey, with his property at Nethercoats, and his august manners, and his reputation at Cambridge, was a most respectable lodger, and Mr. Jones could hardly understand how any one could presume to raise his hand against such a man.

'Dear, dear, sir,—this is a terrible affair!' he said, as he made his way into the room.

'It was very disagreeable, certainly,' said Grey.

'Was the gentleman known to you?' asked the tailor.

'Yes; I know who he is.'

'Any quarrel, sir?'

'Well, yes. I should not have pushed him down stairs had he not quarrelled with me.'

'We can have the police after him if you wish it, sir?'

'I don't wish it at all.'

'Or we might manage to polish him off in any other way, you know.'

It was some time before Mr. Grey could get rid of the tailor, but he did so at last without having told any part of the story to that warlike, worthy, and very anxious individual.

CHAPTER LIII

The Last Will of the Old Squire

IN the meantime Kate Vavasor was living down in Westmoreland, with no other society than that of her grandfather, and did not altogether have a very pleasant life of it. George had been apt to represent the old man to himself as being as strong as an old tower, which, though it be but a ruin, shows no sign of falling. To his eyes the Squire had always seemed to be full of life and power. He could be violent on occasions, and was hardly ever without violence in his eyes and voice. But George's opinion was formed by his wish, or rather by the reverse of his wish. For years he had been longing that his grandfather should die,—had been accusing Fate of gross injustice in that she did not snap the thread; and with such thoughts in his mind he had grudged every ounce which the Squire's vigour had been able to sustain. He had almost taught himself to believe that it would be a good deed to squeeze what remained of life out of that violent old throat. But, indeed, the embers of life were burning low; and had George known all the truth, he would hardly have inclined his mind to thoughts of murder.

He was, indeed, very weak with age, and tottering with unsteady steps on the brink of his grave, though he would still come down early from his room, and would, if possible, creep out about the garden and into the farmyard. He would still sit down to dinner, and would drink his allotted portion of port wine, in the doctor's teeth. The doctor by no means desired to rob him of this last luxury, or even to stint his quantity; but he recommended certain changes in the mode and time of taking it. Against this, however, the old Squire indignantly rebelled, and scolded Kate almost off her legs when she attempted to enforce the doctor's orders. 'What the mischief does it signify,' the old man said to her one evening;—'what difference will it make whether I am dead or alive, unless it is that George would turn you out of the house directly he gets it?'

'I was not thinking of any one but yourself, sir,' said Kate, with a tear in her eye.

'You won't be troubled to think of me much longer,' said the Squire; and then he gulped down the remaining half of his glass of wine.

Kate was, in truth, very good to him. Women always are good under such circumstances; and Kate Vavasor was one who would certainly stick to such duties as now fell to her lot. She was eminently true and loyal to her friends, though she could be as false on their behalf as most false people can be on their own. She was very good to the old man, tending all his wants, taking his violence with good-humour rather than with submission, not opposing him with direct contradiction when he abused his grandson, but saying little words to mitigate his wrath, if it were possible. At such times the Squire would tell her that she also would learn to know her brother's character some day. 'You'll live to be robbed by him, and turned out as naked as you were born,' he said to her one day. Then Kate fired up and declared that she fully trusted her brother's love. Whatever faults he might have, he had been stanch to her. So she said, and the old man sneered at her for saying so.

One morning, soon after this, when she brought him up to his bedroom some mixture of thin porridge which he still endeavoured to swallow for his breakfast, he bade her sit down, and began to talk to her about the property. 'I know you are a fool,' he said, 'about all matters of business;—more of a fool than even women generally are.' To this Kate acceded with a little smile,—acknowledging that her understanding was limited. 'I want to see Gogram,' he said. 'Do you write him a line, telling him to come here to-day,—he or one of his men, —and send it at once by Peter.' Gogram was an attorney who lived at Penrith, and who was never summoned to Vavasor Hall unless the Squire had something to say about his will. 'Don't you think you'd better put it off till you are a little stronger?' said Kate. Whereupon the Squire fired at her such a volley of oaths that she sprang off the chair on which she was sitting, and darted across to a little table at which there was pen and ink, and wrote her note to Mr. Gogram, before she had recovered from the shaking which the battery had given her. She wrote the note, and ran away with it to Peter, and saw Peter on the pony on his way to Penrith, before she dared to return to her grandfather's bedside.

'What should you do with the estate if I left it you?' the Squire said to her the first moment she was again back with him.

This was a question she could not answer instantly. She stood by his bedside for a while thinking,—holding her grandfather's hand and looking down upon the bed. He, with his rough watery old eyes, was gazing up into her face, as though he were trying to read her thoughts. 'I think I should give it to my brother,' she said.

'Then I'm d—— if I'll leave it to you,' said he.

She did not jump now, though he had sworn at her. She still stood, holding his hand softly, and looking down upon the bed. 'If I were you, grandfather,' she said almost in a whisper, 'I would not trust myself to alter family arrangements whilst I was ill. I'm sure you would advise any one else against doing so.'

'And if I were to leave it to Alice, she'd give it him too,' he said, speaking his thoughts out loud. 'What it is you see in him, I never could even guess. He's as ugly as a baboon, with his scarred face. He has never done anything to show himself a clever fellow. Kate, give me some of that bottle the man sent.' Kate handed him his medicine, and then stood again by his bedside.

'Where did he get the money to pay for his election?' the Squire asked, as soon as he had swallowed the draught. 'They wouldn't give such a one as him credit a yard further than they could see him.'

'I don't know where he got it,' said Kate, lying.

'He has not had yours; has he?'

'He would not take it, sir.'

'And you offered it to him?'

'Yes, sir.'

'And he has not had it?'

'Not a penny of it, sir.'

'And what made you offer it to him after what I said to you?'

'Because it was my own,' said Kate, stoutly.

'You're the biggest idiot that ever I heard of, and you'll know it yourself some day. Go away now, and let me know when Gogram comes.'

She went away, and for a time employed herself about her ordinary household work. Then she sat down alone in the dingy old dining-room, to think what had better be done in her present circumstances. The carpet of the room was worn out, as were also the covers of the old chairs and the horsehair sofa which was never moved from its accustomed place along the wall. It was not a comfortable Squire's residence, this old house at Vavasor. In the last twenty years no money had been spent on furniture or embellishments, and for the last ten years there had been no painting, either inside or out. Twenty years ago the Squire had been an embarrassed man, and had taken a turn in his life and had lived sparingly. It could not be said that he had become a miser. His table was kept plentifully, and there had never been want in his house. In some respects, too, he had behaved liberally to Kate and to others, and he had kept up the timber and fences on the property. But the house had become wretched in its dull, sombre, dirty darkness, and the gardens round it were as bad.

What ought she now to do? She believed that her grandfather's last days were coming, and she knew that others of the family should be with him besides herself. For their sakes, for his, and for her own, it would be proper that she should not be alone there when he died. But for whom should she send? Her brother was the natural heir, and would be the head of the family. Her duty to him was clear, and the more so as her grandfather was at this moment speaking of changes in his will. But it was a question to her whether George's presence at Vavasor, even if he would come, would not at this moment do more harm than good to his own interests. It would make some prejudicial change in the old man's will more probable instead of less so. George would not become soft and mild-spoken even by a death-bed side, and it would be likely enough that the Squire would curse his heir with his dying breath. She might send for her uncle John; but if she did so without telling George she would be treating George unfairly; and she knew that it was improbable that her uncle and her brother should act together in anything. Her aunt Greenow, she thought, would come to her, and her presence would not influence the Squire in any way with reference to the property. So she made up her mind at last that she would ask her aunt to come to Vavasor, and that she would tell her brother accurately all that she could tell,—leaving him to come or stay, as he might think. Alice would, no doubt, learn all the facts from him, and her uncle John would hear them from Alice. Then they could do as they pleased. As soon as Mr. Gogram had been there she would write her letters, and they should be sent over to Shap early on the following morning.

Mr. Gogram came and was closeted with the Squire, and the doctor also came. The doctor saw Kate, and, shaking his head, told her that her grandfather was sinking lower and lower every hour. It would be infinitely better for him if he would take that port wine at four doses in the day, or even at two, instead of taking it all together. Kate promised to try again, but stated her conviction that the trial would be useless. The doctor, when pressed on the matter, said that his patient might probably live a week, not improbably a fortnight,—perhaps a month, if he would be obedient,—and so forth. Gogram went away without seeing Kate; and Kate, who looked upon a will as an awful and somewhat tedious ceremony, was in doubt whether her grandfather would live to complete any new operation. But, in truth, the will had been made and signed and witnessed,—the parish clerk and one of the tenants having been had up into the room as witnesses. Kate knew that the men had been there, but still did not think that a new will had been perfected.

That evening when it was dusk the Squire came into the dining-room, having been shuffling about the grand sweep before the house for a quarter of an hour. The day was cold and the wind bleak, but still he would go out, and Kate had wrapped him up carefully in mufflers and great-coats. Now he came in to what he called dinner, and Kate sat down with him. He had drunk no wine that day, although she had brought it to him twice during the morning. Now he attempted to swallow a little soup, but failed; and after that, while Kate was eating her bit of chicken, had the decanter put before him. 'I can't eat, and I suppose it won't hurt you if I take my wine at once,' he said. It went against the grain with him, even yet, that he could not wait till the cloth was gone from the table, but his impatience for the only sustenance that he could take was too much for him.

'But you should eat something, sir; will you have a bit of toast to sop in your wine?'

The word 'sop' was badly chosen, and made the old Squire angry.'Sopped toast! why am I to spoil the only thing I can enjoy?'

'But the wine would do you more good if you would take something with it.'

'Good! Nothing will do me any good any more. As for eating, you know I can't eat. What's the use of bothering me?' Then he filled his second glass, and paused awhile before he put it to his lips. He never exceeded four glasses, but the four he was determined that he would have, as long as he could lift them to his mouth.

Kate finished, or pretended to finish, her dinner within five minutes, in order that the table might be made to look comfortable for him. Then she poked the fire, and brushed up the hearth, and closed the old curtains with her own hands, moving about silently. As she moved his eye followed her, and when she came behind his chair, and pushed the decanter a little more within his reach, he put out his rough, hairy hand, and laid it upon one of hers which she had rested on the table, with a tenderness that was unusual with him. 'You are a good girl, Kate. I wish you had been a boy, that's all.'

'If I had, I shouldn't, perhaps, have been here to take care of you,' she said, smiling.

'No; you'd have been like your brother, no doubt. Not that I think there could have been two so bad as he is.'

'Oh, grandfather, if he has offended you, you should try to forgive him.'

'Try to forgive him! How often have I forgiven him without any trying? Why did he come down here the other day, and insult me for the last time? Why didn't he keep away, as I had bidden him?'

'But you gave him leave to see you, sir.'

'I didn't give him leave to treat me like that. Never mind; he will find that, old as I am, I can punish an insult.'

'You haven't done anything, sir, to injure him?' said Kate.

'I have made another will, that's all. Do you suppose I had that man here all the way from Penrith for nothing?'

'But it isn't done yet?'

'I tell you it is done. If I left him the whole property it would be gone in two years' time. What's the use of doing it?'

'But for his life, sir! You had promised him that he should have it for his life.'

'How dare you tell me that? I never promised him. As my heir, he would have had it all, if he would have behaved himself with common decency. Even though I disliked him, as I always have done, he should have had it.'

'And you have taken it from him altogether?'

'I shall answer no questions about it, Kate.' Then a fit of coughing came upon him, his four glasses of wine having been all taken, and there was no further talk about business. During the evening Kate read a chapter of the Bible out loud. But the Squire was very impatient under the reading, and positively refused permission for a second. 'There isn't any good in so much of it, all at once,' he said, using almost exactly the same words which Kate had used to him about the port wine. There may have been good produced by the small quantity to which he listened as there is good from the physic which children take with wry faces, most unwillingly. Who can say?

For many weeks past Kate had begged her grandfather to allow the clergyman of Vavasor to come to him; but he had positively declined. The vicar was a young man to whom the living had lately been given by the Chancellor, and he had commenced his career by giving instant offence to the Squire. This vicar's predecessor had been an old man, almost as old as the Squire himself, and had held the living for forty years. He had been a Westmoreland man, had read the prayers and preached his one Sunday sermon in a Westmoreland dialect, getting through the whole operation rather within an hour and a quarter. He had troubled none of his parishioners by much advice and had been meek and obedient to the Squire. Knowing the country well, and being used to its habits, he had lived, and been charitable too, on the proceeds of his living, which had never reached two hundred a year. But the new comer was a close-fisted man, with higher ideas of personal comfort, who found it necessary to make every penny go as far as possible, who made up in preaching for what he could not give away in charity; who established an afternoon service, and who had rebuked the Squire for saying that the doing so was trash and nonsense. Since that the Squire had never been inside the church except on the occasion of Christmas-day. For this, indeed, the state of his health gave ample excuse; but he had positively refused to see the vicar, though that gentleman had assiduously called, and had at last desired the servant to tell the clergyman not to come again unless he were sent for. Kate's task was, therefore, difficult, both as regarded the temporal and spiritual wants of her grandfather.

When the reading was finished, the old man dozed in his chair for half an hour. He would not go up to bed before the enjoyment of that luxury. He was daily implored to do so, because that sleep in the chair interfered so fatally with his chance of sleeping in bed. But sleep in his chair he would and did. Then he woke, and after a fit of coughing, was induced, with much ill-humour, to go up to his room. Kate had never seen him so weak. He was hardly able, even with her assistance and that of the old servant, to get up the broad stairs. But there was still some power left to him for violence of language after he got to his room, and he rated Kate and the old woman loudly, because his slippers were not in the proper place. 'Grandfather,' said Kate, 'would you like me to stay in the room with you to-night?' He rated her again for this proposition, and then, with assistance from the nurse, he was gotten into bed and was left alone.

After that Kate went to her own room and wrote her letters. The first she wrote was to her aunt Greenow. That was easily enough written. To Mrs. Greenow it was not necessary that she should say anything about money. She simply stated her belief that her grandfather's last day was near at hand, and begged her aunt to come and pay a last visit to the old man. 'It will be a great comfort to me in my distress,' she said; 'and it will be a satisfaction to you to have seen your father again.' She knew that her aunt would come, and that task was soon done.

But her letter to her brother was much more difficult. What should she tell him, and what should she not tell him? She began by describing her grandfather's state, and by saying to him, as she had done to Mrs. Greenow, that she believed the old man's hours were well-nigh come to a close. She told him that she had asked her aunt to come to her; 'not,' she said, 'that I think her coming will be of material service, but I feel the loneliness of the house will be too much for me at such a time. I must leave it for you to decide,' she said, 'whether you had better be here. If anything should happen,'—people when writing such letters are always afraid to speak of death by its proper name,—'I will send you a message, and no doubt you would come at once.' Then came the question of the will. Had it not occurred to her that her own interests were involved she would have said nothing on the subject; but she feared her brother,—feared even his misconstruction of her motives, even

though she was willing to sacrifice so much on his behalf,— and therefore she resolved to tell him all that she knew. He might turn upon her hereafter if she did not do so, and accuse her of a silence which had been prejudicial to him.

So she told it all, and the letter became long in the telling. 'I write with a heavy heart,' she said, 'because I know it will be a great blow to you. He gave me to understand that in this will he left everything away from you. I cannot declare that he said so directly. Indeed I cannot remember his words; but that was the impression he left on me. The day before he had asked me what I should do if he gave me the estate; but of course I treated that as a joke. I have no idea what he put into this will. I have not even attempted to guess. But now I have told you all that I know.' The letter was a very long one, and was not finished till late; but when it was completed she had the two taken out into the kitchen, as the boy was to start with them before daylight.

Early on the next morning she crept silently into her grandfather's room, as was her habit; but he was apparently sleeping, and then she crept back again. The old servant told her that the Squire had been awake at four, and at five, and at six, and had called for her. Then he had seemed to go to sleep. Four or five times in the course of the morning Kate went into the room, but her grandfather did not notice her. At last she feared he might already have passed away, and she put her hand upon his shoulder, and down his arm. He then gently touched her hand with his, showing her plainly that he was not only alive, but conscious. She then offered him food,—the thin porridge,—which he was wont to take, and the medicine. She offered him some wine too, but he would take nothing.

At twelve o'clock a letter was brought to her, which had come by the post. She saw that it was from Alice, and opening it found that it was very long. At that moment she could not read it, but she saw words in it that made her wish to know its contents as quickly as possible. But she could not leave her grandfather then. At two o'clock the doctor came to him, and remained there till the dusk of the evening had commenced. At eight o'clock the old man was dead.

CHAPTER LIV

Showing how Alice was Punished

POOR Kate's condition at the old Hall on that night was very sad. The presence of death is always a source of sorrow, even though the circumstances of the case are of a kind to create no agony of grief. The old man who had just passed away up-stairs was fully due to go. He had lived his span all out, and had himself known that to die was the one thing left for him to do. Kate also had expected his death, and had felt that the time had come in which it would be foolish even to wish that it should be arrested. But death close to one is always sad as it is solemn.

And she was quite alone at Vavasor Hall. She had no acquaintance within some miles of her. From the young vicar, though she herself had not quarrelled with him, she could receive no comfort, as she hardly knew him; nor was she of a temperament which would dispose her to turn to a clergyman at such a time for comfort, unless to one who might have been an old friend. Her aunt and brother would probably both come to her; but they could hardly be with her for a day or two, and during that day or two it would be needful that orders should be given which it is disagreeable for a woman to have to give. The servants, moreover, in the house were hardly fit to assist her much. There was an old butler, or footman, who had lived at the Hall for more than fifty years, but he was crippled with rheumatism, and so laden with maladies, that he rarely crept out of his own room. He was simply an additional burden on the others. There was a boy who had lately done all the work which the other should have done, and ever so much more beside. There is no knowing how much work such a boy will do when properly drilled, and he was now Kate's best minister in her distress. There was the old nurse,—but she had been simply good for nursing, and there were two rough Westmoreland girls who called themselves cook and housemaid.

On that first evening,—the very day on which her grandfather had died,—Kate would have been more comfortable had she really found something that she could do. But there was in truth nothing. She hovered for an hour or two in and out of the room, conscious of the letter which she had in her pocket, and very desirous in heart of reading it, but restrained by a feeling that at such a moment she ought to think only of the dead. In this she was wrong. Let the living think of the dead, when their thoughts will travel that way whether the thinker wish it or no. Grief taken up because grief is supposed to be proper, is only one degree better than pretended grief. When one sees it, one cannot but think of the lady who asked her friend, in confidence, whether hot roast fowl and bread-sauce were compatible with the earliest state of weeds; or of that other lady,—a royal lady she,—who was much comforted in the tedium of her trouble when assured by one of the lords about the Court that piquet*was mourning.

It was late at night, near eleven, before Kate took out her letter and read it. As something of my story hangs upon it, I will give it at length, though it was a long letter. It had been written with great struggles and with many tears, and Kate, as she read it to the end, almost forgot that her grandfather was lying dead in the room above her.

'Queen Anne Street, April, 186—.

'DEAREST KATE,

'I hardly know how to write to you—what I have to tell, and yet I must tell it. I must tell it to you, but I shall never repeat the story to any one else. I should have written yesterday, when it occurred, but I was so ill that I felt myself unable to make the exertion. Indeed, at one time, after your brother had left me, I almost doubted whether I should ever be able to collect my thoughts again. My dismay was at first so great that my reason for a time deserted me, and I could only sit and cry like an idiot.

'Dear Kate, I hope you will not be angry with me for telling you. I have endeavoured to think about it as calmly as I can, and I believe that I have no alternative. The fact that your brother has quarrelled with me cannot be concealed from you, and I must not leave him to tell you of the manner of it. He came to me yesterday in great anger. His anger then was nothing to what it became afterwards; but even when he first came in he was full of wrath. He stood up before me, and asked me how it had come to pass that I had sent him the money which he had asked of me through the hands of Mr. Grey. Of course I had not done this, and so I told him at once. I had spoken of the matter to no one but papa, and he had managed it for me. Even now I know nothing of it, and as I have not yet spoken to papa I cannot understand it. George at once told me that he disbelieved me, and when I sat quiet under this insult, he used harsher words, and said that I had conspired to lower him before the world.

'He then asked me whether I loved him. Oh, Kate, I must tell it you all, though it is dreadful to me that I should have to write it. You remember how it came to pass when we were in Westmoreland together at Christmas? Do not think that I am blaming you, but I was very rash then in the answers which I made to him. I thought that I could be useful to him as his wife, and I had told myself that it would be good that I should be of use in some way. When he asked me that question yesterday, I sat silent. Indeed, how could I have answered it in the affirmative, when he had just used such language to me,— while he was standing opposite to me, looking at me in that way which he has when he is enraged? Then he spoke again and demanded of me that I should at once send back to Mr. Grey all presents of his which I had kept, and at the same time took up and threw across the table on to the sofa near me, a little paper knife which Mr. Grey once gave me. I could not allow myself to be so ordered by him; so I said nothing, but put the knife back upon the table. He then took it again and threw it beneath the grate. "I have a right to look upon you as my wife," he said, "and, as such, I will not allow you to keep that man's things about you." I think I told him then that I should never become his wife, but though I remember many of his words, I remember none of my own. He swore, I know, with a great oath, that if I went back a second time from my word to him he would leave me no peace,—that he would punish me for my perfidy with some fearful punishment. Oh, Kate, I cannot tell you what he looked like. He had then come quite close to me, and I know that I trembled before him as though he were going to strike me. Of course I said nothing. What could I say to a man who behaved to me in such a manner? Then, as far as I can remember it, he sat down and began to talk about money. I forget what he said at first, but I know that I assured him that he might take what he wanted so long as enough was left to prevent my being absolutely a burden on papa. "That, madam, is a matter of course," he said. I remember those words so well. Then he explained that after what had passed between us, I had no right to ruin him by

141

keeping back from him money which had been promised to him, and which was essential to his success. In this, dear Kate, I think he was mainly right. But he could not have been right in putting it to me in that hard, cruel manner, especially as I had never refused anything that he had asked of me in respect of money. The money he may have while it lasts; but then there must be an end of it all between us, even though he should have the power of punishing me, as he says he will do. Punishing me, indeed! What punishment can be so hard as that which he has already inflicted?

'He then desired me to write a letter to him which he might show to the lawyer,—to our own lawyer, I think he meant,— in order that money might be raised to pay back what Mr. Grey had advanced, and give him what he now required. I think he said it was to be five thousand pounds. When he asked this I did not move. Indeed, I was unable to move. Then he spoke very loud, and swore at me again, and brought me pen and ink, demanding that I should write the letter. I was so frightened that I thought of running to the door to escape, and I would have done so had I not distrusted my own power. Had it been to save my life I could not have written the letter. I believe I was now crying,—at any rate I threw myself back and covered my face with my hands. Then he came and sat by me, and took hold of my arms. Oh, Kate; I cannot tell it you all. He put his mouth close to my ear, and said words which were terrible, though I did not understand them. I do not know what it was he said, but he was threatening me with his anger if I did not obey him. Before he left me, I believe I found my voice to tell him that he should certainly have the money which he required. And so he shall. I will go to Mr. Round myself, and insist on its being done. My money is my own, and I may do with it as I please. But I hope,—I am obliged to hope, that I may never be made to see my cousin again.

'I will not pretend to express any opinion as to the cause of all this. It is very possible that you will not believe all I say,— that you will think that I am mad and have deluded myself. Of course your heart will prompt you to accuse me rather than him. If it is so, and if there must therefore be a division between us, my grief will be greatly increased; but I do not know that I can help it. I cannot keep all this back from you. He has cruelly ill-used me and insulted me. He has treated me as I should have thought no man could have treated a woman. As regards money, I did all that I could do to show that I trusted him thoroughly, and my confidence has only led to suspicion. I do not know whether he understands that everything must be over between us; but, if not, I must ask you to tell him so. And I must ask you to explain to him that he must not come again to Queen Anne Street. If he does, nothing shall induce me to see him. Tell him also that the money that he wants shall assuredly be sent to him as soon as I can make Mr. Round get it.

'Dearest Kate, good-bye. I hope you will feel for me. If you do not answer me I shall presume that you think yourself bound to support his side, and to believe me to have been wrong. It will make me very unhappy; but I shall remember that you are his sister, and I shall not be angry with you.

'Yours always affectionately,

'ALICE VAVASOR.'

Kate, as she read her letter through, at first quickly, and then very slowly, came by degrees almost to forget that death was in the house. Her mind, and heart, and brain, were filled with thoughts and feelings that had exclusive reference to Alice and her brother, and at last she found herself walking the room with quick, impetuous steps, while her blood was hot with indignation.

All her sympathies in the matter were with Alice. It never occurred to her to disbelieve a word of the statement made to her, or to suggest to herself that it had been coloured by any fears or exaggerations on the part of her correspondent. She knew that Alice was true. And, moreover, much as she loved her brother,—willing as she had been and would still be to risk all that she possessed, and herself also, on his behalf,— she knew that it would be risking and not trusting. She loved her brother, such love having come to her by nature, and having remained with her from of old; and in his intellect she still believed. But she had ceased to have belief in his conduct. She feared everything that he might do, and lived with a consciousness that though she was willing to connect all her own fortunes with his, she had much reason to expect that she might encounter ruin in doing so. Her sin had been in this,—that she had been anxious to subject Alice to the same danger,—that she had intrigued, sometimes very meanly, to bring about the object which she had at heart,—that she had used all her craft to separate Alice from Mr. Grey. Perhaps it may be alleged in her excuse that she had thought,—had hoped rather than thought,—that the marriage which she contemplated would change much in her brother that was wrong, and bring him into a mode of life that would not be dangerous. Might not she and Alice together so work upon him, that he should cease to stand ever on the brink of some half-seen precipice? To risk herself for her brother was noble. But when she used her cunning in inducing her cousin to share that risk she was ignoble. Of this she had herself some consciousness as she walked up and down the old dining-room at midnight, holding her cousin's letter in her hand.

Her cheeks became tinged with shame as she thought of the scene which Alice had described,—the toy thrown beneath the grate, the loud curses, the whispered threats, which had been more terrible than curses, the demand for money, made with something worse than a cut-throat's violence, the strong man's hand placed upon that woman's arm in anger and in rage, those eyes glaring, and the gaping horror of that still raw cicatrice, as he pressed his face close to that of his victim! Not for a moment did she think of defending him. She accused him to herself vehemently of a sin over and above those sins which had filled Alice with dismay. He had demanded money from the girl whom he intended to marry! According to Kate's idea, nothing could excuse or palliate this sin. Alice had accounted it as nothing,—had expressed her opinion that the demand was reasonable;—even now, after the ill-usage to which she had been subjected, she had declared that the money should be forthcoming, and given to the man who had treated her so shamefully. It might be well that Alice should so feel and so act, but it behoved Kate to feel and act very differently. She would tell her brother, even in that house of death, should he come there, that his conduct was mean and unmanly. Kate was no coward. She declared to herself that she would do this even though he should threaten her with all his fury,—though he should glare upon her with all the horrors of his countenance.

One o'clock, and two o'clock, still found her in the dark sombre parlour, every now and then pacing the floor of the room. The fire had gone out, and, though it was now the middle of April, she began to feel the cold. But she would not go to bed before she had written a line to Alice. To her brother a message by telegraph would of course be sent the next morning; as also would she send a message to her aunt. But to Alice she would write, though it might be but a line. Cold as she was, she found her pens and paper, and wrote her letter that night. It was very short. 'Dear Alice, to-day I received your letter, and to-day our poor old grandfather died. Tell my uncle John, with my love, of his father's death. You will understand that I cannot write much now about that other matter; but I must tell you, even at such a moment as this, that there shall be no quarrel between you and me. There shall be none at least on my side. I cannot say more till a few days shall have passed by. He is lying up-stairs, a corpse. I have telegraphed to George, and I suppose he will come down. I think my aunt Greenow will come also, as I had written to her before, seeing that I wanted the comfort of having her here. Uncle John will of course come or not as he thinks fitting. I don't know whether I am in a position to say that I shall be glad to see him; but I should be very glad. He and you will know that I can, as yet, tell you nothing further. The lawyer is to see the men about the funeral. Nothing, I suppose, will be done till George comes. Your own cousin and friend, KATE VAVASOR.' And then she added a line below. 'My own Alice,—If you will let me, you shall be my sister, and be the nearest to me and the dearest.'

Alice, when she received this, was at the first moment so much struck, and indeed surprised, by the tidings of her grandfather's death, that she was forced, in spite of the still existing violence of her own feelings, to think and act chiefly with reference to that event. Her father had not then left his room. She therefore went to him, and handed him Kate's letter. 'Papa,' she said, 'there is news from Westmoreland; bad news, which you hardly expected yet.' 'My father is dead,' said John Vavasor. Whereupon Alice gave him Kate's letter, that he might read it. 'Of course I shall go down,' he said, as he came to that part in which Kate had spoken of him. 'Does she think I shall not follow my father to the grave, because I dislike her brother? What does she mean by saying that there shall be no quarrel between you and her?' 'I will explain that at another time,' said Alice. John Vavasor asked no further questions then, but declared at first that he should go to Westmoreland on the following day. Then he altered his purpose. 'I'll go by the mail train to-night,' he said. 'It will be very disagreeable, but I ought to be there when the will is opened.' There was very little more said in Queen Anne Street on the subject till the evening,—till a few moments before Mr. Vavasor left his house. He indeed had thought nothing more about that quarrelling, or rather that promise that there should be no quarrelling, between the girls. He still regarded his nephew George as the man who, unfortunately, was to be his son-in-law, and now, during this tedious sad day, in which he felt himself compelled to remain at home, he busied his mind in thinking of George and Alice, as living together at the old Hall. At six, the father and daughter dined, and soon after dinner Mr. Vavasor went up to his own room to prepare himself for his journey. After a while Alice followed him,—but she did not do so till she knew that if anything was to be told before the journey no further time could be lost. 'Papa,' she said, as soon as she had shut the door behind her, 'I think I ought to tell you before you go that everything is over between me and George.'

'Have you quarrelled with him too?' said her father, with uncontrolled surprise.

'I should perhaps say that he has quarrelled with me. But, dear papa, pray do not question me at present. I will tell you all when you come back, but I thought it right that you should know this before you went.'

'It has been his doing then?'

'I cannot explain it to you in a hurry like this. Papa, you may understand something of the shame which I feel, and you should not question me now.'

'And John Grey?'

'There is nothing different in regard to him.'

'I'll be shot if I can understand you. George, you know, has had two thousand pounds of your money,—of yours or somebody else's. Well, we can't talk about it now, as I must be off. Thinking as I do of George, I'm glad of it,—that's all.' Then he went, and Alice was left alone, to comfort herself as best she might by her own reflections.

George Vavasor had received the message on the day previous to that on which Alice's letter had reached her, but it had not come to him till late in the day. He might have gone down by the mail train of that night, but there were one or two persons, his own attorney especially, whom he wished to see before the reading of his grandfather's will. He remained in town, therefore, on the following day, and went down by the same train as that which took his uncle. Walking along the platform, looking for a seat, he peered into a carriage and met his uncle's eye. The two saw each other, but did not speak, and George passed on to another carriage. On the following morning, before the break of day, they met again in the refreshment room, at the station at Lancaster. 'So my father has gone, George,' said the uncle, speaking to the nephew. They must go to the same house, and Mr. Vavasor felt that it would be better that they should be on speaking terms when they reached it. 'Yes,' said George; 'he has gone at last. I wonder what we shall find to have been his last act of injustice.' The reader will remember that he had received Kate's first letter, in which she had told him of the Squire's altered will. John Vavasor turned away disgusted. His finer feelings were perhaps not very

147

strong, but he had no thoughts or hopes in reference to the matter which were mean. He expected nothing himself, and did not begrudge his nephew the inheritance. At this moment he was thinking of the old Squire as a father who had ever

been kind to him. It might be natural that George should have no such old affection at his heart, but it was unnatural that he should express himself as he had done at such a moment.

The uncle turned away, but said nothing. George followed him with a little proposition of his own. 'We shan't get any conveyance at Shap,' he said. 'Hadn't we better go over in a chaise from Kendal?' To this the uncle assented, and so they finished their journey together. George smoked all the time that they were in the carriage, and very few words were spoken. As they drove up to the old house, they found that another arrival had taken place before them,—Mrs. Greenow having reached the house in some vehicle from the Shap station. She had come across from Norwich to Manchester, where she had joined the train which had brought the uncle and nephew from London.

CHAPTER LV

The Will

THE coming of Mrs. Greenow at this very moment was a great comfort to Kate. Without her she would hardly have known how to bear herself with her uncle and her brother. As it was, they were all restrained by something of the courtesy which strangers are bound to show to each other. George had never seen his aunt since he was a child, and some sort of introduction was necessary between them.

'So you are George,' said Mrs. Greenow, putting out her hand and smiling.

'Yes; I'm George,' said he.

'And a Member of Parliament!' said Mrs. Greenow. 'It's quite an honour to the family. I felt so proud when I heard it!' She said this pleasantly, meaning it to be taken for truth, and then turned away to her brother. 'Papa's time was fully come,' she said, 'though, to tell the truth, I had no idea that he was so weak as Kate described him to have been.'

'Nor I, either,' said John Vavasor. 'He went to church with us here on Christmas-day.'

'Did he, indeed? Dear, dear! He seems at last to have gone off just like poor Greenow.' Here she put her handkerchief up to her face. 'I think you didn't know Greenow, John?'

'I met him once,' said her brother.

'Ah! he wasn't to be known and understood in that way. I'm aware there was a little prejudice, because of his being in trade, but we won't talk of that now. Where should I have been without him, tradesman or no tradesman?'

'I've no doubt he was an excellent man.'

'You may say that, John. Ah, well! we can't keep everything in this life for ever.' It may, perhaps, be as well to explain now that Mrs. Greenow had told Captain Bellfield at their last meeting before she left Norwich, that, under certain circumstances, if he behaved himself well, there might possibly be ground of hope. Whereupon Captain Bellfield had immediately

gone to the best tailor in that city, had told the man of his
coming marriage, and had given an extensive order. But the
tailor had not as yet supplied the goods, waiting for more
credible evidence of the Captain's good fortune. 'We're all
grass of the field,' said Mrs. Greenow, lightly brushing a tear
from her eye, 'and must be cut down and put into the oven in
our turns.' Her brother uttered a slight sympathetic groan,
shaking his head in testimony of the uncertainty of human
affairs, and then said that he would go out and look about the
place. George, in the meantime, had asked his sister to show
him his room, and the two were already together up-stairs.

Kate had made up her mind that she would say nothing about
Alice at the present moment,—nothing, if it could be avoided,
till after the funeral. She led the way up-stairs, almost trembling with fear, for she knew that that other subject of the will
would also give rise to trouble and sorrow,—perhaps, also,
to determined quarrelling.

'What has brought that woman here?' was the first question
that George asked.

'I asked her to come,' said Kate.

'And why did you ask her to come here?' said George,
angrily. Kate immediately felt that he was speaking as though
he were master of the house, and also as though he intended
to be master of her. As regarded the former idea, she had no
objection to it. She thoroughly and honestly wished that he
might be the master; and though she feared that he might find
himself mistaken in his assumption, she herself was not disposed to deny any appearance of right that he might take upon
himself in that respect. But she had already begun to tell herself that she must not submit herself to his masterdom. She had
gradually so taught herself since he had compelled her to write
the first letter in which Alice had been asked to give her money.

'I asked her, George, before my poor grandfather's death,
when I thought that he would linger perhaps for weeks. My
life here alone with him, without any other woman in the
house beside the servants, was very melancholy.'

'Why did you not ask Alice to come to you?'

'Alice could not have come,' said Kate, after a short pause.

'I don't know why she shouldn't have come. I won't have that woman about the place. She disgraced herself by marrying a blacksmith——'

'Why, George, it was you yourself who advised me to go and stay with her.'

'That's a very different thing. Now that he's dead, and she's got his money, it's all very well that you should go to her occasionally; but I won't have her here.'

'It's natural that she should come to her father's house at her father's death-bed.'

'I hate to be told that things are natural. It always means humbug. I don't suppose she cared for the old man any more than I did,—or than she cared for the other old man who married her. People are such intense hypocrites. There's my uncle John, pulling a long face because he has come into this house, and he will pull it as long as the body lies up there; and yet for the last twenty years there's nothing on earth he has so much hated as going to see his father. When are they going to bury him?'

'On Saturday, the day after to-morrow.'

'Why couldn't they do it to-morrow, so that we could get away before Sunday?'

'He only died on **Monday, G**eorge,' said Kate, solemnly.

'Psha! Who has got the will?'

'Mr. Gogram. He was here yesterday, and told me to tell you and uncle John that he would have it with him when he came back from the funeral.'

'What has my uncle John to do with it?' said George, sharply. 'I shall go over to Penrith this afternoon and make Gogram give it up to me.'

'I don't think he'll do that, George.'

'What right has he to keep it? What right has he to it at all? How do I know that he has really got the old man's last will? Where did my grandfather keep his papers?'

'In that old secretary, as he used to call it; the one that stands in the dining-room. It is sealed up.'

'Who sealed it?'

'Mr. Gogram did,—Mr. Gogram and I together.'

'What the deuce made you meddle with it?'

'I merely assisted him. But I believe he was quite right. I think it is usual in such cases.'

'Balderdash! You are thinking of some old trumpery of former days. Till I know to the contrary, everything here belongs to me as heir-at-law, and I do not mean to allow of any interference till I know for certain that my rights have been taken from me. And I won't accept a death-bed will. What a man chooses to write when his fingers will hardly hold the pen, goes for nothing.'

'You can't suppose that I wish to interfere with your rights?'

'I hope not.'

'Oh, George!'

'Well; I say, I hope not. But I know there are those who would. Do you think my uncle John would not interfere with me if he could? By——! if he does, he shall find that he does it to his cost. I'll lead him such a life through the courts, for the next two or three years, that he'll wish that he had remained in Chancery Lane, and had never left it.'

A message was now brought up by the nurse, saying that Mrs. Greenow and Mr. Vavasor were going into the room where the old Squire was lying, 'Would Miss Kate and Mr. George go with them?'

'Mr. Vavasor!' shouted out George, making the old woman jump. She did not understand his meaning in the least. 'Yes, sir; the old Squire,' she said.

'Will you come, George?' Kate asked.

'No; what should I go there for? Why should I pretend an interest in the dead body of a man whom I hated, and who hated me;—whose very last act, as far as I know as yet, was an attempt to rob me? I won't go and see him.'

Kate went, and was glad of an opportunity of getting away from her brother. Every hour the idea was becoming stronger in her mind that she must in some way separate herself from him. There had come upon him of late a hard ferocity which made him unendurable. And then he carried to such a pitch that hatred, as he called it, of conventional rules, that he allowed himself to be controlled by none of the ordinary bonds of society. She had felt this heretofore, with a nervous consciousness that she was doing wrong in endeavouring to bring about a marriage between him and Alice; but this demeanour and mode of talking had now so grown upon him that Kate began to feel herself thankful that Alice had been saved.

Kate went up with her uncle and aunt, and saw the face of her grandfather for the last time. 'Poor, dear old man!' said Mrs. Greenow, as the easy tears ran down her face. 'Do you remember, John, how he used to scold me, and say that I should never come to good? He has said the same thing to you, Kate, I dare say?'

'He has been very kind to me,' said Kate, standing at the foot of the bed. She was not one of those whose tears stand near their eyes.

'He was a fine old gentleman,' said John Vavasor;—'belonging to days that are now gone by, but by no means the less of a gentleman on that account. I don't know that he ever did an unjust or ungenerous act to any one. Come, Kate, we may as well go down.' Mrs. Greenow lingered to say a word or two to the nurse, of the manner in which Greenow's body was treated when Greenow was lying dead, and then she followed her brother and niece.

George did not go into Penrith, nor did he see Mr. Gogram till that worthy attorney came out to Vavasor Hall on the morning of the funeral. He said nothing more on the subject, nor did he break the seals on the old upright desk that stood in the parlour. The two days before the funeral were very wretched for all the party, except, perhaps, for Mrs. Greenow, who affected not to understand that her nephew was in a bad humour. She called him 'poor George,' and treated all his incivility to herself as though it were the effect of his grief. She asked him questions about Parliament, which, of course, he didn't answer, and told him little stories about poor dear Greenow, not heeding his expressions of unmistakable disgust.

The two days at last went by, and the hour of the funeral came. There was the doctor and Gogram, and the uncle and the nephew, to follow the corpse,—the nephew taking upon himself ostentatiously the foremost place, as though he could thereby help to maintain his pretensions as heir. The clergyman met them at the little wicket-gate of the churchyard, having by some reasoning, which we hope was satisfactory to himself, overcome a resolution which he at first formed, that he would not read the burial service over an unrepentant sinner. But he did read it, having mentioned his scruples to none but one confidential clerical friend in the same diocese.

'I'm told that you have got my grandfather's will,' George said to the attorney as soon as he saw him.

'I have it in my pocket,' said Mr. Gogram, 'and purpose to read it as soon as we return from church.'

'Is it usual to take a will away from a man's house in that way?' George asked.

'Quite usual,' said the attorney; 'and in this case it was done at the express desire of the testator.'

'I think it is the common practice,' said John Vavasor.

George upon this turned round at his uncle as though about to attack him, but he restrained himself and said nothing, though he showed his teeth.

The funeral was very plain, and not a word was spoken by George Vavasor during the journey there and back. John Vavasor asked a few questions of the doctor as to the last weeks of his father's life; and it was incidentally mentioned, both by the doctor and by the attorney, that the old Squire's intellect had remained unimpaired up to the last moment that he had been seen by either of them. When they returned to the hall Mrs. Greenow met them with an invitation to lunch. They all went to the dining-room, and drank each a glass of sherry. George took two or three glasses. The doctor then withdrew, and drove himself back to Penrith, where he lived.

'Shall we go into the other room now?' said the attorney.

The three gentlemen then rose up, and went across to the drawing-room, George leading the way. The attorney followed him, and John Vavasor closed the door behind them. Had any observer been there to watch them he might have seen by the faces of the two latter that they expected an unpleasant meeting. Mr. Gogram, as he had walked across the hall, had pulled a document out of his pocket, and held it in his hand as he took a chair. John Vavasor stood behind one of the chairs which had been placed at the table, and leaned upon it, looking across the room, up at the ceiling. George stood on the rug before the fire, with his hands in the pockets of his trousers, and his coat-tails over his arms.

'Gentlemen, will you sit down?' said Mr. Gogram.

John Vavasor immediately sat down.

'I prefer to stand here,' said George.

Mr. Gogram then opened the document before him.

'Before that paper is read,' said George, 'I think it right to say a few words. I don't know what it contains, but I believe it to have been executed by my grandfather only an hour or two before his death.'

'On the day before he died,—early in the day,' said the attorney.

'Well,—the day before he died; it is the same thing,— while he was dying, in fact. He never got out of bed afterwards.'

'He was not in bed at the time, Mr. Vavasor. Not that it would have mattered if he had been. And he came down to dinner on that day. I don't understand, however, why you make these observations.'

'If you'll listen to me you will understand. I make them because I deny my grandfather's fitness to make a will in the last moments of his existence, and at such an age. I saw him a few weeks ago, and he was not fit to be trusted with the management of property then.'

'I do not think this is the time, George, to put forward such objections,' said the uncle.

'I think it is,' said George. 'I believe that that paper purports to be an instrument by which I should be villanously defrauded if it were allowed to be held as good. Therefore I protest against it now, and shall question it at law if action be taken on it. You can read it now, if you please.'

'Oh, yes, I shall read,' said Mr. Gogram; 'and I say that it is as valid a will as ever a man signed.'

'And I say it's not. That's the difference between us.'

The will was read amidst sundry interjections and expressions of anger from George, which it is not necessary to repeat. Nor need I trouble my readers with the will at length. It began by expressing the testator's great desire that his property might descend in his own family, and that the house might be held and inhabited by some one bearing the name of Vavasor. He then declared that he felt himself obliged to pass over his natural heir, believing that the property would not be safe in his hands; he therefore left it in trust to his son John Vavasor, whom he appointed to be sole executor of his will. He devised it to George's eldest son,—should George ever marry and have a son,—as soon as he might reach the age of twenty-five. In the meantime the property should remain in the hands of John Vavasor for his use and benefit, with a lien*on it of five hundred a year to be paid annually to his granddaughter Kate. In the event of George having no son, the property was to go to the eldest son of Kate, or failing that to the eldest son of his other granddaughter who might take the name of Vavasor. All his personal property he left to his son, John Vavasor. 'And, Mr. Vavasor,' said the attorney, as he finished his reading, 'you will, I fear, get very little by that latter clause. The estate now owes nothing; but I doubt whether the Squire had fifty pounds in his banker's hands when he died, and the value of the property about the place is very small. He has been unwilling to spend anything during the last ten years, but has paid off every shilling that the property owed.'

'It is as I supposed,' said George. His voice was very unpleasant, and so was the fire of his eyes and the ghastly rage of his scarred face. 'The old man has endeavoured in his anger to rob me of everything because I would not obey him in his wickedness when I was here with him a short while before he died. Such a will as that can stand nowhere.'

'As to that I have nothing to say at present,' said the attorney.

'Where is his other will,—the one he made before that?'

'If I remember rightly we executed two before this.'

'And where are they?'

'It is not my business to know, Mr. Vavasor. I believe that I saw him destroy one, but I have no absolute knowledge. As to the other, I can say nothing.'

'And what do you mean to do?' said George, turning to his uncle.

'Do! I shall carry out the will. I have no alternative. Your sister is the person chiefly interested under it. She gets five hundred a year for her life; and if she marries and you don't, or if she has a son and you don't, her son will have the whole property.'

George stood for a few moments thinking. Might it not be possible that by means of Alice and Kate together,—by marrying the former,—perhaps, he might still obtain possession of the property? But that which he wanted was the command of the property at once,—the power of raising money upon it instantly. The will had been so framed as to make that impossible in any way. Kate's share in it had not been left to her unconditionally, but was to be received even by her through the hands of her uncle John. Such a will shut him out from all his hopes. 'It is a piece of d—— roguery,' he said.

'What do you mean by that, sir?' said Gogram, turning round towards him.

'I mean exactly what I say. It is a piece of d—— roguery. Who was in the room when that thing was written?'

'The signature was witnessed by——'

'I don't ask as to the signature. Who was in the room when the thing was written?'

'I was here with your grandfather.'

'And no one else?'

'No one else. The presence of any one else at such a time would be very unusual.'

'Then I regard the document simply as waste paper.' After saying this, George Vavasor left the room, and slammed the door after him.

'I never was insulted in such a way before,' said the attorney, almost with tears in his eyes.

'He is a disappointed and I fear a ruined man,' said John Vavasor. 'I do not think you need regard what he says.'

'But he should not on that account insult me. I have only done my duty. I did not even advise his grandfather. It is mean on his part and unmanly. If he comes in my way again I shall tell him so.'

'He probably will not put himself in your way again, Mr. Gogram.'

Then the attorney went, having suggested to Mr. Vavasor that he should instruct his attorney in London to take steps in reference to the proving of the will. 'It's as good a will as ever was made,' said Mr. Gogram. 'If he can set that aside, I'll give up making wills altogether.'

Who was to tell Kate? That was John Vavasor's first thought when he was left alone at the hall-door, after seeing the lawyer start away. And how was he to get himself back to London without further quarrelling with his nephew? And what was he to do at once with reference to the immediate duties of proprietorship which were entailed upon him as executor? It was by no means improbable, as he thought, that George might assume to himself the position of master of the house; that he might demand the keys, for instance, which no doubt were in Kate's hands at present, and that he would take possession with violence. What should he do under such circumstances? It was clear that he could not run away and get back to his club by the night mail train. He had duties there at the Hall, and these duties were of a nature to make him almost regret the position in which his father's will had placed him. Eventually he would gain some considerable increase to his means, but the immediate effect would be terribly troublesome. As he looked up at the melancholy pines which were slowly waving their heads in the wind before the door he declared to himself that he would sell his inheritance and his executorship very cheaply, if such a sale were possible.

In the dining-room he found his sister alone. 'Well, John,' said she; 'well? How is it left?'

'Where is Kate?' he asked.

'She has gone out with her brother.'

'Did he take his hat?'

'Oh, yes. He asked her to walk, and she went with him at once.'

'Then, I suppose, he will tell her,' said John Vavasor. After that he explained the circumstances of the will to Mrs. Greenow. 'Bravo,' exclaimed the widow. 'I'm delighted. I love Kate dearly; and now she can marry almost whom she pleases.'

CHAPTER LVI

Another Walk on the Fells

GEORGE, when he left the room in which he had insulted the lawyer, went immediately across to the parlour in which his aunt and sister were sitting. 'Kate,' said he, 'put on your hat and come and walk with me. That business is over.' Kate's hat and shawl were in the room, and they were out of the house together within a minute.

They walked down the carriage-road, through the desolate, untended grounds, to the gate, before either of them spoke a word. Kate was waiting for George to tell her of the will, but did not dare to ask any question. George intended to tell her of the will, but was not disposed to do so without some preparation. It was a thing not to be spoken of open-mouthed, as a piece of ordinary news. 'Which way shall we go?' said Kate, as soon as they had passed through the old rickety gate, which swang at the entrance of the place. 'Up across the fell,' said George; 'the day is fine, and I want to get away from my uncle for a time.' She turned round, therefore, outside the hill of firs, and led the way back to the beacon wood through which she and Alice had walked across to Haweswater upon a memorable occasion. They had reached the top of the beacon hill, and were out upon the Fell, before George had begun his story. Kate was half beside herself with curiosity, but still she was afraid to ask. 'Well,' said George, when they paused a moment as they stepped over a plank that crossed the boundary ditch of the wood; 'don't you want to know what that dear old man has done for you?' Then he looked into her face very steadfastly. 'But perhaps you know already,' he added. He had come out determined not to quarrel with his sister. He had resolved, in that moment of thought which had been allowed to him, that his best hope for the present required that he should keep himself on good terms with her, at any rate till he had settled what line of conduct he would pursue. But he was, in truth, so sore with anger and disappointment,—he had become so nearly mad with that continued, unappeased wrath in which he now indulged against all the world, that he could not refrain himself from bitter words. He was as one driven by the Furies,* and was no longer able to control them in their driving of him.

'I know nothing of it,' said Kate. 'Had I known I should have told you. Your question is unjust to me.'

'I am beginning to doubt,' said he, 'whether a man can be safe in trusting any one. My grandfather has done his best to rob me of the property altogether.'

'I told you that I feared he would do so.'

'And he has made you his heir.'

'Me?'

'Yes; you.'

'He told me distinctly that he would not do that.'

'But he has, I tell you.'

'Then, George, I shall do that which I told him I should do in the event of his making such a will; for he asked me the question. I told him I should restore the estate to you, and upon that he swore that he would not leave it to me.'

'And what a fool you were,' said he, stopping her in the pathway. 'What an ass! Why did you tell him that? You knew that he would not, on that account, do justice to me.'

'He asked me, George.'

'Psha! now you have ruined me, and you might have saved me.'

'But I will save you still, if he has left the estate to me. I do not desire to take it from you. As God in heaven sees me, I have never ceased to endeavour to protect your interests here at Vavasor. I will sign anything necessary to make over my right in the property to you.' Then they walked on over the Fell for some minutes without speaking. They were still on the same path,—that path which Kate and Alice had taken in the winter,—and now poor Kate could not but think of all that she had said that day on George's behalf;—how had she mingled truth and falsehood in her efforts to raise her brother's character in her cousin's eyes! It had all been done in vain. At this very moment of her own trouble Kate thought of John Grey, and repented of what she had done. Her hopes in that direction were altogether blasted. She knew that her brother had ill-treated Alice, and that she must tell him so if Alice's name were mentioned between them. She could no longer worship her brother, and hold herself at his command in all things. But, as regarded the property to which he was naturally the heir, if any act of hers could give it to him, that act would be done. 'If the will is as you say, George, I will make over my right to you.'

'You can make over nothing,' he answered. 'The old robber has been too cunning for that; he has left it all in the hands of my uncle John. D— him. D— them both.'

'George! George! he is dead now.'

'Dead; of course he is dead. What of that? I wish he had been dead ten years ago,—or twenty. Do you suppose I am to forgive him because he is dead? I'll heap his grave with curses, if that can be of avail to punish him.'

'You can only punish the living that way.'

'And I will punish them;—but not by cursing them. My uncle John shall have such a life of it for the next year or two that he shall bitterly regret the hour in which he has stepped between me and my rights.'

'I do not believe that he has done so.'

'Not done so! What was he down here for at Christmas? Do you pretend to think that that make-believe will was concocted without his knowledge?'

'I'm sure that he knew nothing of it. I don't think my grandfather's mind was made up a week before he died.'

'You'll have to swear that, remember, in a court. I'm not going to let the matter rest, I can tell you. You'll have to prove that. How long is it since he asked you what you would do with the estate if he left it to you?'

Kate thought for a moment before she answered. 'It was only two days before he died, if I remember rightly.'

'But you must remember rightly. You'll have to swear to it. And now tell me this honestly; do you believe, in your heart, that he was in a condition fit for making a will?'

'I advised him not to make it.'

'Why? why? What reason did you give?'

'I told him that I thought no man should alter family arrangements when he was so ill.'

'Exactly. You told him that. And what did he say?'

'He was very angry, and made me send for Mr. Gogram.'

'Now, Kate, think a little before you answer me again. If ever you are to do me a good turn, you must do it now. And, remember this, I don't at all want to take anything away from you. Whatever you think is fair you shall have.'

He was a fool not to have known her better than that.

'I want nothing,' she said, stopping and stamping with her foot upon the crushed heather. 'George, you don't understand what it is to be honest.'

He smiled,—with a slight provoking smile that passed very rapidly from his face. The meaning of the smile was to be read, had Kate been calm enough to read it. 'I can't say that I do.' That was the meaning of the smile. 'Well, never mind about that,' said he; 'you advised my grandfather not to make his will,—thinking, no doubt, that his mind was not clear enough?'

She paused a moment again before she answered him. 'His mind was clear,' she said; 'but I thought that he should not trust his judgment while he was so weak.'

'Look here, Kate; I do believe that you at any rate have no mind to assist in this robbery. That it is a robbery you can't have any doubt. I said he had left the estate to you. That is not what he has done. He has left the estate to my uncle John.'

'Why tell me, then, what was untrue?'

'Are you disappointed?'

'Of course I am; uncle John won't give it you. George, I don't understand you; I don't, indeed.'

'Never mind about that, but listen to me. The estate is left in the hands of John Vavasor; but he has left you five hundred a year out of it till somebody is twenty-five years old who is not yet born, and probably never will be born. The will itself shows the old fool to have been mad.'

'He was no more mad than you are, George.'

'Listen to me, I tell you. I don't mean that he was a raging maniac. Now, you had advised him not to make any new will because you thought he was not in a fit condition?'

'Yes; I did.'

'You can swear to that?'

'I hope I may not be called on to do so. I hope there may be no swearing about it. But if I am asked the question I must swear it.'

'Exactly. Now listen till you understand what it is I mean. That will, if it stands, gives all the power over the estate to John Vavasor. It renders you quite powerless as regards any help or assistance that you might be disposed to give me. But, nevertheless, your interest under the will is greater than his, —or than that of any one else,—for your son would inherit if I have none. Do you understand?'

'Yes; I think so.'

'And your testimony as to the invalidity of the will would be conclusive against all the world.'

'I would say in a court what I have told you, if that will do any good.'

'It will not be enough. Look here, Kate; you must be steadfast here; everything depends on you. How often have you told me that you will stick to me throughout life? Now you will be tried.'

Kate felt that her repugnance towards him,—towards all that he was doing and wished her to do,—was growing stronger within her at every word he spoke. She was becoming gradually aware that he desired from her something which she could not and would not do, and she was aware also that in refusing him she would have to encounter him in all his wrath. She set her teeth firmly together, and clenched her little fist. If a fight was necessary, she would fight with him. As he looked at her closely with his sinister eyes, her love towards him was almost turned to hatred.

'Now you will be tried,' he said again. 'You advised him not to make the will because you thought his intellect was impaired!'

'No; not so.'

'Stop, Kate, stop. If you will think of it, it was so. What is the meaning of his judgment being weak?'

'I didn't say his judgment was weak.'

'But that was what you meant when you advised him not to trust it!'

'Look here, George; I think I know now what you mean. If anybody asks me if his mind was gone, or his intellect deranged, I cannot say that there was anything of the kind.'

'You will not?'

'Certainly not. It would be untrue.'

'Then you are determined to throw me over and claim the property for yourself.' Again he turned towards and looked at her as though he were resolved to frighten her. 'And I am to count you also among my enemies? You had better take care, Kate.'

They were now upon the Fell side, more than three miles away from the Hall; and Kate, as she looked round, saw that they were all alone. Not a cottage,—not a sign of humanity was within sight. Kate saw that it was so, and was aware that the fact pressed itself upon her as being of importance. Then she thought again of her resolution to fight with him, if any fight were necessary; to tell him, in so many words, that she would separate herself from him and defy him. She would not fear him, let his words and face be ever so terrible! Surely her own brother would do her no bodily harm. And even though he should do so,—though he should take her roughly by the arm as he had done to Alice,—though he should do worse than that, still she would fight him. Her blood was the same as his, and he should know that her courage was, at any rate, as high.

And, indeed, when she looked at him, she had cause to fear. He intended that she should fear. He intended that she should dread what he might do to her at that moment. As to what he would do he had no resolve made. Neither had he resolved on anything when he had gone to Alice and had shaken her rudely as she sat beside him. He had been guided by no fixed intent when he had attacked John Grey, nor when he insulted the attorney; but a Fury was driving him, and he was conscious of being so driven. He almost wished to be driven to some act of frenzy. Everything in the world had gone against him, and he desired to expend his rage on some one.

'Kate,' said he, stopping her, 'we will have this out here, if you please. So much, at any rate, shall be settled to-day. You have made many promises to me, and I have believed them. You can now keep them all, by simply saying what you know to be the truth,—that that old man was a drivelling idiot when he made this will. Are you prepared to do me that justice? Think before you answer me, for, by G—, if I cannot have justice among you, I will have revenge.' And he put his hand upon her breast up near to her throat.

'Take your hand down, George,' said she. 'I'm not such a fool that you can frighten me in that way.'

'Answer me!' he said, and shook her, having some part of her raiment within his clutch.

'Oh, George, that I should live to be so ashamed of my brother!'

'Answer me,' he said again; and again he shook her.

'I have answered you. I will say nothing of the kind that you want me to say. My grandfather, up to the latest moment that I saw him, knew what he was about. He was not an idiot. He was, I believe, only carrying out a purpose fixed long before. You will not make me change what I say by looking at me like that, nor yet by shaking me. You don't know me, George, if you think you can frighten me like a child.'

He heard her to the last word, still keeping his hand upon her, and holding her by the cloak she wore; but the violence of his grasp had relaxed itself, and he let her finish her words, as though his object had simply been to make her speak out to him what she had to say. 'Oh,' said he, when she had done, 'That's to be it; is it? That's your idea of honesty. The very name of the money being your own has been too much for you. I wonder whether you and my uncle had contrived it all between you beforehand?'

'You will not dare to ask him, because he is a man,' said Kate, her eyes brimming with tears, not through fear, but in very vexation at the nature of the charge he had brought against her.

'Shall I not? You will see what I dare do. As for you, with all your promises———. Kate, you know that I keep my word. Say that you will do as I desire you, or I will be the death of you.'

'Do you mean that you will murder me?' said she.

'Murder you! yes; why not? Treated as I have been among you, do you suppose that I shall stick at anything? Why should I not murder you—you and Alice, too, seeing how you have betrayed me?'

'Poor Alice!' as she spoke the words she looked straight into his eyes, as though defying him, as far as she herself were concerned.

'Poor Alice, indeed! D—— hypocrite! There's a pair of you; cursed, whining, false, intriguing hypocrites. There; go down and tell your uncle and that old woman there that I threatened to murder you. Tell the judge so, when you're brought into court to swear me out of my property. You false liar!' Then he pushed her from him with great violence, so that she fell heavily upon the stony ground.

He did not stop to help her up, or even to look at her as she

166

lay, but walked away across the heath, neither taking the track on towards Haweswater, nor returning by the path which had brought them thither. He went away northwards across the wild fell; and Kate, having risen up and seated herself on a small cairn of stones which stood there, watched him as he descended the slope of the hill till he was out of sight. He did not run, but he seemed to move rapidly, and he never once turned round to look at her. He went away, down the hill northwards, and presently the curving of the ground hid him from her view.

When she first seated herself her thoughts had been altogether of him. She had feared no personal injury, even when she had asked him whether he would murder her. Her blood had been hot within her veins, and her heart had been full of defiance. Even yet she feared nothing, but continued to think of him and his misery, and his disgrace. That he was gone for ever, utterly and irretrievably ruined, thrown out, as it were, beyond the pale of men, was now certain to her. And this was the brother in whom she had believed; for whom she had not only been willing to sacrifice herself, but for whose purposes she had striven to sacrifice her cousin! What would he do now? As he passed from out of her sight down the hill, it seemed to her as though he were rushing straight into some hell from which there could be no escape.

She knew that her arm had been hurt in the fall, but for a while she would not move it or feel it, being resolved to take no account of what might have happened to herself. But when he had been gone some ten minutes, she rose to her feet, and finding that the movement pained her greatly, and that her right arm was powerless, she put up her left hand and became aware that the bone of her arm was broken below the elbow. Her first thought was given to the telling him of this, or the not telling, when she should meet him below at the house. How should she mention the accident to him? Should she lie, and say that she had fallen as she came down the hill alone? Of course he would not believe her, but still some such excuse as that might make the matter easier for them all. It did not occur to her that she might not see him again at all that day; and that, as far as he was concerned, there might be need for no lie.

She started off to walk down home, holding her right arm steadily against her body with her left hand. Of course she must give some account of herself when she got to the house; but it was of the account to be given to him that she thought. As to the others she cared little for them. 'Here I am; my arm is broken; and you had better send for a doctor.' That would be sufficient for them.

When she got into the wood the path was very dark. The heavens were overcast with clouds, and a few drops began to fall. Then the rain fell faster and faster, and before she had gone a quarter of a mile down the beacon hill, the clouds had opened themselves, and the shower had become a storm of water. Suffering as she was she stood up for a few moments under a large tree, taking the excuse of the rain for some minutes of delay, that she might make up her mind as to what she would say. Then it occurred to her that she might possibly meet him again before she reached the house; and, as she thought of it, she began for the first time to fear him. Would he come out upon her from the trees and really kill her? Had he made his way round, when he got out of her sight, that he might fall upon her suddenly and do as he had threatened? As the idea came upon her, she made a little attempt to run, but she found that running was impracticable from the pain the movement caused her. Then she walked on through the hard rain, steadily holding her arm against her side, but still looking every moment through the trees on the side from which George might be expected to reach her. But no one came near her on her way homewards. Had she been calm enough to think of the nature of the ground, she might have known that he could not have returned upon her so quickly. He must have come back up the steep hill-side which she had seen him descend. No;—he had gone away altogether, across the fells towards Bampton,* and was at this moment vainly buttoning his coat across his breast, in his unconscious attempt to keep out the wet. The Fury was driving him on, and he himself was not aware whither he was driven.

Dinner at the Hall had been ordered at five, the old hour; or rather that had been assumed to be the hour for dinner without any ordering. It was just five when Kate reached the front door. This she opened with her left hand, and turning at once into the dining-room, found her uncle and her aunt standing before the fire.

'Dinner is ready,' said John Vavasor; 'where is George?'

'You are wet, Kate,' said aunt Greenow.

'Yes, I am very wet,' said Kate. 'I must go up-stairs. Perhaps you'll come with me, aunt?'

'Come with you,—of course I will.' Aunt Greenow had seen at once that something was amiss.

'Where's George?' said John Vavasor. 'Has he come back with you, or are we to wait for him?'

Kate seated herself in her chair. 'I don't quite know where he is,' she said. In the meantime her aunt had hastened up to her side just in time to catch her as she was falling from her chair. 'My arm,' said Kate, very gently; 'my arm!' Then she slipped down against her aunt, and had fainted.

'He has done her a mischief,' said Mrs. Greenow, looking up at her brother. 'This is his doing.'

John Vavasor stood confounded, wishing himself back in Queen Anne Street.

CHAPTER LVII

Showing how the Wild Beast got himself back from the Mountains

ABOUT eleven o'clock on that night,—the night of the day on which Kate Vavasor's arm had been broken,—there came a gentle knock at Kate's bedroom door. There was nothing surprising in this, as of all the household Kate only was in bed. Her aunt was sitting at this time by her bedside, and the doctor, who had been summoned from Penrith and who had set her broken arm, was still in the house, talking over the accident with John Vavasor in the dining-room, before he proceeded back on his journey home.

'She will do very well,' said the doctor. 'It's only a simple fracture. I'll see her the day after tomorrow.'

'Is it not odd that such an accident should come from a fall whilst walking?' asked Mr. Vavasor.

The doctor shrugged his shoulders. 'One never can say how anything may occur,' said he. 'I know a young woman who broke the os femoris*by just kicking her cat;—at least, she said she did.'

'Indeed! I suppose you didn't take any trouble to inquire?'

'Not much. My business was with the injury, not with the way she got it. Somebody did make inquiry, but she stuck to her story and nothing came of it. Good night, Mr. Vavasor. Don't trouble her with questions till she has had some hours' sleep, at any rate.' Then the doctor went, and John Vavasor was left alone, standing with his back to the dining-room fire.

There had been so much trouble and confusion in the house since Kate had fainted, almost immediately upon her reaching home, that Mr. Vavasor had not yet had time to make up his mind as to the nature of the accident which had occurred. Mrs. Greenow had at once ascertained that the bone was broken, and the doctor had been sent for. Luckily he had been found at home, and had reached the Hall a little before ten o'clock. In the meantime, as soon as Kate recovered her senses, she volunteered her account of what had occurred.

Her brother had quarrelled with her about the will, she said, and had left her abruptly on the mountain. She had fallen, she went on to say, as she turned from him, and had at once found that she had hurt herself. But she had been too angry with him to let him know it; and, indeed, she had not known the extent herself till he had passed out of her sight. This was her story; and there was nothing in it that was false by the letter, though there was much that was false in the spirit. It was certainly true that George had not known that she was injured. It was true that she had asked him for no help. It was true, in one

170

sense, that she had fallen, and it was true that she had not herself known how severe had been the injury done to her till he had gone beyond the reach of her voice. But she repressed all mention of his violence, and when she was pressed as to the nature of the quarrel, she declined to speak further on that matter.

Neither her uncle nor her aunt believed her. That was a matter of course, and she knew that they did not believe her. George's absence, their recent experience of his moods, and the violence by which her arm must have been broken, made them certain that Kate had more to tell if she chose to tell it. But in her present condition they could not question her. Mrs. Greenow did ask as to the probability of her nephew's return.

'I can only tell you,' said Kate, 'that he went away across the Fell in the direction of Bampton. Perhaps he has gone on to Penrith. He was very angry with us all; and as the house is not his own, he has probably resolved that he will not stay another night under the roof. But, who can say? He is not in his senses when he is angered.'

John Vavasor, as he stood alone after the doctor's departure, endeavoured to ascertain the truth by thinking of it. 'I am sure,' he said to himself, 'that the doctor suspects that there has been violence. I know it from his tone, and I can see it in his eye. But how to prove it? and would there be good in proving it? Poor girl! Will it not be better for her to let it pass as though we believed her story?' He made up his mind that it would be better. Why should he take upon himself the terrible task of calling this insane relation to account for an act which he could not prove? The will itself, without that trouble, would give him trouble enough. Then he began to long that he was back at his club, and to think that the signing-room in Chancery Lane was not so bad. And so he went up to his bed, calling at Kate's door to ask after the patient.

In the meantime there had come a messenger to Mrs. Greenow, who had stationed herself with her niece. One of the girls of the house brought up a scrap of paper to the door, saying that a boy had brought it over with a cart from Shap, and that it was intended for Miss Vavasor, and it was she who

171

knocked at the sick-room door. The note was open and was not
addressed; indeed, the words were written on a scrap of paper
that was crumpled up rather than folded, and were as follows:
'Send me my clothes by the bearer. I shall not return to the
house.' Mrs. Greenow took it in to Kate, and then went away
to see her nephew's things duly put into his portmanteau. This
was sent away in the cart, and Mr. Vavasor, as he went up-
stairs, was told what had been done.

Neither on that night nor on the following day did Mrs.
Greenow ask any further questions; but on the morning after
that, when the doctor had left them with a good account of
the broken limb, her curiosity would brook no further delay.
And, indeed, indignation as well as curiosity urged her on.
In disposition she was less easy, and, perhaps, less selfish,
than her brother. If it were the case that that man had ill-
treated his sister, she would have sacrificed much to bring him
to punishment. 'Kate,' she said, when the doctor was gone, 'I
expect that you will tell me the whole truth as to what occurred
between you and your brother when you had this accident.'

'I have told you the truth.'

'But not the whole truth.'

'All the truth I mean to tell, aunt. He has quarrelled with
me, as I think, most unnecessarily; but you don't suppose that
I am going to give an exact account of the quarrel? We were
both wrong, probably, and so let there be an end of it.'

'Was he violent to you when he quarrelled with you?'

'When he is angry he is always violent in his language.'

'But, did he strike you?'

'Dear aunt, don't be angry with me if I say that I won't be
cross-examined. I would rather answer no more questions
about it. I know that questioning can do no good.'

Mrs. Greenow knew her niece well enough to be aware that
nothing more would be told her, but she was quite sure now
that Kate had not broken her arm by a simple fall. She was
certain that the injury had come from positive violence. Had
it not been so, Kate would not have contented herself with
refusing to answer the last question that had been asked, but

would also have repelled the charge made against her brother with indignation.

'You must have it your own way,' said Mrs. Greenow; 'but let me just tell you this, that your brother George had better keep out of my way.'

'It is probable that he will,' said Kate. 'Especially if you remain here to nurse me.'

Kate's conduct in answering all the questions made to her was not difficult, but she found that there was much difficulty in planning her own future behaviour towards her own brother. Must she abandon him altogether from henceforth; divide herself from him, as it were; have perfectly separate interests, and interests that were indeed hostile? and must she see him ruined and overwhelmed by want of money, while she had been made a rich woman by her grandfather's will? It will be remembered that her life had hitherto been devoted to him; that all her schemes and plans had had his success as their object; that she had taught herself to consider it to be her duty to sacrifice everything to his welfare. It is very sad to abandon the only object of a life! It is very hard to tear out from one's heart and fling away from it the only love that one has cherished! What was she to say to Alice about all this—to Alice whom she had cheated of a husband worthy of her, that she might allure her into the arms of one so utterly unworthy? Luckily for Kate, her accident was of such a nature that any writing to Alice was now out of the question.

But a blow! What woman can bear a blow from a man, and afterwards return to him with love? A wife may have to bear it and to return. And she may return with that sort of love which is a thing of custom. The man is the father of her children, and earns the bread which they eat and which she eats. Habit and the ways of the world require that she should be careful in his interests, and that she should live with him in what amity is possible to them. But as for love,—all that we mean by love when we speak of it and write of it,—a blow given by the defender to the defenceless crushes it all! A woman may forgive deceit, treachery, desertion,—even the preference given to a rival. She may forgive them and forget them; but I do not think that a woman can forget a blow. And as for forgiveness,—it is not the blow that she cannot forgive, but the meanness of spirit that made it possible.

Kate, as she thought of it, told herself that everything in life was over for her. She had long feared her brother's nature, —had feared that he was hard and heartless; but still there had been some hope with her fear. Success, if he could be made to achieve it, would soften him, and then all might be right. But now all was wrong, and she knew that it was so. When he had compelled her to write to Alice for money, her faith in him had almost succumbed. That had been very mean, and the meanness had shocked her. But now he had asked her to perjure herself that he might have his own way, and had threatened to murder her, and had raised his hand against her because she had refused to obey him. And he had accused her of treachery to himself,—had accused her of premeditated deceit in obtaining this property for herself!

'But he does not believe it,' said Kate to herself. 'He said that because he thought it would vex me; but I know he does not think it.' Kate had watched her brother longing for money all his life,—had thoroughly understood the intensity of his wish for it,—the agony of his desire. But so far removed was she from any such longing on her own account, that she could not believe that her brother would in his heart accuse her of it. How often had she offered to give him, on the instant, every shilling that she had in the world! At this moment she resolved, in her mind, that she never wished to see him more; but even now, had it been practicable, she would have made over to him, without any drawback, all her interest in the Vavasor estate.

But any such making over was impossible. John Vavasor remained in Westmoreland for a week, and during that time many discussions were, of course, held about the property. Mr. Round came down from London, and met Mr. Gogram at Penrith. As to the validity of the will Mr. Round said that there was no shadow of a doubt. So an agent was appointed for receiving the rents, and it was agreed that the old Hall should be let in six months from that date. In the meantime Kate was to remain there till her arm should become strong, and she could make her plans for the future. Aunt Greenow promised to remain at the Hall for the present, and offered, indeed, indefinite services for the future, as though she were quite forgetful of Captain Bellfield. Of Mr. Cheesacre she was not forgetful, for she still continued to speak of that gentleman to Kate, as though he were Kate's suitor. But she did not now press upon her niece the acceptance of Mr. Cheesacre's hand as an absolute duty. Kate was mistress of a considerable fortune, and though such a marriage might be comfortable, it was no longer necessary. Mrs. Greenow called him poor Cheesacre, pointing out how easily he might be managed, and how indubitable were his possessions; but she no longer spoke of Kate's chances in the marriage market as desperate, even though she should decline the Cheesacre alliance.

'A young woman, with six hundred a year, my dear, may do pretty nearly what she pleases,' said aunt Greenow. 'It's better than having ten years' grace given you.'

'And will last longer, certainly,' said Kate.

Kate's desire was that Alice should come down to her for a while in Westmoreland, before the six months were over, and this desire she mentioned to her uncle. He promised to carry the message up to Alice, but could not be got to say more than that upon the subject. Then Mr. Vavasor went away, leaving the aunt and niece together at the Hall.

'What on earth shall we do if that wild beast shows himself suddenly among us women?' asked Mrs. Greenow of her brother.

The brother could only say, 'that he hoped the wild beast would keep his distance.'

And the wild beast did keep his distance, at any rate as long as Mrs. Greenow remained at the Hall. We will now go back to the wild beast, and tell how he walked across the mountains, in the rain, to Bampton, a little village at the foot of Haweswater. It will be remembered that after he had struck his sister, he turned away from her, and walked with quick steps down the mountain-side, never turning back to look at

175

her. He had found himself to be without any power of persuasion over her, as regarded her evidence to be given, if the will were questioned. The more he threatened her the steadier she had been in asserting her belief in her grandfather's capacity. She had looked into his eye and defied him, and he had felt himself to be worsted. What was he to do? In truth, there was nothing for him to do. He had told her that he would murder her; and in the state of mind to which his fury had driven him, murder had suggested itself to him as a resource to which he might apply himself. But what could he gain by murdering her,—or, at any rate, by murdering her there, out on the mountain-side? Nothing but a hanging! There would be no gratification even to his revenge. If, indeed, he had murdered that old man, who was now, unfortunately, gone beyond the reach of murder;—if he could have poisoned the old man's cup before that last will had been made—there might have been something in such a deed! But he had merely thought of it, 'letting I dare not wait upon I would'*—as he now told himself, with much self-reproach. Nothing was to be got by killing his sister. So he restrained himself in his passion, and walked away from her, solitary, down the mountain.

The rain soon came on, and found him exposed on the hill-side. He thought little about it, but buttoned his coat, as I have said before, and strode on. It was a storm of rain, so that he was forced to hold his head to one side, as it hit him from the north. But with his hand to his hat, and his head bent against the wind, he went on till he had reached the valley at the foot, and found that the track by which he had been led thither had become a road. He had never known the mountains round the Hall as Kate had known them, and was not aware whither he was going. On one thing only had he made up his mind since he had left his sister, and that was that he would not return to the house. He knew that he could do nothing there to serve his purpose; his threats would be vain impotence; he had no longer any friend in the house. He could hardly tell himself what line of conduct he would pursue, but he thought that he would hurry back to London, and grasp at whatever

176

money he could get from Alice. He was still, at this moment, a Member of Parliament; and as the rain drenched him through and through, he endeavoured to get consolation from the remembrance of that fact in his favour.

As he got near the village he overtook a shepherd boy coming down from the hills, and learned his whereabouts from him. 'Baampton,' said the boy, with an accent that was almost Scotch, when he was asked the name of the place. When Vavasor further asked whether a gig were kept there, the boy simply stared at him, not knowing a gig by that name. At last, however, he was made to understand the nature of his companion's want, and expressed his belief that 'John Applethwaite, up at the Craigs yon, had got a mickle cart.' But the Craigs was a farm-house, which now came in view about a mile off, up across the valley; and Vavasor, hoping that he might still find a speedier conveyance than John Applethwaite's mickle cart, went on to the public-house in the village. But, in truth, neither there, nor yet from John Applethwaite, to whom at last an application was sent, could he get any vehicle; and between six and seven he started off again, through the rain, to make his weary way on foot to Shap. The distance was about five miles, and the little byways, lying between walls, were sticky, and almost glutinous with light-coloured, chalky mud. Before he started he took a glass of hot rum-and-water, but the effect of that soon passed away from him, and then he became colder and weaker than he had been before.

Wearily and wretchedly he plodded on. A man may be very weary in such a walk as that, and yet be by no means wretched. Tired, hungry, cold, wet, and nearly penniless, I have sat me down*and slept among those mountain tracks,—have slept because nature refused to allow longer wakefulness. But my heart has been as light as my purse,* and there has been something in the air of the hills that made me buoyant and happy in the midst of my weariness. But George Vavasor was wretched as well as weary, and every step that he took, plodding through the mud, was a new misfortune to him. What are five miles of a walk to a young man, even though the rain be falling and the ways be dirty? what, though they may come after some other ten that he has already traversed on his feet? His sister Kate would have thought nothing of the distance. But George stopped on his way from time to time, leaning on the loose walls, and cursing the misfortune that had brought him to such a pass. He cursed his grandfather, his uncle, his sister, his cousin, and himself. He cursed the place in which his fore-fathers had lived, and he cursed the whole county. He cursed the rain, and the wind, and his town-made boots, which would not keep out the wet slush. He cursed the light as it faded, and the darkness as it came. Over and over again he cursed the will that had robbed him, and the attorney that had made it. He cursed the mother that had borne him and the father that had left him poor. He thought of Scruby, and cursed him, thinking how that money would be again required of him by that stern agent. He cursed the House of Commons, which had cost him so much, and the greedy electors who would not send him there without his paying for it. He cursed John Grey, as he thought of those two thousand pounds, with double curses. He cursed this world, and all worlds beyond; and thus, cursing everything, he made his way at last up to the inn at Shap.

It was nearly nine when he got there. He had wasted over an hour at Bampton in his endeavour to get John Applethwaite's cart to carry him on, and he had been two hours on his walk from Bampton to Shap,—two hours amidst his cursing. He ordered supper and brandy-and-water, and, as we know, sent off a Mercury for his clothes. But the Mercuries of Westmore-land do not move on quick wings, and it was past midnight before he got his possessions. During all this time he had, by no means, ceased from cursing, but continued it over his broiled ham and while he swallowed his brandy-and-water. He swore aloud, so that the red-armed servant at the inn could not but hear him, that those thieves at the Hall intended to rob him of his clothes;—that they would not send him his property. He could not restrain himself, though he knew that every word he uttered would injure his cause, as regarded the property in Westmoreland, if ever he could make a cause. He knew that he had been mad to strike his sister, and cursed himself for his madness. Yet he could not restrain himself. He told himself that the battle for him was over, and he thought of poison for himself. He thought of poison, and a pistol,—of the pistols he had ever loaded at home, each with six shots, good for a life apiece. He thought of an express train*rushing along at its full career, and of the instant annihilation which it would produce. But if that was to be the end of him, he would not go alone. No, indeed! why should he go alone, leaving those pistols ready loaded in his desk? Among them they had brought him to ruin and to death. Was he a man to pardon his enemies when it was within his power to take them with him, down, down, down——? What were the last words upon his impious lips, as with bloodshot eyes, half drunk, and driven by the Fury, he took himself off to the bed prepared for him, cursing aloud the poor red-haired girl as he went, I may not utter here.

CHAPTER LVIII

The Pallisers at Breakfast

GENTLE reader, do you remember Lady Monk's party, and how it ended,—how it ended, at least as regards those special guests with whom we are concerned? Mr. Palliser went away early, Mrs. Marsham followed him to his house in Park Lane, caught him at home, and told her tale. He returned to his wife, found her sitting with Burgo in the dining-room, under the Argus eyes*of the constant Bott, and bore her away home. Burgo disappeared utterly from the scene, and Mr. Bott, complaining inwardly that virtue was too frequently allowed to be its own reward, comforted himself with champagne, and then walked off to his lodgings. Lady Monk, when Mr. Palliser made his way into her room up-stairs, seeking his wife's scarf,—which little incident, also, the reader may perhaps remember,—saw that the game was up, and thought with regret of the loss of her two hundred pounds. Such was the ending of Lady Monk's party.

Lady Glencora, on her journey home in the carriage with her husband, had openly suggested that Mrs. Marsham had gone to Park Lane to tell of her doings with Burgo, and had declared her resolution never again to see either that lady or Mr. Bott in her own house. This she said with more of defiance in her tone than Mr. Palliser had ever hitherto heard. He was by nature less ready than her, and knowing his own deficiency in that respect, abstained from all answer on the subject. Indeed, during that drive home very few further words were spoken between them. 'I will breakfast with you to-morrow,' he said to her, as she prepared to go up-stairs. 'I have work still to do to-night, and I will not disturb you by coming to your room.'

'You won't want me to be very early?' said his wife.

'No,' said he, with more of anger in his voice than he had yet shown. 'What hour will suit you? I must say something of what has occurred to-night before I leave you to-morrow.'

'I don't know what you can have got to say about to-night, but I'll be down by half-past eleven, if that will do?' Mr. Palliser said that he would make it do, and then they parted.

Lady Glencora had played her part very well before her husband. She had declined to be frightened by him; had been the first to mention Burgo's name, and had done so with no tremor in her voice, and had boldly declared her irreconcilable enmity to the male and female duennas who had dared to take her in charge. While she was in the carriage with her husband she felt some triumph in her own strength; and as she wished him good night on the staircase, and slowly walked up to her room, without having once lowered her eyes before his, something of this consciousness of triumph still supported her. And even while her maid remained with her she held herself up, as it were, inwardly, telling herself that she would not yield,— that she would not be cowed either by her husband or by his spies. But when she was left alone all her triumph departed from her.

She bade her maid go while she was still sitting in her dressing-gown; and when the girl was gone she got close over the fire, sitting with her slippers on the fender, with her elbows on her knees, and her face resting on her hands. In this position she remained for an hour, with her eyes fixed on the altering shapes of the hot coals. During this hour her spirit was by no means defiant, and her thoughts of herself anything but triumphant. Mr. Bott and Mrs. Marsham she had forgotten altogether. After all, they were but buzzing flies, who annoyed her by their presence. Should she choose to leave her husband, they could not prevent her leaving him. It was of her husband and of Burgo that she was thinking,—weighing them one against the other, and connecting her own existence with theirs, not as expecting joy or the comfort of love from either of them, but with an assured conviction that on either side there must be misery for her. But of that shame before all the world which must be hers for ever, should she break her vows and consent to live with a man who was not her husband, she thought hardly at all. That which in the estimation of Alice was everything, to her, at this moment, was almost nothing. For herself, she had been sacrificed; and,—as she told herself with bitter denunciations against herself,—had been sacrificed through her own weakness. But that was done. Whatever way she might go, she was lost. They had married her to a man who cared nothing for a wife, nothing for any woman,—so at least she declared to herself,—but who had wanted a wife that he might have an heir. Had it been given to her to have a child, she thought that she might have been happy,—sufficiently happy in sharing her husband's joy in that respect. But everything had gone against her. There was nothing in her home to give her comfort. 'He looks at me every time he sees me as the cause of his misfortune,' she said to herself. Of her husband's rank, of the future possession of his title and his estates, she thought much. But of her own wealth she thought nothing. It did not occur to her that she had given him enough in that respect to make his marriage with her a comfort to him. She took it for granted that that marriage was now one distasteful to him, as it was to herself, and that he would eventually be the gainer if she should so conduct herself that her marriage might be dissolved.

As to Burgo, I doubt whether she deceived herself much as to his character. She knew well enough that he was a man infinitely less worthy than her husband. She knew that he was a spendthrift, idle, given to bad courses,—that he drank, that he gambled, that he lived the life of the loosest man about the town. She knew also that whatever chance she might have had to redeem him, had she married him honestly before all the world, there could be no such chance if she went to him as his mistress, abandoning her husband and all her duties, and making herself vile in the eyes of all women. Burgo Fitzgerald would not be influenced for good by such a woman as she would then be. She knew much of the world and its ways, and told herself no lies about this. But, as I have said before, she did not count herself for much. What though she were ruined? What though Burgo were false, mean, and untrustworthy? She loved him, and he was the only man she ever had loved!

Lower and lower she crouched before the fire; and then, when the coals were no longer red, and the shapes altered themselves no more, she crept into bed. As to what she should say to her husband on the following morning,—she had not yet begun to think of that.

Exactly at half-past eleven she entered the little breakfast parlour which looked out over the park. It was the prettiest room in the house, and now, at this springtide, when the town trees were putting out their earliest greens, and were fresh and bright almost as country trees, it might be hard to find a prettier chamber. Mr. Palliser was there already, sitting with the morning paper in his hand. He rose when she entered, and, coming up to her, just touched her with his lips. She put her cheek up to him, and then took her place at the breakfast table.

'Have you any headache this morning?' he asked.

'Oh, no,' she said. Then he took his tea and his toast, spoke some word to her about the fineness of the weather, told her some scraps of news, and soon returned to the absorbing interest of a speech made by the leader of the Opposition in the House of Lords. The speech was very interesting to Mr. Palliser, because in it the noble lord alluded to a break-up in the present Cabinet, as to which the rumours were, he said, so rife through the country as to have destroyed all that feeling of security in the existing Government which the country so much valued and desired. Mr. Palliser had as yet heard no official tidings of such a rupture; but if such rupture were to take place, it must be in his favour. He felt himself at this moment to be full of politics,—to be near the object of his ambition, to have affairs upon his hands which required all his attention. Was it absolutely incumbent on him to refer again to the incidents of last night? The doing so would be odious to him. The remembrance of the task now immediately before him destroyed all his political satisfaction. He did not believe that his wife was in any serious danger. Might it not yet be possible for him to escape from the annoyance, and to wash his mind clean of all suspicion? He was not jealous; he was indeed incapable of jealousy. He knew what it would be to be dishonoured, and he knew that under certain circumstances the world would expect him to exert himself in a certain way. But the thing that he had now to do was a great trouble to him. He would rather have to address the House of Commons with ten columns of figures than utter a word of remonstrance to his wife. But she had defied him,—defied him by saying that she would see his friends no more; and it was the remembrance of this, as he sat behind his newspaper, that made him ultimately feel that he could not pass in silence over what had been done.

Nevertheless, he went on reading, or pretending to read, as long as the continuance of the breakfast made it certain that his wife would remain with him. Every now and then he said some word to her of what he was reading, endeavouring to use the tone of voice that was customary to him in his domestic teachings of politics. But through it all there was a certain hesitation,—there were the sure signs of an attempt being made, of which he was himself conscious, and which she understood with the most perfect accuracy. He was deferring the evil moment, and vainly endeavouring to make himself believe that he was comfortably employed the while. She had no newspaper, and made no endeavour to deceive herself. She, therefore, was the first to begin the conversation.

'Plantagenet,' she said, 'you told me last night, as I was going to bed, that you had something to say about Lady Monk's party.'

He put down the newspaper slowly, and turned towards her. 'Yes, my dear. After what happened, I believe that I must say something.'

'If you think anything, pray say it,' said Glencora.

'It is not always easy for a man to show what he thinks by what he says,' he replied. 'My fear is that you should suppose me to think more than I do. And it was for that reason that I determined to sleep on it before I spoke to you.'

'If anybody is angry with me I'd much rather they should have it out with me while their anger is hot. I hate cold anger.'

'But I am not angry.'

'That's what husbands always say when they're going to scold.'

'But I am not going to scold. I am only going to advise you.'

'I'd sooner be scolded. Advice is to anger just what cold anger is to hot.'

'But my dear Glencora, surely if I find it necessary to speak——'

'I don't want to stop you, Plantagenet. Pray, go on. Only it will be so nice to have it over.'

He was now more than ever averse to the task before him. Husbands, when they give their wives a talking, should do it out of hand, uttering their words hard, sharp, and quick,—and should then go. There are some works that won't bear a preface, and this work of marital fault-finding is one of them. Mr. Palliser was already beginning to find out the truth of this. 'Glencora,' he said, 'I wish you to be serious with me.'

'I am very serious,' she replied, as she settled herself in her chair with an air of mockery, while her eyes and mouth were bright and eloquent with a spirit which her husband did not love to see. Poor girl! There was seriousness enough in store for her before she would be able to leave the room.

'You ought to be serious. Do you know why Mrs. Marsham came here from Lady Monk's last night?'

'Of course I do. She came to tell you that I was waltzing with Burgo Fitzgerald. You might as well ask me whether I knew why Mr. Bott was standing at all the doors, glaring at me.'

'I don't know anything about Mr. Bott.'

'I know something about him though,' she said, again moving herself in her chair.

'I am speaking now of Mrs. Marsham.'

'You should speak of them both together as they hunt in couples.'

'Glencora, will you listen to me, or will you not? If you say that you will not, I shall know what to do.'

'I don't think you would, Plantagenet.' And she nodded her little head at him, as she spoke. 'I'm sure I don't know what you would do. But I will listen to you. Only, as I said before, it will be very nice when it's over.'

'Mrs. Marsham came here, not simply to tell me that you were waltzing with Mr. Fitzgerald,—and I wish that when you mention his name you would call him Mr. Fitzgerald.'

'So I do.'

'You generally prefix his Christian name, which it would be much better that you should omit.'

'I will try,' she said, very gently; 'but it's hard to drop an old habit. Before you married me you knew that I had learned to call him Burgo.'

'Let me go on,' said Mr. Palliser.

'Oh, certainly.'

'It was not simply to tell me that you were waltzing that Mrs. Marsham came here.'

'And it was not simply to see me waltzing that Mr. Bott stood in the doorways, for he followed me about, and came down after me to the supper-room.'

'Glencora, will you oblige me by not speaking of Mr. Bott?'

'I wish you would oblige me by not speaking of Mrs. Marsham.' Mr. Palliser rose quickly from his chair with a gesture of anger, stood upright for half a minute, and then sat down again. 'I beg your pardon, Plantagenet,' she said. 'I think I know what you want, and I'll hold my tongue till you bid me speak.'

'Mrs. Marsham came here because she saw that every one in the room was regarding you with wonder.' Lady Glencora twisted herself about in her chair, but she said nothing. 'She saw that you were not only dancing with Mr. Fitzgerald, but that you were dancing with him,—what shall I say?'

'Upon my word I can't tell you.'

'Recklessly.'

'Oh! recklessly, was I? What was I reckless of?'

'Reckless of what people might say; reckless of what I might feel about it; reckless of your own position.'

'Am I to speak now?'

'Perhaps you had better let me go on. I think she was right to come to me.'

'That's of course. What's the good of having spies, if they don't run and tell as soon as they see anything, especially anything—reckless?'

'Glencora, you are determined to make me angry. I am angry now,—very angry. I have employed no spies. When rumours have reached me, not from spies, as you choose to call them, but through your dearest friends and mine——'

'What do you mean by rumours from my dearest friends?'

'Never mind. Let me go on.'

'No; not when you say my dear friends have spread rumours about me. Tell me who they are. I have no dear friends. Do you mean Alice Vavasor?'

'It does not signify. But when I was warned that you had better not go to any house in which you could meet that man, I would not listen to it. I said that you were my wife, and that as such I could trust you anywhere, everywhere, with any person. Others might distrust you, but I would not do so. When I wished you to go to Monkshade, were there to be any spies there? When I left you last night at Lady Monk's, do you believe in your heart that I trusted to Mrs. Marsham's eyes rather than to your own truth? Do you think that I have lived in fear of Mr. Fitzgerald?'

'No, Plantagenet; I do not think so.'

'Do you believe that I have commissioned Mr. Bott to watch your conduct? Answer me, Glencora.'

She paused a moment, thinking what actually was her true belief on that subject. 'He does watch me, certainly,' she said.

'That does not answer my question. Do you believe that I have commissioned him to do so?'

'No; I do not.'

'Then it is ignoble in you to talk to me of spies. I have employed no spies. If it were ever to come to that, that I thought spies necessary, it would be all over with me.'

There was something of feeling in his voice as he said this, —something that almost approached to passion which touched his wife's heart. Whether or not spies would be of any avail, she knew that she had in truth done that of which he had declared that he had never suspected her. She had listened to words of love from her former lover. She had received, and now carried about with her a letter from this man, in which he asked her to elope with him. She had by no means resolved that she would not do this thing. She had been false to her husband; and as her husband spoke of his confidence in her, her own spirit rebelled against the deceit which she herself was practising.

'I know that I have never made you happy,' she said. 'I know that I never can make you happy.'

He looked at her, struck by her altered tone, and saw that her whole manner and demeanour were changed. 'I do not understand what you mean,' he said. 'I have never complained. You have not made me unhappy.' He was one of those men to whom this was enough. If his wife caused him no uneasiness, what more was he to expect from her? No doubt she might have done much more for him. She might have given him an heir. But he was a just man, and knew that the blank he had drawn was his misfortune, and not her fault.

But now her heart was loosed and she spoke out, at first

slowly, but after a while with all the quickness of strong passion. 'No, Plantagenet; I shall never make you happy. You have never loved me, nor I you. We have never loved each other for a single moment. I have been wrong to talk to you about spies; I was wrong to go to Lady Monk's; I have been wrong in everything that I have done; but never so wrong as when I let them persuade me to be your wife!'

'Glencora!'

'Let me speak now, Plantagenet. It is better that I should tell you everything; and I will. I will tell you everything;—everything! I do love Burgo Fitzgerald. I do! I do! I do! How can I help loving him? Have I not loved him from the first,—before I had seen you? Did you not know that it was so? I do love Burgo Fitzgerald, and when I went to Lady Monk's last night, I had almost made up my mind that I must tell him so, and that I must go away with him and hide myself. But when he came to speak to me——'

'He has asked you to go with him, then?' said the husband, in whose bosom the poison was beginning to take effect, thereby showing that he was neither above nor below humanity.

Glencora was immediately reminded that though she might, if she pleased, tell her own secrets, she ought not, in accordance with her ideas of honour, tell those of her lover. 'What need is there of asking, do you think, when people have loved each other as we have done?'

'You wanted to go with him, then?'

'Would it not have been the best for you? Plantagenet, I do not love you;—not as women love their husbands when they do love them. But, before God, my first wish is to free you from the misfortune that I have brought on you.' As she made this attestation she started up from her chair, and coming close to him, took him by the coat. He was startled, and stepped back a pace, but did not speak; and then stood looking at her as she went on.

'What matters it whether I drown myself, or throw myself away by going with such a one as him, so that you might marry again, and have a child? I'd die;—I'd die willingly.

189

How I wish I could die! Plantagenet, I would kill myself if I dared.'

He was a tall man and she was short of stature, so that he stood over her and looked upon her, and now she was looking up into his face with all her eyes. 'I would,' she said. 'I would —I would! What is there left for me that I should wish to live?'

Softly, slowly, very gradually, as though he were afraid of what he was doing, he put his arm round her waist. 'You are wrong in one thing,' he said. 'I do love you.'

She shook her head, touching his breast with her hair as she did so.

'I do love you,' he repeated. 'If you mean that I am not apt at telling you so, it is true, I know. My mind is running on other things.'

'Yes,' she said; 'your mind is running on other things.'

'But I do love you. If you cannot love me, it is a great misfortune to us both. But we need not therefore be disgraced. As for that other thing of which you spoke,—of our having, as yet, no child'—and in saying this he pressed her somewhat closer with his arm—'you allow yourself to think too much of it;—much more of it than I do. I have made no complaints on that head, even within my own breast.'

'I know what your thoughts are, Plantagenet.'

'Believe me that you wrong my thoughts. Of course I have been anxious, and have, perhaps, shown my anxiety by the struggle I have made to hide it. I have never told you what is false, Glencora.'

'No; you are not false!'

'I would rather have you for my wife, childless,—if you will try to love me,—than any other woman, though another might give me an heir. Will you try to love me?'

She was silent. At this moment, after the confession that she had made, she could not bring herself to say that she would even try. Had she said so, she would have seemed to have accepted his forgiveness too easily.

'I think, dear,' he said, still holding her by her waist, 'that we had better leave England for a while. I will give up politics for this season. Should you like to go to Switzerland for the summer, or perhaps to some of the German baths, and then on to Italy when the weather is cold enough?' Still she was silent. 'Perhaps your friend, Miss Vavasor, would go with us?'

He was killing her by his goodness. She could not speak to him yet; but now, as he mentioned Alice's name, she gently put up her hand and rested it on the back of his.

At that moment there came a knock at the door;—a sharp knock, which was quickly repeated.

'Come in,' said Mr. Palliser, dropping his arm from his wife's waist, and standing away from her a few yards.

CHAPTER LIX

The Duke of St. Bungay in Search of a Minister

IT was the butler who had knocked,—showing that the knock was of more importance than it would have been had it been struck by the knuckles of the footman in livery. 'If you please, sir, the Duke of St. Bungay is here.'

'The Duke of St. Bungay!' said Mr. Palliser, becoming rather red as he heard the announcement.

'Yes, sir, his grace is in the library. He bade me tell you that he particularly wanted to see you; so I told him that you were with my lady.

'Quite right; tell his grace that I will be with him in two minutes.' Then the butler retired, and Mr. Palliser was again alone with his wife.

'I must go now, my dear,' he said; 'and perhaps I shall not see you again till the evening.'

'Don't let me put you out in any way,' she answered.

'Oh no;—you won't put me out. You will be dressing, I suppose, about nine.'

'I did not mean as to that,' she answered. 'You must not think more of Italy. He has come to tell you that you are wanted in the Cabinet.'

Again he turned very red. 'It may be so,' he answered, 'but

191

though I am wanted, I need not go. But I must not keep the Duke waiting. Good-bye.' And he turned to the door.

She followed him and took hold of him as he went, so that he was forced to turn to her once again. She managed to get hold of both his hands, and pressed them closely, looking up into his face with her eyes laden with tears. He smiled at her gently, returned the pressure of the hands, and then left her,—without kissing her. It was not that he was minded not to kiss her. He would have kissed her willingly enough had he thought that the occasion required it. 'He says that he loves me,' said Lady Glencora to herself, 'but he does not know what love means.'

But she was quite aware that he had behaved to her with genuine, true nobility. As soon as she was alone and certain of her solitude, she took out that letter from her pocket, and tearing it into very small fragments, without reading it, threw the pieces on the fire. As she did so, her mind seemed to be fixed, at any rate, to one thing,—that she would think no more of Burgo Fitzgerald as her future master. I think, however, that she had arrived at so much certainty as this, at that moment in which she had been parting with Burgo Fitzgerald, in Lady Monk's dining-room. She had had courage enough,—or shall we rather say sin enough,—to think of going with him,—to tell herself that she would do so; to put herself in the way of doing it; nay, she had had enough of both to enable her to tell her husband that she had resolved that it would be good for her to do so. But she was neither bold enough nor wicked enough to do the thing. As she had said of her own idea of destroying herself,—she did not dare to take the plunge. Therefore, knowing now that it was so, she tore up the letter that she had carried so long, and burnt it in the fire.

She had in truth told him everything, believing that in doing so she was delivering her own death-warrant as regarded her future position in his house. She had done this, not hoping thereby for any escape; not with any purpose as regarded herself, but simply because deceit had been grievous to her, and had become unendurable as soon as his words and manner had in them any feeling of kindness. But her confession had no sooner been made than her fault had been forgiven. She had told him that she did not love him. She had told him, even, that she had thought of leaving him. She had justified by her own words any treatment of his, however harsh, which he might choose to practise. But the result had been—the immediate result—that he had been more tender to her than she had ever remembered him to be before. She knew that he had conquered her. However cold and heartless his home might be to her, it must be her home now. There could be no further thought of leaving him. She had gone out into the tilt-yard* and had tilted with him, and he had been the victor.

Mr. Palliser himself had not time for much thought before he found himself closeted with the Duke; but as he crossed the hall and went up the stairs, a thought or two did pass quickly across his mind. She had confessed to him, and he had forgiven her. He did not feel quite sure that he had been right, but he did feel quite sure that the thing had been done. He recognised it for a fact that, as regarded the past, no more was to be said. There were to be no reproaches, and there must be some tacit abandoning of Mrs. Marsham's close attendance. As to Mr. Bott;—he had begun to hate Mr. Bott, and had felt cruelly ungrateful, when that gentleman endeavoured to whisper a word into his ear as he passed through the doorway into Lady Monk's dining-room. And he had offered to go abroad,—to go abroad and leave his politics, and his ambition, and his coming honours. He had persisted in his offer, even after his wife had suggested to him that the Duke of St. Bungay was now in the house with the object of offering him that very thing for which he had so longed! As he thought of this his heart became heavy within him. Such chances,—so he told himself,—do not come twice in a man's way. When returning from a twelvemonth's residence abroad he would be nobody in politics. He would have lost everything for which he had been working all his life. But he was a man of his word, and as he opened the library door he was resolute,—he thought that he could be resolute in adhering to his promise.

'Duke,' he said, 'I'm afraid I have kept you waiting.' And the two political allies shook each other by the hand.

The Duke was in a glow of delight. There had been no waiting. He was only too glad to find his friend at home. He had been prepared to wait, even if Mr. Palliser had been out. 'And I suppose you guess why I'm come?' said the Duke.

'I would rather be told than have to guess,' said Mr. Palliser, smiling for a moment. But the smile quickly passed off his face as he remembered his pledge to his wife.

'He has resigned at last. What was said in the Lords last night made it necessary that he should do so, or that Lord Brock should declare himself able to support him through thick and thin. Of course, I can tell you everything now. He must have gone, or I must have done so. You know that I don't like him in the Cabinet. I admire his character and his genius, but I think him the most dangerous man in England as a statesman. He has high principles,—the very highest; but they are so high as to be out of sight to ordinary eyes. They are too exalted to be of any use for everyday purposes. He is honest as the sun, I'm sure; but it's just like the sun's honesty, —of a kind which we men below can't quite understand or appreciate. He has no instinct in politics, but reaches his conclusions by philosophical deduction. Now, in politics, I would a deal sooner trust to instinct than to calculation. I think he may probably know how England ought to be governed three centuries hence better than any man living, but of the proper way to govern it now, I think he knows less. Brock half likes him and half fears him. He likes the support of his eloquence, and he likes the power of the man; but he fears his restless activity, and thoroughly dislikes his philosophy. At any rate, he has left us, and I am here to ask you to take his place.'

The Duke, as he concluded his speech, was quite contented, and almost jovial. He was thoroughly satisfied with the new political arrangement which he was proposing. He regarded Mr. Palliser as a steady, practical man of business, luckily young, and therefore with a deal of work in him, belonging to the race from which English ministers ought, in his opinion, to be taken, and as being, in some respects, his own pupil. He had been the first to declare aloud that Plantagenet Palliser was the coming Chancellor of the Exchequer; and it had been long known, though no such declaration had been made aloud, that the Duke did not sit comfortably in the same Cabinet with the gentleman who had now resigned. Everything had now gone as the Duke wished; and he was prepared to celebrate some little ovation with his young friend before he left the house in Park Lane.

'And who goes out with him?' asked Mr. Palliser, putting off the evil moment of his own decision; but before the Duke could answer him, he had reminded himself that under his present circumstances he had no right to ask such a question. His own decision could not rest upon that point. 'But it does not matter,' he said; 'I am afraid I must decline the offer you bring me.'

'Decline it!' said the Duke, who could not have been more surprised had his friend talked of declining heaven.

'I fear I must.' The Duke had now risen from his chair, and was standing, with both his hands upon the table. All his contentment, all his joviality, had vanished. His fine round face had become almost ludicrously long; his eyes and mouth were struggling to convey reproach, and the reproach was almost drowned in vexation. Ever since Parliament had met he had been whispering Mr. Palliser's name into the Prime Minister's ear, and now——. But he could not, and would not, believe it. 'Nonsense, Palliser,' he said. 'You must have got some false notion into your head. There can be no possible reason why you should not join us. Finespun himself will support us, at any rate for a time.' Mr. Finespun was the gentleman whose retirement from the ministry the Duke of St. Bungay had now announced.

'It is nothing of that kind,' said Mr. Palliser, who perhaps felt himself quite equal to the duties proposed to him, even though Mr. Finespun should not support him. 'It is nothing of that kind;—it is no fear of that sort that hinders me.'

'Then, for mercy's sake, what is it? My dear Palliser, I

looked upon you as being as sure in this matter as myself; and I had a right to do so. You certainly intended to join us a month ago, if the opportunity offered. You certainly did.'

'It is true, Duke. I must ask you to listen to me now, and I must tell you what I would not willingly tell to any man.' As Mr. Palliser said this a look of agony came over his face. There are men who can talk easily of all their most inmost matters, but he was not such a man. It went sorely against the grain with him to speak of the sorrow of his home, even to such a friend as the Duke; but it was essentially necessary to him that he should justify himself.

'Upon my word,' said the Duke, 'I can't understand that there should be any reason strong enough to make you throw your party over.'

'I have promised to take my wife abroad.'

'Is that it?' said the Duke, looking at him with surprise, but at the same time with something of returning joviality in his face. 'Nobody thinks of going abroad at this time of the year. Of course, you can get away for a time when Parliament breaks up.'

'But I have promised to go at once.'

'Then, considering your position, you have made a promise which it behoves you to break. I am sure Lady Glencora will see it in that light.'

'You do not quite understand me, and I am afraid I must trouble you to listen to matters which, under other circumstances, it would be impertinent in me to obtrude upon you.' A certain stiffness of demeanour, and measured propriety of voice, much at variance with his former manner, came upon him as he said this.

'Of course, Palliser, I don't want to interfere for a moment.'

'If you will allow me, Duke. My wife has told me that, this morning, which makes me feel that absence from England is requisite for her present comfort. I was with her when you came, and had just promised her that she should go.'

'But, Palliser, think of it. If this were a small matter, I would not press you; but a man in your position has public duties. He owes his services to his country. He has no right to go back, if it be possible that he should so do.'

'When a man has given his word, it cannot be right that he should go back from that.'

'Of course not. But a man may be absolved from a promise. Lady Glencora——'

'My wife would, of course, absolve me. It is not that. Her happiness demands it, and it is partly my fault that it is so. I cannot explain to you more fully why it is that I must give up the great object for which I have striven with all my strength.'

'Oh, no!' said the Duke. 'If you are sure that it is imperative——'

'It is imperative.'

'I could give you twenty-four hours, you know.' Mr. Palliser did not answer at once, and the Duke thought that he saw some sign of hesitation. 'I suppose it would not be possible that I should speak to Lady Glencora?'

'It could be of no avail, Duke. She would only declare, at the first word, that she would remain in London; but it would not be the less my duty on that account to take her abroad.'

'Well; I can't say. Of course, I can't say. Such an opportunity may not come twice in a man's life. And at your age too! You are throwing away from you the finest political position that the world can offer to the ambition of any man. No one at your time of life has had such a chance within my memory. That a man under thirty should be thought fit to be Chancellor of the Exchequer, and should refuse it,—because he wants to take his wife abroad! Palliser, if she were dying, you should remain under such an emergency as this. She might go, but you should remain.'

Mr. Palliser remained silent for a moment or two in his chair; he then rose and walked towards the window, as he spoke. 'There are things worse than death,' he said, when his back was turned. His voice was very low, and there was a tear in his eye as he spoke them; the words were indeed whispered, but the Duke heard them, and felt that he could not press him any more on the subject of his wife.

197

'And must this be final?' said the Duke.

'I think it must. But your visit here has come so quickly on my resolution to go abroad,—which, in truth, was only made ten minutes before your name was brought to me,—that I believe I ought to ask for a portion of those twenty-four hours which you have offered me. A small portion will be enough. Will you see me, if I come to you this evening, say at eight? If the House is up in the Lords I will go to you in St. James's Square.'

'We shall be sitting after eight, I think.'

'Then I will see you there. And, Duke, I must ask you to think of me in this matter as a friend should think, and not as though we were bound together only by party feeling.'

'I will,—I will.'

'I have told you what I shall never whisper to any one else.'

'I think you know that you are safe with me.'

'I am sure of it. And, Duke, I can tell you that the sacrifice to me will be almost more than I can bear. This thing that you have offered me to-day is the only thing that I have ever coveted. I have thought of it and worked for it, have hoped and despaired, have for moments been vain enough to think that it was within my strength, and have been wretched for weeks together because I have told myself that it was utterly beyond me.'

'As to that, neither Brock nor I, nor any of us, have any doubt. Finespun himself says that you are the man.'

'I am much obliged to them. But I say all this simply that you may understand how imperative is the duty which, as I think, requires me to refuse the offer.'

'But you haven't refused as yet,' said the Duke. 'I shall wait at the House for you, whether they are sitting or not. And endeavour to join us. Do the best you can. I will say nothing as to that duty of which you speak; but if it can be made compatible with your public service, pray—pray let it be done. Remember how much such a one as you owes to his country.' Then the Duke went, and Mr. Palliser was alone.

He had not been alone before since the revelation which had

been made to him by his wife, and the words she had spoken were still sounding in his ears. 'I do love Burgo Fitzgerald;—I do! I do! I do!' They were not pleasant words for a young husband to hear. Men there are, no doubt, whose nature would make them more miserable under the infliction than it had made Plantagenet Palliser. He was calm, without strong passion, not prone to give to words a stronger significance than they should bear;—and he was essentially unsuspicious. Never for a moment had he thought, even while those words were hissing in his ears, that his wife had betrayed his honour. Nevertheless, there was that at his heart, as he remembered those words, which made him feel that the world was almost too heavy for him. For the first quarter of an hour after the Duke's departure he thought more of his wife and of Burgo Fitzgerald than he did of Lord Brock and Mr. Finespun. But of this he was aware,—that he had forgiven his wife; that he had put his arm round her and embraced her after the hearing of her confession,—and that she, mutely, with her eyes, had promised him that she would do her best for him. Then something of an idea of love came across his heart, and he acknowledged to himself that he had married without loving or without requiring love. Much of all this had been his own fault. Indeed, had not the whole of it come from his own wrong-doing? He acknowledged that it was so. But now,—now he loved her. He felt that he could not bear to part with her, even if there were no question of public scandal, or of disgrace. He had been torn inwardly by that assertion that she loved another man. She had got at his heart-strings at last. There are men who may love their wives, though they never can have been in love before their marriage.

When the Duke had been gone about an hour, and when, under ordinary circumstances, it would have been his time to go down to the House, he took his hat and walked into the Park. He made his way across Hyde Park, and into Kensington Gardens, and there he remained for an hour, walking up and down beneath the elms. The quid-nuncs* of the town, who chanced to see him, and who had heard something of the political movements of the day, thought, no doubt, that he was meditating his future ministerial career. But he had not been there long before he had resolved that no ministerial career was at present open to him. 'It has been my own fault,' he said, as he returned to his house, 'and with God's help I will mend it, if it be possible.'

But he was a slow man, and he did not go off instantly to the Duke. He had given himself to eight o'clock, and he took the full time. He could not go down to the House of Commons because men would make inquiries of him which he would find it difficult to answer. So he dined at home, alone. He had told his wife that he would see her at nine, and before that hour he would not go to her. He sat alone till it was time for him to get into his brougham, and thought it all over. That seat in the Cabinet and Chancellorship of the Exchequer, which he had so infinitely desired, were already done with. There was no doubt about that. It might have been better for him not to have married; but now that he was married, and that things had brought him untowardly to this pass, he knew that his wife's safety was his first duty. 'We will go through Switzerland,' he said to himself, 'to Baden, and then we will get on to Florence and to Rome. She has seen nothing of all these things yet, and the new life will make a change in her. She shall have her own friend with her.' Then he went down to the House of Lords, and saw the Duke.

'Well, Palliser,' said the Duke, when he had listened to him, 'of course I cannot argue it with you any more. I can only say that I am very sorry;—more sorry than perhaps you will believe. Indeed, it half breaks my heart.' The Duke's voice was very sad, and it might almost have been thought that he was going to shed a tear. In truth he disliked Mr. Finespun with the strongest political feeling of which he was capable, and had attached himself to Mr. Palliser almost as strongly. It was a thousand pities! How hard had he not worked to bring about this arrangement, which was now to be upset because a woman had been foolish! 'I never above half liked her,' said the Duke to himself, thinking perhaps a little of the Duchess's complaints of her. 'I must go to Brock at once,' he said aloud, 'and tell him. God knows what we must do now. Good-bye! good-bye! No; I'm not angry. There shall be no quarrel. But I am very sorry.' In this way the two politicians parted.

We may as well follow this political movement to its end. The Duke saw Lord Brock that night, and then those two ministers sent for another minister,—another noble Lord, a man of great experience in Cabinets. These three discussed the matter together, and on the following day Lord Brock got up in the House, and made a strong speech in defence of his colleague, Mr. Finespun. To the end of the Session, at any rate, Mr. Finespun kept his position, and held the seals of the Exchequer while all the quid-nuncs of the nation, shaking their heads, spoke of the wonderful power of Mr. Finespun, and declared that Lord Brock did not dare to face the Opposition without him.

In the meantime Mr. Palliser had returned to his wife, and told her of his resolution with reference to their tour abroad. 'We may as well make up our minds to start at once,' said he. 'At any rate, there is nothing on my side to hinder us.'

CHAPTER LX

Alice Vavasor's Name gets into the Money Market

SOME ten or twelve days after George Vavasor's return to London from Westmoreland he appeared at Mr. Scruby's offices with four small slips of paper in his hand. Mr. Scruby, as usual, was pressing for money. The third election was coming on, and money was already being spent very freely among the men of the River Bank. So, at least, Mr. Scruby declared. Mr. Grimes, of The Handsome Man, had shown signs of returning allegiance. But Mr. Grimes could not afford to be loyal without money. He had his little family to protect. Mr. Scruby, too, had his little family, and was not ashamed to use it on this occasion. 'I'm a family man, Mr. Vavasor, and therefore I never run any risks. I never go a yard further than I can see my way back.' This he had said in answer to a proposition that he should take George's note of hand for the expenses of the next election, payable in three months' time. 'It is so very hard to realize,' said George, 'immediately upon a death, when all the property left is real property.' 'Very hard indeed,' said Mr. Scruby, who had heard with accuracy all the particulars of the old Squire's will. Vavasor understood the lawyer, cursed him inwardly, and suggested to himself that some day he might murder Mr. Scruby as well as John Grey,—and perhaps also a few more of his enemies. Two days after the interview in which his own note of hand had been refused, he again called in Great Marlborough Street. Upon this occasion he tendered to Mr. Scruby for his approval the four slips of paper which have been mentioned. Mr. Scruby regarded them with attention, looking first at one side horizontally, and then at the other side perpendicularly. But before we learn the judgment pronounced by Mr. Scruby as to these four slips of paper, we must go back to their earlier history. As they were still in their infancy, we shall not have to go back far.

One morning, at about eleven o'clock, the parlour-maid came up to Alice, as she sat alone in the drawing-room in Queen Anne Street, and told her there was a 'gentleman' in the hall waiting to be seen by her. We all know the tone in which servants announce a gentleman when they know that the gentleman is not a gentleman.

'A gentleman wanting to see me! What sort of a gentleman?'

'Well, miss, I don't think he's just of our sort; but he's decent to look at.'

Alice Vavasor had no desire to deny herself to any person but one. She was well aware that the gentleman in the hall could not be her cousin George, and therefore she did not refuse to see him.

'Let him come up,' she said. 'But I think, Jane, you ought to ask him his name.' Jane did ask him his name, and came back immediately, announcing Mr. Levy.

This occurred immediately after the return of Mr. John

Vavasor from Westmoreland. He had reached home late on the preceding evening, and at the moment of Mr. Levy's call was in his dressing-room.

Alice got up to receive her visitor, and at once understood the tone of her maid's voice. Mr. Levy was certainly not a gentleman of the sort to which she had been most accustomed. He was a little dark man, with sharp eyes, set very near to each other in his head, with a beaked nose, thick at the bridge, and a black moustache, but no other beard. Alice did not at all like the look of Mr. Levy, but she stood up to receive him, made him a little bow, and asked him to sit down.

'Is papa dressed yet?' Alice asked the servant.

'Well, miss, I don't think he is,—not to say dressed.'

Alice had thought it might be as well that Mr. Levy should know that there was a gentleman in the house with her.

'I've called about a little bit of business, miss,' said Mr. Levy, when they were alone. 'Nothing as you need disturb yourself about. You'll find it all square, I think.' Then he took a case out of his breast-pocket, and produced a note, which he handed to her. Alice took the note, and saw immediately that it was addressed to her by her cousin George. 'Yes, Mr. George Vavasor,' said Mr. Levy. 'I dare say you never saw me before, miss?'

'No, sir; I think not,' said Alice.

'I am your cousin's clerk.'

'Oh, you're Mr. Vavasor's clerk. I'll read his letter, if you please, sir.'

'If you please, miss.'

George Vavasor's letter to his cousin was as follows: —

'DEAR ALICE.

'After what passed between us when I last saw you I thought that on my return from Westmoreland I should learn that you had paid in at my bankers' the money that I require. But I find that this is not so; and of course I excuse you, because women so seldom know when or how to do that which business demands of them. You have, no doubt, heard the injustice which my grandfather has done me, and will probably feel as indignant as I do. I only mention this now, because the nature of his will makes it more than ever incumbent on you that you should be true to your pledge to me.

'Till there shall be some ground for a better understanding between us,—and this I do not doubt will come,—I think it wiser not to call, myself, at Queen Anne Street. I therefore send my confidential clerk with four bills, each of five hundred pounds, drawn at fourteen days' date, across which I will get you to write your name. Mr. Levy will show you the way in which this should be done. Your name must come under the word "accepted," and just above the name of Messrs. Drummonds, where the money must be lying ready, at any rate, not later than Monday fortnight. Indeed, the money must be there some time on the Saturday. They know you so well at Drummonds' that you will not object to call on the Saturday afternoon, and ask if it is all right.

'I have certainly been inconvenienced by not finding the money as I expected on my return to town. If these bills are not properly provided for, the result will be very disastrous to me. I feel, however, sure that this will be done, both for your own sake and for mine.

'Affectionately yours,
'GEORGE VAVASOR.'

The unparalleled impudence of this letter had the effect which the writer had intended. It made Alice think immediately of her own remissness,—if she had been remiss,—rather than of the enormity of his claim upon her. The decision with which he asked for her money, without any pretence at an excuse on his part, did for the time induce her to believe that she had no alternative but to give it to him, and that she had been wrong in delaying to give it. She had told him that he should have it, and she ought to have been as good as her word. She should not have forced upon him the necessity of demanding it.

But the idea of signing four bills was terrible to her, and she felt sure that she ought not to put her name to orders for so large an amount and then intrust them to such a man as Mr. Levy. Her father was in the house, and she might have asked him. The thought that she would do so of course occurred to her. But then it occurred to her also that were she to speak to her father as to this advancing of money to her cousin,—to this giving of money, for she now well understood that it would be a gift;—were she to consult her father in any way about it, he would hinder her, not only from signing the bills for Mr. Levy, but, as far as he could do so, from keeping the promise made to her cousin. She was resolved that George should have the money, and she knew that she could give it to him in spite of her father. But her father might probably be able to delay the gift, and thus rob it of its chief value. If she were to sign the bills, the money must be made to be forthcoming. So much she understood.

Mr. Levy had taken out the four bills from the same case, and had placed them on the table before him. 'Mr. Vavasor has explained, I believe, miss, what it is you have to do?' he said.

'Yes, sir; my cousin has explained.'

'And there is nothing else to trouble you with, I believe. If you will just write your name across them here, I need not detain you by staying any longer.' Mr. Levy was very anxious to make his visit as short as possible, since he had heard that Mr. John Vavasor was in the house.

But Alice hesitated. Two thousand pounds is a very serious sum of money. She had heard much of sharpers,* and thought that she ought to be cautious. What if this man, of whom she had never before heard, should steal the bills after she had signed them? She looked again at her cousin's letter, chiefly with the object of gaining time.

'It's all right, miss,' said Mr. Levy.

'Could you not leave them with me, sir?' said Alice.

'Well; not very well, miss. No doubt Mr. Vavasor has explained it all; but the fact is, he must have them this afternoon. He has got a heavy sum to put down on the nail about this here election, and if it ain't down to-day, them on whom he has to depend will be all abroad.'

'But, sir, the money will not be payable to-day. If I understand it, they are not cheques.'

'No, miss, no; they are not cheques. But your name, miss,
at fourteen days, is the same as ready money;—just the same.'

She paused, and while she paused, he reached a pen for her
from the writing-table, and then she signed the four bills as
he held them before her. She was quick enough at doing this
when she had once commenced the work. Her object, then,
was that the man should be gone from the house before her
father could meet him.

These were the four bits of paper which George Vavasor
tendered to Mr. Scruby's notice on the occasion which we
have now in hand. In doing so, he made use of them after the
manner of a grand capitalist, who knows that he may assume
certain airs as he allows the odours of the sweetness of his
wealth to drop from him.

'You insisted on ready money, with your d—— suspicions,'
said he; 'and there it is. You're not afraid of fourteen days, I
dare say.'

'Fourteen days is neither here nor there,' said Mr. Scruby.
'We can let our payments stand over as long as that, without
doing any harm. I'll send one of my men down to Grimes, and
tell him I can't see him, till,—let me see,' and he looked at
one of the bills, 'till the 15th.'

But this was not exactly what George Vavasor wanted. He
was desirous that the bills should be immediately turned into
money, so that the necessity of forcing payments from Alice,
should due provision for the bills not be made, might fall into
other hands than his.

'We can wait till the 15th,' said Scruby, as he handed the
bits of paper back to his customer.

'You will want a thousand, you say?' said George.

'A thousand to begin with. Certainly not less.'

'Then you had better keep two of them.'

'Well—no! I don't see the use of that. You had better collect
them through your own banker, and let me have a cheque on
the 15th or 16th.'

'How cursed suspicious you are, Scruby.'

'No, I ain't. I'm not a bit suspicious. I don't deal in such articles; that's all!'

'What doubt can there be about such bills as those? Everybody knows that my cousin has a considerable fortune, altogether at her own disposal.'

'The truth is, Mr. Vavasor, that bills with ladies' names on them,—ladies who are no way connected with business,—ain't just the paper that people like.'

'Nothing on earth can be surer.'

'You take them into the City for discount, and see if the bankers don't tell you the same. They may be done, of course, upon your name. I say nothing about that.'

'I can explain to you the nature of the family arrangement, but I can't do that to a stranger. However, I don't mind.'

'Of course not. The time is so short that it does not signify. Have them collected through your own bankers, and then, if it don't suit you to call, send me a cheque for a thousand pounds when the time is up.' Then Mr. Scruby turned to some papers on his right hand, as though the interview had been long enough. Vavasor looked at him angrily, opening his wound at him and cursing him inwardly. Mr. Scruby went on with his paper, by no means regarding either the wound or the unspoken curses. Thereupon Vavasor got up and went away without any word of farewell.

As he walked along Great Marlborough Street, and through those unalluring streets which surround the Soho district, and so on to the Strand and his own lodgings, he still continued to think of some wide scheme of revenge,—of some scheme in which Mr. Scruby might be included. There had appeared something latterly in Mr. Scruby's manner to him, something of mingled impatience and familiarity, which made him feel that he had fallen in the attorney's estimation. It was not that the lawyer thought him to be less honourable, or less clever, than he had before thought him; but that the man was like a rat, and knew a falling house by the instinct that was in him.

So George Vavasor cursed Mr. Scruby, and calculated some method of murdering him without detection.

The reader is not to suppose that the Member for the Chelsea Districts had, in truth, resolved to gratify his revenge by murder,—by murdering any of those persons whom he hated so vigorously. He did not, himself, think it probable that he would become a murderer. But he received some secret satisfaction in allowing his mind to dwell upon the subject, and in making those calculations. He reflected that it would not do to take off Scruby and John Grey at the same time, as it would be known that he was connected with both of them; unless, indeed, he was to take off a third person at the same time,—a third person, as to the expediency of ending whose career he made his calculations quite as often as he did in regard to any of those persons whom he cursed so often. It need hardly be explained to the reader that this third person was the sitting Member for the Chelsea Districts.

As he was himself in want of instant ready money Mr. Scruby's proposition that he should leave the four bills at his own bankers', to be collected when they came to maturity, did not suit him. He doubted much, also, whether at the end of the fourteen days the money would be forthcoming. Alice would be driven to tell her father, in order that the money might be procured, and John Vavasor would probably succeed in putting impediments in the way of the payment. He must take the bills into the City, and do the best there that he could with them. He was too late for this to-day, and therefore he went to his lodgings, and then down to the House. In the House he sat all the night with his hat over his eyes, making those little calculations of which I have spoken.

'You have heard the news; haven't you?' said Mr. Bott to him, whispering in his ear.

'News; no. I haven't heard any news.'

'Finespun has resigned, and Palliser is at this moment with the Duke of St. Bungay in the Lords' library.'

'They may both be at the bottom of the Lords' fishpond, for what I care,' said Vavasor.

'That's nonsense, you know,' said Bott. 'Still, you know Palliser is Chancellor of the Exchequer at this moment. What a lucky fellow you are to have such a chance come to you directly you get in. As soon as he takes his seat down there, of course we shall go up behind him.'

'We shall have another election in a month's time,' said George.

'I'm safe enough,' said Bott. 'It never hurts a man at elections to be closely connected with the Government.'

George Vavasor was in the City by times the next morning, but he found that the City did not look with favourable eyes on his four bills. The City took them up, first horizontally, and then, with a twist of its hand, perpendicularly, and looked at them with distrustful eyes. The City repeated the name, Alice Vavasor, as though it were not esteemed a good name on Change. The City suggested that as the time was so short, the holder of the bills would be wise to hold them till he could collect the amount. It was very clear that the City suspected something wrong in the transaction. The City, by one of its mouths, asserted plainly that ladies' bills never meant business. George Vavasor cursed the City, and made his calculation about murdering it. Might not a river of strychnine be turned on round the Exchange about luncheon time? Three of the bills he left at last with his own bankers for collection, and retained the fourth in his breast-pocket, intending on the morrow to descend with it into those lower depths of the money market which he had not as yet visited. Again, on the next day, he went to work and succeeded to some extent. Among those lower depths he found a capitalist who was willing to advance him two hundred pounds, keeping that fourth bill in his possession as security. The capitalist was to have forty pounds for the transaction, and George cursed him as he took his cheque. George Vavasor knew quite enough of the commercial world to enable him to understand that a man must be in a very bad condition when he consents to pay forty pounds for the use of two hundred for fourteen days.* He cursed the City. He cursed the House of Commons. He cursed his cousin Alice and his sister Kate. He cursed the memory of his grandfather. And he cursed himself.

Mr. Levy had hardly left the house in Queen Anne Street, before Alice had told her father what she had done. 'The money must be forthcoming,' said Alice. To this her father made no immediate reply, but turning himself in his chair away from her with a sudden start, sat looking at the fire and shaking his head. 'The money must be made to be forthcoming,' said Alice. 'Papa, will you see that it is done?' This was very hard upon poor John Vavasor, and so he felt it to be. 'Papa, if you will not promise, I must go to Mr. Round about it myself, and must find out a broker to sell out for me. You would not wish that my name should be dishonoured.'

'You will be ruined,' said he, 'and for such a rascal as that!'

'Never mind whether he is a rascal or not, papa. You must acknowledge that he has been treated harshly by his grand-father.'

'I think that will was the wisest thing my father ever did. Had he left the estate to George, there wouldn't have been an acre of it left in the family in six months' time.'

'But the life interest, papa!'

'He would have raised all he could upon that, and it would have done him no good.'

'At any rate, papa, he must have this two thousand pounds. You must promise me that.'

'And then he will want more.'

'No; I do not think he will ask for more. At any rate, I do not think that I am bound to give him all that I have.'

'I should think not. I should like to know how you can be bound to give him anything?'

'Because I promised it. I have signed the bills now, and it must be done.' Still Mr. Vavasor made no promise. 'Papa, if you will not say that you will do it, I must go down to Mr. Round at once.'

'I don't know that I can do it. I don't know that Mr. Round can do it. Your money is chiefly on mortgage.*Then there was a pause for a moment in the conversation. 'Upon my word, I

never heard of such a thing in my life,' said **Mr.** Vavasor;
'I never did. Four thousand pounds given away to such a man
as that, in three months! Four thousand pounds! And you say
you do not intend to marry him.'

'Certainly not; all that is over.'

'And does he know that it is over?'

'I suppose he does.'

'You suppose so! Things of that sort are so often over with
you!' This was very cruel. Perhaps she had deserved the reproach, but still it was very cruel. The blow struck her with
such force that she staggered under it. Tears came into her
eyes, and she could hardly speak lest she should betray herself
by sobbing.

'I know that I have behaved badly,' she said at last; 'but I
am punished, and you might spare me now!'

'I didn't want to punish you,' he said, getting up from his
chair and walking about the room. 'I don't want to punish you.
But, I don't want to see you ruined!'

'I must go to Mr. Round then, myself.'

Mr. Vavasor went on walking about the room, jingling the
money in his trousers-pockets, and pushing the chairs about as
he chanced to meet them. At last, he made a compromise with
her. He would take a day to think whether he would assist her
in getting the money, and communicate his decision to her on
the following morning.

CHAPTER LXI

The Bills are made all right

Mr. vavasor was at his wits' end about his daughter. She
had put her name to four bills for five hundred pounds
each, and had demanded from him, almost without an apology,
his aid in obtaining money to meet them. And she might put
her name to any other number of bills, and for any amount!
There was no knowing how a man ought to behave to such a
daughter. 'I don't want her money,' the father said to himself;

'and if she had got none of her own, I would make her as comfortable as I could with my own income. But to see her throw her money away in such a fashion as this is enough to break a man's heart.'

Mr. Vavasor went to his office in Chancery Lane, but he did not go to the chambers of Mr. Round, the lawyer. Instead of calling on Mr. Round he sent a note by a messenger to Suffolk Street, and the answer to the note came in the person of Mr. Grey. John Grey was living in town in these days, and was in the habit of seeing Mr. Vavasor frequently. Indeed, he had not left London since the memorable occasion on which he had pitched his rival down the tailor's stairs at his lodgings. He had made himself pretty well conversant with George Vavasor's career, and had often shuddered as he thought what might be the fate of any girl who might trust herself to marry such a man as that.

He had been at home when Mr. Vavasor's note had reached his lodgings, and had instantly walked off towards Chancery Lane. He knew his way to Mr. Vavasor's signing-office very accurately, for he had acquired a habit of calling there, and of talking to the father about his daughter. He was a patient, persevering man, confident in himself, and apt to trust that he would accomplish those things which he attempted, though he was hardly himself aware of any such aptitude. He had never despaired as to Alice. And though he had openly acknowledged to himself that she had been very foolish,—or rather, that her judgment had failed her,—he had never in truth been angry with her. He had looked upon her rejection of himself, and her subsequent promise to her cousin, as the effects of a mental hallucination, very much to be lamented,—to be wept for, perhaps, through a whole life, as a source of terrible sorrow to himself and to her. But he regarded it all as a disease, of which the cure was yet possible,—as a disease which, though it might never leave the patient as strong as she was before, might still leave her altogether. And as he would still have clung to his love had she been attacked by any of those illnesses for which doctors have well-known names, so would he cling to her now that she was attacked by a malady for which no name was known. He had already heard from Mr. Vavasor that Alice had discovered how impossible it was that she should marry her cousin, and, in his quiet, patient, enduring way, was beginning to feel confident that he would, at last, carry his mistress off with him to Nethercoats.

It was certainly a melancholy place, that signing-office, in which Mr. John Vavasor was doomed to spend twelve hours a week, during every term time, of his existence. Whether any man could really pass an existence of work in such a workshop, and not have gone mad,—could have endured to work there for seven hours a day, every week-day of his life, I am not prepared to say. I doubt much whether any victims are so doomed. I have so often wandered*through those gloomy passages without finding a sign of humanity there,—without hearing any slightest tick of the hammer of labour, that I am disposed to think that Lord Chancellors have been anxious to save their subordinates from suicide, and have mercifully decreed that the whole staff of labourers, down to the very message boys of the office, should be sent away to green fields or palatial clubs during, at any rate, a moiety of their existence.

The dismal set of chambers, in which the most dismal room had been assigned to Mr. Vavasor, was not actually in Chancery Lane. Opening off from Chancery Lane are various other small lanes, quiet, dingy nooks, some of them in the guise of streets going no whither, some being thoroughfares to other dingy streets beyond, in which sponging-houses*abound, and others existing as the entrances to so-called Inns of Court,— inns of which all knowledge has for years been lost to the outer world of the laity, and, as I believe, lost almost equally to the inner world of the legal profession. Who has ever heard of Symonds' Inn? But an ancestral Symonds, celebrated, no doubt, in his time, did found an inn, and there it is to this day. Of Staples' Inn,* who knows the purposes or use? Who are its members, and what do they do as such? And Staples' Inn is an inn with pretensions, having a chapel of its own, or, at any rate, a building which, in its external dimensions, is ecclesiastical, having a garden and architectural proportions; and a façade towards Holborn, somewhat dingy, but respectable, with an old gateway, and with a decided character of its own.

The building in which Mr. John Vavasor had a room and a desk was located in one of these side streets, and had, in its infantine days, been regarded with complacency by its founder. It was stone-faced, and strong, and though very ugly, had about it that air of importance which justifies a building in assuming a special name to itself. This building was called the Accountant-General's Record Office, and very probably, in the gloom of its dark cellars, may lie to this day the records of the expenditure of many a fair property which has gotten itself into Chancery, and has never gotten itself out again. It was entered by a dark hall, the door of which was never closed; and which, having another door at its further end leading into another lane, had become itself a thoroughfare. But the passers through it were few in number. Now and then a boy might be seen there carrying on his head or shoulders a huge mass of papers which you would presume to be accounts, or some clerk employed in the purlieus of Chancery Lane who would know the shortest possible way from the chambers of some one attorney to those of some other. But this hall, though open at both ends, was as dark as Erebus;*and any who lingered in it would soon find themselves to be growing damp, and would smell mildew, and would become naturally affected by the exhalations arising from those Chancery records beneath their feet.

Up the stone stairs, from this hall, John Grey passed to Mr. Vavasor's signing-room. The stairs were broad, and almost of noble proportions, but the darkness and gloom which hung about the hall, hung also about them,—a melancholy set of stairs, up and down which no man can walk with cheerful feet. Here he came upon a long, broad passage, in which no sound was, at first, to be heard. There was no busy noise of doors slamming, no rapid sound of shoes, no passing to and fro of men intent on their daily bread. Pausing for a moment, that he might look round about him and realize the deathlike stillness of the whole, John Grey could just distinguish the heavy breathing of a man, thereby learning that there was a captive in, at any rate, one of those prisons on each side of him. As he drew near to the door of Mr. Vavasor's chamber he knew that the breathing came from thence.

On the door there were words inscribed, which were just legible in the gloom—'Signing Room. Mr. Vavasor.'

How John Vavasor did hate those words! It seemed to him that they had been placed there with the express object of declaring his degradation aloud to the world. Since his father's will had been read to him he had almost made up his mind to go down those melancholy stairs for the last time, to shake the dust off his feet as he left the Accountant-General's Record Office for ever, and content himself with half his official income. But how could he give up so many hundreds a year while his daughter was persisting in throwing away thousands as fast as, or faster than, she could lay her hands on them?

John Grey entered the room and found Mr. Vavasor sitting all alone in an arm-chair over the fire. I rather think that that breathing had been the breathing of a man asleep. He was resting himself amidst the labours of his signing. It was a large, dull room, which could not have been painted, I should think, within the memory of man, looking out backwards into some court. The black wall of another building seemed to stand up close to the window,—so close that no direct ray of the sun ever interrupted the signing-clerk at his work. In the middle of the room there was a large mahogany-table, on which lay a pile of huge papers. Across the top of them there was placed a bit of blotting-paper, with a quill pen, the two only tools which were necessary to the performance of the signing-clerk's work. On the table there stood a row of official books, placed lengthways on their edges; the 'Post-Office Directory,' the 'Court Circular,' a 'Directory to the Inns of Court,' a dusty volume of Acts of Parliament, which had reference to Chancery accounts,—a volume which Mr. Vavasor never opened; and there were some others; but there was no book there in which any Christian man or woman could take delight, either for amusement or for recreation. There were three or four chairs round the wall, and there was the one arm-chair which the occupant of the chamber had dragged away from its sacred place to the hearth-rug. There was also an old Turkey carpet on the floor. Other furniture there was none. Can it be a matter of surprise to any one that Mr. Vavasor preferred his club to his place of business? He was not left quite alone in this deathlike dungeon. Attached to his own large room there was a small closet, in which sat the signing-clerk's clerk,—a lad of perhaps seventeen years of age, who spent the greatest part of his time in playing tit-tat-to* by himself upon official blotting-paper. Had I been Mr. Vavasor I should have sworn a bosom friendship with that lad, have told him all my secrets, and joined his youthful games.

'Come in!' Mr. Vavasor had cried when John Grey disturbed his slumber by knocking at the door. 'I'm glad to see you,—very. Sit down; won't you? Did you ever see such a wretched fire? The coals they give you in this place are the worst in all London. Did you ever see such coals?' And he gave a wicked poke at the fire.

It was now the 1st of May, and Grey, who had walked from Suffolk Street, was quite warm. 'One hardly wants a fire at all, such weather as this,' he said.

'Oh; don't you?' said the signing-clerk. 'If you had to sit here all day, you'd see if you didn't want a fire. It's the coldest building I ever put my foot in. Sometimes in winter I have to sit here the whole day in a great-coat. I only wish I could shut old Sugden up here for a week or two, after Christmas.' The great lawyer whom he had named was the man whom he supposed to have inflicted on him the terrible injury of his life, and he was continually invoking small misfortunes on the head of that tyrant.

'How is Alice?' said Grey, desiring to turn the subject from the ten-times-told tale of his friend's wrongs.

Mr. Vavasor sighed. 'She is well enough, I believe,' he said.

'Is anything the matter in Queen Anne Street?'

'You'll hardly believe it when I tell you; and, indeed, I hardly know whether I ought to tell you or not.'

'As you and I have gone so far together, I think that you ought to tell me anything that concerns her nearly.'

'That's just it. It's about her money. Do you know, Grey, I'm beginning to think that I've been wrong in allowing you to advance what you have done on her account?'

'Why wrong?'

'Because I foresee there'll be a difficulty about it. How are we to manage about the repayment?'

'If she becomes my wife there will be no management wanted.'

'But how if she never becomes your wife? I'm beginning to think she'll never do anything like any other woman.'

'I'm not quite sure that you understand her,' said Grey; 'though of course you ought to do so better than any one else.'

'Nobody can understand her,' said the angry father. 'She told me the other day, as you know, that she was going to have nothing more to do with her cousin——'

'Has she——has she become friends with him again?' said Grey. As he asked the question there came a red spot on each cheek, showing the strong mental anxiety which had prompted it.

'No; I believe not;—that is, certainly not in the way you mean. I think that she is beginning to know that he is a rascal.'

'It is a great blessing that she has learned the truth before it was too late.'

'But would you believe it;—she has given him her name to bills for two thousand pounds, payable at two weeks' sight? He sent to her only this morning a fellow that he called his clerk, and she has been fool enough to accept them. Two thousand pounds! That comes of leaving money at a young woman's own disposal.'

'But we expected that, you know,' said Grey, who seemed to take the news with much composure.

'Expected it?'

'Of course we did. You yourself did not suppose that what he had before would have been the last.'

'But after she had quarrelled with him!'

'That would make no difference with her. She had promised him her money, and as it seems that he will be content with that, let her keep her promise.'

'And give him everything! Not if I can help it. I'll expose him. I will indeed. Such a pitiful rascal as he is!'

'You will do nothing, Mr. Vavasor, that will injure your daughter. I'm very sure of that.'

'But, by heavens——. Such sheer robbery as that! Two thousand pounds more in fourteen days!' The shortness of the date at which the bills were drawn seemed to afflict Mr. Vavasor almost as keenly as the amount. Then he described the whole transaction as accurately as he could do so, and also told how Alice had declared her purpose of going to Mr. Round the lawyer, if her father would not undertake to procure the money for her by the time the bills should become due. 'Mr. Round, you know, has heard nothing about it,' he continued. 'He doesn't dream of any such thing. If she would take my advice, she would leave the bills, and let them be dishonoured. As it is, I think I shall call at Drummonds', and explain the whole transaction.'

'You must not do that,' said Grey. 'I will call at Drummonds', instead, and see that the money is all right for the bills. As far as they go, let him have his plunder.'

'And if she won't take you, at last, Grey? Upon my word, I don't think she ever will. My belief is she'll never get married. She'll never do anything like any other woman.'

'The money won't be missed by me if I never get married,' said Grey, with a smile. 'If she does marry me, of course I shall make her pay me.'

'No, by George! that won't do,' said Vavasor. 'If she were your daughter you'd know that she could not take a man's money in that way.'

'And I know it now, though she is not my daughter. I was only joking. As soon as I am certain,—finally certain,—that she can never become my wife, I will take back my money. You need not be afraid. The nature of the arrangement we have made shall then be explained to her.'

In this way it was settled; and on the following morning the father informed the daughter that he had done her bidding, and that the money would be placed to her credit at the bankers' before the bills came due. On that Saturday, the day which her cousin had named in his letter, she trudged down to Drummonds', and was informed by a very courteous senior clerk in that establishment that due preparation for the bills had been made.

So far, I think we may say that Mr. George Vavasor was not unfortunate.

CHAPTER LXII
Going Abroad

ONE morning, early in May, a full week before Alice's visit to the bankers' at Charing Cross, a servant in grand livery, six feet high, got out of a cab at the door in Queen Anne Street, and sent up a note for Miss Vavasor, declaring that he would wait in the cab for her answer. He had come from Lady Glencora, and had been specially ordered to go in a cab and come back in a cab, and make himself as like a Mercury, with wings to his feet, as may be possible to a London footman. Mr. Palliser had arranged his plans with his wife that morning,— or, I should more correctly say, had given her his orders, and she, in consequence, had sent away her Mercury in hot pressing haste to Queen Anne Street. 'Do come;—instantly if you can,' the note said. 'I have so much to tell you, and so much to ask of you. If you can't come, when shall I find you, and where?' Alice sent back a note, saying that she would be in Park Lane as soon as she could put on her bonnet and walk down; and then the Mercury went home in his cab.

Alice found her friend in the small breakfast-room up-stairs, sitting close by the window. They had not as yet met since the evening of Lady Monk's party, nor had Lady Glencora seen Alice in the mourning which she now wore for her grandfather. 'Oh dear, what a change it makes in you,' she said. 'I never thought of your being in black.'

219

'I don't know what it is you want, but shan't I do in mourning as well as I would in colours?'

'You'll do in anything, dear. But I have so much to tell you, and I don't know how to begin. And I've so much to ask of you, and I'm so afraid you won't do it.'

'You generally find me very complaisant.'

'No, I don't, dear. It is very seldom you will do anything for me. But I must tell you everything first. Do take your bonnet off, for I shall be hours in doing it.'

'Hours in telling me!'

'Yes; and in getting your consent to what I want you to do. But I think I'll tell you that first. I'm to be taken abroad immediately.'

'Who is to take you?'

'Ah, you may well ask that. If you could know what questions I have asked myself on that head! I sometimes say things to myself as though they were the most proper and reasonable things in the world, and then within an hour or two I hate myself for having thought of them.'

'But why don't you answer me? Who is going abroad with you?'

'Well; you are to be one of the party.'

'I!'

'Yes; you. When I have named so very respectable a chaperon for my youth, of course you will understand that my husband is to take us.'

'But Mr. Palliser can't leave London at this time of the year?'

'That's just it. He is to leave London at this time of the year. Don't look in that way, for it's all settled. Whether you go with me or not, I've got to go. To-day is Tuesday. We are to be off next Tuesday night, if you can make yourself ready. We shall breakfast in Paris on Wednesday morning, and then it will be to us all just as if we were in a new world. Mr. Palliser will walk up and down the new court of the Louvre,* and you will be on his left arm, and I shall be on his right,— just like English people,—and it will be the most proper thing

that ever was seen in life. Then we shall go on to Basle'—
Alice shuddered as Basle was mentioned, thinking of the balcony over the river—'and so to Lucerne——. But no; that was
the first plan, and Mr. Palliser altered it. He spent a whole
day up here with maps and Bradshaws*and Murray's guide-
books,* and he scolded me so because I didn't care whether we
went first to Baden or to some other place. How could I care?
I told him I would go anywhere he chose to take me. Then he
told me I was heartless;—and I acknowledged that I was heartless. "I am heartless," I said. "Tell me something I don't
know."'

'Oh, Cora, why did you say that?'

'I didn't choose to contradict my husband. Besides, it's true.
Then he threw the Bradshaw away, and all the maps flew
about. So I picked them up again, and said we'd go to Switzerland first. I knew that would settle it, and of course he decided
on stopping at Baden. If he had said Jericho, it would have
been the same thing to me. Wouldn't you like to go to
Jericho?'

'I should have no special objection to Jericho.'

'But you are to go to Baden instead.'

'I've said nothing about that yet. But you have not told me
half your story. Why is Mr. Palliser going abroad in the
middle of Parliament in this way?'

'Ah; now I must go back to the beginning. And indeed,
Alice, I hardly know how to tell you; not that I mind you
knowing it, only there are some things that won't get themselves told. You can hardly guess what it is that he is giving
up. You must swear that you won't repeat what I'm going to
tell you now?'

'I'm not a person apt to tell secrets, but I shan't swear
anything.'

'What a woman you are for discretion! It is you that ought
to be Chancellor of the Exchequer; you are so wise. Only you
haven't brought your own pigs to the best market, after all.'

'Never mind my own pigs now, Cora.'

'I do mind them, very much. But the secret is this. They

have asked Mr. Palliser to be Chancellor of the Exchequer, and he has—refused. Think of that!'

'But why?'

'Because of me,—of me, and my folly, and wickedness, and abominations. Because he has been fool enough to plague himself with a wife;—he who of all men ought to have kept himself free from such troubles. Oh, he has been so good! It is almost impossible to make any one understand it. If you could know how he has longed for this office;—how he has worked for it day and night, wearing his eyes out with figures when everybody else has been asleep, shutting himself up with such creatures as Mr. Bott when other men have been shooting and hunting and flirting and spending their money. He has been a slave to it for years,—all his life I believe,—in order that he might sit in the Cabinet, and be a minister and a Chancellor of the Exchequer. He has hoped and feared, and has been, I believe, sometimes half-mad with expectation. This has been his excitement,—what racing and gambling are to other men. At last, the place was there, ready for him, and they offered it to him. They begged him to take it, almost on their knees. The Duke of St. Bungay was here all one morning about it; but Mr. Palliser sent him away, and refused the place. It's all over now, and the other man, whom they all hate so much, is to remain in.'

'But why did he refuse it?'

'I keep on telling you;—because of me. He found that I wanted looking after, and that Mrs. Marsham and Mr. Bott between them couldn't do it.'

'Oh, Cora! how can you talk in that way?'

'If you knew all, you might well ask how I could. You remember about Lady Monk's ball, that you would not go to, —as you ought to have done. If you had gone, Mr. Palliser would have been Chancellor of the Exchequer at this minute; he would, indeed. Only think of that! But though you did not go, other people did who ought to have remained at home. I went for one,—and you know who was there for another.'

'What difference could that make to you?' said Alice, angrily.

'It might have made a great deal of difference. And, for the matter of that, so it did. Mr. Palliser was there too, but, of course, he went away immediately. I can't tell you all the trouble there had been about Mrs. Marsham,—whether I was to take her with me or not. However, I wouldn't take her, and didn't take her. The carriage went for her first, and there she was when we got there; and Mr. Bott was there too. I wonder whether I shall ever make you understand it all.'

'There are some things I don't want to understand.'

'There they both were, watching me,—looking at me the whole evening; and, of course, I resolved that I would not be put down by them.'

'I think, if I had been you, I would not have allowed their presence to make any difference to me.'

'That is very easily said, my dear, but by no means so easily done. You can't make yourself unconscious of eyes that are always looking at you. I dared them, at any rate, to do their worst, for I stood up to dance with Burgo Fitzgerald.'

'Oh, Cora!'

'Why shouldn't I? At any rate I did; and I waltzed with him for half an hour. Alice, I never will waltz again;—never. I have done with dancing now. I don't think, even in my maddest days, I ever kept it up so long as I did then. And I knew that everybody was looking at me. It was not only Mrs. Marsham and Mr. Bott, but everybody there. I felt myself to be desperate,—mad, like a wild woman. There I was, going round and round and round with the only man for whom I ever cared two straws. It seemed as though everything had been a dream since the old days. Ah! how well I remember the first time I danced with him,—at his aunt's house in Cavendish Square. They had only just brought me out in London then, and I thought that he was a god.'

'Cora! I cannot bear to hear you talk like that.'

'I know well enough that he is no god now; some people say that he is a devil, but he was like Apollo to me then. Did you ever see any one so beautiful as he is?'

'I never saw him at all.'

'I wish you could have seen him; but you will some day. I don't know whether you care for men being handsome.' Alice thought of John Grey, who was the handsomest man that she knew, but she made no answer. 'I do; or, rather, I used to do,' continued Lady Glencora. 'I don't think I care much about anything now; but I don't see why handsome men should not be run after as much as handsome women.'

'But you wouldn't have a girl run after any man, would you; whether handsome or ugly?'

'But they do, you know. When I saw him the other night he was just as handsome as ever;—the same look, half wild and half tame, like an animal you cannot catch, but which you think would love you so if you could catch him. In a little while it was just like the old time, and I had made up my mind to care nothing for the people looking at me.'

'And you think that was right?'

'No, I don't. Yes, I do; that is, it wasn't right to care about dancing with him, but it was right to disregard all the people gaping round. What was it to them? Why should they care who I danced with?'

'That is nonsense, dear, and you must know that it is so. If you were to see a woman misbehaving herself in public, would not you look on and make your comments? Could you help doing so if you were to try?'

'You are very severe, Alice. Misbehaving in public!'

'Yes, Cora. I am only taking your own story. According to that, you were misbehaving in public.'

Lady Glencora got up from her chair near the window, on which she had been crouching close to Alice's knees, and walked away towards the fireplace. 'What am I to say to you, or how am I to talk to you?' said Alice. 'You would not have me tell you a lie?'

'Of all things in the world, I hate a prude the most,' said Lady Glencora.

'Cora, look here. If you consider it prudery on my part to disapprove of your waltzing with Mr. Fitzgerald in the manner you have described,—or, indeed, in any other manner,—

you and I must differ so totally about the meaning of words and the nature of things that we had better part.'

'Alice, you are the unkindest creature that ever lived. You are as cold as stone. I sometimes think that you can have no heart.'

'I don't mind your saying that. Whether I have a heart or not I will leave you to find out for yourself; but I won't be called a prude by you. You know you were wrong to dance with that man. What has come of it? What have you told me yourself this morning? In order to preserve you from misery and destruction, Mr. Palliser has given up all his dearest hopes. He has had to sacrifice himself that he might save you. That, I take it, is about the truth of it,—and yet you tell me that you have done no wrong.'

'I never said so.' Now she had come back to her chair by the window, and was again sitting in that crouching form. 'I never said that I was not wrong. Of course I was wrong. I have been so wrong throughout that I have never been right yet. Let me tell it on to the end, and then you can go away if you like, and tell me that I am too wicked for your friendship.'

'Have I ever said anything like that, Cora?'

'But you will, I dare say, when I have done. Well; what do you think my senior duenna did,—the female one, I mean? She took my own carriage, and posted off after Mr. Palliser as hard as ever she could, leaving the male duenna on the watch. I was dancing as hard as I could, but I knew what was going on all the time as well as though I had heard them talking. Of course Mr. Palliser came after me. I don't know what else he could do, unless, indeed, he had left me to my fate. He came there, and behaved so well,—so much like a perfect gentleman. Of course I went home, and I was prepared to tell him everything, if he spoke a word to me;—that I intended to leave him, and that cart-ropes should not hold me!'

'To leave him, Cora!'

'Yes, and go with that other man whose name you won't let me mention. I had a letter from him in my pocket asking me to go. He asked me a dozen times that night. I cannot think how it was that I did not consent.'

'That you did not consent to your own ruin and disgrace?'

'That I did not consent to go off with him,—anywhere. Of course it would have been my own destruction. I'm not such a fool as not to know that. Do you suppose I have never thought of it;—what it would be to be a man's mistress instead of his wife? If I had not I should be a thing to be hated and despised. When once I had done it I should hate and despise myself. I should feel myself to be loathsome, and, as it were, a beast among women. But why did they not let me marry him, instead of driving me to this? And though I might have destroyed myself, I should have saved the man who is still my husband. Do you know, I told him all that,—told him that if I had gone away with Burgo Fitzgerald he would have another wife, and would have children, and would——?'

'You told your husband that you had thought of leaving him?'

'Yes; I told him everything. I told him that I dearly loved that poor fellow, for whom, as I believe, nobody else on earth cares a single straw.'

'And what did he say?'

'I cannot tell you what he said, only that we are all to go to Baden together, and then to Italy. But he did not seem a bit angry; he very seldom is angry, unless at some trumpery thing, as when he threw the book away. And when I told him that he might have another wife and a child, he put his arm round me and whispered to me that he did not care so much about it as I had imagined. I felt more like loving him at that moment than I had ever done before.'

'He must be fit to be an angel.'

'He's fit to be a cabinet minister, which, I'm quite sure, he'd like much better. And now you know everything; but no,—there is one thing you don't know yet. When I tell you that, you'll want to make him an archangel or a prime minister. "We'll go abroad," he said,—and remember, this was his own proposition, made long before I was able to speak a word;—"We'll go abroad, and you shall get your cousin Alice to go with us." That touched me more than anything. Only think if he had proposed Mrs. Marsham!'

'But yet he does not like me.'

'You're wrong there, Alice. There has been no question of liking or of disliking. He thought you would be a kind of Mrs. Marsham, and when you were not, but went out flirting among the ruins with Jeffrey Palliser, instead——'

'I never went out flirting with Jeffrey Palliser.'

'He did with you, which is all the same thing. And when Plantagenet knew of that,—for, of course, Mr. Bott told him——'

'Mr. Bott can't see everything.'

'Those men do. The worst is, they see more than everything. But, at any rate, Mr. Palliser has got over all that now. Come, Alice; the fact of the offer having come from himself should disarm you of any such objection as that. As he has held out his hand to you, you have no alternative but to take it.'

'I will take his hand willingly.'

'And for my sake you will go with us? He understands himself that I am not fit to be his companion, and to have no companion but him. Now there is a spirit of wisdom about you that will do for him, and a spirit of folly that will suit me. I can manage to put myself on a par with a girl who has played such a wild game with her lovers as you have done.'

Alice would give no promise then. Her first objection was that she had undertaken to go down to Westmoreland and comfort Kate in the affliction of her broken arm. 'And I must go,' said Alice, remembering how necessary it was that she should plead her own cause with George Vavasor's sister. But she acknowledged that she had not intended to stay long in Westmoreland, probably not more than a week, and it was at last decided that the Pallisers should postpone their journey for four or five days, and that Alice should go with them immediately upon her return from Vavasor Hall.

'I have no objection,' said her father, speaking with that voice of resignation which men use when they are resolved to consider themselves injured whatever may be done. 'I can get along in lodgings. I suppose we had better leave the house, as you have given away so much of your own fortune?' Alice

did not think it worth her while to point out to him, in answer
to this, that her contribution to their joint housekeeping should
still remain the same as ever. Such, however, she knew would
be the fact, and she knew also that she would find her father in
the old house when she returned from her travels. To her, in
her own great troubles, the absence from London would be as
serviceable as it could be to Lady Glencora. Indeed, she had
already begun to feel the impossibility of staying quietly at
home. She could lecture her cousin, whose faults were open,
easy to be defined, and almost loud in their nature; but she was
not on that account the less aware of her own. She knew that
she too had cause to be ashamed of herself. She was half afraid
to show her face among her friends, and wept grievously over
her own follies. Those cruel words of her father rang in her
ears constantly;—'Things of that sort are so often over with
you.' The reproach, though cruel, was true, and what reproach
more galling could be uttered to an unmarried girl such as was
Alice Vavasor? She had felt from the first moment in which
the proposition was made to her, that it would be well that she
should for a while leave her home, and especially that drawing-
room in Queen Anne Street, which told her so many tales that
she would fain forget, if it were possible.

Mr. Palliser would not allow his wife to remain in London
for the ten or twelve days which must yet elapse before they
started, nor would he send her into the country alone. He took
her down to Matching Park,* having obtained leave to be
absent from the House for the remainder of the Session, and remained with her there till within two days of their departure.
That week down at Matching, as she afterwards told Alice, was
very terrible. He never spoke a word to rebuke her. He never
hinted that there had been aught in her conduct of which he
had cause to complain. He treated her with a respect that was
perfect, and indeed with more outward signs of affection than
had ever been customary with him. 'But,' as Lady Glencora
afterwards expressed it, 'he was always looking after me. I
believe he thought that Burgo Fitzgerald had hidden himself
among the ruins,' she said once to Alice. 'He never suspected

me, I am sure of that; but he thought that he ought to look
after me.' And Lady Glencora in this had very nearly hit the
truth. Mr. Palliser had resolved, from that hour in which he
had walked out among the elms in Kensington Gardens, that
he would neither suspect his wife, nor treat her as though he
suspected her. The blame had been his, perhaps, more than it
had been hers. So much he had acknowledged to himself, thinking of the confession she had made to him before their marriage.
But it was manifestly his imperative duty,—his duty of duties,
—to save her from that pitfall into which, as she herself had
told him, she had been so ready to fall. For her sake and for
his this must be done. It was a duty so imperative, that in its
performance he had found himself forced to abandon his ambition. To have his wife taken from him would be terrible, but
the having it said all over the world that such a misfortune
had come upon him would be almost more terrible even than
that.

So he went with his wife hither and thither, down at Matching, allowing himself to be driven about behind Dandy and
Flirt. He himself proposed these little excursions. They were
tedious to him, but doubly tedious to his wife, who now found
it more difficult than ever to talk to him. She struggled to talk,
and he struggled to talk, but the very struggles themselves
made the thing impossible. He sat with her in the mornings,
and he sat with her in the evenings; he breakfasted with her,
lunched with her, and dined with her. He went to bed early,
having no figures which now claimed his attention. And so
the week at last wore itself away. 'I saw him yawning sometimes,' Lady Glencora said afterwards, 'as though he would
fall in pieces.'

CHAPTER LXIII

Mr. John Grey in Queen Anne Street

ALICE was resolved that she would keep her promise to Kate, and pay her visit to Westmoreland before she started with the Pallisers. Kate had written to her three lines with her left hand, begging her to come, and those three lines had been more eloquent than anything she could have written had her right arm been uninjured. Alice had learned something of the truth as to that accident from her father; or, rather, had heard her father's surmises on the subject. She had heard, too, how her cousin George had borne himself when the will was read, and how he had afterwards disappeared, never showing himself again at the Hall. After all that had passed she felt that she owed Kate some sympathy. Sympathy may, no doubt, be conveyed by letter; but there are things on which it is almost impossible for any writer to express himself with adequate feeling; and there are things, too, which can be spoken, but which cannot be written. Therefore, though the journey must be a hurried one, Alice sent word down to Westmoreland that she was to be expected there in a day or two. On her return she was to go at once to Park Lane, and sleep there for the two nights which would intervene before the departure of the Pallisers.

On the day before she started for Westmoreland her father came to her in the middle of the day, and told her that John Grey was going to dine with him in Queen Anne Street on that evening.

'To-day, papa?' she asked.

'Yes, to-day. Why not? No man is less particular as to what he eats than Grey.'

'I was not thinking of that, papa,' she said.

To this Mr. Vavasor made no reply, but stood for some minutes looking out of the window. Then he prepared to leave the room, getting himself first as far as the table, where he lifted a book, and then on half-way to the door, before Alice arrested him.

'Perhaps, papa, you and Mr. Grey had better dine alone.'

'What do you mean by alone?'

'I meant without me,—as two men generally like to do.'

'If I wanted that I should have asked him to dine at the club,' said Mr. Vavasor, and then he again attempted to go.

'But, papa——'

'Well, my dear! If you mean to say that because of what has passed you object to meet Mr. Grey, I can only tell you it's nonsense,—confounded nonsense. If he chooses to come there can be no reason why you shouldn't receive him.'

'It will look as though——'

'Look what?'

'As though he were asked as my guest.'

'That's nonsense. I saw him yesterday, and I asked him to come. I saw him again to-day, and he said he would come. He's not such a fool as to suppose after that, that you asked him.'

'No; not that I asked him.'

'And if you run away you'll only make more of the thing than it's worth. Of course I can't make you dine with me if you don't like.'

Alice did not like it, but, after some consideration, she thought that she might be open to the imputation of having made more of the thing than it was worth if she ran away, as her father called it. She was going to leave the country for some six or eight months,—perhaps for a longer time than that, and it might be as well that she should have an opportunity of telling her plans to Mr. Grey. She could do it, she thought, in such a way as to make him understand that her last quarrel with George Vavasor was not supposed to alter the footing on which she stood with him. She did not doubt that her father had told everything to Mr. Grey. She knew well enough what her father's wishes still were. It was not odd that he should be asking John Grey to his house, though such exercises of domestic hospitality were very unusual with him. But,—so she declared to herself,—such little attempts on his part would be altogether thrown away. It was a pity that he had not yet learned to know her better. She would receive Mr. Grey as the mistress of her father's house now, for the last time; and then, on her return in the following year, he would be at Nethercoats, and the whole thing would be over.

She dressed herself very plainly, simply changing one black frock for another, and then sat herself in her drawing-room awaiting the two gentlemen. It was already past the hour of dinner before her father came up-stairs. She knew that he was in the house, and in her heart she accused him of keeping out of the way, in order that John Grey might be alone with her. Whether or no she were right in her suspicions John Grey did not take advantage of the opportunity offered to him. Her father came up first, and had seated himself silently in his arm-chair before the visitor was announced.

As Mr. Grey entered the room Alice knew that she was flurried, but still she managed to carry herself with some dignity. His bearing was perfect. But then, as she declared to herself afterwards, no possible position in life would put him beside himself. He came up to her with his usual quiet smile, —a smile that was genial even in its quietness, and took her hand. He took it fairly and fully into his; but there was no squeezing, no special pressure, no love-making. And when he spoke to her he called her Alice, as though his doing so was of all things the most simply a matter of course. There was no tell-tale hesitation in his voice. When did he ever hesitate at anything? 'I hear you are going abroad,' he said, 'with your cousin, Lady Glencora Palliser.'

'Yes,' said Alice; 'I am going with them for a long tour. We shall not return, I fancy, till the end of next winter.'

'Plans of that sort are as easily broken as they are made,' said her father. 'You won't be your own mistress; and I advise you not to count too surely upon getting further than Baden.'

'If Mr. Palliser changes his mind of course I shall come home,' said Alice, with a little attempt at a smile.

'I should think him a man not prone to changes,' said Grey. 'But all London is talking about his change of mind at this moment. They say at the clubs that he might have been in the Cabinet if he would, but that he has taken up this idea of going abroad at the moment when he was wanted.'

'It's his wife's doing, I take it,' said Mr. Vavasor.

'That's the worst of being in Parliament,' said Grey. 'A man can't do anything without giving a reason for it. There must be men for public life, of course; but, upon my word, I think we ought to be very much obliged to them.'

Alice, as she took her old lover's arm, and walked down with him to dinner, thought of all her former quarrels with him on this very subject. On this very point she had left him. He had never argued the matter with her. He had never asked her to argue with him. He had not condescended so far as that. Had he done so, she thought that she would have brought herself to think as he thought. She would have striven, at any rate, to do so. But she could not become unambitious, tranquil, fond of retirement, and philosophic, without an argument on the matter,—without being allowed even the poor grace of owning herself to be convinced. If a man takes a dog with him from the country up to town, the dog must live a town life without knowing the reason why;—must live a town life or die a town death. But a woman should not be treated like a dog. 'Had he deigned to discuss it with me!' Alice had so often said. 'But, no; he will read his books, and I am to go there to fetch him his slippers, and make his tea for him.' All this came upon her again as she walked down-stairs by his side; and with it there came a consciousness that she had been driven by this usage into the terrible engagement which she had made with her cousin. That, no doubt, was now over. There was no longer to her any question of her marrying George Vavasor. But the fact that she had been mad enough to think and talk of such a marriage, had of itself been enough to ruin her. 'Things of that sort are so often over with you!' After such a speech as that to her from her father, Alice told herself that there could be no more 'things of that sort' for her. But all her misery had been brought about by this scornful superiority to the ordinary pursuits of the world,—this looking down upon humanity. 'It seems to me,' she said, very quietly, while her hand was yet upon his arm, 'that your pity is hardly needed. I should think that no persons can be happier than those whom you call our public men.'

'Ah!' said he, 'that is our old quarrel.' He said it as though the quarrel had simply been an argument between them, or a dozen arguments,—as arguments do come up between friends; not as though it had served to separate for life two persons who had loved each other dearly. 'It's the old story·of the town mouse and the country mouse,—as old as the hills. Mice may be civil for a while, and compliment each other; but when they come to speak their minds freely, each likes his own life best.' She said nothing more at the moment, and the three sat down to their small dinner-table. It was astonishing to Alice that he should be able to talk in this way, to hint at such things, to allude to their former hopes and present condition, without a quiver in his voice, or, as far as she could perceive, without any feeling in his heart.

'Alice,' said her father, 'I can't compliment your cook upon her soup.'

'You don't encourage her, papa, by eating it often enough. And then you only told me at two o'clock to-day.'

'If a cook can't make soup between two and seven, she can't make it in a week.'

'I hope Mr. Grey will excuse it,' said Alice.

'Isn't it good?' said he. 'I won't say that it is, because I should be pretending to have an opinion; but I should not have found out anything against it of myself.'

'Where do you dine usually, now you are in London?' Mr. Vavasor asked.

'At the old club, at the corner of Suffolk Street. It's the oldest club in London, I believe. I never belonged to any other, and therefore can't compare them; but I can't imagine anything much nicer.'

'They give you better soup than ours?' said Alice.

'You've an excellent cook,' said Mr. Vavasor, with great gravity; 'one of the best second-class cooks in London. We

were very nearly getting him, but you nicked him just in time.
I know him well.'

'It's a great deal more than I do, or hope to do. There's
another branch of public life for which I'm quite unfitted. I'd
as soon be called on to choose a Prime Minister for the country, as I would a cook for a club.'

'Of course you would,' said Mr. Vavasor. 'There may be as
many as a dozen cooks about London to be looked up, but
there are never more than two possible Prime Ministers about.
And as one of them must be going out when the other is
coming in, I don't see that there can be any difficulty. Moreover, now-a-days, people do their politics for themselves, but
they expect to have their dinners cooked for them.'

The little dinner went on quietly and very easily. Mr. Vavasor found fault with nearly everything. But as, on this occasion,
the meat and the drink, with the manner of the eating and
drinking, did not constitute the difficulty, Alice was indifferent
to her father's censures. The thing needed was that she and
Mr. Grey should be able to sit together at the same table without apparent consciousness of their former ties. Alice felt that
she was succeeding indifferently well while she was putting in
little mock defences for the cook. And as for John Grey, he
succeeded so well that his success almost made Alice angry
with him. It required no effort with him at all to be successful
in this matter. 'If he can forget all that has passed, so much
the better,' said Alice to herself when she got up into the
drawing-room. Then she sat herself down on the sofa, and
cried. Oh! what had she not lost! Had any woman ever been
so mad, so reckless, so heartless as she had been! And she had
done it, knowing that she loved him! She cried bitterly, and
then went away to wash her eyes, that she might be ready to
give him his coffee when he should come up-stairs.

'She does not look well,' said Grey as soon as she had left
the room.

'Well;—no: how can she look well after what she has gone
through? I sometimes think, that of all the people I ever knew,
she has been the most foolish. But, of course, it is not for me

to say anything against my own child; and, of all people, not to you.'

'Nothing that you could say against her would make any difference to me. I sometimes fancy that I know her better than you do.'

'And you think that she'll still come round again?'

'I cannot say that I think so. No one can venture to say whether or not such wounds as hers may be cured. There are hearts and bodies so organized, that in them severe wounds are incurable, whereas in others no injury seems to be fatal. But I can say that if she be not cured it shall not be from want of perseverance on my part.'

'Upon my word, Grey, I don't know how to thank you enough. I don't, indeed.'

'It doesn't seem to me to be a case for thanking.'

'Of course it isn't. I know that well enough. And in the ordinary way of the world no father would think of thanking a man for wanting to marry his daughter. But things have come to such a pass with us, that, by George! I don't feel like any other father. I don't mind saying anything to you, you know. That claret isn't very good, but you might as well take another glass.'

'Thank you, I will. I should have said that that was rather good wine now.'

'It's not just the thing. What's the use of my having good wine here, when nobody comes to drink it? But, as I was saying about Alice, of course I've felt all this thing very much. I feel as though I were responsible, and yet what could I do? She's her own mistress through it all. When she told me she was going to marry that horrible miscreant, my nephew, what could I do?'

'That's over now, and we need not talk about it.'

'It's very kind of you to say so,—very. I believe she's a good girl. I do, indeed, in spite of it all.'

'I've no doubt of her being what you call a good girl,—none in the least. What she has done to me does not impair her goodness. I don't think you have ever understood how much all this has been a matter of conscience with her.'

236

'Conscience!' said the angry father. 'I hate such conscience. I like the conscience that makes a girl keep her word, and not bring disgrace upon those she belongs to.'

'I shall not think that I am disgraced,' said Grey, quietly, 'if she will come and be my wife. She has meant to do right, and has endeavoured to take care of the happiness of other people rather than her own.'

'She has taken very little care of mine,' said Mr. Vavasor.

'I shall not be at all afraid to trust mine to her,—if she will let me do so. But she has been wounded sorely, and it must take time.'

'And, in the meantime, what are we to do when she tells us that Mr. George Vavasor wants another remittance? Two thousand pounds a quarter comes heavy, you know!'

'Let us hope that he has had enough.'

'Enough! Did such a man ever have enough?'

'Let us hope, then, that she thinks he has had enough. Come; —may I go up-stairs?'

'Oh, yes. I'll follow you. She'll think that I mean something if I leave you together.'

From all this it will be seen that Alice's father and her lover still stood together on confidential terms. Not easily had Mr. Vavasor brought himself to speak of his daughter to John Grey in such language as he had now used; but he had been forced by adverse circumstances to pass the Rubicon*of parental delicacy; he had been driven to tell his wished-for son-in-law that he did wish to have him as a son-in-law; he had been compelled to lay aside those little airs of reserve with which a father generally speaks of his daughter,—and now all was open between them.

'And you really start to-morrow?' said Grey, as he stood close over Alice's work-table. Mr. Vavasor had followed him into the drawing-room, but had seated himself in an easy-chair on the other side of the fire. There was no tone of whispering in Grey's voice, but yet he spoke in a manner which showed that he did not intend to be audible on the other side of the room.

'I start for Westmoreland to-morrow. We do not leave London for the continent till the latter end of next week.'

'But you will not be here again?'

'No; I shall not come back to Queen Anne Street.'

'And you will be away for many months?'

'Mr. Palliser talked of next Easter as the term of his return. He mentioned Easter to Lady Glencora. I have not seen him myself since I agreed to go with him.'

'What should you say if you met me somewhere in your travels?' He had now gently seated himself on the sofa beside her;—not so close to her as to give her just cause to move away, but yet so near as to make his conversation with her quite private.

'I don't think that will be very likely,' she replied, not knowing what to say.

'I think it is very likely. For myself, I hate surprises. I could not bring myself to fall in upon your track unawares. I shall go abroad, but it will not be till the late autumn, when the summer heats are gone,—and I shall endeavour to find you.'

'To find me, Mr. Grey!' There was a quivering in her voice, as she spoke, which she could not prevent, though she would have given worlds to prevent it. 'I do not think that will be quite fair.'

'It will not be unfair, I think, if I give you notice of my approach. I will not fall upon you and your friends unawares.'

'I was not thinking of them. They would be glad to know you, of course.'

'And equally, of course!—or, rather, much more of course, you will not be glad to see me? That's what you mean?'

'I mean that we had better not meet more than we can help.'

'I think differently, Alice,—quite differently. The more we meet the better,—that is what I think. But I will not stop to trouble you now. Good night!' Then he got up and went away, and her father went with him. Mr. Vavasor, as he rose from his chair, declared that he would just walk through a couple of streets; but Alice knew that he was gone to his club.

CHAPTER LXIV

The Rocks and Valleys

DURING these days Mrs. Greenow was mistress of the old Hall down in Westmoreland, and was nursing Kate assiduously through the calamity of her broken arm. There had come to be a considerable amount of confidence between the aunt and the niece. Kate had acknowledged to her aunt that her brother had behaved badly,—very badly; and the aunt had confessed to the niece that she regarded Captain Bellfield as a fit subject for compassion.

'And he was violent to you, and broke your arm? I always knew it was so,' Mrs. Greenow had said, speaking with reference to her nephew. But this Kate had denied. 'No,' said she; 'that was an accident. When he went away and left me, he knew nothing about it. And if he had broken both my arms I should not have cared much. I could have forgiven him that.' But that which Kate could not forgive him was the fault which she had herself committed. For his sake she had done her best to separate Alice and John Grey, and George had shown himself to be unworthy of the kindness of her treachery. 'I would give all I have in the world to bring them together again,' Kate said. 'They'll come together fast enough if they like each other,' said Mrs. Greenow. 'Alice is young still, and they tell me she's as good-looking as ever. A girl with her money won't have far to seek for a husband, even if this paragon from Cambridgeshire should not turn up again.'

'You don't know Alice, aunt.'

'No, I don't. But I know what young women are, and I know what young men are. All this nonsense about her cousin George,—what difference will it make? A man like Mr. Grey won't care about that,—especially not if she tells him all about it. My belief is that a girl can have anything forgiven her, if she'll only tell it herself.'

But Kate preferred the other subject, and so, I think, did Mrs. Greenow herself. 'Of course, my dear,' she would say, 'marriage with me, if I should marry again, would be a very different thing to your marriage, or that of any other young person. As for love, that has been all over for me since poor Greenow died. I have known nothing of the softness of affection since I laid him in his cold grave, and never can again. "Captain Bellfield," I said to him, "if you were to kneel at my feet for years, it would not make me care for you in the way of love."'

'And what did he say to that?'

'How am I to tell you what he said? He talked nonsense about my beauty, as all the men do. If a woman were humpbacked, and had only one eye, they wouldn't be ashamed to tell her she was a Venus.'

'But, aunt, you are a handsome woman, you know.'

'Laws, my dear, as if I didn't understand all about it; as if I didn't know what makes a woman run after! It isn't beauty, —and it isn't money altogether. I've seen women who had plenty of both, and not a man would come nigh them. They didn't dare. There are some of them, a man would as soon think of putting his arm round a poplar tree, they are so hard and so stiff. You know you're a little that way yourself, Kate, and I've always told you it won't do.'

'I'm afraid I'm too old to mend, aunt.'

'Not at all, if you'll only set your wits to work and try. You've plenty of money now, and you're good-looking enough, too, when you take the trouble to get yourself up. But, as I said before, it isn't that that's wanted. There's a stand-off about some women,—what the men call a "nollimy tangere,"* that a man must be quite a furious Orlando*to attempt to get the better of it. They look as though matrimony itself were improper, and as if they believed the little babies were found about in the hedges and ditches. They talk of women being forward! There are some of them a deal too backward, according to my way of thinking.'

'Yours is a comfortable doctrine, aunt.'

'That's just what I want it to be. I want things to be comfortable. Why shouldn't things be nice about one when one's got the means? Nobody can say it's a pleasant thing to live alone. I always thought that man in the song hit it off properly. You remember what he says? "The poker and tongs to each other belongs."*So they do, and that should be the way with men and women.'

'But the poker and tongs have but a bad life of it sometimes.'

'Not so often as the people say, my dear. Men and women ain't like lumps of sugar. They don't melt because the water is sometimes warm. Now, if I do take Bellfield,—and I really think I shall; but if I do, he'll give me a deal of trouble. I know he will. He'll always be wanting my money, and, of course, he'll get more than he ought. I'm not a Solomon, nor yet a Queen of Sheba, no more than anybody else. And he'll smoke too many cigars, and perhaps drink more brandy-and-water than he ought. And he'll be making eyes, too, at some of the girls who'll be fools enough to let him.'

'Dear me, aunt, if I thought all that ill of him, I'm sure I wouldn't marry him;—especially as you say you don't love him.'

'As for love, my dear, that's gone,—clear gone!' Whereupon Mrs. Greenow put up her handkerchief to her eyes. 'Some women can love twice, but I am not one of them. I wish I could,—I wish I could!' These last words were spoken in a tone of solemn regret, which, however, she contrived to change as quickly as she had adopted it. 'But, my dear, marriage is a comfortable thing. And then, though the Captain may be a little free, I don't doubt but what I shall get the upper hand with him at last. I shan't stop his cigars and brandy-and-water, you know. Why shouldn't a man smoke and have a glass, if he don't make a beast of himself? I like to see a man enjoy himself. And then,' she added, speaking tenderly of her absent lover, 'I do think he's fond of me,—I do, indeed.'

'So is Mr. Cheesacre, for the matter of that.'

'Poor Cheesy! I believe he was, though he did talk so much about money. I always like to believe the best I can of them. But then there was no poetry about Cheesy. I don't care about saying it now, as you've quite made up your mind not to have him.'

'Quite, aunt.'

'Your grandfather's will does make a difference, you know. But, as I was saying, I do like a little romance about them,—just a sniff, as I call it, of the rocks and valleys. One knows that it doesn't mean much; but it's like artificial flowers,—it gives a little colour, and takes off the dowdiness. Of course, bread-and-cheese is the real thing. The rocks and valleys are no good at all, if you haven't got that. But enough is as good as a feast. Thanks to dear Greenow,'—here the handkerchief was again used—'Thanks to dear Greenow, I shall never want. Of course I shan't let any of the money go into his hands,—the Captain's, I mean. I know a trick worth two of that, my dear. But, lord love you! I've enough for him and me. What's the good of a woman's wanting to keep it all to herself?'

'And you think you'll really take him, aunt, and pay his washerwoman's bills for him? You remember what you told me when I first saw him?'

'Oh, yes; I remember. And if he can't pay his own washerwoman, isn't that so much more of a reason that I should do it for him? Well; yes; I think I will take him. That is, if he lets me take him just as I choose. Beggars mustn't be choosers, my dear.'

In this way the aunt and niece became very confidential, and Mrs. Greenow whispered into Kate's ears her belief that Captain Bellfield might possibly make his way across the country to Westmoreland. 'There would be no harm in offering him a bed, would there?' Mrs. Greenow asked. 'You see the inn at Shap is a long way off for morning calls.' Kate could not take upon herself to say that there would be any harm, but she did not like the idea of having Captain Bellfield as a visitor. 'After all, perhaps he mayn't come,' said the widow. 'I don't see where he is to raise the money for such a journey, now that he has quarrelled with Mr. Cheesacre.'

'If Captain Bellfield must come to Vavasor Hall, at any rate let him not come till Alice's visit had been completed.' That was Kate's present wish, and so much she ventured to confide to her aunt. But there seemed to be no way of stopping him.

'I don't in the least know where he is, my dear; and as for writing to him, I never did such a thing in my life, and I shouldn't know how to begin.' Mrs. Greenow declared that she had not positively invited the Captain; but on this point Kate hardly gave full credit to her aunt's statement.

Alice arrived, and, for a day or two, the three ladies lived very pleasantly together. Kate still wore her arm in a sling; but she was able to walk out, and would take long walks in spite of the doctor's prohibition. Of course, they went up on the mountains. Indeed, all the walks from Vavasor Hall led to the mountains, unless one chose to take the road to Shap. But they went up, across the beacon hill, as though by mutual consent. There were no questions asked between them as to the route to be taken; and though they did not reach the stone on which they had once sat looking over upon Haweswater, they did reach the spot upon which Kate had encountered her accident. 'It was here I fell,' she said; 'and the last I saw of him was his back, as he made his way down into the valley, there. When I got upon my legs I could still see him. It was one of those evenings when the clouds are dark, but you can see all objects with a peculiar clearness through the air. I stood here ever so long, holding my arm, and watching him; but he never once turned to look back at me. Do you know, Alice, I fancy that I shall never see him again.'

'Do you suppose that he means to quarrel with you altogether?'

'I can hardly tell you what I mean! He seemed to me to be going away from me, as though he went into another world. His figure against the light was quite clear, and he walked quickly, and on he went, till the slope of the hill hid him from me. Of course, I thought that he would return to the Hall. At one time I almost feared that he would come upon me through the woods, as I went back myself. But yet, I had a feeling,—what people call a presentiment,—that I should never see him again.'

'He has never written?'

'No; not a word. You must remember that he did not know that I had hurt myself. I am sure he will not write, and I am sure, also, that I shall not. If he wanted money I would send it to him, but I would not write to him.'

'I fear he will always want money, Kate.'

'I fear he will. If you could know what I suffered when he made me write that letter to you! But, of course, I was a beast. Of course, I ought not to have written it.'

'I thought it a very proper letter.'

'It was a mean letter. The whole thing was mean! He should have starved in the street before he had taken your money. He should have given up Parliament, and everything else! I had doubted much about him before, but it was that which first turned my heart against him. I had begun to fear that he was not such a man as I had always thought him,—as I had spoken of him to you.'

'I had judged of him for myself,' said Alice.

'Of course you did. But I had endeavoured to make you judge kindly. Alice, dear! we have both suffered for him; you more than I, perhaps; but I, too, have given up everything for him. My whole life has been at his service. I have been his creature, to do his bidding, just as he might tell me. He made me do things that I knew to be wrong,—things that were foreign to my own nature; and yet I almost worshipped him. Even now, if he were to come back, I believe that I should forgive him everything.'

'I should forgive him, but I could never do more.'

'But he will never come back. He will never ask us to forgive him, or even wish it. He has no heart.'

'He has longed for money till the Devil has hardened his heart,' said Alice.

'And yet how tender he could be in his manner when he chose it;—how soft he could make his words and his looks! Do you remember how he behaved to us in Switzerland? Do you remember that balcony at Basle, and the night we sat there, when the boys were swimming down the river?'

'Yes;—I remember.'

'So do I! So do I! Alice, I would give all I have in the world, if I could recall that journey to Switzerland.'

'If you mean for my sake, Kate——'

'I do mean for your sake. It made no difference to me. Whether I staid*in Westmoreland or went abroad, I must have found out that my god was made of bricks and clay instead of gold. But there was no need for you to be crushed in the ruins.'

'I am not crushed, Kate!'

'Of course, you are too proud to own it?'

'If you mean about Mr. Grey, that would have happened just the same, whether I had gone abroad or remained at home.'

'Would it, dear?'

'Just the same.'

There was nothing more than this said between them about Mr. Grey. Even to her cousin, Alice could not bring herself to talk freely on that subject. She would never allow herself to think, for a moment, that she had been persuaded by others to treat him as she had treated him. She was sure that she had acted on her own convictions of what was right and wrong; and now, though she had begun to feel that she had been wrong, she would hardly confess as much even to herself.

They walked back, down the hill, to the Hall in silence for the greater part of the way. Once or twice Kate repeated her conviction that she should never again see her brother. 'I do not know what may happen to him,' she said in answer to her cousin's questions; 'but when he was passing out of my sight, into the valley, I felt that I was looking at him for the last time.'

'That is simply what people call a presentiment,' Alice replied.

'Exactly so; and presentiments, of course, mean nothing,' said Kate.

Then they walked on towards the house without further speech; but when they reached the end of the little path which led out of the wood, on to the gravelled sweep before the front door, they were both arrested by a sight that met their eyes. There was a man standing, with a cigar in his mouth, before them, swinging a little cane, and looking about him up at the wood. He had on his head a jaunty little straw-hat, and he wore a jacket with brass buttons, and white trowsers. It was now nearly the middle of May, but the summer does not come to Westmoreland so early as that, and the man, as he stood there looking about him, seemed to be cold and almost uncomfortable. He had not as yet seen the two girls, who stood at the end of the walk, arrested by the sight of him. 'Who is it?' asked Alice, in a whisper.

'Captain Bellfield,' said Kate, speaking with something very like dismay in her voice.

'What! aunt Greenow's Captain?'

'Yes; aunt Greenow's Captain. I have been fearing this, and now, what on earth are we to do with him? Look at him. That's what aunt Greenow calls a sniff of the rocks and valleys.'

The Captain began to move,—just to move, as though it were necessary to do something to keep the life in his limbs. He had finished his cigar, and looked at the end of it with manifest regret. As he threw it away among a tuft of shrubs his eye fell upon the two ladies, and he uttered a little exclamation. Then he came forward, waving his little straw-hat in his hand, and made his salutation. 'Miss Vavasor, I am delighted,' he said. 'Miss Alice Vavasor, if I am not mistaken? I have been commissioned by my dear friend Mrs. Greenow to go out and seek you, but, upon my word, the woods looked so black that I did not dare to venture;—and then, of course, I shouldn't have found you.'

Kate put out her left hand, and then introduced her cousin to the Captain. Again he waved his little straw-hat, and strove to bear himself as though he were at home and comfortable. But he failed, and it was manifest that he failed. He was not the Bellfield who had conquered Mr. Cheesacre on the sands at Yarmouth, though he wore the same jacket and waistcoat, and must now have enjoyed the internal satisfaction of feeling that his future maintenance in life was assured to him. But he was not at his ease. His courage had sufficed to enable him to follow his quarry into Westmoreland, but it did not suffice to make him comfortable while he was there. Kate instantly perceived his condition, and wickedly resolved that she would make no effort to assist him. She went through some ceremony of introduction, and then expressed her surprise at seeing him so far north.

'Well,' said he; 'I am a little surprised myself;—I am, indeed! But I had nothing to do in Norwich,—literally nothing; and your aunt had so often talked to me of the beauties of this place,'—and he waved his hand round at the old house and the dark trees,—'that I thought I'd take the liberty of paying you a flying visit. I didn't mean to intrude in the way of sleeping; I didn't indeed, Miss Vavasor; only Mrs. Greenow has been so kind as to say——'

'We are so very far out of the world, Captain Bellfield, that we always give our visitors beds.'

'I didn't intend it; I didn't indeed, miss!' Poor Captain Bellfield was becoming very uneasy in his agitation. 'I did just put my bag, with a change of things, into the gig, which brought me over, not knowing quite where I might go on to.'

'We won't send you any further to-day, at any rate,' said Kate.

'Mrs. Greenow has been very kind,—very kind, indeed. She has asked me to stay till——Saturday!'

Kate bit her lips in a momentary fit of anger. The house was her house, and not her aunt's. But she remembered that her aunt had been kind to her at Norwich and at Yarmouth, and she allowed this feeling to die away. 'We shall be very glad to see you,' she said. 'We are three women together here, and I'm afraid you will find us rather dull.'

'Oh dear, no,—dull with you! That would be impossible!'

'And how have you left your friend, Mr. Cheesacre?'

'Quite well;—very well, thank you. That is to say, I haven't seen him much lately. He and I did have a bit of a breeze,* you know.'

'I can't say that I did know, Captain Bellfield.'

'I thought, perhaps, you had heard. He seemed to think that I was too particular in a certain quarter! Ha—ha—ha! That's only my joke, you know, ladies.'

They then went into the house, and the Captain straggled in after them. Mrs. Greenow was in neither of the two sitting-rooms which they usually occupied. She, too, had been driven somewhat out of the ordinary composure of her manner by the arrival of her lover,—even though she had expected it, and had retired to her room, thinking that she had better see Kate in private before they met in the presence of the Captain. 'I suppose you have seen my aunt since you have been here?' said Kate.

'Oh dear, yes. I saw her, and she suggested that I had better walk out and find you. I did find you, you know, though I didn't walk very far.'

'And have you seen your room?'

'Yes;—yes. She was kind enough to show me my room. Very nice indeed, thank you;—looking out into the front, and all that kind of thing.' The poor fellow was no doubt thinking how much better was his lot at Vavasor Hall than it had been at Oileymead. 'I shan't stay long, Miss Vavasor,—only just a night or so; but I did want to see your aunt again,—and you, too, upon my word.'

'My aunt is the attraction, Captain Bellfield. We all know that.'

He actually simpered,—simpered like a young girl who is half elated and half ashamed when her lover is thrown in her teeth. He fidgeted with the things on the table, and moved himself about uneasily from one leg to the other. Perhaps he was remembering that though he had contrived to bring himself to Vavasor Hall he had not money enough left to take him back to Norwich. The two girls left him and went to their rooms. 'I will go to my aunt at once,' said Kate, 'and find out what is to be done.'

'I suppose she means to marry him?'

'Oh, yes; she means to marry him, and the sooner the better now. I knew this was coming, but I did so hope it would not be while you were here. It makes me feel so ashamed of myself that you should see it.'

Kate boldly knocked at her aunt's door, and her aunt received her with a conscious smile. 'I was waiting for you to come,' said Mrs. Greenow.

'Here I am, aunt; and, what is more to the purpose, there is Captain Bellfield in the drawing-room.'

'Stupid man! I told him to take himself away about the place till dinner-time. I've half a mind to send him back to Shap at once;—upon my word I have.'

'Don't do that, aunt; it would be inhospitable.'

'But he is such an oaf. I hope you understand, my dear, that I couldn't help it?'

'But you do mean to—to marry him, aunt; don't you?'

'Well, Kate, I really think I do. Why shouldn't I? It's a lonely sort of life being by myself; and, upon my word, I don't think there's very much harm in him.'

'I am not saying anything against him; only in that case you can't very well turn him out of the house.'

'Could not I, though? I could in a minute; and, if you wish it, you shall see if I can't do it.'

'The rocks and valleys would not allow that, aunt.'

'It's all very well for you to laugh, my dear. If laughing would break my bones I shouldn't be as whole as I am now. I might have had Cheesacre if I liked, who is a substantial man, and could have kept a carriage for me; but it was the rocks and valleys that prevented that;—and perhaps a little feeling that I might do some good to a poor fellow who has nobody in the world to look after him.' Mrs. Greenow, as she said this, put her handkerchief up to her eyes, and wiped away the springing moisture. Tears were always easy with her, but on this occasion Kate almost respected her tears. 'I'm sure I hope you'll be happy, aunt.'

'If he makes me unhappy he shall pay for it;' and Mrs. Greenow, having done with her tears, shook her head, as though upon this occasion she quite meant all that she said.

At dinner they were not very comfortable. Either the gloomy air of the place and the neighbourhood of the black pines had depressed the Captain, or else the glorious richness of the prospects before him had made him thoughtful. He had laid aside the jacket with the brass buttons, and had dressed himself for dinner very soberly. And he behaved himself at dinner and after dinner with a wonderful sobriety, being very unlike the Captain who had sat at the head of the table at Mrs. Greenow's picnic. When left to himself after dinner he barely swallowed two glasses of the old Squire's port wine before he sauntered out into the garden to join the ladies, whom he had seen there; and when pressed by Kate to light a cigar he positively declined.

On the following morning Mrs. Greenow had recovered her composure, but Captain Bellfield was still in a rather disturbed state of mind. He knew that his efforts were to be crowned with success, and that he was sure of his wife; but he did not know how the preliminary difficulties were to be overcome, and he did not know what to do with himself at the Hall. After breakfast he fidgeted about in the parlour, being unable to contrive for himself a mode of escape, and was absolutely thrown upon his beam-ends when the widow asked him what he meant to do with himself between that and dinner.

'I suppose I'd better take a walk,' he said; 'and perhaps the young ladies——'

'If you mean my two nieces,' said Mrs. Greenow, 'I'm afraid you'll find they are engaged. But if I'm not too old to walk with——' The Captain assured her that she was just of the proper age for a walking companion, as far as his taste went, and then attempted some apology for the awkwardness of his expression, at which the three women laughed heartily. 'Never mind, Captain,' said Mrs. Greenow. 'We'll have our walk all the same, and won't mind those young girls. Come along.' Then they started, not up towards the mountains, as Kate always did when she walked in Westmoreland, but mildly, and at a gentle place, as beseemed their years, along the road towards Shap. The Captain politely opened the old gate for the widow, and then carefully closed it again,—not allowing it to swing, as he would have done at Yarmouth. Then he tripped up to his place beside her, suggested his arm, which she declined, and walked on for some paces in silence. What on earth was he to say to her? He had done his love-making success-fully, and what was he to do next?

'Well, Captain Bellfield,' said she. They were walking very slowly, and he was cutting the weeds by the roadside with his cane. He knew by her voice that something special was coming so he left the weeds and ranged himself close up alongside of her. 'Well, Captain Bellfield,—so I suppose I'm to be good-natured; am I?'

'Arabella, you'll make me the happiest man in the world.'

'That's all fudge.' She would have said, 'all rocks and val-leys,' only he would not have understood her.

'Upon my word, you will.'

'I hope I shall make you respectable?'

'Oh, yes; certainly. I quite intend that.'

'It is the great thing that you should intend. Of course I am going to make a fool of myself.'

'No, no; don't say that.'

'If I don't say it, all my friends will say it for me. It's lucky for you that I don't much care what people say.'

'It is lucky;—I know that I'm lucky. The very first day I saw you I thought what a happy fellow I was to meet you. Then, of course, I was only thinking of your beauty.'

'Get along with you!'

'Upon my word, yes. Come, Arabella, as we are to be man and wife, you might as well.' At this moment he had got very close to her, and had recovered something of his usual elasti-city; but she would not allow him even to put his arm round her waist. 'Out in the high road!' she said. 'How can you be so impertinent,—and so foolish?'

'You might as well, you know,—just once.'

'Captain Bellfield, I brought you out here not for such fool-ing as that, but in order that we might have a little chat about business. If we are to be man and wife, as you say, we ought to understand on what footing we are to begin together. I'm afraid your own private means are not considerable?'

'Well, no; they are not, Mrs. Greenow.'

'Have you anything?' The Captain hesitated, and poked the

ground with his cane. 'Come, Captain Bellfield, let us have the truth at once, and then we shall understand each other.' The Captain still hesitated, and said nothing. 'You must have had something to live upon, I suppose?' suggested the widow. Then the Captain, by degrees, told his story. He had a married sister by whom a guinea a week was allowed to him. That was all. He had been obliged to sell out of the army, because he was unable to live on his pay as a lieutenant. The price of his commission had gone to pay his debts, and now,—yes, it was too true,—now he was in debt again. He owed ninety pounds to Cheesacre, thirty-two pounds ten to a tailor at Yarmouth, over seventeen pounds at his lodgings in Norwich. At the present moment he had something under thirty shillings in his pocket. The tailor at Yarmouth had lent him three pounds in order that he might make his journey into Westmoreland, and perhaps be enabled to pay his debts by getting a rich wife. In the course of the cross-examination Mrs. Greenow got much information out of him; and then, when she was satisfied that she had learned, not exactly all the truth, but certain indications of the truth, she forgave him all his offences.

'And now you will give a fellow a kiss,—just one kiss,' said the ecstatic Captain, in the height of his bliss.

'Hush!' said the widow, 'there's a carriage coming on the road—close to us.'

CHAPTER LXV

The First Kiss

'HUSH!' said the widow, 'there's a carriage coming on the road—close to us.' Mrs. Greenow, as she spoke these words, drew back from the Captain's arms before the first kiss of permitted ante-nuptial love had been exchanged. The scene was on the high road from Shap to Vavasor, and as she was still dressed in all the sombre habiliments of early widowhood, and as neither he nor his sweetheart were under forty, perhaps it was as well that they were not caught toying together in so very public a place. But they were only just in time to escape the vigilant eyes of a new visitor. Round the corner of the road, at a sharp trot, came the Shap post-horse, with the Shap gig behind him,—the same gig which had brought Bellfield to Vavasor on the previous day,—and seated in the gig, looming large, with his eyes wide awake to everything round him, was —Mr. Cheesacre.

It was a sight terrible to the eyes of Captain Bellfield, and by no means welcome to those of Mrs. Greenow. As regarded her, her annoyance had chiefly reference to her two nieces, and especially to Alice. How was she to account for this second lover? Kate, of course, knew all about it; but how could Alice be made to understand that she, Mrs. Greenow, was not to blame,—that she had, in sober truth, told this ardent gentleman that there was no hope for him? And even as to Kate,— Kate, whom her aunt had absurdly chosen to regard as the object of Mr. Cheesacre's pursuit,—what sort of a welcome would she extend to the owner of Oileymead? Before the wheels had stopped, Mrs. Greenow had begun to reflect whether it might be possible that she should send Mr. Cheesacre back without letting him go on to the Hall; but if Mrs. Greenow was dismayed, what were the feelings of the Captain? For he was aware that Cheesacre knew that of him which he had not told. How ardently did he now wish that he had sailed nearer to the truth in giving in the schedule of his debts to Mrs. Greenow.

'That man's wanted by the police,' said Cheesacre, speaking while the gig was still in motion. 'He's wanted by the police, Mrs. Greenow,' and in his ardour he stood up in the gig and pointed at Bellfield. Then the gig stopped suddenly, and he fell back into his seat in his effort to prevent his falling forward. 'He's wanted by the police,' he shouted out again, as soon as he was able to recover his voice.

Mrs. Greenow turned pale beneath the widow's veil which she had dropped. What might not her Captain have done? He might have procured things, to be sent to him, out of shops on false pretences; or, urged on by want and famine, he might have committed—forgery. 'Oh, my!' she said, and dropped her hand from his arm, which she had taken.

'It's false,' said Bellfield.

'It's true,' said Cheesacre.

'I'll indict you for slander, my friend,' said Bellfield.

'Pay me the money you owe me,' said Cheesacre. 'You're a swindler!'

Mrs. Greenow cared little as to her lover being a swindler in Mr. Cheesacre's estimation. Such accusations from him she had heard before. But she did care very much as to this mission of the police against her Captain. If that were true, the Captain could be her Captain no longer. 'What is this I hear, Captain Bellfield?' she said.

'It's a lie and a slander. He merely wants to make a quarrel between us. What police are after me, Mr. Cheesacre?'

'It's the police, or the sheriff's officer, or something of the kind,' said Cheesacre.

'Oh, the sheriff's officers!' exclaimed Mrs. Greenow, in a tone of voice which showed how great had been her relief. 'Mr. Cheesacre, you shouldn't come and say such things;—you shouldn't, indeed. Sheriff's officers can be paid, and there's an end of them.'

'I'll indict him for the libel—I will, as sure as I'm alive,' said Bellfield.

'Nonsense,' said the widow. 'Don't you make a fool of yourself. When men can't pay their way they must put up with having things like that said of them. Mr. Cheesacre, where were you going?'

'I was going to Vavasor Hall, on purpose to caution you.'

'It's too late,' said Mrs. Greenow, sinking behind her veil.

'Why, you haven't been and married him since yesterday? He only had twenty-four hours' start of me, I know. Or, perhaps you had it done clandestine in Norwich? Oh, Mrs. Greenow!'

He got out of the gig, and the three walked back towards the Hall together, while the boy drove on with Mr. Cheesacre's carpet-bag. 'I hardly know,' said Mrs. Greenow, 'whether we can welcome you. There are other visitors, and the house is full.'

'I'm not one to intrude where I'm not wanted. You may be sure of that. If I can't get my supper for love, I can get it for money. That's more than some people can say. I wonder when you're going to pay me what you owe me, Lieutenant Bellfield?'

Nevertheless the widow had contrived to reconcile the two men before she reached the Hall. They had actually shaken hands, and the lamb Cheesacre had agreed to lie down with the wolf Bellfield. Cheesacre, moreover, had contrived to whisper into the widow's ears the true extent of his errand into Westmoreland. This, however, he did not do altogether in Bellfield's hearing. When Mrs. Greenow ascertained that there was something to be said, she made no scruple in sending her betrothed away from her. 'You won't throw a fellow over, will you, now?' whispered Bellfield into her ear as he went. She merely frowned at him, and bade him begone; so that the walk which Mrs. Greenow began with one lover she ended in company with the other.

Bellfield, who was sent on to the house, found Alice and Kate surveying the newly-arrived carpet-bag. 'He knows 'un,' said the boy who had driven the gig, pointing to the Captain.

'It belongs to your old friend, Mr. Cheesacre,' said Bellfield to Kate.

'And has he come too?' said Kate.

The Captain shrugged his shoulders, and admitted that it was hard. 'And it's not of the slightest use,' said he; 'not the least in the world. He never had a chance in that quarter.'

'Not enough of the rocks and valleys about him, was there, Captain Bellfield?' said Kate. But Captain Bellfield understood nothing about the rocks and valleys, though he was regarded by certain eyes as being both a rock and a valley himself.

In the meantime Cheesacre was telling his story. He first asked, in a melancholy tone, whether it was really necessary that he must abandon all his hopes. 'He wasn't going to say anything against the Captain,' he said, 'if things were really fixed. He never begrudged any man his chance.'

'Things are really fixed,' said Mrs. Greenow.

He could, however, not keep himself from hinting that Oileymead was a substantial home, and that Bellfield had not as much as a straw mattress to lie upon. In answer to this Mrs. Greenow told him that there was so much more reason why some one should provide the poor man with a mattress. 'If you look at it in that light, of course it's true,' said Cheesacre. Mrs. Greenow told him that she did look at it in that light. 'Then I've done about that,' said Cheesacre; 'and as to the little bit of money he owes me, I must give him his time about it, I suppose.' Mrs. Greenow assured him that it should be paid as soon as possible after the nuptial benediction had been said over them. She offered, indeed, to pay it at once if he was in distress for it, but he answered contemptuously that he never was in distress for money. He liked to have his own,— that was all.

After this he did not get away to his next subject quite so easily as he wished; and it must be admitted that there was a difficulty. As he could not have Mrs. Greenow he would be content to put up with Kate for his wife. That was his next subject. Rumours as to the old Squire's will had no doubt reached him, and he was now willing to take advantage of that assistance which Mrs. Greenow had before offered him in this matter. The time had come in which he ought to marry; of that he was aware. He had told many of his friends in Norfolk that Kate Vavasor had thrown herself at his head, and very probably he had thought it true. In answer to all his love speeches to herself, the aunt had always told him what an excellent wife her niece would make him. So now he had come to Westmoreland with this second string to his bow. 'You know you put it into my head your own self,' pleaded Mr. Cheesacre. 'Didn't you, now?'

'But things are so different since that,' said the widow.

'How different? I ain't different. There's Oileymead just where it always was, and the owner of it don't owe a shilling to any man. How are things different?'

'My niece has inherited property.'

'And is that to make a change? Oh! Mrs. Greenow, who would have thought to find you mercenary like that? Inherited property! Is she going to fling a man over because of that?'

Mrs. Greenow endeavoured to explain to him that her niece could hardly be said to have flung him over, and at last pretended to become angry when he attempted to assert his position. 'Why, Mr. Cheesacre, I am quite sure she never gave you a word of encouragement in her life.'

'But you always told me I might have her for the asking.'

'And now I tell you that you mayn't. It's of no use your going on there to ask her, for she will only send you away with an answer you won't like. Look here, Mr. Cheesacre; you want to get married, and it's quite time you should. There's my dear friend Charlie Fairstairs. How could you get a better wife than Charlie?'

'Charlie Fairstairs!' said Cheesacre, turning up his nose in disgust. 'She hasn't got a penny, nor any one belonging to her. The man who marries her will have to find the money for the smock she stands up in.'

'Who's mercenary now, Mr. Cheesacre? Do you go home and think of it; and if you'll marry Charlie, I'll go to your wedding. You shan't be ashamed of her clothing. I'll see to that.'

They were now close to the gate, and Cheesacre paused before he entered. 'Do you think there's no chance at all for me, then?' said he.

'I know there's none. I've heard her speak about it.'

'Somebody else, perhaps, is the happy man?'

'I can't say anything about that, but I know that she wouldn't take you. I like farming, you know, but she doesn't.'

'I might give that up,' said Cheesacre readily,—'at any rate, for a time.'

'No, no, no; it would do no good. Believe me, my friend, that it is of no use.'

He still paused at the gate. 'I don't see what's the use of my going in,' said he. To this she made him no answer. 'There's a pride about me,' he continued, 'that I don't choose to go where I'm not wanted.'

'I can't tell you, Mr. Cheesacre, that you are wanted in that light, certainly,'

'Then I'll go. Perhaps you'll be so good as to tell the boy with the gig to come after me? That's six pound ten it will have cost me to come here and go back. Bellfield did it cheaper, of course; he travelled second class. I heard of him as I came along.'

'The expense does not matter to you, Mr. Cheesacre.'

To this he assented, and then took his leave, at first offering his hand to Mrs. Greenow with an air of offended dignity, but falling back almost into humility during the performance of his adieu. Before he was gone he had invited her to bring the Captain to Oileymead when she was married, and had begged her to tell Miss Vavasor how happy he should be to receive her. 'And, Mr. Cheesacre,' said the widow, as he walked back along the road, 'don't forget dear Charlie Fairstairs.'

They were all standing at the front door of the house when Mrs. Greenow re-appeared,—Alice, Kate, Captain Bellfield, the Shap boy, and the Shap horse and gig. 'Where is he?' Kate asked in a low voice, and everyone there felt how important was the question. 'He has gone,' said the widow. Bellfield was so relieved that he could not restrain his joy, but took off his little straw-hat and threw it up into the air. Kate's satisfaction was almost as intense. 'I am so glad,' said she. 'What on earth should we have done with him?' 'I never was so disappointed in my life,' said Alice. 'I have heard so much of Mr. Cheesacre, but have never seen him.' Kate suggested that she should get into the gig and drive after him. 'He ain't a been and took his-self off?' suggested the boy, whose face became very dismal as the terrible idea struck him. But, with juvenile craft, he put his hand on the carpet-bag, and finding that it did not contain stones, was comforted. 'You drive after him, young gentle-man, and you'll find him on the road to Shap,' said Mrs. Greenow. 'Mind you give him my love,' said the Captain in his glee, 'and say I hope he'll get his turnips in well.'

This little episode went far to break the day, and did more than anything else could have done to put Captain Bellfield at his ease. It created a little joint-stock fund of merriment between the whole party, which was very much needed. The absence of such joint-stock fund is always felt when a small party is thrown together without such assistance. Some bond is necessary on these occasions, and no other bond is so easy or so pleasant. Now, when the Captain found himself alone for a quarter of an hour with Alice, he had plenty of subjects for small-talk. 'Yes, indeed. Old Cheesacre, in spite of his absurdities, is not a bad sort of fellow at bottom;—awfully fond of his money, you know, Miss Vavasor, and always boasting about it.' 'That's not pleasant,' said Alice. 'No; the most unpleasant thing in the world. There's nothing I hate so much, Miss Vavasor, as that kind of talking. My idea is this,—when a man has lots of money, let him make the best use he can of it, and say nothing about it. Nobody ever heard me talking about my money.' He knew that Alice knew that he was a pauper; but, nevertheless, he had the satisfaction of speaking of himself as though he were not a pauper.

In this way the afternoon went very pleasantly. For an hour before dinner Captain Bellfield was had into the drawing-room, and was talked to by his widow on matters of business; but he had of course known that this was necessary. She scolded him soundly about those sheriff's officers. Why had he not told her? 'As long as there's anything kept back, I won't have you,' said she. 'I won't become your wife till I'm quite sure there's not a penny owing that is not shown in the list.' Then I think he did tell her all,—or nearly all. When all was counted it was not so very much. Three or four hundred pounds would make him a new man, and what was such a sum as that to his wealthy widow! Indeed, for a woman wanting a husband of that sort, Captain Bellfield was a safer venture than would be a man of a higher standing among his creditors. It is true Bellfield might have been a forger, or a thief, or a returned convict,— but then his debts could not be large. Let him have done his best, he could not have obtained credit for a thousand pounds;

whereas, no one could tell the liabilities of a gentleman of high standing. Burgo Fitzgerald was a gentleman of high standing, and his creditors would have swallowed up every shilling that Mrs. Greenow possessed; but with Captain Bellfield she was comparatively safe.

Upon the whole I think that she was lucky in her choice; or, perhaps, I might more truly say, that she had chosen with prudence. He was no forger, or thief—in the ordinary sense of the word; nor was he a returned convict. He was simply an idle scamp, who had hung about the world for forty years, doing nothing, without principle, shameless, accustomed to eat dirty puddings, and to be kicked—morally kicked—by such men as Cheesacre. But he was moderate in his greediness, and possessed of a certain appreciation of the comfort of a daily dinner, which might possibly suffice to keep him from straying very wide as long as his intended wife should be able to keep the purse-strings altogether in her own hands. Therefore, I say that Mrs. Greenow had been lucky in her choice, and not altogether without prudence.

'I think of taking this house,' said she, 'and of living here.'

'What, in Westmoreland!' said the Captain, with something of dismay in his tone. What on earth would he do with himself all his life in that gloomy place!

'Yes, in Westmoreland. Why not in Westmoreland as well as anywhere else? If you don't like Westmoreland, it's not too late yet, you know.' In answer to this the poor Captain was obliged to declare that he had no objection whatever to Westmoreland.

'I've been talking to my niece about it,' continued Mrs. Greenow, 'and I find that such an arrangement can be made very conveniently. The property is left between her and her uncle,—the father of my other niece, and neither of them want to live here.'

'But won't you be rather dull, my dear?'

'We could go to Yarmouth, you know, in the autumn.' Then the Captain's visage became somewhat bright again. 'And, perhaps, if you are not extravagant, we could manage a month or so in London during the winter, just to see the plays and do a little shopping.' Then the Captain's face became very bright. 'That will be delightful,' said he. 'And as for being dull,' said the widow, 'when people grow old they must be dull. Dancing can't go on for ever.' In answer to this the widow's Captain assured the widow that she was not at all old; and now, on this occasion, that ceremony came off successfully which had been interrupted on the Shap road by the noise of Mr. Cheesacre's wheels. 'There goes my cap,' said she. 'What a goose you are! What will Jeannette say?' 'Bother Jeannette,' said the Captain in his bliss. 'She can do another cap, and many more won't be wanted.' Then I think the ceremony was repeated.

Upon the whole the Captain's visit was satisfactory—at any rate to the Captain. Everything was settled. He was to go away on Saturday morning, and remain in lodgings at Penrith till the wedding, which they agreed to have celebrated at Vavasor Church. Kate promised to be the solitary bridesmaid. There was some talk of sending for Charlie Fairstairs, but the idea was abandoned. 'We'll have her afterwards,' said the widow to Kate, 'when you are gone, and we shall want her more. And I'll get Cheesacre here, and make him marry her. There's no good in paying for two journeys.' The Captain was to be allowed to come over from Penrith twice a week previous to his marriage; or perhaps, I might more fairly say, that he was commanded to do so. I wonder how he felt when Mrs. Greenow gave him his first five-pound note, and told him that he must make it do for a fortnight?—whether it was all joy, or whether there was about his heart any touch of manly regret?

'Captain Bellfield, of Vavasor Hall, Westmoreland. It don't sound badly,' he said to himself, as he travelled away on his first journey to Penrith.

CHAPTER LXVI
Lady Monk's Plan

O<small>N</small> the night of Lady Monk's party, Burgo Fitzgerald disappeared; and when the guests were gone and the rooms were empty, his aunt inquired for him in vain. The old butler and factotum of the house, who was employed by Sir Cosmo to put out the lamps and to see that he was not robbed beyond a certain point on these occasions of his wife's triumphs, was interrogated by his mistress, and said that he thought Mr. Burgo had left the house. Lady Monk herself knocked at her nephew's door, when she went up-stairs, ascending an additional flight of stairs with her weary old limbs in order that she might do so; she even opened the door and saw the careless débris of his toilet about the room. But he was gone. 'Perhaps, after all, he has arranged it,' she said to herself, as she went down to her own room.

But Burgo, as we know, had not 'arranged it.' It may be remembered that when Mr. Palliser came back to his wife in the supper-room at Lady Monk's, bringing with him the scarf which Lady Glencora had left up-stairs, Burgo was no longer with her. He had become well aware that he had no chance left, at any rate for that night. The poor fool, acting upon his aunt's implied advice rather than his own hopes, had secured a post-chaise, and stationed it in Bruton Street, some five minutes' walk from his aunt's house. And he had purchased feminine wrappings, cloaks, &c.—things that he thought might be necessary for his companion. He had, too, ordered rooms at the new hotel near the Dover Station,—the London Bridge Station,—from whence was to start on the following morning a train to catch the tidal boat for Boulogne. There was a dressing-bag there for which he had paid twenty-five guineas out of his aunt's money, not having been able to induce the tradesman to grant it to him on credit; and there were other things, —slippers, collars, stockings, handkerchiefs, and what else might, as he thought, under such circumstances be most necessary. Poor thoughtful, thoughtless fool!

The butler was right. He did leave the house. He saw Lady Glencora taken to her carriage from some back hiding-place in the hall, and then slipped out, unmindful of his shining boots, and dress coat and jewelled studs. He took a Gibus hat,*—his own, or that of some other unfortunate,—and slowly made his way down to the place in Bruton Street. There was the carriage and pair of horses, all in readiness; and the driver, when he had placed himself by the door of the vehicle, was not long in emerging from the neighbouring public-house. 'All ready, your honour,' said the man. 'I shan't want you to-night,' said Burgo, hoarsely;—'go away.' 'And about the things, your honour?' 'Take them to the devil. No; stop. Take them back with you, and ask somebody to keep them till I send for them. I shall want them and another carriage in a day or two.' Then he gave the man half a sovereign, and went away, not looking at the little treasures which he had spent so much of his money in selecting for his love. When he was gone, the waterman and the driver turned them over with careful hands and gloating eyes. 'It's a 'eiress, I'll go bail,' said the waterman. 'Pretty dear! I suppose her parints was too many for her,' said the driver. But neither of them imagined the enormity which the hirer of the chaise had in truth contemplated.

Burgo from thence took his way back into Grosvenor Square, and from thence down Park Street, and through a narrow passage and a mews which there are in those parts, into Park Lane. He had now passed the position of Mr. Palliser's house, having come out on Park Lane at a spot nearer to Piccadilly; but he retraced his steps, walking along by the rails of the Park, till he found himself opposite to the house. Then he stood there, leaning back upon the railings, and looking up at Lady Glencora's windows. What did he expect to see? Or was he, in truth, moved by love of that kind which can take joy in watching the slightest shadow that is made by the one loved object, —that may be made by her, or, by some violent conjecture of the mind, may be supposed to have been so made? Such love as that is, I think, always innocent. Burgo Fitzgerald did not love like that. I almost doubt whether he can be said to have loved at all. There was in his breast a mixed, feverish desire, which he took no trouble to analyze. He wanted money. He wanted the thing of which this Palliser had robbed him. He wanted revenge,—though his desire for that was not a burning desire. And among other things, he wanted the woman's beauty of the woman whom he coveted. He wanted to kiss her again as he had once kissed her, and to feel that she was soft, and lovely, and loving for him. But as for seeing her shadow, unless its movement indicated some purpose in his favour,—I do not think that he cared much about that.

And why then was he there? Because in his unreasoning folly he did not know what step to take, or what step not to take. There are men whose energies hardly ever carry them beyond looking for the thing they want. She might see him from the window, and come to him. I do not say that he thought that it would be so. I fancy that he never thought at all about that or about anything. If you lie under a tree, and open your mouth, a plum may fall into it. It was probably an undefined idea of some such chance as this which brought him against the railings in the front of Mr. Palliser's house; that, and a feeling made up partly of despair and partly of lingering romance that he was better there, out in the night air, under the gas-lamps, than he could be elsewhere. There he stood and looked, and cursed his ill-luck. But his curses had none of the bitterness of those which George Vavasor was always uttering. Through it all there remained about Burgo one honest feeling,—one conviction that was true,—a feeling that it all served him right, and that he had better, perhaps, go to the devil at once, and give nobody any more trouble. If he loved no one sincerely, neither did he hate any one; and whenever he made any self-inquiry into his own circumstances, he always told himself that it was all his own fault. When he cursed his fate, he only did so because cursing is so easy. George Vavasor would have ground his victims up to powder if he knew how; but Burgo Fitzgerald desired to hurt no one.

There he stood till he was cold, and then, as the plum did not drop into his mouth, he moved on. He went up into Oxford

Street, and walked along it the whole distance to the corner of Bond Street, passing by Grosvenor Square, to which he intended to return. At the corner of Bond Street, a girl took hold of him, and looked up into his face. 'Ah!' she said, 'I saw you once before.'—'Then you saw the most miserable devil alive,' said Burgo. 'You can't be miserable,' said the girl. 'What makes you miserable? You've plenty of money.'—'I wish I had,' said Burgo. 'And plenty to eat and drink,' exclaimed the girl; 'and you are so handsome! I remember you. You gave me supper one night when I was starving. I ain't hungry now. Will you give me a kiss?'—'I'll give you a shilling, and that's better,' said Burgo. 'But give me a kiss too,' said the girl. He gave her first the kiss, and then the shilling, and after that he left her and passed on. 'I'm d——d if I wouldn't change with her!' he said to himself. 'I wonder whether anything really ails him?' thought the girl 'He said he was wretched before. Shouldn't I like to be good to such a one as him!'

Burgo went on, and made his way into the house in Grosvenor Square, by some means probably unknown to his aunt, and certainly unknown to his uncle. He emptied his pockets as he got into bed, and counted a roll of notes which he had kept in one of them. There were still a hundred and thirty pounds left. Lady Glencora had promised that she would see him again. She had said as much as that quite distinctly. But what use would there be in that if all his money should then be gone? He knew that the keeping of money in his pocket was to him quite an impossibility. Then he thought of his aunt. What should he say to his aunt if he saw her in the course of the coming day? Might it not be as well for him to avoid his aunt altogether?

He breakfasted up-stairs in his bedroom,—in his bed, indeed, eating a small paté de foie gras from the supper-table, as he read a French novel. There he was still reading his French novel in bed when his aunt's maid came to him, saying that his aunt wished to see him before she went out. 'Tell me, Lucy,' said he, 'how is the old girl?'

'She's as cross as cross, Mr. Burgo. Indeed, I shan't;—not

a minute longer. Don't, now; will you? I tell you she's waiting for me.' From which it may be seen that Lucy shared the general feminine feeling in favour of poor Burgo.

Thus summoned Burgo applied himself to his toilet; but as he did so, he recruited his energies from time to time by a few pages of the French novel, and also by small doses from a bottle of curaçoa*which he had in his bedroom. He was utterly a pauper. There was no pauper poorer than he in London that day. But, nevertheless, he breakfasted on paté de foie gras and curaçoa, and regarded those dainties very much as other men regard bread and cheese and beer.

But though he was dressing at the summons of his aunt, he had by no means made up his mind that he would go to her. Why should he go to her? What good would it do him? She would not give him more money. She would only scold him for his misconduct. She might, perhaps, turn him out of the house if he did not obey her,—or attempt to do so; but she would be much more likely to do this when he had made her angry by contradicting her. In neither case would he leave the house, even though its further use were positively forbidden him, because his remaining there was convenient; but as he could gain nothing by seeing 'the old girl,' as he had called her, he resolved to escape to his club without attending to her summons.

But his aunt, who was a better general than he, out-manœuvred him. He crept down the back stairs; but as he could not quite condescend to escape through the area, he was forced to emerge upon the hall, and here his aunt pounced upon him, coming out of the breakfast-parlour. 'Did not Lucy tell you that I wanted to see you?' Lady Monk asked, with severity in her voice.

Burgo replied, with perfect ease, that he was going out just to have his hair washed and brushed. He would have been back in twenty minutes. There was no energy about the poor fellow, unless, perhaps, when he was hunting; but he possessed a readiness which enabled him to lie at a moment's notice with the most perfect ease. Lady Monk did not believe him; but she could not confute him, and therefore she let the lie pass.

'Never mind your hair now,' she said. 'I want to speak to you. Come in here for a few minutes.'

As there was no way of escape left to him, he followed his aunt into the breakfast-parlour.

'Burgo,' she said, when she had seated herself, and had made him sit in a chair opposite to her, 'I don't think you will ever do any good.'

'I don't much think I shall, aunt.'

'What do you mean, then, to do with yourself?'

'Oh,—I don't know. I haven't thought much about it.'

'You can't stay here in this house. Sir Cosmo was speaking to me about you only yesterday morning.'

'I shall be quite willing to go down to Monkshade, if Sir Cosmo likes it better;—that is, when the season is a little more through.'

'He won't have you at Monkshade. He won't let you go there again. And he won't have you here. You know that you are turning what I say into joke.'

'No, indeed, aunt.'

'Yes, you are;—you know you are. You are the most ungrateful, heartless creature I ever met. You must make up your mind to leave this house at once.'

'Where does Sir Cosmo mean that I should go, then?'

'To the workhouse, if you like. He doesn't care.'

'I don't suppose he does;—the least in the world,' said Burgo, opening his eyes, and stretching his nostrils, and looking into his aunt's face as though he had great ground for indignation.

But the turning of Burgo out of the house was not Lady Monk's immediate purpose. She knew that he would hang on there till the season was over. After that he must not be allowed to return again, unless he should have succeeded in a certain enterprise. She had now caught him in order that she might learn whether there was any possible remaining chance of success as to that enterprise. So she received his indignation in silence, and began upon another subject. 'What a fool you made of yourself last night, Burgo!'

'Did I;—more of a fool than usual?'

'I believe that you will never be serious about anything. Why did you go on waltzing in that way when every pair of eyes in the room was watching you?'

'I couldn't help going on, if she liked it.'

'Oh, yes;—say it was her fault. That's so like a man!'

'Look here, aunt; I'm not going to sit here and be abused. I couldn't take her in my arms, and fly away with her out of a crowd.'

'Who wants you to fly away with her?'

'For the matter of that, I suppose that you do.'

'No, I don't.'

'Well, then, I do.'

'You! you haven't spirit to do that, or anything else. You are like a child that is just able to amuse itself for the moment, and never can think of anything further. You simply disgraced yourself last night, and me too,—and her; but, of course, you care nothing about that.'

'I had a plan all ready;—only he came back.'

'Of course he came back. Of course he came back, when they sent him word how you and she were going on. And now he will have forgiven her, and after that, of course, the thing will be all over.'

'I tell you what, aunt; she would go if she knew how. When I was forced to leave her last night, she promised to see me again. And as for being idle, and not doing anything;—why, I was out in Park Lane last night, after you were in bed.'

'What good did that do?'

'It didn't do any good, as it happened. But a fellow can only try. I believe, after all, it would be easier down in the country,—especially now that he has taken it into his head to look after her.'

Lady Monk sat silent for a few moments, and then she said in a low voice, 'What did she say to you when you were parting? What were her exact words?' She, at any rate, was not deficient in energy. She was anxious enough to see her purpose accomplished. She would have conducted the matter with discretion, if the running away with Mr. Palliser's wife could, in very fact, have been done by herself.

'She said she would see me again. She promised it twice.'

'And was that all?'

'What could she say more, when she was forced to go away?'

'Had she said that she would go with you?'

'I had asked her,—half a dozen times, and she did not once refuse. I know she means it, if she knew how to get away. She hates him;—I'm sure of it. A woman, you know, wouldn't absolutely say that she would go, till she was gone.'

'If she really meant it, she would tell you'

'I don't think she could have told me plainer. She said she would see me again. She said that twice over.'

Again Lady Monk sat silent. She had a plan in her head,— a plan that might, as she thought, give to her nephew one more chance. But she hesitated before she could bring herself to explain it in detail. At first she had lent a little aid to this desired abduction of Mr. Palliser's wife, but in lending it had said no word upon the subject. During the last season she had succeeded in getting Lady Glencora to her house in London, and had taken care that Burgo should meet her there. Then a hint or two had been spoken, and Lady Glencora had been asked to Monkshade. Lady Glencora, as we know, did not go to Monkshade, and Lady Monk had then been baffled. But she did not therefore give up the game. Having now thought of it so much, she began to speak of it more boldly, and had procured money for her nephew that he might thereby be enabled to carry off the woman. But though this had been well understood between them, though words had been spoken which were sufficiently explicit, the plan had not been openly discussed. Lady Monk had known nothing of the mode in which Lady Glencora was to have been carried off after her party, nor whither she was to have been taken. But now,— now she must arrange it herself, and have a scheme of her own, or else the thing must fail absolutely. Even she was almost reluctant to speak out plainly to her nephew on such a subject. What if he should be false to her, and tell of her? But when a woman has made such schemes, nothing distresses her so sadly as their failure. She would risk all rather than that Mr. Palliser should keep his wife.

'I will try and help you,' she said at last, speaking hoarsely, almost in a whisper, 'if you have courage to make an attempt yourself.'

'Courage!' said he. 'What is it you think I am afraid of? Mr. Palliser? I'd fight him,—or all the Pallisers, one after another, if it would do any good.'

'Fighting! There's no fighting wanted, as you know well enough. Men don't fight now-a-days. Look here! If you can get her to call here some day,—say on Thursday, at three o'clock, —I will be here to receive her; and instead of going back into her carriage, you can have a cab for her somewhere near. She can come, as it were, to make a morning call.'

'A cab!'

'Yes; a cab won't kill her, and it is less easily followed than a carriage.'

'And where shall we go?'

'There is a train to Southampton at four, and the boat sails for Jersey at half-past six; you will be in Jersey the next morning, and there is a boat goes on to St. Malo, almost at once. You can go direct from one boat to the other,—that is, if she has strength and courage.' After that, who will say that Lady Monk was not a devoted aunt?

'That would do excellently well,' said the enraptured Burgo.

'She will have a difficulty in getting away from me, out of the house. Of course I shall say nothing about it, and shall know nothing about it. She had better tell her coachman to drive somewhere to pick some one up, and to return;—out somewhere to Tyburnia,* or down to Pimlico.* Then she can leave me, and go out on foot, to where you have the cab. She can tell the hall-porter that she will walk to her carriage. Do you understand?' Burgo declared that he did understand.

'You must call on her, and make your way in, and see her, and arrange all this. It must be a Thursday, because of the boats.' Then she made inquiry about his money, and took from him the notes which he had, promising to return them, with something added, on the Thursday morning; but he asked, with a little whine, for a five-pound note, and got it. Burgo then told her about the travelling-bags and the stockings, and they were quite pleasant and confidential. 'Bid her come in a stout travelling-dress,' said Lady Monk. 'She can wear some lace or something over it, so that the servants won't observe it. I will take no notice of it.' Was there ever such an aunt?

After this, Burgo left his aunt, and went away to his club, in a state of most happy excitement.

CHAPTER LXVII

The Last Kiss

ALICE, on her return from Westmoreland, went direct to Park Lane, whither Lady Glencora and Mr. Palliser had also returned before her. She was to remain with them in London one entire day, and on the morning after that they were to start for Paris. She found Mr. Palliser in close attendance upon his wife. Not that there was anything in his manner which at all implied that he was keeping watch over her, or that he was more with her, or closer to her than a loving husband might wish to be with a young wife; but the mode of life was very different from that which Alice had seen at Matching Priory!

On her arrival Mr. Palliser himself received her in the hall, and took her up to his wife before she had taken off her travelling hat. 'We are so much obliged to you, Miss Vavasor,' he said. 'I feel it quite as deeply as Glencora.'

'Oh, no,' she said; 'it is I that am under obligation to you for taking me.'

He merely smiled, and shook his head, and then took her up-stairs. On the stairs he said one other word to her: 'You must forgive me if I was cross to you that night she went out among the ruins.' Alice muttered something,—some little fib of courtesy as to the matter having been forgotten, or never

271

borne in mind; and then they went on to Lady Glencora's room. It seemed to Alice that he was not so big or so much to be dreaded as when she had seen him at Matching. His descent from an expectant, or more than an expectant, Chancellor of the Exchequer, down to a simple, attentive husband, seemed to affect his gait, his voice, and all his demeanour. When he received Alice at the Priory he certainly loomed before her as something great, whereas now his greatness seemed to have fallen from him. We must own that this was hard upon him, seeing that the deed by which he had divested himself of his greatness had been so pure and good!

'Dear Alice, this is so good of you! I am all in the midst of packing, and Plantagenet is helping me.' Plantagenet winced a little under this, as the hero of old must have winced when he was found with the distaff.*Mr. Palliser had relinquished his sword of state for the distaff which he had assumed, and could take no glory in the change. There was, too, in his wife's voice the slightest hint of mockery, which, slight as it was, he perhaps thought she might have spared. 'You have nothing left to pack,' continued Glencora, 'and I don't know what you can do to amuse yourself.'

'I will help you,' said Alice.

'But we have so very nearly done. I think we shall have to pull all the things out, and put them up again, or we shall never get through to-morrow. We couldn't start to-morrow; —could we, Plantagenet?'

'Not very well, as your rooms are ordered in Paris for the next day.'

'As if we couldn't find rooms at every inn on the road. Men are so particular. Now in travelling I should like never to order rooms,—never to know where I was going or when I was going, and to carry everything I wanted in a market-basket.' Alice, who by this time had followed her friend along the passage to her bedroom, and had seen how widely the packages were spread about, bethought herself that the market-basket should be a large one. 'And I would never travel among Christians. Christians are so slow, and they wear chimney-pot hats everywhere. The further one goes from London among Christians, the more they wear chimney-pot hats. I want Plantagenet to take us to see the Kurds, but he won't.'

'I don't think that would be fair to Miss Vavasor,' said Mr. Palliser, who had followed them.

'Don't put the blame on her head,' said Lady Glencora. 'Women have always pluck for anything. Wouldn't you like to see a live Kurd, Alice?'

'I don't exactly know where they live,' said Alice.

'Nor I. I have not the remotest idea of the way to the Kurds. You see my joke, don't you, though Plantagenet doesn't? But one knows that they are Eastern, and the East is such a grand idea!'

'I think we'll content ourselves with Rome, or perhaps Naples, on this occasion,' said Mr. Palliser.

The notion of Lady Glencora packing anything for herself was as good a joke as that other one of the Kurds and whey. But she went flitting about from room to room, declaring that this thing must be taken, and that other, till the market-basket would have become very large indeed. Alice was astonished at the extent of the preparations, and the sort of equipage with which they were about to travel. Lady Glencora was taking her own carriage. 'Not that I shall ever use it,' she said to Alice, 'but he insists upon it, to show that I am not supposed to be taken away in disgrace. He is so good;—isn't he?'

'Very good,' said Alice. 'I know no one better.'

'And so dull!' said Lady Glencora. 'But I fancy that all husbands are dull from the nature of their position. If I were a young woman's husband, I shouldn't know what to say to her that wasn't dull.'

Two women and two men servants were to be taken. Alice had received permission to bring her own maid—'or a dozen, if you want them,' Lady Glencora had said. 'Mr. Palliser in his present mood would think nothing too much to do for you. If you were to ask him to go among the Kurds, he'd go at once;—or on to Crim Tartary, if you made a point of it.' But as both Lady Glencora's servants spoke French, and as her own did not, Alice trusted herself in that respect to her cousin. 'You shall have one all to yourself,' said Lady Glencora. 'I only take two for the same reason that I take the carriage,—just as you let a child go out in her best frock, for a treat, after you've scolded her.'

When Alice asked why it was supposed that Mr. Palliser was so specially devoted to her, the thing was explained to her. 'You see, my dear, I have told him everything. I always do tell everything. Nobody can say I am not candid. He knows about your not letting me come to your house in the old days. Oh, Alice!—you were wrong then; I shall always say that. But it's done and gone; and things that are done and gone shall be done and gone for me. And I told him all that you said,—about you know what. I have had nothing else to do but make confessions for the last ten days, and when a woman once begins, the more she confesses the better. And I told him that you refused Jeffrey.'

'You didn't?'

'I did indeed, and he likes you the better for that. I think he'd let Jeffrey marry you now if you both wished it;—and then, oh dear!—supposing that you had a son and that we adopted it?'

'Cora, if you go on in that way I will not remain with you.'

'But you must, my dear. You can't escape now. At any rate, you can't when we once get to Paris. Oh dear! you shouldn't grudge me my little naughtinesses. I have been so proper for the last ten days. Do you know I got into a way of driving Dandy and Flirt at the rate of six miles an hour, till I'm sure the poor beasts thought they were always going to a funeral. Poor Dandy and poor Flirt! I shan't see them now for another year.'

On the following morning they breakfasted early, because Mr. Palliser had got into an early habit. He had said that early hours would be good for them. 'But he never tells me why,' said Lady Glencora. 'I think it is pleasant when people are travelling,' said Alice. 'It isn't that,' her cousin answered; 'but we are all to be such particularly good children. It's hardly fair, because he went to sleep last night after dinner while you and I kept ourselves awake: but we needn't do that another night, to be sure.' After breakfast they all three went to work to do nothing. It was ludicrous and almost painful to see Mr. Palliser wandering about and counting the boxes, as though he could do any good by that. At this special crisis of his life he hated his papers and figures and statistics, and could not apply himself to them. He, whose application had been so un-remitting, could apply himself now to nothing. His world had been brought to an abrupt end, and he was awkward at making a new beginning. I believe that they all three were reading novels before one o'clock. Lady Glencora and Alice had deter-mined that they would not leave the house throughout the day. 'Nothing has been said about it, but I regard it as part of the bond that I'm not to go out anywhere. Who knows but what I might be found in Gloucester Square?' There was, however, no absolute necessity that Mr. Palliser should remain with them; and, at about three, he prepared himself for a solitary walk. He would not go down to the House. All interest in the House was over with him for the present. He had the Speaker's leave to absent himself for the season. Nor would he call on any one. All his friends knew, or believed they knew, that he had left town. His death and burial had been already chronicled, and were he now to reappear, he could reappear only as a ghost. He was being talked of as the departed one;—or rather, such talk on all sides had now come nearly to an end. The poor Duke of St. Bungay still thought of him with regret when more than ordinarily annoyed by some special grievance coming to him from Mr. Finespun; but even the Duke had become almost reconciled to the present order of things. Mr. Palliser knew better than to disturb all this by showing himself again in public; and prepared himself, therefore, to take another walk under the elms in Kensington Gardens.

He had his hat on his head in the hall, and was in the act of putting on his gloves, when there came a knock at the front door. The hall-porter was there, a stout, plethoric personage, not given to many words, who was at this moment standing with his master's umbrella in his hand, looking as though he would fain be of some use to somebody, if any such utility were compatible with the purposes of his existence. Now had come this knock at the door, while the umbrella was still in his hand, and the nature of his visage changed, and it was easy to see that he was oppressed by the temporary multiplicity of his duties. 'Give me the umbrella, John,' said Mr. Palliser. John gave up the umbrella, and opening the door disclosed Burgo Fitzgerald standing upon the door-step. 'Is Lady Glencora at home?' asked Burgo, before he had seen the husband. John turned a dismayed face upon his master, as though he knew that the comer ought not to be making a morning call at that house,—as no doubt he did know very well,—and made no instant reply. 'I am not sure,' said Mr. Palliser, making his way out as he had originally purposed. 'The servant will find out for you.' Then he went on his way across Park Lane and into the Park, never once turning back his face to see whether Burgo had effected an entrance into the house. Nor did he return a minute earlier than he would otherwise have done. After all, there was something chivalrous about the man.

'Yes; Lady Glencora was at home,' said the porter, not stirring to make any further inquiry. It was no business of his if Mr. Palliser chose to receive such a guest. He had not been desired to say that her ladyship was not at home. Burgo was therefore admitted and shown direct up into the room in which Lady Glencora was sitting. As chance would have it, she was alone. Alice had left her and was in her own chamber, and Lady Glencora was sitting at the window of the small room up-stairs that overlooked the Park. She was seated on a foot-stool with her face between her hands when Burgo was admitted, thinking of him, and of what the world might have been to her had 'they left her alone,' as she was in the habit of saying to Alice and to herself.

She rose quickly, so that he saw her only as she was rising. 'Ask Miss Vavasor to come to me,' she said, as the servant left the room; and then she came forward to greet her lover.

'Cora,' he said, dashing at once into his subject—hopelessly, but still with a resolve to do as he had said that he would do. 'Cora, I have come to you, to ask you to go with me.'

'I will not go with you,' said she.

'Do not answer me in that way, without a moment's thought. Everything is arranged——'

'Yes, everything is arranged,' she said. 'Mr. Fitzgerald, let me ask you to leave me alone, and to behave to me with generosity. Everything is arranged. You can see that my boxes are all prepared for going. Mr. Palliser and I, and my friend, are starting to-morrow. Wish me God-speed and go, and be generous.'

'And is this to be the end of everything?' He was standing close to her, but hitherto he had only touched her hand at greeting her. 'Give me your hand, Cora,' he said.

'No;—I will never give you my hand again. You should be generous to me and go. This is to be the end of everything,— of everything that is common to you and to me. Go, when I ask you.'

'Cora; did you ever love me?'

'Yes; I did love you. But we were separated, and there was no room for love left between us.'

'You are as dear to me now,—dearer than ever you were. Do not look at me like that. Did you not tell me when we last parted that I might come to you again? Are we children, that others should come between us and separate us like that?'

'Yes, Burgo; we are children. Here is my cousin coming. You must leave me now.' As she spoke the door was opened and Alice entered the room. 'Miss Vavasor, Mr. Fitzgerald,' said Lady Glencora. 'I have told him to go and leave me. Now that you have come, Alice, he will perhaps obey me.'

Alice was dumb-founded, and knew not how to speak either to him or to her; but she stood with her eyes riveted on the face of the man of whom she had heard so much. Yes; certainly he was very beautiful. She had never before seen man's beauty such as that. She found it quite impossible to speak a word to him then—at the spur of the moment, but she acknowledged the introduction with a slight inclination of the head, and then stood silent, as though she were waiting for him to go.

'Mr. Fitzgerald, why do you not leave me and go?' said Lady Glencora.

Poor Burgo also found it difficult enough to speak. What could he say? His cause was one which certainly did not admit of being pleaded in the presence of a strange lady; and he might have known from the moment in which he heard Glencora's request that a third person should be summoned to their meeting—and probably did know, that there was no longer any hope for him. It was not on the cards that he should win. But there remained one thing that he must do. He must get himself out of that room; and how was he to effect that?

'I had hoped,' said he, looking at Alice, though he addressed Lady Glencora—'I had hoped to be allowed to speak to you alone for a few minutes.'

'No, Mr. Fitzgerald; it cannot be so. Alice, do not go. I sent for my cousin when I saw you, because I did not choose to be alone with you. I have asked you to go——'

'You perhaps have not understood me?'

'I understand you well enough.'

'Then, Mr. Fitzgerald,' said Alice, 'why do you not do as Lady Glencora has asked you? You know—you must know, that you ought not to be here.'

'I know nothing of the kind,' said he, still standing his ground.

'Alice,' said Lady Glencora, 'we will leave Mr. Fitzgerald here, since he drives us from the room.'

In such contests, a woman has ever the best of it at all points. The man plays with a button to his foil, while the woman uses a weapon that can really wound. Burgo knew that he must go, —felt that he must skulk away as best he might, and perhaps hear a low titter of half-suppressed laughter as he went. Even that might be possible. 'No, Lady Glencora,' he said, 'I will not drive you from the room. As one must be driven out, it shall be I. I own I did think that you would at any rate have been—less hard to me.' He then turned to go, bowing again very slightly to Miss Vavasor.

He was on the threshold of the door before Glencora's voice recalled him. 'Oh my God!' she said, 'I am hard,—harder than flint. I am cruel. Burgo!' And he was back with her in a moment, and had taken her by the hand.

'Glencora,' said Alice, 'pray,—pray let him go. Mr. Fitzgerald, if you are a man, do not take advantage of her folly.'

'I will speak to him,' said Lady Glencora. 'I will speak to him, and then he shall leave me.' She was holding him by the hand now and turning to him, away from Alice, who had taken her by the arm. 'Burgo,' she said, repeating his name twice again, with all the passion that she could throw into the word, —'Burgo, no good can come of this. Now, you must leave me. You must go. I shall stay with my husband as I am bound to do. Because I have wronged you, I will not wrong him also. I loved you;—you know I loved you.' She still held him by the hand, and was now gazing up into his face, while the tears were streaming from her eyes.

'Sir,' said Alice, 'you have heard from her all that you can care to hear. If you have any feeling of honour in you, you will leave her.'

'I will never leave her, while she tells me that she loves me!'

'Yes, Burgo, you will;—you must! I shall never tell you that again, never. Do as she bids you. Go, and leave us;—but I could not bear that you should tell me that I was hard.'

'You are hard;—hard and cruel, as you said, yourself.'

'Am I? May God forgive you for saying that of me!'

'Then why do you send me away?'

'Because I am a man's wife, and because I care for his honour, if not for my own. Alice, let us go.'

He still held her, but she would have been gone from him had he not stooped over her, and put his arm round her waist. In doing this, I doubt whether he was quicker than she would have been had she chosen to resist him. As it was, he pressed her to his bosom, and, stooping over her, kissed her lips. Then he left her, and making his way out of the room, and down the stairs, got himself out into the street.

'Thank God, that he is gone!' said Alice.

'You may say so,' said Lady Glencora, 'for you have lost nothing!'

'And you have gained everything!'

'Have I? I did not know that I had ever gained anything, as yet. The only human being to whom I have ever yet given my whole heart,—the only thing that I have ever really loved, has just gone from me for ever, and you bid me thank God that I have lost him. There is no room for thankfulness in any of it; —either in the love or in the loss. It is all wretchedness from first to last!'

'At any rate, he understands now that you meant it when you told him to leave you.'

'Of course I meant it. I am beginning to know myself by degrees. As for running away with him, I have not the courage to do it. I can think of it, scheme for it, wish for it;—but as for doing it, that is beyond me. Mr. Palliser is quite safe. He need not try to coax me to remain.'

Alice knew that it was useless to argue with her, so she came and sat over her,—for Lady Glencora had again placed herself on the stool by the window,—and tried to sooth her by smoothing her hair, and nursing her like a child.

'Of course I know that I ought to stay where I am,' she said, breaking out, almost with rage, and speaking with quick, eager voice. 'I am not such a fool as to mistake what I should be if I left my husband, and went to live with that man as his mistress. You don't suppose that I should think that sort of life very blessed. But why have I been brought to such a pass as this? And as for female purity! Ah! What was their idea of purity when they forced me, like ogres, to marry a man for whom they knew I never cared? Had I gone with him,—had I now eloped with that man who ought to have been my husband,—whom would a just God have punished worst,—me, or those two old women and my uncle, who tortured me into this marriage?'

'Come, Cora,—be silent.'

'I won't be silent! You have had the making of your own lot. You have done what you liked, and no one has interfered with you. You have suffered, too; but you, at any rate, can respect yourself.'

'And so can you, Cora,—thoroughly, now.'

'How;—when he kissed me, and I could hardly restrain myself from giving him back his kiss tenfold, could I respect myself? But it is all sin. I sin towards my husband, feigning that I love him; and I sin in loving that other man, who should have been my husband. There;—I hear Mr. Palliser at the door. Come away with me; or rather, stay, for he will come up here, and you can keep him in talk while I try to recover myself.'

Mr. Palliser did at once as his wife had said, and came upstairs to the little front room, as soon as he had deposited his hat in the hall. Alice was, in fact, in doubt what she should do as to mentioning, or omitting to mention, Mr. Fitzgerald's name. In an ordinary way, it would be natural that she should name any visitor who had called, and she specially disliked the idea of remaining silent because that visitor had come as the lover of her host's wife. But, on the other hand, she owed much to Lady Glencora; and there was no imperative reason, as things had gone, why she should make mischief. There was no further danger to be apprehended. But Mr. Palliser at once put an end to her doubts. 'You have had a visitor here?' said he.

'Yes,' said Alice.

'I saw him as I went out,' said Mr. Palliser. 'Indeed, I met him at the hall-door. He, of course, was wrong to come here; —so wrong, that he deserves punishment, if there were any punishment for such offences.'

'He has been punished, I think,' said Alice.

'But as for Glencora,' continued Mr. Palliser, without any apparent notice of what Alice had said, 'I thought it better that she should see him or not, as she should herself decide.'

'She had no choice in the matter. As it turned out, he was

shown up here at once. She sent for me, and I think she was right to do that.'

'Glencora was alone when he came in?'

'For a minute or two,—till I could get to her.'

'I have no questions to ask about it,' said Mr. Palliser, after waiting for a few moments. He had probably thought that Alice would say something further. 'I am very glad that you were within reach of her, as otherwise her position might have been painful. For her, and for me perhaps, it may be as well that he has been here. As for him, I can only say, that I am forced to suppose him to be a villain. What a man does when driven by passion, I can forgive; but that he should deliberately plan schemes to ruin both her and me, is what I can hardly understand.' As he made this little speech I wonder whether his conscience said anything to him about Lady Dumbello, and a certain evening in his own life, on which he had ventured to call that lady, Griselda.

The little party of three dined together very quietly, and after dinner they all went to work with their novels. Before long Alice saw that Mr. Palliser was yawning, and she began to understand how much he had given up in order that his wife might be secure. It was then, when he had left the room for a few minutes, in order that he might wake himself by walking about the house, that Glencora told Alice of his yawning down at Matching. 'I used to think that he would fall in pieces. What are we to do about it?'

'Don't seem to notice it,' said Alice.

'That's all very well,' said the other; 'but he'll set us off yawning as bad as himself, and then he'll notice it. He has given himself up to politics, till nothing else has any salt in it left for him. I cannot think why such a man as that wanted a wife at all?'

'You are very hard upon him, Cora.'

'I wish you were his wife, with all my heart. But, of course, I know why he got married. And I ought to feel for him as he has been so grievously disappointed.' Then Mr. Palliser having walked off his sleep, returned to the room, and the remainder of the evening was passed in absolute tranquillity.

Burgo Fitzgerald, when he left the house, turned back into Grosvenor Square, not knowing, at first, whither he was going. He took himself as far as his uncle's door, and then, having paused there for a moment, hurried on. For half an hour, or thereabouts, something like true feeling was at work within his heart. He had once more pressed to his bosom the woman he had, at any rate, thought that he had loved. He had had his arm round her, and had kissed her, and the tone with which she had called him by his name was still ringing in his ears, 'Burgo!' He repeated his own name audibly to himself, as though in this way he could recall her voice. He comforted himself for a minute with the conviction that she loved him. He felt,—for a moment,—that he could live on such consolation as that! But among mortals there could, in truth, hardly be one with whom such consolation would go a shorter way. He was a man who required to have such comfort backed by patés and curaçoa to a very large extent, and now it might be doubted whether the amount of patés and curaçoa at his command would last him much longer.

He would not go in and tell his aunt at once of his failure, as he could gain nothing by doing so. Indeed, he thought that he would not tell his aunt at all. So he turned back from Grosvenor Square, and went down to his club in St. James's Street, feeling that billiards and brandy-and-water might, for the present, be the best restorative. But, as he went back, he blamed himself very greatly in the matter of those bank-notes which he had allowed Lady Monk to take from him. How had it come to pass that he had been such a dupe in her hands? When he entered his club in St. James's Street his mind had left Lady Glencora, and was hard at work considering how he might best contrive to get that spoil out of his aunt's possession.

CHAPTER LXVIII

From London to Baden

ON the following morning everybody was stirring by times at Mr. Palliser's house in Park Lane, and the master of that house yawned no more. There is some life in starting for a long journey, and the life is the stronger and the fuller if the things and people to be carried are numerous and troublesome. Lady Glencora was a little troublesome, and would not come down to breakfast in time. When rebuked on account of this manifest breach of engagement, she asserted that the next train would do just as well; and when Mr. Palliser proved to her, with much trouble, that the next train could not enable them to reach Paris on that day, she declared that it would be much more comfortable to take a week in going than to hurry over the ground in one day. There was nothing she wanted so much as to see Folkestone.

'If that is the case, why did not you tell me so before?' said Mr. Palliser, in his gravest voice. 'Richard and the carriage went down yesterday, and are already on board the packet.'

'If Richard and the carriage are already on board the packet,' said Lady Glencora, 'of course we must follow them, and we must put off the glories of Folkestone till we come back. Alice, haven't you observed that, in travelling, you are always driven on by some Richard or some carriage, till you feel that you are a slave?'

All this was trying to Mr. Palliser; but I think that he enjoyed it, nevertheless, and that he was happy when he found that he did get his freight off from the Pimlico Station in the proper train.

Of course Lady Glencora and Alice were very ill crossing the Channel; of course the two maids were worse than their mistresses; of course the men kept out of their master's way when they were wanted, and drank brandy-and-water with the steward down-stairs; and of course Lady Glencora declared that she would not allow herself to be carried beyond Boulogne

284

that day;—but, nevertheless, they did get on to Paris. Had
Mr. Palliser become Chancellor of the Exchequer, as he had
once hoped, he could hardly have worked harder than he did
work. It was he who found out which carriage had been taken
for them, and who put, with his own hands, the ladies' dress-
ing-cases and cloaks on to the seats,—who laid out the novels,
which, of course, were not read by the road,—and made preparations as though this stage of their journey was to take
them a week, instead of five hours and a half.

'Oh, dear! how I have slept!' said Lady Glencora, as they
came near to Paris.

'I think you've been tolerably comfortable,' said Mr. Palliser, joyfully.

'Since we got out of that horrid boat I have done pretty
well. Why do they make the boats so nasty? I'm sure they do
it on purpose.'

'It would be difficult to make them nice, I suppose,' said
Alice.

'It is the sea that makes them uncomfortable,' said Mr.
Palliser.

'Never mind; we shan't have any more of it for twelve
months, at any rate. We can get to the Kurds, Alice, without
getting into a packet again. That, to my way of thinking, is
the great comfort of the Continent. One can go everywhere
without being sea-sick.'

Mr. Palliser said nothing, but he sighed as he thought of
being absent for a whole year. He had said that such was his
intention, and would not at once go back from what he himself
had said. But how was he to live for twelve months out of the
House of Commons? What was he to do with himself, with
his intellect and his energy, during all these coming dreary
days? And then,—he might have been Chancellor of the Exchequer! He might even now, at this very moment, have been
upon his legs, making a financial statement of six hours' dura-
tion, to the delight of one-half of the House, and bewilderment
of the other, instead of dragging cloaks across that dingy,
dull, dirty waiting-room at the Paris Station, in which British

subjects are kept in prison while their boxes are being tumbled out of the carriages.

'But we are not to stop here;—are we?' said Lady Glencora, mournfully.

'No, dear;—I have given the keys to Richard. We will go on at once.'

'But can't we have our things?'

'In about half an hour,' pleaded Mr. Palliser.

'I suppose we must bear it, Alice?' said Lady Glencora as she got into the carriage that was waiting for her.

Alice thought of the last time in which she had been in that room,—when George and Kate had been with her,—and the two girls had been quite content to wait patiently while their trunks were being examined. But Alice was now travelling with great people,—with people who never spoke of their wealth, or seemed ever to think of it, but who showed their consciousness of it at every turn of their lives. 'After all,' Alice had said to herself more than once, 'I doubt whether the burden is not greater than the pleasure.'

They staid in Paris for a week, and during that time Alice found that she became very intimate with Mr. Palliser. At Matching she had, in truth, seen but little of him, and had known nothing. Now she began to understand his character, and learned how to talk to him. She allowed him to tell her of things in which Lady Glencora resolutely persisted in taking no interest. She delighted him by writing down in a little pocket-book the number of eggs that were consumed in Paris every day, whereas Glencora protested that the information was worth nothing unless her husband could tell her how many of the eggs were good, and how many bad. And Alice was glad to find that a hundred and fifty thousand female operatives were employed in Paris, while Lady Glencora said it was a great shame, and that they ought all to have husbands. When Mr. Palliser explained that that was impossible, because of the redundancy of the female population, she angered him very much by asserting that she saw a great many men walking about who, she was quite sure, had not wives of their own.

'I do so wish you had married him!' Glencora said to Alice that evening. 'You would always have had a pocket-book ready to write down the figures, and you would have pretended to care about the eggs, and the bottles of wine, and the rest of it. As for me, I can't do it. If I see an hungry woman, I can give her my money; or if she be a sick woman, I can nurse her; or if I hear of a very wicked man, I can hate him;—but I cannot take up poverty and crime in the lump. I never believe it all. My mind isn't big enough.'

They went into no society at Paris, and at the end of a week were all glad to leave it.

'I don't know that Baden will be any better,' Lady Glencora said; 'but, you know, we can leave that again after a bit,—and so we shall go on getting nearer to the Kurds.'

To this, Mr. Palliser demurred. 'I think we had better make up our mind to stay a month at Baden.'

'But why should we make up our minds at all?' his wife pleaded.

'I like to have a plan,' said Mr. Palliser.

'And so do I,' said his wife,—'if only for the sake of not keeping it.'

'There's nothing I hate so much as not carrying out my intentions,' said Mr. Palliser.

Upon this, Lady Glencora shrugged her shoulders, and made a mock grimace to her cousin. All this her husband bore for a while meekly, and it must be acknowledged that he behaved very well. But, then, he had his own way in everything. Lady Glencora did not behave very well,—contradicting her husband, and not considering, as, perhaps, she ought to have done, the sacrifice he was making on her behalf. But, then, she had her own way in nothing.

She had her own way in almost nothing; but on one point she did conquer her husband. He was minded to go from Paris back to Cologne, and so down the Rhine to Baden. Lady Glencora declared that she hated the Rhine,—that, of all rivers, it was the most distasteful to her; that, of all scenery, the scenery of the Rhine was the most over-praised; and that she would be wretched all the time if she were carried that way. Upon this, Mr. Palliser referred the matter to Alice; and she, who had last been upon the Rhine with her cousins Kate and George Vavasor, voted for going to Baden by way of Strasbourg.

'We will go by Strasbourg, then,' said Mr. Palliser, gallantly.

'Not that I want to see that horrid church again,' said Glencora.

'Everything is alike horrid to you, I think,' said her husband. 'You are determined not to be contented, so that it matters very little which way we go.'

'That's the truth,' said his wife. 'It does matter very little.'

They got on to Baden,—with very little delay at Strasbourg, and found half an hotel prepared for their reception. Here the carriage was brought into use for the first time, and the mistress of the carriage talked of sending home for Dandy and Flirt. Mr. Palliser, when he heard the proposition, calmly assured his wife that the horses would not bear the journey. 'They would be so out of condition,' he said, 'as not to be worth anything for two or three months.'

'I only meant to ask for them if they could come in a balloon,' said Lady Glencora.

This angered Mr. Palliser, who had really, for a few minutes, thought of pacifying his wife by sending for the horses.

'Alice,' she asked, one morning, 'how many eggs are eaten in Baden every morning before ten o'clock?'

Mr. Palliser, who at the moment was in the act of eating one, threw down his spoon, and pushed his plate from him.

'What's the matter, Plantagenet?' she asked.

'The matter!' he said. 'But never mind; I am a fool to care for it.'

'I declare I didn't know that I had done anything wrong,' said Lady Glencora. 'Alice, do you understand what it is?'

Alice said that she did understand very well.

'Of course she understands,' said Mr. Palliser. 'How can she help it? And, indeed, Miss Vavasor, I am more unhappy than I can express myself, to think that your comfort should be disturbed in this way.'

'Upon my word I think Alice is doing very well,' said Lady Glencora. 'What is there to hurt her comfort? Nobody scolds her. Nobody tells her that she is a fool. She never jokes, or does anything wicked, and, of course, she isn't punished.'

Mr. Palliser, as he wandered that day alone through the gambling-rooms at the great Assembly House,* thought that, after all, it might have been better for him to have remained in London, to have become Chancellor of the Exchequer, and to have run all risks.

'I wonder whether it would be any harm if I were to put a few pieces of money on the table, just once?' Lady Glencora said to her cousin, on the evening of the same day, in one of those gambling salons. There had been some music on that evening in one side of the building, and the Pallisers had gone to the rooms. But as neither of the two ladies would dance, they had strayed away into the other apartments.

'The greatest harm in the world!' said Alice; 'and what on earth could you gain by it? You don't really want any of those horrid people's money?'

'I'll tell you what I want,—something to live for,—some excitement. Is it not a shame that I see around me so many people getting amusement, and that I can get none? I'd go and sit out there, and drink beer and hear the music, only Plantagenet wouldn't let me. I think I'll throw one piece on to the table to see what becomes of it.'

'I shall leave you if you do,' said Alice.

'You are such a prude! It seems to me as if it must have been my special fate,—my good fate, I mean,—that has thrown me so much with you. You look after me quite as carefully as Mr. Bott and Mrs. Marsham ever did; but as I chose you myself, I can't very well complain, and I can't very well get rid of you.'

'Do you want to get rid of me, Cora?'

'Sometimes. Do you know, there are moments when I almost make up my mind to go headlong to the devil,—when I think it is the best thing to be done. It's a hard thing for a woman to do, because she has to undergo so much obloquy before she

289

gets used to it. A man can take to drinking, and gambling and all the rest of it, and nobody despises him a bit. The domestic old fogies give him lectures if they can catch him, but he isn't fool enough for that. All he wants is money, and he goes away and has his fling. Now I have plenty of money,—or, at any rate, I had,—and I never got my fling yet. I do feel so tempted to rebel, and go ahead, and care for nothing.'

'Throwing one piece on to the table wouldn't satisfy that longing.'

'You think I should be like the wild beast that has tasted blood, and can't be controlled Look at all these people here. There are husbands gambling, and their wives don't know it; and wives gambling, and their husbands don't know it. I wonder whether Plantagenet ever has a fling? What a joke it would be to come and catch him!'

'I don't think you need be afraid.'

'Afraid! I should like him all the better for it. If he came to me, some morning, and told me that he had lost a hundred thousand pounds, I should be so much more at my ease with him.'

'You have no chance in that direction, I'm quite sure.'

'None the least. He 'd make a calculation that the chances were nine to seven against him, and then the speculation would seem to him to be madness '

'I don't suppose he'd wish to try, even though he were sure of winning.'

'Of course not. It would be a very vulgar kind of thing then. Look,—there 's an opening there. I'll just put on one napoleon.'*

'You shall not. If you do, I'll leave you at once. Look at the women who are playing. Is there one there whom it would not disgrace you to touch? Look what they are. Look at their cheeks, and their eyes, and their hands. Those men who rake about the money are bad enough, but the women look like fiends.'

'You're not going to frighten me in that hobgoblin sort of way, you know. I don't see anything the matter with any of the people.'

290

'What do you think of that young woman who has just got a handful of money from the man next to her?'

'I think she is very happy. I never get money given to me by handfuls, and the man to whom I belong gives me no encouragement when I want to amuse myself.' They were now standing near to one end of the table, and suddenly there came to be an opening through the crowd up to the table itself. Lady Glencora, leaving Alice's side, at once stepped up and deposited a piece of gold on one of the marked compartments. As soon as she placed it she retreated again with flushed face, and took hold of Alice's arm. 'There,' she said, 'I have done it.' Alice, in her dismay, did not know what step to take. She could not scold her friend now, as the eyes of many were turned upon them, nor could she, of course, leave her, as she had threatened. Lady Glencora laughed with her peculiar little low laughter, and stood her ground. 'I was determined you shouldn't frighten me out of it,' she said.

One of the ministers at the table had in the meantime gone on with the cards, and had called the game; and another minister had gently pushed three or four more pieces of gold up to that which Lady Glencora had flung down, and had then cunningly caught her eye, and, with all the courtesy of which he was master, had pushed them further on towards her. She had supposed herself to be unknown there in the salon, but no doubt all the croupiers and half the company knew well enough who was the new customer at the table. There was still the space open, near to which she stood, and then some one motioned to her to come and take up the money which she had won. She hesitated, and then the croupier asked her, in that low, indifferent voice which these men always use, whether she desired that her money should remain. She nodded her head to him, and he at once drew the money back again to the spot on which she had placed the first napoleon. Again the cards were turned up softly, again the game was called, and again she won. The money was dealt out to her,—on this occasion with a full hand. There were lying there between twenty and thirty napoleons, of which she was the mistress.

Her face had flushed before, but now it became very red. She caught hold of Alice, who was literally trembling beside her, and tried to laugh again. But there was that in her eye which told Alice that she was really frightened. Some one then placed a chair for her at the table, and in her confusion, not knowing what she was to do, she seated herself. 'Come away,' said Alice, taking hold of her, and disregarding everything but her own purpose, in the agony of the moment. 'You must come away! You shall not sit there!' 'I must get rid of that money,' said Glencora, trying to whisper her words, 'and then I will come away.' The croupier again asked her if the money was to remain, and she again nodded her head. Everybody at the table was now looking at her. The women especially were staring at her,—those horrid women with vermilion cheeks, and loud bonnets half off their heads, and hard, shameless eyes, and white gloves, which, when taken off in the ardour of the game, disclosed dirty hands. They stared at her with that fixed stare which such women have, and Alice saw it all, and trembled.

Again she won. 'Leave it,' said Alice, 'and come away.' 'I can't leave it,' said Glencora. 'If I do, there'll be a fuss. I'll go the next time.' What she said was, of course, in English, and was probably understood by no one near her; but it was easy to be seen that she was troubled, and, of course, those around her looked at her the more because of her trouble. Again that little question and answer went on between her and the croupier, and on this occasion the money was piled up on the compartment—a heap of gold which made envious the hearts of many who stood around there. Alice had now both her hands on the back of the chair, needing support. If the devil should persist, and increase that stock of gold again, she must go and seek for Mr. Palliser. She knew not what else to do. She understood nothing of the table, or of its laws; but she supposed all those ministers of the game to be thieves, and believed that all villanous contrivances were within their capacity. She thought that they might go on adding to that heap so long as Lady Glencora would sit there, presuming that they might thus get her into their clutches. Of course, she did not sift her suspicions.

Who does at such moments? 'Come away at once, and leave it,' she said, 'or I shall go.' At that moment the croupier raked it all up, and carried it all away; but Alice did not see that this had been done. A hand had been placed on her shoulder, and as she turned round her face her eyes met those of Mr. Palliser. 'It is all gone,' said Glencora, laughing. And now she, turning round, also saw her husband. 'I am so glad that you are come,' said Alice. 'Why did you bring her here?' said Mr. Palliser. There was anger in his tone, and anger in his eye. He took his wife's arm upon his own, and walked away quickly, while Alice followed them alone. He went off at once, down the front steps of the building, towards the hotel. What he said to his wife, Alice did not hear; but her heart was swelling with the ill-usage to which she herself was subjected. Though she might have to go back alone to England, she would tell him that he was ill-treating her. She followed him on, up into their drawing-room, and there he stood with the door open in his hand for her, while Lady Glencora threw herself upon a sofa, and burst out into affected laughter. 'Here's a piece of work,' she said, 'about a little accident.'

'An accident!' said Mr. Palliser.

'Yes, an accident. You don't suppose that I sat down there meaning to win all that money?' Whereupon he looked at her with scorn.

'Mr. Palliser,' said Alice, 'you have treated me this evening in a manner I did not expect from you. It is clear that you blame me.'

'I have not said a word, Miss Vavasor.'

'No; you have not said a word. You know well how to show your anger without speaking. As I do not choose to undergo your displeasure, I will return to England by myself.'

'Alice! Alice!' said Glencora, jumping up, 'that is nonsense! What is all this trumpery thing about? Leave me, because he chooses to be angry about nothing?'

'Is it nothing that I find my wife playing at a common gambling-table, surrounded by all that is wretched and vile,—established there, seated, with heaps of gold before her?'

'You wrong me, Plantagenet,' said Glencora. 'There was only one heap, and that did not remain long. Did it, Alice?'

'It is impossible to make you ashamed of anything,' he said.

'I certainly don't like being ashamed,' she answered; 'and don't feel any necessity on this occasion.'

'If you don't object, Mr. Palliser,' said Alice. 'I will go to bed. You can think over all this at night,—and so can I. Good-night, Glencora.' Then Alice took her candle, and marched off to her own room, with all the dignity of which she was mistress.

CHAPTER LXIX

From Baden to Lucerne

THE second week in July saw Mr. Palliser's party, carriage and all, established at Lucerne, in Switzerland, safe beyond the reach of the German gambling-tables. Alice Vavasor was still with them; and the reader will therefore understand that that quarrel about Lady Glencora's wickedness had been settled without any rupture. It had been settled amicably, and by the time that they had reached Lucerne, Alice was inclined to acknowledge that the whole thing was not worth notice; but for many days her anger against Mr. Palliser had not been removed, and her intimacy with him had been much checked. It was now a month since the occurrence of that little scene in the salon at Baden, which was described in the last chapter, —since Mr. Palliser had marched off with his wife, leaving Alice to follow as she best could by herself. After that, as the reader may remember, he had almost told her that she was to be blamed because of his wife's indiscretion; and when she had declared her intention of leaving him, and making her way home to England by herself, he had answered her not at all, and had allowed her to go off to her own room under the full ban of his displeasure. Since that he had made no apology to her; he had not, in so many words, acknowledged that he had wronged her; but Alice had become aware that he intended to apologize by his conduct, and she had been content so far to indulge his obstinacy as to accept this conduct on his part in lieu of any outspoken petition for pardon. The acknowledgment of a mistake and the asking for grace is almost too much for any woman to expect from such a man as Mr. Palliser.

Early on the morning after the scene in question, Lady Glencora had gone into Alice's bedroom, and had found her cousin in her dressing-gown, packing up her things, or looking as though she intended to do so. 'You are not such a fool,' she said, 'as to think anything of what occurred yesterday?' Alice assured her that, whether fool or not, she did think a great deal of it. 'In point of fact,' said Alice, 'I can't stand it. He expects me to take care of you, and chooses to show himself offended if you don't do just what he thinks proper; whereas, as you know well enough, I have not the slightest influence over you.' All these positions Lady Glencora contradicted vigorously. Of course, Mr. Palliser had been wrong in walking out of the Assembly Rooms as he had done, leaving Alice behind him. So much Lady Glencora admitted. But this had come of his intense anxiety. 'And you know what a man he is,' said his wife—'how stiff, and hard, and unpleasant he can be without meaning it.'—'There is no reason why I should bear his unpleasantness,' said Alice. 'Yes, there is,—great reason. You are to do it for the sake of friendship. And as for my not doing what you tell me, you know that's not true.'

'Did I not beg you to keep away from the table?'

'Of course you did, and of course I was naughty; but that was only once. Alice, I want you more than I ever wanted you before. I cannot tell you more now, but you must stay with me.'

Alice consented to come down to breakfast without any immediate continuance of her active preparations for going, and at last, of course, she staid. When she entered the breakfast room Mr. Palliser came up to her, and offered her his hand. She had no alternative but to take it, and then seated herself. That there was an intended apology in the manner in which he offered her toast and butter, she was convinced; and the special courtesy with which he handed her to the carriage, when she and Lady Glencora went out for their drive, after dinner, was almost as good as a petition for pardon. So the thing went on, and by degrees Mr. Palliser and Miss Vavasor were again friends.

But Alice never knew in what way the matter was settled between Mr. Palliser and his wife, or whether there was any such settling. Probably there was none. 'Of course, he understands that it didn't mean anything,' Lady Glencora had said. 'He knows that I don't want to gamble.' But let that be as it might, their sojourn at Baden was curtailed, and none of the party went up again to the Assembly Rooms before their departure.

Before establishing themselves at Lucerne they made a little tour round by the Falls of the Rhine and Zurich. In their preparations for this journey, Alice made a struggle, but a struggle in vain, to avoid a passage through Basle. It was only too clear to her that Mr. Palliser was determined to go by Basle. She could not bring herself to say that she had recollections connected with that place which would make a return to it unpleasant to her. If she could have said as much, even to Glencora, Mr. Palliser would no doubt have gone round,—round by any more distant route that might have been necessary to avoid that eternal gateway into Switzerland. But she could not say it. She was very averse to talking about herself and her own affairs, even with her cousin. Of course Lady Glencora knew the whole story of Mr. John Grey and his rejection,—and knew much also of that other story of Mr. George Vavasor. And, of course, like all Alice's friends, she hated George Vavasor, and was prepared to receive Mr. John Grey with open arms, if there were any possibility that her cousin would open her arms to him also. But Alice was so stubborn about her own affairs that her friend found it almost impossible to speak of them. 'It is not that you trouble me,' Alice once said, 'but that you trouble yourself about that which is of no use. It is all done and over; and though I know that I have behaved badly,—very badly,—yet I believe that everything has been done for the best. I am inclined to think that I can live alone, or perhaps with my cousin Kate, more happily than I could with any husband.'

'That is such nonsense.'

'Perhaps so; but, at any rate, I mean to try. We Vavasors don't seem to be good at marrying.'

'You want some one to break your heart for you; that's what you want,' said Lady Glencora. In saying this she knew but little of the state of her friend's heart, and perhaps was hardly capable of understanding it. With all the fuss that Lady Glencora made to herself,—with all the tears that she had shed about her lost lover, and was so often shedding,—with all her continual thinking of the matter, she had never loved Burgo Fitzgerald as Alice Vavasor had loved Mr. Grey. But her nature was altogether different to that of Alice. Love with her had in it a gleam of poetry, a spice of fun, a touch of self-devotion, something even of hero-worship; but with it all there was a dash of devilry, and an aptitude almost for wickedness. She knew Burgo Fitzgerald to be a scapegrace, and she liked him the better on that account. She despised her husband because he had no vices. She would have given everything she had to Burgo,—pouring her wealth upon him with a total disregard of herself, had she been allowed to do so. She would have forgiven him sin after sin, and might perhaps have brought him round, at last, to some life not absolutely reckless and wretched. But in all that she might have done, there would have been no thoughtfulness,—no true care either for him or for herself. And now that she was married there was no thoughtfulness, or care either for herself or for her husband. She was ready to sacrifice herself for him, if any sacrifice might be required of her. She believed herself to be unfit for him, and would have submitted to be divorced,—or smothered out of the way, for the matter of that,—if the laws of the land would have permitted it. But she had never for a moment given to herself the task of thinking what conduct on her part might be the best for his welfare.

But Alice's love had been altogether of another kind,—and

I am by no means sure that it was better suited for the work of this work-a-day world than that of her cousin. It was too thoughtful. I will not say that there was no poetry in it, but I will say that it lacked romance. Its poetry was too hard for romance. There was certainly in it neither fun nor wickedness; nor was there, I fear, so large a proportion of hero-worship as there always should be in a girl's heart when she gives it away. But there was in it an amount of self-devotion which none of those near to her had hitherto understood,—unless it were that one to whom the understanding of it was of the most importance. In all the troubles of her love, of her engagements, and her broken promises, she had thought more of others than of herself,—and, indeed, those troubles had chiefly come from that self-devotion. She had left John Grey because she feared that she would do him no good as his wife, —that she would not make him happy; and she had afterwards betrothed herself for a second time to her cousin, because she believed that she could serve him by marrying him. Of course she had been wrong. She had been very wrong to give up the man she did love, and more wrong again in suggesting to herself the possibility of marrying the man she did not love. She knew that she had been wrong in both, and was undergoing repentance with very bitter inward sackcloth. But she said little of all this even to her cousin.

They went to Lucerne by Basle, and put up at the big hotel with the balcony over the Rhine, which Alice remembered so well. On the first evening of her arrival she found herself again looking down upon the river, as though it might have been from the same spot which she had occupied together with George and Kate. But, in truth, that house is very large, and has many bedrooms over the water. Who has ever been through Basle, and not stood in one of them, looking down upon the father of waters? Here, on this very spot, in one of these balconies, was brought to her a letter from her cousin Kate, which was filled with tidings respecting her cousin George. Mr. Palliser brought it to her with his own hands, and she had no other alternative but to read it in his presence.

'George has lost his election,' the letter began. For one moment Alice thought of her money, and the vain struggle in which it had been wasted. For one moment, something like regret for the futility of the effort she had made came upon her. But it passed away at once. 'It was worth our while to try it,' she said to herself, and then went on with her letter. 'I and Aunt Greenow are up in London,' the letter went on to say, 'and have just heard the news. Though I have been here for three days, and have twice sent word to him to say so, he has not been near me. Perhaps it is best that he should stay away, as I do not know how any words could pass between us that would be pleasant. The poll was finished this afternoon, and he lost his election by a large majority. There were five candidates altogether for the two seats—three Liberals, and two Conservatives. The other two Liberals were seated, and he was the last of the five. I continue to hear tidings about him from day to day,—or rather, my aunt hears them and tells them to me,—which fill me full of fears as to his future career. I believe that he has abandoned his business, and that he has now no source of income. I would willingly share what I have with him; or I would do more than that. After keeping back enough to repay you gradually what he owes you, I would give him all my share of the income out of the estate. But I cannot do this while we are presumed to be enemies. I am up here to see a lawyer as to some steps which he is taking to upset grandpapa's will. The lawyer says that it is all nonsense, and that George's lawyer is not really in earnest; but I cannot do anything till the matter is settled. Dear Alice, though so much of your money is for a time gone, I am bound to congratulate you on your safety,—on what I may more truly call your escape. You will understand what my own feelings must be in writing this, after all that I did to bring you and him together,—after all my hopes and ambition respecting him. As for the money, it shall be repaid. I do not think I shall ever dare to indulge in any strong desire again. I think you will forgive me the injury I have done you;—and I know that you will pity me.

'I am here to see the London lawyer,—but not only for that. Aunt Greenow is buying her wedding clothes, and Captain Bellfield is in lodgings near to us, also buying his trousseau; or, as I should more properly say, having it bought for him. I am hardly in a mood for much mirth, but it is impossible not to laugh inwardly when she discusses before me the state of his wardrobe, and proposes economical arrangements—greatly to his disgust. At present, she holds him very tightly in hand, and makes him account for all his hours as well as all his money. "Of course, he'll run wild directly he's married," she said to me, yesterday; "and, of course, there'll always be a fight about it; but the more I do to tame him now, the less wild he'll be by-and-by. And though I dare say, I shall scold him sometimes, I shall never quarrel with him." I have no doubt all that is true; but what a fool she is to trouble herself with such a man. She says she does it for an occupation. I took courage to tell her once that a caged tiger would give her as much to do, and be less dangerous. She was angry at this, and answered me very sharply. I had tried my hand on a tiger, she said, and had felt his claws. She chose to sacrifice herself,—if a sacrifice it were to be,—when some good result might be possible. I had nothing further to say; and from that time to this we have been on the pleasantest terms possible as to the Captain. They have settled with your father to take Vavasor Hall for three years, and I suppose I shall stay with them till your return. What I may do then will depend entirely upon your doings. I feel myself to be a desolate, solitary being, without any tie to any person, or to any place. I never thought that I should feel the death of my grandfather to be such a loss to me as it has been. Except you, I have nothing left to me; and, as regards you, I have the pleasant feeling that I have for years been endeavouring to do you the worst possible injury, and that you must regard me as an enemy from whom you have escaped indeed, but not without terrible wounds.'

Alice was always angered by any assumption that her conduct to Mr. Grey had been affected by the advice or influence of her cousin Kate. But this very feeling seemed to preserve

Kate from the worse anger, which might have been aroused against her, had Alice acknowledged the injury which her cousin had in truth done to her. It was undoubtedly true that had Alice neither seen nor heard from Kate during the progress of John Grey's courtship, John Grey would not have lost his wife. But against this truth Alice was always protesting within her own breast. She had been weak, foolish, irresolute, —and had finally acted with false judgment. So much she now admitted to herself. But she would not admit that any other woman had persuaded her to such weakness. 'She mistakes me,' Alice thought, as she put up her letter. 'She is not the enemy who has wounded me.'

Mr. Palliser, who had brought her the letter, was seated in the same balcony, and while Alice had been reading, had almost buried himself in newspapers which conveyed intelligence as to the general elections then in progress. He was now seated with a sheet of 'The Times' in his hand, opened to its full extent,—for he had been too impatient to cut the paper,—and as he held it up in his hands before his eyes, was completely hidden beneath it. Five or six other open papers were around him, and he had not spoken a word since he had commenced his present occupation. Lady Glencora was standing on the other side of him, and she also had received letters. 'Iphy tells me that you are returned for Silverbridge,' she said at last.

'Who? I! yes; I'm returned,' said Mr. Palliser, speaking with something like disdain in his voice as to the possibility of anybody having stood with a chance of success against him in his own family borough.* For a full appreciation of the advantages of a private seat in the House of Commons let us always go to those great Whig families who were mainly instrumental in carrying the Reform Bill. The house of Omnium had been very great on that occasion. It had given up much, and had retained for family use simply the single seat at Silverbridge. But that that seat should be seriously disputed hardly suggested itself as possible to the mind of any Palliser. The Pallisers and the other great Whig families have been right in this. They have kept in their hands, as rewards for their own services to the country, no more than the country is manifestly willing to give them. 'Yes; I have been returned,' said Mr. Palliser. 'I'm sorry to see, Miss Vavasor, that your cousin has not been so fortunate.'

'So I find,' said Alice. 'It will be a great misfortune to him.'

'Ah! I suppose so. Those Metropolitan elections cost so much trouble and so much money, and under the most favourable circumstances, are so doubtful. A man is never sure there till he has fought for his seat three or four times.'

'This has been the third time with him,' said Alice, 'and he is a poor man.'

'Dear, dear,' said Mr. Palliser, who himself knew nothing of such misfortunes. 'I have always thought that those seats should be left to rich commercial men who can afford to spend money upon them. Instead of that, they are generally contested by men of moderate means. Another of my friends in the House has been thrown out.'

'Who is that unfortunate?' asked Lady Glencora.

'Mr. Bott,' said the unthinking husband.

'Mr. Bott out!' exclaimed Lady Glencora. 'Mr. Bott thrown out! I am so glad. Alice, are you not glad? The red-haired man, that used to stand about, you know, at Matching;—he has lost his seat in Parliament. I suppose he'll go and stand about somewhere in Lancashire, now.'

A very indiscreet woman was poor Lady Glencora. Mr. Palliser's face became black beneath 'The Times' newspaper. 'I did not know,' said he, 'that my friend Mr. Bott and Miss Vavasor were enemies.'

'Enemies! I don't suppose they were enemies,' said Glencora. 'But he was a man whom no one could help observing,— and disliking.'

'He was a man I specially disliked,' said Alice, with great courage. 'He may be very well in Parliament; but I never met a man who could make himself so disagreeable in society. I really did feel myself constrained to be his enemy.'

'Bravo, Alice!' said Lady Glencora.

'I hope he did nothing at Matching, to—to—to——,' began Mr. Palliser, apologetically.

'Nothing especially to offend me, Mr. Palliser,—except that he had a way that I especially dislike of trying to make little secret confidences.'

'And then he was so ugly,' said Lady Glencora.

'I felt certain that he endeavoured to do mischief,' said Alice.

'Of course he did,' said Lady Glencora; 'and he had a habit of rubbing his head against the papers in the rooms, and leaving a mark behind him that was quite unpardonable.'

Mr. Palliser was effectually talked down, and felt himself constrained to abandon his political ally. Perhaps he did this the easier as the loss which Mr. Bott had just suffered would materially interfere with his political utility. 'I suppose he will remain now among his own people,' said Mr. Palliser.

'Let us hope he will,' said Lady Glencora,—'and that his own people will appreciate the advantage of his presence.' Then there was nothing more said about Mr. Bott.

It was evening, and while they were still sitting among their letters and newspapers, there came a shout along the water, and the noise of many voices from the bridge. Suddenly, there shot down before them in the swift running stream the heads of many swimmers in the river, and with the swimmers came boats carrying their clothes. They went by almost like a glance of light upon the waters, so rapid was the course of the current. There was the shout of the voices,—the quick passage of the boats,—the uprising, some half a dozen times, of the men's hands above the surface; and then they were gone down the river, out of sight—like morsels of wood thrown into a cataract, which are borne away instantly.

'Oh, how I wish I could do that!' said Lady Glencora.

'It seems to be very dangerous,' said Mr. Palliser. 'I don't know how they can stop themselves.'

'Why should they want to stop themselves?' said Lady Glencora. 'Think how cool the water must be; and how beautiful to be carried along so quickly; and to go on, and on, and on! I suppose we couldn't try it?'

As no encouragement was given to this proposition, Lady Glencora did not repeat it; but stood leaning on the rail of the balcony, and looking enviously down upon the water. Alice was, of course, thinking of that other evening, when perhaps the same swimmers had come down under the bridge and before the balcony, and when George Vavasor was sitting in her presence. It was, I think, on that evening, that she made up her mind to separate herself from Mr. Grey.

On the day after that, Mr. Palliser and his party went on to Lucerne, making that journey, as I have said, by slow stages; taking Shaffhausen and Zurich in their way. At Lucerne, they established themselves for some time, occupying nearly a dozen rooms in the great hotel which overlooks the lake. Here there came to them a visitor, of whose arrival I will speak in the next chapter.

CHAPTER LXX

At Lucerne

I AM inclined to think that Mr. Palliser did not much enjoy this part of his tour abroad. When he first reached Lucerne there was no one there with whom he could associate pleasantly, nor had he any occupation capable of making his time run easily. He did not care for scenery. Close at his elbow was the finest to be had in Europe; but it was nothing to him. Had he been simply journeying through Lucerne at the proper time of the year for such a journey, when the business of the Session was over, and a little change of air needed, he could have enjoyed the thing in a moderate way, looking about him, passing on, and knowing that it was good for him to be there at that moment. But he had none of that passion for mountains and lakes, none of that positive joy in the heather, which would have compensated many another man for the loss of all that Mr. Palliser was losing. His mind was ever at home in the House of Commons, or in that august assembly which men call the Cabinet, and of the meetings of which he read from week to week the simple records. Therein were mentioned the names of those heroes to whom Fortune had been so much kinder than she had been to him; and he envied them. He took short, solitary walks, about the town, over the bridges, and along the rivers, making to himself the speeches which he would have made to full houses, had not his wife brought ruin upon all his hopes. And as he pictured to himself the glorious successes which probably never would have been his had he remained in London, so did he prophesy to himself an absolute and irremediable downfall from all political power as the result of his absence,—having, in truth, no sufficient cause for such despair. As yet, he was barely thirty, and had he been able to judge his own case as keenly as he could have judged the case of another, he would have known that a short absence might probably raise his value in the estimation of others rather than lower it. But his personal annoyance was too great to allow of his making such calculations aright. So he became fretful and unhappy; and though he spoke no word of rebuke to his wife, though he never hinted that she had robbed him of his glories, he made her conscious by his manner that she had brought him to this miserable condition.

Lady Glencora herself had a love for the mountains and lakes, but it was a love of that kind which requires to be stimulated by society, and which is keenest among cold chickens, picnic-pies, and the flying of champagne corks. When they first entered Switzerland she was very enthusiastic, and declared her intention of climbing up all the mountains, and going through all the passes. She endeavoured to induce her husband to promise that she should be taken up Mont Blanc. And I think she would have carried this on, and would have been taken up Mont Blanc, had Mr. Palliser's aspirations been congenial. But they were not congenial, and Lady Glencora soon lost all her enthusiasm. By the time that they were settled at Lucerne she had voted the mountains to be bores, and had almost learned to hate the lake, which she declared always made her wet through when she got into a small boat, and sea-sick when she put her foot in a large one. At Lucerne they made no acquaintances, Mr. Palliser being a man not apt to new friendships. They did not even dine at the public table, though Lady Glencora had expressed a wish to do so. Mr. Palliser did not like it, and of course Lady Glencora gave way. There were, moreover, some marital passages which were not pleasant to a third person. They did not scold each other; but Lady Glencora would make little speeches of which her husband disapproved. She would purposely irritate him by continuing her tone of badinage, and then Mr. Palliser would become fretful, and would look as though the cares of the world were too many for him. I cannot, therefore, say that Alice had much to make the first period of her sojourn at Lucerne a period of enjoyment.

But when they had been there about a fortnight, a stranger arrived, whose coming at any rate lent the grace of some excitement to their lives. Their custom was to breakfast at nine,—or as near nine as Lady Glencora could be induced to appear,—and then Mr. Palliser would read till three. At that hour he would walk forth by himself, after having handed the two ladies into their carriage, and they would be driven about for two hours. 'How I do hate this carriage,' Lady Glencora said one day. 'I do so wish it would come to grief, and be broken to pieces. I wonder whether the Swiss people think that we are going to be driven about here for ever.' There were moments, however, which seemed to indicate that Lady Glencora had something to tell her cousin, which, if told, would alter the monotony of their lives. Alice, however, would not press her for her secret.

'If you have anything to tell, why don't you tell it?' Alice once said.

'You are so hard,' said Lady Glencora.

'So you tell me very often,' Alice replied; 'and it is not complimentary. But hard or soft, I won't make a petition for your confidence.' Then Lady Glencora said something savage, and the subject was dropped for a while.

But we must go back to the stranger. Mr. Palliser had put the ladies into their carriage, and was standing between the front door of the hotel and the lake on a certain day, doubting whether he would walk up the hill to the left or turn into the town on the right, when he was accosted by an English gentleman, who, raising his hat, said that he believed that he spoke to Mr. Palliser.

'I am Mr. Palliser,' said our friend, very courteously, returning the salute, and smiling as he spoke. But though he smiled, and though he was courteous, and though he raised his hat, there was something in his look and voice which would not have encouraged any ordinary stranger to persevere. Mr. Palliser was not a man with whom it was easy to open an acquaintance.

'My name is John Grey,' said the stranger.

Then the smile was dropped, the look of extreme courtesy disappeared, the tone of Mr. Palliser's voice was altered, and he put out his hand. He knew enough of Mr. John Grey's history to be aware that Mr. John Grey was a man with whom he might permit himself to become acquainted. After the inter-change of a very few words, the two men started off for a walk together.

'Perhaps you don't wish to meet the carriage?' said Mr. Palliser. 'If so, we had better go through the town and up the river.'

They went through the town, and up the river, and when Mr. Palliser, on his return, was seen by Alice and Lady Glen-cora, he was alone. They dined together, and nothing was said. Together they sauntered out in the evening, and together came in and drank their tea; but still nothing was said. At last, Alice and her cousin took their candles from Mr. Palliser's hands and left the sitting-room for the night.

'Alice,' said Lady Glencora, as soon as they were in the passage together, 'I have been dying for this time to come. I could not speak before, or I should have made blunders, and so would you. Let us go into your room at once. Who do you think is here, at Lucerne, in this house, at this very moment?'

Alice knew at once who it was. She knew, immediately, that Mr. Grey had followed her, though no word had been written to her or spoken to her on the subject since that day on which he himself had told her that they would meet abroad. But though she was quite sure, she did not mention his name. 'Who is it, Glencora?' she asked, very calmly.

'Whom in all the world would you best like to see?' said Glencora.

'My cousin Kate, certainly,' said Alice.

'Then it is not your cousin Kate. And I don't believe you;— or else you're a fool.'

Alice was accustomed to Lady Glencora's mode of talking, and therefore did not think much of this. 'Perhaps I am a fool,' she said.

'Only I know you are not. But I am not at all so sure as to your being no hypocrite. The person I mean is a gentleman, of course. Why don't you show a little excitement, at any rate? When Plantagenet told me, just before dinner, I almost jumped out of my shoes. He was going to tell you himself after dinner, in the politest way in the world, no doubt, and just as the servants were carrying away the apples. I thought it best to save you from that; but, I declare, I believe I might have left him to do it; it would have had no effect upon you. Who is it that has come, do you suppose?'

'Of course I know now,' said Alice, very calmly, 'that Mr. John Grey has come.'

'Yes, Mr. John Grey has come. He is here in this house at this minute;—or, more probably, waiting outside by the lake till he shall see a light in your bedroom.' Then Lady Glencora paused for a moment, waiting that Alice might say something. But Alice said nothing. 'Well?' said Lady Glencora, rising up from her chair. 'Well?'

'Well?' said Alice.

'Have you nothing to say? Is it the same to you as though Mr. Smith had come?'

'No; not exactly the same. I am quite alive to the importance of Mr. Grey's arrival, and shall probably lie awake all night thinking about it,—if it will do you any good to know that; but I don't feel that I have much to say about it.'

'I wish I had let Mr. Palliser tell you, in an ordinary way, before all the servants. I do indeed.'

'It would not have made much difference.'

'Not the least, I believe. I wonder whether you ever did care for anybody in your life,—for him, or for that other one, or for anybody. For nobody, I believe;—except your cousin Kate. Still waters, they say, run deep; and sometimes I think your waters run too deep for me to fathom. I suppose I may go now, if you have got nothing more to say?'

'What do you want me to say? Of course I know why he has come here. He told me he should come.'

'And you have never said a word about it.'

'He told me he should come, and I thought it better not to say a word about it. He might change his mind, or anything might happen. I told him not to come; and it would have been much better that he should have remained away.'

'Why;—why;—why would it be better?'

'Because his being here will do no good to any one.'

'No good! It seems to me impossible but that it should do all the good in the world. Look here, Alice. If you do not altogether make it up with him before to-morrow evening, I shall believe you to be utterly heartless. Had I been you I should have been in his arms before this. I'll go now, and leave you to lie awake, as you say you will.' Then she left the room, but returned in a moment to ask another question. 'What is Plantagenet to say to him about seeing you to-morrow? Of course he has asked permission to come and call?'

'He may come if he pleases. You don't think I have quarrelled with him, or would refuse to see him!'

'And may we ask him to dine with us?'

'Oh, yes.'

'And make up a picnic, and all the rest of it. In fact, he is to be regarded as only an ordinary person. Well;—good night. I don't understand you, that's all.'

It may be doubted whether Alice understood herself. As soon as her friend was gone, she put out her candle and seated herself at the open window of her room, looking out upon the moonlight as it played upon the lake. Would he be there, thinking of her, looking up, perhaps, as Glencora had hinted, to see if he could distinguish her light among the hundred that would be flickering across the long front of the house? If it were so, at any rate he should not see her; so she drew the curtain, and sat there watching the lake. It was a pity that he should have come, and yet she loved him dearly for coming. It was a pity that he should have come, as his coming could lead to no good result. Of this she assured herself over and over again, and yet she hardly knew why she was so sure of it. Glencora had called her hard; but her conviction on that matter had not come from hardness. Now that she was alone, her heart was full of love, of the soft romance of love towards this man; and yet she felt that she ought not to marry him, even though he might still be willing to take her. That he was still willing to take her, that he desired to have her for his wife in

spite of all the injury she had done him, there could be no
doubt. Why else had he followed her to Switzerland? And she
remembered, now at this moment, how he had told her at
Cheltenham that he would never consider her to be lost to
him, unless she should, in truth, become the wife of another
man. Why, then, should it not be as he wished it?

She asked herself the question, and did not answer it; but
still she felt that it might not be so. She had no right to such
happiness after the evil that she had done. She had been driven
by a frenzy to do that which she herself could not pardon; and
having done it, she could not bring herself to accept the position which should have been the reward of good conduct. She
could not analyze the causes which made her feel that she must
still refuse the love that was proffered to her; she could not
clearly read her own thoughts; but the causes were as I have
said, and such was the true reading of her thoughts. Had she
simply refused his hand after she had once accepted it,—had
she refused it, and then again changed her mind, she could
have brought herself to ask him to forgive her. But she had
done so much more than this, and so much worse! She had
affianced herself to another man since she had belonged to him,
—since she had been his, as his future wife. What must he not
think of her, and what not suspect? Then she remembered
those interviews which she had had with her cousin since she
had written to him, accepting his offer. When he had been
with her in Queen Anne Street she had shrunk from all outward signs of a love which she did not feel. There had been
no caress between them. She had not allowed him to touch her
with his lips. But it was impossible that the nature of that mad
engagement between her and her cousin George should ever
be made known to Mr. Grey. She sat there wiping the tears
from her eyes as she looked for his figure among the figures
by the lake-side; but, as she sat there, she promised herself no
happiness from his coming. Oh! reader, can you forgive her
in that she had sinned against the softness of her feminine
nature? I think that she may be forgiven, in that she had never
brought herself to think lightly of her own fault.

If he were there, by the lake-side, she did not see him. I think we may say that John Grey was not a man to console himself in his love by looking up at his lady's candle. He was one who was capable of doing as much as most men in the pursuit of his love,—as he proved to be the case when he followed Alice to Cheltenham, and again to London, and now again to Lucerne; but I doubt whether a glimmer from her bedroom-window, had it been unmistakably her own glimmer, and not that of some ugly old French woman who might chance to sleep next to her, would have done him much good. He had come to Lucerne with a purpose, which purpose, if it might be possible, he meant to carry out; but I think he was already in bed, being tired with long travel, before Lady Glencora had left Alice's room.

At breakfast the next morning nothing was said for awhile about the new arrival. At last Mr. Palliser ventured to speak. 'Glencora has told you, I think, that Mr. Grey is here? Mr. Grey is an old friend of yours, I believe?'

Alice, keeping her countenance as well as she was able, said Mr. Grey had been, and, indeed, was, a very dear friend of hers. Mr. Palliser knew the whole story, and what was the use of any little attempt at dissimulation? 'I shall be glad to see him,—if you will allow me?' she went on to say.

'Glencora suggests that we should ask him to dinner,' said Mr. Palliser; and then that matter was settled.

But Mr. Grey did not wait till dinner-time to see Alice. Early in the morning his card was brought up, and Lady Glencora, as soon as she saw the name, immediately ran away.

'Indeed you need not go,' said Alice.

'Indeed I shall go,' said her ladyship. 'I know what's proper on these occasions, if you don't.'

So she went, whisking herself along the passages with a little run; and Mr. Grey, as he was shown into her ladyship's usual sitting-room, saw the skirt of her ladyship's dress as she whisked herself off towards her husband.

'I told you I should come,' he said, with his ordinary sweet smile. 'I told you that I should follow you, and here I am.'

He took her hand, and held it, pressing it warmly. She hardly knew with what words first to address him, or how to get her hand back from him.

'I am very glad to see you,—as an old friend,' she said; 'but I hope——'

'Well;—you hope what?'

'I hope you have had some better cause for travelling than a desire to see me?'

'No, dearest; no. I have had no better cause, and, indeed, none other. I have come on purpose to see you; and had Mr. Palliser taken you off to Asia or Africa, I think I should have felt myself compelled to follow him. You know why I follow you?'

'Hardly,' said she,—not finding at the moment any other word that she could say.

'Because I love you. You see what a plain-spoken John Bull I am, and how I come to the point at once. I want you to be my wife; and they say that perseverance is the best way when a man has such a want as that.'

'You ought not to want it,' she said, whispering the words as though she were unable to speak them out loud.

'But I do, you see. And why should I not want it?'

'I am not fit to be your wife.'

'I am the best judge of that, Alice. You have to make up your mind whether I am fit to be your husband.'

'You would be disgraced if you were to take me, after all that has passed;—after what I have done. What would other men say of you when they knew the story?'

'Other men, I hope, would be just enough to say, that when I had made up my mind, I was tolerably constant in keeping to it. I do not think they could say much worse of me than that.'

'They would say that you had been jilted, and had forgiven the jilt.'

'As far as the forgiveness goes, they would tell the truth. But, indeed, Alice, I don't very much care what men do say of me.

'But I care, Mr. Grey;—and though you may forgive me, I cannot forgive myself. Indeed I know now, as I have known all along, that I am not fit to be your wife. I am not good enough. And I have done that which makes me feel that I have no right to marry any one.' These words she said, jerking out the different sentences almost in convulsions; and when she had come to the end of them, the tears were streaming down her cheeks. 'I have thought about it, and I will not. I will not. After what has passed, I know that it will be better,—more seemly, that I should remain as I am.'

Soon after that she left him, not, however, till she had told him that she would meet him again at dinner, and had begged him to treat her simply as a friend. 'In spite of everything, I hope that we may always be friends,—dear friends,' she said.

'I hope we may,' he answered;—'the very dearest.' And then he left her.

In the afternoon he again encountered Mr. Palliser, and having thought over the matter since his interview with Alice, he resolved to tell his whole story to his new acquaintance,— not in order that he might ask for counsel from him, for in this matter he wanted no man's advice,—but that he might get some assistance. So the two men walked off together, up the banks of the clear-flowing Reuss,* and Mr. Palliser felt the comfort of having a companion.

'I have always liked her,' said Mr. Palliser, 'though, to tell the truth, I have twice been very angry with her.'

'I have never been angry with her,' said the lover.

'And my anger was in both instances unjust. You may imagine how great is my confidence in her, when I have thought she was the best companion my wife could have for a long journey, taken under circumstances that were—that were——; but I need not trouble you with that.'

So great had been the desolation of Mr. Palliser's life since his banishment from London that he almost felt tempted to tell the story of his troubles to this absolute stranger. But he bethought himself of the blood of the Pallisers, and refrained. There are comforts which royalty may never enjoy, and lux- uries in which such men as Plantagenet Palliser may not per- mit themselves to indulge.

'About her and her character I have no doubt in the world,'

said Grey. 'In all that she has done I think that I have seen her motives; and though I have not approved of them, I have always known them to be pure and unselfish. She has done nothing that I did not forgive as soon as it was done. Had she married that man, I should have forgiven her even that,—though I should have known that all her future life was destroyed, and much of mine also. I think I can make her happy if she will marry me, but she must first be taught to forgive herself. Living as she is with you, and with your wife, she may, perhaps, just now be more under your influence and your wife's than she can possibly be under mine.' Whereupon, Mr. Palliser promised that he would do what he could. 'I think she loves me,' said Mr. Grey.

Mr. Palliser said that he was sure she did, though what ground he had for such assurance I am quite unable to surmise. He was probably desirous of saying the most civil thing which occurred to him.

The little dinner-party that evening was pleasant enough, and nothing more was said about love. Lady Glencora talked nonsense to Mr. Grey, and Mr. Palliser contradicted all the nonsense which his wife talked. But this was all done in such a way that the evening passed away pleasantly. It was tacitly admitted among them that Mr. Grey was to be allowed to come among them as a friend, and Lady Glencora managed to say one word to him aside, in which she promised to give him her most cordial co-operation.

CHAPTER LXXI

Showing how George Vavasor received a Visit

WE must go back for a few pages to scenes which happened in London during this summer, so that the reader may understand Mr. Grey's position when he reached Lucerne. He had undergone another quarrel with George Vavasor, and something of the circumstances of that quarrel must be told.

It has been already said that George Vavasor lost his election for the Chelsea Districts, after all the money which he had spent,—money which he had been so ill able to spend, and on which he had laid his hands in a manner so disreputable! He had received two thousand pounds from the bills which Alice had executed on his behalf,—or rather, had received the full value of three out of the four bills, and a part of the value of the fourth, on which he had been driven to raise what immediate money he had wanted by means of a Jew bill-discounter. One thousand pounds he had paid over at once into the hands of Mr. Scruby, his Parliamentary election agent, towards the expenses of his election; and when the day of polling arrived had exactly in his hands the sum of five hundred pounds. Where he was to get more when this was gone he did not know. If he were successful,—if the enlightened constituents of the Chelsea Districts, contented with his efforts on behalf of the River Bank, should again send him to Parliament, he thought that he might still carry on the war. A sum of ready money he would have in hand; and, as to his debts, he would be grandly indifferent to any consideration of them. Then there might be pickings in the way of a Member of Parliament of his calibre. Companies,—mercantile companies,—would be glad to have him as a director, paying him a guinea a day, or perhaps more, for his hour's attendance. Railways in want of vice-chairmen might bid for his services; and in the City he might turn that 'M.P.' which belonged to him to good account in various ways. With such a knowledge of the City world as he possessed, he thought that he could pick up a living in London, if only he could retain his seat in Parliament.

But what was he to do if he could not retain it? No sooner had Mr. Scruby got the thousand pounds into his clutches than he pressed for still more money. George Vavasor, with some show of justice on his side, pointed out to this all-devouring agent that the sum demanded had already been paid. This Mr. Scruby admitted, declaring that he was quite prepared to go on without any further immediate remittance, although by doing so he might subject himself to considerable risk. But another five hundred pounds, paid at once, would add greatly to the safety of the seat; whereas eight hundred judiciously thrown in at the present moment would make the thing quite secure. But Vavasor swore to himself that he would not part with another shilling. Never had he felt such love for money as he did for that five hundred pounds which he now held in his pocket. 'It's no use,' he said to Mr. Scruby. 'I have done what you asked, and would have done more had you asked for more at that time. As it is, I cannot make another payment before the election.' Mr. Scruby shrugged his shoulders, and said that he would do his best. But George Vavasor soon knew that the man was not doing his best,—that the man had, in truth, abandoned his cause. The landlord of The Handsome Man jeered him when he went there canvassing. 'Laws, Mr. Vavasor!' said the landlord of The Handsome Man, 'you're not at all the fellow for us chaps along the river,—you ain't. You're afraid to come down with the stumpy,*—that's what you are.' George put his hand upon his purse, and acknowledged to himself that he had been afraid to come down with the stumpy.

For the last five days of the affair George Vavasor knew that his chance was gone. Mr. Scruby's face, manner, and words, told the result of the election as plainly as any subsequent figures could do. He would be absent when Vavasor called, or the clerk would say that he was absent. He would answer in very few words, constantly shrugging his shoulders. He would even go away and leave the anxious candidate while he was in the middle of some discussion as to his plans. It was easy to see that Mr. Scruby no longer regarded him as a successful man, and the day of the poll showed very plainly how right Mr. Scruby had been.

George Vavasor was rejected, but he still had his five hundred pounds in his pocket. Of course he was subject to that mortification which a man feels when he reflects that some little additional outlay would have secured his object. Whether it might have been so, or not, who can say? But there he was, with the gateway between the lamps barred against him, ex-Member of Parliament for the Chelsea Districts, with five hundred pounds in his pocket, and little or nothing else that he could call his own. What was he to do with himself?'

After trying to make himself heard upon the hustings when he was rejected, and pledging himself to stand again at the next election, he went home to his lodgings in Cecil Street, and endeavoured to consider calmly his position in the world. He had lost his inheritance. He had abandoned one profession after another, and was now beyond the pale of another chance in that direction. His ambition had betrayed him, and there were no longer possible to him any hopes of political activity. He had estranged from himself every friend that he had ever possessed. He had driven from him with violence the devotion even of his sister. He had robbed the girl whom he intended to marry of her money, and had so insulted her that no feeling of amity between them was any longer possible. He had nothing now but himself and that five hundred pounds, which he still held in his pocket. What should he do with himself and his money? He thought over it all with outer calmness for awhile, as he sat there in his arm-chair.

From the moment in which he had first become convinced that the election would go against him, and that he was therefore ruined on all sides, he had resolved that he would be calm amidst his ruin. Sometimes he assumed a little smile, as though he were laughing at his own position. Mr. Bott's day of rejection had come before his own, and he had written to Mr. Bott a drolling note of consolation and mock sympathy. He had shaken hands with Mr. Scruby, and had poked his fun at the agent, bidding him be sure to send in his little bill soon. To all who accosted him, he replied in a subrisive tone; and he bantered Calder Jones, whose seat was quite sure, till Calder Jones began to have fears that were quite unnecessary. And now, as he sat himself down, intending to come to some final decision as to what he would do, he maintained the same calmness. He smiled in the same way, though there was no one there to see the smile. He laughed even audibly once or twice, as he vainly endeavoured to persuade himself that he was able to regard the world and all that belonged to it as a bubble.

There came to him a moment in which he laughed out very audibly. 'Ha! ha!' he shouted, rising up from his chair, and he walked about the room, holding a large paper-knife in his hand. 'Ha! ha!' Then he threw the knife away from him, and thrusting his hands into his trousers-pockets, laughed again—'Ha! ha!' He stood still in the centre of the room, and the laughter was very plainly visible on his face, had there been anybody there to see it.

But suddenly there was a change upon his face, as he stood there all alone, and his eyes became fierce, and the cicatrice that marred his countenance grew to be red and ghastly, and he grinned with his teeth, and he clenched his fists as he still held them within his pockets. 'Curse him!' he said out loud. 'Curse him, now and for ever!' He had broken down in his calmness, when he thought of that old man who had opposed him during his life, and had ruined him at his death. 'May all the evils which the dead can feel cling to him for ever and ever!' His laughter was all gone, and his assumed tranquillity had deserted him. Walking across the room, he struck his foot against a chair; upon this, he took the chair in his hands, and threw it across the room. But he hardly arrested the torrent of his maledictions as he did so. What good was it that he should lie to himself by that mock tranquillity, or that false laughter? He lied to himself no longer, but uttered a song of despair that was true enough. What should he do? Where should he go? From what fountain should he attempt to draw such small draughts of the water of comfort as might support him at the present moment? Unless a man have some such fountain to which he can turn, the burden of life cannot be borne. For the moment, Vavasor tried to find such fountain in a bottle of brandy which stood near him. He half-filled a tumbler, and then, dashing some water on it, swallowed it greedily. 'By ——!' he said, 'I believe it is the best thing a man can do.'

But where was he to go? to whom was he to turn himself? He went to a high desk which stood in one corner of the room, and unlocking it, took out a revolving pistol, and for a while carried it about with him in his hand. He turned it up, and looked at it, and tried the lock, and snapped it without caps, to see that the barrel went round fairly. 'It's a beggarly thing to do,' he said, and then he turned the pistol down again; 'and if I do do it, I'll use it first for another purpose.' Then he poured out for himself more brandy-and-water, and having drunk it, he threw himself upon the sofa, and seemed to sleep.

But he did not sleep, and by-and-by there came a slight single knock at the door, which he instantly answered. But he did not answer it in the usual way by bidding the comer to come in. 'Who's there?' he said. Then the comer attempted to enter, turning the handle of the door. But the door had been locked, and the key was on Vavasor's side. 'Who's there?' he asked again, speaking out loudly, but in an angry voice. 'It is I,' said a woman's voice. 'D——ation!' said George Vavasor.

The woman heard him, but she made no sign of having heard him. She simply remained standing where she was till something further should be done within. She knew the man well, and knew that she must bide his time. She was very patient,—and for the time was meek, though it might be that there would come an end to her meekness. Vavasor, when he had heard her voice, and knew who was there, had again thrown himself on to the sofa. There flashed across his mind another thought or two as to his future career,—another idea about the pistol, which still lay upon the table. Why should he let the intruder in, and undergo the nuisance of a disagreeable interview, if the end of all things might come in time to save him from such trouble? There he lay for ten minutes thinking, and then the low single knock was heard again. He jumped upon his feet, and his eyes were full of fire. He knew that it was useless to bid her go and leave him. She would sit there, if it were through the whole night. Should he open the door and strangle her, and pass out over her with the pistol in his hand, so that he might make that other reckoning which he desired to accomplish, and then never come back any more?

He took a turn through the room, and then walked gently up to the door, and undid the lock. He did not open the door, nor did he bid his visitor enter, but having made the way easy for her if she chose to come in, he walked back to the sofa and threw himself on it again. As he did so, he passed his hand across the table so as to bring the pistol near to himself at the place where he would be lying. She paused a moment after she had heard the sound of the key, and then she made her way into the room. He did not at first speak to her. She closed the door very gently, and then, looking around, came up to the foot of the sofa. She paused a moment, waiting for him to address her; but as he said nothing, but lay there looking at her, she was the first to speak. 'George,' she said, 'what am I to do?'

She was a woman of about thirty years of age, dressed poorly, in old garments, but still with decency, and with some attempt at feminine prettiness. There were flowers in the bonnet on her head, though the bonnet had that unmistakable look of age which is quite as distressing to bonnets as it is to women, and the flowers themselves were battered and faded. She had long black ringlets on each cheek, hanging down much below her face, and brought forward so as to hide in some degree the hollowness of her jaws. Her eyes had a peculiar brightness, but now they left on those who looked at her cursorily no special impression as to their colour. They had been blue,— that dark violet blue, which is so rare, but is sometimes so lovely. Her forehead was narrow, her mouth was small, and her lips were thin; but her nose was perfect in its shape, and, by the delicacy of its modelling, had given a peculiar grace to her face in the days when things had gone well with her, when her cheeks had been full with youth and good living, and had been dimpled by the softness of love and mirth. There were no dimples there now, and all the softness which still remained was that softness which sorrow and continual melancholy give to suffering women. On her shoulders she wore a light shawl, which was fastened on her bosom with a large clasp brooch. Her faded dress was supported by a wide crinoline, but the under garment had lost all the grace of its ancient shape, and now told that woman's tale of poverty and taste for dress which is to be read in the outward garb of so many of Eve's daughters.* The whole story was told so that those who ran might read it. When she had left her home this afternoon, she had struggled hard to dress herself so that something of the charm of apparel might be left to her; but she had known of her own failure at every twist that she had given to her gown, and at every jerk with which she had settled her shawl. She had despaired at every push she had given to her old flowers, vainly striving to bring them back to their old forms; but still she had persevered. With long tedious care she had mended the old gloves which would hardly hold her fingers. She had carefully hidden the rags of her sleeves. She had washed her little shrivelled collar, and had smoothed it out painfully. It had been a separate grief to her that she could find no cuffs to put round her wrists;—and yet she knew that no cuffs could have availed her anything. Nothing could avail her now. She expected nothing from her visit; yet she had come forth anxiously, and would have waited there throughout the whole night had access to his room been debarred to her. 'George,' she said, standing at the bottom of the sofa, 'what am I to do?'

As he lay there with his face turned towards her, the windows were at her back, and he could see her very plainly. He saw and appreciated the little struggles she had made to create by her appearance some reminiscence of her former self. He saw the shining coarseness of the long ringlets which had once been softer than silk. He saw the sixpenny brooch on her bosom where he had once placed a jewel, the price of which would now have been important to him. He saw it all, and lay there for a while, silently reading it.

'Don't let me stand here,' she said, 'without speaking a word to me.'

'I don't want you to stand there,' he said.

'That's all very well, George. I know you don't want me to stand here. I know you don't want to see me ever again.'

'Never.'

'I know it. Of course I know it. But what am I to do? Where am I to go for money? Even you would not wish that I should starve.'

'That's true, too. I certainly would not wish it. I should be delighted to hear that you had plenty to eat and plenty to drink, and plenty of clothes to wear. I believe that's what you care for the most, after all.'

'It was only for your sake,—because you liked it.'

'Well;—I did like it; but that has come to an end, as have all my other likings. You know very well that I can do nothing more for you. What good do you do yourself by coming here to annoy me? Have I not told you over and over again that you were never to look for me here? It is likely that I should give you money now, simply because you have disobeyed me!'

'Where else was I to find you?'

'Why should you have found me at all? I don't want you to find me. I shall give you nothing;—not a penny. You know very well that we've had all that out before. When I put you into business I told you that we were to see no more of each other.'

'Business!' she said. 'I never could make enough out of the shop to feed a bird.'

'That wasn't my fault. Putting you there cost me over a hundred pounds, and you consented to take the place.'

'I didn't consent. I was obliged to go there because you took my other home away from me.'

'Have it as you like, my dear. That was all I could do for you;—and more than most men would have done, when all things are considered.' Then he got up from the sofa, and stood himself on the hearthrug, with his back to the fireplace. 'At any rate, you may be sure of this, Jane;—that I shall do nothing more. You have come here to torment me, but you shall get nothing by it.'

'I have come here because I am starving.'

'I have nothing for you. Now go;' and he pointed to the door. Nevertheless, for more than three years of his life this woman had been his closest companion, his nearest friend, the being with whom he was most familiar. He had loved her according to his fashion of loving, and certainly she had loved him. 'Go,' he said, repeating the word very angrily. 'Do as I bid you, or it will be the worse for you.'

'Will you give me a sovereign?'

'No;—I will give you nothing. I have desired you not to come to me here, and I will not pay you for coming.'

'Then I will not go;' and the woman sat down upon a chair at the foot of the table. 'I will not go till you have given me something to buy food. You may put me out of the room if you can, but I will lie at the door of the stairs. And if you get me out of the house, I will sit upon the door-step.'

'If you play that game, my poor girl, the police will take you.'

'Let them. It has come to that with me, that I care for nothing. Out of this I will not go till you give me money,—unless I am put out.'

And for this she had dressed herself with so much care, mending her gloves, and darning her little fragments of finery! He stood looking at her, with his hands thrust deep into his pockets,—looking at her and thinking what he had better do to rid himself of her presence. If he even quite resolved to take that little final journey of which we have spoken, with the pistol in his hand, why should he not go and leave her there? Or, for the matter of that, why should he not make her his heir to all remainder of his wealth? What he still had left was sufficient to place her in a seventh heaven of the earth. He cared but little for her, and was at this moment angry with her; but there was no one for whom he cared more, and no friend with whom he was less angry. But then his mind was not quite made up as to that final journey. Therefore he desired to rid himself and his room of the nuisance of her presence.

'Jane,' he said, looking at her again with that assumed tranquillity of which I have spoken, 'you talk of starving and of being ruined,——'

'I am starving. I have not a shilling in the world.'

'Perhaps it may be a comfort to you in your troubles to know that I am, at any rate, as badly off as you are? I won't say that I am starving, because I could get food to eat at this moment if I wanted it; but I am utterly ruined. My property, —what should have been mine,—has been left away from me. I have lost the trumpery seat in Parliament for which I have paid so much. All my relations have turned their backs upon me——'

'Are you not going to be married?' said she, rising quickly from her chair and coming close to him.

'Married! No;—but I am going to blow my brains out. Look at that pistol, my girl. Of course you won't think that I am in earnest,—but I am.'

She looked up into his face piteously. 'Oh! George,' she said, 'you won't do that?'

'But I shall do that. There is nothing else left for me to do. You talk to me about starving. I tell you that I should have no objection to be starved, and so be put an end to in that way. It's not so bad as some other ways when it comes gradually. You and I, Jane, have not played our cards very well. We have staked all that we had, and we've been beaten. It's no good whimpering after what's lost. We'd better go somewhere else and begin a new game.'

'Go where?' said she.

'Ah!—that's just what I can't tell you.'

'George,' she said, 'I'll go anywhere with you. If what you say is true,—if you're not going to be married, and will let me come to you, I will work for you like a slave. I will indeed. I know I'm poorly looking now——'

'My girl, where I'm going, I shall not want any slave; and as for your looks,—when you go there too,—they'll be of no matter, as far as I am able to judge.'

'But, George, where are you going?'

'Wherever people do go when their brains are knocked out of them; or, rather, when they have knocked out their own brains,—if that makes any difference.'

'George,'—she came up to him now, and took hold of him by the front of his coat, and for the moment he allowed her to do so,—'George, you frighten me. Do not do that. Say that you will not do that!'

'But I am just saying that I shall.'

'Are you not afraid of God's anger? You and I have been very wicked.'

'I have, my poor girl. I don't know much about your wickedness. I've been like Topsey;—indeed I am a kind of second Topsey myself. But what's the good of whimpering when it's over?'

'It isn't over; it isn't over,—at any rate for you.'

'I wish I knew how I could begin again. But all this is nonsense, Jane, and you must go.'

'You must tell me, first, that you are not going to—kill yourself.'

'I don't suppose I shall do it to-night,—or, perhaps, not to-morrow. Very probably I may allow myself a week, so that your staying here can do no good. I merely wanted to make you understand that you are not the only person who has come to grief.'

'And you are not going to be married?'

'No; I'm not going to be married, certainly.'

'And I must go now?'

'Yes; I think you'd better go now.' Then she rose and went, and he let her leave the room without giving her a shilling! His bantering tone, in speaking of his own position, had been successful. It had caused her to take herself off quietly. She knew enough of his usual manner to be aware that his threats of self-destruction were probably unreal; but, nevertheless, what he had said had created some feeling in her heart which had induced her to yield to him, and go away in peace.

CHAPTER LXXII

Showing how George Vavasor paid a Visit

IT was nearly seven o'clock in the evening,—a hot, July evening,—when the woman went from Vavasor's room, and left him there alone. It was necessary that he should immediately do something. In the first place he must dine, unless he meant to carry out his threat, and shoot himself at once. But he had no such intention as that, although he stood for some minutes with the pistol in his hand. He was thinking then of shooting some one else. But he resolved that, if he did so at all, he would not do it on that evening, and he locked up the pistol again in the standing desk. After that, he took up some papers, referring to steam packets, which were lying on his table. They contained the programmes of different companies, and showed how one vessel went on one day to New York, and another on another day would take out a load of emigrants for New Zealand and Australia. 'That's a good line,' said he, as he read a certain prospectus. 'They generally go to the bottom, and save a man from any further trouble on his own account.' Then he dressed himself, putting on his boots and coat, and went out to his club for his dinner.

London was still fairly full,—that is to say, the West-End was not deserted, although Parliament had been broken up two months earlier than usual, in preparation for the new elections. Many men who had gone down into the country were now back again in town, and the dining-room at the club was crowded. Men came up to him condoling with him, telling him that he was well rid of a great nuisance, that the present Members for the Chelsea Districts would not sit long, or that there would be another general election in a year or two. To all these little speeches he made cheerful replies, and was declared by his acquaintance to bear his disappointment well. Calder Jones came to him and talked hunting talk, and Vavasor expressed his intention of being at Roebury in November. 'You had better join our club,' said Calder Jones. In answer to which Vavasor said that he thought he would join the club. He remained in the smoking-room till nearly eleven; then he took himself home, and remained up half the night destroying papers. Every written document on which he could lay his hands he destroyed. All the pigeon-holes of his desk were emptied out, and their contents thrown into the flames. At first he looked at the papers before he burned them; but the trouble of doing so soon tired him, and he condemned them all, as he came to them, without examination. Then he selected a considerable amount of his clothes, and packed up two portmanteaus, folding his coats with care, and inspecting his boots narrowly, so that he might see which, out of the large number before him, it might be best worth his while to take with him. When that was done, he took from his desk a bag of sovereigns, and, pouring them out upon the table, he counted them out into parcels of twenty-five each, and made them up carefully into rouleaus*with paper. These, when complete, he divided among the two portmanteaus and a dressing-bag which he also packed and a travelling desk, which he filled with papers, pens, and the like. But he put into it no written document. He carefully looked through his linen, and anything that had been marked with more than his initials he rejected. Then he took out a bundle of printed cards, and furnished a card-case with them. On these cards was inscribed the name of Gregory Vance. When all was finished, he stood for awhile with his back to the fireplace contemplating his work. 'After all,' he said to himself, 'I know that I shall never start; and, if I do, nobody can hinder me, and my own name would be as good as any other. As for a man with such a face as mine not being known, that is out of the question.' But still he liked the arrangements which he had made, and when he had looked at them for awhile he went to bed.

He was up early the next morning, and had some coffee brought to him by the servant of the house, and as he drank it he had an interview with his landlady. 'He was going,' he said;—'going that very day.' It might be possible that he would change his mind; but as he would desire to start without delay, if he did go, he would pay her then what he owed her, and what would be due for her lodgings under a week's notice. The woman stared, and curtseyed, and took her money. Vavasor, though he had lately been much pressed for money, had never been so foolish as to owe debts where he lived. 'There will be some things left about, Mrs. Bunsby,' he said, 'and I will get you to keep them till I call or send.' Mrs. Bunsby said that she would, and then looked her last at him. After that interview she never saw him again.

When he was left alone he put on a rough morning coat, and taking up the pistol, placed it carefully in his pocket, and sallied forth. It was manifest enough that he had some decided scheme in his head, for he turned quickly towards the West when he reached the Strand, went across Trafalgar Square to Pall Mall East, and then turned up Suffolk Street. Just as he reached the club-house at the corner he paused and looked back, facing first one way and then the other. 'The chances are that I shall never see anything of it again,' he said to himself. Then he laughed in his own silent way, shook his head slightly, and turning again quickly on his heel, walked up the street till he reached the house of Mr. Jones, the pugilistic tailor. The reader, no doubt, has forgotten all he ever knew of Mr. Jones, the pugilistic tailor. It can soon be told again. At Mr. Jones's house John Grey lodged when he was in London, and he was in London at this moment.

Vavasor rang the bell, and as soon as the servant came he went quickly into the house, and passed her in the passage. 'Mr. Grey is at home,' he said. 'I will go up to him.' The girl said that Mr. Grey was at home, but suggested that she had better announce the gentleman. But Vavasor was already half-way up the stairs, and before the girl had reached the first landing-place, he had entered Mr. Grey's room and closed the door behind him.

Grey was sitting near the open window, in a dressing-gown, and was reading. The breakfast things were on the table, but he had not as yet breakfasted. As soon as he saw George Vavasor, he rose from his chair quickly, and put down his book. 'Mr. Vavasor,' he said, 'I hardly expected to see you in my lodgings again!'

'I dare say not,' said Vavasor; 'but, nevertheless, here I am.' He kept his right hand in the pocket which held the pistol, and held his left hand under his waistcoat.

'May I ask why you have come?' said Grey.

'I intend to tell you, at any rate, whether you ask me or not. I have come here to declare in your own hearing,—as I am in the habit of doing occasionally behind your back,—that you are a blackguard;—to spit in your face, and defy you.' As he said this he suited his action to his words, but without any

serious result. 'I have come here to see if you are man enough
to resent any insult that I can offer you; but I doubt whether
you are.'

'Nothing that you can say to me, Mr. Vavasor, will have any
effect upon me;—except that you can, of course, annoy me.'

'And I mean to annoy you, too, before I have done with you.
Will you fight me?'

'Fight a duel with you,—with pistols? Certainly not.'

'Then you are a coward, as I supposed.'

'I should be a fool if I were to do such a thing as that.'

'Look here, Mr. Grey. You managed to worm yourself into
an intimacy with my cousin, Miss Vavasor, and to become
engaged to her. When she found out what you were, how
paltry, and mean, and vile, she changed her mind, and bade
you leave her.'

'Are you here at her request?'

'I am here as her representative.'

'Self-appointed, I think.'

'Then, sir, you think wrong. I am at this moment her

330

affianced husband; and I find that, in spite of all that she has said to you,—which was enough, I should have thought, to keep any man of spirit out of her presence,—you still persecute her by going to her house, and forcing yourself upon her presence. Now, I give you two alternatives. You shall either give me your written promise never to go near her again, or you shall fight me.'

'I shall do neither one nor the other,—as you know very well yourself.'

'Stop till I have done, sir. If you have courage enough to fight me, I will meet you in any country. I will fight you here in London, or, if you are afraid of that, I will go over to France, or to America, if that will suit you better.'

'Nothing of the kind will suit me at all. I don't want to have anything to do with you.'

'Then you are a coward.'

'Perhaps I am;—but your saying so will not make me one.'

'You are a coward, and a liar, and a blackguard. I have given you the option of behaving like a gentleman, and you have refused it. Now, look here. I have come here with arms, and I do not intend to leave this room without using them, unless you will promise to give me the meeting that I have proposed.' And he took the pistol out of his pocket.

'Do you mean that you are going to murder me?' Grey asked. There were two windows in the room, and he had been sitting near to that which was furthest removed from the fireplace, and consequently furthest removed from the bell, and his visitor was now standing immediately between him and the door. He had to think what steps he might best take, and to act upon his decision instantly. He was by no means a timid man, and was one, moreover, very little prone to believe in extravagant action. He did not think, even now, that this disappointed, ruined man had come there with any intention of killing him. But he knew that a pistol in the hands of an angry man is dangerous, and that it behoved him to do his best to rid himself of the nuisance which now encumbered him. 'Do you mean that you are going to murder me?' he had said.

331

'I mean that you shall not leave this room alive unless you promise to meet me, and fight it out.' Upon hearing this, Grey turned himself towards the bell. 'If you move a step, I will fire at you,' said Vavasor. Grey paused a moment, and looked him full in the face. 'I will,' said Vavasor again.

'That would be murder,' said Grey.

'Don't think that you will frighten me by ugly words,' said Vavasor, 'I am beyond that.'

Grey had stopped for a moment to fix his eyes on the other man's face; but it was only for a moment, and then he went on to the bell. He had seen that the pistol was pointed at himself, and had once thought of rushing across the room at his adversary, calculating that a shot fired at him as he did so might miss him, and that he would then have a fair chance of disarming the madman. But his chief object was to avoid any personal conflict, to escape the indignity of a scramble for the pistol,—and especially to escape the necessity of a consequent appearance at some police-office, where he would have to justify himself, and answer the questions of a lawyer hired to cross-question him. He made, therefore, towards the bell, trusting that Vavasor would not fire at him, but having some little thought also as to the danger of the moment. It might be that everything was over for him now,—that the fatal hour had come, and that eternity was close upon him. Something of the spirit of a prayer flashed across his mind as he moved. Then he heard the click of the pistol's hammer as it fell, and was aware that his eyes were dazzled, though he was unconscious of seeing any flame. He felt something in the air, and knew that the pistol had been fired;—but he did not know whether the shot had struck him or had missed him. His hand was out for the bell-handle, and he had pulled it, before he was sure that he was unhurt.

'D——ation!' exclaimed the murderer. But he did not pull the trigger again. Though the weapon had of late been so often in his hands, he forgot, in the agitation of the moment, that his missing once was but of small matter if he chose to go on with his purpose. Were there not five other barrels for him, each making itself ready by the discharge of the other? But he had paused, forgetting, in his excitement, the use of his weapon, and before he had bethought himself that the man was still in his power, he heard the sound of the bell. 'D——ation!' he exclaimed. Then he turned round, left the room, hurried down the stairs, and made his way out into the street, having again passed the girl on his way.

Grey, when he perceived that his enemy was gone, turned round to look for the bullet or its mark. He soon found the little hole in the window-shutter, and probing it with the point of his pencil, came upon the morsel of lead which might now just as readily have been within his own brain. There he left it for the time, and then made some not inaccurate calculation as to the narrowness of his own escape. He had been standing directly between Vavasor and the shutter, and he found, from the height of the hole, that the shot must have passed close beneath his ear. He remembered to have heard the click of the hammer, but he could not remember the sound of the report, and when the girl entered the room, he perceived at once from her manner that she was unaware that fire-arms had been used.

'Has that gentleman left the house?' Grey asked. The girl said that he had left the house. 'Don't admit him again,' said he;—'that is, if you can avoid it. I believe he is not in his right senses.' Then he asked for Mr. Jones, his landlord, and in a few minutes the pugilistic tailor was with him.

During those few minutes he had been called upon to resolve what he would do now. Would he put the police at once upon the track of the murderer, who was, as he remembered too well, the first cousin of the woman whom he still desired to make his wife? That cross-examination which he would have to undergo at the police-office, and again probably in an assize court, in which all his relations with the Vavasor family would be made public, was very vivid to his imagination. That he was called upon by duty to do something he felt almost assured. The man who had been allowed to make such an attempt once with impunity, might probably make it again. But he resolved that he need not now say anything about the pistol to the pugilistic tailor, unless the tailor said something to him.

'Mr. Jones,' he said, 'that man whom I had to put out of the room once before, has been here again.'

'Has there been another tussle, sir?'

'No;—nothing of that kind. But we must take some steps to prevent his getting in again, if we can help it.'

Jones promised his aid, and offered to go at once to the police. To this, however, Mr. Grey demurred, saying that he should himself seek assistance from some magistrate. Jones promised to be very vigilant as to watching the door; and then John Grey sat down to his breakfast. Of course he thought much of what had occurred. It was impossible that he should not think much of so narrow an escape. He had probably been as near death as a man may well be without receiving any injury; and the more he thought of it, the more strongly he was convinced that he could not allow the thing to pass by without some notice, or some precaution as to the future.

At eleven o'clock he went to Scotland Yard, and saw some officer great in power over policemen, and told him all the circumstances,—confidentially. The powerful officer recommended an equally confidential reference to a magistrate; and towards evening a very confidential policeman in plain clothes paid a visit to Vavasor's lodgings in Cecil Street. But Vavasor lodged there no longer. Mrs. Bunsby, who was also very confidential,—and at her wits' end because she could not learn the special business of the stranger who called,—stated that Mr. George Vavasor left her house in a cab at ten o'clock that morning, having taken with him such luggage as he had packed, and having gone, 'she was afraid, for good,' as Mrs. Bunsby expressed it.

He had gone for good, and at the moment in which the policeman was making the inquiry in Cecil Street, was leaning over the side of an American steamer which had just got up her steam and weighed her anchor in the Mersey. He was on board at six o'clock, and it was not till the next day that the cabman was traced who had carried him to the Euston Square

Station.* Of course, it was soon known that he had gone to America, but it was not thought worth while to take any further steps towards arresting him. Mr. Grey himself was decidedly opposed to any such attempt, declaring his opinion that his own evidence would be insufficient to obtain a conviction. The big men in Scotland Yard were loath to let the matter drop. Their mouths watered after the job, and they had very numerous and very confidential interviews with John Grey. But it was decided that nothing should be done. 'Pity!' said one enterprising superintendent, in answer to the condolings of a brother superintendent. 'Pity's no name for it. It's the greatest shame as ever I knew since I joined the force. A man as was a Member of Parliament only last Session,—as belongs to no end of swell clubs, a gent as well known in London as any gent about the town! And I'd have had him back in three months, as sure as my name's Walker.' And that superintendent felt that his profession and his country were alike disgraced.

And now George Vavasor vanishes from our pages, and will be heard of no more. Roebury knew him no longer, nor Pall Mall, nor the Chelsea Districts. His disappearance was a nine days' wonder, but the world at large knew nothing of the circumstances of that attempt in Suffolk Street. Mr. Grey himself told the story to no one, till he told it to Mr. Palliser at Lucerne. Mr. Scruby complained bitterly of the way in which Vavasor had robbed him; but I doubt whether Scruby, in truth, lost much by the transaction. To Kate, down in Westmoreland, no tidings came of her brother, and her sojourn in London with her aunt had nearly come to an end before she knew that he was gone. Even then the rumour reached her through Captain Bellfield, and she learned what few facts she knew from Mrs. Bunsby in Cecil Street.

'He was always mysterious,' said Mrs. Greenow, 'and now he has vanished. I hate mysteries, and, as for myself, I think it will be much better that he should not come back again.' Perhaps Kate was of the same opinion; but, if so, she kept it to herself.

CHAPTER LXXIII

In which come Tidings of Great Moment to all the Pallisers

IT was not till they had been for a day or two together at Lucerne that Mr. Grey told Mr. Palliser the story of George Vavasor's visit to him in Suffolk Street. Having begun the history of his connection with Alice, he found himself obliged to go with it to the end, and as he described the way in which the man had vanished from the sight of all who had known him,—that he had in truth gone, so as no longer to be a cause of dread, he could not without dissimulation keep back the story of that last scene. 'And he tried to murder you!' said Mr. Palliser. 'He should be caught and,—and——' Mr. Palliser hesitated, not liking to say boldly that the first cousin of the lady who was now living with him ought to be hung.

'It is better as it is,' said Grey.

'He actually walked into your rooms in the day time, and fired a pistol at you as you were sitting at your breakfast! He did that in London, and then walked off and went abroad, as though he had nothing to fear!'

'That was just it,' said Grey.

Mr. Palliser began to think that something ought to be done to make life more secure in the metropolis of the world. Had he not known Mr. Grey, or been accustomed to see the other man in Parliament, he would not have thought so much about it. But it was almost too much for him when he reflected that one man whom he now called his friend had been nearly murdered in daylight, in the heart of his own part of London, by another man whom he had reckoned among his Parliamentary supporters. 'And he has got your money too!' said Palliser, putting all the circumstances of the case together. In answer to this Mr. Grey said that he hoped the loss might eventually be his own; but that he was bound to regard the money which had been taken as part of Miss Vavasor's fortune. 'He is simply the greatest miscreant of whom I ever heard in my life,' said Mr. Palliser. 'The wonder is that Miss

Vavasor should ever have brought herself to—to like him.' Then Mr. Grey apologised for Alice, explaining that her love for her cousin had come from her early years; that the man himself was clever and capable of assuming pleasant ways, and that he had not been wholly bad till ruin had come upon him. 'He attempted public life and made himself miserable by failing, as most men do who make that attempt,' said Grey. This was a statement which Mr. Palliser could not allow to pass without notice. Whereupon the two men got away from George Vavasor and their own individual interests, and went on seriously discussing the merits and demerits of public life. 'The end of it all is,' said Grey at last, 'that public men in England should be rich like you, and not poor like that miserable wretch, who has now lost everything that the Fates had given him.'

They continued to live at Lucerne in this way for a fortnight. Mr. Grey, though he was not unfrequently alone with Alice, did not plead his suit in direct words; but continued to live with her on terms of close and easy friendship. He had told her that her cousin had left England,—that he had gone to America immediately after his disappointment in regard to the seat in Parliament, and that he would probably not return. 'Poor George!' Alice had said; 'he is a man very much to be pitied.' 'He is a man very much to be pitied,' Grey had replied. After that, nothing more was said between them about George Vavasor. From Lady Glencora, Alice did hear something; but Lady Glencora herself had not heard the whole story. 'I believe he misbehaved himself, my dear,' Lady Glencora said; 'but then, you know, he always does that. I believe that he saw Mr. Grey and insulted him. Perhaps you had better not ask anything about it till by-and-by. You'll be able to get anything out of him then.' In answer to this Alice made her usual protest, and Lady Glencora, as was customary, told her that she was a fool.

I am inclined to think that Mr. Grey knew what he was about. Lady Glencora once scolded him very vehemently for not bringing the affair to an end. 'We shall be going on to Italy before it's settled,' she said; 'and I don't suppose you can go with us, unless it is settled.' Mr. Grey protested that he had no intention of going to Italy in either case.

'Then it will be put off for another year or two, and you are both of you as old as Adam and Eve already.'

'We ancient people are never impatient,' said Grey, laughing.

'If I were you I would go to her and tell her, roundly, that she should marry me, and then I would shake her. If you were to scold her, till she did not know whether she stood on her head or her heels, she would come to reason.'

'Suppose you try that, Lady Glencora!'

'I can't. It's she that always scolds me,—as you will her, when she's your wife. You and Mr. Palliser are very much alike. You're both of you so very virtuous that no woman would have a chance of picking a hole in your coats.'

But Lady Glencora was wrong. Alice would, no doubt, have submitted herself patiently to her lover's rebukes, and would have confessed her own sins towards him with any amount of self-accusation that he might have required; but she would not, on that account, have been more willing to obey him in that one point, as to which he now required present obedience. He understood that she must be taught to forgive herself for the evil she had done,—to forgive herself, at any rate in part,—before she could be induced to return to her old allegiance to him. Thus they went on together at Lucerne, passing quiet, idle days,—with some pretence of reading, with a considerable amount of letter-writing, with boat excursions and pony excursions,—till the pony excursions came to a sudden end by means of a violent edict, as to which, and the cause of it, a word or two must be said just now. During these days of the boats and the ponies, the carriage which Lady Glencora hated so vehemently was shut up in limbo, and things went very pleasantly with her. Mr. Palliser received political letters from England, which made his mouth water sadly, and was often very fidgety. Parliament was not now sitting, and the Government would, of course, remain intact till next February. Might it not be possible that when the rent came in the Cabinet, he might yet be present at the darning? He was a constant man, and had once declared his intention of being absent for a year. He continued to speak to Grey of his coming travels, as though it was impossible that they should be over until after the next Easter. But he was sighing for Westminster, and

regretting the blue-books which were accumulating themselves at Matching;—till on a sudden, there came to him tidings which upset all his plans, which routed the ponies, which made everything impossible, which made the Alps impassable and the railways dangerous, which drove Burgo Fitzgerald out of Mr. Palliser's head, and so confused him that he could no longer calculate the blunders of the present Chancellor of the Exchequer. All the Palliser world was about to be moved from its lowest depths, to the summits of its highest mountains. Lady Glencora had whispered into her husband's ear that she thought it probable——; she wasn't sure;—she didn't know. And then she burst out into tears on his bosom as he sat by her on her bedside.

He was beside himself when he left her, which he did with the primary intention of telegraphing to London for half a dozen leading physicians. He went out by the lake side, and walked there alone for ten minutes in a state of almost unconscious exaltation. He did not quite remember where he was, or what he was doing. The one thing in the world which he had lacked; the one joy which he had wanted so much, and which is so common among men, was coming to him also. In a few minutes it was to him as though each hand already rested on the fair head of a little male Palliser, of whom one should rule in the halls at Gatherum, and the other be eloquent among the Commons of England. Hitherto,—for the last eight or nine months, since his first hopes had begun to fade,—he had been a man degraded in his own sight amidst all his honours. What good was all the world to him if he had nothing of his own to come after him? We must give him his due, too, when we speak of this. He had not had wit enough to hide his grief from his wife; his knowledge of women and of men in social life had not been sufficient to teach him how this should be done; but he had wished to do it. He had never willingly rebuked her for his disappointment, either by a glance of his eye, or a tone of his voice; and now he had already forgiven everything. Burgo Fitzgerald was a myth. Mrs. Marsham should never again come near her. Mr. Bott was, of course, a thing abolished;—he had not even had the sense to keep his seat in Parliament. Dandy and Flirt should feed on gilded corn, and there should be an artificial moon always ready in the ruins. If only those d——able saddle-ponies of Lucerne had not come across his wife's path! He went at once into the yard and ordered that the ponies should be abolished;—sent away, one and all, to the furthest confines of the canton; and then he himself inspected the cushions of the carriage. Were they dry? As it was August in those days, and August at Lucerne is a warm month, it may be presumed that they were dry.

He then remembered that he had promised to send Alice up to his wife, and he hurried back into the house. She was alone in the breakfast-room, waiting for him and for his wife. In these days, Mr. Grey would usually join them at dinner; but he seldom saw them before eleven or twelve o'clock in the day. Then he would saunter in and join Mr. Palliser, and they would all be together till the evening. When the expectant father of embryo dukes entered the room, Alice perceived at once that some matter was astir. His manner was altogether changed, and he showed by his eye that he was eager and moved beyond his wont. 'Alice,' he said, 'would you mind going up to Glencora's room? She wishes to speak to you.' He had never called her Alice before, and as soon as the word was spoken, he remembered himself and blushed.

'She isn't ill, I hope?' said Alice.

'No;—she isn't ill. At least I think she had better not get up quite yet. Don't let her excite herself, if you can help it.'

'I'll go to her at once,' said Alice rising.

'I'm so much obliged to you;—but, Miss Vavasor——'

'You called me Alice just now, Mr. Palliser, and I took it as a great compliment.'

He blushed again. 'Did I? Very well. Then I'll do it again—if you'll let me. But, if you please, do be as calm with her as you can. She is so easily excited, you know. Of course, if there's anything she fancies, we'll take care to get it for her; but she must be kept quiet.' Upon this Alice left him, having had no moment of time to guess what had happened, or was about to happen; and he was again alone, contemplating the future glories of his house. Had he a thought for his poor cousin Jeffrey, whose nose was now so terriby out of joint? No, indeed. His thoughts were all of himself, and the good things that were coming to him,—of the new world of interest that was being opened for him. It would be better to him, this, than being Chancellor of the Exchequer. He would rather have it in store for him to be father of the next Duke of Omnium, than make half a dozen consecutive annual speeches in Parliament as to the ways and means, and expenditure of the British nation! Could it be possible that this foreign tour had produced for him this good fortune? If so, how luckily had things turned out! He would remember even that ball at Lady Monk's with gratitude. Perhaps a residence abroad would be best for Lady Glencora at this particular period of her life. If so, abroad she should certainly live. Before resolving, however, on anything permanently on this head, he thought that he might judiciously consult those six first-rate London physicians, whom, in the first moment of his excitement, he had been desirous of summoning to Lucerne.

In the meantime Alice had gone up to the bedroom of the lady who was now to be the subject of so much anxious thought. When she entered the room, her friend was up and in her dressing-gown, lying on a sofa which stood at the foot of the bed. 'Oh, Alice, I'm so glad you've come,' said Lady Glencora. 'I do so want to hear your voice.' Then Alice knelt beside her, and asked her if she were ill.

'He hasn't told you? But of course he wouldn't. How could he? But, Alice, how did he look? Did you observe anything about him? Was he pleased?'

'I did observe something, and I think he was pleased. But what is it? He called me Alice. And seemed to be quite unlike himself. But what is it? He told me that I was to come to you instantly.'

'Oh, Alice, can't you guess?' Then suddenly Alice did guess the secret, and whispered her guess into Lady Glencora's ear. 'I suppose it is so,' said Lady Glencora. 'I know what they'll do. They'll kill me by fussing over me. If I could go about my work like a washerwoman, I should be all right.'

'I am so happy,' she said, some two or three hours afterwards. 'I won't deny that I am very happy. It seemed as though I were destined to bring nothing but misery to everybody, and I used to wish myself dead so often. I shan't wish myself dead now.'

'We shall all have to go home, I suppose?' said Alice.

'He says so;—but he seems to think that I oughtn't to travel above a mile and a half a day. When I talked of going down the Rhine in one of the steamers, I thought he would have gone into a fit. When I asked him why, he gave me such a look. I know he'll make a goose of himself;—and he'll make geese of us, too; which is worse.'

On that afternoon, as they were walking together, Mr. Palliser told the important secret to his new friend, Mr. Grey. He could not deny himself the pleasure of talking about this great event. 'It is a matter, you see, of such immense importance to me,' Mr. Palliser said.

'Indeed, it is,' said Grey. 'Every man feels that when a child is about to be born to him.' But this did not at all satisfy Mr. Palliser.

'Yes,' said he. 'That's of course. It is an important thing to everybody;—very important, no doubt. But, when a man ——. You see, Grey, I don't think a man is a bit better because he is rich, or because he has a title; nor do I think he is likely to be in any degree the happier. I am quite sure that he has no right to be in the slightest degree proud of that which he has had no hand in doing for himself.'

'Men usually are very proud of such advantages,' said Grey.

'I don't think that I am; I don't, indeed. I am proud of some things. Whenever I can manage to carry a point in the House, I feel very proud of it. I don't think I ever knocked under to any one, and I am proud of that.' Perhaps, Mr. Palliser was thinking of a certain time*when his uncle the Duke had threatened him, and he had not given way to the Duke's threats. 'But I don't think I'm proud because chance has made me my uncle's heir.'

'Not in the least, I should say.'

'But I do feel that a son to me is of more importance than it is to most men. A strong anxiety on the subject, is, I think, more excusable in me than it might be in another. I don't know whether I quite make myself understood?'

'Oh, yes! When there's a dukedom and heaven knows how many thousands a year to be disposed of, the question of their future ownership does become important.'

'This property is so much more interesting to one, if one feels that all one does to it is done for one's own son.'

'And yet,' said Grey, 'of all the great plunderers of property throughout Europe, the Popes have been the most greedy.'

'Perhaps it's different, when a man can't have a wife,' said Mr. Palliser.

From all this it may be seen that Mr. Palliser and Mr. Grey had become very intimate. Had chance brought them together in London they might have met a score of times before Mr. Palliser would have thought of doing more than bowing to such an acquaintance. Mr. Grey might have spent weeks at Matching, without having achieved anything like intimacy with its noble owner. But things of that kind progress more quickly abroad than they do at home. The deck of an ocean steamer, is perhaps the most prolific hotbed for the growth of sudden friendships; but an hotel by the side of a Swiss lake does almost as well.

For some time after this Lady Glencora's conduct was frequently so indiscreet as to drive her husband almost to frenzy. On the very day after the news had been communicated to him, she proposed a picnic, and made the proposition not only in the presence of Alice, but in that of Mr. Grey also! Mr. Palliser, on such an occasion, could not express all that he thought; but he looked it.

'What is the matter, now, Plantagenet?' said his wife.

'Nothing,' said he;—'nothing. Never mind.'

'And shall we make this party up to the chapel?'

The chapel in question was Tell's chapel,*—ever so far up the lake. A journey in a steam-boat would have been necessary.

'No!' said he, shouting out his refusal at her. 'We will not.'

'You needn't be angry about it,' said she;—as though he could have failed to be stirred by such a proposition at such a time. On another occasion she returned from an evening walk, showing on her face some sign of the exercise she had taken.

'Good G—! Glencora,' said he, 'do you mean to kill yourself?'

He wanted her to eat six or seven times a day; and always told her that she was eating too much, remembering some ancient proverb about little and often. He watched her now as closely as Mrs. Marsham and Mr. Bott had watched her before; and she always knew that he was doing so. She made the matter worse by continually proposing to do things which she knew he would not permit, in order that she might enjoy the fun of seeing his agony and amazement. But this, though it was fun to her at the moment, produced anything but fun, as its general result.

'Upon my word, Alice, I think this will kill me,' she said. 'I am not to stir out of the house now, unless I go in the carriage, or he is with me.'

'It won't last long.'

'I don't know what you call long. As for walking with him, it's out of the question. He goes about a mile an hour. And then he makes me look so much like a fool. I had no idea that he would be such an old coddle.'

'The coddling will all be given to some one else, very soon.'

'No baby could possibly live through it, if you mean that. If there is a baby——'

'I suppose there will be one, by-and-by,' said Alice.

'Don't be a fool! But if there is, I shall take that matter into my own hands. He can do what he pleases with me, and I can't help myself; but I shan't let him or anybody do what they please with my baby. I know what I'm about in such matters a great deal better than he does. I've no doubt he's a very clever man in Parliament; but he doesn't seem to me to understand anything else.'

Alice was making some very wise speech in answer to this, when Lady Glencora interrupted her.

'Mr. Grey wouldn't make himself so troublesome, I'm quite sure.' Then Alice held her tongue.

When the first consternation arising from the news had somewhat subsided,—say in a fortnight from the day in which Mr. Palliser was made so triumphant,—and when tidings had been duly sent to the Duke, and an answer from his Grace had come, arrangements were made for the return of the party to England. The Duke's reply was very short:—

'MY DEAR PLANTAGENET,—Give my kind love to Glencora. If it's a boy, of course I will be one of the godfathers. The Prince, who is very kind, will perhaps oblige me by being the other. I should advise you to return as soon as convenient.

'Your affectionate uncle,
'OMNIUM.'

That was the letter; and short as it was, it was probably the longest that Mr. Palliser had ever received from the Duke.

There was great trouble about the mode of their return.

'Oh, what nonsense,' said Glencora. 'Let us get into an express train, and go right through to London.' Mr. Palliser looked at her with a countenance full of rebuke and sorrow. He was always so looking at her now. 'If you mean, Plantagenet, that we are to be dragged all across the Continent in that horrible carriage, and be a thousand days on the road, I for one won't submit to it.' 'I wish I had never told him a word about it,' she said afterwards to Alice. 'He would never have found it out himself, till this thing was all over.'

Mr. Palliser did at last consent to take the joint opinion of a Swiss doctor and an English one who was settled at Berne; and who, on the occasion, was summoned to Lucerne. They suggested the railway; and as letters arrived for Mr. Palliser, —medical letters,—in which the same opinion was broached, it was agreed, at last, that they should return by railway; but they were to make various halts on the road, stopping at each halting-place for a day. The first was, of course, Basle, and from Basle they were to go on to Baden.

'I particularly want to see Baden again,' Lady Glencora said; 'and perhaps I may be able to get back my napoleon.'

CHAPTER LXXIV

Showing what happened in the Churchyard

THESE arrangements as to the return of Mr. Palliser's party to London did not, of course, include Mr. Grey. They were generally discussed in Mr. Grey's absence, and communicated to him by Mr. Palliser. 'I suppose we shall see you in England before long?' said Mr. Palliser. 'I shall be able to tell you that before you go,' said Grey. 'Not but that in any event I shall return to England before the winter.'

'Then come to us at Matching,' said Mr. Palliser. 'We shall be most happy to have you. Say that you'll come for the first fortnight in December. After that we always go to the Duke, in Barsetshire. Though, by-the-by, I don't suppose we shall go anywhere this year,' Mr. Palliser added, interrupting the warmth of his invitation, and reflecting that, under the present circumstances, perhaps, it might be improper to have any guests at Matching in December. But he had become very fond of Mr. Grey, and on this occasion, as he had done on some others, pressed him warmly to make an attempt at Parliament. 'It isn't nearly so difficult as you think,' said he, when Grey declared that he would not know where to look for a seat. 'See the men that get in. There was Mr. Vavasor. Even he got a seat.'

'But he had to pay for it very dearly.'

'You might easily find some quiet little borough.'

'Quiet little boroughs have usually got their own quiet little Members,' said Grey.

'They're fond of change; and if you like to spend a thousand pounds, the thing isn't difficult. I'll put you in the way of it.' But Mr. Grey still declined. He was not a man prone to be talked out of his own way of life, and the very fact that George Vavasor had been in Parliament would of itself have gone far towards preventing any attempt on his part in that direction. Alice had also wanted him to go into public life, but he had put aside her request as though the thing were quite out of the question,—never giving a moment to its consideration. Had she asked him to settle himself and her in Central Africa, his manner and mode of refusal would have been the same. It was this immobility on his part,—this absolute want of any of the weakness of indecision, which had frightened her, and driven her away from him. He was partly aware of this; but that which he had declined to do at her solicitation, he certainly would not do at the advice of any one else. So it was that he argued the matter with himself. Had he now allowed himself to be so counselled, with what terrible acknowledgments of his own faults must he not have presented himself before Alice?

'I suppose books, then, will be your object in life?' said Mr. Palliser.

'I hope they will be my aids,' Grey answered. 'I almost doubt whether any object such as that you mean is necessary for life, or even expedient. It seems to me that if a man can so train himself that he may live honestly and die fearlessly, he has done about as much as is necessary.'

'He has done a great deal, certainly,' said Mr. Palliser, who was not ready enough to carry on the argument as he might have done had more time been given to him to consider it. He knew very well that he himself was working for others, and not for himself; and he was aware, though he had not analyzed his own convictions on the matter, that good men struggle as they do in order that others, besides themselves, may live honestly, and, if possible, die fearlessly. The recluse of Nethercoats had thought much more about all this than the rising star of the House of Commons; but the philosophy of the rising star was the better philosophy of the two, though he was by far the less brilliant man. 'I don't see why a man should not live honestly and be a Member of Parliament as well,' continued Mr. Palliser, when he had been silent for a few minutes.

'Nor I either,' said Grey. 'I am sure that there are such men, and that the country is under great obligation to them. But they are subject to temptations which a prudent man like myself may perhaps do well to avoid.' But though he spoke with an assured tone, he was shaken, and almost regretted that he did not accept the aid which was offered to him. It is astonishing how strong a man may be to those around him,—how impregnable may be his exterior, while within he feels himself to be as weak as water, and as unstable as chaff.

But the object which he had now in view was a renewal of his engagement with Alice, and he felt that he must obtain an answer from her before they left Lucerne. If she still persisted in refusing to give him her hand, it would not be consistent with his dignity as a man to continue his immediate pursuit of her any longer. In such case he must leave her, and see what future time might bring forth. He believed himself to be aware that he would never offer his love to another woman;

and if Alice were to remain single, he might try again, after the lapse of a year or two. But if he failed now,—then, for that year or two, he would see her no more. Having so resolved, and being averse to anything like a surprise, he asked her, as he left her one evening, whether she would walk with him on the following morning. That morning would be the morning of her last day at Lucerne; and as she assented she knew well what was to come. She said nothing to Lady Glencora on the subject, but allowed the coming prospects of the Palliser family to form the sole subject of their conversation that night, as it had done on every night since the great news had become known. They were always together for an hour every evening before Alice was allowed to go to bed, and during this hour the anxieties of the future father and mother were always discussed till Alice Vavasor was almost tired of them. But she was patient with her friend, and on this special night she was patient as ever. But when she was released and was alone, she made a great endeavour to come to some fixed resolution as to what she would do on the morrow,—some resolution which should be absolutely resolute, and from which no eloquence on the part of any one should move her. But such resolutions are not easily reached, and Alice laboured through half the night almost in vain. She knew that she loved the man. She knew that he was as true to her as the sun is true to the earth. She knew that she would be, in all respects, safe in his hands. She knew that Lady Glencora would be delighted, and her father gratified. She knew that the countesses would open their arms to her,—though I doubt whether this knowledge was in itself very persuasive. She knew that by such a marriage she would gain all that women generally look to gain when they give themselves away. But, nevertheless, as far as she could decide at all, she decided against her lover. She had no right of her own to be taken back after the evil that she had done, and she did not choose to be taken back as an object of pity and forgiveness.

'Where are you going?' said her cousin, when she came in with her hat on, soon after breakfast.

'I am going to walk,—with Mr. Grey.'

'By appointment?'

'Yes, by appointment. He asked me yesterday.'

'Then it's all settled, and you haven't told me!'

'All that is settled I have told you very often. He asked me yesterday to walk with him this morning, and I could not well refuse him.'

'Why should you have wished to refuse him?'

'I haven't said that I did wish it. But I hate scenes, and I think it would have been pleasanter for us to have parted without any occasion for special words.'

'Alice, you are such a fool!'

'So you tell me very often.'

'Of course he is now going to say the very thing that he has come all this way for the purpose of saying. He has been wonderfully slow about it; but then slow as he is, you are slower. If you don't make it up with him now, I really shall think you are very wicked. I am becoming like Lady Midlothian;—I can't understand it. I know you want to be his wife, and I know he wants to be your husband, and the only thing that keeps you apart is your obstinacy,—just because you have said you wouldn't have him. My belief is that if Lady Midlothian and the rest of us were to pat you on the back, and tell you how right you were, you'd ask him to take you, out of defiance. You may be sure of this, Alice; if you refuse him now, it'll be for the last time.'

This, and much more of the same kind, she bore before Mr. Grey came to take her, and she answered to it all as little as she could. 'You are making me very unhappy, Glencora,' she said once. 'I wish I could break you down with unhappiness,' Lady Glencora answered, 'so that he might find you less stiff, and hard, and unmanageable.' Directly upon that he came in, looking as though he had no business on hand more exciting than his ordinary morning's tranquil employments. Alice at once got up to start with him. 'So you and Alice are going to make your adieux,' said Lady Glencora. 'It must be done sooner or later,' said Mr. Grey; and then they went off.

Those who know Lucerne,—and almost everybody now does know Lucerne,—will remember the big hotel which has been built close to the landing-pier of the steamers, and will remember also the church that stands upon a little hill or rising ground, to the left of you, as you come out of the inn upon the lake. The church*is immediately over the lake, and round the church there is a burying-ground, and skirting the burying-ground there are cloisters, through the arches and apertures of which they who walk and sit there look down immediately upon the blue water, and across the water upon the frowning menaces of Mount Pilate.* It is one of the prettiest spots in that land of beauty; and its charm is to my feeling enhanced by the sepulchral monuments over which I walk, and by which I am surrounded, as I stand there. Up here, into these cloisters, Alice and John Grey went together. I doubt whether he had formed any purpose of doing so. She certainly would have gone without a question in any direction that he might have led her. The distance from the inn up to the church-gate did not take them ten minutes, and when they were there their walk was over. But the place was solitary, and they were alone; and it might be as well for Mr. Grey to speak what words he had to say there as elsewhere. They had often been together in those cloisters before, but on such occasions either Mr. Palliser or Lady Glencora had been with them. On their slow passage up the hill very little was spoken, and that little was of no moment. 'We will go in here for a few minutes,' he said. 'It is the prettiest spot about Lucerne, and we don't know when we may see it again.' So they went in, and sat down on one of the embrasures that open from the cloisters over the lake.

'Probably never again,' said Alice. 'And yet I have been here now two years running.'

She shuddered as she remembered that in that former year George Vavasor had been with her. As she thought of it all she hated herself. Over and over again she had told herself that she had so mismanaged the latter years of her life that it was impossible for her not to hate herself. No woman had a clearer idea of feminine constancy than she had, and no woman had sinned against that idea more deeply. He gave her time to think of all this as he sat there looking down upon the water.

'And yet I would sooner live in Cambridgeshire,' were the first words he spoke.

'Why so?'

'Partly because all beauty is best enjoyed when it is sought for with some trouble and difficulty, and partly because such beauty, and the romance which is attached to it, should not make up the staple of one's life. Romance, if it is to come at all, should always come by fits and starts.'

'I should like to live in a pretty country.'

'And would like to live a romantic life,—no doubt; but all those things lose their charm if they are made common. When a man has to go to Vienna or St. Petersburg two or three times a month, you don't suppose he enjoys travelling?'

'All the same, I should like to live in a pretty country,' said Alice.

'And I want you to come and live in a very ugly country.' Then he paused for a minute or two, not looking at her, but gazing still on the mountain opposite. She did not speak a word, but looked as he was looking. She knew that the request was coming, and had been thinking about it all night; but now that it had come she did not know how to bear herself. 'I don't think,' he went on to say, 'that you would let that consideration stand in your way, if on other grounds you were willing to become my wife.'

'What consideration?'

'Because Nethercoats is not so pretty as Lucerne.'

'It would have nothing to do with it,' said Alice.

'It should have nothing to do with it.'

'Nothing; nothing at all,' repeated Alice.

'Will you come, then? Will you come and be my wife, and help me to be happy amidst all that ugliness? Will you come and be my one beautiful thing, my treasure, my joy, my comfort, my counsellor?'

'You want no counsellor, Mr. Grey.'

'No man ever wanted one more. Alice, this has been a bad year to me, and I do not think that it has been a happy one for you.'

'Indeed, no.'

'Let us forget it,—or rather, let us treat it as though it were forgotten. Twelve months ago you were mine. You were, at any rate, so much mine that I had a right to boast of my possession among my friends.'

'It was a poor boast.'

'They did not seem to think so. I had but one or two to whom I could speak of you, but they told me that I was going to be a happy man. As to myself, I was sure that I was to be so. No man was ever better contented with his bargain than I was with mine. Let us go back to it, and the last twelve months shall be as though they had never been.'

'That cannot be, Mr. Grey. If it could, I should be worse even than I am.'

'Why cannot it be?'

'Because I cannot forgive myself what I have done, and because you ought not to forgive me.'

'But I do. There has never been an hour with me in which there has been an offence of yours rankling in my bosom unforgiven. I think you have been foolish, misguided,—led away by a vain ambition, and that in the difficulty to which these things brought you, you endeavoured to constrain yourself to do an act, which, when it came near to you,—when the doing of it had to be more closely considered, you found to be contrary to your nature.' Now, as he spoke thus, she turned her eyes upon him, and looked at him, wondering that he should have had power to read her heart so accurately. 'I never believed that you would marry your cousin. When I was told of it, I knew that trouble had blinded you for awhile. You had driven yourself to revolt against me, and upon that your heart misgave you, and you said to yourself that it did not matter then how you might throw away all your sweetness. You see that I speak of your old love for me with the frank conceit of a happy lover.'

'No;—no, no!' she ejaculated.

'But the storm passes over the tree and does not tear it up by the roots or spoil it of all its symmetry. When we hear the winds blowing, and see how the poor thing is shaken, we think that its days are numbered and its destruction at hand. Alice, when the winds were shaking you, and you were torn and buffeted, I never thought so. There may be some who will forgive you slowly. Your own self-forgiveness will be slow. But I, who have known you better than any one,—yes, better than any one,—I have forgiven you everything, have forgiven you instantly. Come to me, Alice, and comfort me. Come to me, for I want you sorely.' She sat quite still, looking at the lake and the mountain beyond, but she said nothing. What could she say to him? 'My need of you is much greater now,' he went on to say, 'than when I first asked you to share the world with me. Then I could have borne to lose you, as I had never boasted to myself that you were my own,—had never pictured to myself the life that might be mine if you were always to be with me. But since that day I have had no other hope,—no other hope but this for which I plead now. Am I to plead in vain?'

'You do not know me,' she said; 'how vile I have been! You do not think what it is,—for a woman to have promised herself to one man while she loved another.'

'But it was me you loved. Ah! Alice, I can forgive that. Do I not tell you that I did forgive it the moment that I heard it? Do you not hear me say that I never for a moment thought that you would marry him? Alice, you should scold me for my vanity, for I have believed all through that you loved me, and me only. Come to me, dear, and tell me that it is so, and the past shall be only as a dream.'

'I am dreaming it always,' said Alice.

'They will cease to be bitter dreams if your head be upon my shoulder. You will cease to reproach yourself when you know that you have made me happy.'

'I shall never cease to reproach myself. I have done that which no woman can do and honour herself afterwards. I have been——a jilt.'

'The noblest jilt that ever yet halted between two minds! There has been no touch of selfishness in your fickleness. I think I could be hard enough upon a woman who had left me for greater wealth, for a higher rank,—who had left me even that she might be gay and merry. It has not been so with you.'

'Yes, it has. I thought you were too firm in your own will, and——'

'And you think so still. Is that it?'

'It does not matter what I think now. I am a fallen creature, and have no longer a right to such thoughts. It will be better for us both that you should leave me,—and forget me. There are things which, if a woman does them, should never be forgotten;—which she should never permit herself to forget.'

'And am I to be punished then, because of your fault? Is that your sense of justice?' He got up, and standing before her, looked down upon her. 'Alice, if you will tell me that you do not love me, I will believe you, and will trouble you no more. I know that you will say nothing to me that is false. Through it all you have spoken no word of falsehood. If you love me, after what has passed, I have a right to demand your hand. My happiness requires it, and I have a right to expect your compliance. I do demand it. If you love me, Alice, I tell you that you dare not refuse me. If you do so, you will fail hereafter to reconcile it to your conscience before God.'

Then he stopped his speech, and waited for a reply; but Alice sat silent beneath his gaze, with her eyes turned upon the tombstones beneath her feet. Of course she had no choice but to yield. He, possessed of power and force infinitely greater than hers, had left her no alternative but to be happy. But there still clung to her what I fear we must call a perverseness of obstinacy, a desire to maintain the resolution she had made, —a wish that she might be allowed to undergo the punishment she had deserved. She was as a prisoner who would fain cling to his prison after pardon has reached him, because he is conscious that the pardon is undeserved. And it may be that there was still left within her bosom some remnant of that feeling of rebellion which his masterful spirit had ever produced in her. He was so imperious in his tranquillity, he argued his question of such love with a manifest preponderance of right on his side, that she had always felt that to yield to him would be to confess the omnipotence of his power. She knew now that she must yield to him,—that his power over her was omnipotent. She was pressed by him as in some countries the prisoner is pressed by the judge,—so pressed that she acknowledged to herself silently that any further antagonism to him was impossible. Nevertheless, the word which she had to speak still remained unspoken, and he stood over her, waiting for her answer. Then slowly he sat down beside her, and gradually he put his arm round her waist. She shrank from him, back against the stonework of the embrasure, but she could not shrink away from his grasp. She put up her hand to impede his, but his hand, like his character and his words, was full of power. It would not be impeded. 'Alice,' he said, as he pressed her close with his arm, 'the battle is over now, and I have won it.'

'You win everything,—always,' she said, whispering to him, as she still shrank from his embrace.

'In winning you I have won everything.' Then he put his face over her and pressed his lips to hers. I wonder whether he was made happier when he knew that no other touch had profaned those lips since last he had pressed them?

CHAPTER LXXV

Rouge et Noir*

ALICE insisted on being left up in the churchyard, urging that she wanted to 'think about it all,' but, in truth, fearing that she might not be able to carry herself well, if she were to walk down with her lover to the hotel. To this he made no objection, and, on reaching the inn, met Mr. Palliser in the hall. Mr. Palliser was already inspecting the arrangement of certain large trunks which had been brought down-stairs, and was preparing for their departure. He was going about the house, with a nervous solicitude to do something, and was flattering himself that he was of use. As he could not be Chancellor of the Exchequer, and as, by the nature of his disposition, some employment was necessary to him, he was looking to the cording of the boxes. 'Good morning! good morning!' he said to Grey, hardly looking at him, as though time were too precious with him to allow of his turning his eyes upon his friend. 'I am going up to the station to see after a carriage for to-morrow. Perhaps you'll come with me.' To this proposition Mr. Grey assented. 'Sometimes, you know,' continued Mr. Palliser, 'the springs of the carriages are so very rough.' Then, in a very few words, Mr. Grey told him what had been his own morning's work. He hated secrets and secrecy, and as the Pallisers knew well what had brought him upon their track, it was, he thought, well that they should know that he had been successful. Mr. Palliser congratulated him very cordially, and then, running up-stairs for his gloves or his stick, or, more probably, that he might give his wife one other caution as to her care of herself, he told her also that Alice had yielded at last. 'Of course she has,' said Lady Glencora.

'I really didn't think she would,' said he.

'That's because you don't understand things of that sort,' said his wife. Then the caution was repeated, the mother of the future duke was kissed, and Mr. Palliser went off on his mission about the carriage, its cushions, and its springs. In the course of their walk Mr. Palliser suggested that, as things were settled so pleasantly, Mr. Grey might as well return with them to England, and to this suggestion Mr. Grey assented.

Alice remained alone for nearly an hour, looking out upon the rough sides and gloomy top of Mount Pilate. No one disturbed her in the churchyard;—no steps were heard along the tombstones,—no voice sounded through the cloisters. She was left in perfect solitude to think of the past, and form her plans of the future. Was she happy, now that the manner of her life to come was thus settled for her; that all further question as to the disposal of herself was taken out of her hands, and that her marriage with a man she loved was

so firmly arranged that no further folly of her own could disarrange it? She was happy, though she was slow to confess her
happiness to herself. She was happy, and she was resolute in
this,—that she would now do all she could to make him happy
also. And there must now, she acknowledged, be an end to her
pride,—to that pride which had hitherto taught her to think
that she could more wisely follow her own guidance than that
of any other who might claim to guide her. She knew now
that she must follow his guidance. She had found her master,
as we sometimes say, and laughed to herself with a little inward laughter as she confessed that it was so. She was from
henceforth altogether in his hands. If he chose to tell her that
they were to be married at Michaelmas, or at Christmas, or on
Lady Day, they would, of course, be married accordingly. She
had taken her fling at having her own will, and she and all her
friends had seen what had come of it. She had assumed the
command of the ship, and had thrown it upon the rocks, and
she felt that she never ought to take the captain's place again.
It was well for her that he who was to be captain was one
whom she respected as thoroughly as she loved him.

She would write to her father at once,—to her father and
Lady Macleod,—and would confess everything. She felt that
she owed it to them that they should be told by herself that
they had been right and that she had been wrong. Hitherto
she had not mentioned to either of them the fact that Mr. Grey
was with them in Switzerland. And, then, what must she do
as to Lady Midlothian? As to Lady Midlothian, she would do
nothing. Lady Midlothian, of course, would triumph;—would
jump upon her, as Lady Glencora had once expressed it, with
very triumphant heels,—would try to patronise her, or, which
would be almost worse, would make a parade of her forgiveness. But she would have nothing to do with Lady Midlothian,
unless, indeed, Mr. Grey should order it. Then she laughed at
herself again with that inward laughter, and, rising from her
seat, proceeded to walk down the hill to the hotel.

'Vanquished at last!' said Lady Glencora, as Alice entered
the room.

'Yes, vanquished; if you like to call it so,' said Alice.

'It is not what I call it, but what you feel it,' said the other. 'Do you think that I don't know you well enough to be sure that you regard yourself now as an unfortunate prisoner,—as a captive taken in war, to be led away in triumph, without any hope of a ransom? I know that it is quite a misery to you that you should be made a happy woman of at last. I understand it all, my dear, and my heart bleeds for you.'

'Of course; I knew that was the way you would treat me.'

'In what way would you have me treat you? If I were to hug you with joy, and tell you how good he is, and how fortunate you are,—if I were to praise him, and bid you triumph in your success, as might be expected on such an occasion,— you would put on a long face at once, and tell me that though the thing is to be, it would be much better that the thing shouldn't be. Don't I know you, Alice?'

'I shouldn't have said that;—not now.'

'I believe in my heart you would;—that, or something like it. But I do wish you joy all the same, and you may say what you please. He has got you in his power now, and I don't think even you can go back.'

'No; I shall not go back again.'

'I would join with Lady Midlothian in putting you into a mad-house, if you did. But I am so glad; I am, indeed. I was afraid to the last,—terribly afraid; you are so hard and so proud. I don't mean hard to me, dear. You have never been half hard enough to me. But you are hard to yourself, and, upon my word, you have been hard to him. What a deal you will have to make up to him!'

'I feel that I ought to stand before him always as a penitent, —in a white sheet.'

'He will like it better, I dare say, if you will sit upon his knee. Some penitents do, you know. And how happy you will be! He'll never explain the sugar-duties*to you, and there'll be no Mr. Bott at Nethercoats.' They sat together the whole morning,—while Mr. Palliser was seeing to the springs and cushions,—and by degrees Alice began to enjoy her happiness.

As she did so her friend enjoyed it with her, and at last they had something of the comfort and excitement which such an occasion should give. 'I'll tell you what, Alice; you shall come and be married at Matching, in August, or perhaps September. That's the only way in which I can be present; and if we can bespeak some sun, we'll have the breakfast out in the ruins.'

On the following morning they all started together, a first-class compartment having been taken for the Palliser family, and a second-class compartment close to them for the Palliser servants. Mr. Palliser, as he slowly handed his wife in, was a triumphant man; as was also Mr. Grey, as he handed in his lady-love, though, in a manner, much less manifest. We may say that both the gentlemen had been very fortunate while at Lucerne. Mr. Palliser had come abroad with a feeling that all the world had been cut from under his feet. A great change was needed for his wife, and he had acknowledged at once that everything must be made to yield to that necessity. He certainly had his reward,—now in his triumphant return. Terrible troubles had afflicted him as he went, which seemed now to have dissipated themselves altogether. When he thought of Burgo Fitzgerald he remembered him only as a poor, unfortunate fellow, for whom he should be glad to do something, if the doing of anything were only in his power; and he had in his pocket a letter which he had that morning received from the Duke of St. Bungay, marked private and confidential, which was in its nature very private and confidential, and in which he was told that Lord Brock and Mr. Finespun were totally at variance about French wines.* Mr. Finespun wanted to do something, now in the recess,—to send some political agent over to France,—to which Lord Brock would not agree; and no one knew what would be the consequence of this disagreement. Here might be another chance,—if only Mr. Palliser could give up his winter in Italy! Mr. Palliser, as he took his place opposite his wife, was very triumphant.

And Mr. Grey was triumphant, as he placed himself gently in his seat opposite to Alice. He seemed to assume no right, as he took that position apparently because it was the one which came naturally to his lot. No one would have been made aware that Alice was his own simply by seeing his arrangements for her comfort. He made no loud assertion as to his property and his rights, as some men do. He was quiet and subdued in his joy, but not the less was he triumphant. From

the day on which Alice had accepted his first offer,—nay, from an earlier day than that; from the day on which he had first resolved to make it, down to the present hour, he had never been stirred from his purpose. By every word that he had said, and by every act that he had done, he had shown himself to be unmoved by that episode in their joint lives, which Alice's other friends had regarded as so fatal. When she first rejected him, he would not take his rejection. When she told him that she intended to marry her cousin, he silently declined to believe that such marriage would ever take place. He had never given her up for a day, and now the event proved that he had been right. Alice was happy, very happy; but she was still disposed to regard her lover as Fate, and her happiness as an enforced necessity.

They stopped a night at Basle, and again she stood upon

the balcony. He was close to her as she stood there,—so close that, putting out her hand for his, she was able to take it and press it closely. 'You are thinking of something, Alice,' he said. 'What is it?'

'It was here,' she said—'here, on this very balcony, that I first rebelled against you, and now you have brought me here that I should confess and submit on the same spot. I do confess. How am I to thank you for forgiving me?'

On the following morning they went on to Baden-Baden, and there they stopped for a couple of days. Lady Glencora had positively refused to stop a day at Basle, making so many objections to the place that her husband had at last yielded. 'I could go from Vienna to London without feeling it,' she said, with indignation; 'and to tell me that I can't do two easy days' journey running!' Mr. Palliser had been afraid to be imperious, and therefore, immediately on his arrival at one of the stations in Basle, he had posted across the town, in the heat and the dust, to look after the cushions and the springs at the other.

'I've a particular favour to ask of you,' Lady Glencora said to her husband, as soon as they were alone together in their rooms at Baden. Mr. Palliser declared that he would grant her any particular favour,—only promising that he was not to be supposed to have thereby committed himself to any engagement under which his wife should have authority to take any exertion upon herself. 'I wish I were a milkmaid,' said Lady Glencora.

'But you are not a milkmaid, my dear. You haven't been brought up like a milkmaid.'

But what was the favour? If she would only ask for jewels, —though they were the Grand Duchess's diamond eardrops, he would endeavour to get them for her. If she would have quaffed molten pearls, like Cleopatra, he would have procured the beverage,—having first fortified himself with a medical opinion as to the fitness of the drink for a lady in her condition. There was no expenditure that he would not willingly incur for her, nothing costly that he would grudge. But when she asked for a favour, he was always afraid of an imprudence.

Very possibly she might want to drink beer in an open garden.

And her request was, at last, of this nature! 'I want you to take me up to the gambling-rooms,' said she.

'The gambling-rooms!' said Mr. Palliser in dismay.

'Yes, Plantagenet; the gambling-rooms. If you had been with me before, I should not have made a fool of myself by putting my piece of money on the table. I want to see the place; but then I saw nothing, because I was so frightened when I found that I was winning.'

Mr. Palliser was aware that all the world of Baden,—or rather the world of the strangers at Baden,—assembles itself in those salons. It may be also that he himself was curious to see how men looked when they lost their own money, or won that of others. He knew how a Minister looked when he lost or gained a tax. He was familiar with millions and tens of millions in a committee of the whole House. He knew the excitement of a near division upon the estimates. But he had never yet seen a poor man stake his last napoleon, and rake back from off the table a small hatful of gold. A little exercise after an early dinner was, he had been told, good for his wife; and he agreed therefore that, on their second evening at Baden, they would all walk up and see the play.

'Perhaps I shall get back my napoleon,' said Glencora to Alice.

'And perhaps I shall be forgiven when somebody sees how difficult it is to manage you,' said Alice, looking at Mr. Palliser.

'She isn't in earnest,' said Mr. Palliser, almost fearing the result of the experiment.

'I don't know that,' said Lady Glencora.

They started together, Mr. Palliser with his wife, and Mr. Grey with Alice on his arm, and found all the tables at work. They at first walked through the different rooms, whispering to each other their comments on the people that they saw, and listening to the quick, low, monotonous words of the croupiers as they arranged and presided over the games. Each table was closely surrounded by its own crowd, made up of players, embryo players, and simple lookers-on, so that they could not see much as they walked. But this was not enough for Lady Glencora. She was anxious to know what these men and women were doing,—to see whether the croupiers wore horns on their heads and were devils indeed,—to behold the faces of those who were wretched and of those who were triumphant, —to know how the thing was done, and to learn something of that lesson in life. 'Let us stand here a moment,' she said to her husband, arresting him at one corner of the table which had the greatest crowd. 'We shall be able to see in a few minutes.' So he stood with her there, giving way to Alice, who went in front with his wife; and in a minute or two an aperture was made, so that they could all see the marked cloth, and the money lying about, and the rakes on the table, and the croupier skilfully dealing his cards, and,—more interesting than all the rest, the faces of those who were playing. Grey looked on, over Alice's shoulder, very attentively,—as did Palliser also,—but both of them kept their eyes upon the ministers of the work. Alice and Glencora did the same at first, but as they gained courage they glanced round upon the gamblers.

It was a long table, having, of course, four corners, and at the corner appropriated by them they were partly opposite to the man who dealt the cards. The corner answering to theirs at the other end was the part of the table most removed from their sight, and that on which their eyes fell last. As Lady Glencora stood she could hardly see,—indeed, at first she could not see,—one or two who were congregated at this spot. Mr. Palliser, who was behind her, could not see them at all. But to Alice,—and to Mr. Grey, had he cared about it,—every face at the table was visible except the faces of those who were immediately close to them. Before long Alice's attention was riveted on the action and countenance of one young man who sat at that other corner. He was leaning, at first listlessly, over the table, dressed in a velveteen jacket, and with his round-topped hat brought far over his eyes, so that she could not fully see his face. But she had hardly begun to observe him before he threw back his hat, and taking some pieces of gold from under his left hand, which lay upon the table, pushed three or four of them on to one of the divisions marked on the cloth. He seemed to show no care, as others did, as to the special spot which they should occupy. Many were very particular in this respect, placing their ventures on the lines, so as to share the fortunes of two compartments, or sometimes of four; or they divided their coins, taking three or four numbers, selecting the numbers with almost grotesque attention to some imagined rule of their own. But this man let his gold go all together, and left it where his half-stretched rake deposited it by chance. Alice could not but look at his face. His eyes she could see were bloodshot, and his hair, when he pushed back his hat, was rough and dishevelled; but still there was that in his face which no woman could see and not regard. It was a face which at once prepossessed her in his favour,—-as it had always prepossessed all others. On this occasion he had won his money, and Alice saw him drag it in as lazily as he had pushed it out.

'Do you see that little Frenchman?' said Lady Glencora. 'He has just made half a napoleon, and has walked off with it. Isn't it interesting? I could stay here all the night.' Then she turned round to whisper something to her husband, and Alice's eyes again fell on the face of the man at the other end of the table. After he had won his money, he had allowed the game to go on for a turn without any action on his part. The gold again went under his hand, and he lounged forward with his hat over his eyes. One of the croupiers had said a word, as though calling his attention to the game, but he had merely shaken his head. But when the fate of the next turn had been decided, he again roused himself, and on this occasion, as far as Alice could see, pushed his whole stock forward with the rake. There was a little mass of gold, and, from his manner of placing it, all might see that he left its position to chance. One piece had got beyond its boundary, and the croupier pushed it back with some half-expressed inquiry as to his correctness. 'All right,' said a voice in English. Then Lady Glencora started and clutched Alice's arm with her hand. Mr. Palliser was explaining to Mr. Grey, behind them, something about German finance as connected with gambling-tables, and did not hear the voice, or see his wife's motion. I need hardly tell the reader that the gambler was Burgo Fitzgerald.

But Lady Glencora said not a word,—not as yet. She looked forward very gently, but still with eager eyes, till she could just see the face she knew so well. His hat was now pushed back, and his countenance had lost its listlessness. He watched narrowly the face of the man as he told out the amount of the cards as they were dealt. He did not try to hide his anxiety, and when, after the telling of some six or seven cards, he heard a certain number named, and a certain colour called, he made some exclamation which even Glencora could not hear. And then another croupier put down, close to Burgo's money, certain rolls of gold done up in paper, and also certain loose napoleons.

'Why doesn't he take it?' said Lady Glencora.

'He is taking it,' said Alice, not at all knowing the cause of her cousin's anxiety.

Burgo had paused a moment, and then prepared to rake the money to him; but as he did so, he changed his mind, and pushed it all back again,—now, on this occasion, being very careful to place it on its former spot. Both Alice and Glencora could see that a man at his elbow was dissuading him,—had even attempted to stop the arm which held the rake. But Burgo shook him off, speaking to him some word roughly, and then again he steadied the rolls upon their appointed place. The croupier who had paused for a moment now went on quickly with his cards, and in two minutes the fate of Burgo's wealth was decided. It was all drawn back by the croupier's unimpassioned rake, and the rolls of gold were restored to the tray from whence they had been taken.

Burgo looked up and smiled at them all round the table. By this time most of those who stood around were looking at him. He was a man who gathered eyes upon him wherever he might be, or whatever he was doing; and it had been clear that he was very intent upon his fortune, and on the last occasion the amount staked had been considerable. He knew that men and women were looking at him, and therefore he smiled faintly as he turned his eyes round the table. Then he got up, and, putting his hands in his trousers pockets, whistled as he walked away. His companion followed him, and laid a hand upon his shoulder; but Burgo shook him off, and would not turn round. He shook him off, and walked on whistling, the length of the whole salon.

'Alice,' said Lady Glencora, 'it is Burgo Fitzgerald.' Mr. Palliser had gone so deep into that question of German finance that he had not at all noticed the gambler. 'Alice, what can we do for him? It is Burgo,' said Lady Glencora.

Many eyes were now watching him. Used as he was to the world and to misfortune, he was not successful in his attempt to bear his loss with a show of indifference. The motion of his head, the position of his hands, the tone of his whistling, all told the tale. Even the unimpassioned croupiers furtively cast an eye after him, and a very big Guard, in a cocked hat, and uniform, and sword, who hitherto had hardly been awake, seemed evidently to be interested by his movements. If there is to be a tragedy at these places,—and tragedies will sometimes occur,—it is always as well that the tragic scene should be as far removed as possible from the salons, in order that the public eye should not suffer.

Lady Glencora and Alice had left their places, and had shrunk back, almost behind a pillar. 'Is it he, in truth?' Alice asked.

'In very truth,' said Glencora. 'What can I do? Can I do anything? Look at him, Alice. If he were to destroy himself, what should I do then?'

Burgo, conscious that he was the regarded of all eyes, turned round upon his heel and again walked the length of the salon. He knew well that he had not a franc left in his possession, but still he laughed and still he whistled. His companion, whoever he might be, had slunk away from him, not caring to share the notoriety which now attended him.

'What shall I do, Alice?' said Lady Glencora, with her eyes still fixed on him who had been her lover.

'Tell Mr. Palliser,' whispered Alice.

Lady Glencora immediately ran up to her husband, and took him away from Mr. Grey. Rapidly she told her story,—with such rapidity that Mr. Palliser could hardly get in a word. 'Do something for him;—do, do. Unless I know that something is done, I shall die. You needn't be afraid.'

'I'm not afraid,' said Mr. Palliser.

Lady Glencora, as she went on quickly, got hold of her husband's hand, and caressed it. 'You are so good,' said she. 'Don't let him out of your sight. There; he is going. I will go home with Mr. Grey. I will be ever so good; I will, indeed. You know what he'll want, and for my sake you'll let him have it. But don't let him gamble. If you could only get him home to England, and then do something. You owe him something, Plantagenet; do you not?'

'If money can do anything, he shall have it.'

'God bless you, dearest! I shall never see him again; but if you could save him! There;—he is going now. Go;—go.' She pushed him forward, and then retreating, put her arm within Mr. Grey's, still keeping her eye upon her husband.

Burgo, when he first got to the door leading out of the salon, had paused a moment, and, turning round, had encountered the big gendarme close to him. 'Well, old Buffer, what do you want?' said he, accosting the man in English. The big gendarme simply walked on through the door, and said nothing. Then Burgo also passed out, and Mr. Palliser quickly went after him. They were now in the large front salon, from whence the chief door of the building opened out upon the steps. Through this door Burgo went without pausing, and Mr. Palliser went after him. They both walked to the end of the row of buildings, and then Burgo, leaving the broad way, turned into a little path which led up through the trees to the hills. That hill-side among the trees is a popular resort at Baden, during the day; but now, at nine in the evening, it was deserted. Palliser did not press on the other man, but followed him, and did not accost Burgo till he had thrown himself on the grass beneath a tree.

'You are in trouble, I fear, Mr. Fitzgerald,' said Mr. Palliser, as soon as he was close at Burgo's feet.

'We will go home. Mr. Palliser has something to do,' said Lady Glencora to Mr. Grey, as soon as the two men had disappeared from her sight.

'Is that a friend of Mr. Palliser?' said Mr. Grey.

'Yes;—that is, he knows him, and is interested about him. Alice, shall we go home? Oh! Mr. Grey, you must not ask any questions. He,—Mr. Palliser, will tell you everything when he sees you,—that is, if there is anything to be told.' Then they all went home, and soon separated for the night. 'Of course I shall sit up for him,' said Lady Glencora to Alice, 'but I will do it in my own room. You can tell Mr. Grey, if you like.' But Alice told nothing to Mr. Grey, nor did Mr. Grey ask any questions.

CHAPTER LXXVI

The Landlord's Bill

'You are in trouble, Mr. Fitzgerald, I fear,' said Mr. Palliser, standing over Burgo as he lay upon the ground. They were now altogether beyond the gas-lights, and the evening was dark. Burgo, too, was lying with his face to the ground, expecting that the footsteps which he had heard would pass by him.

'Who is that?' said he, turning round suddenly; but still he was not at once able to recognise Mr. Palliser, whose voice was hardly known to him.

'Perhaps I have been wrong in following you,' said Mr. Palliser, 'but I thought you were in distress, and that probably I might help you. My name is Palliser.'

'Plantagenet Palliser?' said Burgo, jumping up on to his legs and looking close into the other's face. 'By heavens! it is Plantagenet Palliser! Well, Mr. Palliser, what do you want of me?'

'I want to be of some use to you, if I can. I and my wife saw
you leave the gaming-table just now.'

'Is she here too?'

'Yes;—she is here. We are going home, but chance brought
us up to the salon. She seemed to think that you are in distress,
and that I could help you. I will, if you will let me.'

Mr. Palliser, during the whole interview, felt that he could
afford to be generous. He knew that he had no further cause
for fear. He had no lingering dread of this poor creature who
stood before him. All that feeling was over, though it was as
yet hardly four months since he had been sent back by Mrs.
Marsham to Lady Monk's house to save his wife, if saving
her were yet possible.

'So she is here, is she;—and saw me there when I staked my
last chance? I should have had over twenty thousand francs
now, if the cards had stood to me.'

'The cards never do stand to any one, Mr. Fitzgerald.'

'Never;—never,—never!' said Burgo. 'At any rate, they
never did to me. Nothing ever does stand to me.'

'If you want twenty thousand francs,—that's eight hundred pounds, I think,—I can let you have it without any
trouble.'

'The devil you can!'

'Oh, yes. As I am travelling with my family——' I wonder
whether Mr. Palliser considered himself to be better entitled
to talk of his family than he had been some three or four weeks
back—'As I am travelling with my family, I have been obliged
to carry large bills with me, and I can accommodate you without any trouble.'

There was something pleasant in this, which made Burgo
Fitzgerald laugh. Mr. Palliser, the husband of Lady Glencora M'Cluskie, and the heir of the Duke of Omnium happen-
ing to have money with him! As if Mr. Palliser could not bring
down showers of money in any quarter of the globe by simply
holding up his hand. And then to talk of accommodating him,
—him, Burgo Fitzgerald, as though it were simply a little
matter of convenience,—as though Mr. Palliser would of

course find the money at his bankers' when he next examined his book! Burgo could not but laugh.

'I was not in the least doubting your ability to raise the money,' said he; 'but how would you propose to get it back again?'

'That would be at your convenience,' said Mr. Palliser, who hardly knew how to put himself on a proper footing with his companion, so that he might offer to do something effectual for the man's aid.

'I never have any such convenience,' said Burgo. 'Who were those women whose tubs always had holes at the bottom of them? My tub always has such a hole.'

'You mean the daughters of Danaus,'*said Mr. Palliser.

'I don't know whose daughters they were, but you might just as well lend them all eight hundred pounds apiece.'

'There were so many of them,' said Mr. Palliser, trying a little joke. 'But as you are the only one I shall be most happy, as I said before, to be of service.'

They were now walking slowly together up towards the hills, and near to them they heard a step. Upon this, Burgo turned round.

'Do you see that fellow?' said he. Mr. Palliser, who was somewhat short-sighted, said that he did not see him. 'I do, though. I don't know his name, but they have sent him out from the hotel with me, to see what I do with myself. I owe them six or seven hundred francs, and they want to turn me out of the house and not let me take my things with me.'

'That would be very uncomfortable,' said Mr. Palliser.

'It would be uncomfortable, but I shall be too many for them. If they keep my traps they shall keep me. They think I'm going to blow my brains out. That's what they think. The man lets me go far enough off to do that,—so long as it's nowhere about the house.'

'I hope you're not thinking of such a thing?'

'As long as I can help it, Mr. Palliser, I never think of anything.' The stranger was now standing near to them,—almost so near that he might hear their words. Burgo, perceiving this, walked up to him, and, speaking in bad French, desired him to leave them. 'Don't you see that I have a friend with me?'

'Oh! a friend,' said the man, answering in bad English. 'Perhaps de friend can advance moneys?'

'Never mind what he can do,' said Burgo. 'You do as you are bid, and leave me.'

Then the gentleman from the hotel retreated down the hill, but Mr. Palliser, during the rest of the interview, frequently fancied that he heard the man's footfall at no great distance.

They continued to walk on up the hill very slowly, and it was some time before Mr. Palliser knew how to repeat his offer.

'So Lady Glencora is here?' Burgo said again.

'Yes, she is here. It was she who asked me to come to you,' Mr. Palliser answered. Then they both walked on a few steps in silence, for neither of them knew how to address the other.

'By George!—isn't it odd,' said Burgo, at last, 'that you and I, of all men in the world, should be walking together here at Baden? It's not only that you're the richest man in London, and that I'm the poorest, but——; there are other things, you know, which make it so funny.'

'There have been things which make me and my wife very anxious to give you aid.'

'And have you considered, Mr. Palliser, that those things make you the very man in the world,—indeed, for the matter of that, the only man in the world,—from whom I can't take aid? I would have taken it all if I could have got it,—and I tried hard.'

'I know you have been disappointed, Mr. Fitzgerald.'

'Disappointed! By G—! yes. Did you ever know any man who had so much right to be disappointed as I have? I did love her, Mr. Palliser. Nay, by heavens! I do love her. Out here I will dare to say as much even to you. I shall never try to see her again. All that is over, of course. I've been a fool about her as I have been about everything. But I did love her.'

'I believe it, Mr. Fitzgerald.'

'It was not altogether her money. But think what it would have been to me, Mr. Palliser. Think what a chance I had, and what a chance I lost. I should have been at the top of everything,—as now I am at the bottom. I should not have spent that. There would have been enough of it to have saved me. And then I might have done something good instead of crawling about almost in fear of that beast who is watching us.'

'It has been ordered otherwise,' said Mr. Palliser, not knowing what to say.

'Yes; it has been ordered, with a vengeance! It seems to have been ordered that I'm to go to the devil; but I don't know who gave the orders, and I don't know why.'

Mr. Palliser had not time to explain to his friend that the orders had been given, in a very peremptory way, by himself, as he was anxious to bring back the conversation to his own point. He wished to give some serviceable, and, if possible, permanent aid to the poor ne'er-do-well; but he did not wish to talk more than could be helped about his own wife.

'There is an old saying, which you will remember well,' said he, 'that the way to good manners is never too late.'

'That's nonsense,' said Burgo. 'It's too late when the man feels the knot round his neck at the Old Bailey.'

'Perhaps not, even then, Indeed, we may say, certainly not, if the man be still able to take the right way. But I don't want to preach to you.'

'It wouldn't do any good, you know.'

'But I do want to be of service to you. There is something of truth in what you say. You have been disappointed; and I, perhaps, of all men am the most bound to come to your assistance now that you are in need.'

'How can I take it from you?' said Burgo, almost crying.

'You shall take it from her!'

'No;—that would be worse; twenty times worse. What! take her money, when she would not give me herself!'

'I do not see why you should not borrow her money,—or mine. You shall call it which you will.'

'No; I won't have it.'

'And what will you do then?'

'What will I do? Ah! that's the question. I don't know what I will do. I have the key of my bedroom in my pocket, and I will go to bed to-night. It's not very often that I look forward much beyond that.'

'Will you let me call on you, to-morrow?'

'I don't see what good it will do? I shan't get up till late, for fear they should shut the room against me. I might as well have as much out of them as I can. I think I shall say I'm ill, and keep my bed.'

'Will you take a few napoleons?'

'No; not a rap. Not from you. You are the first man from whom I ever refused to borrow money, and I should say that you'll be about the last to offer to lend it me.'

'I don't know what else I can offer?' said Mr. Palliser.

'You can offer nothing. If you will say to your wife from me that I bade her adieu;—that is all you can do for me. Good night, Mr. Palliser; good night.'

Mr. Palliser left him and went his way, feeling that he had no further eloquence at his command. He shook Burgo's hand, and then walked quickly down the hill. As he did so, he passed, or would have passed, the man who had been dodging them.

'Misther, Misther!' said the man in a whisper.

'What do you want of me?' asked Mr. Palliser, in French.

Then the man spoke in French, also. 'Has he got any money? Have you given him any money?'

'I have not given him any money,' said Mr. Palliser, not quite knowing what he had better do or say under such circumstances.

'Then he will have a bad time with it,' said the man. 'And he might have carried away two thousand francs just now! Dear, dear, dear! Has he got any friends, sir?'

'Yes, he has friends. I do not know that I can assist him, or you.'

'Fitzgerald;—his name is Fitzgerald?'

'Yes,' said Mr. Palliser; 'his name is Fitzgerald.'

374

'Ah! There are so many Fitzgeralds in England. Mr. Fitz-gerald, London;—he has no other address?'

'If he had, and I knew it, I should not give it you without his sanction.'

'But what shall we do? How shall we act? Perhaps with his own hand he will himself kill. For five weeks his pension he owes; yes, for five weeks. And for wine, oh so much! There came through Baden a my lord, and then, I think he got money. But he went and played. That was of course. But; oh my G—! he might have carried away this night two thousand francs; yes, two thousand francs!'

'Are you the hotelkeeper?'

'His friend, sir; only his friend. That is, I am the head Commissionaire. I look after the gentlemen who sometimes are not all—not all——' exactly what they should be, the commissioner intended to explain; and Mr. Palliser understood him although the words were not quite spoken. The interview was ended by Mr. Palliser taking the name of the hotel, and promising to call before Mr. Fitzgerald should be up in the morning—a purposed visit, which we need not regard as requiring any very early energy on Mr. Palliser's part, when we remember Burgo's own programme for the following day.

Lady Glencora received her husband that night with infinite anxiety, and was by no means satisfied with what had been done. He described to her as accurately as he could the nature of his interview with Burgo, and he described to her also his other interview with the head commissioner.

'He will; he will,' said Lady Glencora, when she heard from her husband the man's surmise that perhaps he might destroy himself. 'He will; he will; and if he does, how can you expect that I shall bear it?' Mr. Palliser tried to soothe her by telling her of his promised visit to the landlord; and Lady Glencora, accepting this as something, strove to instigate her husband to some lavish expenditure on Burgo's behalf. 'There can be no reason why he should not take it,' said Glencora. 'None the least. Had it not been promised to him? Had he not a right to it?' The subject was one which Mr. Palliser found it very hard to discuss. He could not tell his wife that Fitzgerald ought to accept his bounty; but he assured her that his money should be forthcoming, almost to any extent, if it could be made available.

On the following morning he went down to the hotel, and saw the real landlord. He found him to be a reasonable, tranquil, and very good-natured man,—who was possessed by a not irrational desire that his customers' bills should be paid; but who seemed to be much less eager on the subject than are English landlords in general. His chief anxiety seemed to arise from the great difficulty of doing anything with the gentleman who was now lying in his bed up-stairs. 'Has he had any breakfast?' Mr. Palliser asked.

'Breakfast! Oh yes;' and the landlord laughed. He had been very particular in the orders he had given. He had desired his cutlets to be dressed in a particular way,—with a great deal of cayenne pepper, and they had been so dressed. He had ordered a bottle of Sauterne; but the landlord had thought, or the head-waiter acting for him had thought, that a bottle of ordinary wine of the country would do as well. The bottle of ordinary wine of the country had just that moment been sent up-stairs.

Then Mr. Palliser sat down in the landlord's little room, and had Burgo Fitzgerald's bill brought to him. 'I think I might venture to pay it,' said Mr. Palliser.

'That was as monsieur pleased,' said the landlord, with something like a sparkle in his eye.

What was Mr. Palliser to do? He did not know whether, in accordance with the rules of the world in which he lived, he ought to pay it, or ought to leave it; and certainly the landlord could not tell him. Then he thought of his wife. He could not go back to his wife without having done something; so, as a first measure, he paid the bill. The landlord's eyes glittered, and he receipted it in the most becoming manner.

'Should he now send up the bottle of Sauterne?'—but to this Mr. Palliser demurred.

'And to whom should the receipted bill be given?' Mr.

Palliser thought that the landlord had better keep it himself for a while.

'Perhaps there is some little difficulty?' suggested the landlord.

Mr. Palliser acknowledged that there was a little difficulty. He knew that he must do something more. He could not simply pay the bill and go away. That would not satisfy his wife. He knew that he must do something more; but how was he to do it? So at last he let the landlord into his confidence. He did not tell the whole of Burgo's past history. He did not tell that little episode in Burgo's life which referred to Lady Glencora. But he did make the landlord understand that he was willing to administer money to Mr. Fitzgerald, if only it could be administered judiciously.

'You can't keep him out of the gambling salon, you know, sir; that is, not if he has a franc in his pocket.' As to that the landlord was very confident.

It was at last arranged, that the landlord was to tell Burgo that his bill did not signify at present, and that the use of the hotel was to be at Burgo's command for the next three months. At the end of that time he was to have notice to quit. No money was to be advanced to him;—but the landlord, even in this respect, had a discretion.

'When I get home, I will see what can be done with his relations there,' said Mr. Palliser. Then he went home and told his wife.

'But he'll have no clothes,' said Lady Glencora.

Mr. Palliser said that the judicious landlord would manage that also; and in that way Lady Glencora was appeased,—appeased, till something final could be done for the young man, on Mr. Palliser's return home.

Poor Burgo! He must now be made to end his career as far as these pages are concerned.* He soon found that something had been done for him at the hotel, and no doubt he must have made some guess near the truth. The discreet landlord told him nothing,—would tell him nothing; but that his bill did not signify as yet. Burgo thinking about it, resolved to write

377

about it in an indignant strain to Mr. Palliser; but the letter did not get itself written. When in England, Mr. Palliser saw Sir Cosmo Monk, and with many apologies, told him what he had done.

'I regret it,' said Sir Cosmo, in anger. 'I regret it; not for the money's sake, but I regret it.' The amount expended, was however repaid to Mr. Palliser, and an arrangement was made for remitting a weekly sum of fifteen pounds to Burgo, through a member of the diplomatic corps, as long as he should remain at a certain small German town which was indicated, and in which there was no public gambling-table. Lady Glencora expressed herself satisfied for the present; but I much doubt whether poor Burgo lived long in comfort on the allowance made to him.

Here we must say farewell to Burgo Fitzgerald.

CHAPTER LXXVII

The Travellers return Home

MR. PALLISER did not remain long in Baden after the payment of Burgo's bill. Perhaps I shall not throw any undeserved discredit on his courage if I say that he was afraid to do so. What would he have said,—what would he have been able to say, if that young man had come to him demanding an explanation? So he hurried away to Strasbourg the same day, much to his wife's satisfaction.

The journey home from thence was not marked by any incidents. Gradually Mr. Palliser became a little more lenient to his wife and slightly less oppressive in his caution. If he still inquired about the springs of the carriages, he did so in silence, and he ceased to enjoin the necessity of a day's rest after each day's journey. By the time that they reached Dover he had become so used to his wife's condition that he made but little fluttering as she walked out of the boat by that narrow gangway which is so contrived as to make an arrival there a serious inconvenience to a lady, and a nuisance even to a man. He was somewhat staggered when a big man, in the middle of the night, insisted on opening the little basket which his wife carried, and was uncomfortable when obliged to stop her on the plank while he gave up the tickets which he thought had been already surrendered; but he was becoming used to his position, and bore himself like a man.

During their journey home Mr. Palliser had by no means kept his seat opposite to Lady Glencora with constancy. He had soon found that it was easier to talk to Mr. Grey than to his wife, and, consequently, the two ladies had been much together, as had also the two gentlemen. What the ladies discussed may be imagined. One was about to become a wife and the other a mother, and that was to be their fate after each had made up her mind that no such lot was to be hers. It may, however, be presumed that for every one word that Alice spoke Lady Glencora spoke ten. The two men, throughout these days of close intimacy, were intent upon politics. Mr. Palliser, who may be regarded as the fox who had lost his tail,—the tail being, in this instance, the comfort of domestic privacy,—was eager in recommending his new friend to cut off his tail also. 'Your argument would be very well,' said he, 'if men were to be contented to live for themselves only.'

'Your argument would be very well,' said the other, 'if it were used to a man who felt that he could do good to others by going into public life. But it is wholly inefficacious if it recommends public life simply or chiefly because a man may gratify his own ambition by public services.'

'Of course there is personal gratification, and of course there is good done,' said Mr. Palliser.

'Is,—or should be,' said Mr. Grey.

'Exactly; and the two things must go together. The chief gratification comes from the feeling that you are of use.'

'But if you feel that you would not be of use?'

We need not follow the argument any further. We all know its nature, and what between two such men would be said on both sides. We all know that neither of them would put the matter altogether in a true light. Men never can do so in words, let the light within themselves be ever so clear. I do not think that any man yet ever had such a gift of words as to make them a perfect exponent of all the wisdom within him. But the effect was partly that which the weaker man of the two desired,—the weaker in the gifts of nature, though art had in some respects made him stronger. Mr. Grey was shaken in his quiescent philosophy, and startled Alice,—startled her as much as he delighted her,—by a word or two he said as he walked with her in the courts of the Louvre. 'It's all hollow here,' he said, speaking of French politics.

'Very hollow,' said Alice, who had no love for the French mode of carrying on public affairs.

'Of all modes of governing*this seems to me to be the surest of coming to a downfall. Men are told that they are wise enough to talk, but not wise enough to have any power of action. It is as though men were cautioned that they were walking through gunpowder, and that no fire could be allowed them, but were at the same time enjoined to carry lucifer matches*in their pockets. I don't believe in the gunpowder, and I think there should be fire, and plenty of it; but if I didn't want the fire I wouldn't have the matches.'

'It's so odd to hear you talk politics,' said Alice, laughing.

After this he dropped the subject for a while, as though he were ashamed of it, but in a very few minutes he returned to it manfully. 'Mr. Palliser wants me to go into Parliament.' Upon hearing this Alice said nothing. She was afraid to speak. After all that had passed she felt that it would not become her to show much outward joy on hearing such a proposition, so spoken by him, and yet she could say nothing without some sign of exultation in her voice. So she walked on without speaking, and was conscious that her fingers trembled on his arm. 'What do you say about it?' he asked.

'What do I say? Oh, John, what right can I have to say anything?'

'No one else can have so much right,—putting aside of course myself, who must be responsible for my own actions.

He asked me whether I could afford it, and he seems to think that a smaller income suffices for such work now than it did a few years since. I believe that I could afford it, if I could get a seat that was not very expensive at the first outset. He could help me there.'

'On that point, of course, I can have no opinion.'

'No; not on that point. I believe we may take that for granted. Living in London for four or five months in the year might be managed. But as to the mode of life!'

Then Alice was unable to hold her tongue longer, and spoke out her thoughts with more vehemence than discretion. No doubt he combated them with some amount of opposition. He seldom allowed out-spoken enthusiasm to pass by him without some amount of hostility. But he was not so perverse as to be driven from his new views by the fact that Alice approved them, and she, as she drew near home, was able to think that the only flaw in his character was in process of being cured.

When they reached London they all separated. It was Mr. Palliser's purpose to take his wife down to Matching with as little delay as possible. London was at this time nearly empty, and all the doings of the season were over. It was now the first week of August, and as Parliament had not been sitting for nearly two months, the town looked as it usually looks in September. Lady Glencora was to stay but one day in Park Lane, and it had been understood between her and Alice that they were not to see each other.

'How odd it is parting in this way, when people have been together so long,' said Lady Glencora. 'It always seems as though there had been a separate little life of its own which was now to be brought to a close. I suppose, Mr. Grey, you and I, when we next meet, will be far too distant to fight with each other.'

'I hope that may never be the case,' said Mr. Grey.

'I suppose nothing would prevent his fighting; would it, Alice? But, remember, there must be no fighting when we do meet next, and that must be in September.'

'With all my heart,' said Mr. Grey. But Alice said nothing.

Then Mr. Palliser made his little speech. 'Alice,' he said, as he gave his hand to Miss Vavasor, 'give my compliments to your father, and tell him that I shall take the liberty of asking him to come down to Matching for the early shooting in September, and that I shall expect him to bring you with him. You may tell him also that he will have to stay to see you off, but that he will not be allowed to take you away.' Lady Glencora thought that this was very pretty as coming from her husband, and so she told him on their way home.

Alice insisted on going to Queen Anne Street in a cab by herself. Mr. Palliser had offered a carriage; and Mr. Grey, of course, offered himself as a protector; but she would have neither the one nor the other. If he had gone with her he might by chance have met her father, and she was most anxious that she should not be encumbered by her lover's presence when she first received her father's congratulations. They had slept at Dover, and had come up by a mid-day train. When she reached Queen Anne Street, the house was desolate, and she might therefore have allowed Mr. Grey to attend her. But she found a letter waiting for her which made her for the moment forget both him and her father. Lady Macleod, at Cheltenham, was very ill, and wished to see her niece, as she said, before she died. 'I have got your letter,' said the kind old woman, 'and am now quite happy. It only wanted that to reconcile me to my departure. I thought through it all that my girl would be happy at last. Will she forgive me if I say that I have forgiven her?' The letter then went on to beg Alice to come to Cheltenham at once. 'It is not that I am dying now,' said Lady Macleod, 'though you will find me much altered and keeping my bed. But the doctor says he fears the first cold weather. I know what that means, my dear; and if I don't see you now, before your marriage, I shall never see you again. Pray get married as soon as you can. I want to know that you are Mrs. Grey before I go. If I were to hear that it was postponed because of my illness, I think it would kill me at once.'

There was another letter for her from Kate, full, of course, of congratulations, and promising to be at the wedding; 'that is,' said Kate, 'unless it takes place at the house of some one of your very grand friends;' and telling her that aunt Greenow was to be married in a fortnight;—telling her of this, and begging her to attend that wedding. 'You should stand by your family,' said Kate. 'And only think what my condition will be if I have no one here to support me. Do come. Journeys are nothing now-a-days. Don't you know I would go seven times the distance for you? Mr. Cheesacre and Captain Bellfield are friends after all, and Mr. Cheesacre is to be best man. Is it not beautiful? As for poor me, I'm told I haven't a chance left of becoming mistress of Oileymead and all its wealth.'

Alice began to think that her hands were almost too full. If she herself were to be married in September, even by the end of September, her hands were very full indeed. Yet she did not know how to refuse any of the requests made to her. As to Lady Macleod, her visit to her was a duty which must of course be performed at once. She would stay but one day in London, and then go down to Cheltenham. Having resolved upon this she at once wrote to her aunt to that effect. As to that other affair down in Westmoreland, she sighed as she thought of it, but she feared that she must go there also. Kate had suffered too much on her behalf to allow of her feeling indifferent to such a request.

Then her father came in. 'I didn't in the least know when you might arrive,' said he, beginning with an apology for his absence. 'How could I, my dear?' Alice scorned to remind him that she herself had named the precise hour of the train by which they had arrived. 'It's all right, papa,' said she. 'I was very glad to have an hour to write a letter or two. Poor Lady Macleod is very ill. I must go to her the day after to-morrow.'

'Dear, dear, dear! I had heard that she was poorly. She is very old, you know. So, Alice, you've made it all square with Mr. Grey at last?'

'Yes, papa;—if you call that square.'

'Well; I do call it square. It has all come round to the proper thing.'

'I hope he thinks so.'

'What do you think yourself, my dear?'

'I've no doubt it's the proper thing for me, papa.'

'Of course not; of course not; and I can tell you this, Alice, he is a man in a thousand. You've heard about the money?'

'What money, papa?'

'The money that George had.' As the reader is aware, Alice had heard nothing special about this money. She only knew, or supposed she knew, that she had given three thousand pounds to her cousin. But now her father explained to her the whole transaction. 'We couldn't have realised your money for months, perhaps,' said he; 'but Grey knew that some men must have rope enough before they can hang themselves.'

Alice was unable to say anything on this subject to her father, but to herself she did declare that not in that way or with that hope had John Grey produced his money. 'He must be paid, papa,' she said. 'Paid!' he answered; 'he can pay himself now. It may make some difference in the settlements, perhaps, but he and the lawyers may arrange that. I shan't think of interfering with such a man as Grey. If you could only know, my dear, what I've suffered!' Alice in a penitential tone expressed her sorrow, and then he too assured her that he had forgiven her. 'Bless you, my child!' he said, 'and make you happy, and good, and—and—and very comfortable.' After that he went back to his club.

Alice made her journey down to Cheltenham without any adventure, and was received by Lady Macleod with open arms. 'Dearest Alice, it is so good of you.' 'Good!' said Alice, 'would I not have gone a thousand miles to you?'

Lady Macleod was very eager to know all about the coming marriage. 'I can tell you now, my dear, though I couldn't do it before, that I knew he'd persist for ever. He told me so himself in confidence.'

'He has persisted, aunt; that is certain.'

'And I hope you'll reward him. A beautiful woman without discretion is like a pearl in a swine's snout; but a good wife is a crown of glory to her husband. Remember that, my dear, and choose your part for his sake.'

'I won't be that unfortunate pearl, if I can help it, aunt.'

'We can all help it, if we set about it in the right way. And, Alice, you must be careful to find out all his likes and his dislikes. Dear me! I remember how hard I found it, but then I don't think I was so clever as you are.'

'Sometimes I think nobody has ever been so stupid as I have.'

'Not stupid, my dear; if I must say the word, it is self-willed. But, dear, all that is forgiven now. Is it not?'

'There is a forgiveness which it is rather hard to get,' said Alice.

There was something said then as to the necessity of looking for pardon beyond this world, which I need not here repeat. To all her old friend's little sermons Alice was infinitely more attentive than had been her wont, so that Lady Macleod was comforted and took heart of grace, and at last brought forth from under her pillow a letter from the Countess of Midlothian, which she had received a day or two since, and which bore upon Alice's case. 'I was not quite sure whether I'd show it you,' said Lady Macleod, 'because you wouldn't answer her when she wrote to you. But when I'm gone, as I shall be soon, she will be the nearest relative you have on your mother's side, and from her great position, you know, Alice——' But here Alice became impatient for the letter. Her aunt handed it to her, and she read as follows:—

'Castle Reekie, July, 186—.

'DEAR LADY MACLEOD,—I am so sorry to hear of the symptoms you speak about. I strongly advise you to depend chiefly on beef-tea. They should be very careful to send it up quite free from grease, and it should not be too strong of the meat. There should be no vegetables in it. Not soup, you know, but beef-tea. If any thing acts upon your strength, that will. I need not tell one who has lived as you have done where to look for that other strength which alone can support you at such a time as this. I would go to you if I thought that my presence would be any comfort to you, but I know how sensitive you are, and the shock might be too much for you.

'If you see Alice Vavasor on her return to England, as you

385

probably will, pray tell her from me that I give her my warmest congratulations, and that I am heartily glad that matters are arranged. I think she treated my attempts to heal the wound in a manner that they did not deserve; but all that shall be forgiven, as shall also her original bad behaviour to poor Mr. Grey.' Alice was becoming weary of so much forgiveness, and told herself, as she was reading the letter, that that of Lady Midlothian was at any rate unnecessary. 'I trust that we may yet meet and be friends,' continued Lady Midlothian. 'I am extremely gratified at finding that she has been thought so much of by Mr. Palliser. I'm told that Mr. Palliser and Mr. Grey have become great friends, and if this is so, Alice must be happy to feel that she has had it in her power to confer so great a benefit on her future husband as he will receive from this introduction.' 'I ain't a bit happy, and I have conferred no benefit on Mr. Grey,' exclaimed Alice, who was unable to repress the anger occasioned by the last paragraph.

'But it is a great benefit, my dear.'

'Mr. Palliser has every bit as much cause to be gratified for that as Mr. Grey, and perhaps more.'

Poor Lady Macleod could not argue the matter in her present state. She merely sighed, and moved her shrivelled old hand up and down upon the counterpane. Alice finished the letter without further remarks. It merely went on to say how happy the writer would be to know something of her cousin as Mrs. Grey, as also to know something of Mr. Grey, and then gave a general invitation to both Mr. and Mrs. Grey, asking them to come to Castle Reekie whenever they might be able. The Marchioness, with whom Lady Midlothian was staying, had expressly desired her to give this message. Alice, however, could not but observe that Lady Midlothian's invitation applied only to another person's house.

'I'm sure she means well,' said Alice.

'Indeed she does,' said Lady Macleod, 'and then you know you'll probably have children; and think what a thing it will be for them to know the Midlothian family. You shouldn't rob them of their natural advantages.'

Alice remained a week with her aunt, and went from thence direct to Westmoreland. Some order as to bridal preparations we must presume she gave on that single day which she passed in London. Much advice she had received on this head from Lady Glencora, and no inconsiderable amount of assistance was to be rendered to her at Matching during the fortnight she would remain there before her marriage. Something also, let us hope, she might do at Cheltenham. Something no doubt she did do. Something also might probably be achieved among the wilds in Westmoreland, but that something would necessarily be of a nature not requiring fashionable tradespeople. While at Cheltenham she determined that she would not again return to London before her marriage. This resolve was caused by a very urgent letter from Mr. Grey, and by another, almost equally urgent, from Lady Glencora. If the marriage did not take place in September she would not be present at it. The gods of the world,—of Lady Glencora's world,—had met together and come to a great decision. Lady Glencora was to be removed in October to Gatherum Castle, and remain there till the following spring, so that the heir might, in truth, be born in the purple. 'It is such a bore,' said Lady Glencora, 'and I know it will be a girl. But the Duke isn't to be there, except for the Christmas week.' An invitation for the ceremony at Matching had been sent from Mr. Palliser to Mr. Vavasor, and another from Lady Glencora to Kate, 'whom I long to know,' said her ladyship, 'and with whom I should like to pick a crow,* if I dared, as I'm sure she did all the mischief.'

CHAPTER LXXVIII

Mr. Cheesacre's Fate

IT must be acknowledged that Mrs. Greenow was a woman of great resources, and that she would be very prudent for others, though I fear the verdict of those who know her must go against her in regard to prudence in herself. Her marriage with Captain Bellfield was a rash act,—certainly a rash act, although she did take so much care in securing the payment of her own income into her own hands; but the manner in which she made him live discreetly for some months previous to his marriage, the tact with which she renewed the friendship which had existed between him and Mr. Cheesacre, and the skill she used in at last providing Mr. Cheesacre with a wife, oblige us all to admit that, as a general, she had great powers.

When Alice reached Vavasor Hall she found Charlie Fairstairs established there on a long visit. Charlie and Kate were to be the two bridesmaids, and, as Kate told her cousin in their first confidential intercourse on the evening of Alice's arrival, there were already great hopes in the household that the master of Oileymead might be brought to surrender. It was true that Charlie had not a shilling, and that Mr. Cheesacre had set his heart on marrying an heiress. It was true that Miss Fairstairs had always stood low in the gentleman's estimation, as being connected with people who were as much without rank and fashion as they were without money, and that the gentleman loved rank and fashion dearly. It was true that Charlie was no beauty, and that Cheesacre had an eye for feminine charms. It was true that he had despised Charlie, and had spoken his contempt openly;—that he had seen the girl on the sands at Yarmouth every summer for the last ten years, and about the streets of Norwich every winter, and had learned to regard her as a thing poor and despicable, because she was common in his eyes. It is thus that the Cheesacres judge of people. But in spite of all these difficulties Mrs. Greenow had taken up poor Charlie's case, and Kate Vavasor expressed a strong opinion that her aunt would win.

'What has she done to the man?' Alice asked.

'Coaxed him; simply that. She has made herself so much his master that he doesn't know how to say no to her. Sometimes I have thought that he might possibly run away, but I have abandoned that fear now. She has little confidences with him from day to day, which are so alluring to him that he cannot tear himself off. In the middle of one of them he will find himself engaged.'

'But, the unfortunate girl! Won't it be a wretched marriage for her?'

'Not at all. She'll make him a very good wife. He's one of those men to whom any woman, after a little time, will come to be the same. He'll be rough with her once a month or so, and perhaps tell her that she brought no money with her; but that won't break any bones, and Charlie will know how to fight her own battles. She'll save his money if she brings none, and in a few years' time they will quite understand each other.'

Mr. Cheesacre and Captain Bellfield were at this time living in lodgings together, at Penrith, but came over and spent every other day at Vavasor, returning always to their lodgings in the evening. It wanted but eight days to the marriage when Alice arrived, and preparations for that event were in progress. 'It's to be very quiet, Alice,' said her aunt; 'as quiet as such a thing can be made. I owe that to the memory of the departed one. I know that he is looking down upon me, and that he approves all that I do. Indeed, he told me once that he did not want me to live desolate for his sake. If I didn't feel that he was looking down and approving it, I should be wretched indeed.' She took Alice up to see her trousseau, and gave the other expectant bride some little hints which, under present circumstances, might be useful. 'Yes, indeed; only three-and-sixpence a piece, and they're quite real. Feel them. You wouldn't get them in the shops under six.' Alice did feel them, and wondered whether her aunt could have saved the half-crown honestly. 'I had my eyes about me when I was up in town, my dear. And look here, these are quite new,—have never been on yet, and I had them when I was married before. There is nothing like being careful, my dear. I hate meanness, as everybody knows who knows me; but there is nothing like being careful. You have a lot of rich people about you just now, and will have ever so many things given you which you won't want. Do you put them all by, and be careful. They may turn out useful, you know.' Saying this, Mrs. Greenow folded up, among her present bridal belongings, sundries of the wealth which had accrued to her in an earlier stage of her career.

And then Mrs. Greenow opened her mind to Alice about the Captain, 'He's as good as gold, my dear; he is, indeed,— in his own way. Of course, I know that he has faults, and I should like to know who hasn't. Although poor dear Greenow certainly was more without them than anybody else I ever knew.' As this remembrance came upon Mrs. Greenow she put her handkerchief to her eyes, and Alice observed that that which she held still bore the deepest hem of widowhood. They would be used, no doubt, till the last day, and then put by in lavender for future possible occasions. 'Bellfield may have been a little extravagant. I dare say he has. But how can a man help being extravagant when he hasn't got any regular income? He has been ill-treated in his profession; very. It makes my blood curdle when I think of it. After fighting his country's battles through blood, and dust, and wounds;—but I'll tell you about that another time.'

'I suppose a man seldom does make a fortune, aunt, by being a soldier?'

'Never, my dear; much better be a tailor. Don't you ever marry a soldier. But as I was saying, he is the best-tempered creature alive, and the stanchest friend I ever met. You should hear what Mr. Cheesacre says of him! But you don't know Mr. Cheesacre?'

'No, aunt, not yet. If you remember, he went away before I saw him when he came here before.'

'Yes, I know, poor fellow! Between you and me, Kate might have had him if she liked; but perhaps Kate was right.'

'I don't think he would have suited Kate at all.'

'Because of the farmyard, you mean? Kate shouldn't give herself airs. Money's never dirty, you know. But perhaps it's all for the best. There's a sweet girl here to whom he is violently attached, and who I hope will become Mrs. Cheesacre. But as I was saying, the friendship between these two men is quite wonderful, and I have always observed that when a man can create that kind of affection in the bosom of another man, he invariably is,—is the sort of man,—the man, in fact, who makes a good husband.'

Alice knew the story of Charlie Fairstairs and her hopes; knew of the quarrels between Bellfield and Cheesacre; knew almost as much of Bellfield's past life as Mrs. Greenow did herself; and Mrs. Greenow was no doubt aware that such was the case. Nevertheless, she had a pleasure in telling her own story, and told it as though she believed every word that she spoke.

On the following day the two gentlemen came over, according to custom, and Alice observed that Miss Fairstairs hardly spoke to Mr. Cheesacre. Indeed her manner of avoiding that gentleman was so very marked that it was impossible not to observe it. They drank tea out of doors, and when Mr. Cheesacre on one occasion sauntered across towards the end of the bench on which Charlie was sitting, Charlie got up and walked away. And in strolling about the place afterwards, and in going up through the wood, she was at great pains to attach herself to some other person, so that there should be no such attaching between her and the owner of Oileymead. At one time Mr. Cheesacre did get close up to her and spoke some word, some very indifferent word. He knew that he was being cut and he wanted to avoid the appearance of a scene. 'I don't know, sir,' said Charlie, again moving away with excellent dignity, and she at once attached herself to Alice who was close by. 'I know you have just come home from Switzerland,' said Charlie. 'Beautiful Switzerland! My heart pants for Switzerland. Do tell me something about Switzerland!' Mr. Cheesacre had heard that Alice was the dear friend of a lady who would probably some day become a duchess. He therefore naturally held her in awe, and slunk away. On this occasion Mrs. Greenow clung lovingly to her future husband, and the effect was that Mr. Cheesacre found himself to be very much alone and unhappy. He had generally enjoyed these days at Vavasor Hall, having found himself, or fancied himself, to be the dominant spirit there. That Mrs. Greenow was always in truth the dominant spirit I need hardly say; but she knew how to make a companion happy, and well also how to make him wretched. On the whole of this day poor Cheesacre was very wretched.

'I don't think I shall go there any more,' he said to Bellfield, as he drove the gig back to Penrith that evening.

'Not go there any more, Cheesy,' said Bellfield; 'why, we are to have the dinner out in the field on Friday. It's your own bespeak.'*

'Well, yes; I'll go on Friday, but not after that.'

'You'll stop and see me turned off, old fellow?'

'What's the use? You'll get your wife, and that's enough for you. The truth is, that since that girl came down from London with her d——d airs;'—the girl from London with the airs was poor Alice,—'the place is quite changed. I'm blessed if the whole thing isn't as dark as ditch-water. I'm a plain man, I am; and I do hate your swells.' Against this view of the case Captain Bellfield argued stoutly; but Cheesacre had been offended, and throughout the next day he was cross and touchy. He wouldn't play billiards, and on one occasion hinted that he hoped he should get that money soon.

'You did it admirably, my dear,' said Mrs. Greenow that night to Charlie Fairstairs. The widow was now on terms almost more confidential with Miss Fairstairs than with her own niece, Kate Vavasor. She loved a little bit of intrigue; and though Kate could intrigue, as we have seen in this story, Kate would not join her aunt's intrigues. 'You did it admirably. I really did not think you had so much in you.'

'Oh, I don't know,' said Charlie, blushing at the praise.

'And it's the only way, my dear;—the only way, I mean, for you with such a one as him. And if he does come round, you'll find him an excellent husband.'

'I don't think he cares for me a bit,' said Charlie whimpering.

'Pooh, nonsense! Girls never know whether men care for them or not. If he asks you to marry him, won't that be a sign that he cares for you? and if he don't, why, there'll be no harm done.'

'If he thinks it's his money——' began Charlie.

'Now, don't talk nonsense, Charlie,' said Mrs. Greenow, 'or you'll make me sick. Of course it's his money, more or less.

You don't mean to tell me you'd go and fall in love with him if he was like Bellfield, and hadn't got a rap? I can afford that sort of thing; you can't. I don't mean to say you ain't to love him. Of course, you're to love him; and I've no doubt you will, and make him a very good wife. I always think that worldliness and sentimentality are like brandy-and-water. I don't like either of them separately, but taken together they make a very nice drink. I like them warm, with——, as the gentlemen say.'
To this little lecture Miss Fairstairs listened with dutiful patience, and when it was over she said nothing more of her outraged affections or of her disregard for money. 'And now, my dear, mind you look your best on Friday. I'll get him away immediately after dinner, and when he's done with me you can contrive to be in his way, you know.'

The next day was what Kate called the blank day at the Hall. The ladies were all alone, and devoted themselves, as was always the case on the blank days, to millinery and household cares. Mrs. Greenow, as has before been stated, had taken a lease of the place, and her troubles extended beyond her mere bridal wardrobe. Large trunks of household linen had arrived, and all this linen was marked with the name of Greenow; Greenow, 5.58; Greenow, 7.52; and a good deal had to be done before this ancient wealth of housewifery could be properly converted to Bellfield purposes. 'We must cut out the pieces, Jeannette, and work 'em in again ever so carefully,' said the widow, after some painful consideration. 'It will always show,' said Jeannette, shaking her head. 'But the other would show worse,' said the widow; 'and if you fine-draw it, not one person in ten will notice it. We'd always put them on with the name to the feet, you know.'

It was not quite true that Cheesacre had bespoke the dinner out in the field, although no doubt he thought he had done so. The little treat, if treat it was, had all been arranged by Mrs. Greenow, who was ever ready to create festivities. There was not much scope for a picnic here. Besides their own party, which, of course, included the Captain and Mr. Cheesacre, no guest could be caught except the clergyman;—that low-church clergyman, who was so anxious about his income, and with whom the old Squire had quarrelled. Mrs. Greenow had quickly obtained the advantage of his alliance, and he, who was soon to perform on her behalf the marriage ceremony, had promised to grace this little festival. The affair simply amounted to this, that they were to eat their dinner uncomfortably in the field instead of comfortably in the dining-room. But Mrs. Greenow knew that Charlie's charms would be much strengthened by a dinner out-of-doors. 'Nothing,' she said to Kate, 'nothing makes a man come forward so well as putting him altogether out of his usual tack. A man who wouldn't think of such a thing in the drawing-room would be sure to make an offer if he spent an evening with a young lady down-stairs in the kitchen.'

At two o'clock the gig from Penrith arrived at the Hall, and for the next hour both Cheesacre and the Captain were engaged in preparing the tables and carrying out the viands. The Captain and Charlie Fairstairs were going to lay the cloth. 'Let me do it,' said Cheesacre, taking it out of the Captain's hands. 'Oh, certainly,' said the Captain, giving up his prize. 'Captain Bellfield would do it much better,' said Charlie, with a little toss of her head; 'he's as good as a married man, and they always do these things best.'

The day was fine, and although the shade was not perfect, and the midges were troublesome, the dinner went off very nicely. It was beautiful to see how well Mrs. Greenow remembered herself about the grace, seeing that the clergyman was there. She was just in time, and would have been very angry with herself, and have thought herself awkward, had she forgotten it. Mr. Cheesacre sat on her right hand, and the clergyman on her left, and she hardly spoke a word to Bellfield. Her sweetest smiles were all given to Cheesacre. She was specially anxious to keep her neighbour, the parson, in good-humour, and therefore illuminated him once in every five minutes with a passing ray; but the full splendour of her light was poured out upon Cheesacre, as it never had before been poured. How she did flatter him, and with what a capacious gullet did he swallow her flatteries! Oileymead was the only paradise she had ever seen. 'Ah, me; when I think of it sometimes,—but never mind.' A moment came to him when he thought that even yet he might win the race, and send Bellfield away howling into outer darkness. A moment came to him, and the widow saw the moment well. 'I know I have done for the best,' said she, 'and therefore I shall never regret it; at any rate, it's done now.'

'Not done yet,' said he plaintively.

'Yes; done, and done, and done. Besides, a man in your position in the county should always marry a wife younger than yourself,—a good deal younger.' Cheesacre did not understand the argument, but he liked the allusion to his position in the county, and he perceived that it was too late for any changes in the present arrangements. But he was happy; and all that feeling of animosity to Alice had vanished from his breast. Poor Alice! she, at any rate, was innocent. With so much of her own to fill her mind, she had been but little able to take her share in the Greenow festivities; and we may safely say, that if Mr. Cheesacre's supremacy was on any occasion attacked, it was not attacked by her. His supremacy on this occasion was paramount, and during the dinner, and after the dinner, he was allowed to give his orders to Bellfield in a manner that must have gratified him much. 'You must have another glass of champagne with me, my friend,' said Mrs. Greenow; and Mr. Cheesacre drank the other glass of champagne. It was not the second nor the third that he had taken.

After dinner they started off for a ramble through the fields, and Mrs. Greenow and Mr. Cheesacre were together. I think that Charlie Fairstairs did not go with them at all. I think she went into the house and washed her face, and brushed her hair, and settled her muslin. I should not wonder if she took off her frock and ironed it again. Captain Bellfield, I know, went with Alice, and created some astonishment by assuring her that he fully meant to correct the error of his ways. 'I know what it is,' he said, 'to be connected with such a family as yours, Miss Vavasor.' He too had heard about the future duchess, and wished to be on his best behaviour. Kate fell to the lot of the parson.

'This is the last time we shall ever be together in this way,' said the widow to her friend.

'Oh, no,' said Cheesacre; 'I hope not.'

'The last time. On Wednesday I become Mrs. Bellfield, and I need hardly say that I have many things to think of before that; but, Mr. Cheesacre, I hope we are not to be strangers hereafter?' Mr. Cheesacre said that he hoped not. Oileymead would always be open to Captain and Mrs. Bellfield.

'We all know your hospitality,' said she; 'it is not to-day nor to-morrow that I or my husband,—that is to be,—will have to learn that. He always declares that you are the very beau ideal of an English country gentleman.'

'Merely a poor Norfolk farmer,' said Cheesacre. 'I never want to put myself beyond my own place. There has been some talk about the Commission of the Peace, but I don't think anything of it.'

'It has been the greatest blessing in the world for him that he has ever known you,' said Mrs. Greenow, still talking about her future husband.

'I've tried to be good-natured; that's all. D—me, Mrs. Greenow, what's the use of living if one doesn't try to be good-natured? There isn't a better fellow than Bellfield living. He and I ran for the same plate, and he has won it. He's a lucky fellow, and I don't begrudge him his luck.'

'That's so manly of you, Mr. Cheesacre! But, indeed, the plate you speak of was not worth your running for.'

'I may have my own opinion about that, you know.'

'It was not. Nobody knows that as well as I do, or could have thought over the whole matter so often. I know very well what my mission is in life. The mistress of your house, Mr. Cheesacre, should not be any man's widow.'

'She wouldn't be a widow then, you know.'

'A virgin heart should be yours; and a virgin heart may be yours, if you choose to accept it.'

'Oh, bother!'

'If you choose to take my solicitude on your behalf in that way, of course I have done. You were good enough to say just now that you wished to see me and my husband in your hospitable halls. After all that has passed, do you think that I could be a visitor at your house unless there is a mistress there?'

'Upon my word, I think you might.'

'No, Mr. Cheesacre; certainly not. For all our sakes, I should decline. But if you were married——'

'You are always wanting to marry me, Mrs. Greenow.'

'I do, I do. It is the only way in which there can be any friendship between us, and not for worlds would I lose that advantage for my husband,—let alone what I may feel for myself.'

'Why didn't you take me yourself, Mrs. Greenow?'

'If you can't understand, it is not for me to say anything more, Mr. Cheesacre. If you value the warm affection of a virgin heart——'

'Why, Mrs. Greenow, all yesterday she wouldn't say a word to me.'

'Not say a word to you? Is that all you know about it? Are you so ignorant that you cannot see when a girl's heart is breaking beneath her stays?' This almost improper allusion had quite an effect on Mr. Cheesacre's sensitive bosom. 'Did you say a word to her yesterday? And if not, why have you said so many words before?'

'Oh, Mrs. Greenow; come!'

'It is, oh, Mrs. Greenow. But it is time that we should go back to them.' They had been sitting all this time on a bank, under a hedge. 'We will have our tea, and you shall have your pipe and brandy-and-water, and Charlie shall bring it to you. Shall she, Mr. Cheesacre?'

'If she likes she shall, of course.'

'Do you ask her, and she'll like it quick enough. But remember, Mr. Cheesacre, I'm quite serious in what I say about your having a mistress for your house. Only think what an age you'll be when your children grow up, if you don't marry soon now.'

They returned to the field in which they had dined, and found Charlie under the trees, with her muslin looking very fresh. 'What, all a-mort?'*said Mrs. Greenow. Charlie did not quite understand this, but replied that she preferred being alone. 'I have told him that you should fill his pipe for him,' said Mrs. Greenow. 'He doesn't care for ladies to fill his pipe for him,' said Charlie. 'Do you try,' said the widow, 'while I go indoors and order the tea.'

It had been necessary to put the bait very close before Cheesacre's eyes, or there would have been no hope that he might take it. The bait had been put so very close that we must feel sure that he saw the hook. But there are fish so silly that they will take the bait although they know the hook is there. Cheesacre understood it all. Many things he could not see, but he could see that Mrs. Greenow was trying to catch him as a husband for Charlie Fairstairs; and he knew also that he had always despised Charlie, and that no worldly advantage whatever would accrue to him by a marriage with such a girl. But there she was, and he didn't quite know how to avoid it. She did look rather nice in her clear-starched muslin frock, and he felt that he should like to kiss her. He needn't marry her because he kissed her. The champagne which had created the desire also gave him the audacity. He gave one glance around him to see that he was not observed, and then he did kiss Charlie Fairstairs under the trees. 'Oh, Mr. Cheesacre,' said Charlie. 'Oh, Mr. Cheesacre,' echoed a laughing voice; and poor Cheesacre, looking round, saw that Mrs. Greenow, who ought to have been inside the house looking after the boiling water, was moving about for some unknown reason within sight of the spot which he had chosen for his dalliance.

'Mr. Cheesacre,' said Charlie sobbing, 'how dare you do that?—and where all the world could see you?'

'It was only Mrs. Greenow,' said Cheesacre.

'And what will she think of me?'

'Lord bless you;—she won't think anything about it.'

'But I do;—I think a great deal about it. I don't know what to do, I don't;—I don't.' Whereupon Charlie got up from her

seat under the trees and began to move away slowly. Cheesacre thought about it for a moment or two. Should he follow
her or should he not? He knew that he had better not follow
her. He knew that she was bait with a very visible hook. He
knew that he was a big fish for whom these two women were
angling. But after all, perhaps it wouldn't do him much harm
to be caught. So he got up and followed her. I don't suppose
she meant to take the way towards the woods,—towards the
little path leading to the old summer-house up in the trees.
She was too much beside herself to know where she was going,
no doubt. But that was the path she did take, and before long
she and Cheesacre were in the summer-house together. 'Don't,
Sam, don't! Somebody really will be coming. Well, then, there.
Now I won't do it again.' 'Twas thus she spoke when the last
kiss was given on this occasion;—unless there may have been
one or two later in the evening, to which it is not necessary
more especially to allude here. But on the occasion of that last
kiss in the summer-house Miss Fairstairs was perfectly justified by circumstances, for she was then the promised bride of
Mr. Cheesacre.

But how was he to get down again among his friends? That
consideration troubled Mr. Cheesacre as he rose from his
happy seat after that last embrace. He had promised Charlie,
and perhaps he would keep his promise, but it might be as
well not to make it all too public at once. But Charlie wasn't
going to be thrown over;—not if she knew it, as she said to
herself. She returned therefore triumphantly among them all,
—blushing indeed, and with her eyes turned away, and her
hand now remained upon her lover's arm;— but still so close
to him that there could be no mistake. 'Goodness, gracious,
Charlie! where have you and Mr. Cheesacre been?' said Mrs.
Greenow. 'We got up into the woods and lost ourselves,' said
Charlie. 'Oh, indeed,' said Mrs. Greenow.

It would be too long to tell now, in these last pages of our
story, how Cheesacre strove to escape, and with what skill
Mrs. Greenow kept him to his bargain. I hope that Charlie
Fairstairs was duly grateful. Before that evening was over,

under the comfortable influence of a glass of hot brandy-and-water,—the widow had, I think, herself mixed the second glass for Mr. Cheesacre, before the influence became sufficiently comfortable,—he was forced to own that he had made himself the happy possessor of Charlie Fairstairs' heart and hand. 'And you are a lucky man,' said the widow with enthusiasm; 'and I congratulate you with all my heart. Don't let there be any delay now, because a good thing can't be done too soon.' And indeed, before that night was over, Mrs. Greenow had the pair together in her own presence, and then fixed the day. 'A fellow ought to be allowed to turn himself,' Cheesacre said to her, pleading for himself in a whisper. But no; Mrs. Greenow would give him no such mercy. She knew to what a man turning himself might probably lead. She was a woman who was quite in earnest when she went to work, and I hope that Miss Fairstairs was grateful. Then, in that presence, was in truth the last kiss given on that eventful evening. 'Come, Charlie, be good-natured to him. He's as good as your own now,' said the widow. And Charlie was good-natured. 'It's to be as soon as ever we come back from our trip,' said Mrs. Greenow to Kate, the next day, 'and I'm lending her money to get all her things at once. He shall come to the scratch, though I go all the way to Norfolk by myself and fetch him by his ears. He shall come, as sure as my name's Greenow,—or Bellfield, as it will be then, you know.'

'And I shouldn't wonder if she did have to go to Norfolk,' said Kate to her cousin. That event, however, cannot be absolutely concluded in these pages. I can only say that, when I think of Mrs. Greenow's force of character and warmth of friendship, I feel that Miss Fairstairs' prospects stand on good ground.

Mrs. Greenow's own marriage was completed with perfect success. She took Captain Bellfield for better or for worse, with a thorough determination to make the best of his worst, and to put him on his legs, if any such putting might be possible. He, at any rate, had been in luck. If any possible stroke of fortune could do him good, he had found that stroke.

He had found a wife who could forgive all his past offences,—
and also, if necessary, some future offences; who had money
enough for all his wants, and kindness enough to gratify them,
and who had, moreover,—which for the Captain was the most
important,—strength enough to keep from him the power of
ruining them both. Reader, let us wish a happy married life
to Captain and Mrs. Bellfield!

The day after the ceremony Alice Vavasor and Kate Vavasor
started for Matching Priory.

CHAPTER LXXIX

Diamonds are Diamonds

KATE and Alice, as they drew near to their journey's end,
were both a little flurried, and I cannot but own that
there was cause for nervousness. Kate Vavasor was to meet
Mr. Grey for the first time. Mr. Grey was now staying at
Matching and was to remain there until a week of his marriage.
He was then to return to Cambridgeshire for a day or two,
and after that was to become a guest at the rector's house at
Matching the evening before the ceremony. 'Why not let him
come here at once?' Lady Glencora had said to her husband.
'It is such nonsense, you know.' But Mr. Palliser would not
hear of it. Mr. Palliser, though a Radical in public life, would
not for worlds transgress the social laws of his ancestors; and
so the matter was settled. Kate on this very day of her arrival
at Matching would thus see Mr. Grey for the first time, and
she could not but feel that she had been the means of doing Mr.
Grey much injury. She had moreover something,—not much
indeed, but still something,—of that feeling which made the
Pallisers terrible to the imagination, because of their rank and
wealth. She was a little afraid of the Pallisers, but of Mr. Grey
she was very much afraid. And Alice also was not at her ease.
She would fain have prevented so very quick a marriage had
she not felt that now,—after all the trouble that she had caused,
—there was nothing left for her but to do as others wished.

When a day had been named she had hardly dared to demur, and had allowed Lady Glencora to settle everything as she had wished. But it was not only the suddenness of her marriage which dismayed her. Its nature and attributes were terrible to her. Both Lady Midlothian and the Marchioness of Auld Reekie were coming. When this was told to her by letter she had no means of escape. 'Lady Macleod is right in nearly all that she says,' Lady Glencora had written to her. 'At any rate, you needn't be such a fool as to run away from your cousins, simply because they have handles to their names. You must take the thing as it comes.' Lady Glencora, moreover, had settled for her the list of bridesmaids. Alice had made a petition that she might be allowed to go through the ceremony with only one,—with none but Kate to back her. But she ought to have known that when she consented to be married at Matching,—and indeed she had had very little power of resisting that proposition,—all such questions would be decided for her. Two daughters therefore of Lady Midlothian were to act, Lady Jane and Lady Mary, and the one daughter of the Marchioness, who was also a Lady Jane, and there were to be two Miss Howards down from London,—girls who were known both to Alice and to Lady Glencora, and who were in some distant way connected with them both. A great attempt was made to induce the two Miss Pallisers to join the bevy, but they had frankly pleaded their age. 'No woman should stand up as a bridesmaid,' said the strong-minded Iphy, 'who doesn't mean to get married if she can. Now I don't mean to get married, and I won't put myself among the young people.' Lady Glencora was therefore obliged to submit to do the work with only six. But she swore that they should be very smart. She was to give all the dresses, and Mr. Palliser was to give a brooch and an armlet to each. 'She is the only person in the world I want to pet, except yourself,' Lady Glencora had said to her husband, and he had answered by giving her *carte blanche* as regards expense.

All this was very terrible to Kate, who had not much feminine taste for finery. Of the dress she had heard,—of the dress which was waiting at Matching to be made up after her arrival, —though as yet she knew nothing of the trinkets. There are many girls who could submit themselves at a moment to the kindness of such a woman as Lady Glencora. Perhaps most girls would do so, for of all such women in the world, Lady Glencora was the least inclined to patronize or to be condescending in her kindnesses. But Kate Vavasor was one to whom such submission would not come easily.

'I wish I was out of this boat,' she said to Alice in the train.

'So that I might be shipwrecked alone!'

'No; there can be no shipwreck to you. When the day of action comes you will be taken away, up to heaven, upon the clouds. But what am I to do with all these Lady Janes and Lady Marys? Or what are they to do with me?'

'You'll find that Glencora will not desert you. You can't conceive what taste she has.'

'I'd sooner be bridesmaid to Charlie Fairstairs. I would indeed. My place in the world is not among Cabinet Ministers and old countesses.'

'Nor mine.'

'Yes; it seems that yours is to be there. They are your cousins, and you have made at any rate one great friend among them,—one who is to be the biggest of them all.'

'And you are going to throw me over, Kate?'

'To tell the truth, Alice, I sometimes think you had better throw me over. I know it would be sad,—sad for both, but perhaps it would be better. I have done you much harm and no good; and now where I am going I shall disgrace you.' She talked even of getting out at some station and returning, and would have done so had not Alice made it impossible. As it was, the evening found her and Alice together entering the park-gate at Matching, in Lady Glencora's carriage. Lady Glencora had sent a note to the station. 'She could not come herself,' she said, 'because Mr. Palliser was a little fussy. You'll understand, dear, but don't say a word.' Alice didn't say a word, having been very anxious not to lower Mr. Palliser in her cousin's respect.

403

None of the Lady Janes and Lady Marys were at Matching when they arrived. Indeed, there was no guest there but Mr. Grey, for which Kate felt herself to be extremely grateful. Mr. Grey came into the hall, standing behind Mr. Palliser, who stood behind his wife. Alice passed by them both, and was at once in her lover's arms. 'Then I must introduce myself,' said Lady Glencora to Kate, 'and my husband also.' This she did, and no woman in England could have excelled her in the manner of doing it. 'I have heard so much about you,' said she, still keeping Kate's hand, 'and I know how good you've been;——and how wicked you have been,' she added in a whisper. Then Mr. Grey was brought up to her, and they were introduced. It was not till some days had passed over them that she felt herself at all at her ease with Mr. Grey, and I doubt whether she ever reached that point with Mr. Palliser; but Lady Glencora she knew, and liked, and almost loved, from the first moment of their meeting.

'Have you heard the news?' said Lady Glencora to Alice, the first minute that they were alone. Alice, of course, had not heard the news. 'Mr. Bott is going to marry Mrs. Marsham. There is such a row about it. Plantagenet is nearly mad. I never knew him so disgusted in my life. Of course I don't dare to tell him so, but I am so heartily rejoiced. You know how I love them both, and I could not possibly wish any better reward for either.' Alice, who had personally known more of Mr. Bott than of Mrs. Marsham, said that she couldn't but be sorry for the lady. 'She's old enough to be his mother,' said Lady Glencora, 'otherwise I really don't know any people better suited to each other. The best is, that Mr. Bott is doing it to regain his footing with Mr. Palliser! I am sure of that;—and Plantagenet will never speak to him again. But, Alice, there is other news.'

'What other news?'

'It is hardly news yet, and of course I am very wicked to tell you. But I feel sure Mr. Grey knows all about it, and if I didn't tell, he would.'

'He hasn't told me anything yet.'

404

'He hasn't had time; and when he does, you mustn't pretend to know. I believe Mr. Palliser will certainly be Chancellor of the Exchequer before next month, and, if so, he'll never come in for Silverbridge again.'

'But he'll be in Parliament; will he not?'

'Oh, yes; he'll be in Parliament. I don't understand all about it. There is a man going out for the county,*—for Barsetshire, —some man whom the Duke used to favour, and he wants Plantagenet to come in for that. I can't understand what difference it makes.'

'But he will be in the Cabinet?'

'Oh, yes. But who do you suppose is to be the new Member for Silverbridge?'

'I can't guess,' said Alice. Though, of course, she did guess.

'Mind, I don't know it. He has never told me. But he told me that he had been with the Duke, and asked the Duke to let Jeffrey have the seat. The Duke became as black as thunder, and said that Jeffrey had no fortune. In short, he wouldn't hear of it. Poor Jeffrey! we must try to do something for him, but I really don't know how. Then the Duke said that Plantagenet should put in for Silverbridge some friend who would support himself; and I fancy,—mind it's only fancy,—but I fancy that Plantagenet mentioned to his Grace—one Mr. Grey.'

'Oh, Glencora!'

'They've been talking together till sometimes I think Mr. Grey is worse than Plantagenet. When Mr. Grey began to say something the other night in the drawing-room about sugar, I knew it was all up with you. He'll be a financial Secretary; you see if he isn't; or a lord of something, or an under-some-body of State; and then some day he'll go mad, either because he does or because he doesn't get into the Cabinet.' Lady Glencora, as she said all this, knew well that the news she was giving would please her cousin better than any other tidings that could be told.

By degrees the guests came. The two Miss Howards were the first, and they expressed themselves as delighted with Lady Glencora's taste and with Mr. Palliser's munificence,—

for at that time the brooches and armlets had been produced. Kate had said very little about these matters, but the Miss Howards were loud in their thanks. But they were good-humoured, merry girls, and the house was pleasanter after their arrival than it had been before. Then came the dreaded personage,—the guest,—Lady Midlothian! On the subject of Lady Midlothian Kate had really become curious. She had a real desire to see the face and gait of the woman, and to hear her voice. Lady Midlothian came, and with her came Lady Jane and Lady Mary. I am by no means sure that Lady Jane and Lady Mary were not nearly as old as the two Miss Pallisers; but they were not probably so fully resolved as to the condition of their future modes of living as were those two ladies, and if so, they were not wrong to shine as bridesmaids. With them Alice had made some slight acquaintance during the last spring in London, and as they were now to attend upon her as the bride they were sufficiently gracious. To Kate, too, they were civil enough, and things, in public, went on very pleasantly at Matching.

A scene there was, of course, between Alice and Lady Midlothian;—a scene in private. 'You must go through it,' Lady Glencora had said, with jocose mournfulness; 'and why should you not let her jump upon you a little? It can't hurt you now.'

'But I don't like people to jump upon me,' Alice said.

'And why are you to have everything just as you like it? You are so unreasonable. Think how I've been jumped on! Think what I have borne from them! If you knew the things she used to say to me, you would not be such a coward. I was sent down to her for a week, and had no power of helping myself. And the Marchioness used to be sent for to look at me, for she never talks. She used to look at me, and groan, and hold up her hands till I hated her the worst of the two. Think what they did to me, and yet they are my dear friends now. Why should you escape altogether?'

Alice could not escape altogether, and therefore was closeted with Lady Midlothian for the best part of an hour. 'Did Lady Macleod read to you what I wrote?' the Countess asked.

'Yes,—that is, she gave me the letter to read.'

'And I hope you understand me, Alice?'

'Oh, yes, I suppose so.'

'You suppose so, my dear! If you only suppose so I shall not be contented. I want you to appreciate my feelings towards you thoroughly. I want you to know that I am most anxious as to your future life, and that I am thoroughly satisfied with the step you are now taking.' The Countess paused, but Alice said nothing. Her tongue was itching to tell the old woman that she cared nothing for this expression of satisfaction; but she was aware that she had done much that was deserving of punishment, and resolved to take this as part of her penance. She was being jumped upon, and it was unpleasant; but, after all that had happened, it was only fitting that she should undergo much unpleasantness. 'Thoroughly satisfied,' continued the Countess; 'and now, I only wish to refer, in the slightest manner possible, to what took place between us when we were both of us under this roof last winter.'

'Why refer to it at all, Lady Midlothian?'

'Because I think it may do good, and because I cannot make you understand that I have thoroughly forgiven everything, unless I tell you that I have forgiven that also. On that occasion I had come all the way from Scotland on purpose to say a few words to you.'

'I am so sorry that you should have had the trouble.'

'I do not regret it, Alice. I never do regret doing anything which I believe to have been my duty. There is no knowing how far what I said then may have operated for good.' Alice thought that she knew very well, but she said nothing. 'I must confess that what I then understood to be your obstinacy,— and I must say also, if I tell the truth, your indifference to—to —to all prudential considerations whatever, not to talk of appearances and decorum, and I might say, anything like a high line of duty or moral conduct,—shocked me very much. It did, indeed, my dear. Taking it altogether, I don't know that I was ever more shocked in my life. The thing was so inscrutable!' Here Lady Midlothian held up one hand in a manner that was truly imposing; 'so inscrutable! But that is all over now. What was personally offensive to myself I could easily forgive, and I do forgive it. I shall never think of it any more.' Here Lady Midlothian put up both her hands gently, as though wafting the injury away into the air. 'But what I wish specially to say to you is this; your own conduct is forgiven also!' Here she paused again, and Alice winced. Who was this dreadful old Countess;—what was the Countess to her, that she should be thus tormented with the old woman's forgiveness? John Grey had forgiven her, and of external forgiveness that was enough. She had not forgiven herself,— would never forgive herself altogether; and the pardon of no old woman in England could assist her in doing so. She had sinned, but she had not sinned against Lady Midlothian. 'Let her jump upon you, and have done with it,' Lady Glencora had said. She had resolved that it should be so, but it was very hard to keep her resolution.

'The Marchioness and I have talked it over,' continued Lady Midlothian, 'and she has asked me to speak for both her and myself.' There is comfort at any rate in that, thought Alice, who had never yet seen the Marchioness. 'We have resolved that all those little mistakes should be as though they had never been committed. We shall both be most happy to receive you and your husband, who is, I must say, one of the most gentlemanlike looking men I ever saw. It seems that he and Mr. Palliser are on most friendly,—I may say, most confidential terms, and that must be quite a pleasure to you.'

'It's a pleasure to him, which is more to the purpose,' said Alice.

'Exactly so. And now, my dear, everything is forgiven and shall be forgotten. Come and give me a kiss, and let me wish you joy.' Alice did as she was bidden, and accepted the kiss and the congratulations, and a little box of jewellery which Lady Midlothian produced from out of her pocket. 'The diamonds are from the Marchioness, my dear, whose means, as you doubtless are aware, greatly exceed my own. The garnets are from me. I hope they may both be worn long and happily.'

I hardly know which was the worst, the lecture, the kiss, or the present. The latter she would have declined, had it been possible; but it was not possible. When she had agreed to be married at Matching she had not calculated the amount of punishment which would thereby be inflicted on her. But I think that, though she bore it impatiently, she was aware that she had deserved it. Although she fretted herself greatly under the infliction of Lady Midlothian, she acknowledged to herself, even at the time, that she deserved all the lashes she received. She had made a fool of herself in her vain attempt to be greater and grander than other girls, and it was only fair that her folly should be in some sort punished before it was fully pardoned. John Grey punished it after one fashion; by declining to allude to it, or to think of it, or to take an account of it. And now Lady Midlothian had punished it after another fashion, and Alice went out of the Countess's presence with sundry inward exclamations of 'mea culpa,' and with many unseen beatings of the breast.

Two days before the ceremony came the Marchioness and her august daughter. Her Lady Jane was much more august than the other Lady Jane;—very much more august indeed. She had very long flaxen hair, and very light blue eyes, which she did not move frequently, and she spoke very little,—one may almost say not at all, and she never seemed to do anything. But she was very august, and was, as all the world knew, engaged to marry the Duke of Dumfriesshire, who, though twice her own age, was as yet childless, as soon as he should have completed his mourning for his first wife. Kate told her cousin that she did not at all know how she should ever stand up as one in a group with so august a person as this Lady Jane, and Alice herself felt that such an attendant would quite obliterate her. But Lady Jane and her mother were both harmless. The Marchioness never spoke to Kate and hardly spoke to Alice, and the Marchioness's Lady Jane was quite as silent as her mother.

On the morning of this day,—the day on which these very august people came,—a telegram arrived at the Priory calling for Mr. Palliser's immediate presence in London. He came to Alice full of regret, and behaved himself very nicely. Alice now regarded him quite as a friend. 'Of course I understand,' she said, 'and I know that the business which takes you up to London pleases you.' 'Well; yes;—it does please me. I am glad,—I don't mind saying so to you. But it does not please me to think that I shall be away at your marriage. Pray make your father understand that it was absolutely unavoidable. But I shall see him, of course, when I come back. And I shall see you too before very long.'

'Shall you?'

'Oh yes.'

'And why so?'

'Because Mr. Grey must be at Silverbridge for his election. —But perhaps I ought not tell you his secrets.' Then he took her into the breakfast-parlour and showed her his present. It was a service of Sèvres china,—very precious and beautiful. 'I got you these things because Grey likes china.'

'So do I like china,' said she, with her face brighter than he had ever yet seen it.

'I thought you would like them best,' said he. Alice looking up at him with her eyes full of tears told him that she did like them best; and then, as he wished her all happiness, and as he was stooping over her to kiss her, Lady Glencora came in.

'I beg pardon,' said she, 'I was just one minute too soon; was I not?'

'She would have them sent here and unpacked,' said Mr. Palliser, 'though I told her it was foolish.'

'Of course I would,' said Lady Glencora. 'Everything shall be unpacked and shown. It's easy to get somebody to pack them again.'

Much of the wedding tribute had already been deposited with the china, and among other things there were the jewels that Lady Midlothian had brought.

'Upon my word, her ladyship's diamonds are not to be sneezed at,' said Lady Glencora.

'I don't care for diamonds,' said Alice.

Then Lady Glencora took up the Countess's trinkets, and shook her head and turned up her nose. There was a wonderfully comic expression on her face as she did so.

'To me they are just as good as the others,' said Alice.

'To me they are not, then,' said Lady Glencora. 'Diamonds are diamonds, and garnets are garnets; and I am not so romantic but what I know the difference.'

On the evening before the marriage Alice and Lady Glencora walked for the last time through the Priory ruins. It was now September, and the evenings were still long, so that the ladies could get out upon the lawn after dinner. Whether Lady Glencora would have been allowed to walk through the ruins so late as half-past eight in the evening if her husband had been there may be doubtful, but her husband was away and she took this advantage of his absence.

'Do you remember that night we were here?' said Lady Glencora.

'When shall I forget it; or how is it possible that such a night should ever be forgotten?'

'No; I shall never forget it. Oh dear, what wonderful things have happened since that! Do you ever think of Jeffrey?'

'Yes;—of course I think of him. I did like him so much. I hope I shall see him some day.'

'And he liked you too, young woman; and, what was more, young woman, I thought at one time that, perhaps, you were going to like him in earnest.'

'Not in that way, certainly.'

'You've done much better, of course; especially as poor Jeffrey's chance of promotion doesn't look so good now. If I have a boy, I wonder whether he'll hate me?'

'Why should he hate you?'

'I can't help it, you know, if he does. Only think what it is to Plantagenet. Have you seen the difference it makes in him already?'

'Of course it makes a difference;—the greatest difference in the world.'

'And think what it will be to me, Alice. I used to lie in bed

411

and wish myself dead, and make up my mind to drown myself, —if I could only dare. I shan't think any more of that poor fellow now.' Then she told Alice what had been done for Burgo; how his uncle had paid his bills once again, and had agreed to give him a small income. 'Poor fellow!' said Lady Glencora, 'it won't do more than buy him gloves, you know.'

The marriage was magnificent, greatly to the dismay of Alice and to the discomfort of Mr. Vavasor, who came down on the eve of the ceremony,—arriving while his daughter and Lady Glencora were in the ruins. Mr. Grey seemed to take it all very easily, and, as Lady Glencora said, played his part exactly as though he were in the habit of being married, at any rate, once a year. 'Nothing on earth will ever put him out, so you need not try, my dear,' she said, as Alice stood with her a moment alone in the dressing-room up-stairs before her departure.

'I know that,' said Alice, 'and therefore I shall never try.'

CHAPTER LXXX

The Story is finished within the Halls of the Duke of Omnium

MR. GREY and his wife were duly carried away from Matching Priory by post horses, and did their honeymoon, we may be quite sure, with much satisfaction. When Alice was first asked where she would go, she simply suggested that it should not be to Switzerland. They did, in truth, go by slow stages to Italy, to Venice, Florence, and on to Rome; but such had not been their intention when they first started on their journey. At that time Mr. Grey believed that he would be wanted again in England, down at Silverbridge in Barsetshire, very shortly. But before he had been married a week he learned that all that was to be postponed. The cup of fruition had not yet reached Mr. Palliser's lips. 'There will be no vacancy either in the county or in the borough till Parliament meets.' That had been the message sent by Mr. Palliser to Mr. Grey.

Lady Glencora's message to Alice had been rather more full, having occupied three pages of note-paper, the last of which had been crossed, but I do not know that it was more explicit. She had abused Lord Brock, had abused Mr. Finespun, and had abused all public things and institutions, because the arrangements as now proposed would be very comfortable to Alice, but would not, as she was pleased to think, be very comfortable to herself. 'You can go to Rome and see everything and enjoy yourself, which I was not allowed to do; and all this noise and bother, and crowd of electioneering, will take place down in Barsetshire just when I am in the middle of all my trouble.' There were many very long letters came from Lady Glencora to Rome during the winter,—letters which Alice enjoyed thoroughly, but which she could not but regard as being very indiscreet. The Duke was at the Castle during the Christmas week, and the descriptions of the Duke and of his solicitude as to his heir were very comic. 'He comes and bends over me on the sofa in the most stupendous way, as though a woman to be the mother of his heir must be a miracle in nature. He is quite awful when he says a word or two, and more awful in his silence. The devil prompted me the other day, and I said I hoped it would be a girl. There was a look came over his face which nearly frightened me. If it should be, I believe he will turn me out of the house; but how can I help it? I wish you were going to have a baby at the same time. Then, if yours was a boy and mine a girl, we'd make a change.' This was very indiscreet. Lady Glencora would write indiscreet letters like this, which Alice could not show to her husband. It was a thousand pities.

But December and January wore themselves away, and the time came in which the Greys were bound to return to England. The husband had very fully discussed with his wife that matter of his parliamentary ambition, and found in her a very ready listener. Having made up his mind to do this thing, he was resolved to do it thoroughly, and was becoming almost as full of politics, almost as much devoted to sugar, as Mr. Palliser himself. He at any rate could not complain that his wife would not interest herself in his pursuits. Then, as they returned, came letters from Lady Glencora, written as her troubles grew nigh. The Duke had gone, of course; but he was to be there at the appointed time. 'Oh, I do so wish he would have a fit of the gout in London,—or at Timbuctoo,' said Lady Glencora. When they reached London they first heard the news from Mr. Vavasor, who on this occasion condescended to meet them at the railway. 'The Duke has got an heir,' he said, before the carriage-door was open;—'born this morning!' One might have supposed that it was the Duke's baby, and not the baby of Lady Glencora and Mr. Palliser. There was a note from Mr. Palliser to Mr. Grey. 'Thank God!' said the note, 'Lady Glencora and the boy'—Mr. Palliser had scorned to use the word child—'Lady Glencora and the boy are quite as well as can be expected. Both the new writs were moved for last night.' Mr. Palliser's honours, as will be seen, came rushing upon him all at once.

Wondrous little baby,—purpureo-genitus!*What have the gods not done for thee, if thou canst only manage to live till thy good things are all thine own,—to live through all the terrible solicitude with which they will envelope thee! Better than royal rank will be thine, with influence more than royal, and power of action fettered by no royalty. Royal wealth which will be really thine own, to do with it as it beseemeth thee. Thou wilt be at the top of an aristocracy in a country where aristocrats need gird themselves with no buckram.* All that the world can give will be thine; and yet when we talk of thee religiously, philosophically, or politico-economically, we are wont to declare that thy chances of happiness are no better,— no better, if they be no worse,—than are those of thine infant neighbour just born, in that farmyard cradle. Who shall say that they are better or that they are worse? Or if they be better, or if they be worse, how shall we reconcile to ourselves that seeming injustice?*

And now we will pay a little visit to the small one born in the purple, and the story of that visit shall be the end of our history. It was early in April, quite early in April, and Mr.

and Mrs. Grey were both at Gatherum Castle. Mrs. Grey was there at the moment of which we write, but Mr. Grey was absent at Silverbridge with Mr. Palliser. This was the day of the Silverbridge election, and Mr. Grey had gone to that ancient borough, to offer himself as a candidate to the electors, backed by the presence and aid of a very powerful member of the Cabinet. Lady Glencora and Alice were sitting up-stairs with the small, purple-born one in their presence, and the small, purple-born one was lying in Alice's lap.

'It is such a comfort that it is over,' said the mother.

'You are the most ungrateful of women.'

'Oh, Alice,—if you could have known? Your baby may come just as it pleases. You won't lie awake trembling how on earth you will bear your disgrace if one of the vile weaker sex should come to disturb the hopes of your lords and masters;—for I had two, which made it so much more terrible.'

'I'm sure Mr. Palliser would not have said a word.'

'No, he would have said nothing,—nor would the Duke. The Duke would simply have gone away instantly, and never have seen me again till the next chance comes,—if it ever does come. And Mr. Palliser would have been as gentle as a dove; —much more gentle than he is now, for men are rarely gentle in their triumph. But I should have known what they both thought and felt.'

'It's all right now, dear.'

'Yes, my bonny boy,—you have made it all right for me;— have you not?' And Lady Glencora took her baby into her own arms. 'You have made everything right, my little man. But oh, Alice, if you had seen the Duke's long face through those three days; if you had heard the tones of the people's voices as they whispered about me; if you had encountered the oppressive cheerfulness of those two London doctors,—doctors are such bad actors,—you would have thought it impossible for any woman to live throughout. There's one comfort;—if my mannikin lives, I can't have another eldest. He looks like living;—don't he, Alice?' Then were perpetrated various mysterious ceremonies of feminine idolatry which were continued

415

till there came a grandly dressed old lady, who called herself
the nurse, and who took the idol away.

In the course of that afternoon Lady Glencora took Alice
all over the house. It was a castle of enormous size, quite new,
—having been built by the present proprietor,—very cold,
very handsome, and very dull. 'What an immense place!' said
Alice, as she stood looking round her in the grand hall, which
was never used as an entrance except on very grand occasions.
'Is it not? And it cost—oh, I can't tell you how much it cost.
A hundred thousand pounds or more. Well;—that would be
nothing, as the Duke no doubt had the money in his pocket
to do what he liked with at the time. But the joke is, nobody
ever thinks of living here. Who'd live in such a great, over-
grown place such as this, if they could get a comfortable house
like Matching? Do you remember Longroyston and the hot-
water pipes? I always think of the poor Duchess when I come
through here. Nobody ever lives here, or ever will. The Duke
comes for one week in the year, and Plantagenet says he hates
to do that. As for me, nothing on earth shall ever make me
live here. I was completely in their power and couldn't help
their bringing me here the other day;—because I had, as it
were, disgraced myself.'

'How disgraced yourself?'

'In being so long, you know, before that gentleman was
born. But they shan't play me the same trick again. I shall
dare to assert myself, now. Come,—we must go away. There
are some of the British public come to see one of the British
sights. That's another pleasure here. One has to run about to
avoid being caught by the visitors. The housekeeper tells me
they always grumble because they are not allowed to go into
my little room upstairs.'

On the evening of that day Mr. Palliser and Mr. Grey
returned home from Silverbridge together. The latter was
then a Member of Parliament, but the former at that moment
was the possessor of no such dignity. The election for the
borough was now over, whereas that for the county had not
yet taken place. But there was no rival candidate for the posi-

tion, and Mr. Palliser was thoroughly contented with his fate. He was at this moment actually Chancellor of the Exchequer, and in about ten days' time would be on his legs in the House proposing for his country's use his scheme of finance. The two men were seated together in an open carriage, and were being whirled along by four horses. They were both no doubt happy in their ambition, but I think that of the two, Mr. Palliser showed his triumph the most. Not that he spoke even to his friend a word that was triumphant in its tone. It was not thus that he rejoiced. He was by nature too placid for that. But there was a nervousness in his contentment which told the tale to any observer who might know how to read it.

'I hope you'll like it,' he said to Grey.

'I shall never like it as you do,' Grey answered.

'And why not;—why not?'

'In the first place, I have not begun it so young.'

'Any time before thirty-five is young enough.'

'For useful work, yes,—but hardly for enjoyment in the thing. And then I don't believe it all as you do. To you the British House of Commons is everything.'

'Yes;—everything,' said Mr. Palliser with unwonted enthusiasm;—'everything, everything. That and the Constitution are everything.'

'It is not so to me.'

'Ah, but it will be. If you really take to the work, and put yourself into harness, it will be so. You'll get to feel it as I do. The man who is counted by his colleagues as number one on the Treasury Bench in the English House of Commons is the first of living men. That's my opinion. I don't know that I ever said it before; but that's my opinion.'

'And who is the second;—the purse-bearer to this great man?'

'I say nothing about the second. I don't know that there is any second. I wonder how we shall find Lady Glencora and the boy.' They had then arrived at the side entrance to the Castle, and Mr. Grey ran up-stairs to his wife's room to receive her congratulations.

'And you are a Member of Parliament?' she asked.

'They tell me so, but I don't know whether I actually am one till I've taken the oaths.'

'I am so happy. There's no position in the world so glorious!'

'It's a pity you are not Mr. Palliser's wife. That's just what he has been saying.'

'Oh, John, I am so happy. It is so much more than I have deserved. I hope,—that is, I sometimes think——'

'Think what, dearest?'

'I hope nothing that I have ever said has driven you to it.'

'I'd do more than that, dear, to make you happy,' he said, as he put his arm round her and kissed her; 'more than that, at least if it were in my power.'

Probably my readers may agree with Alice, that in the final adjustment of her affairs she had received more than she had deserved. All her friends, except her husband, thought so. But as they have all forgiven her, including even Lady Midlothian herself, I hope that they who have followed her story to its close will not be less generous.

EXPLANATORY NOTES

T ROLLOPE never intended to create difficulties for his audience
and there is little in his work to perplex unduly the modern
reader. Nevertheless, he does belong very much to his age and
his novels reflect topical interests and matters of a particular
historical period. I have tried in the following notes to give some
indication of these whilst avoiding a burdensome and irritating
documentation of trivia. Some of my notes draw upon material
to be found in R. W. Chapman's addenda to the original Oxford
edition and in Stephen Wall's Penguin edition of *Can You
Forgive Her?* (1972).

VOLUME I

CHAPTER I

Page 1. (1) *Upper Ten Thousand*: the American writer Nathaniel
Willis (1806–67) coined the phrase in his *Necessity for a Promen-
ade Drive* and by the 1860s it seems to have been in popular
use.

(2) *and had failed*: John Vavasor's condition bears a close
resemblance to Trollope's father, himself a failing London
barrister who finally gave up his profession during Trollope's
boyhood.

Page 2. *à l'outrance* (Fr.): excessively, beyond measure.

Page 3. (1) *Chancery*: the court which, until the fusion of the
courts in 1875 into the High Court of Justice and the Court of
Appeal, administered the rules of equity as distinct from the
rules of common law. It dealt with such matters as the administration of the estates of deceased persons, the execution of trusts,
foreclosures of mortgages, partnerships, and the estates of
infants. By the Judicature Act of 1873 it was established as a
division.

(2) *Lord Chancellor*: the highest judiciary functionary in
England, ranking after princes of the blood and the archbishop

of Canterbury. He presides in the Chancery Division of the Supreme Court and appoints all justices of the peace.

(3) *Westminster Hall, and Lincoln's Inn*: until 1820 the Hall was used as a court of justice; Lincoln's Inn is one of the four Inns of Court having the exclusive right of admitting persons to practise at the bar.

Page 5. K.C.B.: Knight Commander (of the Order) of the Bath (so called after the bath rites which preceded installation).

Page 6. (1) *Calvinistic Sabbatarian*: one whose observance of Sunday is excessively strict.

(2) *comitatus*: literally, a retinue of warriors or nobles attached to a king or chieftain.

(3) *Queen Anne Street*: to the west of Portland Place and north of Oxford Street, it was built around 1760.

CHAPTER II

Page 9. cantle: segment or portion.

Page 11. (1) *King Street, Saint James's*: this runs parallel to Pall Mall, to the north of St. James's Park.

(2) *the modern Babylon*: the mystical Babylon of the Apocalypse; hence, any sinful and luxurious city.

CHAPTER III

Page 21. Paynim: pagan, heathen; especially Muslim or Saracen.

Page 25. an idol of clay: 'As for this image, his head was of fine gold, his breast and his arms of silver, his belly and his thighs of brass, his legs of iron, his feet part of iron, and part of clay.' (Dan. 2: 33)

Page 27. flys: light, speedy, covered carriages drawn by a single horse, hired from a livery stable rather than in the streets.

Page 31. adhesion: support, approval.

CHAPTER IV

Page 36. (1) *Cremorne*: Chelsea pleasure gardens, notorious for irregularities, closed in 1877. Trollope also refers to them in *The Small House at Allington*, Chapter IV.

(2) *unentailed*: i.e. the estate had not been settled on a number of persons in succession, none of them having the right to dispose of it as absolute owner.

Page 37. *the metropolitan borough of Chelsea* was, by reputation, Radical in its political character, although it became entitled to parliamentary representation as a borough only in 1868. Until then it was part of the county constituency of Middlesex, which in the 1857 general election returned a Liberal member.

Page 38. *mite*: 'And there came a poor widow, and she cast in two mites, which make a farthing' (Mark 12: 42). Also a Flemish coin of very little value.

Page 41. *the proper witching hour of night*: Trollope misquotes Shakespeare, *Hamlet*, III. ii. 413: "Tis now the very witching time of night'.

Page 42. (1) *jobbed*: stabbed or speared.

(2) *Volunteers*: the volunteer movement was begun in 1859 to strengthen defences against the aggression of Napoleon III.

CHAPTER V

Page 44. (1) *Retro age, Satanas* (Lat.): 'Get thee behind me, Satan' (Matt. 16: 23).

(2) *Grimsell . . . Gemmi . . . Jungfrau*: travel articles abounded in the popular periodicals; Trollope himself travelled widely and published numerous accounts in periodical and book form. The Jungfrau is a mountain in the northern Bernese Alps; the Grimsell and the Gemmi are passes in the same range.

(3) *Alpine Club*: Trollope took some interest in the club, which was established in 1857 to stimulate exploration of the Alps.

Page 46. (1) *the big hotel*: this has been identified as the Hôtel Trois Rois, referred to in Murray's *Handbook for Travellers in Switzerland*. In the early 1850s Trollope submitted a handbook on Ireland to John Murray which was rejected.

(2) *meed*: one's merited portion (of praise, honour, etc.).

Page 52. *duenna*: chaperon (usually elderly).

421

CHAPTER VI

Page 55. the little inn at Handek: Murray refers to the delights of this inn, situated near the Grimsell.

Page 64. It is Hyperion to a Satyr: Kate is recalling Hamlet's comparison of his father with Claudius: 'So excellent a king, that was to this / Hyperion to a Satyr . . . ' (II. i, 139–40). Hyperion, according to Hesiod, was a sun-god; in Keats's poem he is about to be deposed by Apollo. In early mythology satyrs were sinister, half-bestial spirits of woods and hills.

CHAPTER VII

Page 68. (1) *. . . it is not so*: towards the end of 1859 Trollope was appointed Surveyor of the Eastern District for the Post Office. His area of responsibility included Suffolk and as his post entailed much travelling he had first-hand knowledge of Yarmouth.

(2) *Shoreditch*: also known as Bishopsgate, the London terminus of the Great Eastern Railway until November 1875 when Liverpool Street Station superseded it.

(3) *beyond the stones*: streets were unpaved beyond the metropolitan boundary.

Page 70. manes (Lat.): shade of a departed person. Mrs. Greenow pronounces it as one syllable.

Page 71. cynosure: the constellation of the Lesser Bear, containing the Pole Star; hence, an object of special attraction. Trollope may be recalling Milton, whom he read assiduously: 'Where perhaps some beauty lies / The cynosure of neighbouring eyes' (*L'Allegro*, 79–80).

Page 74. sold out: military commissions could be disposed of by sale under a purchase system.

CHAPTER VIII

Page 77. (1) *Dance on the sand . . . and yet no footing seen*:
> 'Bid me discourse, I will enchant thine ear,
> Or like a fairy trip upon the green,

Or like a nymph, with long dishevell'd hair,
Dance on the sands, and yet no footing seen.'
(Shakespeare, *Venus and Adonis*, ll. 145–8.)

Trollope makes further play with this throughout the episode.

(2) *éclat* (Fr.): radiance, renown; in the nineteenth century the word had disparaging connotations.

Page 83. the West Indian Station: Trollope visited the West Indies on Post Office business and his subsequent account, *The West Indies and the Spanish Main* (1859), he always regarded very highly.

Page 85. (1) *pour passer le temps* (Fr.): to idle away the time.

(2) *Lord Nelson*: Horatio Nelson (1758–1805), educated at Norwich and elsewhere in the region, was born at Burnham-Thorpe in Norfolk and descended from a well-established Norfolk family.

CHAPTER IX

Page 93. Sir Roger de Coverley: an English country-dance (and tune), more stately than the polka and waltz.

Page 96. (1) *paper*: promissory note undertaking to pay a stated sum to a particular person (or to the bearer), either at a date specified or on demand.

(2) *mangels*: a variety of beet, with a root larger than that of the garden beet, cultivated as a food for cattle.

CHAPTER X

Page 100. Cambridgeshire: as surveyor of the Eastern District, Trollope was familiar with the county.

Page 101. prebendal stall: literally, a canon or other prebend's seat in a cathedral: hence, the stipend due to an ecclesiastical office-holder. Reforms in the late 1830s reduced some of these incomes.

Page 104. steeple: at 465 feet the steeple of Strasbourg cathedral is amongst the tallest in Europe.

CHAPTER XI

Page 110. *a flock of learned ladies*: Victorian feminists were active in promoting women's rights, publishing the *English-woman's Journal* from Langham Place, near Queen Anne Street. In *North America* (1862) Trollope had discussed the problem of women's employment; in the 1850s the relationship between women's independence and marriage was a topical issue.

Page 111. (1) *Augustus*: the title taken by Octavian, first Emperor of Rome (27 BC–AD 14) who attempted, in the face of great opposition, to reform the Roman Senate.

(2) *the Girondists*: a moderate republican party in the French Assembly of 1791–2 and the Convention of 1792–5. They obstructed the policies of Robespierre (1758–94) who was among the promoters of the Reign of Terror and exercised a kind of dictatorship before his overthrow and execution.

(3) *Manchester and its cares*: a reference to the emergence of the manufacturing class in English politics, led particularly by John Bright (1811–89) and Richard Cobden (1804–65) both of whom had close associations with Manchester.

Page 120. *Charles Kemble*: manager of Covent Garden between 1815 and 1840, Charles Kemble (1775–1854) was noted for his great range of acting and particularly for his comic roles.

CHAPTER XII

Page 124. *Bicester*: Trollope referred earlier to the stables at Roebury; hence it seems that, in his imagination at least, Roebury is to be found near Bicester in Oxfordshire.

Page 125. *Sybarite*: originally a native of Sybaris, an ancient Greek city of southern Italy noted for its luxury; hence, a voluptuary or sensualist.

Page 128. (1) *birds'-eye fogle*: a spotted, probably silken neckerchief.

(2) *spigot*: a device to regulate the flow of liquor from its container.

EXPLANATORY NOTES

CHAPTER XIII

Page 130. *to my own cheek*: i.e. for my own benefit.

Page 131. *a family . . . in the vale of Taunton*: like the lawyer, Mr. Vholes, in Dickens's *Bleak House*. The book contains a satire on the abuses of the old court of Chancery, the delays and costs of which brought misery and ruin on its suitors. The point is naturally lost on Grimes.

Page 133. *charge*: the reference is to extortionate interest charges, fixed according to the date of settlement.

Page 134. (1) *stanch*: staunch.

(2) *You can't do it cheap*: contemporary figures bear this out: in 1857 the authorized election expenses in Lambeth amounted to £5,300. Bribery and other electoral abuses had by no means been prevented by the 1832 Reform Bill.

Page 135. *sheriff's officers*: officials employed to execute the sheriff's writ, with powers to arrest. The sheriff was nominally responsible for detaining prisoners in safe custody, preparing jurors, the execution of writs and death sentences.

CHAPTER XIV

Page 145. (1) *Nimrods*: 'The mighty hunter before the Lord' (Gen. 10: 9). Also the pseudonym of Charles Apperley (1778–1843), author of popular sporting books and articles.

(2) *Capel Court*: located in Bartholomew Lane, it housed the Stock Exchange.

Page 149. *. . . when at Tibur she regretted Rome*: cf. Horace, *Epistles*, i, viii. Tibur was a town sixteen miles north-east of ancient Rome.

CHAPTER XVI

Page 162. *a sporting literary gentleman*: named Pollock, this character has a strong element of authorial self-portraiture. Trollope's *Autobiography* bears witness to his own fondness for hunting: '. . . it has been for more than thirty years a duty to me to ride hounds . . . Nothing has ever been allowed to stand in the way of hunting.' (Ed. Sadleir and Page, O.U.P., The World's Classics, 1980, p. 64.) His *Hunting Sketches* appeared in 1865.

Page 163. *chaffed*: teased, railed at (in a light-hearted fashion).

Page 165. (1) *Edgehill*: a village 7 miles N.W. of Banbury, site of a Civil War battle in 1642.

(2) . . . *I will not change the name*: Trollope's note testifies to his admiration of Thackeray, also expressed in his *Auto-biography* and in his English Men of Letters volume on him (1879). In 1859, as editor of the *Cornhill Magazine*, Thackeray had invited Trollope to contribute a serialized novel and the first issue carried the opening of *Framley Parsonage*. Thackeray died in December 1863; Trollope wrote a glowing tribute in the *Cornhill*. Cinqbars is a profligate character to be found in a number of Thackeray's works.

Page 166. *cover hack*: actually a covert-hack, a horse used for riding to the meet.

Page 167. (1) *Tattersall's*: an auction-room for horses founded near Hyde Park Corner in 1766.

(2) '*make un break*': i.e. the gathering of hounds and the fox's bolting.

Page 169. . . . *those who domineered and those who submitted*: in the early pages of his *Autobiography* Trollope recalls with similar feeling the misery of his schooldays at Harrow, Sunbury, and Winchester.

CHAPTER XVII

Page 173. *dog-carts*, *gigs*, *and waggonettes*: dog-carts were open vehicles, with two transverse seats back to back, the hinder of these originally made to box in dogs; gigs were light, two-wheeled, one-horse carriages; waggonettes were four-wheeled, made open or with a removable cover and furnished with a bench at each side facing inwards, with one or two seats arranged crosswise in front.

Page 174. *trap*: a small carriage on springs, usually two-wheeled.

Page 175. *saddle-bows*: the arched front of the saddle.

Page 181. *quickset*: live slips or cuttings of plants, especially of whitethorn or other shrub, grown to create a hedge.

Page 183. *ten minutes' law*: in this sense, an allowance in time or distance granted to an animal that is to be hunted.

Page 186. *rowels*: the rotating disc with sharp radial points at the extremity of the spur.

CHAPTER XVIII

Page 188. *St. George's Square*: this is in the manuscript and all editions; doubtless Trollope means St. George's, Hanover Square.

Page 191. *Gatherum Castle*: Trollope's comic nomenclatures can be preposterous. The tradition of giving allegorical names probably derives from the Morality plays, but in the nineteenth-century novel they were generally used to confirm personality traits. Gatherum Castle is described in *Doctor Thorne*, Chapter XIX.

CHAPTER XIX

Page 202. *poult*: the young of the domestic fowl and various game-birds.

CHAPTER XX

Page 208. (1) *Caffres*: Caffres, or Kaffirs, was originally a term applied to all black aboriginal inhabitants of Southern Africa other than Hottentots and Bushmen. Derived from the Arabic, the word signifies a non-believer. Although Zululand is in northern Natal, and Caffres were particularly associated with the south-east region of Cape Province, Bellfield is using the word in its most general sense.

(2) *Kitchyhomy River*: the mouth of the Essequibo River is indeed to be found on the coast of Guiana where African slaves were deported, but the Kitchyhomy River exists only in Bellfield's imagination.

Page 209. *the heights of Inkerman*: the battle fought in the Crimea on 5 November 1854 in which British troops besieging Sebastopol repulsed a Russian attack.

Page 210. *laurestinus*: actually Laurustinus, an evergreen winter-flowering shrub.

CHAPTER XXI

Page 216. (1) *the Great Western . . . the Great Northern*: their two contemporary counterparts are Paddington (opened in 1854) and King's Cross (opened in 1852).

(2) *tuft-hunting*: the term derives from the tuft, a gold tassel worn by a peer's son or a fellow commoner at Oxford University; hence, one who tries to curry favour with the powerful.

Page 220. *blue books*: official reports of Parliament and the Privy Council, issued in a blue paper cover, synonymous with nineteenth-century public scrutiny of administration, etc.

CHAPTER XXII

Page 222. *Whitechapel*: a light, two-wheeled spring-cart.

Page 223. *Mrs. Grundy*: a symbol of conventional propriety, she was created by the dramatist Thomas Morton (1764?–1838) in *Speed the Plough*, a comedy produced in 1798. Significantly, she never actually appears, her supposed opinions being constantly invoked as the guide to correct behaviour.

Page 224. *branch*: a privately owned (and financed) branch-line.

Page 225. *Reform Bill*: a bill for widening the parliamentary franchise and removing inequalities and abuses in the system of representation, introduced by Lord John Russell in 1831 and carried after an intense struggle in 1832. (Others were passed in 1867 and 1884.) It entailed, amongst other things, the reorganization of constituency boundaries. It would seem that Matching, eliminated by the bill, must have been a rotten borough.

Page 233. *that woman's travels*: this has been hesitantly identified as *Recollections of Tartar Steppes and their Inhabitants* (1863) by Mrs. Lucy Atkinson, which described her encounters with wolves and tigers.

CHAPTER XXIII

Page 236. *the ballot*: Trollope himself opposed the introduction of secret voting (it became law in 1872); the Radicals generally supported it as part of the programme of electoral reform.

Page 238. (1) *Rowland Hill*: considered the architect of the modern postal service, Hill (1795–1879) was the originator of cheap postage. Although Trollope was pleased to call himself an 'anti-Hillite' he recognized his superior's administrative skill and reforming brilliance.

(2) *crosses*: i.e. inserts new material across the lines of a letter by turning it sideways.

(3) *I do hate the Americans*: Jeffrey Palliser's views are contrary to Trollope's own. His mother visited America between 1827 and 1831 and launched her own literary career with *The Domestic Manners of the Americans* (1832). Trollope briefly visited the southern states during the Civil War in 1861 and published in the following year his *North America*, predicting a just victory for the North. He returned on a number of occasions and in his *Autobiography* plainly declares his view of Americans: 'Who can but love their personal generosity, their active and far-seeking philanthropy, their love of education, their hatred of ignorance, the general conviction on the minds of all of them that a man should be enabled to walk upright, fearing no one and conscious that he is responsible for his own actions?' (p. 314).

Page 239. (1) *Topsy*: the little slave girl in Harriet Beecher Stowe's *Uncle Tom's Cabin* (1852).

(2) *Mudie's*: the circulating library begun in 1842 by Charles Mudie (1818–90) and formed into a company in 1862. It closed in 1937.

Page 241. . . . *as long as he could get any cotton*: in 1864 the Northern States blockaded the Southern ports and the supply of cotton to England, already severely restricted, came to a virtual standstill.

Page 242. (1) *mace*: a cue with a flat square head.

(2) *cannon*: billiards is played with 3 balls, 1 red and 2 white. Points can be scored by the cannon, i.e. by the player's ball hitting the other two balls successively.

CHAPTER XXIV

Page 248. *Idoneus puellis* (Lat.): this, and the previous sentence, refer to Horace: 'Though that life is past, I was but now still meet for ladies' love, and fought my battles not without glory. Now my armour and the lute, whose campaigns are over, will hang here on yonder wall.' (*Odes*, III. xxvi. 1–4; tr. Wickham.)

Page 253. (1) *St. Helens* did not become a constituency until 1868.

(2) *the Manchester school*: the name was first applied by Disraeli in 1846 to those who, led by Cobden and Bright, advocated the principles of free trade and later supported them on other policies.

CHAPTER XXV

Page 261. *Hecuba*: wife of King Priam of Troy and mother of many of his children, including Hector, Paris, Cassandra, and Polyxena. According to Homer, Priam fathered fifty sons and fifty daughters by his wife and concubines.

Page 262. . . . *the source of all progress*: Plantagenet, not unnaturally, utters Trollope's own sentiments here which are restated in his *Autobiography*: 'All material progress has come from man's desire to do the best he can for himself and those about him . . . ' (p. 105).

CHAPTER XXVI

Page 273. *Bacchus* . . . *Ariadne*: daughter of Minos, King of Crete, who guided Theseus through the labyrinth after his destruction of the Minotaur. She was later abandoned by him on the island of Dia (Naxos) where, according to one legend, she was found by Bacchus (Dionysus) who married her and gave her a crown of seven stars which became a constellation after her death.

CHAPTER XXVII

Page 282. *clerestory windows*: in the upper part of the nave, choir, and transepts of any large church, these admit light to the central parts of the building.

CHAPTER XXVIII

Page 292. *female emigration*: a topical problem from the 1840s was the surplus of women; emigration was thought a useful contingency for them, as also for fallen women. Lady Baldock in *Phineas Finn* (Chapter XL) supports the 'Female Protestant Unmarried Woman's Emigration Society'.

CHAPTER XXIX

Page 302. *curricle*: a running-course, or a light, two-wheeled carriage drawn by two horses abreast; either fits the meaning here.

Page 303. (1) *Juan and Haidee . . . Lambro*: Haidee, the beautiful daughter of a Greek pirate, restored Don Juan to life and the pair fell in love; but her father, Lambro, discovered them and captured Juan. See Byron's *Don Juan*, Canto III.

(2) *Foundling Hospital*: founded in 1739 for the reception of neglected and deserted children; the hospital stands near Gray's Inn Lane.

Page 304. (1) *went to smash*: i.e. become insolvent or bankrupt. Trollope recounts a very similar experience in his *Autobiography* (Chapter III).

(2) *. . . at two months for five hundred*: Burgo is proposing that, on his behalf, George should sign a promissory note for £500; the money-lender will then release £150 with payment, including interest, to be made in two months.

Page 309. *ruffler*: a proud, swaggering, or arrogant fellow.

CHAPTER XXX

Page 317. *Do tell him to be punctual*: Trollope is recalling the habit of the money-lender who would call on him daily with the same injunction when he began his Post Office career. (See *Autobiography*, Chapter III.) A similar character is Mr. Clarkson in *Phineas Finn* (Chapter XXI).

CHAPTER XXXI

Page 320. (1) *Beacon Hill*: although there is no generally known Beacon Hill near Haweswater, the name might well have been given locally to any suitable eminence with a conspicuous summit.

(2) *Naddale*: an area of forest bordering the south-eastern shore of Haweswater.

(3) *Bowness and Windermere*: as the crow flies, some 13 miles S.W. of Haweswater.

(4) . . . *from Lancaster to Carlisle*: the principal travelling route across Shap Fells.

Page 321. *inside jaunting-car*: a light two-wheeled vehicle popular in Ireland, seating four persons arranged in pairs facing inwards. (A back-to-back arrangement was described as 'outside'.)

Page 322. *Swindale Fell*: the eastern slopes of Naddale Forest. According to Lewis's *Topographical Dictionary* (1848), Swindale was a chapelry of 73 inhabitants.

Page 326. (1) *Vavaseurs*: feudal tenants ranking immediately below a baron. In the General Prologue to the *Canterbury Tales* Chaucer says of the Franklin: 'Was nowher such a worthy vavasour' (360).

(2) *Helvellyn . . . Kidsty Pyk . . . Scaw Fell*: Helvellyn (3,118 ft.) is 9 miles S.E. of Keswick; Kidsty Pike (2,560 ft.) is near the southern shore of Haweswater. Scaw Fell (3,162 ft.) is 11 miles S.W. of Keswick.

Page 327. *Hawes Water*: as the lake has been dammed to provide Manchester's water supply, Trollope's description is now inaccurate in certain details.

Page 330. *Crichton*: James Crichton (1560–85?) was a formidably learned Scot who travelled Europe as a soldier and scholar. His title of Admirable originated in Sir Thomas Urquhart's narrative of his career (1652); William Ainsworth's novel *Crichton* (1837) and James Barrie's play *The Admirable Crichton* (1902) are also based upon his life.

CHAPTER XXXII

Page 331. *Shap*: between Kendal and Penrith.

Page 335. *spuds*: small garden tools for digging.

CHAPTER XXXIII

Page 342. . . . *Mr. Hawthorne has described as beefy*: in *The Scarlet Letter* Nathaniel Hawthorne describes a group of 'wives and maidens of old English birth . . . and the beef and ale of their native land . . . entered largely into their composition' (Chapter 2). Hawthorne offered in 1860 a similar and very fine description of Trollope's novels: 'solid and substantial, written on the strength of beef and through the inspiration of ale, and just as real as if some giant had hewn a great lump out of the earth and put it under a glass case, with all its inhabitants going about their daily business, and not suspecting that they were being made a show of'. (Quoted in *Autobiography*, p. 144.)

CHAPTER XXXV

Page 362. . . . *as old as Enoch*: 'And the days of Enoch were three hundred and sixty-five years' (Gen. 5: 23). The sixth in descent from Adam and father of Methuselah, he did not die but was translated to heaven.

CHAPTER XXXVI

Page 371. (1) '*Look here, upon this picture—and on this*': Shakespeare, *Hamlet*, III. iv. 53.

(2) *Pandemonium*: ' . . . Pandaemonium, the high capital / Of Satan, and his peers . . . ' (Milton, *Paradise Lost*, I, 1.756).

Page 372. *Quarterly*: the *Quarterly Review*, founded in 1809 by John Murray as a Tory rival to the *Edinburgh Review*.

Page 374. *college tutorship*: at this period it was obligatory to resign from college tutorships at Oxford and Cambridge upon marriage.

CHAPTER XXXVII

Page 384. . . . *for many years*: the basic plot of *Can You Forgive Her?* was first created by Trollope in 1850 in his play *The Noble Jilt*, a comedy written partly in blank verse and partly in prose. It was sent to the actor George Bartley, who rejected it for reasons Trollope understood but found hurtful. See *Autobiography*, pp. 85–6.

Page 385. *Doctors' Commons*: originally the common table and dining-hall of the College of Doctors of Civil Law in London; hence, the name is applied to the buildings (demolished in 1867) occupied by these, and now to their site, to the south of St. Paul's Cathedral. See Dickens's description in *David Copperfield*, Chapters XXII and XXVI.

Page 391. *cankery chiels*: presumably Trollope's Cumbrian dialect for 'spiteful fellows'.

Page 396. . . . *readjusting the payment*: i.e. arrangements concerning the rate and date of repayment.

Page 402. (1) *augean*: Augeas, king of Elis, had an immense herd of oxen whose stables had never been cleansed. To clean them in a single day was one of the labours imposed on Hercules.

(2) *Tombland*: to the west of Norwich Cathedral, it is the site of an annual medieval market.

(3) *brougham*: a one-horse, closed carriage, with two or four wheels, for up to four persons.

Page 404. . . . *by which young Irish ladies allure their lovers*: Trollope may be drawing on personal experience. In 1841 he arrived in Ireland as deputy to a Post Office inspector in Connaught. A year later he met Rose Heseltine, an English girl, at Kingstown, near Dublin; they were married in 1844.

CHAPTER XL

Page 413. *weepers*: the long, black crepe veils of a widow.

Page 419. *sun's portraiture*: contemporary term for a photographic image.

Page 421. *trivet*: a three-footed stand or support; hence thoroughly or perfectly right (in reference to a trivet's stability).

VOLUME II

CHAPTER XLI

Page 6. *writ*: a document issued by the Crown directing a sheriff to hold an election of a Member or Members of Parliament.

Page 9. (1) *cut a purse*: steal money.

(2) *Globe*: an evening newspaper.

CHAPTER XLII

Page 9. . . . *what were left of the direct taxes*: as Chancellor of the Exchequer, Gladstone had cut income tax by over half in his budgets between 1861 and 1866, and planned to abolish the tax entirely.

Page 10. (1) *Juno and Venus*: Juno (Hera), Venus (Aphrodite), and Minerva (Athene) competed for the golden apple which Paris awarded to Venus. Juno pursued with inexorable jealousy the mistresses of her husband Zeus and their children, which brought her into frequent conflict with Venus.

(2) . . . *when Oxford embraces Manchester*: until 1865 Gladstone sat for Oxford University; his espousal of free-trade won the loyalty of some of the Manchester school.

Page 12. . . . *pulled his hat*: hats were frequently worn in the House.

Page 25. *It's only just a step*: Mrs. Marsham has made more effort than she cares to admit: Norfolk Street is some distance from Park Lane.

Page 26. Argus: a monster with a hundred eyes sent by the jealous Hera to watch her priestess and rival Io, whom Zeus changed into a heifer.

Page 27. Cerberus: the dog of Pluto stationed at the entrance of Hades to prevent the living from entering and the dead from escaping.

Page 28. Doctor Fell: a type of vaguely unamiable person against whom no precise grounds for dislike can be adduced. Dr. John Fell (1625–86) was bishop of Oxford and a considerable benefactor of the University, particularly of the University Press. It is curious that he should be principally associated with the jingle, 'I do not love you, Dr. Fell; / But why I cannot tell; / But this I know full well, / I do not love you, Dr. Fell' (a translation of Martial, *Epigrams*, I. xxxii, by Thomas Browne).

Page 32. doit: originally, a small Dutch coin; hence, in this phrase, a bit or jot.

CHAPTER XLIV

Page 37. (1) . . . *the other day in Russia*: the Russian serfs were liberated in 1861.

(2) *embanking the river . . . to . . . Pimlico*: the embankment of the Thames between Westminster and Blackfriars Bridge was discussed in 1860 and undertaken in 1864. Pimlico, though, lies in the opposite direction and at this time there was no proposal to extend the embankment.

Page 39. (1) *the Reach*: part of the Thames known as Chelsea Reach.

(2) *Metropolitan Board*: the Metropolitan Board of Works was responsible for major improvements of, amongst other things, public waterways and thoroughfares.

(3) *Cheapside*: in medieval London a busy market area and a place for pageants, sports, and occasional executions.

Page 43. . . . *the expense of a petition*: in 1868 Trollope failed to be elected as a Liberal candidate for Beverley, Yorkshire, and knew well the miseries and expense of canvassing. After the election, the town brought a petition alleging bribery and corruption and the town was disenfranchised, to Trollope's satisfaction. See *Autobiography*, Chapter XVI.

CHAPTER XLV

Page 44. (1) *Somerset House*: this houses the offices of the Revenue Department, the principal Probate Registry, and the Registrar General of Births, Marriages, and Deaths.

(2) . . . *which they shall one day possess*: the Houses of Parliament were rebuilt after the fire of 1834; the new House of Lords began to be used in 1847, the House of Commons in 1852.

(3) . . . *which it most becomes an Englishman to have achieved*: Trollope's paean on the glories of parliamentary service is echoed in his *Autobiography* (see Chapter XVI). This esteem is evident throughout the novel, particularly in the figure of Plantagenet Palliser.

Page 46. . . . *a party was forming itself*: party groupings were an almost nominal discipline at this time; shifting loyalties were pledged to individuals or factions.

Page 50. (1) *'count out'*: the House was declared inquorate when the Speaker was alerted to the presence of fewer than forty Members.

(2) . . . *the privilege of that House*: MPs have long been immune from certain kinds of prosecution because of their position.

CHAPTER XLVI

Page 58. *Chatham*: William Pitt, first earl of Chatham (1708–78) celebrated as a great Whig statesman, administrator, and orator.

CHAPTER XLVII

Page 66. *ticket-of-leave*: an order of licence giving a convict his liberty under certain restrictions before his sentence had expired. That such convicts were widely feared is illustrated by the success of Tom Taylor's play *The Ticket-of-Leave Man* which ran for over 400 performances in 1863–4.

CHAPTER XLVIII

Page 82. fifty thousand a year: the sum had a certain topical significance: in 1863 Parliament granted it as the income of the Prince of Wales on his marriage.

Page 85. (1) *like the proud young porter*: the reference confuses the porter with the heroine in 'The Loving Ballad of Lord Bateman': 'O when she arrived at Lord Bateman's castle, / How boldly then she rang the bell! / "Who's there? who's there?" cries the proud young porter, / "O come unto me pray quickly tell." '

(2) *the whole tenor of my life's way*: 'Along the cool sequester'd vale of life / They kept the noiseless tenor of their way' (Thomas Grey 'Elegy Written in a Country Churchyard', 75–6).

Page 94. Marchioness of Hartletop: formerly Griselda Grantly, whose father, Archdeacon Grantly, figures largely in *The Warden* and other Barsetshire novels. Plantagenet Palliser's brief flirtation with her is described in *The Small House at Allington*, published in 1864 as *Can You Forgive Her?* began to appear in instalments.

CHAPTER LI

Page 111. Rush and Palmer: two infamous Victorian murderers, hanged in 1849 and 1856.

CHAPTER LII

Page 119. Picture Galleries: the National Gallery in Trafalgar Square, opened in 1838.

CHAPTER LIV

Page 140. piquet: a card game for two players with a pack of 32 cards.

CHAPTER LV

Page 150. grass of the field: 'Wherefore, if God so clothe the grass of the field, which today is, and tomorrow is cast into the oven, shall he not much more clothe you, O ye of little faith?' (Matt. 6: 30).

Page 156. *lien*: in law, a right to retain possession of property until a debt due to the person detaining it is satisfied. Trollope may here be using it in the looser sense of 'bond'.

CHAPTER LVI

Page 160. *the Furies*: in Greek mythology, the avenging deities, Alecto, Megaera, and Tisiphone who executed the curses pronounced upon criminals, tortured the guilty with the stings of conscience, or inflicted famine and pestilences.

Page 168. *Bampton*: a village a few miles to the N.E. of Haweswater.

CHAPTER LVII

Page 170. *os femoris* (Lat.): thigh bone.

Page 176. *letting I dare not . . .* ': 'Letting "I dare not" wait upon "I would" ' (Shakespeare, *Macbeth*, I. vii. 44).

Page 177. (1) *I have sat me down*: in 1839 Trollope's sister Cecelia married John Tilley, who was to achieve a high position in the Post Office, and settled at Penrith. In the early 1840s Trollope's mother lived in the same area for a short time. Hence, Trollope would have been familiar with the topography which serves as such a contrast to the metropolitan settings.

(2) *as light as my purse*: Trollope's early career in the Post Office was punctuated by skirmishes with his superiors; his salary rose only very slowly and he was frequently in debt.

Page 179. *express train*: Ferdinand Lopez in *The Prime Minister* is killed by an express train (Chapter LX).

CHAPTER LVIII

Page 180. *Argus eyes*: slain by Hermes, his eyes were transferred by Hera to the tail of the peacock.

CHAPTER LIX

Page 193. *tilt-yard*: the lists in which medieval combatants challenged each other with lances, on horseback.

Page 199. *quid-nuncs* (Lat.): literally, 'what now?'; hence, gossips.

CHAPTER LX

Page 205. *sharpers*: cheats, swindlers.

Page 207. . . . *when the time is up*: the promissory notes signed by Alice could not be used, unlike cheques, as ready money; 14 days (in this case) had to elapse before George could be credited with the sum by a bank.

Page 209. . . . *the use of two hundred for fourteen days*: depending on the reputation of a bill's signatory, a discount-broker in the City would cash a bill, charging interest.

Page 210. . . . *on mortgage*: i.e. secured by land or property.

CHAPTER LXI

Page 213. (1) *I have so often wandered* . . . : Trollope's father occupied 'dingy, almost suicidal chambers, at No. 23 Old Square, Lincoln's Inn,—chambers which on one melancholy occasion did become absolutely suicidal' when a pupil destroyed himself in his rooms. (*Autobiography*, pp. 2–3.)

(2) *sponging-houses*: a house kept by a bailiff or sheriff's officer, formerly in regular use as a place of preliminary confinement for debtors.

(3) *Symonds' Inn* . . . *Staples' Inn*: the Inns of Court (the Inner and Middle Temples, Lincoln's Inn and Gray's Inn) and of Chancery were originally residences of associations of law students. The Inns of Chancery were formerly attached to one of the Inns of Court, but have ceased to exist as corporate bodies. Some buildings have been destroyed; others, such as Staple Inn, survive in private ownership.

Page 214. *Erebus*: a place of nether darkness, on the way to Hades.

Page 216. *tit-tat-to*: a game resembling noughts and crosses.

CHAPTER LXII

Page 220. *the new court of the Louvre*: the ancient palace of the Kings of France was entirely rebuilt in the reign of Philip II and enlarged by Francis I and his successors down to Napoleon III, who added new pavilions between 1852 and 1857.

Page 221. (1) *Bradshaws*: 'Bradshaw's Railway Guide' was first published in 1839; it became a monthly guide in 1841 and continued publication until May 1961.

(2) *Murray's guide-books*: in 1820 John Murray (1778–1843) published Mrs. Mariana Starke's *Guide for Travellers on the Continent*, which led to a series of Murray's guide-books, several written by his son John Murray (1808–92).

Page 228. *Matching Park*: Trollope's slip for Matching Priory.

CHAPTER LXIII

Page 237. *to pass the Rubicon*: by crossing the Rubicon (the river separating Italy from Cisalpine Gaul) Caesar overstepped the boundaries of his province and committed himself to war against the Senate and Pompey (49 BC); hence, to take a perilously decisive step.

CHAPTER LXIV

Page 240. (1) *nollimy tangere*: a corruption of 'noli me tangere' (Lat.): 'touch me not'. The phrase is to be found in the Vulgate and in John 20: 17.

(2) *a furious Orlando*: Ariosto's epic *Orlando Furioso* (published in its entirety in 1532) tells of Orlando's love for Angelica; thwarted, Orlando is for a time seized by a furious and grotesque madness.

Page 241. *The poker and tongs* . . . : a slight misquotation from the song 'Widow Machree' by the Irish novelist and songwriter Samuel Lover (1797–1868): 'Sure the shovel and tongs / To each other belongs.'

Page 245. *staid*: variant of 'stayed'.

Page 247. *a bit of a breeze*: slang for argument, row.

CHAPTER LXV

Page 252. . . . *coming on the road—close to us*: the repetition at this point begins a new monthly instalment.

CHAPTER LXVI

Page 263. Gibus hat: an opera or crush hat, so called after its first maker.

Page 266. curaçoa: a liqueur flavoured with peel of bitter oranges.

Page 270. (1) *Tyburnia*: a residential quarter of London to the north of Hyde Park, in the neighbourhood of Portman Square.

(2) *Pimlico*: Pimlico Station, on the south side of the Thames, was replaced by Victoria Station in 1860 as the terminus of the London, Brighton and South Coast Railway; the former name may have continued in use to refer to its successor.

CHAPTER LXVII

Page 272. the hero of old . . . found with the distaff: a cleft stick holding wool or flax wound for spinning by hand; hence, woman's work. Hercules was sold as a slave to Omphale, a queen of Lydia, and set to menial tasks whilst his mistress assumed his lion's skin and club.

CHAPTER LXVIII

Page 289. the great Assembly House: the Conversationhaus, particularly well known for its gaming tables.

Page 290. napoleon: a gold coin issued by Napoleon I, worth 20 francs.

CHAPTER LXIX

Page 301. his own family borough: whilst the 1832 Reform Bill widened the franchise and altered constituency boundaries, aristocratic families continued to monopolize certain seats.

CHAPTER LXX

Page 314. Reuss: the river which flows into the Lake of Lucerne at Lucerne.

CHAPTER LXXI

Page 317. stumpy: slang for cash.

EXPLANATORY NOTES

Page 321. *Eve's daughters*: i.e. a fallen woman. Trollope may be recalling Milton: 'Adam, the goodliest man of men since born / His sons; the fairest of her daughters Eve' (*Paradise Lost*, IV 323–4).

CHAPTER LXXII

Page 328. *rouleaus*: gold coins made up into cylindrical packets.
Page 335. *Euston Square Station*: at this period the station was referred to indifferently as 'Euston' and 'Euston Square'.

CHAPTER LXXIII

Page 343. *a certain time*: see *The Small House at Allington*, Chapter XLIII.
Page 344. *Tell's chapel*: William Tell died in 1357; a commemorative chapel was built 31 years later.

CHAPTER LXXIV

Page 351. (1) *the church*: the church of St. Leger or Stiftskirche.
   (2) *Mount Pilate*: otherwise called Mount Pilatus, the name derives from a tradition that the corpse of Pontius Pilate found its final resting-place there (or that Pilate was banished or committed suicide there). The name is perhaps a corruption of 'pileatus', i.e. 'capped' with clouds.

CHAPTER LXXV

Page 356. *Rouge et Noir* (Fr.): a card game; stakes are placed on red and black marks on the table.
Page 359. *sugar-duties*: tax on sugar was reduced by Gladstone in 1864.
Page 360. *French wines*: an Anglo-French trade agreement in 1860 included a reduction of duty on French wine, and imports doubled during the following decade.

CHAPTER LXXVI

Page 371. *the daughters of Danaus*: the fifty Danaïdes, all but one of whom were condemned to Hades after slaying their

husbands on their wedding night. Their punishment was to
fill a leaky jar by means of a sieve.

Page 377. . . . *as far as these pages are concerned*: Burgo Fitzgerald reappears in *The Duke's Children*.

CHAPTER LXXVII

Page 380. (1) *modes of governing*: under the Second Empire
(1852–70) the powers of both the Senate and the lower house
were severely restricted, particularly in the choice of members.

(2) *lucifer matches*: precursor of the modern matchstick,
ignited in the same way.

Page 387. *to pick a crow*: the usual phrase was to 'pull' or
'pluck' a crow: to find fault with, or to have some awkward
matter to settle.

CHAPTER LXXVIII

Page 392. *It's your own bespeak*: i.e. your own arrangement.

Page 398. *all a-mort*: i.e. spiritless.

Page 400. *He shall come to the scratch* . . .: literally, to the starting
line (of a race).

CHAPTER LXXIX

Page 405. *going out for the county*: elected on a narrower franchise
than borough members, county members were seen as representing the aristocratic landed interest. A county seat would be more
in keeping with Palliser's status.

CHAPTER LXXX

Page 414. (1) *purpureo-genitus* (Lat.): born in the purple.

(2) *buckram*: a kind of coarse linen or cloth stiffened with
gum or paste; hence, having a false appearance of strength.

(3) *that seeming injustice*: in his *Autobiography* Trollope addresses himself to the same question. As an 'advanced conservative Liberal' he supports a gradual tendency towards
equality, but suggests that inequality is ultimately an ordi-
nance of the Creator and not to be forcibly altered.

WHO'S WHO

IN

CAN YOU FORGIVE HER?

[Characters whose names are in capital letters appear also in the other novels indicated.]

Applethwaite, John, farmer in Westmoreland, ii. 176.

Auld Reekie, Marchioness of, i. 12; of Castle Reekie, i. 192; aunt of Lady Glencora Palliser, i. 192; her daughter Lady Jane, ii. 402. *See* Macleod, Midlothian.

Bellfield, 'Captain' Gustavus, late of the 97th regiment, i. 74, 80; forty, i. 139; m. Arabella Greenow, ii. 400.

Blowehard, a musician, i. 79.

BOTT, ——, cotton spinner, M.P. (Radical) for St. Helens, Lancashire, i. 240, 253; loses his seat, ii. 302; m. Mrs. Marsham, q.v., ii. 404. See also *P.M.*

BROCK, Lord, Liberal Chancellor of the Exchequer, Prime Minister, ii. 17.
  See *Ph.R.*, *P.M.*

Bunratty, Marquis of, i. 126, ii. 6.

Bunsby, Mrs., George Vavasor's landlady, ii. 328.

Calder Jones, M.P., of the Roebury Club, i. 163.

Cheesacre, Samuel, of Oileymead, Norfolk, i. 75, 96; about forty-five, i. 77; m. Charlotte Fairstairs, ii. 400.

Cinquebars (i.e. 'Five-barred Gate'), Lord, M.P., of the Roebury Club, i. 165 note, ii. 11.

Conway Sparkes, Mrs., poetess, i. 240.

Drummonds, Messrs., bankers, ii. 204.

Dumfriesshire, Duke of, ii. 409.

Duncombe, ——, M.P. for Chelsea Districts, i. 134.

Fairstairs, Charlotte ('Charlie') and Fanny, i. 82; Joe, i. 83; *see* Cheesacre.

Farringcourt, M.P., ii. 47, 50.

Finespun, ——, Liberal Chancellor of the Exchequer, ii. 195.

FITZGERALD, BURGO, i. 179, 187; thirty, i. 187; his married sister, i. 188, 217; his aunt Lady Monk, q.v.
  See also *D.C.*

Flutey, a musician, i. 79.

Gogram, ——, Squire Vavasor's lawyer, ii. 130.

Graham, Colonel, ii. 81.

Grant, Miss ——, George Vavasor's fiancée, i. 38.

GRANTLY, THEOPHILUS, Archdeacon of Barchester, ii. 94. For his daughter GRISELDA, Lady Dumbello (later Hartletop), *see* Hartletop and s.v. Palliser.
  See *The Warden* and other Barchester books.

Green, Mrs., i. 83.

Greenow, Mrs.: Arabella, o.d. and youngest child (i. 66) of Squire Vavasor, widow of Samuel G. of Lancashire, i. 209; £40,000, i. 101; m. 'Captain' Bellfield, q.v.

GREY, JOHN, of Nethercoats, Cambridgeshire, i. 20; £1,500 p.a., o.s. of Prebendary of Ely, i. 101; Cambridge University, i. 101; m. Alice Vavasor, q.v.
  See also *Pb.F., E.D., P.M.*

Grimes, ——, landlord of 'The Handsome Man', Chelsea, i. 125.

Grimsby, a hunting man, i. 78.

Grindley, ('Grindems'), of the Roebury Club, i. 163.

Gubbins, i. 157.

HARTLETOP, Marquis and Marchioness of, ii. 94, 98. *See* Grantly, Palliser. (Before succeeding his father Lord H. was styled Lord Dumbello).
  See also *Pb.F.*

Hock and Block, bankers in Lombard St., ii. 114.

Jane, Alice Vavasor's maid, i. 232.

Jenny, 'Jeannette', Mrs. Greenow's maid, i. 68.

Jones, pugilistic tailor and lodging-house keeper, ii. 123

Jones, Mrs., of Montpelier Parade, Yarmouth, i. 69.

Kilfenora, Lord, e.s. of the Marquis of Bunratty; M.P., Chelsea Districts, i. 126.

Levy, George Vavasor's 'confidential clerk', ii. 202.

VAVASOR, ALICE, o.d. of John Vavasor; £400 p.a., i. 43; m. John Grey, q.v. For her 'great relations' see Auld Reekie, Macleod, Midlothian, Palliser (Glencora).

Vavasor, Arabella, Mrs. Greenow, q.v.

Vavasor, George, only grandson and natural heir of Squire V., i. 16; Alice Vavasor's first cousin, i. 16; 'a year or two over thirty', i. 35; of Cecil Street, Strand; Oxfordshire; and 'a third establishment, which shall be nameless', i. 120–1; M.P. (Liberal) for the Chelsea Districts, ii. 43; his discarded mistress Jane ——, ii. 320.

Vavasor, John, younger but only surviving son of the squire, i. 1; m. Alice Macleod (£400 a year), i. 2; widower; fifty, i. 4; of Queen Anne Street, i. 6; assistant commissioner ('signer') to the Accountant General, i. 2, ii. 215.

Vavasor, Kate, Alice Vavasor's first cousin, grand-daughter of the squire, i. 15; nearly thirty, i. 57.

Walker, of Scotland Yard, ii. 335.

Walker, Mrs., her dd. Maria and Ophelia, i. 87–90, 96–8.

Walker, Sir William, Bart., M.F.H., i. 173.

GEORGE ELIOT	Daniel Deronda
	The Lifted Veil and Brother Jacob
	Middlemarch
	The Mill on the Floss
	Silas Marner
SUSAN FERRIER	Marriage
ELIZABETH GASKELL	Cranford
	The Life of Charlotte Brontë
	Mary Barton
	North and South
	Wives and Daughters
GEORGE GISSING	New Grub Street
	The Odd Woman
THOMAS HARDY	Far from the Madding Crowd
	Jude the Obscure
	The Mayor of Casterbridge
	The Return of the Native
	Tess of the d'Urbervilles
	The Woodlanders
WILLIAM HAZLITT	Selected Writings
JAMES HOGG	The Private Memoirs and Confessions of a Justified Sinner
JOHN KEATS	The Major Works
	Selected Letters
CHARLES MATURIN	Melmoth the Wanderer
WALTER SCOTT	The Antiquary
	Ivanhoe
	Rob Roy
MARY SHELLEY	Frankenstein
	The Last Man

ÉMILE ZOLA

L'Assommoir
The Attack on the Mill
La Bête humaine
La Débâcle
Germinal
The Kill
The Ladies' Paradise
The Masterpiece
Nana
Pot Luck
Thérèse Raquin

American Literature

British and Irish Literature

Children's Literature

Classics and Ancient Literature

Colonial Literature

Eastern Literature

European Literature

History

Medieval Literature

Oxford English Drama

Poetry

Philosophy

Politics

Religion

The Oxford Shakespeare